Oracle RMAN 11g Backup and Recovery

Robert G. Freeman
Matthew Hart

New York   Chicago   San Francisco
Lisbon   London   Madrid   Mexico City   Milan
New Delhi   San Juan   Seoul   Singapore   Sydney   Toronto

The *McGraw·Hill* Companies

Cataloging-in-Publication Data is on file with the Library of Congress

McGraw-Hill books are available at special quantity discounts to use as premiums and sales promotions, or for use in corporate training programs. To contact a representative, please e-mail us at bulksales@mcgraw-hill.com.

Oracle RMAN 11*g* Backup and Recovery

1234567890 DOC DOC 109876543210

ISBN 978-0-07-162860-0
MHID   0-07-162860-6

Sponsoring Editor	**Copy Editor**	**Illustration**
Lisa McClain	Jan Jue	Lyssa Wald
Editorial Supervisor	**Proofreader**	**Art Director, Cover**
Janet Walden	Paul Tyler	Jeff Weeks
Project Editor	**Indexer**	**Cover Designer**
Emilia Thiuri	Jack Lewis	Pattie Lee
Acquisitions Coordinator	**Production Supervisor**	
Meghan Riley	Jean Bodeaux	
Technical Editor	**Composition**	
Matthew Arrocha	Apollo Publishing Service	

This book is dedicated to all the people who make my life great. My kids, my wife, my cat, my father, my friends, co-workers past and present.
—Robert

This book is dedicated to the team of professionals around the globe that I have the privilege of working with every day.
—Matthew

About the Authors

Robert G. Freeman has been an Oracle DBA for so long he can't remember now when he actually entered SQL*Plus for the first time. In his spare time (what's that?) Robert flies airplanes and loves to ride trains. Robert has written a number of books, including previous titles for Oracle Press on *Oracle Database 11g New Features*.

Matthew Hart is the coauthor of six books for Oracle Press, most recently *Oracle 10g High Availability with RAC, Flashback, and DataGuard, Oracle Enterprise Manager 10g Handbook*, and the tome you now hold in your hands. He has worked with high availability technologies in Oracle since version 7.3, and has worked with RMAN since its inception. Matthew currently works and lives in Kansas City, Missouri.

About the Contributors

Emre Baransel received his B.S. degree from Istanbul University in Electric and Electronic Engineering. He started his career in information technology and became an Oracle addict. He worked for Turkey's leading Telco and GSM operators as an Oracle DBA. His special focus is on grid technologies, disaster recovery, and security. He writes articles on his Oracle blog and also supervises a web page that publishes Oracle-related writings in Turkish. He's an OCP (Oracle Certified Professional) and CCNP (Cisco Certified Network Professional).

Scott Black has worked in information technology for over ten years, mostly in the e-commerce, and healthcare industries. His main areas of focus were networking and server administration when he started his career, and he has spent the last six years in database administration focusing on Oracle and SQL Server. With Oracle, his main interests are large-scale database performance tuning, RAC, and enterprise management of large numbers of databases.

Alan Bort started working as first-line support for Oracle customers before the support model switched to web-based Oracle support. In the beginning, his area of interest was Linux System Administration, Oracle Database, and Oracle Applications, but later focused only on Oracle Database with a special interest in large-scale high availability and disaster recovery scenarios. He currently works for IBM's Service Delivery structure for several companies and has worked on several projects to overhaul their Disaster Recovery capabilities.

Jeremiah Wilton has over fifteen years of Oracle administration and architecture experience. As Amazon.com's first DBA, he helped lead Amazon.com's database group from pre-IPO times through the years of exponential growth. He now directs education and emergency support services for Blue Gecko, a leader in remote database administration and managed hosting for Oracle, Oracle Applications, and MySQL. Jeremiah is a recognized expert in scalability, high availability, stability, and complex recoveries. He also teaches the Oracle Certificate Program at the University of Washington and independent seminars on a variety of Oracle subjects. In 2001 at Oracle Openworld, Oracle Education honored Jeremiah as one of the first eight Oracle Certified Masters in the world. Jeremiah is a member of the Oak Table and has presented at numerous conferences including Oracle Openworld, Collaborate, and UKOUG. He is the author of a variety of technical whitepapers and articles available at www.bluegecko.net.

Alisher Yuldashev has been an Oracle DBA for more than twelve years. Currently, he is a Senior Oracle DBA at The Pythian Group, a global industry leader in remote database administration services and consulting for Oracle and Oracle Applications. Alisher is an Oracle Certified Professional DBA and is responsible for all aspects of database administration for Pythian's wide range of multinational clients, from migrations and performance tuning to disaster recovery, and data warehousing. Alisher lives in Ottawa, Canada, with his wife, Anna, and their child, Rihanna.

When he is not working with Oracle, he spends his time with his wonderful family, and enjoys snowboarding the Canadian mountains and reading books.

About the Technical Editor

Matt Arrocha started in the computer industry as a hardware technician. He spent 5 years at NASA in Florida repairing hardware for all manned and unmanned space flight. He worked for 2 years with Seagate in their tape backup division (previously Conner/Maynard). He has been with Oracle now since 1996 and has been working with Recovery Manager since its release in Oracle Database 8.0.3. He is currently the Advanced Resolution Lead for Backup & Recovery in the United States and Canada and the RMAN Global Technical Lead.

Contents at a Glance

PART IV

RMAN in the Oracle Ecosystem

PART V

Appendixes

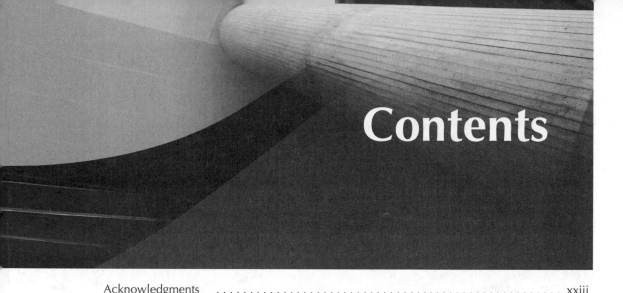

Contents

PART I
Getting Started with RMAN in Oracle Database 11*g*

PART II
Setup Principles and Practices

PART III
Using RMAN Effectively

PART IV
RMAN in the Oracle Ecosystem

PART V
Appendixes

Acknowledgments

As we bring this book to a close, I stand in Hobbit land…also known as New Zealand, doing a presentation on RMAN. How amazing is it that I get to do things like this. My life has been very positively impacted by the Oracle Database product. I feel so lucky to be doing what I'm doing, and to have the opportunities that I have. There are so many people to thank who have helped me along on this journey and if I took the time to name each one, we would have yet another voluminous book on our hands that would cost at least twenty-five dollars just in shipping charges. So I'll refrain from the typical naming of names, you know who you are and I thank you for everything you have done for me.

As for this book, there are a few people to thank. I want to thank my wife, Lisa, for putting up with me during the writing and editing process. I want to thank Lisa McClain and Meghan Riley for putting up with my terrible schedule, and Matthew as well. They really deserve a reward. Thanks to the rest of the team at McGraw-Hill Professional, including Janet Walden, Emilia Thiuri, Jan Jue, and Paul Tyler. Also thanks to you, the reader, for reading/buying this book.

—Robert G. Freeman

It seems to be getting harder and harder to get these books out the door, given the complex nature of the products, and the ever-changing landscape of the authors and contributors' lives. Therefore, I want to first thank both Lisa McClain, and especially Meghan Riley, for not saying all of the completely deserved things I'm sure they wanted to say to me, and instead remaining focused on the outcome and driving us all toward it. You both deserved better.

Second big thanks goes to Matt Arrocha, for, again, playing the part of the person who actually knows the most about RMAN and keeping us on track.

The contributors on this book, as always, worked hard to create extremely valuable chapters on media management that complete the book (and give it some of its legendary heft). Thanks to Emre Baransel, Scott Black, Alan Bort, Jeremiah Wilton, and Alisher Yuldashev for making this a complete book.

No book is complete without the sharp eyes and controlling hand of the copy editor, and Jan Jue had both in spades. Emilia Thiuri, the project editor, also suffered at the hands of this very-tardy author, and deserves special thanks for her patience.

This is Robert and my third collaboration, and I remain impressed with his enthusiasm and desire for completeness. Robert, good luck over there at the mothership. As always, my good friend Martin Ingram continues to provide the kind of personal and professional support that keeps me pushing hard, every day.

This book came at a time when I had no business writing another book, and to muscle it through to completion meant the kinds of sacrifices for which I must stand in awe of my wife and my kids, who have learned the hard way what it takes to make this sort of thing happen. I owe everything I've ever done well or right to them.

Thanks to you, the reader, for making the RMAN books such a great success and for reading yet another version.

—Matthew Hart

Introduction

o, yet another edition of our RMAN backup and recovery book has hit the shelves! Oracle Database 11*g* has proven to be quite the release to be sure. RMAN has new functionality and whizbang new features that improve an already awesome product. RMAN has certainly evolved over the years, as anyone who started working with it in Oracle version 8 can attest to.

Answering the Question ... and Asking a New One

In *Oracle9i RMAN Backup & Recovery*, we posed the following question in this same space: how can I balance availability with recoverability? We hoped to answer that question with a full coverage of Oracle's backup and recovery solution, and the number of copies sold tells us that many people liked the answer. We introduced *Oracle9i RMAN Backup & Recovery* at a time when people were really starting to adopt RMAN as a backup and recovery solution.

With the release of *Oracle Database 10g RMAN Backup & Recovery*, we found an audience of people more familiar with RMAN. At the same time, this audience was asking more complex questions, and trying to keep up with all the new features offered with Oracle Database 10*g*. With databases growing ever faster, and mean-time-to-recovery becoming the buzzword of the day, RMAN became an indispensable tool in the DBA's day-to-day toolkit.

With the release of Oracle Database 11*g*, the trend continues. Complexity is an understatement these days, and DBAs struggle to keep up with the changes occurring. From Grid computing to high availability and mean-time-to-recovery, the questions get more complex and so to do the answers. Still, we feel like RMAN comes out as the answer to such questions.

If you are not aware, RMAN comes with the Oracle database license. It's installed when the database is installed and generally ready to go (with some minimal configuration which we talk about in depth in this book!). RMAN is ready to back up the smallest Oracle Database or the largest, most complex Oracle database. It can back up your single instance database sitting on a small server or your multinode RAC clustered database sitting on multiple servers. RMAN still has the old bells and whistles you are used to, but Oracle Database 11*g* offers a range of new features that improve its capabilities several fold.

A Book for the DBA and the Sys Admin

Perhaps the most frustrating part of formulating a solid, reliable backup strategy for an Oracle database is that it usually overlaps two different kinds of people: the database administrator and the system administrator. Formulating an RMAN strategy is no different. Its tight integration with the Oracle RDBMS means a system administrator must establish a working knowledge of an Oracle database. But, the reliance on external tape storage systems and the network topology makes it critical that the DBA be able to administer networked computer systems. This makes for an interesting separation of duties and for headaches on each side.

Furthermore, business demands are fusing the role descriptions of the DBA and the system administrator. Or, more precisely, DBAs are finding their work increasingly expanding into system administrator work, and system administrators find themselves spending more time learning SQL commands.

This book addresses this overlap by offering how-to advice in the areas where the overlap is most acute: database backups.

RMAN: An Evolution into Excellence

RMAN was introduced in version 8.0.3, the first production release of Oracle8. Prior to this, the Oracle-provided interface for streaming backups directly to tape involved logical backups using the Export utility, or use of the Enterprise Backup Utility (EBU). Ah, EBU. May it rest in peace, and we promise this is the last time we will ever mention it. *Ever.*

As an initial release, RMAN had its pratfalls and quirks. But with every release since its rollout, new features have been added, bugs have been fixed, and the interface has been polished. The best way to visualize the progress is to think of the traditional poster showing the evolution of humans: at the far left, we see a monkey, walking on all fours. Then, moving to the right, we see an increasingly upright version of a human, until we arrive at the far right, where we see a fully upright, modern homo sapiens.

With the release of Oracle9*i*, RMAN reached a fully upright walking position. It has truly become a necessary component in any serious strategy for a highly available database system.

Now that RMAN has been through two 10*g* releases, it has moved beyond a simple upright position, and has picked up a tablet and learned to read. Belabored metaphor aside, RMAN has continued its evolution into a fully functional availability partner.

What This Book Covers

This handbook was written to utilize the latest features included in Oracle Database 11*g* Release 2. It therefore takes advantage of the latest enhancements to the RMAN interface and explains the newest features available. All code examples and architectural explanations are based on the 11*g*R2 release of RMAN.

If you are still using earlier versions of Oracle and RMAN (Oracle8*i*, Oracle9*i*, Oracle Database 10*g*) this book will still be helpful, but you will find a number of features missing. You might want to also reference our previous RMAN books (*Oracle9*i *RMAN Backup & Recovery* or *Oracle Database 10*g *RMAN Backup & Recovery*). The book you are currently reading makes no attempt to cover functionality as it existed in previous versions.

Using This Book Effectively

Like all technical manuals worth their weight, this book is meant to be readable, cover to cover, as a way to familiarize yourself with RMAN and its role in any high availability or disaster recovery solution. The topics are approached in a format that allows each complex subject to build on previous chapters, slowly working forward from principles, to setup, to backups, and then beyond backups to advanced functionality and practices.

As such, Part I is dedicated to an introduction to backup and recovery principles in the Oracle RDBMS. It gives an important conceptual understanding of RMAN and how it does that mojo that it does. These two chapters lay the foundation for all future chapters, and we encourage you to read them carefully and understand the concepts being discussed. If you can understand the concepts and internal workings, then the rest of the book will be a breeze.

Part II is dedicated to setting up RMAN for initial usage. We cover all possible RMAN configuration options. Then, we discuss the integration with a media manager, the layer that allows you to write your backups directly to a tape device. While there are many products on the market, we will discuss four of the media management products: Oracle's own Secure Backup, VERITAS NetBackup, EMC NetWorker Module for Oracle, and IBM Tivoli Storage Manager.

In Part III, we provide the basics for RMAN usage, from the most basic backup operation to the most advanced recovery option. We discuss catalog maintenance and how to keep an eye on the catalog so that you can effectively manage the backups that are accumulating. Here is where we discuss using Oracle's redesigned Enterprise Manager product and cover Flashback Technology for recovery from logical errors. Finally, there is a discussion on tuning RMAN backups and restores for optimal performance when it counts.

Part IV moves past backup and recovery, discussing how RMAN can assist you in tasks other than just simple backups. In this part, we run through how to use the RMAN backups to make a cloned copy of your database and how to use the backups to create a standby database for Oracle Data Guard. Then, we discuss using RMAN in a Real Application Clusters (RAC) environment, with its special needs and requirements. We end the section with a series of RMAN case studies that delve into common (and not so common) situations that require RMAN.

The appendixes in Part V include an RMAN syntax reference, for building a successful RMAN command, and an exploration of the RMAN catalog, both in v$views in the database and rc_* views in the recovery catalog. In addition, Appendix C goes into some detail about how to set up an RMAN test environment to put this book to work with minimal busywork.

RMAN Workshops

Not everyone reads a book cover to cover. We know this. Sometimes that's not the higher calling of a good technical book. A good book lives next to the computer, with pages dog-eared, sections highlighted, and little yellow Post-its hanging off the side.

This book is meant to be a reference guide in addition to a conceptual explanation. We've packed this thing with useful techniques and timesaving practices that you can implement now, even if you're a little spotty on the architecture. Sometimes you just need to know *how to do it*, right? Especially when it comes to backup and recovery. No one wants to get stuck in the middle of a weekend recovery binge, trying to figure out the exact syntax for a particular restore operation while the production database sits idly by, bleeding revenue at a spectacular rate.

So, to help with the highlighting and dog-earing of pages, we utilize RMAN Workshop sections, which readers of our previous RMAN books will recognize. Whenever we provide useful code for performing a specific operation, or a series of steps to complete a certain project, we put it in an RMAN Workshop box. When you see this box, you know the following pages will be filled with the actual steps you need to follow to get your job done fast. Think of RMAN Workshops as recipes, providing the ingredients and the mixing instructions for a quick and easy meal. And to make your life even easier, we've highlighted each RMAN Workshop, with its descriptive title and the page number, in the main Contents.

Again, we encourage you to read the book chapter for chapter. Nothing can replace a conceptual understanding of a product, especially when that product is protecting your most valuable asset: the database.

So, enjoy the book! RMAN is a challenging and rewarding product to dig into and utilize. It can save you time and energy, and help avoid health problems related to insomnia, outage stress, and paranoia. We haven't got a Surgeon General's label yet, but we're working on it.

PART
I

Getting Started with RMAN in Oracle Database 11*g*

CHAPTER
1

Oracle Database 11*g*
Backup and Recovery
Architecture Tour

elcome to *Oracle Database 11g RMAN Backup and Recovery.* If you purchased our previous RMAN books, you have an idea of what to expect from this text. However, this book is more than just a simple revision. RMAN in Oracle Database 11*g* has so many new features that this book has a lot of new and revised content. We hope you find it useful. We have also listened to you and acted on some of your feedback. We hope you will find the results make this book the best yet!

If you are already using RMAN and are concerned that the changes in Oracle Database 11*g* will adversely affect your backup and recovery strategies, don't worry. RMAN is fully backward compatible, so your existing backup and recovery strategies will not have to change when you move to Oracle Database 11*g*.

If you are just starting with RMAN, then welcome aboard! RMAN is a great choice for Oracle database backup and recovery. In this book, we give you all the information you need to use RMAN successfully. The book is designed to help you get started using RMAN as quickly as possible.

Before we get deep into RMAN, though, we thought you would like to tour the base Oracle backup and recovery landscape, which actually has not changed a great deal in Oracle Database 11*g*. So, for some of you, the landscape may be familiar, in which case you can either ride along to refresh your memory or proceed straight to Chapter 2. If you are new to Oracle, this tour will really help you prepare for the onslaught of RMAN information you will be getting in subsequent chapters. So, jump on the bus, keep your feet and hands inside at all times, and we will be off.

In this tour of the Oracle database backup and recovery architecture, you will encounter the following:

■ Backup and recovery essentials

■ A few Oracle terms to know

■ Oracle database physical architecture

■ Oracle operational internals

■ ARCHIVELOG versus NOARCHIVELOG mode operations

■ Oracle recovery modes

■ Manual backup operations in Oracle

■ Manual recovery operations in Oracle

As we proceed, you will learn the importance of understanding how the Oracle product works, so that you can properly apply the techniques that will be documented in this book to bring your wayward database back to life. You will also see that there is more to backing up and recovering a database than just entering a few commands and putting tapes in the tape drive.

The direct results of misapplying a technique, or not understanding a principle of the architecture, may be an extended outage or even loss of data. In fact, one of us just had a case where a restore took ten hours, when, after reviewing the facts, it should have only taken two hours. The difference in this case was that the DBA doing the restore lacked some basic understanding of the database he was recovering. This led to a grave mistake in his selected form of recovery. The old adage that you must walk before you can run certainly applies when it comes to backup and recovery. Finally, we are going to cover only basics and any additional information that you need to know with regard to RMAN and recovering your database. If you need more information on these subject areas, several good Oracle Press titles can help you. You can find these titles at www.oraclepressbooks.com.

Backup and Recovery Essentials

Our first stop is backup and recovery essentials. Two different areas need to be dealt with when crafting plans to execute in the event your database goes bottom up. The first architectural question is one of high availability, which is loosely coupled with the second question, which is one of backup and recovery. Let's look at these questions of high availability and backup and recovery in more detail.

High Availability

High availability (HA) implies an architecture that prevents the users from being aware of partial or total system (database, network, hardware, and so forth) failure. HA solutions can include such elements as mirrored drives, RAID architectures, database clustering, database failover schemes, and, of course, backup and recovery. HA adds costs to the overall database architectural solution, over and above the costs of the backup and recovery solution selected. RMAN is really not an HA solution, but it is part of an overall database solution that can include HA. Backup and recovery of your database is not superseded by HA solutions. Rather, how you will back up and recover your database is one of a collection of HA decisions you need to make.

If you are interested in looking at HA solutions, a number of them include

- Data Guard/Stand-by Database

- Real Application Clusters

- Oracle Replication/Streams

- RAID and mirrored drives

Various other vendors provide HA solutions as well. Because HA options are really a separate topic from RMAN, we do not cover them in this book. Oracle Press does offer a book that includes coverage on HA solutions: *Oracle Database 10g High Availability with RAC, Flashback, & Data Guard* (McGraw-Hill/Osborne, 2004) by Matthew Hart, one of the authors of this very text!

Backup and Recovery

As we continue our tour (anyone want to stop at the snack bar?), we move to backup and recovery, which is getting us close to the main topic of this book, RMAN. We will talk in detail throughout this chapter about the different kinds of backups that can be done in Oracle, but for now, let's talk about the primary types of backups: offline (cold) and online (hot).

Offline backups are done with the database down, which means that it is also unavailable to users. *Online* backups, on the other hand, are done with the database up and running, so users can continue with their business. RMAN supports both types of backups. In fact, as you will see in later chapters, some of the features of RMAN make it the preferable method for performing online database backups.

You shouldn't just "decide" that it's time to back up your database. This is particularly true in the case of production databases, where the users have certain levels of expectations for protection of their data. Before you decide when and how to back up your database, you should gather some of your users' requirements and consider your company's general backup policy. Only after you have gathered those requirements can you craft that backup plan. Let's look in some more detail at how you gather those requirements.

Backup and Recovery Strategy Requirements Gathering

In gathering user requirements, you really want to find out from them what their needs are. Users need to be asked a number of questions, and as the database administrator (DBA), you should take the lead in asking them. To collect backup and recovery requirements, you need to ask your customers a few questions like the following:

- How much data loss can you afford in the event of a database failure?

- What is the maximum length of time you are able to allow for recovery of your database?

- How much are you willing to spend to ensure that your data is recoverable?

- Can the system be down during the backup?

- How much time will it take to get damaged hardware replaced?

Let's quickly look at each of these questions in more detail.

How Much Data Loss Can You Afford?   This is probably the most important question of all. All backup and recovery plans have some risk of data loss associated with them, and as you move closer to a zero data loss solution, the costs of the backup and recovery plan can skyrocket. Just as was the case with HA, the organization needs to quantify the cost of data loss and, based on that cost, craft a cost-effective backup and recovery plan. It is critical that the customer understand how much data loss risk they are taking with the chosen backup and recovery plan. Of course, each database has an allowable amount of loss, too, and one database may be much more tolerant of data loss than another.

What Is the Maximum Length of Time You Are Able to Allow for Recovery?   Different technologies perform in different ways and vary widely in price. Generally, the faster you wish your recovery to go, the more expensive the technology ends up being. For example, recoveries directly from disk tend to be a bit more expensive than recoveries from tape, but also tend to be faster. It is important that the customer understand how long recovery of the database will take in the event of a complete outage. Some cases have little tolerance for recovery, and you may need to consider technologies such as Oracle Stand-by Database.

How Much Can You Spend on Recovery?   There is a direct relationship between how much data loss you can tolerate, how long it will take to actually recover the database, and how much it will cost to provide a given level of protection. It is important, early on, to understand just how much the customer is willing to spend on architecture to support your proposed backup and recovery plan. Nothing is more embarrassing than proposing a massive architecture with a high dollar cost, and having the customer look at you and laugh at the projected expense.

Can the System Be Down During the Backup?   Another key piece of information to determine is what the state of the database needs to be during the backup. Can an outage be afforded to do backups, or do those backups need to be done online? The answer to this question impacts your total overall cost and your decisions in choosing a backup strategy.

How Much Time Will It Take to Get Damaged Hardware Replaced?   This is a key consideration. Often it's not the database that fails, but some piece of hardware. Hardware failure can considerably impact the time it takes to get your database running again. You need to make sure the system stakeholders understand the impact of hardware failures and consider architectures that can help protect them from hardware failures, such as Oracle Real Application Clusters.

Backup and Recovery: Crafting the Plan

Now that you have gathered your requirements, you can begin to craft your backup and recovery plan. You need to make a number of decisions:

- Based on the user (and business) requirements, do you need to do offline or online backups of the database?

- If you are going to use online backups, how often do you need to back up archived redo logs? How will you protect the archived redo logs from loss between backup sessions?

- What are the company policies and standards with regard to recoverability?

- How are you going to ensure that your system is recoverable in the event of a disaster?

- Are there any architectural decisions that need to be made?

Each of these questions is important. Disasters are important to plan for, and they do happen. Company policies may well supersede the needs of the users. Backup policies and standards are important to implement and enforce. Managing one database backup and recovery policy is easy. Managing many different databases with different methods of doing backup and recovery becomes cumbersome and dangerous.

Managing archived redo logs is important because they are critical to recovery, and you want to be able to support your users as much as you can. After all, the users are the reason you are there! To really determine how to craft your backup strategy, you need to understand how Oracle works and how Oracle backup and recovery works; we will talk about that shortly. First, just to make sure we are all on the same page, let's discuss some basic Oracle terms.

A Few Oracle Terms to Know

It is always a bit hard to decide where to start when discussing the Oracle architecture, because so many of the different components are interrelated. This makes it hard to talk about one without referring to the other. So that we can have a common point of reference for some basic terms, in this section we quickly define those terms. We will be using these terms throughout the rest of this book, so it is really important that you clearly understand them (we also define them in more depth as this chapter progresses). So, if you are a bit hazy on Oracle internal terms, please review the following until you know without hesitation what they are:

- **Alert log**   A text log file in which the database maintains error and status messages. The alert log can be a critical structure when trying to determine the nature of a database failure. Typically, the alert log is in the background dump destination directory, as defined by the database parameter BACKGROUND_DUMP_DEST, and is called alert<sid>.log.

- **Archived redo logs**   When the database is in ARCHIVELOG mode, archived redo logs are generated each time Oracle switches online redo logs by the LGWR process. Archived redo logs are used during database recovery. Copies of the archived redo logs can be written to as many as ten different directories, defined by the Oracle parameter LOG_ARCHIVE_DEST_*n* in the database parameter file. Also, Oracle Database 11*g* allows you to store archived redo logs in a new location called the flash recovery area, which we discuss in more detail in Chapter 3.

■ **Backup control file** A backup of the control file generated as the result of using the **alter database backup controlfile to 'file_name'** command or the **alter database backup control file to trace** command.

■ **Block** The most atomic unit of storage in Oracle. The default block size is determined by the parameter DB_BLOCK_SIZE in the database parameter file, and it is set permanently when a database is created. Oracle Database 11*g* allows tablespaces to be different block sizes than the default.

■ **Checkpoint** A database event that causes the database to flush dirty (used) blocks from memory and write them to disk.

■ **Database** Consists of the different components that make up an Oracle database (tablespaces, redo logs, and so forth). A database is much different from an instance. A database is where the data lives, and what you will be backing up and recovering with RMAN.

■ **Database consistency** Implies that each object in the database is consistent to the same point in time. This means that the data in the database datafiles is consistent to the same point in time. This also means that the database control files are synchronized with the database datafile headers.

■ **Database control file** A database control file stores several kinds of metadata related to the database. This includes information on the database datafiles, archived redo logs, RMAN backups, and other internal database information.

■ **Database datafile** A physical entity that is related to a tablespace. A database consists of at least one database datafile (which would be assigned to the SYSTEM tablespace), and most databases consist of many different database datafiles. Whereas a tablespace can have many different database datafiles associated with it, a given database datafile can have only one tablespace associated with it.

■ **Database parameter file** Contains instance and database configuration information and comes in two mutually exclusive flavors: init.ora, which is a text file, and spfile .ora, which allows for persistent settings of database parameters via the **alter system** command.

■ **Flash recovery area (FRA)** An optionally configured area of disk that is used to store various recovery-related files. RMAN backup files, archived redo logs, online redo logs, and control files can be stored in this area. You can find more details on the FRA in Chapter 2 and find setup information in Chapter 3. You'll see examples of the use of the FRA in most chapters of this book.

■ **Granule** A unit of Oracle contiguous memory. All System Global Area (SGA) memory allocations are rounded to the nearest granule units. The size of a granule depends on the overall expected size of the SGA, and it may be 4MB or 16MB. An SGA size of greater than 128MB tends to be the break point when Oracle uses the larger granule sizes. The number of granules allocated to the database is determined at database startup.

■   **Instance**   The collection of Oracle memory and processes. When the SGA (memory) is allocated and each of the required Oracle processes is up and running successfully, then the Oracle instance is considered started. Note that just because the Oracle instance is running, this does not mean that the database itself is open. An instance is associated with one, and only one, database at any given time.

■   **Online redo logs**   When redo is generated, it is physically stored in the online redo logs of the database. Oracle requires that at least two online redo logs be created for a database to operate. These online redo logs can have multiple mirrored copies for protection of the redo. This is known as *multiplexing* the redo log. As an online redo log fills with redo, Oracle switches to the next online redo log, which is known as a *log switch* operation.

Each online redo log file has a unique *log sequence number* associated with it that uniquely identifies it and, if it's archived, its associated archived redo log file. You can find the log sequence number of the online redo logs by querying the V$LOG view. The sequence number of a given archived redo log can be found in the V$ARCHIVED_LOG view or the V$LOG_HISTORY view.

Additionally, an online redo log (and an archived redo log) contains a range of database System Change Numbers (SCNs) that is unique to that redo log. During recovery, Oracle applies the undo in the archived/online redo logs in order of log sequence number.

■   **Processes**   The programs that do the actual work of the Oracle database. Oracle Database 11*g* has five required processes among others.

■   **Redo**   A record of all changes made to a given database. For almost any change in the database, an associated redo record is generated.

■   **Schema**   Owns the various logical objects in Oracle, such as tables and indexes, and is synonymous with the user.

■   **SGA (System Global Area)**   An area of shared memory that is allocated by Oracle as it is started. Memory in the SGA can be shared by all Oracle processes.

■   **System Change Number (SCN)**   A counter that represents the current state of the database at a given time. As with the counter on a VCR, as time progresses, the SCN increases. Each SCN atomically represents a point in the life of the database. Thus, at 11 A.M., the database SCN might be 10ffx0 (4351 decimal), and at 12 P.M., it might be 11f0x0 (4592 decimal).

■   **Tablespace**   A physi-logical entity. It is a logical entity because it is the place that Oracle logical objects (such as tables and indexes) are stored. It is a physical entity because it is made up of one or more database datafiles. A database must contain at least one tablespace, the SYSTEM tablespace, but most databases consist of many different tablespaces.

■   **Trace files**   Generated by the database in a number of different situations, including process errors. Each database process also generates its own trace file. Trace files can be important when trying to resolve the nature of a database failure.

Controlling the Database Software

During various recovery operations, you need to control the state of the Oracle database and its associated instance. Let's quickly review how to start and stop Oracle databases.

To start the Oracle Database 11*g* database, you use the SQL*Plus Oracle utility. Log in as the user system by using the SYSDBA login ID. At the SQL*Plus prompt, issue the **startup** command, as you can see in this example:

```
/usr/oracle>sqlplus / as sysdba
SQL*Plus: Release 11.2.0.1.0 Production on Mon Jan 26 10:55:49 2010
Copyright (c) 1982, 2009, Oracle.  All rights reserved.
Connected to:
Oracle Database 11g Enterprise Edition Release 11.2.0.1.0 - Production
With the Partitioning, Real Application Clusters, Automatic Storage Management,
OLAP, Dada Mining and Real Application Testing options
Connected to an idle instance.
SQL> startup
```

When you start an Oracle database with the **startup** command, the operation goes through three different phases:

- **Instance startup** The Oracle database instance is started.

- **Database mount** The Oracle database is mounted.

- **Database open** The Oracle database is opened for user activity.

NOTE
*You should be aware that the RMAN client, which we will discuss in later chapters, has the ability to shut down and start up the Oracle database on its own. You will not need to move from RMAN to SQL*Plus during a recovery operation in most cases.*

The **startup** command has several different variations (which are important to know for several different RMAN operations), some of which include the following:

- **startup** Causes Oracle to go through each of the three startup phases, and to open to the user community.

- **startup restrict** Causes Oracle to go through each of the three startup phases, and to open in restricted mode. Only those users with restricted privileges can access the database.

- **startup nomount** Causes the startup process to stop after it has successfully started the database instance. You will often use this command to start the database instance prior to actually creating a database. This command is also handy to have if you need to re-create the control file. Note that to use RMAN with a given database, you must be able to successfully start the instance with the **startup nomount** command.

- **startup mount** Causes the startup process to stop after it has successfully started the database instance and then mounted it. This command is helpful if you need to recover the SYSTEM tablespace.

- **startup read only**   Causes your Oracle database (or standby database) to open in READ ONLY mode. Thus, DML operations are not supported, but you can query the database. This is handy if you are doing point-in-time recovery and you want to make sure you have recovered the database to the correct point in time before you commit to the new database incarnation with the **resetlogs** command.

- **startup force**   Causes the database to be shut down with a **shutdown abort** (discussed in the next list). This command can be followed by the mode you wish the database to be opened in again. Examples include

    - startup force restrict

    - startup force mount

    - startup force nomount

Of course, now that you know how to start up the database, you need to know how to shut it down. Again, from SQL*Plus, you can use the **shutdown** command, which comes in these flavors:

- **shutdown** (also **shutdown normal**)   Causes Oracle to wait for all user processes to disconnect from the database. Once this has occurred, the database will be completely shut down. Use of this option avoids instance recovery. After the **shutdown** command is executed, no new user processes are able to connect to the database.

- **shutdown immediate**   Kills all existing user sessions and rolls back all uncommitted transactions. Use of this option avoids instance recovery. After **shutdown immediate** is executed, no new user processes are able to connect to the database.

- **shutdown abort**   Basically, crashes the database. Use of this option requires instance (but not media) recovery. After **shutdown abort** is executed, no new user processes are able to connect to the database.

- **shutdown transactional**   Causes Oracle to wait for all user processes to commit their current transactions and then disconnects the user processes and shuts down the database. While it is waiting for these transactions to complete, no new user sessions are allowed to connect to the database.

As we proceed through this book, we use many of these commands, and it is important to understand what state the database and its associated instance are in when the command has completed.

Oracle Architecture

Our tour continues as we begin looking at the physical components of Oracle. First, we take a look at the processes that make up an Oracle database. Then, we look at Oracle memory structures and the different logical, physical, and physi-logical structures that make up an Oracle database. Finally, we discuss the differences between an instance and an Oracle database.

The Oracle Processes

When the **startup nomount** command is issued, Oracle attempts to start an Oracle *instance.* An Oracle instance is started after several required operating system processes (programs) are started and the SGA memory area is allocated. In this section, we are going to look at the processes that get Oracle started. First, we look at the basic five Oracle processes required for any Oracle database to be functional. Next, we look at user and server processes. Finally, we look at other, optional Oracle processes that you might see from time to time.

NOTE
This is just a basic introduction to the Oracle processes. If you want more in-depth detail on them, please refer to the Oracle documentation.

The Five Required Oracle Processes

If an Oracle Database 11*g* instance has successfully started, a minimum of five different processes will start. Of course, on certain systems (such as Microsoft-based OSs), the five different processes are really just threads of a single Oracle process, but the basic idea is still the same. These required processes are as follows:

- **PMON**   Also known as the process monitor process (and one of what some call the "Jamaican processes").

- **SMON**   Also known as the system monitor process (and the other "Jamaican process").

- **DBW***n*   Known as the database writer processes. An instance can be configured with up to nine of these processes in Oracle Database 11*g* (but generally no more than one is required). DBWn is responsible for writing information to the database datafiles from the database buffer cache structure in the SGA.

- **LGWR**   The log writer process is responsible for writing generated redo to the database online redo logs from the log buffer. LGWR is signaled to do these writes when a user session is committed, when the redo log buffer is nearly full, and at other times as required.

- **CKPT**   During a checkpoint operation, the CKPT process notifies DBWn of the checkpoint. The CKPT process also updates database datafile headers with current checkpoint information.

The User and Server Processes

When a user connects to the database, a user process is spawned (or a new thread is started on Windows NT) that connects to a separately spawned server process. These processes communicate with each other using various protocols, such as Bequeath or TCP/IP.

Other Optional Oracle Processes

A number of other Oracle processes may be launched as well when the Oracle instance is started (and in some cases, optional processes may actually be started much later on demand), depending on the configuration of the Oracle database parameter file. Most of these processes have little bearing on RMAN and database backup and recovery (unless the failure of one of the processes causes the database to crash, which is rare), so we won't spend much time on them. All of the optional processes are described in the Oracle documentation, online at otn.oracle.com, as well as in several Oracle Press books.

One set of optional processes that does have some bearing on RMAN and backup and recovery are the ARCH*n* processes. These processes (one or many of them) are critical to the backup and recovery process if you are doing online backups. See the section titled "ARCHIVELOG Mode vs. NOARCHIVELOG Mode," later in the chapter, for more on the ARCHn process(es).

Oracle Memory and RMAN

In this section, we look at the memory areas that we need to be concerned with in relationship to RMAN. As with any process, RMAN does require memory for its own operations and as a part of its database interactions. First, we describe the Oracle SGA in more detail, and then we look at the Private Global Area (PGA).

The Oracle System Global Area

The principal memory structure that we are concerned with in terms of RMAN and backup and recovery is the System Global Area (SGA). The SGA consists of one large allocation of shared memory that can be broken down into several memory substructures:

- The database buffer cache

- The shared pool

- The redo log buffer

- The large pool

- The Java pool

- The Streams pool

Of particular interest to the RMAN user are the shared pool and the large pool. RMAN uses several Oracle PL/SQL packages as it goes through its paces (as you will read in Chapter 2). These packages are like any other Oracle PL/SQL packages in that they must be loaded into the shared pool. If the shared pool is not large enough, or if it becomes fragmented, it is possible that the RMAN packages will not be able to execute. Thus, it is important to allocate enough memory to the shared pool for RMAN operations.

The large pool is used by RMAN in specific cases and is not used by default, even if it is configured. RMAN allows you to duplex RMAN backups (or to make concurrent copies of the same backup in different places) if either of the database parameters, BACKUP_TAPE_IO_SLAVES or DBWR_IO_SLAVES, is set to TRUE. These parameters are typically set to TRUE if you wish to simulate asynchronous IO. If these two parameters are set, Oracle can use the large pool memory rather than local memory (PGA). The use of the PGA is the default, so don't get confused and allocate tons of memory to the large pool when it will never get used.

Defining Memory Allocations in the SGA

The individual sizes of the SGA components are allocated based on the settings of parameters in the database parameter file. Depending on the version of the database you are using, these parameters include MEMORY_MAX_SIZE, MEMORY_TARGET, SGA_MAX_SIZE, SGA_TARGET, SHARED_POOL_SIZE, DB_CACHE_SIZE, DB_*n*K_CACHE_SIZE, LOG_BUFFER, LARGE_POOL_SIZE, and JAVA_POOL_SIZE (and several others). Each of these is defined in the Oracle documentation, so refer to it if you need more information on them. In Chapter 2, we will cover in detail the main parameters that have some bearing in terms of RMAN usage.

To recap quickly, we have discussed the makings of an Oracle instance in the last several pages. We have talked about the different Oracle processes and the different Oracle memory structures. When the processes and the memory all come together, an Oracle instance is formed. Now that we have an instance, we are ready for a database. In the next section, we discuss the various structures that make up an Oracle database.

The Oracle Database

Our tour now turns its attention to the Oracle database architecture itself. An Oracle database is made up of a number of different structures—some physical, some logical, and some physi-logical. In this section, we look at each of these types of structures and discuss each of the individual components of the Oracle database. We will conclude this section by looking at the flash recovery area (FRA) and Automatic Storage Management (ASM).

Oracle Physical Components

The Oracle database physical architecture includes the following components:

- Database datafiles

- Online redo logs

- Archived redo logs

- Database control files

- Oracle tablespaces

- Flashback logs (optional)

Each of these items is physically located on a storage device that is connected to your computer. These objects make up the physical existence of your Oracle database, and to recover your database, you may need to restore and recover one or more of these objects from a backup (except the flashback log). Let's look at each of these objects in a bit more detail.

Database Datafiles   The database datafiles are the data storage medium of the database and are related to tablespaces, as you will see shortly. When information is stored in the database, it ultimately gets stored in these physical files. Each database datafile contains a *datafile header* that contains information to help track the current state of that datafile. This datafile header is updated during checkpoint operations to reflect the current state of the datafile.

Database datafiles can have a number of different statuses assigned to them. The primary statuses we are interested in are ONLINE, which is the normal status, and OFFLINE, which is generally an abnormal status. A database datafile might take on the RECOVER status, as well, indicating that there is a problem with the datafile and that recovery is required.

If the database is in ARCHIVELOG mode (more on this later), you can take a datafile offline, which may be required for certain recovery operations. If the database is in NOARCHIVELOG mode, then you can only take the database datafile offline by dropping it. Offline dropping of a datafile can have some nasty effects on your database (such as loss of data), so drop datafiles with care.

Online Redo Logs   If the Oracle SCN can be likened to the counter on a VCR, then the redo logs can be likened to the videotape. (This analogy becomes harder and harder as DVRs replace

VCRs!) The online redo logs are responsible for recording every single atomic change that occurs in the database. Each Oracle database must have a minimum of two different online redo log groups, and most databases generally have many more than that, for performance and data preservation reasons.

Each online redo log group can have multiple members located on different disk drives for protection purposes. Oracle writes to the different members in parallel, making the write process more efficient. Oracle writes to one redo log group at a time, in round-robin fashion. When the group has been filled, the LGWR process closes those redo logs and then opens the next online redo log for processing.

Within redo logs are records called *change vectors*. Each change vector represents an atomic database change, in SCN order. During recovery (RMAN or manual), Oracle applies those change vectors to the database. This has the effect of applying all change records to the database in order, thus recovering it to the point in time of the failure (or another, earlier time if required). The LGWR process is responsible for writing the change vectors (cumulatively known as redo) to the online redo logs from the redo log buffer. We discuss this in more detail shortly in the section, "The Combined Picture."

Archived Redo Logs   A *log switch* occurs when Oracle stops writing to one online redo log and begins to write to another. As the result of a log switch, if the database is in ARCHIVELOG mode and the ARCH process is running, a copy of the online redo log will be made. This copy of the online redo log is called an archived redo log. Oracle can actually copy the archived redo log files to up to ten different destinations. During media recovery, the archived redo logs are applied to the database to recover it. We discuss this in more detail shortly, in "The Combined Picture."

Database Control Files   Each Oracle database has one or more database control files. The control file contains various database information, such as the current SCN, the state of the database datafiles, and the status of the database. Of interest to the RMAN DBA is the fact that the control file also stores critical information on various RMAN operations, such as the backup status of each database datafile. If you lose your control file, you will need to follow specific procedures to re-create the RMAN catalog within it. Also of interest might be the fact that the checkpoint SCN (or the SCN of the last update of a given datafile) is stored in the control file. Oracle will cross-check this checkpoint SCN with the checkpoint SCNs stored in the datafile headers. If they all match, the database requires no recovery whatsoever. If the SCNs do not match, then some form of recovery will be required. Typically this will be crash recovery, which is automated. Sometimes, for example if a data file is missing, media recovery will be required.

Oracle Tablespaces   Our tour continues into a somewhat metaphysical part of Oracle. Tablespaces are the link between the physical world of Oracle, in the form of the database datafiles, and the logical world, in the form of the Oracle tablespace. Often, we refer to a tablespace as a physi-logical structure. Oracle stores objects within tablespaces, such as tables and indexes.

A tablespace is physically made up of one or more Oracle database datafiles. Thus, the overall space allocation available in a tablespace depends on the overall allocated size of these database datafiles. A tablespace can be OFFLINE or ONLINE, and may also be in either READ WRITE or READ ONLY mode. If a tablespace is in READ ONLY mode, the contents of the tablespace will not change. Because the contents of a READ ONLY tablespace do not change, DBAs often only back up READ ONLY tablespace database datafiles once, immediately after they are made read only. Of course, if the tablespace is ever taken out of READ ONLY mode, you need to start backing up the tablespace again.

Flashback Logs   Oracle Database 10*g* introduced the capability to flashback the Oracle database to a time other than the current time. This capability is facilitated through the use of flashback logs. Flashback logs are stored in the FRA. Oracle is solely responsible for the management of flashback logs, so it will create, remove, and resize them as required. Also note that flashback logs are not archived by Oracle and are not needed for recovery. RMAN supports flashback recovery.

The Flash Recovery Area

Oracle Database 10*g* introduced the concept of the FRA, which allows you to define a central area of disk space for recovery-related files such as RMAN backups and archived redo logs. The flash recovery area should not be confused with Oracle's Flashback Database features, though the FRA does participate in Flashback Database operations. The FRA is so much more than Flashback Database, though. The following structures can be stored in the FRA:

- Archived redo logs

- RMAN backup set pieces

- RMAN datafile copies

- Flashback logs

- A copy of the database control file

- One member of each redo log group

- Control file autobackups and copies

We will discuss the FRA in much more detail in Chapters 2 and 3.

Oracle Automatic Storage Management

Oracle ASM is Oracle's answer to the need for an integrated system to manage database files. ASM supports a number of different file system types, from cooked disk drives, to raw disk drives, to NetFiler devices. The idea of ASM is to simplify the life of the DBA by making Oracle responsible for basic disk management operations such as load balancing and data protection. RMAN supports the ASM infrastructure in that you can place your database FRA on ASM disks, or you can back up directly to ASM disks.

While ASM has its place, we feel that it is mega-overkill for most Oracle installations. If you have a single, non-RAC server with two or three databases, you do not need ASM. In this book, we provide ASM coverage so that if you are using RMAN and ASM, you can back up and recover using ASM.

More About the Oracle Redo Logs

We have talked about the Oracle redo logs somewhat already, but they are such important things, even when talking about RMAN, that we wanted to dive into a bit more detail. You might ask, "But doesn't RMAN take care of everything for me?" RMAN certainly tries to take care of everything for you, but you will find times that it's your knowledge that will give you the insight to truly save the day. Indeed, just having a recipe to follow might well not be enough. You need to understand the whys and mechanics behind Oracle backup and recovery. As Carl Jung said: "The shoe that fits one person pinches another; there is no recipe for living that suits all cases." Just knowing the rudiments of backup and recovery does not prepare you for all potential problems you will face.

Redo logs are typically created when the database is first created, and as the database changes, you may find that you need to modify the online redo log files by creating more of them, making them larger, or perhaps renaming them. Since you are an enlightened DBA and want to know everything you can about backup and recovery of your database, you will want to understand online and archived redo logs. In this section, we will talk about redo logs in a bit more detail. First, we will look at redo logs in general. Next, we will look at the multiplexing of online redo log groups and the redo log sequence number. Finally, we will address administration of online redo logs.

An Overview of Redo Logs

Oracle redo logs come in two flavors:

■ Online redo logs

■ Archived redo logs

Redo logs are one of the most critical components when restoring and recovering an Oracle database. This is because redo logs store a history of almost everything that happens in your database. During normal database operations, the Oracle LGWR process will write to an online redo log, creating a change record that you really hope you never have to use.

The LGWR process will write information called redo to the online redo log files as the redo is generated by Oracle transactions. *Redo* is simply a record of what occurs in the database and the order that those events happen in. Redo is generated by almost every Oracle operation including DML, DDL, and transactional commit operations. During recovery, Oracle will read the redo and essentially replay the redo in the order it was generated to recover the database. Sometimes this recovery is behind the covers and requires no DBA activity (as with crash recovery), but sometimes, such as in the case of database or datafile recovery, the DBA has to get involved.

Online redo log files are fixed in size. Once the LGWR process has reached the end of a given online redo log file, it will close that file and try to find another online redo log file to write to. This process is called a *log switch*. A log switch is a serial process, and potentially very expensive from a performance point of view. This isn't a performance book though, so we won't go into the performance aspects of a log switch.

During a log switch, LGWR will look for an available online redo log file that it can write to. If it finds an available online redo log file, it will open that file and begin to write to it. If LGWR cannot find an available file, then it will wait for an online redo log to become available. While it's waiting, LGWR will be busy writing complaining messages to the alert log and other places, and database operations will be suspended. Database managers typically are not too happy if your databases stop, so we want to avoid that if at all possible!

Each online redo log file that is created is assigned to an *online redo log group.* In a non-clustered configuration, Oracle will only write to one redo log group at a time. If you are running Real Application Clusters (RAC), each RAC instance will write to its own set of redo log groups.

Online redo log groups can have one of several different statuses:

■ **Current**   This is the online redo log that is in use.

■ **Active**   This is an online redo log that is not in the current redo log file group, but it's still waiting for the ARCH process to finish copying redo to the archived redo logs.

■ **Inactive**   This is an online redo log that isn't active and has been archived.

■ **Unused**   This is an online redo log that has yet to be used by the Oracle database.

The status of an online redo log group can be seen by querying the V$LOG view as seen here:

```
SQL> select group#, status from v$Log;
    GROUP# STATUS
---------- ----------------
         1 INACTIVE
         2 INACTIVE
         3 INACTIVE
         4 CURRENT
```

Multiplexing Online Redo Logs

If you want to have a really bad day, then just try losing your active online redo log. If you do, it's pretty likely that your database is about to come crashing down and that you will have experienced some data loss. This is because recovery to the point of failure in an Oracle database is dependent on the availability of the online redo log. As you can see, the online redo log makes the database vulnerable to loss of a disk device, mistaken administrative delete commands, or other kinds of errors. To address this concern, you can create mirrors of each online redo log. When you have created more than one copy of an online redo log, the group that log is a member of is called a *multiplexed online redo log group.* Typically these multiplexed copies are put on different physical devices to provide additional protection for the online redo log groups. For highest availability, we recommend that you separate the members of each online redo log group onto different disk devices, different everything… Here is an example of creating a multiplexed online redo log group:

```
alter database add logfile group 4
('C:\ORACLE\ORADATA\BETA1\REDO04a.LOG','C:\ORACLE\ORADATA\BETA1\REDO04b.LOG')
size 100m reuse;
```

Each member of a multiplexed online redo log group is written to in parallel, and having multiple members in each group rarely causes performance problems.

The Log Sequence Number

As each online redo log group is written to, that group is assigned a number. This is the *log sequence number.* The first log sequence number for a new database is always 1. As the online redo log groups are written to, the number will increment by one during each log switch operation. So, the next online redo log being written to will be log sequence 2, and so on.

During normal database operations, Oracle will open an available online redo log, write redo to it, and then close it once it has filled the online redo log. Once the online redo log has filled, the LGWR process switches to another online redo log group. At that time, if the database is in ARCHIVELOG mode, LGWR also signals ARCH to wake up and start working. This round-robin style of writing to online redo logs is shown in Figure 1-1.

ARCH responds to the call from LGWR by making copies of the online redo log in the locations defined by the Oracle database parameter LOG_ARCHIVE_DEST_*n* and/or to the defined flash recovery area. Until the ARCH process has successfully completed the creation of at least one archived redo log, then the related online redo log file cannot be reused by Oracle. Depending

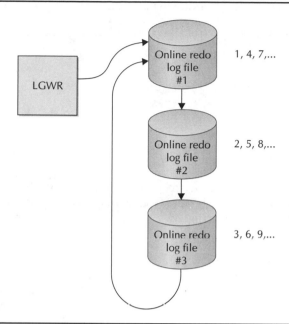

FIGURE 1-1   *Writing to online redo logs*

on your system configuration, more than one archived redo log may need to be created before the associated online redo log can be reused. As archived redo logs are created, they maintain the log sequence number assigned to the parent online redo log. That log sequence number will remain unique for that database until the database is opened using the **resetlogs** operation. Once a **resetlogs** operation is executed, then the log sequence number is reset to 1.

One final note about opening the database using the **resetlogs** command when performing recovery. If you are using Oracle Database 10*g* and later Oracle provides the ability to restore the database using a backup taken before the point in time that you issued the **resetlogs** command, when you issue the **resetlogs** command, Oracle will archive any remaining unarchived online redo logs, before the online redo logs are reset. This provides the ability to restore the database from a backup taken before the issuance of the **resetlogs** command. Using these backup files, and all the archived redo logs, you can now restore beyond the point of the **resetlogs** command. The ability to restore past the point of the **resetlogs** command relieves the DBA from the urgency of performing a backup after a **resetlogs**-based recovery (though such a backup is still important). This also provides for reduced mean-time-to-recover, as you can open the database to users after the restore, rather than having a requirement to back up the database first.

Management of Online Redo Logs

The **alter database** command is used to add or remove online redo logs. In this example, we are adding a new online redo log group to the database. The new logfile group will be group 4, and we define its size as 100m:

```
alter database add logfile group 4
'C:\ORACLE\ORADATA\BETA1\REDO04.LOG' size 100m;
```

You can see the resulting logfile group in the V$LOG and V$LOGFILE views:

```
SQL> select group#, sequence#, bytes, members from v$log
  2  where group#=4;
    GROUP#  SEQUENCE#        BYTES     MEMBERS
---------- ---------- ---------- ----------
         4          0 104,857,600           1
SQL> select group#, member from v$logfile
  2  where group#=4;
    GROUP# MEMBER
---------- ------------------------------------------------------------
         4 C:\ORACLE\ORADATA\BETA1\REDO04.LOG
```

In this next example, we remove redo log file group 4 from the database. Note that this does not physically remove the physical files. You will still have to perform this function after removing the log file group. This can be dangerous, so be careful when doing so:

```
alter database drop logfile group 4;
```

NOTE
If you are using the FRA or have set the DB_CREATE_ONLINE_LOG_DEST_n, then Oracle will remove online redo logs for you after you drop them.

To resize a logfile group, you will need to drop and then re-create it with the bigger file size.

ARCHIVELOG Mode vs. NOARCHIVELOG Mode

An Oracle database can run in one of two modes. By default, the database is created in NOARCHIVELOG mode. This mode permits normal database operations, but does not provide the capability to perform point-in-time recovery operations or online backups. If you want to do online (or hot) backups, then run the database in ARCHIVELOG mode. In ARCHIVELOG mode, the database makes copies of all online redo logs via the ARCH process, to one or more archive log destination directories.

The use of ARCHIVELOG mode requires some configuration of the database beyond simply putting it in ARCHIVELOG mode. You must also configure the ARCH process and prepare the archived redo log destination directories. Note that once an Oracle database is in ARCHIVELOG mode, that database activity will be suspended once all available online redo logs have been used. The database will remain suspended until those online redo logs have been archived. Thus, incorrect configuration of the database when it is in ARCHIVELOG mode can eventually lead to the database suspending operations because it cannot archive the current online redo logs. This might sound menacing, but really it just boils down to a few basic things:

- Configure your database properly (we cover configuration of your database for backup and recovery in this book quite well).

- Make sure you have enough space available.

■ Make sure that things are working as you expect them to. For example, if you define a flash recovery area in your ARCHIVELOG mode database, make sure the archived redo logs are being successfully written to that directory.

More coverage on the implications of ARCHIVELOG mode, how to implement it (and disable it), and configuration for ARCHIVELOG operations can be found in Chapter 3.

Oracle Logical Structures

There are several different logical structures within Oracle. These structures include tables, indexes, views, clusters, user-defined objects, and other objects within the database. Schemas own these objects, and if storage is required for the objects, that storage is allocated from a tablespace.

It is the ultimate goal of an Oracle backup and recovery strategy to be able to recover these logical structures to a given point in time. Also, it is important to recover the data in these different objects in such a way that the state of the data is consistent to a given point in time. Consider the impact, for example, if you were to recover a table as it looked at 10 A.M., but only recover its associated index as it looked at 9 A.M. The impact of such an inconsistent recovery could be awful. It is this idea of a consistent recovery that really drives Oracle's backup and recovery mechanism, and RMAN fits nicely into this backup and recovery architectural framework.

The Combined Picture

Now that we have introduced you to the various components of the Oracle database, let's quickly put together a couple of narratives that demonstrate how they all work together. First, we look at the overall database startup process, which is followed by a narrative of the basic operational use of the database.

Startup and Shutdown of the Database

Our DBA, Eliza, has just finished some work on the database, and it's time to restart it. She starts SQL*Plus and connects as SYS using the SYSDBA account. At the SQL prompt, Eliza issues the **startup** command to open the database. The following shows an example of the results of this command:

```
SQL> startup
ORACLE instance started.
Total System Global Area     84700976 bytes
Fixed Size                     282416 bytes
Variable Size                71303168 bytes
Database Buffers             12582912 bytes
Redo Buffers                   532480 bytes
Database mounted.
Database opened.
```

Recall the different phases that occur after the **startup** command is issued: instance startup, database mount, and then database open. Let's look at each of these stages now in a bit more detail.

Instance Startup (startup nomount)

The first thing that occurs when starting the database is instance startup. It is here that Oracle parses the database parameter file and makes sure that the instance is not already running by trying to acquire an instance lock. Then, the various database processes (as described in "The Oracle Processes," earlier in this chapter), such as DBWn and LGWR, are started. Also, Oracle allocates memory needed for the SGA. Once the instance has been started, Oracle reports to the user who has started it that the instance has been started back, and how much memory has been allocated to the SGA.

Had Eliza issued the command **startup nomount**, then Oracle would have stopped the database startup process after the instance was started. She might have started the instance in order to perform certain types of recovery, such as control file re-creation.

Mounting the Database (startup mount)

The next stage in the startup process is the mount stage. As Oracle passes through the mount stage, it opens the database control file. Having done that successfully, Oracle extracts the database datafile names from the control file in preparation for opening them. Note that Oracle does not actually check for the existence of the datafiles at this point, but only identifies their location from the control file. Having completed this step, Oracle reports back that it has mounted the database.

At this point, had Eliza issued the command **startup mount**, Oracle would have stopped opening the database and waited for further direction. When the Oracle instance is started and the database is mounted but not open, certain types of recovery operations may be performed, including renaming the location of database datafiles and recovery system tablespace datafiles.

Opening the Database

Eliza issued the **startup** command, however, so Oracle moves on and tries to open the database. During this stage, Oracle verifies the presence of the database datafiles and opens them. As it opens them, it checks the datafile headers and compares the SCN information contained in those headers with the SCN stored in the control files. Let's talk about these SCNs for a second.

SCNs are Oracle's method of tracking the state of the database. As changes occur in the database, they are associated with a given SCN. As these changes are flushed to the database datafiles (which occurs during a *checkpoint* operation), the headers of the datafiles are updated with the current SCN. The current SCN is also recorded in the database control file.

When Oracle tries to open a database, it checks the SCNs in each datafile and in the database control file. If the SCNs are the same and the bitmapped flags are set correctly, then the database is considered to be consistent, and the database is opened for use.

NOTE
Think of SCNs as being like the counter on a VCR. As time goes on, the counter continues to increment, indicating a temporal point in time where the tape currently is. So, if you want to watch a program on the tape, you can simply rewind (or fast forward) the tape to the counter number, and there is the beginning of the program. SCNs are the same way. When Oracle needs to recover a database, it "rewinds" to the SCN it needs to start with and then replays all of the transactions after that SCN until the database is recovered.

If the SCNs are different, then Oracle automatically performs *crash or instance recovery,* if possible. Crash or instance recovery occurs if the redo needed to generate a consistent image is in the online redo log files. If crash or instance recovery is not possible, because of a corrupted datafile or because the redo required to recover is not in the online redo logs, then Oracle requests that the DBA perform *media recovery.* Media recovery involves recovering one or more database datafiles from a backup taken of the database and is a manual process, unlike instance recovery. Assisting in media recovery is where RMAN comes in, as you will see in later chapters. Once the database open process is completed successfully (with no recovery, crash recovery, or media recovery), then the database is open for business.

Shutting Down the Database

Of course, Eliza will probably want to shut down the database at some point in time. To do so, she could issue the **shutdown** command. This command closes the database, unmounts it, and then shuts down the instance in almost the reverse order as the startup process already discussed. There are several options to the **shutdown** command.

Note in particular that a **shutdown abort** of a database is basically like simulating a database crash. This command is used often, and it rarely causes problems. Oracle generally recommends that your database be shut down in a consistent manner, if at all possible.

If you must use the **shutdown abort** command to shut down the database (and in the real world, this does happen frequently because of outage constraints), then you should reopen the database with the **startup** command (or even better, **startup restrict**). Following this, do the final shutdown on the database using the **shutdown immediate** command before performing any offline backup operations. Note that even this method may result in delays shutting down the database because of the time it takes to roll back transactions during the shutdown process.

NOTE
As long as your backup and recovery strategy is correct, it really doesn't matter whether the database is in a consistent state (as with a normal **shutdown***) or an inconsistent state (as with a* **shutdown abort***) when an offline backup occurs. Oracle does recommend that you do cold backups with the database in a consistent state, and we recommend that, too (because the online redo logs will not be getting backed up by RMAN). Finally, note that online backups eliminate this issue completely!*

Using the Database and Internals

In this section, we are going to follow some users performing different transactions in an Oracle database. First, we provide you with a graphical roadmap that puts together all the processes, memory structures, and other components of the database for you. Then, we follow a user as the user makes changes to the database. We then look at commits and how they operate. Finally, we look at database checkpoints and how they work.

Process and Database Relationships

We have discussed a number of different processes, memory structures, and other objects that make up the Oracle database. Figure 1-2 provides a graphic that might help you better understand the interrelationships between the different components in Oracle.

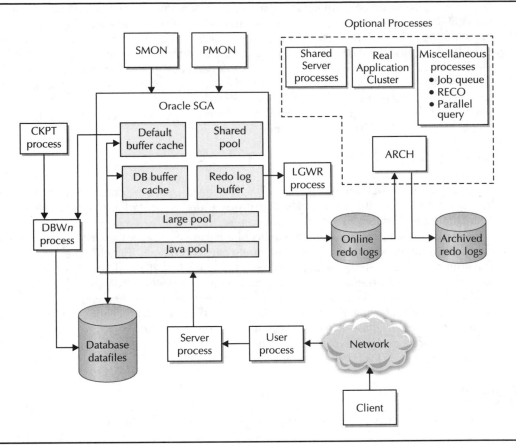

FIGURE 1-2 *A typical Oracle database*

Changing Data in the Database

Now, assume the database is open. Let's say that Fred needs to add a new record to the DEPT table for the janitorial department. So, Fred might issue a SQL statement like this:

```
INSERT INTO DEPT VALUES (60, 'JANITOR','DALLAS');
```

The **insert** statements (as well as **update** and **delete** commands) are collectively known as Data Manipulation Language (DML). As a statement is executed, redo is generated and stored in the redo log buffer in the Oracle SGA. Note that redo is generated by this command, regardless of the presence of the **commit** command. The **delete** and **update** commands work generally the same way with respect to redo generation.

One of the results of DML is that **undo** is generated and stored in *rollback segments.* **Undo** consists of instructions that allow Oracle to undo (or roll back) the statement being executed. Using **undo**, Oracle can roll back the database changes and provide *read consistent images* (also known as read consistency) to other users. Let's look a bit more at the **commit** command and read consistency.

Committing the Change

Having issued the **insert** command, Fred wants to ensure that this change is committed to the database, so he issues the **commit** command:

```
COMMIT;
```

The effects of issuing the **commit** command include the following:

- The change becomes visible to all users who query the table at a point in time after the commit occurs. If Eliza queries the DEPT table after the commit occurs, then she will see department 60. However, if Eliza had already started a query before the commit, then this query would not see the changes to the table.

- The change is recoverable if the database is in NOARCHIVELOG mode and if crash or instance recovery is required.

- The change is recoverable if the database is in ARCHIVELOG mode (assuming a valid backup and recovery strategy) and media recovery is required and if all archived and online redo logs are available.

The **commit** command causes the Oracle LGWR process to flush the online redo log buffer to the online redo logs. Uncommitted redo is flushed to the online redo logs regardless of a commit (in fact, uncommitted changes can be written to the datafiles, too). When a commit is issued, Oracle writes a *commit vector* to the redo log buffer, and the buffer is flushed to disk before the commit returns. It is this commit vector, and the fact that the commit issued by Fred's session will not return until his redo has been flushed to the online redo logs successfully, that will ensure that Fred's changes will be recoverable.

The commit Command and Read Consistency   Did you notice that Eliza was not able to see Fred's change until he issued the **commit** command? This is known as *read consistency.* Another example of read consistency would be a case where Eliza started a report before Fred committed his change. Assume that Fred committed the change during Eliza's report. In this case, it would be inconsistent for department 60 to show up in Eliza's report, since it did not exist at the time that her report started. As Eliza's report continues to run, Oracle checks the start SCN of the report query against the SCNs of the blocks being read in Oracle to produce the report output. If the time of the report is earlier than the current SCN on the data block, then Oracle goes to the rollback segments and finds undo for that block that will allow Oracle to construct an image consistent with the time that the report started.

As Fred continues other work on the database, the LGWR process writes to the online redo logs on a regular basis. At some point in time, an online redo log will fill up, and LGWR will close that log file, open the next log file, and begin writing to it. During this transition period, LGWR also signals the ARCH process to begin copying the log file that it just finished using to the archive log backup directories.

Checkpoints

Now, you might be wondering, when does this data actually get written out to the database datafiles? Recall that a checkpoint is an event in which Oracle (through DBWR) writes data out to the datafiles. There are several different kinds of checkpoints. Some of the events that result in a checkpoint are the following:

- A redo log switch

- Normal database shutdowns

- When a tablespace is taken in or out of online backup mode (see "Oracle Physical Backup and Recovery" later in this chapter)

Note that ongoing incremental checkpoints occur throughout the lifetime of the database, providing a method for Oracle to decrease the overall time required when performing crash recovery. As the database operates, Oracle is constantly writing out streams of data to the database datafiles. These writes occur in such a way as to not impede performance of the database. Oracle provides certain database parameters to assist in determining how frequently Oracle must process incremental checkpoints.

Oracle Backup and Recovery Primer

Before you use RMAN, you should understand some general backup and recovery concepts in Oracle. Backups in Oracle come in two general categories, logical and physical. In the following sections, we quickly look at logical backup and recovery and then give Oracle physical backup and recovery a full treatment.

Logical Backup and Recovery

Oracle Database 11*g* uses the Oracle Data Pump architecture to support logical backup and recovery. These utilities include the Data Pump Export program (**expdp**) and the Data Pump Import program (**impdp**). With logical backups, point-in-time recovery is not possible. RMAN does not do logical backup and recovery, so this topic is beyond the scope of this book.

Oracle Physical Backup and Recovery

Physical backups are what RMAN is all about. Before we really delve into RMAN in the remaining chapters of this book, let's first look at what is required to manually do physical backups and recoveries of an Oracle database. While RMAN removes you from much of the work involved in backup and recovery, some of the principles remain the same. Understanding the basics of manual backup and recovery will help you understand what is going on with RMAN and will help us contrast the benefits of RMAN versus previous methods of backing up Oracle.

We have already discussed ARCHIVELOG mode and NOARCHIVELOG mode in Oracle. In either mode, Oracle can do an offline backup. Further, if the database is in ARCHIVELOG mode, then Oracle can do offline or online backups. We will cover the specifics of these operations with RMAN in later chapters of this book.

Of course, if you back up a database, it would be nice to be able to recover it. Following the sections on online and offline backups, we will discuss the different Oracle recovery options available. Finally, in these sections, we take a very quick, cursory look at Oracle manual backup and recovery.

NOARCHIVELOG Mode Physical Backups

We have already discussed NOARCHIVELOG mode in the Oracle database. This mode of database operations supports backups of the database only when the database is shut down. Also, only full recovery of the database up to the point of the backup is possible in NOARCHIVELOG mode. To perform a manual backup of a database in NOARCHIVELOG mode, follow these steps (note that these steps are different if you are using RMAN, which we will cover in later chapters):

1. Shut down the database completely.
2. Back up all database datafiles, the control files, and the online redo logs.
3. Restart the database.

ARCHIVELOG Mode Physical Backups

If you are running your database in ARCHIVELOG mode, you can continue to perform full backups of your database with the database either running or shut down. Even if you perform the backup with the database shut down, you will want to use a slightly different cold backup procedure:

1. Shut down the database completely.
2. Back up all database datafiles.
3. Restart the database.
4. Force an online redo log switch with the **alter system switch logfile** command. Once the online redo logs have been archived, back up all archived redo logs.
5. Create a backup of the control file using the **alter database backup control file to trace** and **alter database backup controlfile to 'file_name'** commands.

Of course, with your database in ARCHIVELOG mode, you may well want to do online, or hot, backups of your database. With the database in ARCHIVELOG mode, Oracle allows you to back up each individual tablespace and its datafiles while the database is up and running. The nice thing about this is that you can back up selective parts of your database at different times. To do an online backup of your tablespaces, follow this procedure:

1. Use the **alter tablespace begin backup** command to put the tablespaces and datafiles that you wish to back up in online backup mode. If you want to back up the entire database, you can use the **alter database begin backup** command to put all the database tablespaces in hot backup mode.
2. Back up the datafiles associated with the tablespace you have just put in hot backup mode. (You can opt to just back up specific datafiles.)
3. Take the tablespaces out of hot backup mode by issuing the **alter tablespace end backup** command for each tablespace you put in online backup mode in Step 1. If you want to take all tablespaces out of hot backup mode, use the **alter database end backup** command.
4. Force an online redo log switch with the **alter system switch logfile** command.
5. Once the log switch has completed and the current online redo log has been archived, back up all the archived redo logs.

Note the log switch and backup of archived redo logs in Step 5. This is required, because all redo generated during the backup must be available to apply should a recovery be required. While Oracle continues to physically update the datafiles during the online backup (except for the datafile headers), there is a possibility of block splitting during backup operations, which will make the backed up datafile inconsistent. Further, since a database datafile might be written after it has been backed up but before the end of the overall backup process, it is important to have the redo generated during the backup to apply during recovery because each datafile on the backup might well be current as of a different SCN, and thus the datafile backup images will be inconsistent.

Redo generation changes when you issue the **alter tablespace begin backup** command or **alter database begin backup** command. Typically, Oracle only stores change vectors as redo records. These are small records that just define the change that has taken place. When a datafile is in online backup mode, Oracle will record the entire block that is being changed rather than just the change vectors. This means total redo generation during online backups can increase significantly. This can impact disk space requirements and CPU overhead during the hot backup process. RMAN enables you to perform hot backups without having to put a tablespace in hot backup mode, thus eliminating the additional I/O you would otherwise experience. Things return to normal when you end the online backup status of the datafiles.

Note that in both backups in ARCHIVELOG mode (online and offline), we do not back up the online redo logs, and instead back up the archived redo logs of the database. In addition, we do not back up the control file, but rather create backup control files. We do this because we never want to run the risk of overwriting the online redo logs or control files during a recovery.

You might wonder why we don't want to recover the online redo logs. During a recovery in ARCHIVELOG mode, the most current redo is likely to be available in the online redo logs, and thus the current online redo log will be required for full point-in-time recovery. Because of this, we do not overwrite the online redo logs during a recovery of a database that is in ARCHIVELOG mode. If the online redo logs are lost as a result of the loss of the database (and hopefully this will not be the case), then you will have to do point-in-time recovery with all available archived redo logs.

For much the same reason that we don't back up the online redo logs, we don't back up the control files. Because the current control file contains the latest online and archived redo log information, we do not want to overwrite that information with earlier information on these objects. In case we lose all of our control files, we will use a backup control file to recover the database.

Finally, consider performing supplemental backups of archived redo log files and other means of protecting the archived redo logs from loss. Loss of an archived redo log directly impacts your ability to recover your database to the point of failure. If you lose an archived redo log and that log sequence number is no longer part of the online redo log groups, then you will not be able to recover your database beyond the archived redo log sequence prior to the sequence number of the lost archived redo log.

NOARCHIVELOG Mode Recoveries

If you need to recover a backup taken in NOARCHIVELOG mode, doing so is as simple as recovering all the database datafiles, the control files, and the online redo logs and starting the database. Of course, a total recovery may require such things as recovering the Oracle RDBMS software, the parameter file, and other required Oracle items, which we will discuss in the last section of this chapter.

Note that a recovery in NOARCHIVELOG mode is only possible to the point in time that you took your last backup. If you are recovering a database backed up in NOARCHIVELOG mode, you can only recover the database to the point of the backup. No database changes after the point of the backup can be recovered if your database is in NOARCHIVELOG mode.

ARCHIVELOG Mode Recoveries

A database that is in ARCHIVELOG mode can be backed up using online or offline backups. The fortunate thing about ARCHIVELOG mode, as opposed to NOARCHIVELOG mode, is that you can recover the database to the point of the failure that occurred. In addition, you can choose to recover the database to a specific point in time, or to a specific point in time based on the change number.

ARCHIVELOG mode recoveries also allow you to do specific recoveries on datafiles, tablespaces, or the entire database. In addition, you can do point-in-time recovery or recovery to a specific SCN. Let's quickly look at each of these options.

In this section, we briefly cover full database recoveries in ARCHIVELOG mode. We then look at tablespace and datafile recoveries, followed by point-in-time recoveries.

ARCHIVELOG Mode Full Recovery   You can recover a database backup in ARCHIVELOG mode up to the point of failure, assuming that the failure of the database did not compromise at least one member of each of your current online redo log groups and any archived redo logs that were not backed up. If you have lost your archived redo logs or online redo logs, then you will need to perform some form of point-in-time recovery, as discussed later in this section. Also, if you have lost all copies of your current control file, you will need to recover it and perform incomplete recovery.

To perform full database recovery from a backup of a database in ARCHIVELOG mode, follow this procedure:

1.   Restore all the database datafiles from your backup.
2.   Restore all backed up archived redo logs.
3.   Mount the database (**startup mount**).
4.   Recover the database (**recover database**).
5.   Oracle prompts you to apply redo from the archived redo logs. Simply enter **AUTO** at the prompt, and Oracle will automatically apply all redo logs.
6.   Once all redo logs have been applied, open the recovered database (**alter database open**).

ARCHIVELOG Tablespace and Datafile Recovery   Tablespace and datafile recovery can be performed with the database mounted or open. To perform a recovery of a tablespace in Oracle with the database open, follow these steps:

1.   Take the tablespace offline (**alter tablespace offline**).
2.   Restore all datafiles associated with the tablespace to be recovered.
3.   Recover the tablespace (**recover tablespace**) online.
4.   Once recovery has completed, bring the tablespace online (**alter tablespace online**).

Just as you can recover a tablespace, you can also recover specific datafiles. This has the benefit of leaving the tablespace online. Only data that resides in the offline datafiles will be unavailable during the recovery process. The rest of the database will remain available during the recovery. Here is a basic outline of a datafile recovery:

1. Take the datafile offline (**alter database datafile 'file_name' offline**).

2. Restore all datafiles to be recovered.

3. Recover the tablespace (**recover datafile**) online.

4. Once recovery has completed, bring the datafile online (**alter database datafile 'file_name' online**).

ARCHIVELOG Point-In-Time Recoveries   Another benefit of ARCHIVELOG mode is the capability to recover a database to a given point in time rather than to the point of failure. This capability is used often when creating a clone database (perhaps for testing or reporting purposes) or in the event of major application or user error. You can recover a database to either a specific point in time or a specific database SCN.

If you want to recover a tablespace to a point in time, you need to recover the entire database to the same point in time (unless you perform tablespace point-in-time recovery, which is a different topic). For example, assume that you have an accounting database, that most of your data is in the ACCT tablespace, and that you wish to recover the database back in time two days. You cannot just restore the ACCT tablespace and recover it to a point in time two days ago, because the remaining tablespaces (SYSTEM, TEMP, and RBS, for example) will still be consistent to the current point in time, and the database will fail to open because it will be inconsistent.

To recover a database to a point in time, follow these steps:

1. Recover all database datafiles from a backup that ended before the point in time that you want to recover the database to.

2. Recover the database to the point in time that you wish it to be recovered to. Use the command **recover database until time '01-01-2010 21:00:00'** and apply the redo logs as required.

3. Once the recovery is complete, open the database using the **alter database open resetlogs** command.

You can also choose to recover the database using an SCN number:

1. Recover all database datafiles from a backup that ended before the point in time that you want to recover the database to.

2. Recover the database to the SCN that you wish it to be recovered to. Use the command **recover database until change '221122'** and apply the redo logs as required.

3. Once the recovery is complete, open the database.

Further, you can apply changes to the database and manually cancel the process after a specific archived redo log has been applied:

1. Recover all database datafiles from a backup that ended before the point in time that you want to recover the database to.

2. Recover the database to the point in time that you wish it to be recovered to. Use the command **recover database until cancel** and apply the redo logs as required. When you have applied the last archived redo log, simply issue the **cancel** command to finish applying redo.

3. Once the recovery is complete, open the database.

Keep in mind the concept of database consistency when doing point-in-time recovery (or any recovery, for that matter). If you are going to recover a database to a given point in time, you must do so with a backup that finished before the point in time that you wish to recover to. Also, you must have all the archived redo logs (and possibly the remaining online redo logs) available to complete recovery.

A Word About Flashback Database   Another recovery method available to you is the use of Oracle's flashback features. We will cover Oracle's flashback features in more depth in Chapter 13, but know that with the various flashback functionality, you can significantly reduce the overall time it takes to recover your database from user- and application-level errors. RMAN supports some of the Oracle Database 11*g* flashback features, so it is most appropriate to cover those in this book.

Backing Up Other Oracle Components

We have quickly covered the essentials of backup and recovery for Oracle. One last issue that remains to be covered are the things that need to be backed up. These are items that generally are backed up with less frequency because they change rarely. These items include

- The Oracle RDBMS software (Oracle Home and the Oracle Inventory).

- Network parameter files (names.ora, sqlnet.ora, and tnsnames.ora).

- Database parameter files (init.ora, INI files, and so forth). Note that RMAN does allow you to back up the database parameter file (only if it's a SPFILE) along with the control file!

- The system oratab file and other system Oracle-related files (for example, all rc startup scripts for Oracle).

It is important that these items be backed up regularly as a part of your backup and recovery process. You need to plan to back up these items regardless of whether you do manual backups or RMAN backups, because RMAN does not back up these items either.

As you can see, the process of backup and recovery of an Oracle database can involve a number of steps. Since DBAs want to make sure they do backups correctly every time, they generally write a number of scripts for this purpose. There are a few problems with this practice. First of all, scripts can break. When the script breaks, who is going to support it, particularly when the DBA who wrote it moves to a new position somewhere in the inaccessible tundra in northern Alaska? Second, either you have to write the script to keep track of when you add or remove datafiles, or you have to manually add or remove datafiles from the script as required.

With RMAN, you get a backup and recovery product that is included with the base database product for free, and that reduces the complexity of the backup and recovery process. Also, you get the benefit of Oracle support when you run into a problem. Finally, with RMAN, you get additional features that no other backup and recovery process can match. We will look at those in coming chapters.

RMAN solves all of these problems and adds features that make its use even more beneficial for the DBA. In this book, we will look at these features and how they can help make your life easier and make your database backups more reliable.

Summary

We didn't discuss RMAN much in this chapter, but we laid some important groundwork for future discussions of RMAN that you will find in later chapters. As promised, we covered some essential backup and recovery concepts, such as high availability and backup and recovery planning, that are central to the purpose of RMAN. We then defined several Oracle terms that you need to be familiar with later in this text. We then reviewed the Oracle database architecture and internal operations. We cannot stress enough how important it is to have an understanding of how Oracle works inside when it comes time to actually recover your database in an emergency situation. Finally, we discussed manual backup and recovery operations in Oracle. Contrast these to the same RMAN operations in later chapters, and you will find that RMAN is ultimately an easy solution to backup and recovery of your Oracle database.

CHAPTER
2

Introduction to the
RMAN Architecture

his chapter will take you through each of the components in the RMAN architecture one by one, explaining the role each plays in a successful backup or recovery of the Oracle database. Most of this discussion assumes that you have a good understanding of the Oracle RDBMS architecture. If you are not familiar at a basic level with the different components of an Oracle database, you might want to read the brief introduction in Chapter 1, or pick up a beginner's guide to database administration, before continuing. After we discuss the different components for backup and recovery, we walk through a simple backup procedure to disk and talk about each component in action.

Server-Managed Recovery

In the previous chapter, you learned the principles and practices of backup and recovery in the old world. It involved creating and running scripts to capture the filenames, associate them with tablespaces, get the tablespaces into backup mode, get an OS utility to perform the copy, and then stop backup mode.

But this book is really about using Recovery Manager (RMAN). Recovery Manager implements a type of *server-managed recovery* (SMR). SMR refers to the ability of the database to perform the operations required to keep itself backed up successfully. It does so by relying on built-in code in the Oracle RDBMS kernel. Who knows more about the schematics of the database than the database itself?

The power of SMR comes from what details it can eliminate on your behalf. As the degree of enterprise complexity increases, and the number of databases that a single DBA is responsible for increases, personally troubleshooting dozens or even hundreds of individual scripts becomes too burdensome. In other words, as the move to "grid computing" becomes more mainstreamed, the days of personally eyeballing all the little details of each database backup become a thing of the past. Instead, many of the nitpicky details of backup management get handled by the database itself, allowing us to take a step back from the day-to-day upkeep and to concentrate on more important things. Granted, the utilization of RMAN introduces certain complexities that overshadow the complete level of ease that might be promised by SMR—why else would you be reading this book? But the blood, sweat, and tears you pour into RMAN will give you huge payoffs. You'll see.

The RMAN Utility

RMAN is the specific implementation of SMR provided by Oracle. RMAN is a stand-alone application that makes a client connection to the Oracle database to access internal backup and recovery packages. It is, at its very core, nothing more than a command interpreter that takes simplified commands you type and turns those commands into remote procedure calls (RPCs) that are executed at the database.

We point this out primarily to make one thing very clear: RMAN does very little work. Sure, the coordination of events is important, but the real work of actually backing up and recovering a database is performed by processes at the target database itself. The *target database* refers to the database that is being backed up. The Oracle database has internal packages that actually take the PL/SQL blocks passed from RMAN and turn them into system calls to read from, and write to, the disk subsystem of your database server.

The RMAN utility is installed as part of the Database Utilities suite of command-line utilities. This suite includes Data Pump, SQL*Loader, DBNEWID, and dbverify. During a typical Oracle installation, RMAN will be installed. It is included with Enterprise and Standard Editions, although there are restrictions if you have a license only for Standard Edition: without Enterprise Edition,

RMAN can only allocate a single channel for backups. If you are performing a client installation, it will be installed if you choose the Administrator option instead of the Runtime client option.

The RMAN utility is made up of two pieces: the executable file and the recover.bsq file. The recover.bsq file is essentially the library file, from which the executable file extracts code for creating PL/SQL calls to the target. The recover.bsq file is the brains of the whole operation. These two files are invariably linked and logically make up the RMAN client utility. It is worth pointing out that the recover.bsq file and the executable file must be the same version or nothing will work.

The RMAN utility serves a distinct, orderly, and predictable purpose: it interprets commands you provide into PL/SQL calls that are remotely executed at the target database. The command language is unique to RMAN, and using it takes a little practice. It is essentially a stripped-down list of all the things you need to do to back up, restore, or recover databases, or to manipulate those backups in some way. These commands are interpreted by the executable translator, then matched to PL/SQL blocks in the recover.bsq file. RMAN then passes these RPCs to the database to gather information based on what you have requested. If your command requires an I/O operation (in other words, a backup command or a restore command), then when this information is returned, RMAN prepares another block of procedures and passes it back to the target database. These blocks are responsible for engaging the system calls to the OS for specific read or write operations.

RMAN and Database Privileges

RMAN needs to access packages at the target database that exist in the SYS schema. In addition, RMAN requires the privileges necessary to start up, shut down, and—during restore operations—create the target database. Therefore, RMAN always connects to the target database as a sysdba user. Don't worry, you do not need to specify this as you would from SQL*Plus; because RMAN requires it for every target database connection, it is assumed. Therefore, when you connect to the target, RMAN automatically supplies the "as sysdba" to the connection:

```
RMAN> connect target sys/password
connected to target database: PROD (DBID=4159396170)
```

If you try to connect as someone who does not have sysdba privileges, RMAN will give you an error:

```
RMAN> connect target /
RMAN-00571: ===========================================================
RMAN-00569: =============== ERROR MESSAGE STACK FOLLOWS =============
RMAN-00571: ===========================================================
ORA-01031: insufficient privileges
```

This is a common error during the setup and configuration phase of RMAN. It is encountered when you are not logged into your server as a member of the dba group. This OS group controls the authentication of sysdba privileges to all Oracle databases on the server. (The name dba is the default and is not required. Some OS installs use a different name, and you are by no means obligated to use dba.) Typically, most Unix systems have a user named oracle that is a member of the group dba. This is the user that installs the Oracle software to begin with, and in most modern configurations, you will have sudo set up so that you can **'sudo oracle'**—still logged in as yourself, but assuming oracle privileges. It doesn't matter who you connect as within RMAN—you will always be connected as a sysdba user, with access to the SYS schema and the ability to start up and shut down the database. On Windows platforms, Oracle creates a local group called ORA_DBA and adds the installing user to the group.

If you are logged in as a user who does not have dba group membership and you will need to use RMAN, then you must create and use a password file for your target database. If you will be connecting RMAN from a client system across the network, you need to create and use a password file. The configuration steps for this can be found in Chapter 3.

The Network Topology of RMAN Backups

The client/server architecture of RMAN inevitably leads to hours of confusion. This confusion typically comes from where RMAN is being executed, versus where the backup work is actually being done. RMAN is a client application that attaches to the target database via an Oracle Net connection. If you are running the RMAN executable in the same ORACLE_HOME as your target database, then this Oracle Net connection can be a bequeath, or local, connection and won't require you to provide an Oracle Net alias—so long as you have the appropriate ORACLE_SID variable set in your environment. Otherwise, you will need to configure your tnsnames.ora file with an entry for your target database, and you will need to do this from the location where you will be running RMAN. Figure 2-1 provides an illustration of the network topology of different RMAN locations.

Running RMAN Remotely

If you are responsible for many databases spread over the enterprise, one option is to consolidate your RMAN application at a single client system, where you can better manage your tnsnames.ora entries. All your RMAN scripts can be consolidated, and you have no confusion later on where RMAN is running. You know exactly where it is running: on your laptop, your desktop, or your Linux workstation. This client/server model makes sense, as well, if you will be using a recovery catalog in your RMAN configuration, as you will be making more than one Oracle Net connection each time you operate RMAN. On the other hand, running RMAN from a different system (or even from a different ORACLE_HOME) than the target database means you will be required to set up a password file, leading to more configuration and management at each of your target databases.

FIGURE 2-1 *Five different locations (and versions) for the RMAN executable*

> ### Who Uses a Recovery Catalog?
> A recovery catalog is a repository for RMAN's backup history, with metadata about when the backups were taken, what was backed up, and how big the backups are. It includes crucial information about these backups that is necessary for recovery. This metadata is extracted from the default location, the target database control file, and held in database tables within a user's schema. Do you need a recovery catalog? Not really—only stored scripts functionality actually requires the catalog. If you end up configuring a more complex environment with standby configurations (Chapter 20), or sync/split configurations (Chapter 22), you will need one. Does a recovery catalog come in handy? Usually. Does a recovery catalog add a layer of complexity? Indubitably. Chapter 3, which discusses the creation and setup of a recovery catalog, goes into greater depth about why you should or should not use a recovery catalog. We provide a discussion of the recovery catalog architecture later in this chapter.

If you will be making a remote connection from RMAN to the target database, you need to create a tnsnames.ora entry that can connect you to the target database with a dedicated server process. RMAN cannot use Shared Servers (formerly known as Multi-Threaded Servers, or MTS) to make a database connection. So if you use Shared Servers, which is the default setup on all new installations, then you need to create a separate Oracle Net alias that uses a dedicated server process. The difference between the two can be seen in the following sample tsnames.ora file. Note that the first alias entry is for dedicated server processes, and the second uses the Shared Servers architecture.

```
PROD_RMAN =
  (DESCRIPTION =
    (ADDRESS_LIST =
      (ADDRESS = (PROTOCOL = TCP)(HOST = cervantes)(PORT = 1521))
    )
    (CONNECT_DATA =
      (SERVER = DEDICATED)
      (SERVICE_NAME = prod)
    )
  )
PROD =
  (DESCRIPTION =
    (ADDRESS_LIST =
      (ADDRESS = (PROTOCOL = TCP)(HOST = cervantes)(PORT = 1521))
    )
    (CONNECT_DATA =
      (SERVER = SHARED)
      (SERVICE_NAME = prod)
    )
  )
```

Running RMAN Locally from the Target Database's ORACLE_HOME

In our opinion, running RMAN locally from each target database is the best way to manage a large enterprise with hundreds (or thousands) of database targets. Because of RMAN's legendary compatibility headaches, keeping the rman.exe bundled tightly to the target database will save you time in the long run. There are drawbacks to deploying your RMAN backups in this fashion, but with many deployments under our belt, we feel that it is the best way to go.

Running RMAN locally means you can always make a bequeath connection to the database, requiring no password file setup and no tnsnames.ora configuration. Bear in mind that the simplicity of this option is also its drawback: as soon as you want to introduce a recovery catalog, or perform a database duplication operation, you introduce all the elements that you are trying to avoid in the first place. This option can also lead to confusion during usage: because you always make a local connection to the database, it is easy to connect to the wrong target database. It can also be confusing to know which environment you are connecting from; if you have more than one Oracle software installation on your system (and who doesn't?), then you can go down a time-sucking rat hole if you assume you are connecting to your PROD instance, when in fact you set up your ORACLE_HOME and ORACLE_SID environment variables for the TEST instance.

Perhaps the true difference between running RMAN from your desktop workstation and running it locally at each target database server comes down to OS host security. To run RMAN locally, you always have to be able to log into each database server as the oracle user at the OS level and to have privileges defined for such. However, if you always make an Oracle Net connection to the database from a remote RMAN executable, you need never have host login credentials.

Choose your option wisely. We've stated our preference, and then given you its bad news. As Figure 2-2 depicts, even our simplification into two options—client RMAN or server RMAN—can be tinkered with, giving you a hybrid model that fits your needs. Figure 2-2 shows five different scenarios:

1. RMAN runs as a client connection from the DBA's workstation, because the DBA in charge of backing up PRODWB and DW_PROD does not have the oracle user password on the production database server.

FIGURE 2-2 *Running different versions of the RMAN executable in the enterprise*

2. RMAN backs up DW_PROD remotely, as with PRODWB, due to security restrictions on the database production server.

3. The 10.2 TEST database is backed up with a local RMAN executable that runs from the TEST $ORACLE_HOME.

4. The 11.1.0 DEV database is backed up locally. Because the DBA has oracle user privileges on the Test and Dev Server, this is feasible, and it minimizes the number of client installs to maintain at the local workstation.

5. The 11.2.0 DEV database is backed up locally as well, for the same reasons as the 11.1.0 DEV database.

Remember to remain flexible in your RMAN topology. At times you will need to run your backups in NOCATALOG mode, using the local RMAN executable. And there may come a time when you need to run a remote RMAN job as well.

The Database Control File

So far, we have discussed the RMAN executable and its role in the process of using server-managed recovery with Oracle 11g. As we said, the real work is being done at the target database—it's backing itself up. Next, we must discuss the role of the control file in an RMAN backup or recovery process.

The control file has a day job already; it is responsible for the physical schematics of the database. The name says it all: the control file controls where the physical files of a database can be found, and what header information each file currently contains (or should contain). Its contents include datafile information, redo log information, and archive log information. It has a snapshot of each file header for the critical files associated with the database. Because of this wealth of information, the control file has been the primary component of any recovery operation prior to RMAN (Chapter 1 discusses this in greater detail).

Because of the control file's role as the repository of database file information, it makes sense that RMAN would utilize the control file to pull information about what needs to be backed up. And that's just what it does: RMAN uses the control file to compile file lists, obtain checkpoint information, and determine recoverability. By accessing the control file directly, RMAN can compile file lists without a user having to create the list herself, eliminating one of the most tiresome steps of backup scripting. And RMAN does not require that the script be modified when a new file is added. It already knows about your new file. RMAN knows this because the control file knows this.

The control file also moonlights as an RMAN data repository. After RMAN completes a backup of any portion of the database, it writes a record of that backup to the control file, along with checkpoint information about when the backup was started and completed. This is one of the primary reasons that the control file grew exponentially in size between Oracle version 7 and Oracle version 8—RMAN tables in the control file. These records are often referred to as *metadata*—data about the data recorded in the actual backup. This metadata will also be stored in a recovery catalog when one is used (see Chapter 3).

Record Reuse in the Control File

The control file can grow to meet space demands. When a new record is added for a new datafile, a new log file, or a new RMAN backup, the control file can expand to meet these demands. However, there are limitations. As most databases live for years, in which thousands of redo logs switch and thousands of checkpoints occur, the control file has to be able to eliminate some data that is no longer necessary. So, it ages out information as it needs space and reuses certain "slots" in tables in round-robin fashion. However, some information cannot be eliminated—for instance, the list of datafiles. This information is critical for the minute-to-minute database operation, and new space *must* be made available for these records.

The control file thus separates its internal data into two types of records: circular reuse records and noncircular reuse records. *Circular reuse records* are records that include information that can be aged out of the control file if push comes to shove. This includes, for instance, archive log history information, which can be removed without affecting the production database. *Noncircular reuse records* are those records that cannot be sacrificed. If the control file runs out of space for these records, the file expands to make more room. These records include datafile and log file lists.

The record of RMAN backups in the control file falls into the category of circular reuse records, meaning that the records will get aged out if the control file section that contains them becomes full. This can be catastrophic to a recovery situation: without the record of the backups in the control file, it is as though the backups never took place. Remember this: if the control file does not have a record of your RMAN backup, the backup cannot easily be used by RMAN for recovery (we'll explain how to re-add backups to the control file records in Chapter 12). This makes the control file a critical piece in the RMAN equation. Without one, we have nothing. If records get aged out, then we have created a lot of manual labor to rediscover the backups.

Fear not, though. Often, it is unimportant when records get aged out; it takes so long for the control file to fill up, the backups that are removed are obsolete. You can also set a larger timeframe for when the control file will age out records. This is controlled by the init.ora parameter CONTROL FILE_RECORD_KEEP_TIME. By default, this parameter is set to 7 (in days). This means that if a record is less than seven days old, the control file will not delete it, but rather expand the control file section. You can set this to a higher value, say, 30 days, so that the control file always expands, until only records older than a month will be overwritten when necessary. Setting this to a higher day value is a good idea, but the reverse is not true. Setting this parameter to 0 means that the record section never expands, in which case you are flirting with disaster.

In addition, if you will be implementing a recovery catalog, you need not worry about circular reuse records. As long as you resync your catalog at least once within the timeframe specified by the CONTROL FILE_RECORD_KEEP_TIME parameter, then let those records age out—the recovery catalog never ages out records.

The Snapshot Control File

As you can tell, the control file is a busy little file. It's responsible for schematic information about the database, which includes checkpoint SCN information for recovery. This constant SCN and file management is critical to the livelihood of your database, so the control file must be available for usage by the RDBMS on a constant basis.

This poses a problem for RMAN. RMAN needs to get a consistent view of the control file when it sets out to make a backup of every datafile. It only needs to know the most recent checkpoint information and file schematic information at the time the backup begins. After the backup starts, RMAN needs this information to stay consistent for the duration of the backup operation; in other words, it needs a *read consistent* view of the control file. With the constant updates from the database, this is nearly impossible—unless RMAN were to lock the control file for the duration of the backup. But that would mean the database could not advance the checkpoint or switch logs or produce new archive logs. Impossible.

To get around this, RMAN uses the *snapshot control file,* an exact copy of your control file that is only used by RMAN during backup and resync operations. At the beginning of these

Re-Creating the Control File: RMAN Users Beware!

It used to be that certain conditions required the occasional rebuild of the database control file, such as resetting the MAXLOGFILES parameter or the MAXLOGHISTORY parameter. Certain parameters cannot be set unless you rebuild the control file, because these parameters define the size of the internal control file tables that hold noncircular reuse records. Therefore, if you need that section to be larger, you have to rebuild the control file.

If you use RMAN and you do not use a recovery catalog, be very careful of the control file rebuild. When you issue the command

```
alter database backup control file to trace;
```

the script that is generated does not include the information in the control file that identifies your backups. *Without these backup records, you cannot access the backups when they are needed for recovery.* All RMAN information is lost, and you cannot get it back. The only RMAN information that gets rebuilt when you rebuild the control file is any permanent configuration parameters you have set with RMAN. In Oracle 10g and higher, a new mechanism generates limited backup metadata within a control file, but you are still building in a lot of manual work that never used to exist. Therefore, we encourage you to avoid a control file rebuild at all costs.

If you back up the control file to a binary file, instead of to trace, then all backup information is preserved. This command looks like the following:

```
alter database backup controlfile to '/u01/backup/bkup_cfile.ctl';
```

operations, RMAN refreshes the snapshot control file from the actual control file, thus putting a momentary lock on the control file. Then, RMAN switches to the snapshot and uses it for the duration of the backup; in this way, it has read consistency without holding up database activity.

By default, the snapshot control file exists in the ORACLE_HOME/dbs directory on Unix platforms and in the ORACLE_HOME/database directory on Windows. It has a default name of SNCF<ORACLE_SID>.ORA. This can be modified or changed at any time by using the **configure snapshot controlfile** command:

```
configure snapshot controlfile name to '<location\file_name>';
```

Certain conditions might lead to the following error on the snapshot control file, which is typically the first time a person ever notices the file even exists:

```
RMAN-08512: waiting for snapshot controlfile enqueue
```

This error happens when the snapshot control file header is locked by a process other than the one requesting the enqueue. If you have multiple backup jobs, it may be that you are trying to run two backup jobs simultaneously from two different RMAN sessions. To troubleshoot this error, open a SQL*Plus session and run the following SQL statement:

```
SELECT s.sid, username AS "User", program, module, action, logon_time
"Logon", l.*
FROM v$session s, v$enqueue_lock l
WHERE l.sid = s.sid and l.type = 'CF' AND l.id1 = 0 and l.id2 = 2;
```

The RMAN Server Processes

RMAN makes a client connection to the target database, and two server processes are spawned. The primary process is used to make calls to packages in the SYS schema in order to perform the backup or recovery operations. This process coordinates the work of the channel processes during backups and restores.

The secondary, or shadow, process polls any long-running transactions in RMAN and then logs the information internally. You can view the results of this polling in the view V$SESSION_LONGOPS:

```
SELECT SID, SERIAL#, CONTEXT, SOFAR, TOTALWORK,
       ROUND(SOFAR/TOTALWORK*100,2) "%_COMPLETE"
FROM V$SESSION_LONGOPS
WHERE OPNAME LIKE 'RMAN%'
AND OPNAME NOT LIKE '%aggregate%'
AND TOTALWORK != 0
AND SOFAR <> TOTALWORK
/
```

You can also view these processes in the V$SESSION view. When RMAN allocates a channel, it provides the session ID information in the output:

```
allocated channel: ORA_DISK_1
channel ORA_DISK_1: sid=16 devtype=DISK
```

The "sid" information corresponds to the SID column in V$SESSION. So you could construct a query such as this:

```
SQL> column client_info format a30
SQL> column program format a15
SQL> select sid, saddr, paddr, program, client_info
     from v$session where sid=16;
     SID SADDR    PADDR    PROGRAM         CLIENT_INFO
---------- -------- -------- --------------- ------------------------
      16 682144E8 681E82BC RMAN.EXE        rman channel=ORA_DISK_1
```

RMAN Channel Processes

In addition to the two default processes, an individual process is created for every channel that you allocate during a backup or restore operation. In RMAN lingo, the *channel* is the server process at the target database that coordinates the reads from the datafiles and the writes to the specified location during backup. During a restore, the channel coordinates reads from the backup location and the writing of data blocks to the datafile locations. There are only two kinds of channels: disk channels and tape channels. You cannot allocate both kinds of channels for a single backup operation—you are writing the backup either to disk or to tape. Like the background RMAN process, the channel processes can be tracked from the data dictionary, and then correlated with a SID at the OS level. It is the activity of these channel processes that gets logged by the polling shadow process into the V$SESSION_LONGOPS view.

RMAN and I/O Slaves

RMAN can utilize I/O slaves if they are configured on the target database. For the purposes of RMAN backups and restores, two kinds of slaves are used: disk I/O slaves and tape I/O slaves.

Disk I/O slaves are configured using the parameter DBWR_IO_SLAVES. This parameter can be set to any number of values, and its primary use in life is to wake up extra DBWR slaves for disk writes when the dirty buffers are flushed to disk from the buffer cache. However, if this parameter is set to any non-zero value, be it 1 or 12 or 32, RMAN throws a switch that will automatically engage four I/O slaves per channel to assist with reading data blocks into RMAN memory buffers. This is a nice feature, but it changes considerably the way in which RMAN allocates memory. Using DBWR_IO_SLAVES is only important if your OS platform does not support native asynchronous I/O, or if you have disabled asynchronous I/O for the Oracle RDBMS. If you have asynchronous I/O enabled, then you do not need to use disk I/O slaves.

Tape I/O slaves assist with server process access to the tape device. If you have the parameter BACKUP_TAPE_IO_SLAVES set to TRUE, then RMAN will allocate a single I/O slave per tape channel process to assist with writes to the tape location. Unlike disk I/O slaves, this parameter affects no part of the database other than RMAN tape backups. Because there is no native asynchronous I/O to tape devices, we recommend you set this parameter to TRUE. It will help keep your tape drives streaming, meaning better performance on backups and restores. Chapter 16 discusses tape streaming in more depth.

The SYS Packages Used by RMAN

The RMAN server process that coordinates the work of the channels has access to two packages in the SYS schema: DBMS_RCVMAN and DBMS_BACKUP_RESTORE. These two packages compose the entirety of the RMAN functionality in the target database.

SYS.DBMS_RCVMAN

DBMS_RCVMAN is the package that is used to access the tables in the control file and pass this information to RMAN so it can build backup and restore operations that accurately reflect the database schematics. This package is responsible for setting TIME operators and verifying checkpoint information in the datafile headers prior to running any operation. It also checks file locations and sizes, along with other information concerning node affinity (in a RAC environment) and disk affinity. This kind of information affects performance, and RMAN has automatic load-balancing and performance-enhancing algorithms that it runs through prior to building the actual backup/restore commands. Chapter 16 talks in depth about these performance gains. Stay tuned.

SYS.DBMS_BACKUP_RESTORE

SYS.DBMS_RCVMAN accesses the control file and verifies all the requisite information. It passes this information back to the RMAN server process, which can then create PL/SQL blocks based on code in the recover.bsq file. These PL/SQL blocks are made up of calls to the package DBMS_BACKUP_RESTORE, the true workhorse of RMAN. DBMS_BACKUP_RESTORE is the actual package that creates system calls to back up datafiles, control files, and archived redo logs. RMAN takes the information returned from DBMS_RCVMAN, divvies out the work among the channels based on the load-balancing algorithm, and then creates a series of calls to DBMS_BACKUP_RESTORE.

It is the work of DBMS_BACKUP_RESTORE that you can track in V$SESSION_LONGOPS. It performs the backup and restore operations. In addition, it accesses the control file, but only in a very limited way. It accesses it to back it up (actually, it backs up the snapshot control file), and to write backup information to it after backups have completed. Once it has completed a backup set, it writes to tables in the control file the information about when the backup was taken, how long it took to complete, and the size and name of the backup.

RMAN Packages in the Kernel

Both of these RMAN packages are installed by default by running the catproc.sql script when the database is created. There is no way to omit them during database creation, and therefore they exist in every Oracle database since version 8.0.3. What this means to you is that no configuration by you is required for RMAN to work. You can run RMAN right now and start backing up your database.

These packages have another important trait: they are hard-coded into the Oracle software library files, so they can be called even when the database is not open. Most packages, as you know, would only be available when the database is open. However, RMAN can write calls to DBMS_BACKUP_RESTORE when the database instance is in nomount or mount mode. This is a critical element, and the reason is clear: we need to be able to back up and restore the database even when it is not open.

Which brings us to an interesting point: what state must the target be in if we are to connect to it using RMAN? Does the instance need to be started, or do we need to mount it, or must it be open? The answer is that RMAN can connect to the target database in any of these three states, but it must at least be in nomount mode (otherwise, there's no *there* there!).

Backing Up the Data Block

As you learned in Chapter 1, even when you used advanced techniques for backups, the units you were backing up were files. The OS utility that ultimately made the backup was looking at the entire file and backing it up, and because of this, you had to go to extraordinary lengths to protect the integrity of the Oracle data blocks within the files. RMAN, however, is different. Because RMAN is integrated into the RDBMS, it has access to your data at the same level that the database itself uses: the data block.

Block-level access is what distinguishes RMAN from any other backup utility, and even if you didn't already know this, it's why you are reading this book and implementing an RMAN backup strategy. This is an extremely powerful level of access that provides nearly all the benefits that you will get from using RMAN. It is because of this access that we can utilize the data block for more efficient backup and recovery.

The Data Block Backup Overview

Here's how it works: RMAN compiles the list of files to be backed up, based on the backup algorithm rules. Based on the number of channels and the number of files being simultaneously backed up, RMAN creates memory buffers in the Oracle shared memory segment. This is typically in the Private Global Area (PGA), but there are circumstances that push the memory buffers into the Shared Global Area (SGA). The channel server process then begins reading the datafiles and filling the RMAN buffers with these blocks. When a buffer is full, it pushes the blocks from an input buffer into an output buffer. This memory-to-memory write occurs for each individual data block in the datafile. If the block meets the criteria for being backed up and the memory-to-memory write detected no corruption, then the block remains in the output buffer until the output buffer is full. Once full, the output buffer is pushed to the backup location—a disk or a tape, whichever it may be.

Once the entire set of files has been filtered through the memory buffers, the backup piece is finished, and RMAN writes the completion time and name of the backup piece to the target database control file.

The Benefits of Block-Level Backups

Memory-to-memory writes occur for each block that is moved from disk into memory. During this operation, the block can be checked for corruption. Corruption checking is one of the nicest features of RMAN, and we discuss it in more detail in Chapter 12. Be aware that block checking is not used if you are performing a proxy copy.

Null Block Compression

Null block compression becomes an option when we have access to the data block. We can eliminate blocks that have never been used (have a zeroed header) and discard them during the memory-to-memory write. Therefore, we only back up blocks that have been used and that have a more efficient backup.

This is a good place to mention the different misconceptions related to null block compression. The first misconception is that null compression eliminates empty blocks. The null compression algorithm has only two access points that RMAN has to the database: the file header and the block header. RMAN can only draw conclusions about the contents of a block from its header or from the file header information. Why no space management information? Space management information is only available when the database is open, and RMAN null compression cannot rely on the database being open. We must rely only on that information that we can get without an open database: namely, file headers and block headers. So, if you truncate a table, all the blocks that had information in them but are now empty will be backed up, because RMAN only knows that the block has been initialized by a segment. It does not know that the block is empty.

The second common misconception about null block compression is that null compression saves time during the backup, as less is being backed up. This is true, to a certain extent, but only if your backup device is an extremely bad bottleneck. If you stream very quickly to your disk or tape backup location, then the act of eliminating blocks in memory saves little time, because RMAN is still reading every block in the file into memory—it just is not writing every block to the output device. Even during incremental backups, which eliminate blocks based on an incremental checkpoint SCN, we still have to check the header of each block to discover if it has changed since the last incremental backup. Incremental backups, then, save space in our backup location, and they provide a faster form of recovery, but they are not meant to be a significant or reliable time-saver during the actual backup.

Unused Block Compression

Unused block compression is the second mechanism for skipping unused blocks. It matches null block compression in its outcome: namely, never-initialized blocks will not be backed up. However, after version 10.2.0.3, it also can exclude used but empty blocks. This algorithm lends itself to saved time during backup, because it accesses space management information and checks the bitmaps for each segment. From this information, it builds the lists of initialized blocks and does not even attempt to back up the others. This means there is less total data read into memory, which translates into saved time.

Unused block compression is automatically used, but it cannot be used for all blocks in a database. There are architectural limits to the approach, and it requires the following be true:

- The backup requested is a full or level 0 incremental backup.

- The backup is going to disk (or Oracle Secure Backup).

- COMPATIBLE init parameter is set to 10.2 or higher.

- There are no guaranteed restore points for the database.

- The datafile is locally managed (that is, the space management info is in the file header, not in the data dictionary).

It is this final element, locally managed datafiles, that allows RMAN to get the bitmap info it requires for successful unused block compression, as it does not require a round-trip through the (perhaps unavailable) data dictionary.

Binary Compression

In version 10*g*, RMAN finally made available a version of whitespace compression, as would be done by a ZIP utility. This provides actual compression of the backed up blocks themselves. In addition, the new block-change tracking file allows RMAN to skip some blocks during backup without reading them into a memory buffer—so incremental backups begin to save time, if the change tracking is turned on. For more on compression and block-change tracking, see the full coverage in Chapter 9.

In 11*g*R2, you can enable Oracle Advanced Compression, which provides three different levels of compression, so you can match the binary compression to your environment. The levels are High, Medium, and Low: High, for bandwidth-bound environments where limiting access to the network resources is the highest priority; Medium, for a combination of compression ratio to CPU utilization; and Low, where CPU utilization is the limiting factor over network bandwidth or total size of the backup piece.

Backup Performance with Block-Level Backup

Block-level backup also provides performance gains from the perspective of redo generation. As you learned in Chapter 1, if you use old-school hot backup methodology, the amount of redo that you generate while you are running with a tablespace in hot backup mode can sometimes grow exponentially. This causes excess redo log switching, checkpoint failure, and massive amounts of archive log generation that can further cascade into space management challenges in your log archive destination.

RMAN, on the other hand, does not require hot backup mode, because it does not need to guarantee block consistency during a backup. RMAN's access to the data block allows it to coordinate with DBWR processes writing dirty buffers, and it can wait until the block is consistent before it reads the block into memory. So, blocks aren't being dumped to redo, and we always have consistent blocks in our backup.

RMAN does require ARCHIVELOG mode, of course. In fact, RMAN will not allow you to back up a datafile while the database is open unless you are in ARCHIVELOG mode. It gives you the following polite error:

```
ORA-19602: cannot backup or copy active file in NOARCHIVELOG mode
```

RMAN also leverages block-level backups to provide an often-overlooked but extremely useful recovery option: block media recovery. Now, if you were to receive the stomach-turning "ora-1578: block corruption detected" error, instead of recovering the entire file and performing recovery, RMAN can simply recover the bad block and perform recovery, meaning the rest of the data in the datafile is available during the recovery. More information on this appears in Chapter 12.

This just touches the surface of all the benefits you get from RMAN, but you get the point. The payoff is enormous when RMAN is utilized for block-level backups. The rest of this book is dedicated to utilizing this to your advantage.

RMAN in Memory

RMAN builds buffers in memory through which it streams data blocks for potential backup. This memory utilization counts against the total size of the PGA and, sometimes, the SGA. There are two kinds of memory buffers. *Input buffers* are the buffers that are filled with data blocks read from files that are being backed up. *Output buffers* are the buffers that are filled when the memory-to-memory write occurs to determine whether a particular block needs to be backed up. When the output buffer is filled, it is written to the backup location. The memory buffers differ depending on whether you are backing up to or restoring from disk or tape. Figure 2-3 illustrates input and output buffer allocation. It illustrates a backup of two datafiles being multiplexed into a single backup set.

FIGURE 2-3 *Input and output buffers in memory*

Input Memory Buffers

When you are backing up the database, the size and number of input memory buffers depend on the exact backup command being executed. Primarily, they depend on the number of files being multiplexed into a single backup. *Multiplexing* refers to the number of files that will have their blocks backed up to the same backup piece. To keep the memory allocation within reason, the following rules are applied to the memory buffer sizes based on the number of files being backed up together:

- If the number of files going into the backup set is four or less, then RMAN allocates four buffers per file at 1MB per buffer. The total will be 16MB or less.

- If the number of files going into the backup set is greater than four, but no greater than eight, then each file gets four buffers, each of 512KB. This ensures that the total remains at 16MB or less.

- If the number of files being multiplexed is greater than eight, then RMAN allocates four buffers of size 128KB. This ensures that each file being backed up will account for 512KB of buffer memory.

Bear in mind that these memory amounts are on a per-channel basis. So, if you allocate two channels to back up a database with 32 datafiles, for instance, then RMAN will load-balance the files between the two channels and may not end up with 16 files per channel. If some files are significantly larger than others, you may end up with only 8 files going into one backup set and 24 files going into the other. If this were the case, then the buffers for the first channel with 8 files would allocate 16MB of memory for input buffers (four buffers multiplied by 512KB each, multiplied by 8 files), and the second channel would allocate 12MB of memory buffers (512KB per file multiplied by 24 files).

You can use the following query to monitor the size of buffers on a per-file basis while the backup is running:

```
SELECT set_count, device_type, type, filename,
buffer_size, buffer_count, open_time, close_time
FROM v$backup_async_io
ORDER BY set_count,type, open_time, close_time;
```

Output Buffers When Backing Up to Disk

In addition to input buffers, RMAN allocates output buffers, depending on what the output source is. If you are backing up to disk, then RMAN allocates output buffers that must fill up with data blocks from the input buffers before being flushed to the backup piece on your file system. Per channel, there will be four output buffers, each of which is 1MB. So, the memory footprint per channel will always be 4MB.

Output Memory Buffers When Backing Up to Tape

Memory allocation is different when backing up to tape, to account for the slower I/O rates that we expect from tape devices. When you are backing up to or restoring from tape, RMAN allocates four buffers per channel process, each of which is 256KB, so that the total memory footprint per channel is 1MB.

Memory Buffers on Restore

Memory utilization during restore operations is slightly different than during backups. This is due to the fact that the roles are reversed: instead of reading from the datafiles and writing to the backup location, we are reading from the backup location and writing to the datafiles. During a restore from a disk backup, the input buffers will be 1MB, and RMAN will allocate four buffers per channel. When restoring from tape, RMAN allocates four input buffers with a size of BLKSIZE, which defaults to 256KB. The output buffers on restore are always 128KB, and there will be four of them per channel.

Multisection Backups and Memory

In 11*g,* Oracle introduced a new feature that allows RMAN to use multiple channels to back up a single, large file. This means that the memory input/output buffer conversation earlier still holds true, but the buffers are per channel, not necessarily per file. So, each channel opens the four input buffers for each section of the file it will be backing up. The output buffers remain the same as the preceding algorithm per backup piece.

RMAN Memory Utilization: PGA vs. SGA

Backups to disk use PGA memory space for backup buffers, which is allocated out of the memory space for the channel processes. If your operating system is not configured for native asynchronous I/O, then you can utilize the parameter DBWR_IO_SLAVES to use I/O slaves for filling up the input buffers in memory. If this parameter is set to any non-zero value, RMAN automatically allocates four I/O slaves to coordinate the load of blocks into the input memory buffer. To coordinate this work, RMAN must utilize a shared memory location. So, the memory buffers for disk backups are pushed into the shared pool, or the large pool if one exists.

Memory for tape output buffers is allocated in the PGA, unless you are using tape I/O slaves. To enable tape I/O slaves, you set the init.ora parameter BACKUP_TAPE_IO_SLAVES to TRUE. This can be done dynamically and set in the SPFILE if you desire. When this is set to TRUE, RMAN creates a single slave process per channel to assist with the backup workload. To coordinate this work, RMAN pushes the memory allocation into the SGA.

If either of these I/O slave options is configured, memory will be pulled from the shared pool area in the SGA, unless you have a large pool configured. If you do not have a large pool configured, and you expect to use I/O slaves, we highly recommend that you create a large pool with a size based on the total number of channels you expect to allocate for your backups, plus 1MB for overhead. Allocating how many channels makes sense? Chapter 16 will tell you. If you already have a large pool for Shared Servers (formerly MTS), JDBC connection pooling, or because you have PARALLEL_AUTOMATIC_TUNING set to TRUE, then increase the size of the pool to account for the RMAN memory buffers.

This introduction to the RMAN memory architecture does not include much information on tuning your system to cope with RMAN backups. Obviously, a resource hit takes place while RMAN is running. In fact, you can tune RMAN to use more or less resources, depending on your needs. Chapter 16 discusses how to do this in greater detail.

One last note on memory utilization: If you are backing up to tape, you will be using a media management server product. If you are running your media manager from the same system as your target database, you will need additional system resources for the tape subsystem. Be sure to factor this in when tuning for backups.

> **The Large Pool in the Oracle SGA**
>
> The large pool is a specific area in the SGA of Oracle's memory space. It is configured using the LARGE_POOL_SIZE parameter in your init.ora or SPFILE, and the value is specified in bytes. The large pool is utilized for certain memory activities that require shared space but tend to walk all over the usual operations in the shared pool. Its occupants are primarily restricted to RMAN memory buffers if I/O slaves are used, and Shared Servers for connection pooling. Sometimes the large pool is used for Java connections, and it will also house parallel query slaves if you set PARALLEL_AUTOMATIC_TUNING to TRUE (this is deprecated in 10*g*).
>
> Do you need a large pool? No. Without one, all of its potential occupants simply take up space in the shared pool. This is not the end of the world, but it's highly desirable to separate out RMAN buffers into their own space in the PGA. That way, SQL and PL/SQL parsing and other normal shared pool operations are not affected by RMAN backups, and vice versa. It also makes tuning the Oracle memory space for RMAN simpler and more straightforward.

The Recovery Catalog

So far, we have discussed the two most important RMAN components: the RMAN client utility and the internal database packages. However, another component is involved with RMAN backups, although its usage is entirely optional: the recovery catalog.

The recovery catalog is a repository for metadata about RMAN backups. In a sense, you can think of the recovery catalog as merely a copy of the pertinent information out of the control file that RMAN requires for backup and recovery purposes. You create the recovery catalog in a user's schema in an Oracle database, and it is no more than a few packages, tables, indexes, and views. These tables contain data that is refreshed from the target database control file upon a resync command from within RMAN. The difference, of course, is that the recovery catalog can contain information about all the databases in your enterprise—and the control file holds only information about its own database.

To use a recovery catalog, you first connect from RMAN to the target database. Then, you make a second Net connection to the recovery catalog from within RMAN, like this:

```
rman>connect target /
rman>connect catalog rman/password@rcat
```

In the connect string to the catalog, you pass the username and password for the user that owns the RMAN catalog. Unlike with the target, the connection to the catalog is not a sysdba connection and does not need this privilege granted to it.

Once connected, you can manually resync the catalog, or it will be implicitly resynchronized on any backup operation. A *resync* refers to the refreshing of the information from the target database control file to the tables in the recovery catalog.

A recovery catalog can serve as a repository for more than one target database, and as such can help centralize the administration of backups of many different databases. It has views that can be queried from SQL*Plus to determine the number, size, and range of backups for each target database that has been registered in that catalog.

Figure 2-4 details the network topology when a catalog is used. Inside of the recovery catalog are two packages: DBMS_RCVMAN and DBMS_RCVCAT. The first one, DBMS_RCVMAN, is identical in form to that same package in the SYS schema. It is in this way that the RMAN utility

FIGURE 2-4 *Connecting to a recovery catalog*

can use either the recovery catalog or the target database control file for information about backup and recovery, and not worry about different implementations.

The package name DBMS_RCVMAN in the recovery catalog can lead to some confusion on the database that houses the recovery catalog. This database is usually referred to as the *catalog database.* The catalog database is also a potential target database, so it also has a package in the SYS schema called DBMS_RCVMAN; thus, if you select from DBA_OBJECTS on your catalog database, there are two packages with the same name, in two different schemas. This is not a mistake or a problem. One of them is built by the catproc.sql at the time of database creation (in the SYS schema), and the other is built when we create the recovery catalog (in a regular user schema).

The second package in the recovery catalog is DBMS_RCVCAT, and it is only used to perform operations specific to the recovery catalog during RMAN operations. In essence, you can think of this package as being the recovery catalog implementation of DBMS_BACKUP_RESTORE; whereas DBMS_BACKUP_RESTORE writes backup completion information to the target database control file, DBMS_RCVCAT does this in the recovery catalog.

The base tables that contain information in the recovery catalog are unimportant, as you do not want to manually modify them. Instead, for the catalog's protection, Oracle created a series of views, all prefixed with RC_, that can be used to extract information from the catalog. Manually issuing any DML against catalog objects is a dangerous prospect, and we don't recommend it. The RC_* views, and what you can get from them, are outlined in Chapter 10. As noted there, these views are different implementations of corresponding v$views in the database control file.

The Auxiliary Database

The *auxiliary database* refers to the instance that will become host to restored files from the target database in the event of a tablespace point-in-time recovery (TSPITR), a duplication operation (cloning the database), or the creation of a standby database using RMAN backups. When you perform any of these tasks, you will be connecting to the target database and the auxiliary database at the same time from within RMAN. In this way, you can utilize the information about the backups in the target database control file to coordinate the restore of those backups to the auxiliary database location. The following shows the connection to both the target database (locally) and the auxiliary database (using an Oracle Net connection):

```
rman>connect target /
rman>connect auxiliary sys/pwd@aux1
```

RMAN makes a simultaneous connection to each database and requires access to the SYS. DBMS_BACKUP_RESTORE and SYS.DBMS_RCVMAN packages in both the target database and the auxiliary database. As such, RMAN requires sysdba privileges at the auxiliary, just as it does at the target. Because RMAN must make a sysdba connection to two separate databases, you are required to configure at least one of them with a password file and make an Oracle Net connection to it—there is no way to connect locally to two different databases.

We discuss the exact auxiliary database setup in great detail in Chapter 19. Figure 2-5 shows the network topology of an RMAN configuration when an auxiliary database is used. In Oracle8*i*, a recovery catalog was required in order to perform any actions at the auxiliary database, so this figure shows the topology with a catalog, as well.

FIGURE 2-5 *Network topology with an auxiliary database in the mix*

Compatibility Issues

Given the number of different components that we have to work with, you must stick with database version restrictions when working with RMAN. There are five different pieces to the compatibility puzzle, each of which has a version number:

- The RMAN executable version (the client utility)

- The target database

- The recovery catalog schema

- The recovery catalog database

- The auxiliary database (for duplication, TSPITR, and standby creation)

The easiest answer, of course, is to make sure all of these components are on the latest version, 11.2. If they are all at the same level, then there is no problem, right? Of course, in the world where all of your databases are at the same level, everyone has their very own pony, fairies roam the earth, babies never cry, and no one ever has to take backups because failures never occur. But for the world we live in, there are some things to understand about RMAN version compatibility.

The Target and the RMAN Executable

The first general rule to stick with is to ensure that the target database and the RMAN executable are the same version. This is easy, if you will always be running RMAN from the target database environment. It gets trickier if you will be running all of your RMAN jobs from a centralized client interface. It means your client system will have to have an ORACLE_HOME client installation that corresponds in version to every database version that you will need to connect to and back up. The level of complexity is pretty high with this solution. This can also be avoided by using Oracle Enterprise Manager Grid Control. This allows a centralized interface so you can use the remote RMAN executables from a single console, or more consoles if the backup tasks are divided among DBAs. We discuss the Enterprise Manager interface in Chapter 11.

The Catalog Database and Catalog Schema

There are essentially three tiers to worry about with compatibility: Oracle9*i,* Oracle 10*g,* and Oracle 11*g.* From the perspective of the catalog database and the catalog schema, there's a simpler answer: If you create a 11.2 recovery catalog in a 11.2 database, all databases down to 8.1.7.4 can be registered in it. If that is not possible, then read closely: All Oracle8 versions can be registered in an 8.1.*x* catalog. However, a 9.0.1 or 9.2.0 database cannot be registered in an 8*i* catalog, nor a 10.*x* in a 9*x* catalog, nor an 11*g* database in a lower version catalog. So, if you do not have an available database to use for the 11*g* recovery catalog, you will need to run it in NOCATALOG mode until one becomes available. Don't even think about running multiple-versions catalogs—it's just not worth it. Remember, as soon as you introduce a new version of the RDBMS into production anywhere in your ecosystem, then you need to get your RMAN catalog to that version as well.

The Auxiliary Database

From a compatibility standpoint, the auxiliary database must be the same version as the target database that it will be cloned from. In fact, we would go so far as to encourage you to match the ORACLE_HOME to which you will duplicate to the same level as the target database's ORACLE_HOME. In Chapter 17, we discuss in greater detail the use of an auxiliary database.

The RMAN Process: From Start to Finish

So far, we have discussed the different architectural components of taking a backup using Recovery Manager. As you may have noticed, there are a number of pieces to keep straight. To put it into a little perspective, we will run through a typical backup operation and explain the underlying RMAN activity at every step. That way, you should be able to associate the lengthy exposition in this chapter to the actual steps that you will take to perform a backup.

The following example illustrates a backup of a database called PROD. The backup will be going to a disk location; the discussion of setting up and utilizing a media manager for backups to tape will be deferred to Chapters 4 through 8. The target database PROD has 20 datafiles and is running in ARCHIVELOG mode. The database is up and running during this operation. Here is our backup command:

```
C$>rman
rman>connect target /
rman>backup database;
```

That's it. That's all it takes. The following discussion explains what happens.

RMAN makes the bequeath connection to the target database that we have set up in our environment. This means it checks the variable ORACLE_SID for an instance name, then spawns a server process at that instance, logging in as a sysdba user. This connects as the internal database user SYS. RMAN immediately spawns the channel processes that will be used to perform the backup. In this case, we are using default settings, so only one channel is allocated. We are not using I/O slaves, so the process allocates memory in the PGA.

Next, RMAN compiles a call to SYS.DBMS_RCVMAN to request database schematic information from the target database control file, starting with a determination of the target database version. It gathers version information from the control file, along with control file information itself: What type of control file is it? What is the sequence number current in it? When was it created?

Because we have specified a full database backup, RMAN requests information for each datafile in the database and determines if any files are offline. As part of this information, it gathers which disk each file is on and how to dole out the work. Because we are using default settings, there will be only one channel and only one backup set. Therefore, RMAN ignores all disk affinity information and concentrates on compiling the list of files for inclusion in the backup set.

After the list is compiled, RMAN is ready to begin the backup process itself. To guarantee consistency, it then builds the snapshot control file. If one already exists, it overwrites it with a new one. Then RMAN creates the call to the DBMS_BACKUP_RESTORE package to create the backup piece. The backup piece will be built in the default file location; on Unix, this is ORACLE_HOME/dbs, and on Windows, it is ORACLE_HOME/database. RMAN has the file list, so it can allocate the memory buffers for performing the read from disk. With 20 files, RMAN allocates input buffers of size 128KB. There will be four buffers per file, for a total memory utilization of 10MB for input buffers. RMAN will only allocate four output buffers, each of 1MB. This brings our total memory utilization to 14MB for the backup.

After the memory is allocated, RMAN initializes the backup piece. The backup piece will be given a default name that guarantees uniqueness. RMAN then begins the backup. In database versions 9.2, 10.1, and 10.2, RMAN allocates disk space in 50MB increments: 50MB is allocated on disk and filled with output buffers; when full, another 50MB is grabbed, until the last block is dumped to the backup piece. When the backup is complete, any remaining space in the final 50MB chunk is freed. It is worth pointing out that RMAN no longer does a check to see if there is enough space to complete the entire backup at the onset. This is due to the fact that null compression, and new 10*g* whitespace compression, will significantly reduce the backup from being the size of the datafiles. Instead, RMAN will run its backup until it runs out of space, and then fail.

Once the backup piece is initiated, the channel process can begin the database backup process. RMAN determines if you are using an SPFILE, and if so, it backs it up automatically as part of your backup set. Then RMAN will back up the current control file to the backup set. This control file backup is automatic whenever the SYSTEM tablespace is backed up; this behavior is changed if you have control file autobackup turned on (see Chapter 9).

So, we have the SPFILE and the control file backed up, and it is time to begin the datafile reads to pull data blocks into memory. The channel process does this by doing a read-ahead on the disk and pulling several blocks into memory at the same time. Then, the memory-to-memory write from input buffer to output buffer occurs. During this write, RMAN determines if the block has ever been initialized, or if the block header information is still zeroed out. If it is an unused block, the write to the output buffer never occurs and the block is discarded. If the block has been used, RMAN performs a checksum on the block. If the header and footer of the block do not match, RMAN indicates a corrupt block and aborts the backup. If the block has been initialized, and it passes the checksum, then that block is written to the output buffer.

Once the output buffer fills to capacity, we dump the buffer to the backup file location. The RMAN buffers are being filled up with blocks from all of the datafiles, so there is no order to the blocks in the dump file. The file is merely a bucket, and only RMAN will be able to restore the blocks to their proper location upon restore. While the blocks are being written out to the backup piece, the status of the backup is being polled by the RMAN shadow process. It checks in on the RPCs at the target and passes that information to V$SESSION_LONGOPS for your review. Based on the information gathered at the beginning of the backup operation, RMAN has an estimated completion percentage for each channel process. This can be viewed in V$SESSION_LONGOPS:

```
SELECT SID, SERIAL#, CONTEXT, SOFAR, TOTALWORK,
       ROUND(SOFAR/TOTALWORK*100,2) "%_COMPLETE"
FROM V$SESSION_LONGOPS
WHERE OPNAME LIKE 'RMAN%'
AND OPNAME NOT LIKE '%aggregate%'
AND TOTALWORK != 0
AND SOFAR <> TOTALWORK
/
       SID    SERIAL#    CONTEXT      SOFAR  TOTALWORK %_COMPLETE
---------- ---------- ---------- ---------- ---------- ----------
        17        167          1       4784     116328       4.11
```

You can reissue this query throughout the backup process to get an update on the work still needing to be completed:

```
       SID    SERIAL#    CONTEXT      SOFAR  TOTALWORK %_COMPLETE
---------- ---------- ---------- ---------- ---------- ----------
        17        167          1      96999     116328      83.38
```

Once every block in a datafile has been read into an input buffer and its status determined, then RMAN completes the file backup by writing the datafile header out to the backup piece. After all the files have their file headers written to the backup piece, RMAN makes a final call to SYS.DBMS_BACKUP_RESTORE, which writes backup information to the control file. This information includes the name of the backup piece, the checkpoint SCN at the time it started, and the time it completed.

And that is the entire process. Obviously, it gets more complex if we exercise more backup options, such as using multiple channels, using the FILESPERSET parameter, and backing up to tape. But each of these configurations shares the same fundamental process as previously described. If at any time during your study or testing of RMAN you want a more intimate look at the internal steps RMAN takes during backup, you can turn the debug option on for the backup and get a complete list of the entire process:

```
rman target / debug trace=/u02/oradata/trace/rmanbkup.out
```

Be warned, though, that this output is extremely verbose, and it can hamper backup performance. Only use debug for learning purposes on TEST instances, unless otherwise instructed to do so by Oracle Support Services when you are troubleshooting a production backup problem.

The Flash Recovery Area

The flash recovery area (FRA) is not a requirement for using RMAN, but it should be. New in 10*g*, the FRA is a specific location on disk that you set up to house all the Oracle recovery files. *Recovery files* refers to all files that might be required for a media recovery operation: full datafile backups, incremental backups, datafile copies, backup control files, and archive logs. The FRA also functions as a repository for mirrored copies of online redo log files, the block-change tracking file, and for a current control file. If set up, flashback logs for using the flashback database option also live in the FRA. (We discuss flashback technologies in Chapter 13.)

The concept behind the FRA is to simplify the management of your backup and recovery duties by consolidating the requisite files into a single location that Oracle and RMAN can then micromanage, while the DBA moves on to other important duties. This simplification is based on some underlying principles of a solid backup strategy that focuses on availability:

- At least one copy of important datafiles, if not the entire database, should be kept on disks that are locally accessible to the database.

- Backups past a certain age should be moved to tape based on storage pressure on local disks.

- Long-term backup management should be almost completely automatic, based on business rules.

The FRA that you set up can be either a directory on a normal disk volume or an Automatic Storage Management (ASM) disk group. The FRA is determined by two initialization parameters: DB_RECOVERY_FILE_DEST and DB_RECOVERY_FILE_DEST_SIZE. The first determines the location and the second, the size. These can be set in your init.ora file, if you still use one, or in the SPFILE via an **alter system set** command.

With an FRA configured, you are not required to set any other LOG_ARCHIVE_DEST_*n* parameter for archive logs; by default, with an FRA, Oracle will default LOG_ARCHIVE_DEST_10 to the FRA. It should also be noted that with an FRA in use, you cannot use LOG_ARCHIVE_DEST or LOG_ARCHIVE_DUPLEX_DEST—but, of course, you rid yourself of these outdated parameters long ago…right?

The FRA manages recovery files internally, first based on database name, then on types of files, and then by the dates the files are generated. The files themselves are named according to the Oracle Managed Files (OMF) format. As such, the files are hard to decipher (except for archive logs, which still maintain the structure you give them with the LOG_ARCHIVE_FORMAT parameter). Significant internal directory structures exist for file management. However, the point of an FRA is that you don't need to spend much time worrying about the files. That being said, it's worth taking note of the internal structure and familiarizing yourself with where the files go. Sooner or later, you will end up digging for a particular file manually. Trust us.

The same FRA can be used by multiple databases. This can provide significant advantages, particularly for a Data Guard configuration, but also if you have a large ASM disk group and multiple databases on the same system. It can come in handy, as well, when it comes time to clone production for test purposes. Here's the catch: all the databases that share the FRA either have a different value for DB_NAME or have a different name for the value DB_UNIQUE_NAME.

Summary

In this chapter, we discussed the underlying architecture employed by RMAN to perform backups of an Oracle Database 11*g* database. We covered the RMAN executable, the target database packages, and the control file. We discussed in detail the process architecture and how memory is allocated for RMAN backups. We discussed the usage of an RMAN recovery catalog and how to connect to an auxiliary database. After discussing the different architectural components, we gave a brief run-through of a typical backup operation to show the different components in use.

PART
II

Setup Principles and Practices

CHAPTER
3

RMAN Setup and Configuration

et's get started with this RMAN thing, shall we? Let's just reach down, pull on the handle, I said, pull on the handle…and, it doesn't start. We first need to set up RMAN and our database for backup and recovery operations before we can actually do anything. In this chapter, we look at initial RMAN setup requirements and options. First, we dive into Oracle redo logs a little deeper than we did in Chapter 1. These are critical structures in the Oracle database for recovery. Building on that discussion, we look at putting the database in ARCHIVELOG mode, in case you want to do online backups. We then look at the basic RMAN interface, so that you can get into RMAN itself. Next, we discuss configuring RMAN for database backup operations. Finally, we discuss the RMAN recovery catalog, including why you might want to use it and how to configure it.

Configuring Your Database to Run in ARCHIVELOG Mode

Now that you have learned about ARCHIVELOG mode and NOARCHIVELOG mode in Chapter 1 and learned how important redo is to your database, you probably understand why many DBAs run their databases in ARCHIVELOG mode. If you are content with running in NOARCHIVELOG mode, then much of this section's discussion will not apply to you. If you are going to run in ARCHIVELOG mode, you will need to do some basic configuration, which is the topic of this section.

When running in ARCHIVELOG mode, you have two choices in configuring where the archived redo logs are copied. In fact, you can choose to use both choices. The first choice is to configure for ARCHIVELOG destination directories, and the second is to configure the Oracle flash recovery area (FRA). We will discuss those two topics next. Afterward, we will discuss actually putting the database in ARCHIVELOG mode.

ARCHIVELOG Destination Directories

When configuring ARCHIVELOG mode, you will need to decide where you want Oracle to create archived redo logs. The option that has been available for the longest is to use archive log destination directories. To use archive log destination directories, you set some specific parameters in Oracle to configure this option. First, you use the LOG_ARCHIVE_DEST_n (where n is a number in the range of 1 to 10) parameter to define up to ten different archive log destinations. These destinations can be local directories, network directories (for example, NT folders), NAS (network-attached storage), or even a defined database service name if you are using standby database/Data Guard. Note that there is no default location defined for LOG_ARCHIVE_DEST_n.

If you are using SPFILES, you use the **alter system** command to set the LOG_ARCHIVE_DEST_n parameter as seen here:

```
alter system set log_archive_dest_1='location=c:\oracle\oraarc\beta1';
```

NOTE
Setting the LOG_ARCHIVE_DEST directory to a directory location that does not exist, or that Oracle cannot write to, is a common mistake. Just make sure that after you set the parameter and put the database in ARCHIVELOG mode, you issue an **alter system switch logfile** *command to make sure that ARCH is writing the archived redo logs properly.*

Each LOG_ARCHIVE_DEST_n location can be defined as either a mandatory or optional location. By default, all LOG_ARCHIVE_DEST_n locations are optional in Oracle Database 11g.

Mandatory locations mean just that—the archived redo logs have to be written to that location. Failure of the ARCH process to write to mandatory locations will result in suspension of database activities fairly quickly (after you have cycled through all the online redo logs). Optional locations will have no impact on database operations.

```
alter system set log_archive_dest_1='location=c:\oracle\oraarc\beta1 mandatory';
```

In Oracle Database 11*g*, all LOG_ARCHIVE_DEST_*n* locations are optional by default (though one location must always succeed since the minimum setting of LOG_ARCHIVE_MIN_SUCCEED_ DEST is 1). The parameter LOG_ARCHIVE_MIN_SUCCEED_DEST indicates how many archive log destination directories must have successful copies for an online redo log to be considered successfully archived. The default setting for LOG_ARCHIVE_MIN_SUCCEED_DEST is 1, and this is the minimum setting for this parameter. Here is an example of setting this parameter to a value of 2:

```
alter system set log_archive_min_succeed_dest=2;
```

Other parameters are related to archived redo logs, the ARCH process, and the LOG_ ARCHIVE_DEST series of parameters:

- **LOG_ARCHIVE_STATE_*n***   Defines one of two different states for each archive log destination. If set to ENABLE, the ARCH process will consider the destination associated with this state as a valid archive log destination. If set to DEFER, the ARCH process will not archive logs to the related LOG_ARCHIVE_DEST_*n* location.

- **LOG_ARCHIVE_FORMAT**   Provides a template for Oracle to use when naming archived redo logs. As Oracle creates the archived redo logs, it renames them in such a way that each of the archived redo logs has a unique name assigned to it. Using the LOG_ ARCHIVE_FORMAT parameter, you can manipulate the default naming standard as you require. This parameter has no effect for archived redo logs being created in the FRA.

- **LOG_ARCHIVE_START**   This parameter is obsolete in Oracle Database 10*g* and later versions. Oracle will now start the ARCH process for you automatically.

- **LOG_ARCHIVE_MAX_PROCESSES**   This parameter defines the number of ARCH processes that Oracle initially starts when the database is started.

NOTE
If you are running Oracle Database 9i or earlier, you will need to make sure you set the LOG_ARCHIVE_START parameter to TRUE when configuring your database for ARCHIVELOG mode. This is no longer required in Oracle Database 10g and later.

Each of the different parameters mentioned thus far is defined in the *Oracle Database 11*g *Reference Manual* (which is part of the overall Oracle documentation), should you need further information on them.

In the following example, we have a database we want to put in ARCHIVELOG mode. We will create three different archive log destination directories, including one to a service name that supports an Oracle standby database. We will also enforce the requirements that at least two of these destinations must be written to in order for the movement of the archived redo log to be considered complete, and that the standby database must be one of those two locations. Here is an example of the use of the various database parameter file parameters related to ARCHIVELOG mode operations:

```
log_archive_dest_1='location=d:\oracle\oraarc\robt mandatory'
log_archive_dest_2='location=z:\oracle\oraarc\robt optional'
log_archive_dest_3='service=recover1 mandatory'
log_archive_min_succeed_dest=2
log_archive_format="robt_%s_%t.arc"
```

In this example, our first archive log destination goes to d:\oracle\oraarc\robt. The second archive log destination is to a secondary location on the Z: drive. We have made this an optional archiving location because it is a networking device (which may not be all that reliable). The third destination is to an Oracle Net service (probably a standby database) called recover1. This will cause Oracle to send the archived redo logs through Oracle Net as they are generated.

Proceeding through the example, by using the LOG_ARCHIVE_MIN_SUCCEED_DEST parameter, we have indicated that the archived redo logs must be successfully copied to at least two different locations. The format of the archived redo log is defined with the LOG_ARCHIVE_FORMAT parameter.

The Flash Recovery Area

The flash recovery area (FRA) allows you to centralize storage of all recovery-related files. The FRA can use locally attached storage, the Oracle Cluster File System (OCFS), or Automatic Storage Management (ASM) features. Table 3-1 lists the file types that can be contained within the FRA. The FRA helps with the management of overall disk space allocation and provides a centralized storage area for all recovery-related files.

Retention of files in the FRA is determined by the RMAN retention policy. This is set via the RMAN **configure retention policy** command. This command and RMAN retention will be discussed in much more detail later in this chapter. If a file does not have a retention policy associated with it or it's a permanent file, then it will never be deleted. If a file is not yet obsolete under the RMAN retention policy, then it will not be deleted. Finally, archived logs are eligible for deletion once they are obsolete.

The FRA is created in a specific location defined by the parameter DB_RECOVERY_FILE_DEST. This location can be a file system or an ASM volume. You define the quota of space allocated to the database's FRA by using the DB_RECOVERY_FILE_DEST_SIZE parameter. This is a logical, database-specific, Oracle-controlled file space limitation, independent of the overall space available in the file system itself. Oracle monitors the space available in the FRA used by the database, and once the amount of available space in the FRA starts to diminish to unsafe levels, Oracle generates a warning in the alert log. In Oracle Database 11*g*, these warnings occur when reclaimable space is less than 15 percent of the DB_RECOVERY_FILE_DEST_SIZE value. A critical alert is also signaled when the database is at less than 3 percent of reclaimable space. These alerts appear in OEM, in the alert log, or you can review the DBA_OUTSTANDING_ALERTS table. Several views are available for you to reference when trying to determine if your flash recovery area is running out of space. We address those views later in this chapter in the section titled "Flash Recovery Area Views."

NOTE
Running out of space in the FRA can be troublesome if that area is your only archive log destination, as this can cause your database to eventually halt. If the FRA is going to be your only archive log destination, monitor space availability carefully.

File Type	Notes
Archived redo logs	Archived redo logs will be stored in the FRA.
Control file	One copy of the control file is created in the FRA when the database is created.
Control file autobackups	The default location for the RMAN control file autobackups will be the FRA, if it is defined.
Flashback logs	Flashback logs (discussed later in this chapter) will be stored in the FRA, if it is defined.
Redo log	One copy of each redo log group member can be stored in the FRA.
RMAN datafile copies	The default location for the RMAN datafile copies will be the FRA, if it is defined.
RMAN backup and other related files	The default location for the RMAN files in general (backup set pieces, etc.) will be the FRA, if it is defined.

TABLE 3-1 *File Types Found in the Flash Recovery Area*

Figuring out how much space to allocate to the FRA can be a bit challenging. Typically you have to monitor space usage and adjust the size of the FRA as required. If the database already exists, you can review the amount of archive log space consumed by checking the DBA_HIST_LOG view. This view derives its data from Oracle's AWR infrastructure. It will tell you the average size of the archived redo logs and the time of the log switch. Here is an example of a query against the DBA_HIST_LOG view:

```
SQL> alter session set nls_date_format='mm/dd/yyyy hh24:mi:ss';
Session altered.

SQL> select sequence#, first_time Log_started
  2  ,lead(first_time, 1,NULL) over (order by first_time) Log_ended
  3  from (select distinct sequence#, first_time
  4  from  dba_hist_log
  5  where archived='YES'
  6  and sequence#!=0
  7  order by first_time)
  8  order by sequence#;

SEQUENCE# LOG_STARTED         LOG_ENDED
---------- ------------------- -------------------
        82 05/18/2009 22:02:56 05/19/2009 12:52:06
        83 05/19/2009 12:52:06 05/19/2009 22:01:24
        84 05/19/2009 22:01:24 05/20/2009 15:25:39
        85 05/20/2009 15:25:39 05/21/2009 10:00:58
        86 05/21/2009 10:00:58 05/21/2009 17:02:00
        87 05/21/2009 17:02:00 05/21/2009 22:01:28
        88 05/21/2009 22:01:28

7 rows selected.
```

Many large systems run more than one Oracle database. Each of these databases will use archive log storage space, and typically these archived redo logs will all be stored on the same file system. On occasion, a single database can consume all the space on that storage device. This can impact all databases using that storage device, since they will no longer be able to create archived redo logs. One benefit of the FRA is that it provides the ability to allocate a specific space quota to each database. Thus, with an FRA, you can reduce the risk that one database will consume all archive log space and negatively impact other databases.

If you find that the FRA has run out of space, you can respond to the problem as follows:

1. If the problem is one of insufficient space allocation via the parameter DB_RECOVERY_FILE_DEST_SIZE and sufficient physical disk space exists to increase the space allocated to the FRA, increase the size of the parameter. This will immediately add space to the FRA. Of course, you cannot increase this parameter to a value that is greater than the amount of space that is physically available on the file system.

2. If you need more physical space, allocate additional physical space to the file system, and then increase the size of the DB_RECOVERY_FILE_DEST_SIZE parameter.

3. If additional space is not available, you can move the FRA to another file system where more space is available.

4. You can also make room in the FRA by using the RMAN **backup recovery area** command to move the contents of the FRA to another location. We will cover the **backup recovery area** command and its limitations during discussions on performing RMAN backups.

5. As a last-ditch effort, physically remove older backup set pieces and/or archived redo logs from the FRA, and then use the RMAN **crosscheck** command to get the database to recognize that the files have been removed.

NOTE
If you find yourself queasy at the idea of removing physical files from the FRA, then your gut instincts are good. Essentially this means either that your retention policy is not correct or that you have not allocated enough space to support the retention policy established for your database. Also, removing files potentially compromises the recoverability of your database, so exercise extreme caution when removing files.

Setting Up the Flash Recovery Area

To set up the FRA, you will want to configure the following parameters:

Parameter	DB_RECOVERY_FILE_DEST_SIZE	DB_RECOVERY_FILE_DEST
Example	`Alter system set db_recovery_file_dest_size=20G scope=both;`	`Alter system set db_recovery_file_dest='/u01/oracle/flash_recovery' scope=both;`
Purpose	Sets the allocated size of the FRA, in bytes, and must be defined in order to enable the FRA. This allows you to control how much disk space is allocated to the FRA. You should not set this value to a size greater than the total amount of available disk space.	Specifies the location of the FRA. This can be a file system, an ASM disk location, or an OMF location.

Note that you must specify the DB_RECOVERY_FILE_DEST_SIZE parameter before you specify the DB_RECOVERY_FILE_DEST parameter. Failure to do so will result in an ORA-32001 error message. In a similar fashion, you must disable the DB_RECOVERY_FILE_DEST parameter before you reset the DB_RECOVERY_FILE_DEST_SIZE parameter. Leaving DB_RECOVERY_FILE_ DEST empty will disable the FRA. Here is an example of disabling the FRA by resetting the DB_ RECOVERY_FILE_DEST parameter:

```
alter system set db_recovery_file_dest=' ' scope=both;
```

Oracle allows you to archive to both the FRA and to one or more additional locations through the use of the LOG_ARCHIVE_DEST_*n* parameters. One case when you would want to do this is if you were configuring standby databases and you still wanted to take advantage of the features of the FRA.

To configure both FRA and archive log destination directories, you set the standard FRA parameter DB_RECOVERY_FILE_DEST, defining the location of the FRA. You will also define the various LOG_ARCHIVE_DEST_*n* parameters that are required. By default, when a LOG_ ARCHIVE_DEST_n parameter is defined, that location will be used instead of the FRA. To get Oracle to use the FRA when a LOG_ARCHIVE_DEST_*n* parameter is set, you need to define an additional LOG_ARCHIVE_DEST_*n* parameter for the FRA. Typically, this will be LOG_ARCHIVE_ DEST_10, and you will use the Oracle-supplied constant USE_DB_RECOVERY_FILE_DEST to indicate that this destination is the FRA. Here is an example where we configure Oracle to use the FRA and a regular archive log destination directory:

```
alter system set log_archive_dest_10='LOCATION=USE_DB_RECOVERY_FILE_DEST';
alter system set log_archive_dest_1='location=c:\oracle\oraarc\beta1 mandatory';
```

In this example, the ARCH process will now create archived redo logs in both LOG_ ARCHIVE_DEST_1 and LOG_ARCHIVE_DEST_10, which is the FRA.

Flash Recovery Area Views
Several views are available to help you manage the FRA. These views include the following:

- DBA_OUTSTANDING_ALERTS

- V$RECOVERY_FILE_DEST

- V$FLASH_RECOVERY_AREA_USAGE

Also, columns are available in several other views that help you to manage the FRA. Let's look at each of these views and columns in more detail.

The DBA_OUTSTANDING_ALERTS View   As files are added or removed from the FRA, records of these events are logged in the database alert log. You can check the new DBA view, DBA_OUTSTANDING_ALERTS, for information on outstanding issues with the FRA. Note that there is somewhat of a lag between the time a space-related issue occurs and when the warning appears in the DBA_OUTSTANDING_ALERTS view.

The following is an example where the FRA has run out of space and is posting an alert to the DBA_OUTSTANDING_ALERTS view. You would need to deal with this situation quickly or risk the database coming to a complete halt. In this case, we used the **alter system** command to increase the amount of space allocated to the FRA.

```
SQL> select reason from dba_outstanding_alerts;
REASON
----------------------------------------------------------------
db_recovery_file_dest_size of 524288000 bytes is 100.00% used
and has 0 remaining bytes available.

SQL> alter system set db_recovery_file_dest_size=800m;
```

The V$RECOVERY_FILE_DEST View   The V$RECOVERY_FILE_DEST view provides an overview of the FRA that is defined in your database. It provides the size that the FRA is configured for, the amount of space used, how much space can be reclaimed, and the number of files in the FRA. In the following example, we can see that the increase in space to the FRA to 800MB has been recorded (SPACE_LIMIT). However, we still have used too much space (SPACE_USED), and the FRA is still full.

```
SQL> select * from v$recovery_file_dest;
NAME
-----------------------------------------------------------------------
    SPACE_LIMIT             SPACE_USED  SPACE_RECLAIMABLE NUMBER_OF_FILES
-------------- ---------------------- ------------------ ---------------
c:\oracle\product\10.2.0\flash_recovery_area
    838,860,800            1,057,116,672        338,081,280              11
```

One nice thing about Oracle is that it manages the FRA space for us as much as it can, and if there is reclaimable space available, it will free it as required. Note that in the previous query, Oracle indicated we were out of FRA space. Did you notice the SPACE_RECLAIMABLE column, though? This column indicates that there is reclaimable space available. This is space that is taken up by archived redo logs or backup set pieces that are no longer needed by virtue of whatever retention criteria we have selected (we will discuss retention criteria and setting those criteria later in this chapter). When Oracle needs space in the FRA (say, for example, we force a log switch), it will remove any files that are reclaimable and free up space. In the next query, we can see that this has occurred. After we ran the previous query that indicated we were out of FRA space, we forced a log switch. This caused Oracle to reclaim space from the FRA for reuse, and it then was able to write out the archived redo log. We can query the V$RECOVERY_FILE_DEST view and see that this has indeed occurred:

```
SQL> alter system switch logfile;
System altered.
SQL> select * from v$recovery_file_dest;
NAME
-----------------------------------------------------------------------
    SPACE_LIMIT             SPACE_USED  SPACE_RECLAIMABLE NUMBER_OF_FILES
-------------- ---------------------- ------------------ ---------------
c:\oracle\product\10.2.0\flash_recovery_area
    838,860,800             719,412,736             64,000               7
```

The V$FLASH_RECOVERY_AREA_USAGE View   The V$FLASH_RECOVERY_AREA_USAGE view provides more detailed information on which types of files are occupying space in the FRA. This view groups the file types and then provides the percentage of space that is used by each file type, the percentage of the total FRA reclaimable space that comes from that group, and the number of files in the FRA that come from that group. Here is a query of the V$FLASH_RECOVERY_AREA_ USAGE view:

```
SQL> SELECT * FROM V$FLASH_RECOVERY_AREA_USAGE;

FILE_TYPE      PERCENT_SPACE_USED  PERCENT_SPACE_RECLAIMABLE  NUMBER_OF_FILES
------------   ------------------  -------------------------  ---------------
CONTROLFILE                     0                          0                0
ONLINELOG                       0                          0                0
ARCHIVELOG                  17.14                      17.09                7
BACKUPPIECE                108.88                      23.22                4
IMAGECOPY                       0                          0                0
FLASHBACKLOG                    0                          0                0
```

In this example, we notice a few things:

■ We are over our defined space allocation (the PERCENT_SPACE_USED of all the rows exceeds 100 percent). This is probably because the size of the FRA was recently changed and Oracle has not yet reclaimed enough space to bring the total used below 100 percent.

■ The backup set pieces are consuming most of that space, and 23.22 percent of that space is reclaimable.

■ The archived redo logs consume only 17 percent of the space allocated to the FRA, and even if we were to remove all of the archived redo logs, we would not free up enough space to bring the FRA under the amount of space allocated to it.

Other Views with FRA Columns   The column IS_RECOVERY_DEST_FILE can be found in a number of Oracle Database V$ views such as V$CONTROLFILE, V$LOGFILE, V$ARCHIVED_ LOG, V$DATAFILE_COPY, V$DATAFILE, and V$BACKUP_PIECE. This column is a Boolean that indicates whether the file is in the FRA.

Another column, BYTES, can be found in the V$BACKUP_PIECE and RC_BACKUP_PIECE (an RMAN recovery catalog view) views. This column indicates the size of the backup set piece in bytes.

> **NOTE**
> *Manually removing fixed files from the FRA can have unexpected consequences. Oracle does not immediately detect the removal of these files, and thus the space is not reclaimed. If you end up manually removing files (or lose a disk perhaps), use the RMAN* **crosscheck** *command along with the* **delete** *command to cause Oracle to update the current control file information on the FRA. The folks at Oracle recommend that you not manually remove files managed by Oracle if at all possible.*

Other Flash Recovery Area Features

The **alter database add logfile** and **alter database add standby logfile** commands create an online redo log member in the FRA if the OMF-related DB_CREATE_ONLINE_LOG_DEST_*n* parameter is not set. The **alter database drop logfile** and **alter database rename file** commands also support files in the FRA. The nice thing about using these OMF-related features is that Oracle will manage the physical files for you. Thus, if you drop an online redo log group, and the physical files of that group were created by Oracle based on the setting of DB_CREATE_ONLINE_LOG_DEST_*n,* then Oracle will remove those physical files for you.

During database creation, Oracle can use the FRA to store the database control file and online redo logs. If the OMF-related parameter DB_CREATE_ONLINE_LOG_DEST_*n* is defined, then the control file and redo logs will be created in those locations, but will not be created in the FRA, even if the FRA is defined. If DB_CREATE_ONLINE_LOG_DEST_*n* is not defined, but CREATE_FILE_DEST is defined, then the control file and online redo logs will be created in the location defined by CREATE_FILE_DEST. If DB_RECOVERY_FILE_DEST is also defined, then a copy of the control file and online redo logs will get created there as well. The result is a multiplexed online redo log. Finally, if only DB_RECOVERY_FILE_DEST is defined, then the control file will get created in that location. If none of these parameters is defined, then the control file and online redo logs will be created to a default location, which is OS specific.

An additional use of the FRA has to do with Flashback Database–related features. We discuss Oracle's Flashback Database features in more detail in Chapter 15.

The FRA and ASM

RMAN supports the use of Automatic Storage Management (ASM) for the storage of RMAN backups. What is ASM? ASM is a disk management tool that eliminates the need for the DBA to manage the physical files associated with a given database. ASM is somewhat like the logical volume groups you might be used to in Unix. ASM uses *ASM disk groups,* which are logical units of storage. Physical disks are assigned to an ASM disk group, providing the overall storage capability of that ASM disk group. ASM disk groups can exist on previously allocated file systems or on raw disks. Combined with OCFS, clustered servers can share ASM disks in RAC configurations. Having configured ASM and having defined the various disk groups, you can then assign datafiles, control files, online redo logs, and various RMAN backup files to the ASM disk groups.

ASM offers a number of features including load balancing, data redundancy, and easy addition and removal of new disks to the ASM disk groups. It is beyond the scope of this book to discuss configuration of ASM in general. However, be aware that RMAN does support ASM disk groups should you wish to use them. We are not necessarily recommending ASM in this book. Most non-RAC sites probably will find little value in an ASM implementation. However, if you are a RAC site, you might want to consider ASM coupled with OCFS as an alternative to other clustering options, depending on your platform.

If you are using ASM, you can configure the FRA such that it will be created in the ASM file system, as shown in this example:

```
alter system set db_recovery_file_dest='+ASMV01';
```

In this case, Oracle will use the ASM disk volume ASMV01 for the FRA. We can then use RMAN to back up to the FRA. We will discuss backups in Chapter 11.

Should You Use the FRA?

We think the idea behind the FRA is a good one. We also like to copy those backups to some other media, such as tape, so we can send them offsite for disaster recovery purposes (nothing like a good flood, bomb, or tornado to make your disaster recovery planning seem really important).

We also like the FRA for the archived redo logs, but we also like the idea of copying archived redo logs to more than one location (and more specifically, to more than one disk). Keep in mind that the archived redo logs are critical to database recovery, and if you lose one, all the others after that one are pretty much worthless. So, we tend to configure our databases using FRA and at least one other archive log destination that is on a different disk. This means that we use the LOG_ARCHIVE_DEST_*n* parameters to configure the database to use both the FRA and another, separate file system to store our archived redo logs.

Another benefit of the FRA we like is the implementation of space quotas. Many database servers these days run more than one database. We have seen cases where one database has consumed all of the physical disk space with archived redo logs. This caused problems not only for the database that filled up the archived redo log destination directory, but also for all of the other databases on the system. By using a quota system, you can limit one database's ability to impact others.

We could go beyond this and tell you how much we like things such as standby databases and the like, but that's not what this book is about. The bottom line is that you need to protect the data in your charge, because there is no worse feeling than coming into work on Monday morning and finding out that the system crashed over the weekend and that the entire database is lost…along with all your backups.

Switching Between ARCHIVELOG Modes

Once you have configured the database to run in ARCHIVELOG mode, you can switch it between NOARCHIVELOG and ARCHIVELOG mode quite easily. To put the database in ARCHIVELOG mode, you must first shut down the database in a consistent state using one of these commands: **shutdown**, **shutdown immediate**, or **shutdown transactional**. Once the database has been cleanly shut down, mount the database by issuing the **startup mount** command. Once the database is mounted, issue the command **alter database archivelog** to put the database in ARCHIVELOG mode. You can then open the database with the **alter database open** command.

If you wish to take the database out of ARCHIVELOG mode, reverse the process. First shut down the database. Once the database has been shut down, mount the database by issuing the **startup mount** command. Once the database is mounted, issue the command **alter database noarchivelog** to put the database in NOARCHIVELOG mode. You can then open the database with the **alter database open** command.

If You Created Your Database with the Oracle Database Configuration Assistant

If you created your database with the Oracle Database Configuration Assistant (ODBCA), it is likely that Oracle has configured much of RMAN for you. ODBCA will configure the database in ARCHIVELOG mode, configure the FRA, and even offer you the chance to schedule RMAN backups. For smaller installations, this may well be all that is needed, and you will not need to worry about any other basic RMAN configuration issues. Still, it's a good idea to be aware of all the options that RMAN offers. For example, encryption of backups is not enabled when you create a database with the ODBCA, and you might want to enable that feature.

RMAN Workshop: *Put the Database in ARCHIVELOG Mode*

Workshop Notes

For this workshop, you need an installation of the Oracle software, and a database that is up and running in NOARCHIVELOG mode. Before you start the workshop, determine where you want the flash recovery area to reside. You will also need to decide where a second archive log destination directory will be, as this workshop will have you archiving to two locations.

Step 1. Configure both the FRA and a separate archive log destination for the archived redo logs. First, set the FRA parameters DB_RECOVERY_FILE_DEST_SIZE and DB_RECOVERY_FILE_DEST:

```
SQL> alter system set db_recovery_file_dest_size=2G;
System altered.
SQL> alter system set
db_recovery_file_dest='c:\oracle\product\10.2.0\flash_recovery_area';
System altered.
```

Step 2. Now, define two archive log destination directories, one of which will be the FRA. Set the database parameter file, and set the LOG_ARCHIVE_DEST_1 parameter so that it is pointing to a predefined file system that will be our first archive log directory. Since we are configuring LOG_ARCHIVE_DEST_1 and we want to use the FRA, we need to set the LOG_ARCHIVE_DEST_10 parameter to point to the FRA by using the parameter USE_DB_RECOVERY_FILE_DEST. Use the **show parameter** command to verify that the settings are correct:

```
SQL> alter system set log_archive_dest_1='location=d:\archive\rob10R2';
System altered.
SQL> alter system set
log_archive_dest_10='LOCATION=USE_DB_RECOVERY_FILE_DEST';
SQL> show parameter log_archive_dest
NAME                    TYPE         VALUE
--------------------- ----------- --------
log_archive_dest_1      string
location=d:\archive\rob10R2
log_archive_dest_10     string
LOCATION=USE_DB_RECOVERY_FILE_DEST
```

Step 3. Shut down the database:

```
SQL> shutdown immediate
Database closed.
Database dismounted.
ORACLE instance shut down.
```

Step 4. Mount the database:

```
SQL> startup mount
ORACLE instance started.
Total System Global Area    84700976 bytes
Fixed Size                    282416 bytes
Variable Size               71303168 bytes
Database Buffers            12582912 bytes
Redo Buffers                  532480 bytes
Database mounted.
```

Step 5. Put the database in ARCHIVELOG mode:

```
SQL> alter database archivelog ;
Database altered.
```

Step 6. Open the database:

```
SQL> alter database open;
Database altered.
```

Although it is not part of the workshop, the process of taking the database out of ARCHIVELOG mode is as simple as reversing the process described in the workshop. Shut down the database, restart the database instance by issuing the **startup mount** command, and put the database in NOARCHIVELOG mode by issuing the command **alter database noarchivelog**. Note that you are not required to shut down the database in a consistent manner when moving from ARCHIVELOG mode to NOARCHIVELOG mode. Here is an example of switching back into NOARCHIVELOG mode:

```
SQL> shutdown
ORACLE instance shut down.
SQL> startup mount
ORACLE instance started.
Total System Global Area    84700976 bytes
Fixed Size                    282416 bytes
Variable Size               71303168 bytes
Database Buffers            12582912 bytes
Redo Buffers                  532480 bytes
Database mounted.
SQL> alter database noarchivelog;
Database altered.
SQL> alter database open;
Database altered.
```

Finally, you should do a backup of the database once you have completed either task.

The Oracle Database 11*g* Fault Diagnosability Infrastructure

One of the major new features in Oracle Database 11*g* is the new Fault Diagnosability Infrastructure. We will cover various features associated with the new Fault Diagnosability throughout this book. This infrastructure is designed to help prevent, detect, diagnose, and resolve problems such as database bugs and various forms of corruption. This new infrastructure changes some things, such as where the alert log is generated, and adds a great deal of new functionality to the Oracle Database. Throughout this text we will discuss the Fault Diagnosability Infrastructure in more detail. In Chapter x, we will discuss the Support Workbench, which provides for automated responses to database problems. Chapter 13 will also discuss the health checkers, another new component associated with the Oracle Automatic Diagnostic Repository (ADR). In Chapters 12 and 13, we will talk about using the Recovery Advisor, closely linked to the ADR, during database restores.

For the purposes of setting up the Fault Diagnosability Infrastructure for an Oracle Database, what we are concerned with in this chapter is the setting of the new parameter DIAGNOSTIC_DEST. The new DIAGNOSTIC_DEST parameter defines the root of the ADR and deprecates several parameters including USER_DUMP_DEST, CORE_DUMP_DEST, and BACKGROUND_DUMP_DEST. As a result, if you create a new Oracle Database 11g database with the DBCA, you will not find the alert log or user trace files where you previously would have expected them.

By default, the DIAGNOSTIC_DEST parameter is set to $ORACLE_BASE. If $ORACLE_BASE is not set, then it is set to the value of $ORACLE_HOME. The root directory of the ADR directory structure starts with a directory called diag, under which is a subdirectory that references the product type. For example, for the database, the product is called rdbms. Under rdbms is a directory for each database, followed by a directory for each individual instance.

For example, if $ORACLE_BASE is /u01/oracle, the database name is mydb, and the database instance is mydb1, then the structure of the ADR directory for that database will be /u01/oracle/diag/rdbms/mydb/mydb1. This directory structure is called the ADR home, and each instance has its own ADR home. If you are using RAC, you can use shared storage for ADR, or individual storage on each node. We would recommend shared storage in a RAC environment since you can see the aggregate diagnostic data from any node. Also, a shared ADR allows for more robust recovery options for the Data Recovery Advisor.

Under this directory structure will be a number of other directories. Some of the most common directories include the following:

- **Alert**   This is the location of the XML-formatted alert log.

- **cdump**   This is the location of the core dumps for the database.

- **Trace**   This contains trace files generated by the system, as well as a text copy of the alert log.

- **Incident**   This directory contains multiple subdirectories, one for each incident.

Here is diagram of the ADR Base structure:

A new view, V$DIAG_INFO, provides information on the various ADR locations, as well as information related to ADR, such as active incidents. Here is an example of a query against the V$DIAG_INFO view:

```
SQL> select * from v$diag_info;
   INST_ID NAME                           VALUE
---------- ------------------------       ----------------------------------------
         1 Diag Enabled                   TRUE
         1 ADR Base                       C:\ORACLE\PRODUCT
         1 ADR Home                       C:\ORACLE\PRODUCT\diag\rdbms\rob11gr4\
                                          rob11gr4
         1 Diag Trace                     C:\ORACLE\PRODUCT\diag\rdbms\rob11gr4\
                                          rob11gr4\trace
         1 Diag Alert                     C:\ORACLE\PRODUCT\diag\rdbms\rob11gr4\
                                          rob11gr4\alert
         1 Diag Incident                  C:\ORACLE\PRODUCT\diag\rdbms\rob11gr4\
                                          rob11gr4\incident
         1 Diag Cdump                     C:\ORACLE\PRODUCT\diag\rdbms\rob11gr4\
                                          rob11gr4\cdump
         1 Health Monitor                 C:\ORACLE\PRODUCT\diag\rdbms\rob11gr4\
                                          rob11gr4\hm
         1 Default Trace File             C:\ORACLE\PRODUCT\diag\rdbms\rob11gr4\
                                          rob11gr4\trace\rob11gr4_ora_7832.trc
         1 Active Problem Count           1
         1 Active Incident Count          1
11 rows selected.
```

The RMAN Command Line

Now that the database is in ARCHIVELOG mode (if you are going to do online backups), you are ready to configure RMAN and your database for backups. Before you can do that, it would be nice to actually know how to use the RMAN executable. So, let's take a slight detour in our setup discussion to look at the RMAN command-line interface (CLI) and how to use it.

There are two different ways to get to RMAN. The first is from the command line, and the second is by using OEM (Oracle Enterprise Manager). We will deal with the OEM interface in more detail in Chapter 11. Most of the examples you will see in this book, however, will be done using the CLI. We figure that if you can do it from the command line, you can do it from anywhere. In the next sections, we will look at how to connect to databases with the RMAN command line and also how to use the **connect** command.

Connecting via the RMAN Command Line

You can start RMAN from the OS prompt simply by typing the command **rman**. Once you have started the RMAN command interpreter, you can perform whatever operations you might need to perform. Often, it's much easier to get some of the preliminary work done by using command-line parameters. Thus, when we start RMAN, we can pass several command-line parameters. You can use the command-line parameters to connect RMAN to the database you are going to back up (known as the *target database*), to the recovery catalog, or for a number of other tasks. Table 3-2 provides a list of the command-line parameters, the data type for the argument of the parameter (if there is one), and the purpose of the parameter.

RMAN Command-Line Parameter	Parameter Argument Type	Purpose
target	Character string	Defines the username, password, and service name of the target database to connect to.
catalog	Character string	Defines the username, password, and service name of the recovery catalog.
nocatalog	No arguments	Indicates that no recovery catalog is going to be used by this session. This parameter is the default parameter in Oracle8*i* and Oracle9*i*.
cmdfile	Character string	Indicates the name of a command file script to execute.
log	Character string	Indicates that the RMAN session should be logged. The log file will take the name of the argument to this parameter. Also causes all RMAN messages to the screen to be suppressed (except the RMAN prompt).
trace	Character string	Indicates that the RMAN session should be traced. The trace file will take the name of the argument to this parameter.

TABLE 3-2 *RMAN Command-Line Parameters*

RMAN Command-Line Parameter	Parameter Argument Type	Purpose
append	No arguments	Indicates that the log file (defined by the log parameter) should be appended to.
debug	Various arguments	Indicates that RMAN should be started in debug mode.
msgno	No arguments	Indicates that the RMAN- prefix should be shown with each error message. If this option is not selected, then certain non-error messages will not include a message number with them.
send	Character string	Sends the character string message to the media management layer.
pipe	String	Invokes the RMAN pipe interface.
timeout	Integer	Indicates the number of seconds to wait for pipe input.
auxiliary	Character string	Defines the username, password, and service name of the auxiliary database to connect to.
checksyntax	None	Checks the command file listed for syntax errors.
slaxdebug	None	Checks for command line and RMAN prompt parsing errors.

TABLE 3-2   *RMAN Command-Line Parameters* (continued)

Here are some examples of starting RMAN with some command-line parameters (and you will see others later):

```
RMAN target=system/manager@robt nocatalog
RMAN target='sys/robert as sysdba@robt' nocatalog
RMAN target=system/manager@robt
catalog=system/manager@catalog log="RMAN.log"
RMAN target system/manager@robt nocatalog log "RMAN.log"
```

NOTE
The = sign between the command-line parameter and the value of that parameter is optional. Also, if you are running Oracle Database 11g Real Application Clusters, you can connect to only one instance of that cluster.

Note that RMAN *always* connects as SYSDBA to the target database. This is good to know because it implies that the account we connect to has to have the SYSDBA privileges.

If you forget the command-line arguments to RMAN (and somehow manage to leave this book and your documentation at home), there is a way to get RMAN to display the valid command-line parameters. Simply start RMAN with an invalid parameter. As you can see in the following example, RMAN will return an error, but will also provide you with a list of valid command-line parameters (we removed some of the errors at the bottom of the listing for brevity):

```
C:\Documents and Settings\Robert>rman help
Argument     Value          Description
-----------------------------------------------------------------------
target       quoted-string  connect-string for target database
catalog      quoted-string  connect-string for recovery catalog
nocatalog    none           if specified, then no recovery catalog
cmdfile      quoted-string  name of input command file
log          quoted-string  name of output message log file
trace        quoted-string  name of output debugging message log file
append       none           if specified, log is opened in append mode
debug        optional-args  activate debugging
msgno        none           show RMAN-nnnn prefix for all messages
send         quoted-string  send a command to the media manager
pipe         string         building block for pipe names
timeout      integer        number of seconds to wait for pipe input
checksyntax  none           check the command file for syntax errors
-----------------------------------------------------------------------
Both single and double quotes (' or ") are accepted for a quoted-string.
Quotes are not required unless the string contains embedded white-space.
```

RMAN offers the **checksyntax** parameter, which allows you to check the RMAN commands you want to issue for errors. Here is an example of the use of the **checksyntax** parameter:

```
C:\Documents and Settings\Robert>rman checksyntax
Recovery Manager: Release 11.2.0.1.0 - Production on Thu Nov 5 04:03:03 2009
Copyright (c) 1982, 2009, Oracle and/or its affiliates.  All rights reserved.
RMAN> backup database pls archivelog;
RMAN-00571: ===========================================================
RMAN-00569: =============== ERROR MESSAGE STACK FOLLOWS ===============
RMAN-00571: ===========================================================
RMAN-00558: error encountered while parsing input commands
RMAN-01009: syntax error: found "identifier": expecting one of: "archivelog,
auxiliary, backupset, backup, channel, controlfilecopy, copy, current, database,
datafilecopy, datafile, db_recovery_file_dest, delete, diskratio, filesperset,
force, format, from, include, keep, maxsetsize, noexclude, nokeep, not, plus,
pool, recovery, reuse, section, skip readonly, skip, spfile, tablespace, tag, to,
(, ;"
RMAN-01008: the bad identifier was: pls
RMAN-01007: at line 1 column 17 file: standard input

RMAN> backup database plus archivelog;
The command has no syntax errors
```

Note that a lot can be divined from RMAN error messages. Often, within the message, you can see that RMAN was expecting a particular keyword or phrase.

RMAN Client Compatibility

When using the RMAN client, you will want to consider the compatibility of that client with the target database that you are connecting to. You will also need to consider the compatibility of the recovery catalog, which we will discuss in more detail in Chapter 9. In general, the version of the RMAN client should be the same or higher than the version of the target database that you will be connecting to. Here is a table that provides guidelines on RMAN compatibility between the target and auxiliary databases and the RMAN client:

Target/Auxiliary Database	Client Version Requirement
8.0.6	8.0.6 only
8.1.7	8.0.6.1 or 8.1.7 only
8.1.7.4	8.1.7.4 only
9.0.1	9.0.1 only
9.2.0	>= 9.0.1.3 and <= target database executable version
10.1.0	>= 9.0.1.3 and <= target database executable version
10.2.0	>= 9.0.1.3 and <= target database executable version
11.1.0	>= 9.0.1.3 and <= target database executable version
11.2.0	>= 9.0.1.3 and <= target database executable version

RMAN is stored in the $ORACLE_HOME/bin directory, and this directory should be in the PATH on the OS Oracle is running on. If you have several ORACLE_HOME directories, then you will want to be cautious. Make sure that the OS PATH is pointing to the correct ORACLE_HOME before you start RMAN. If you do not set the PATH correctly, you could be using the wrong ORACLE_HOME directory. Also be cautious that there is not some other rman executable in the path before the RMAN executable. For example, an rman command in some versions of Unix sometimes ends up running instead of RMAN because it comes first in the path. In cases like this, you will need to adjust the path, or you may need to change to the $ORACLE_HOME/bin directory and run rman directly from that location.

Typically, RMAN will generate an error if you are using an incompatible client version. You can use OS-level utilities (such as oraenv) to determine if you are using the correct ORACLE_ HOME, or you can check the banner of the RMAN client.

Using the RMAN connect Command

If you start RMAN and realize that you either have not connected to the correct database or wish to connect to a different database (target, catalog, or auxiliary), you can use the **connect** command to change which database RMAN is connected to. To change to another target database, use the **connect target** command. To change to a different recovery catalog, use the **connect catalog** command. To connect to a different auxiliary database, use the **connect auxiliary** command. Here are some examples of the use of the **connect** command:

```
connect target sys/password@testdb;
connect catalog rcat_user/password@robdb;
```

Exiting the RMAN Client

When you are done with RMAN, it's time to get out of the client. RMAN offers two commands, **quit** and **exit**. These commands will return you to the OS prompt. RMAN also allows you to shell out to the OS with the **host** command. Here are some examples:

```
C:\>rman target=/
Recovery Manager: Release 11.2.0.1.0-Production on Wed Oct 4 22:49:14 2006
Copyright (c) 1982, 2005, Oracle. All rights reserved.
connected to target database: ORCL2 (DBID=582838926)

RMAN> host;
Microsoft Windows XP [Version 5.1.2600]
(C) Copyright 1985-2001 Microsoft Corp.
C:\>exit
host command complete
RMAN> exit
Recovery Manager complete.
```

Configuring the Database for RMAN Operations

Now that you know how to start RMAN, we need to deal with some configuration issues. While it is possible to just fire up RMAN and do a backup, it's a better idea to deal with some configuration questions before you do so. First, you need to set up the database user that RMAN will be using. Next, you can configure RMAN to use several settings by default, so we will look at those settings as well.

Setting Up the Database User

By default, you can use RMAN with the SYS account (as sysdba) without any configuration required. Of course, that's probably not the best account to use when you are doing production backups. We recommend, before you use RMAN to do a backup, that you create a separate account that is designated for RMAN backups. The following workshop helps you do just that.

RMAN Workshop: *Create the Target Database RMAN Backup Account*

Workshop Notes

For this workshop, you need an installation of the Oracle software and a database that is up and running. You need administrative privileges on this database.

Step 1. Determine the user account name that you want to use, and create it with the database **create user** command:

```
CREATE USER backup_admin IDENTIFIED BY backupuserpassword
DEFAULT TABLESPACE users;
```

Step 2. Grant the sysdba privilege to the BACKUP_ADMIN user. You need to grant this privilege because RMAN always connects to the database by using the sysdba login. Here is an example of granting the sysdba privilege to the BACKUP_ADMIN account:

```
GRANT sysdba TO backup_admin;
```

NOTE
*If you created your database with the **dbca**, you were offered an option to set up automated daily backups. If you selected this option, Oracle will do some initial RMAN configuration for you (it will configure the FRA, for example). While this RMAN configuration is sufficient for databases that are not of consequence, if you are managing databases that are mission critical, you should still follow the steps outlined in this chapter and ensure that your database is properly configured for RMAN operations.*

So, what happens if you try to connect RMAN to an account that is not properly created? The following error will occur:

```
D:\oracle\oradata\robt>RMAN target=backup/backup@robt
Recovery Manager: Release 11.2.0.1.0
Production on Tue Aug 22 21:40:51 2006
Copyright (c) 1982, 2005, Oracle.  All rights reserved.
RMAN-00571: ===========================================================
RMAN-00569: =============== ERROR MESSAGE STACK FOLLOWS ===============
RMAN-00571: ===========================================================
RMAN-00554: initialization of internal recovery manager package failed
RMAN-04005: error from target database:
ORA-01031: insufficient privileges
```

Now that we have created the user and granted it the privileges it will need, we are a step closer to being ready to use RMAN. Still, we have some RMAN default settings we need to configure, so let's look at those next.

Setting Up Database Security

We need to discuss briefly the differences between connecting to RMAN on the local server and connecting to it via Oracle Net. When you start RMAN, you might be logged onto the same server as the database. In this case, if you are logged on using a privileged OS user account, you do not need to do anything beyond the two steps in the preceding RMAN Workshop. How do you know whether your user account is a privileged one? It depends on the OS you are using. If you are using Unix, there is generally a Unix group called dba (though it may be called something else) that is created when the Oracle-owning account (usually called Oracle) is created. If your Unix user account is assigned to this group, then you will be able to connect to a target database without any additional work. If you are using Windows platforms, then the privileged users are assigned to an NT group, generally called ORA_DBA.

If you are not logging onto the local server using a privileged account, or if you are connecting to the target database using Oracle Net from a client workstation (for example, you are connecting using system/manager@testdb), then you need to configure your database to use a password file. To do so, you first need to create the password file, and then need to configure the database so that it knows to use it. Let's look at each of these steps in detail.

Create the Password File

To create the database password file, you use the Oracle utility **orapwd**. This command takes three parameters:

■ **file**   The password filename

- **password**   The password for the sys user

- **entries**   Any number of entries to reserve for additional privileged Oracle user accounts

By default, the Oracle database (on NT) will expect the password file to take on the naming standard PWD*sid*.ora, where *sid* is your database name. Here is an example of the creation of a password file:

```
orapwd file=PWDrobt.ora password=robert entries=20
```

So, now that we have created the password file, we need to configure the database to use it, and thus to allow us to do remote backups via Oracle Net.

Configure the Database to Use the Password File

By default, an Oracle database is not configured to use the password file (unless you have used the ODBCA to create your database). To configure the database, edit the parameter file (init.ora) in your favorite editor. The parameter we are interested in is REMOTE_LOGIN_PASSWORDFILE. This parameter can be set to one of three values in Oracle Database 11*g*:

- **none**   The default value. In this case, Oracle will ignore the password file, and only local privileged logins will be recognized for sysdba access.

- **shared**   This parameter indicates that multiple databases can use the same password file. When in this mode, only the SYS user account password can be stored.

- **exclusive**   This parameter indicates that the password file is used by only one database. In this mode, the password file can contain passwords for several privileged Oracle accounts. This is the recommend mode of operation, particularly when running RMAN. If you wish to connect RMAN to your database from a remote client, you must use this parameter setting.

If you are using an SPFILE instead of a text-based parameter file, then use the **alter system** command to modify this parameter setting:

```
alter system set REMOTE_LOGIN_PASSWORDFILE=EXCLUSIVE scope=spfile;
```

Finally, the REMOTE_LOGIN_PASSWORDFILE parameter is not dynamic, so you cannot change it with the database up and running. Instead you will have to change the SPFILE (using the **scope=spfile** parameter of the **alter system** command) and then shut down the database and restart it.

Setting the CONTROL_FILE_RECORD_KEEP_TIME Parameter

When configuring your database for RMAN, you should consider how long you wish backup records to be stored in the control file. This includes records of full database backups and of specific datafile, control file, parameter file, and archive log backups. The database parameter CONTROL_FILE_RECORD_KEEP_TIME is defined in days (the default is **7**). Thus, by default, Oracle will maintain RMAN backup and recovery records for seven days. You can set this parameter to any value between 0 and 365 days.

This parameter can have a number of operational database impacts. First, it directly impacts the size of the database control file, because as RMAN backups occur, records relating to these backups are stored in the control file. As records are saved in the control file, the control file might well run out of space. In this case, Oracle will expand the control file to accommodate the storage of the required number of backup records. Setting this parameter to **0** will disallow any control file growth, but has the negative effect of making the RMAN backup history retention period uncertain.

We suggest that you set CONTROL_FILE_RECORD_KEEP_TIME to a value no less than your selected database backup retention period. Otherwise, you risk having database backups available on your backup media without related backup records available in the control file. This can cause serious complications if you need to recover these older backups for some reason!

CAUTION
There are a number of places where incorrectly set file retention can cause your backup's retention strategy to fail. These include incorrectly setting CONTROL_FILE_RECORD_KEEP_TIME, RMAN retention policies, or retention policies on your tape vendor products. Make sure all retention policies are aligned so you don't wake up someday and find you are unable to restore your backups.

Configuring RMAN Default Settings

RMAN allows you to perform automated database backup and recovery, as you will see in later chapters. To support this feature, RMAN allows you to define default values for a number of settings, such as channel configuration. In this section, we look at the configuration of default RMAN settings. Of course, if you can configure something, you will want to be able to change that configuration, and even to remove it completely if required. We will look at that, too. So, what will be the benefit of all of this configuration work? It will make the process of actually doing backups much easier in the end. First, we will quickly examine the **configure** command in RMAN and all that it provides us. Then, we will look at several of the different defaults you might want to configure by using the **configure** command.

Throughout this section, we use a number of terms that you might not yet be familiar with because they are covered in later chapters. Many of the terms were introduced in Chapter 2, though others may not be quite clear to you yet. That's okay, because to use RMAN, none of the default configuration options are really required. We suggest that you skim this section to get a feel for the various default values that you can set, and then, after you have read later chapters, return here and reread this section. At that point, you will be ready to decide what defaults you want to apply to your Oracle database.

Introducing the configure Command

RMAN provides the **configure** command, which allows you to define default values to be applied when executing backup and recovery sessions. Using the **configure** command, RMAN allows you to make changes to the default values of the various parameters that are persistent until cleared or changed again. The ability to customize default configuration settings allows you to execute automated RMAN operations. The following are several of the different settings that you can configure:

- A default device type, such as disk or SBT (system backup tape), to use for RMAN jobs.

- The number of channels that are automatically allocated when performing automated backup and restore jobs.

- A tablespace exclusion policy to configure specific tablespaces to be excluded during full database backup operations.

- The maximum size for any given backup piece and the size of any backup set when doing an automated backup.

- Backup optimization to default to ON or OFF. Backup optimization eliminates duplicate backups of identical datafiles (for example, those associated with read-only tablespaces) and archived redo logs.

- The default filename for the snapshot control file (refer to Chapter 2 for more details on the snapshot control file).

- The default for automated backups of the control file to ON or OFF, as well as the default format for the control file backup output files and the default device on which to create these backups.

- The default filenames for files of an auxiliary database.

- A default retention policy, which determines which backups and copies are eligible for deletion because they are no longer needed.

- The default encryption value and the associated encryption algorithm.

- The default compression algorithm to use if compression is to be used.

- A deletion policy for archived redo logs.

Each configurable setting has a default value assigned to it. The defaults are stored in the database control file (as are any configured values). This is true even if you are connecting to a recovery catalog. You can see the currently configured values for the various RMAN parameters by using the **show** command. Any nondefault RMAN-configured settings are also listed in the V$RMAN_CONFIGURATION database view. Here are some examples of the **show** command's use:

```
show default device type;
show maxsetsize;
show retention policy;
show all;
```

Configuring Various RMAN Default Settings

This section looks at setting RMAN defaults. First, let's look at configuration of channel default settings. You can configure channels in different ways. You can configure defaults for all channels with the **configure channel device type** command, or configure defaults for specific default channels with the **configure channel _n_ device type** command.

You can clear channel defaults for all channels with the **configure channel device type clear** command, and clear channel defaults for specific default channels with the **configure channel *n* device type clear** command.

When you allocate a channel with the **allocate channel** command, you can specify the assigned names to the channels that you allocate. For example, the **allocate channel d1 device type disk** command will create a channel called d1. When automated channels are allocated, Oracle assigns default names to these channels. These default names depend on the type of default device used. The following table provides an example of the default name format that will be used.

Device Type	Default Name Format	Example
Disk	ORA_DISK_*n*	*ORA_DISK_1* *ORA_DISK_2*
Tape	ORA_SBT_TAPE_*n*	*ORA_SBT_TAPE_1* *ORA_SBT_TAPE_2*

The number of channels that are automatically allocated depends on the default level of parallelism defined (which we will discuss later in this chapter).

When you issue the **configure** command, Oracle displays the previous configuration settings, followed by the new configuration setting. Now, let's look at some of the ways that you can use the **configure** command to automate the backup and restore process with RMAN.

Examples of Using the configure Command

This section presents some examples of using the **configure** command to define default values. In this section, we cover a number of topics revolving around the **configure** command, including:

- Configuring channel default settings

- Using the format string

- Configuring default automated backups of the control file and the SPFILE

- Configuring default retention policies

- Configuring default levels of encryption

- Configuring archive log deletion policies

Configuring Channel Default Settings

Let's start with an example of configuring the default backup/restore device to tape or to disk. In this case, all channels assigned to backups will be allocated to disk:

```
CONFIGURE DEFAULT DEVICE TYPE TO SBT;
CONFIGURE DEFAULT DEVICE TYPE TO DISK;
```

When default device types are configured, Oracle will use that default channel unless you override the default using the **backup device type** parameter. Maintenance channels for **delete** commands and auxiliary channels for duplicate operations will also be automatically allocated.

Once we have configured a default device type, we can configure defaults for the specific type of backup that should occur when that device is used. For example, when doing backups to disk, we can opt to have Oracle back up the database by default using the standard Oracle backup set methodology, or we can have it default to using copies (which can only go to disk). You can also indicate that backup sets should be compressed by default and indicate the degree of parallelism (which represents the number of channels that will be allocated for that backup). Here are examples of configuring for these different options:

```
CONFIGURE DEVICE TYPE DISK BACKUP TYPE TO BACKUPSET;
CONFIGURE DEVICE TYPE DISK BACKUP TYPE TO COMPRESSED BACKUPSET;
CONFIGURE DEVICE TYPE DISK BACKUP TYPE TO COPY;
CONFIGURE DEVICE TYPE DISK PARALLELISM 2;
```

One word about compression, which was a new feature of RMAN in Oracle Database 10*g*. Compression provides real compression of your Oracle backup sets, not unlike zip compression. This can make your backup sets much smaller. Of course, the compression itself consumes resources and will make the backups take longer to complete or restore.

Now, let's look at an example of configuring the number of channels to be allocated during an automated backup or recovery operation. Also in this example, we have set the default level of parallelism for disk operations to two. Thus, if you start an automated backup, two channels will be allocated to perform the backup in parallel.

```
CONFIGURE CHANNEL 1 DEVICE TYPE DISK FORMAT 'd:\backup\robt\backup_%U';
CONFIGURE CHANNEL 2 DEVICE TYPE DISK FORMAT 'e:\backup\robt\backup_%U';
```

NOTE
Generally, when setting the default level of parallelism, you should set it to the number of tape drives you will be backing up to. When using disks, some trial and error might be called for. Since disks have multiple heads and may be stripped, it may be that multiple channels will result in better throughput. Test parallelism to your disks and act accordingly on the results.

Several options are available when configuring channels. With the **maxpiecesize** parameter, you can control the size of a backup set piece. You can control the maximum number of files that RMAN can open at one time with the **maxopenfiles** parameter. The **rate** parameter allows you to throttle RMAN and to control the rate at which a backup occurs in either bytes, kilobytes, megabytes, or gigabytes per second.

In this example, we put all these options to use. We limit channel 1 to creating each individual backup piece at a maximum size of 100MB, and we limit RMAN to opening a maximum of eight files on this channel. Finally, we have constrained the channel such that it cannot have a throughput of more than 100MB.

```
CONFIGURE CHANNEL 1 DEVICE TYPE DISK MAXPIECESIZE 100m maxopenfiles 8
rate 100MB;
```

NOTE
Don't get confused about the difference between the **maxpiecesize**
parameter and the **maxsetsize** *parameter:* **maxpiecesize** *limits the size*
of the individual backup set pieces and has no impact on the overall
cumulative size of the backup. The **maxsetsize** *parameter, on the other*
hand, can and will limit the overall size of your backup, so use it
carefully!

If we had wished to limit all channels, we could have issued the command slightly differently:

```
CONFIGURE CHANNEL DEVICE TYPE DISK MAXPIECESIZE 100m;
```

So, why might we want to change the maximum size that a given backup set piece can be? First, we might have some specific file size limitations that we have to deal with. Tapes can only handle so much data, and some disk file systems have limits on how large a given datafile can be.

We might also want to set a tape device as the default device for all channels, along with some specific parameter settings. In this case, our **configure** command might look like this:

```
-- Note that we could have used the - sign after the PARMS clause if
-- we preferred like this:
-- PARMS='ENV=(NB_ORA_CLASS=RMAN_rs100_tape).
-- This is true with many parameters.
CONFIGURE CHANNEL DEVICE TYPE sbt MAXPIECESIZE 100m
PARMS 'ENV=(NB_ORA_CLASS=RMAN_rs100_tape)';
```

When using the **configure** command, you may find that you need to clear a given configuration so that you can use the default. To do this, use the **configure** command with the **clear** option. In this example, we are clearing out the default options set for default channel 1:

```
CONFIGURE CHANNEL 1 DEVICE TYPE DISK CLEAR;
```

Configuring Backup Set–Related Settings
You may wish to configure a default maximum size for an entire backup set, in which case you would use this slightly modified syntax (it is followed by an example of resetting this value back to the default, which is unlimited):

```
CONFIGURE MAXSETSIZE TO 7500K;
CONFIGURE MAXSETSIZE CLEAR;
```

CAUTION
Be careful when using **maxsetsize** *to limit the size of the entire backup*
that is being created. While your database might be smaller than
the **maxsetsize** *defined initially, it could quickly grow beyond the*
maxsetsize, *causing your database backups to fail.*

As you will see in later chapters, you can configure the backup process to create duplexed backups; in other words, multiple copies of the backup can be created at different locations. You can also configure database default settings such that automatic backups will be duplexed using the **configure** command. Here is an example where we have defined that all backups to disk by default will be duplexed, with two copies:

```
configure datafile backup copies for device type disk to 2;
```

You may wish to exclude specific tablespaces during an automated backup, which Oracle allows you to do with the **configure** command. Here is an example of excluding a tablespace by default:

```
configure exclude for tablespace old_data;
```

The **configure** command allows you to enable or disable backup optimization. When enabled, *backup optimization* will cause Oracle to skip backups of files that already have identical backups on the device being backed up to. Here is an example of configuring backup optimization:

```
configure backup optimization on;
```

Note that for optimization to occur, you must have enabled it. In addition, you must issue the **backup database** or **backup archivelog** command with the **like** or **all** option. Alternatively, you can use the **backup backupset all** command (more information on these types of backups is provided in later chapters). Finally, you can disable the setting for backup optimization by using the **force** parameter of the **backup** command.

Configuring Snapshot Control File Settings

We discussed the snapshot control file in Chapter 2. This file is a point-in-time copy of the database control file that is taken during RMAN backup operations. The snapshot control file ensures that the backup is consistent to a given point in time. Thus, if you add a tablespace or datafile to a database after the backup has started (assuming an online backup, of course), that tablespace or datafile will not be included in the backup. Sometimes it is desirable to have RMAN create the backup control file in a location other than the default location. In this event, you can use the **configure** command to define a new default location for the snapshot control file:

```
configure snapshot controlfile name to 'd:\oracle\backup\scontrolf_mydb';
```

Note that Oracle does not create the snapshot control file in the FRA even if the FRA is configured. Also note in this example, we include the name of the database (or database instance if running RAC) to ensure the snapshot control filenames are unique.

Using the Format String

Note in previous examples that in several places we defined one or more disk locations and filename formats. This is known as the *format string specification*. You will see the format string specification used a great deal in this book, and you will often use it when working with RMAN unless you are using the FRA. The FRA uses Oracle's own file-naming conventions, so using a format string when backing up to the FRA is not recommended or required (and can cause problems with file maintenance). Since the FRA is the default location for backups, there is no need to configure a backup device to point to the FRA. You may need to configure channels for other reasons, but do not configure them such that they have a format string pointing to the FRA.

The format string is platform independent (though directory structures will be platform specific). A format string on Windows will look pretty much the same on Unix or on any other platform. For example, if we were using a Unix system, our format string might look like this:

```
CONFIGURE CHANNEL 1 DEVICE TYPE DISK FORMAT
'/u01/opt/oracle/backup/robt/backup_%U';
CONFIGURE CHANNEL 2 DEVICE TYPE DISK FORMAT
'/u01/opt/oracle/backup/robt/backup_%U';
```

NOTE
Oracle will not manage your backup files if you use the **format** *parameter, even if you are backing up to the FRA, because the backup is not managed by Oracle. If the* **format** *parameter is used, then the retention policy will have to remove the formatted backups. If* **format** *is not used, then OMF names are used, and the files are created in the FRA. Do not use the* **format** *option when backing up to the FRA.*

The format string is used a lot in the **configure** command. You will also see it in other RMAN commands such as the **backup**, **restore**, and **allocate channel** commands. RMAN offers several *syntax elements* associated with the format string specification. These elements are placeholders that will cause RMAN to replace the format string with the associated defined values. For example, the %U syntax element in the previous example tells RMAN to substitute a system-generated unique identifier for the filename. %U then keeps each backup filename unique. Table 3-3 lists the valid syntax elements and gives a quick description of their use.

Element	Description
%a	Indicates that the activation ID of the database should be substituted.
%b	Specifies the filename without any directory paths. This can only be used with the **set newname** command or for creating a backup using image copies.
%c	Specifies that the copy number of the backup piece within a set of duplexed backup pieces, with a maximum value of 256, should be substituted. This number will be 1 for nonduplexed backup sets and 0 for proxy copies.
%d	Indicates that the name of the database should be substituted.
%D	Indicates that the current day of the month from the Gregorian calendar in the format DD should be substituted.
%e	Indicates that the archived log sequence number should be substituted.
%f	Indicates that the absolute file number should be substituted.
%F	Provides a unique and repeatable name that combines the database ID (DBID), day, month, year, and sequence.
%h	Indicates that the archived redo log thread number should be substituted.
%I	Indicates that the DBID should be substituted.

TABLE 3-3 *Format String Specification Descriptions*

Element	Description
%M	Indicates that the month in the Gregorian calendar in the format MM should be substituted.
%N	Indicates that the tablespace name should be substituted.
%n	Indicates that the name of the database, padded on the right with x characters to a total length of eight characters, should be substituted. For example, if ROBDB is the database name, then the padded name is ROBDBxxx.
%p	Indicates that the piece number within the backup set should be substituted. This value starts at 1 for each backup set and is incremented by 1 as each backup piece is created.
%s	Indicates that the backup set number should be substituted. This number is a counter in the control file that is incremented for each backup set. The counter value starts at 1. This number will be unique for the lifetime of the control file (thus, it is reset at RESETLOGS or when the control file is restored or re-created).
%t	Indicates that the backup set timestamp, which is a 4-byte value derived as the number of seconds elapsed since a fixed reference time, should be substituted. %s and %t combined can be used to form a unique name for the backup set.
%T	Indicates that the year, month, and day from the Gregorian calendar in the format YYYYMMDD should be substituted.
%u	Indicates that an eight-character name, consisting of compressed representations of the backup set or image copy number and the time the backup set or image copy was created, should be substituted.

%U	This is the default file-naming pattern and provides a system-generated unique filename for RMAN-related files. The meaning of this substitution string differs when dealing with image copies or backup pieces.
	When using backup set pieces, %U specifies a convenient shorthand for `%u_%p_%c` that guarantees uniqueness in generated backup filenames.
	The meaning differs when using image copies, and depending on the type of image copy.
	Meaning when used with an image copy of datafiles:
	`data-D-%d_id-%I_TS-%N_FNO-%f_%u`
	Meaning when used with an image copy of an archived redo log:
	`arch-D_%d-id-%I_S-%e_T-%h_A-%a_%u`
	Meaning when used with an image copy of a control file:
	`cf-D_%d-id-%I_%u`

%Y	Indicates that the year in the format YYYY should be substituted.
%%	Indicates that you wish to actually use the % character; for example, %%Y.

TABLE 3-3 *Format String Specification Descriptions* (continued)

Configuring Default Automated Backups of the Control File and the SPFILE

RMAN in Oracle Database 10*g* and later offers the ability to back up the control file and the database parameter file, and you can configure these backups to take place by default. Again, you can use the **configure** command to configure this automated backup process to happen automatically during a backup. Here is an example of configuring automated backups of these important database files, and an example of turning off the default configuration:

```
configure controlfile autobackup on;
configure controlfile autobackup off;
```

When autobackup of the control and parameter files is configured, the following rules apply:

■ The control file and the server parameter file will be automatically backed up with each RMAN **backup** or **copy** command issued that is not included in a **run** block.

■ If a **run** block is used, then the control files and parameter files will be backed up at the end of the **run** block if the last command is not **backup** or **copy**.

NOTE
If you are not going to use a recovery catalog and the following conditions apply:

■ *You wish to be able to recover your control file after an automated control file backup.*

■ *You are not using the FRA.*

In addition to the last two types of automated control file backups, a special type of control file backup can be configured to occur as a direct result of database changes such as adding new tablespaces, adding datafiles, adding online redo logs, and so on. This type of automatic backup can only happen to disk. A special option of the **configure controlfile autobackup** command can be used to facilitate this backup. Here is an example:

```
RMAN> configure controlfile autobackup format for device type
disk to 'd:\backup\contf\robt_%F'
```

When this option is used, the Oracle RDBMS will automatically back up the control file during database structure changes that impact the control file. These changes might include adding a new tablespace, altering the state of a tablespace or datafile (for example, bringing it online), adding a new online redo log, renaming a file, adding a new redo thread, and so forth. Note that this automated backup can only be to disk, because tape is not supported. These backups can get a bit large (since the control file contains a history of many of the past backups), so make sure you allocate enough disk space to the backup directory. In spite of the additional space that will be required, these backups can be incredibly handy to have for recovery. Finally, be aware that if the backup fails for any reason, the database operation itself will not fail.

NOTE
You must know the DBID of the database. You should, as a part of your initial setup and configuration of RMAN, note the DBIDs of the databases that you will be backing up and save that list somewhere safe. The DBID of the database is available from the V$DATABASE view in the DBID column. The DBID of the database is also displayed when you start RMAN and connect to a target database, as shown in this example:

```
[oracle@robertgfreeman ~]$ rman target=/
Recovery Manager: Release 11.2.0.1.0 - Production on Thu Nov 5 04:04:06 2009
Copyright (c) 1982, 2009, Oracle and/or its affiliates.  All rights reserved.
connected to target database: ROB1(DBID=1854903786)
```

Configuring Default Retention Policies

So, how long do you want to keep your database backups? RMAN enables you to configure a backup retention policy by using the **configure retention policy** command. If you configure a retention policy and are using the FRA, then RMAN and Oracle will take care of automatically removing backups when they become obsolete. If you are not using the FRA, then configuring a retention policy will not cause backups to be deleted automatically, but will cause expired backup sets to appear when the **report obsolete** command is executed. See Chapter 15 for more on **report obsolete**.

There are really three kinds of retention policies in Oracle: recovery window–based, redundancy-based, and none. Let's look at each of these in more detail next.

Recovery Window–Based Retention Policies   The recovery window–based retention policy is designed to ensure that your database can be recovered to a specific point in time. For example, if you wanted to make sure that you could recover your database back to any point in time up to three days ago (assuming you were running in ARCHIVELOG mode, of course), you would set a recovery window–based retention policy of three days. The command to configure such a retention policy would be as follows:

```
RMAN> configure retention policy to recovery window of 3 days;
old RMAN configuration parameters:
CONFIGURE RETENTION POLICY TO RECOVERY WINDOW OF 7 DAYS;
new RMAN configuration parameters:
CONFIGURE RETENTION POLICY TO RECOVERY WINDOW OF 3 DAYS;
new RMAN configuration parameters are successfully stored
```

Note that the recovery window–based retention criteria can result in backups actually being maintained longer than the stated recovery window. For example, if your recovery window is three days, but your last full backup was five days ago, then that backup will remain valid until it is no longer needed to restore your database. Even if you back up your database today, five days later, the backup that is five days ago is still needed because it is the only source of recovery back to day 3. Figure 3-1 provides a graphical demonstration of this.

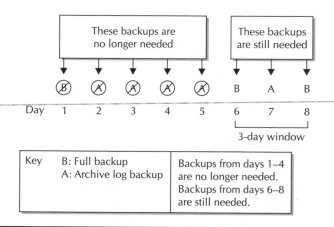

Figure 3-1 *Recovery window maintaining older backups*

Now that we have configured our retention policy, let's see which previous backups are reported to be obsolete:

```
RMAN> report obsolete;
RMAN retention policy will be applied to the command
RMAN retention policy is set to recovery window of 3 days
Report of obsolete backups and copies
```

```
Type                    Key    Completion Time    Filename/Handle
--------------------    ------ ------------------ --------------------
Archive Log             12     08-SEP-09
/oracle/app/oracle/flash_recovery_area/ROB1/archivelog/2009_09_08/
o1_mf_1_9_5bd8qv45_.arc
Backup Set              24     08-SEP-09
  Backup Piece          34     08-SEP-09
/oracle/app/oracle/flash_recovery_area/ROB1/backupset/2009_09_08/
o1_mf_annnn_TAG20090908T202600_5bg4kr90_.bkp
Backup Set              25     08-SEP-09
  Backup Piece          35     08-SEP-09
/oracle/app/oracle/flash_recovery_area/ROB1/backupset/2009_09_08/
o1_mf_nnnd0_TAG20090908T202601_5bg4ktk1_.bkp
```

In this example, we have two backup sets and two related backup pieces that are obsolete based on our backup retention policy. Additionally, we have an archived redo log that is ready to be removed as well. If these backups are in a defined FRA (which these are), Oracle will remove them as required. If you are not using an FRA, or if these backups were created before you converted to using an FRA, you will need to use the **delete obsolete** command to remove them. More information on the **delete obsolete** command can be found in Chapter 15, and an example is provided here, too:

```
RMAN> delete obsolete;
RMAN retention policy will be applied to the command
RMAN retention policy is set to recovery window of 3 days
using channel ORA_DISK_1
using channel ORA_DISK_2
Deleting the following obsolete backups and copies:
Type                    Key    Completion Time    Filename/Handle
--------------------    ------ ------------------ --------------------
Archive Log             12     08-SEP-09
/oracle/app/oracle/flash_recovery_area/ROB1/archivelog/2009_09_08/
o1_mf_1_9_5bd8qv45_.arc
Backup Set              24     08-SEP-09
  Backup Piece          34     08-SEP-09
/oracle/app/oracle/flash_recovery_area/ROB1/backupset/2009_09_08/
o1_mf_annnn_TAG20090908T202600_5bg4kr90_.bkp
Backup Set              25     08-SEP-09
  Backup Piece          35     08-SEP-09
/oracle/app/oracle/flash_recovery_area/ROB1/backupset/2009_09_08/
o1_mf_nnnd0_TAG20090908T202601_5bg4ktk1_.bkp
Do you really want to delete the above objects (enter YES or NO)? yes
```

Note in the preceding example that the system will ask you to confirm that you really want to remove the objects that are slated to be removed. If any of the listed objects are not available to be removed, then you will need to run the **crosscheck** command (discussed in Chapter 14). Otherwise, each item listed as deleted in the **delete obsolete** output will be deleted by Oracle.

Redundancy-Based Retention Policies   This kind of retention policy is based on the total number of backups maintained by RMAN and is more typically used if you are backing up your database infrequently. This is the default retention policy, with a default value of 1. If you were to set this value to 3, then Oracle would consider the last three backups as current, and any other backups would be considered obsolete. Here is an example of configuring a redundancy retention policy of 3:

```
RMAN> configure retention policy to redundancy 3;
old RMAN configuration parameters:
CONFIGURE RETENTION POLICY TO REDUNDANCY 3;
new RMAN configuration parameters:
CONFIGURE RETENTION POLICY TO REDUNDANCY 3;
new RMAN configuration parameters are successfully stored
```

Note in the output that RMAN displays both the old and new settings for the retention policy.

No Retention Policy   If you want to disable the retention policy, you use the command **configure retention policy to none**, and no retention policy will be applicable. Use the **configure retention policy clear** command to reset the retention policy to the default value, which is a redundancy of 1.

NOTE
If you are using a tape management system, it may have its own retention policy. If the tape management system's retention policy conflicts with the backup retention policy that you have defined in RMAN, the tape management system's retention policy will take precedence, and your ability to recover a backup will be in jeopardy.

Configuring Default Levels of Encryption

RMAN can create encrypted backups starting with Oracle Database 10*g* Release 2 and later. During the backup, the backup sets are encrypted as they are created. When the backups are restored, Oracle will decrypt the backup sets. In this section, we discuss the types of encryption that are available and then look at how to configure RMAN so that it can use encryption.
Oracle offers three different encryption modes:

- **Transparent mode**   Transparent mode encryption requires no DBA interaction. To use this mode, you must have configured the Oracle Encryption Wallet.

- **Password mode**   Password mode encryption requires that a password be supplied when creating backups to be encrypted or when restoring backups that were encrypted when they were created. The password is supplied by using the command **set encryption on identified by password only** in your RMAN backup scripts. This is the encryption mode we will use in this text.

- **Dual mode**   Dual mode backups can be restored either by password or by the presence of the Oracle Encryption Wallet. This makes offsite restores of backups easier, since the install of the Oracle Encryption Wallet is not required. To create a dual mode encrypted backup, you use the **set encryption on identified by password** command (note that the **only** keyword is missing).

Use the **configure** command to configure various persistent settings related to RMAN encryption of backups. You can use the RMAN **configure** command to indicate the following:

- Whether all database files should be encrypted

■ Whether specific tablespaces should be encrypted

■ Which of the available encryption algorithms should be used to encrypt your backups

If you are using Oracle Encryption Wallet–based security, then you only need to set the persistent RMAN settings required by the **configure** command. If you wish to use password mode encryption or dual mode encryption, you need to configure the persistent security defaults with the configure **command**, and then use the **set** command when starting your backups to set the correct password for the backup. RMAN does not persistently set the backup password, so it must be entered for each RMAN backup or recovery session. The **set** command, and how to use it during backups, is covered in much more detail in Chapter 9. In the following command, we configure and enable backup encryption for the entire database. Notice that if we have not configured the Oracle Encryption Wallet, any subsequent backups will fail unless we use the **set** command to establish an encryption password for the session (we are jumping the gun just a bit, but we provide an example of using the **set** command to set the backup password in appropriate context).

```
-- Configures default encryption.
-- Uses transparent mode encryption by default.
RMAN> CONFIGURE ENCRYPTION FOR DATABASE ON;
-- For this session, we want password mode encryption,
-- so we have to set the
-- password. This is good only for this session, until we exit RMAN or
-- issue another connect command.
RMAN> SET ENCRYPTION ON IDENTIFIED BY robert ONLY;
-- Way ahead of ourselves, but this backs up the database!
RMAN> BACKUP DATABASE PLUS ARCHIVELOG;
```

Archived redo log backups are backed up using encryption if the following are true:

■ The **set encryption on** command is in effect at the time that the backup of the archived redo logs is occurring.

■ Encryption has been configured for the entire database, or for at least one tablespace of the database.

The **configure** command also provides the ability to determine the encryption algorithm you wish to use. The available algorithms can be seen in the V$RMAN_ENCRYPTION_ALGORITHMS view as seen in this example:

```
SQL> select algorithm_name from V$RMAN_ENCRYPTION_ALGORITHMS;
ALGORITHM_NAME
------------------------------------------------------------
AES128
AES192
AES256
```

Knowing the algorithms available, we can now configure a default encryption algorithm we wish to use, as seen here:

```
RMAN> Configure encryption algorithm 'AES128';
using target database control file instead of recovery catalog
new RMAN configuration parameters:
CONFIGURE ENCRYPTION ALGORITHM 'AES128';
new RMAN configuration parameters are successfully stored
```

Configuring Archive Log Deletion Policies

You can configure RMAN to manage your archived redo log deletion policy for you. By default, Oracle applies the configured backup retention policy to the archived redo logs. In Oracle Database 11g, you can also configure a separate deletion policy for archived redo logs. This policy will get applied to archived redo logs in both the FRA and in those stored outside the FRA. Only those in the FRA will be removed by Oracle, however. If logs are in the FRA, Oracle will try to keep them as long as possible, only removing them when additional space is required. If you are using a non-FRA location, then you will need to use the **delete obsolete** or **delete archivelog** command to remove archived redo logs marked as obsolete. In this example we use the **configure** command to configure an archive log deletion policy. In this case, all archived redo logs that are backed up three times will be eligible for removal:

```
RMAN> Configure archivelog deletion policy to backed up 3 times to device type disk;
new RMAN configuration parameters:
CONFIGURE ARCHIVELOG DELETION POLICY TO BACKED UP 3 TIMES TO DISK;
new RMAN configuration parameters are successfully stored
```

In versions of Oracle before Oracle Database 11g, the archived redo log deletion policy applied only to archived redo logs being applied on a standby database. In these versions, you could configure RMAN to mark archived redo logs as eligible for removal after they have been applied to a mandatory standby database by using the **configure archivelog deletion policy to applied on standby** command. In this case, once the archived redo log has been successfully applied to a mandatory standby database location, it is eligible for removal from the FRA by Oracle. This functionality remains in Oracle Database 11g and later.

If You Are Using Shared Servers

If you are using Oracle's Shared Servers option (known as Multi-Threaded Server, or MTS, in previous Oracle versions), then you have to configure a dedicated server for use with RMAN because RMAN cannot use a Shared Servers session to connect to the database. If you are using a Shared Servers architecture, refer to Chapter 5 of the *Oracle Database Backup and Recovery Advanced Users Guide (11g Release 2)* for more information on how to configure RMAN for use with the Oracle Database 11g Shared Servers option.

Essentially, you must configure a dedicated connection in Oracle Net for your server by using the **SERVER=dedicated** syntax, as shown in this example (note that Oracle Net configurations vary greatly, so what may be required of you might differ):

```
Rob1_ded =
    (DESCRIPTION=
       (ADDRESS=(PROTOCOL=tcp)(HOST=robpc)(port1521))
       (CONNECT_DATA=(SERVICE_NAME=rob1_ded)(SERVER=dedicated)))
```

Summary of RMAN Configuration Tasks

We have thrown a great deal of information at you in this chapter. The following summarizes the tasks that you will need to perform to get set up to do database backups with RMAN. We also provide a few suggestions along the way. Each of the steps listed here has detailed instructions included earlier in this chapter:

1. Determine whether you wish to run the database in ARCHIVELOG mode or NOARCHIVELOG mode. Configure the database accordingly. In most cases, we would recommend ARCHIVELOG mode since it provides a large number of recovery options.

2. We recommend that you configure and use the FRA.

3. Set up a separate database user account (not sys) for use with RMAN.

4. In the database parameter file, set the CONTROL_FILE_RECORD_KEEP_TIME parameter to a number of days equivalent to or greater than the number of days you wish to retain database backups. Retention is one area within RMAN that can have "gotchas." Make sure that your retention policies in RMAN, the CONTROL_FILE_RECORD_KEEP_TIME parameter, and any retention policies established by your tape administrators (if you are backing up to tape) are aligned.

5. If you are using shared servers, set up a dedicated server address for RMAN to connect to.

6. Using RMAN, connect to the target database to ensure that the database is set up correctly (error messages will appear if your RMAN account is not correctly set up).

7. Use the **configure** command to establish your default RMAN values. In particular, consider configuring the following:

   - Configure the default degree of parallelism for tape or disk backups. Set it to a default value equivalent to the number of disks or tape drives that you will be backing up to. If you are backing up to a SAN with many disk drives, consider using parallel channels to back up to those disk devices.

   - Configure automatic channels and device types. The number of channels that you configure should equal the degree of parallelism that you have configured. Configure as many channels as you have individual devices, and configure the same number of channels as you have.

   - Configure automated control file/database parameter file autobackups.

   - If you own ASO (Advanced Security Option, which is the license required to use encryption), then configure automated database backup encryption.

8. Configure the retention policy as required. Make sure this retention policy is in sync with any other retention policies, such as those associated with tape management systems. Also, if required, consider retention criteria for your archived redo logs.

9. Configure RMAN for control file and SPFILE automatic backups.

10. Before you use it for production database backups, test your RMAN configuration by doing a backup and recovery as demonstrated in later chapters.

Other Backup and Recovery Setup and Configuration Considerations

Finally, let's consider the other backup and recovery implications of your database. RMAN will not back up certain things that you need to consider as a part of your overall backup and recovery strategy planning. These include such things as the base Oracle RDBMS software and the parameter files (tnsnames.ora, names.ora, sqlnet.ora, and so on). You need to make plans to back up and recover these files as a part of your overall backup and recovery planning.

You also need to consider your disaster planning with regard to RMAN and non-RMAN backups. How will you protect these backups from flood, fire, and earthquake? In advance is a very good time to consider these questions, not when the fire is burning two flights below!

Summary

Whew! We have covered a great deal of ground in this chapter, and, indeed, there are several things you need to do before you start using RMAN. First, we described how to set up the database in ARCHIVELOG mode if that is what you wish to do. Next, we looked at the RMAN command line and at how to configure your database for use with RMAN, including setting up the password file and configuring a user account for use with RMAN. We also looked at configuring RMAN default settings. We strongly suggest you take advantage of this feature in RMAN, because it can make your life much easier. Finally, we provided you with a summary of RMAN configuration tasks and talked about other backup and recovery considerations.

CHAPTER
4

Media Management
Considerations

he RMAN utility in Oracle Database 11*g* focuses on the best way to leverage disk backups as the media recovery solution. With the price of disks falling, massive storage area networks (SANs) have found a permanent place in many data centers. With the business evolving toward cheaper and larger disks, upgrades in RMAN functionality (such as the flash recovery area) were implemented to make best use of the available storage space.

It's a logical progression for the RMAN backup utility, and, of course, writing to disk is something that the Oracle Database is extremely good at. So, anytime it gets to leverage its disk-writing muscle, the RDBMS will do so for performance improvements.

But, for many customers, the world of unlimited disk storage has not arrived. For many, the size of the database, or its location, keeps it from being backed up to disk. Or, there still may be a business requirement to make a copy of the data and archive it offsite. So, what does RMAN do if it needs to write to good, old-fashioned tape?

Tape backups of the Oracle database require third-party assistance. This is primarily due to the disparate nature of the different sequential media subsystems that are on the market and that are used every day. Instead of trying to employ different system calls for each different type of tape device, RMAN's development team decided to employ those software vendors that already earn a living by selling products that can read and write from tape.

Oracle has its own media management software solution, Oracle Secure Backup (OSB). OSB is a fully integrated, RMAN-to-tape solution that does not require any third-party vendor software plug-in, and OSB has come a long way since its introduction in 10*g*R2. However, many customers will continue to purchase a license from any of the number of certified backup providers that have an Oracle RMAN plug-in (more on this in a minute).

This chapter covers the conceptual architecture of employing a media manager to back up your database directly to disk. It does so from a generic standpoint, by staying focused on the RMAN side of the equation and speaking in sweeping generalizations about the media management products themselves. We will talk about the setup from the RMAN side, how it all works, and what changes when you use tape for your output device. Chapters 6, 7, and 8 go into detail about four of the most popular media management products on the market, and talk about configuring and using them specifically. Chapter 5 provides an overview of the new Oracle-produced media management product, Oracle Secure Backup (OSB).

In Oracle 10*g*R2 and Oracle 11*g*, you can utilize OSB to provide free backup to tape functionality, provided that you have a single tape head and it is attached directly to the server that contains the Oracle database that you want to back up. In other words, you will pay for centralized tape farms. To get additional backup-to-tape functionality, you will have to purchase the full version of OSB, or to buy a product from a media management vendor.

Tape Backups in a Disk Backup World

In the world of Oracle databases, size does matter. In fact, less than a decade ago, a database of a few gigabytes was considered very large. Now, databases range upward into the terabytes, the first pedabyte database has been reported, and the average database is 100GB and growing. So when it comes to backups, trying to find enough contiguous space on disk to get the thing backed up can be difficult, even with the massive number of SANs being deployed in the enterprise.

Thus, the first reason for considering tape backups is the size of the database. The size of a database determines whether you need to back up to tape: buying more hard drives can get pricey. But even with disk prices dropping radically, tapes are still cheaper and reliable, considering their purpose is to hold copies of data—copies that likely will rarely get used. Of course, sometimes disk backups become a critical piece of a strategy that stresses quick recovery, and using tape backups is much slower than using disks on both the backup and the restore. The price point of a tape, compared with disks, remains a compelling reason for tape backups.

The second reason to use tape backups is manageability. Typically, enterprise-wide backup strategies are implemented and executed by one person on a centralized system. And this allows your company to invest in large tape storage jukeboxes that can stream data from multiple sources. Then, the data backups can be catalogued and removed without having someone trek all over the enterprise distributing tapes, troubleshooting individual tape devices, or training users on new software rollouts.

A third and frequently disregarded reason for tape backups is their portability. A pile of tapes can easily be moved offsite for archiving and disaster-proofing. Hard drives just don't transport that well.

The drawback to pooling backup resources is that it leads to complications, especially in regard to Oracle databases. The complexity of Oracle datafiles, log files, and control files means that we cannot simply let an OS job step in and copy the files at its leisure. Instead, we have to prepare the database for the backup job, signal the copy to begin, and afterward reconfigure the database. Or, so it was in the old-school world (refer to Chapter 1).

Using RMAN means that this kind of database configuration is eliminated and that backups can occur anytime, under any circumstances. However, to get the backups to stream to your centralized tape backup location, you have to do some RMAN-specific configuration.

RMAN and the Media Manager: An Overview

RMAN streams backups to tape by engaging a media manager. A *media manager* is software provided by a third-party vendor that takes the data stream of blocks passed from the RMAN channel process and redirects it to the appropriate tape. Most often, a media management server exists in an enterprise network. A *media management server* is a centralized system that handles all enterprise-wide backup operations to tape devices that it manages.

To engage a media manager, a computer system must have the corresponding media management client software installed on it. This is the software that makes the connection to the media management server and passes the data to it over the network. For RMAN to engage the media management server, an additional software component is needed. After you install the client software, you must also install the Oracle module for the media manager. The *Oracle module* is a software plug-in for the Oracle RDBMS that connects RMAN to the client media management software, which can then make the pass to the media management server. This plug-in for Oracle is referred to as the *Media Management Library* (MML). Figure 4-1 shows a generalized overview of the backup topology when a media manager is used to back up to tape.

The Media Manager Catalog

The media manager is a separate subsystem in the overall backup system you will use. It has three essential components, as previously described: the Media Management Library that integrates with Oracle, the media management client, and the media management server. The media management server has multiple components, the specifics of which depend upon the vendor. But all media management servers must have a few similar components, the most important of which (from the perspective of this chapter) is the media manager catalog.

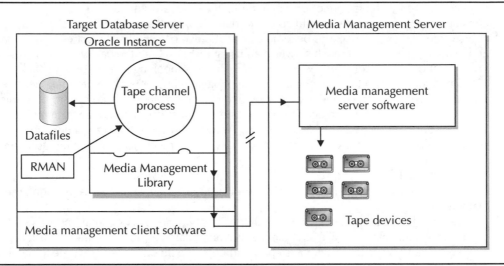

FIGURE 4-1 *Network topology when backing up to tape*

The media manager catalog is the database at the media management server that holds information about the physical tapes, who has access to those tapes, and what is being stored on those tapes. This catalog records the RMAN file handle when a backup is complete. The *handle* refers to the name of the backup piece that gets created when you perform a backup with RMAN. When you back up to disk, the handle is the physical filename. When you back up to tape, the handle is used in the media manager catalog to refer to the location on tape where the backups can be located.

RMAN completes a backup to tape by providing the handle name to the media manager, which records that handle in the catalog. When a restore is required, RMAN requests a specific handle (based on its own catalog) from the media manager. The media manager looks for that handle, associates it with a specific tape, and determines if that tape is available. If the tape is available, the media manager engages the tape and begins to stream the data back to RMAN so that you can rebuild the datafiles.

The Media Manager: Other Software Components

In addition to the catalog, the media management server comprises two essential pieces:

- **Device agent** The component responsible for engaging the actual tape device and passing data to and from it.

- **Robotic interface** The software that controls any robotics that are responsible for changing tapes when they are full or for retrieving a tape that was been filled.

From the Oracle perspective, RMAN is blind to these components. RMAN simply sends a command request to its MML, and the media management software handles the coordination of all events after that. However, it is important to be familiar with these software components because your backup and recovery success depends on them. Many problems that come from using RMAN are related to the device agent or the robotic interface, but from the RMAN interface these problems are nearly impossible to discern.

Media Management Library

The MML is simply a library file that interprets generic requests from RMAN for a particular backup or restore operation, and translates that request into the specific system call necessary at the media management server to turn that request into reality. The MML is provided by the same vendor that supplies the media management client and server software, but you purchase and license the MML separately from the client and server software.

The MML is loaded into the Oracle memory space as an integrated library file when a tape channel is first allocated; it is logically part of the Oracle RDBMS software, so that RMAN can make the correct calls to the media management client software. The integration is simple: When a channel to tape is allocated, Oracle loads a file called libobk.so. This file, located in the ORACLE_HOME/lib directory, is just a symbolic link to whichever MML file you will be using. On the Windows platform, Oracle looks for a file called orasbt.dll in the searchable path. Regardless of which media management provider you use, its media management DLL will be named orasbt.dll, and media management providers usually write it to the WINDOWS\system32 directory. If your media management provider does not do this, it will append to the system path environment variable a searchable path that leads to orasbt.dll.

In the next four chapters, we discuss the linking process by which you can establish your vendor's MML file as the one RMAN initiates when a channel is allocated. For testing purposes, Oracle provides a test MML file. This library file allows you to allocate a channel to tape but then to write the backup to disk. In the following RMAN Workshop, we show you how to use this test MML.

RMAN Workshop: *Test Tape Channels with the Oracle Default SBT Interface*

Workshop Notes

You need access to a sufficient amount of disk space, and you need to create a directory in which to place the backup piece. In our example, we use the mount point u04, on which we created a directory called *backup*. Make sure you have sufficient memory available for the backup, as outlined in Chapter 2, and be aware of the disk I/O that goes to the backup location. Try to allocate space on a controller other than those that house your actual database.

Step 1.   Build your backup directory:

```
$>cd /u04
mkdir backup
```

Step 2.   Make sure permissions are established so that the Oracle Database, which operates as the user that installed the software, can write to this location:

```
ls -l backup
```

Step 3.   Initiate RMAN and connect to the target. In the following example, we are connecting locally to the target PROD. This means that an env command shows us that ORACLE_SID=PROD.

```
$>Rman
Rman> connect target
```

Step 4. Run your backup by using the PARMS parameter during channel allocation to specify the oracle test library file. You also need to specify a BACKUP_DIR directory, which is the location that RMAN will write the backup to. Here, we specify this as /u04/backup:

```
<RMAN> run {
2> allocate channel x1 type 'sbt_tape'
3> PARMS="SBT_LIBRARY=oracle.disksbt,
4> ENV=(BACKUP_DIR=/u04/backup)";
5> backup datafile 1 format='%U';}
```

Alternatively, you can use a permanent configuration command to set the oracle library (but remember that you've done it, and don't leave it lying around for too long):

```
CONFIGURE CHANNEL DEVICE TYPE 'SBT_TAPE' PARMS
'SBT_LIBRARY=oracle.disksbt,ENV=(BACKUP_DIR=/u04/backup)';
```

Here's the output from the preceding command:

```
allocated channel: x1
channel x1: SID=27 device type=SBT_TAPE
channel x1: WARNING: Oracle Test Disk API
Starting backup at 25-SEP-09
channel x1: starting full datafile backup set
channel x1: specifying datafile(s) in backup set
input datafile file number=00001 name=/home/oracle/app/oracle/oradata/v112/system01.dbf
channel x1: starting piece 1 at 25-SEP-09
channel x1: finished piece 1 at 25-SEP-09
piece handle=04kq4cbe_1_1 tag=TAG20090925T102902 comment=API Version 2.0,MMS Version 8.1.3.0
channel x1: backup set complete, elapsed time: 00:02:07
channel x1: starting full datafile backup set
channel x1: specifying datafile(s) in backup set
including current control file in backup set
including current SPFILE in backup set
channel x1: starting piece 1 at 25-SEP-09
channel x1: finished piece 1 at 25-SEP-09
piece handle=05kq4cfd_1_1 tag=TAG20090925T102902 comment=API Version 2.0,MMS Version 8.1.3.0
channel x1: backup set complete, elapsed time: 00:00:02
Finished backup at 25-SEP-09
released channel: x1
```

This is a great test if you are trying to troubleshoot possible problems with your media manager backup solution and cannot get the backups to work. By allocating a "fake" tape channel, you can see that RMAN is configured correctly.

CAUTION
Do not use the test MML file for production backups. If you will be backing up to disk in a production environment, allocate a disk channel. The performance of the fake MML is terrible, because RMAN is allocating memory buffers for tape, not disk, and therefore is not taking advantage of the speed of disk writes versus tape writes.

If you have not successfully loaded your vendor's MML file and you do not specify in the PARMS section of the channel allocation that you want to use Oracle's disk SBT interface, you will receive an error when you try to allocate a channel to tape:

```
RMAN-00571: ====================================================
RMAN-00569: =============== ERROR MESSAGE STACK FOLLOWS =====
RMAN-00571: ====================================================
RMAN-03009: failure of allocate command on x channel
       at 12/05/2005 21:26:43
ORA-19554: error allocating device, device type: SBT_TAPE, device name
ORA-27211: Failed to load Media Management Library
```

Interfacing with the MML

When you are linking Oracle and the MML, you are establishing the means by which RMAN can pass a command that engages the MML and, by extension, the media management client software installed on the database server. But how do you know which media management server to engage?

To specify the media management server, you must pass an environment variable within the RMAN session to specify the server name. We specify the server name as an environment variable when we allocate our tape channel. As you saw in the previous RMAN Workshop, you pass the environment variable by using the PARMS option of the **allocate channel** command. Different media management products have different environment variables that they accept. VERITAS NetBackup, for example, requires the parameter NB_ORA_SERV:

```
Allocate channel t1 type 'sbt_tape'
PARMS="ENV=(NB_ORA_SERV=storage1)";
```

In the preceding example, the name of the media management server is storage1, and our database server has already been registered in this server and has permission to write to its tape devices.

In addition to passing the name of the server, we can pass numerous other parameters at the time of the channel allocation to take advantage of management functions at the server. For instance, NetBackup offers the ability to specify the class or the schedule to use for this backup, whereas EMC Networker allows you to specify the resource pool. More details on these parameters are given in Chapters 6 and 7.

The SBT API

RMAN can engage different media managers with impunity because it sends the same marching orders no matter what MML has been loaded. Oracle developed RMAN with a generic API called the SBT API, which is provided to third-party vendors that wish to write integration products for Oracle database backups. This API is the means by which RMAN sends commands to the media manager.

The SBT API is responsible for sending the commands to the media management server to initiate the creation of backup files on tape. It also sends commands to search for previous backups based on the file handle in the media manager catalog. It can send commands to remove these backups, as well as write new backups and, of course, read from the backup location. There are two versions of the Oracle RMAN SBT API: 1.1 and 2.0. Version 1.1 was published and used with Oracle 8.0.*x*, and that's it. Since then, RMAN has made calls to the media manager by using the specifications of version 2.0. You can see this version in RMAN's output when you run a backup:

```
channel x1: finished piece 1 at 25-SEP-09
piece handle=05kq4cfd_1_1 tag=TAG20090925T102902 comment=API Version 2.0,MMS Version 8.1.3.0
channel x1: backup set complete, elapsed time: 00:00:02
Finished backup at 25-SEP-09
```

RMAN also returns the version of the MML that it initializes at channel allocation time. This is seen during channel allocation in the RMAN output:

```
allocated channel: x
channel x: sid=12 devtype=SBT_TAPE
channel x: VERITAS NetBackup for Oracle8 - Release 3.4GA (030800)
```

Not only is this a good way to determine your MML version, but it also means that you have successfully linked in your MML with RMAN—otherwise, it would not be able to extract the version information.

Back Up to Tape: From Start to Finish

In this section, we do a walk-through of a backup to tape and show the different calls made to the SBT API and how they are handled by the media manager. Again, please note that we are giving you a very generic overview, and the specifics are handled by the vendor that writes the integration MML.

When you allocate a tape channel, RMAN spawns a server process at your target database. This server process then makes a call to the SBT API of sbtinit(). This call initializes the MML file and loads it into memory. It also returns to RMAN the version of SBT API supported by that MML. After calling sbtinit(), RMAN calls sbtinit2(), which supplies further configuration details to the media manager software.

After RMAN has parsed your backup command, it executes the RPC that makes the call to sys.dbms_backup_restore.backuppiececreate. At this time, the channel process calls sbtbackup(), which handles the creation of the backup piece at the specified tape location. This call informs the media manager that Oracle will begin pushing the flow of data blocks to it, so it should prepare the tape device for the onslaught.

The RMAN input buffers fill up and make the memory-to-memory write to the output buffer. When the output buffer fills, the channel process calls sbtwrite2(), which performs the write of filled output buffers to the tape location (for more on input buffers, see Chapter 2). Typically, this means engaging the device agent at the media management server in order to access the tape itself.

When all the output buffers for a particular backup set have been cleared out and there is no more work for sbtwrite2(), the channel session calls sbtclose2(). This flushes out any media manager buffers and commits the backup piece to tape.

After we complete the backup piece, the channel process invokes sbtinfo2(), to make sure the media manager catalog has documented the backup piece. It requests the tape, the tape location, and the expiration time of the backup from the catalog. Then, it writes the backup piece handle to the catalog.

After confirming the backup piece location, the channel process calls sbtend(), which cleans up any remaining resources and releases them for other database use. The final action performed is the deallocation of the channel process, which is terminated at the target database.

Restore from Tape: From Start to Finish

Of course, sooner or later all that backing up you've been doing will get put to the test, and you will need to perform a restore. As with a backup, the SBT API has a specific series of steps that it goes through during a restore operation in order to get the backups on tape back into place for your database. In this section, we briefly run through the SBT API during a restore operation.

When you allocate the tape channel for restore, RMAN creates a server process at the target database. This channel then calls sbtinit() to initialize the media manager software. This is identical to the initialization that would take place for a backup: the MML file is loaded into memory.

Based on the parameters of our **restore** command in RMAN, RMAN will have checked its catalog to determine the handle name of the backup required for the restore. It then takes this requested backup piece handle and passes it to the media manager by using sbtrestore(). The sbtrestore() function instructs the media manager to prepare the appropriate tape for a restore operation. This means engaging the media manager catalog and finding the appropriate tape, and then (if necessary) passing the command to the robotic instruction set to get the tape. After the tape is loaded, it will need to be rewound to the backup piece starting point.

After preparing the tape for the restore, the channel process calls the sbtread2() function to read the data from the tape device and stream it to the Oracle process. This data is loaded into the input buffers, written to the output buffers, and finally written to the datafile locations as specified by the control file.

When the end of a backup piece is detected on tape, the tape channel process calls the sbtclose() function to disengage the particular tape that had that piece on it. This signals that Oracle is done with the tape. If there are more backup pieces that need to be read for the restore operation, then the channel process returns to the second step and calls sbtrestore() for a different backup piece.

After the restore is complete and RMAN requests no more backup pieces, the channel process calls the sbtend() function, which cleans up the channel resources and releases them for other use. Then the channel process is terminated, after which the media manager is free to unload any tapes that had been requested.

Using sbttest and loadsbt.exe

As we mentioned previously, there are always indications as to whether you have successfully linked your MML with Oracle. The information from the channel allocation shows the MML version, for instance. However, these sorts of indicators do not guarantee success, because a failure may occur farther down the topology: at the media management client level or at the media management server. Oracle provides a utility called sbttest that can test to make sure that RMAN will be able to perform backups to tape by using your media management configuration. This utility is called from a command line and performs a complete test: it writes a block to tape and then requests a read of that block. In this way, it runs through the entire gamut of SBT API functions that would occur during backup and makes sure they will all be successful.

Using sbttest is simple. After making sure that you have completed the full configuration of your media management configuration, go to the command prompt within the environment from which you will run RMAN and type **sbttest** and a test filename. The following code walks you through each of the sbt() calls previously listed in the "Restore from Tape: From Start to Finish" section and provides output on whether each call succeeded:

```
/u02/home/usupport> sbttest oratest_061902
The sbt function pointers are loaded from libobk.so library.
NetWorker: Cannot contact nsrexecd service on horatio.hadba.com,
Service not available.-- sbtinit succeeded
NetWorker: Cannot contact nsrexecd service on horatio.hadba.com,
Service not available.-- sbtinit (2nd time) succeeded
sbtinit: Media manager supports SBT API version 2.0
sbtinit: vendor description string=NMO v3.5.0.1
sbtinit: allocated sbt context area of 536 bytes
sbtinit: Media manager is version 3.5.0.1
sbtinit: proxy copy is supported
sbtinit: maximum concurrent proxy copy files is 0
-- sbtinit2 succeeded
-- regular_backup_restore starts ...........................
MMAPI error from sbtbackup: 7501, nwora_index_ssinfo:
index connect to cervantes.windba.com failed for client
horatio.hadba.com: Program not registered
-- sbtbackup failed
```

The sbttest utility has matured impressively since its inception as a simple binary indicator of success or failure. Now, a number of parameters can be passed to tweak the exact test you would like to take your media management system through. This includes naming the database you want to test, changing the number of blocks that are written by sbttest, and specifying how to further handle the file that sbttest writes to tape. Simply typing **sbttest** at the command prompt will give you all the switches you can use, along with simple text descriptions.

The sbttest utility is only available for Unix platforms; on Windows, you can request the utility loadsbt.exe from Oracle Support. Unfortunately, this utility does not have the same capabilities as sbttest and instead simply checks the searchable path for a file called orasbt.dll. If it finds this file, it will try to load it the same way that Oracle will during a tape backup. It will tell you if it can be loaded, but it will not attempt to write a block to tape, so it does not "swim downstream" very far to see if the entire configuration works. As such, it is not as useful as sbttest.

Media Management Errors

Error reporting in RMAN looks much the same when reporting media management problems as it does when reporting any other problem, and this can lead to some confusion. It is critical when troubleshooting RMAN errors to be able to determine where exactly the error is coming from: is it RMAN, the target database, the catalog database, or the media manager?

There are specific ways to determine if an error that is being returned in RMAN is related to the media manager. Some of them are obvious, particularly if you have not linked the MML correctly. We've shown examples of these errors already. However, if you have properly linked the MML with your Oracle installation, how can you tell if an error is related to the MML?

There are a number of different errors, but the most common error you will see related to the media manager is ORA-19511. This error is actually a *blank error,* meaning that Oracle supplies no text; instead, Oracle provides this as an error trap for media management errors. So if you see the following error, there is no doubt that you have linked your MML correctly and that the problem you are having is irrefutably a problem with the media manager:

```
ORA-19511: sbtbackup: Failed to process backup file
```

Other indicators of media management problems are not so clear, but just as telling. For instance, if you ever see in the error stack RMAN referring to a "sequential file," then you are dealing with a tape backup, and the problem is due to a failed read or write to the sequential file on tape. Another common error is ORA-27206:

```
RMAN-10035: exception raised in RPC: ORA-27206: requested file
not found in media management catalog
```

Again, the wording indicates a problem communicating with the media management catalog, which is where you would need to look to resolve the problem.

In addition to actual errors, any hang you might encounter in RMAN is *usually* related to media management problems. *Usually.* When RMAN makes an sbtwrite() call to the media manager, for instance, RMAN cannot possibly know how long this will take to complete. Therefore, RMAN does not provide any sort of time-out for the operation—it will wait indefinitely for the media manager to return with either a successful write or an error. If the media manager is waiting on a particular event that has no time out, such as a tape switch or a tape load, the media manager waits, and so RMAN waits. And so you wait. And wait. As we said, RMAN will not time out, so if you notice that RMAN is taking a particularly long time to complete and you see no progress in V$SESSION_LONGOPS (see Chapter 2), then your first instinct should be to check the media manager for an untrapped error or for an event such as a tape load or tape switch

Summary

In this chapter, we discussed the concepts behind how RMAN utilizes the media management software of a third-party vendor to make backups to tape. We walked through the specific steps that RMAN makes using the SBT API. We also briefly discussed media management errors in RMAN.

CHAPTER
5

Oracle Secure Backup

racle Secure Backup (OSB) is a reliable, complete, and centralized tape backup management solution. OSB provides heterogeneous data protection in distributed, mixed-platform environments. It protects Oracle Database and file system data, such as the contents of Oracle Home. In addition to tape backup, OSB delivers an integrated Oracle database backup to third-party cloud (Internet) storage, through the Oracle Secure Backup Cloud Module. Oracle Secure Backup offers two tape management editions: OSB and OSB Express.

This chapter discusses features of OSB, its interfaces, components of OSB, and how to install and configure OSB.

Features of Oracle Secure Backup

- Provides support for all major tape drives and tape libraries in SAN (storage area network), Gigabit Ethernet, and SCSI (Small Computer System Interface) environments

- Supports Internet Protocol v4 (IPv4), Internet Protocol v6 (IPv6), and mixed IPv4/IPv6 environments on all platforms that support IPv6

- Accesses local and remote file systems and any tape device from any location in a network without using NFS (network file system) or CIFS (Common Internet File System)

- Supports Fibre-attached devices

- Backs up to and restores data from Oracle Cluster File System (OCFS) on Linux and Microsoft Windows systems

- Allows use of wildcards and exclusion lists to specify the files for backup

- Performs multilevel incremental backups, duplexed database backups, and backups that span multiple volumes

- Offers automatic tape-drive sharing to reduce idle tape-drive write periods

- Uses direct-to-block positioning and direct access restore to avoid unnecessarily reading tape blocks to locate files

- Features highly configurable encryption of Oracle9*i* forward and file system backups

- Supports fast backup compression starting with Oracle Database 11.1.0.6

- Supports ACSLS (Automated Cartridge System Library Software) and vaulting

- Reports progress of backup or restore jobs during the operations

- Offers tight RMAN integration

- Integrated with Oracle Enterprise Manager Database and Grid Control, starting with Oracle Database 10*g* Release 2

- Allows direct backup to cloud storage using the Oracle Secure Backup Cloud Module

- Acts as single point of contact for issues involving Recovery Manager (RMAN) and the media manager

- Includes Oracle Secure Backup Express, available free with the Oracle Database and Oracle Applications, which may be employed for backup and restore of one server to a single tape drive

Oracle Secure Backup and Recovery Manager

Oracle Secure Backup is a media management layer for RMAN, and it supplies an SBT interface that RMAN can use to back up database files to tape. The OSB SBT library is the only interface that supports RMAN encrypted backups and unused block compression directly to tape. The RMAN ability to eliminate backup of committed undo is exclusive to OSB and is not available with other media management products. In Oracle Database 11*g*, CPU overhead is reduced by using a shared buffer for SBT (System Backup to Tape) and tape to eliminate the copy process from SBT to the tape buffer. OSB is better integrated with Oracle Enterprise Manager (OEM) as compared with other media managers, and managing tapes, media servers, and tape devices using OEM is exclusive to OSB.

Differences Between OSB and OSB Express

The following are the common features for Oracle Secure Backup and Oracle Secure Backup Express:

- Integrated with RMAN for online tape backup and restore of Oracle Database

- Backs up and restores file system data

- Integrated with Oracle Enterprise Manager (Oracle Database 10*g*R2 and higher)

These features are available only with Oracle Secure Backup:

- Backs up Real Application Clusters (RAC) environments

- Integrated with Oracle Enterprise Manager Grid Control (Oracle Database 10*g*R2 and higher)

- Enables multiple tape drive usage within the backup environment

- Provides Fibre-attached device support

- Offers backup encryption to tape

- Includes Oracle fast backup compression (Oracle Database 11*g*R1 and higher)

- Supports ACSLS and vaulting

- Features networked backup of distributed servers and/or tape devices

Backup Encryption

Oracle Secure Backup encryption is available for both RMAN and file system backup operations. The data is encrypted on the server before transport over the network, or written to a locally attached tape device. Database data is encrypted after RMAN has passed the data through the

SBT to OSB. If the RMAN data from the SBT is encrypted, then no further encryption occurs. Backup encryption is normally available only with the purchase of the Oracle Advanced Security Option (ASO).

Fast Database Backup Compression

Fast database backup compression is normally available only with the purchase of the Oracle Advanced Compression Option (ACO).

Oracle Secure Backup Cloud Module

The Oracle Secure Backup Cloud Module is independent of the OSB tape management editions. The module has been qualified only with Amazon S3 (Simple Storage Service) for now, but it might be expanded to other cloud storage vendors in the future. The number of Oracle Secure Backup Cloud Module licenses depends on the number of RMAN channels for backup to the cloud and does not depend on the number of Oracle database backups. For example, four OSB Cloud Module licenses could be used to back up two Oracle databases using two RMAN channels for each or used to back up one Oracle database using four RMAN channels.

Oracle Secure Backup Interfaces

Figure 5-1 illustrates the interfaces you may use to access Oracle Secure Backup, described here:

- **Oracle Enterprise Manager Database Control and Grid Control**   This is the preferred graphical user interface (GUI) for managing OSB. Most of OSB tasks can be performed via OEM. The OSB administrative server can be configured as a target in OEM Grid Control and can be used to perform file system backup and restore operations.

FIGURE 5-1   *OSB interfaces*

■ **Oracle Secure Backup Web tool**   This interface is a browser-based GUI that enables you to configure an administrative domain, browse the backup catalog, manage backup and restore of file system data, and perform certain other tasks not possible in OEM. It exposes all functions of obtool. The Web tool employs an Apache web server running on the administrative server.

■ **Oracle Secure Backup command-line interface (obtool)**   This command-line program is the primary interface to OSB and is in the bin subdirectory of the OSB home. Using obtool, you may log into the administrative domain to back up and restore file system data as well as to perform configuration and administrative tasks. You may run obtool on any host within the administrative domain.

■ **Recovery Manager command-line interface**   The RMAN command-line interface may be used to configure and initiate database backup and restore operations for utilization of OSB. The RMAN utility is located in the bin directory of an ORACLE_HOME directory. The RMAN command-line client will run on any database host, as long as the client is able to connect to the target database. The OSB SBT library must exist on the same host as the target database in order for RMAN to make backups using OSB.

Oracle Secure Backup Components

An administrative domain is a group of hosts managed as a common unit for performing backup and restore operations. When configuring OSB, roles are assigned to each host in the domain. A single host may consist of one or more of the following roles:

■ **Administrative server**   Starting and monitoring backup and recovery jobs is accomplished by the administrative server running within an administrative domain. The administrative server may also run other applications in addition to OSB.

■ **Media server**   Houses secondary storage devices such as tape drives or tape libraries. At least one media server will be defined for each administrative domain.

■ **Client**   A host whose local data is backed up by OSB. One or more clients will be defined in each administrative domain. Most hosts in the administrative domain are clients.

Figure 5-2 illustrates an OSB administrative domain. The domain includes an administrative server, a media server with an attached tape library, three clients, and five hosts.

Figure 5-3 demonstrates an OSB administrative domain containing a single Linux host. This Linux host assumes the roles of administrative server, media server, and client. An Oracle database and a locally attached tape library are configured for the Linux host.

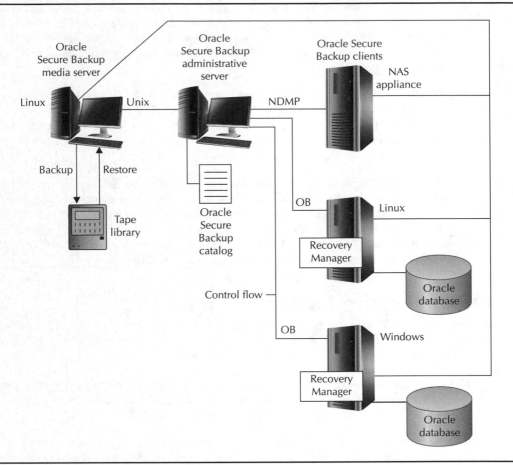

FIGURE 5-2 *OSB administrative domain*

FIGURE 5-3 *OSB administrative domain with a single host*

Oracle Secure Backup Daemons

An administrative domain uses seven types of OSB daemons:

- **Service daemon**   This daemon runs on the administrative server, media server, and client. Access to OSB configuration data on the administrative server is provided by the service daemon. It also runs jobs requested by the schedule daemon. On a media server or a client, the daemon handles membership in an administrative domain.

- **Schedule daemon**   This runs only on the administrative server. It is the OSB scheduler.

- **Index daemon**   This daemon runs only on the administrative server, to manage the backup catalog. It starts when a backup is completed or the catalog is accessed for restore or browsing operations.

- **Apache web server daemon**   This runs only on the administrative server and provides the Web tool interface.

- **NDMP daemon**   This daemon runs on a media server and a client, and provides data communication between them.

- **Robot daemon**   This runs on a media server and manipulates tapes in a tape library. The service daemon starts one robot daemon for each tape library when a tape manipulation is needed.

- **Proxy daemon**   This daemon runs on a client to verify user access for SBT backup and restore operations.

Host Access Modes

Communicating to a host in an administrative domain is possible through two access modes:

- **Primary**   For primary access mode, OSB is installed on a host. The access mode is used by OSB daemons. An Oracle database typically exists on a host accessed via this mode. In OEM, it is referred to as "native" access mode. In OSB Web tool, it is called "OB" access mode.

- **NDMP**   The Network Data Management Protocol host is a storage appliance provided by third-party vendors, such as DinoStor, Mirapoint, and Network Appliance. Using a vendor-specific implementation, the NDMP host uses the NDMP protocol to back up and restore file systems. OSB is accessible via NDMP, although OSB software is not installed on an NDMP host.

Administrative Data

OSB arranges information for the administrative domain as a hierarchy of files in the OSB home on the administrative server. The directory that OSB installed into is the OSB home.

Figure 5-4 illustrates the directory structure for an OSB home. All platforms have the same directory structure, although the default home is /usr/local/oracle/backup for Unix and Linux systems, but is C:\Program Files\Oracle\Backup for Microsoft Windows systems.

Domain-wide entities, such as media families, classes, and devices, are included within the administrative data. Figure 5-4 illustrates how the config directory contains several subdirectories.

FIGURE 5-4 *Administrative server directories*

These subdirectories each represent an object maintained by OSB. For each object directory, OSB creates files describing the characteristics for the corresponding object.

Only in rare circumstances would it be necessary to access the administrative database directly from the file system. The OEM, Web tool, and obtool interfaces are commonly used to access catalogs and configuration data.

Oracle Secure Backup Users and Classes

To enable OSB to maintain consistent user identities across the administrative domain, OSB saves information for OSB users, as well as their rights, on the administrative server.

On the administrative server, each OSB user has an account and an encrypted password. Using Web tool or obtool, operating system users may enter their username and password. Using an encrypted SSL connection, the client program transmits the password to the administrative server.

The admin user is created by default during OSB installation on the administrative server. Also during the installation, you can create the oracle user to back up and recover Oracle databases. The installer assigns a random password to the oracle user. Usually, it is unnecessary to log into OSB by using this user.

Operating System Accounts

For OSB users, the namespace is distinct from the namespaces for Linux, Unix, and Microsoft Windows users. Therefore, if you access a host in the administrative domain as, for example, the operating system user backup_usr, and if the OSB user in the domain is named backup_usr, these accounts will be managed separately, though the names are identical. You may find it convenient to create the OSB user with the same name and password as an operating system user.

At the time you create an OSB user, you may associate the user with Unix and Microsoft Windows accounts. Accounts of this type are used with an unprivileged backup, which is a backup that is not run with root privileges. Privileged backup and restore operations use a client with root (Unix) or Local System (Microsoft Windows) permissions.

If you were to create an OSB user named backup_usr and associate it with Unix account ubackup_usr and Microsoft Windows account wbackup_usr, when backup_usr uses the **backup -- unprivileged** command to back up a client, the jobs will run under the operating system account associated with backup_usr. Therefore, backup_usr is only able to back up files on a Unix client accessible to ubackup_usr, and able to back up files on a Microsoft Windows client accessible to wbackup_usr.

With the "modify administrative domain's configuration" right, you may configure the preauthorization attribute for an OSB user. This right allows you to preauthorize operating system users to create RMAN backups or to access the OSB command-line utilities.

NDMP Hosts

When setting up an OSB user account, you may configure user access to NDMP. You may set up the host to use a user-defined text password, a null password, or the default NDMP password. A password for an NDMP host is associated with the host, not the user. You may configure a password authentication method such as MD5-encrypted or text.

Oracle Secure Backup Rights and Classes

A defined set of rights granted to an OSB user is considered an OSB class. Though similar to a Unix group, an OSB class has a finer granularity of access rights specific for the needs of OSB. As shown in Figure 5-5, multiple users may be assigned to a class, while each user is a member of a single class.

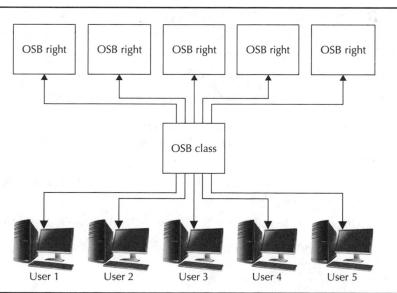

FIGURE 5-5   *Rights and classes*

These classes are important to understanding the rights of an OSB user:

- **admin** Utilized for overall administration of a domain, it consists of all rights necessary to change domain configurations and to complete backup and restore operations.

- **monitor** Does not allow users to receive e-mail notifications, change domain configurations, or to complete backup and restore operations. The users can only access backups, see information about storage devices and domain configuration, and list scheduled jobs.

- **operator** For standard day-to-day operations, it has no configuration rights, but consists of all the rights needed for backup and restore operations. This class allows the user to control and query the state of primary and secondary storage devices.

- **oracle** Much like the operator class, but with rights enabling the user to change Oracle database configuration settings and to perform Oracle database backups. Members of this class usually are OSB users mapped to operating system accounts of an Oracle database installation.

- **reader** Allows members to browse the OSB catalog. Readers may modify only the name and password for their OSB user accounts.

- **user** Assigned to users to allow them rights to interact in limited ways with their domains. This class allows users to browse their own data within the OSB catalog and to perform user-based restores.

Installing and Configuring Oracle Secure Backup

OSB is available for delivery on CD-ROM or may be downloaded from the Oracle Technology Network (OTN) web site at the following address:

http://www.oracle.com/technology/products/secure-backup/index.html

The following are requirements for installing and configuring OSB:

- Each host in the OSB administrative domain must run TCP/IP. Static IP addresses should be assigned to all hosts, or it should be ensured that the DHCP server always assigns the same IP address.

- There should be no duplicate host names in the OSB administrative domain, because index catalog data is based on the client host name.

- For Linux media servers, the SCSI Generic (SG) driver needs to be installed.

- Each node of a RAC cluster using OSB requires an installation of OSB.

RMAN Workshop: *Install and Configure Oracle Secure Backup*

Workshop Notes

The following example uses the Linux operating system. OSB is downloaded from OTN. The recommended directory for the installation of OSB on Linux is /usr/local/oracle/backup. To simplify the example, the administrative server, media server, and client are all installed on the same machine.

Step 1. As the root user, check if the uncompress utility is installed on the system. If it is not, create a symbolic link pointing to the gunzip utility:

```
[root@lin32 ~]# uncompress
-bash: uncompress: command not found
[root@lin32 ~]# ln -s /bin/gunzip /bin/uncompress
```

Step 2. Create a directory for the download, and then issue the **change directory** command to that directory:

```
[root@lin32 ~]# mkdir download
[root@lin32 ~]# cd download/
```

Step 3. Download OSB into the download directory and then unzip the product:

```
[root@lin32 download]# ls -l
total 43864
-rw-r--r-- 1 root root 44866571 Jan 19 20:31 osb-10.3.0.1.0_linux32_release.zip
[root@lin32 download]# unzip osb-10.3.0.1.0_linux32_release.zip
Archive:  osb-10.3.0.1.0_linux32_release.zip
   creating: osb-10.3.0.1.0_linux32_cdrom090504/
 extracting: osb-10.3.0.1.0_linux32_cdrom090504/OSB.10.3.0.1.0_LINUX32.rel
   creating: osb-10.3.0.1.0_linux32_cdrom090504/doc/
   creating: osb-10.3.0.1.0_linux32_cdrom090504/doc/dcommon/
   creating: osb-10.3.0.1.0_linux32_cdrom090504/doc/dcommon/css/
   inflating: osb-10.3.0.1.0_linux32_cdrom090504/doc/dcommon/css/blafdoc.css
   inflating: osb-10.3.0.1.0_linux32_cdrom090504/doc/dcommon/css/bp_layout.css
...
   inflating: osb-10.3.0.1.0_linux32_cdrom090504/welcome.html
   inflating: osb-10.3.0.1.0_linux32_cdrom090504/doc.tar
```

Step 4. Create the directory where the install will place OSB files:

```
[root@lin32 download]# mkdir -p /usr/local/oracle/backup
```

Step 5. Issue the change **directory** command to the OSB destination and run setup:

```
[root@lin32 download]# cd /usr/local/oracle/backup/
[root@lin32 backup]# /root/download/osb-10.3.0.1.0_linux32_cdrom090504/setup
```

The following output is returned:

```
Welcome to Oracle's setup program for Oracle Secure Backup. This program loads
Oracle Secure Backup software from the CD-ROM to a filesystem directory of your
choosing.
This CD-ROM contains Oracle Secure Backup version 10.3.0.1.0_LINUX32.
Please wait a moment while I learn about this host... done.
- - - - - - - - - - - - - - - - - - - - - - - - - - - - - - - - - -
    1. linux32
       administrative server, media server, client
- - - - - - - - - - - - - - - - - - - - - - - - - - - - - - - - - -
Loading Oracle Secure Backup installation tools... done.
Loading linux32 administrative server, media server, client... done.
- - - - - - - - - - - - - - - - - - - - - - - - - - - - - - - - - -
Oracle Secure Backup has installed a new obparameters file.
Your previous version has been saved as install/obparameters.savedbysetup.
Any changes you have made to the previous version must be made to the new obparameters file.
Would you like the opportunity to edit the obparameters file
Please answer 'yes' or 'no' [no]:
```

Step 6. Leaving the default parameters for now, press ENTER to choose the default answer. The following output is returned:

```
- - - - - - - - - - - - - - - - - - - - - - - - - - - - - - - - - -
Loading of Oracle Secure Backup software from CD-ROM is complete.
You may unmount and remove the CD-ROM.
Would you like to continue Oracle Secure Backup installation with 'installob' now?
(The Oracle Secure Backup Installation Guide contains complete information about
installob.)
Please answer 'yes' or 'no' [yes]:
```

Step 7. Again, press ENTER to choose the default answer. The following output is returned:

```
- - - - - - - - - - - - - - - - - - - - - - - - - - - - - - - - - -
Welcome to installob, Oracle Secure Backup's installation program.
For most questions, a default answer appears enclosed in square brackets.
Press Enter to select this answer.
Please wait a few seconds while I learn about this machine... done.
Have you already reviewed and customized install/obparameters for your Oracle
Secure Backup installation [yes]?
```

Step 8. Again, press ENTER to choose the default answer and to leave the default parameters. The following output is returned:

```
- - - - - - - - - - - - - - - - - - - - - - - - - - - - - - - - - -
Oracle Secure Backup is not yet installed on this machine.
Oracle Secure Backup's Web server has been loaded, but is not yet configured.
Choose from one of the following options. The option you choose defines the
software components to be installed.
```

```
Configuration of this host is required after installation completes.
You can install the software on this host in one of the following ways:
     (a) administrative server, media server and client
     (b) media server and client
     (c) client
If you are not sure which option to choose, please refer to the Oracle Secure
Backup Installation Guide. (a,b or c) [a]?
```

Step 9.   You are going to install all three components of OSB on the same server, so again press ENTER to choose the default answer. The following output is returned:

```
Beginning the installation.  This will take just a minute and will produce
several lines of informational output.
Installing Oracle Secure Backup on lin32 (Linux version 2.6.18-53.el5)
You must now enter a password for the Oracle Secure Backup encryption key store.
Oracle suggests you choose a password of at least 8 characters in length,
containing a mixture of alphabetic and numeric characters.
Please enter the key store password:
Re-type password for verification:
```

Step 10.   Enter the OSB encryption key twice. The key is not displayed. You will see the following output:

```
You must now enter a password for the Oracle Secure Backup 'admin' user. Oracle
suggests you choose a password of at least 8 characters in length, containing a
mixture of alphabetic and numeric characters.
Please enter the admin password:
Re-type password for verification:
```

Step 11.   Enter the admin password twice. The password is not displayed. You will see the following output:

```
You should now enter an email address for the Oracle Secure Backup 'admin' user.
Oracle Secure Backup uses this email address to send job summary reports and to
notify the user when a job requires input. If you leave this blank, you can set it
later using the obtool's 'chuser' command.
Please enter the admin email address:
```

Step 12.   Leave the e-mail address blank for now. The following output is returned:

```
     generating links for admin installation with Web server
     updating /etc/ld.so.conf
     checking Oracle Secure Backup's configuration file (/etc/obconfig)
     setting Oracle Secure Backup directory to /usr/local/oracle/backup in /etc/obconfig
     setting local database directory to /usr/etc/ob in /etc/obconfig
     setting temp directory to /usr/tmp in /etc/obconfig
     setting administrative directory to /usr/local/oracle/backup/admin in /etc/obconfig
     protecting the Oracle Secure Backup directory
     creating /etc/rc.d/init.d/observiced
     activating observiced via chkconfig
     initializing the administrative domain
******************************* N O T E *******************************
On Linux systems Oracle recommends that you answer no to the next two questions.
The preferred mode of operation on Linux systems is to use the /dev/sg devices for
```

```
attach points as described in the 'ReadMe' and in the 'Installation and
Configuration Guide'.
Is lin32 connected to any tape libraries that you'd like to use with Oracle Secure Backup [no]?
Is lin32 connected to any tape drives that you'd like to use with Oracle Secure
Backup [no]?
```

Step 13. Since, in this example, you use a Linux system, answer "no," as recommended by Oracle, and configure the media server later. The following summary is returned:

```
Installation summary:
    Installation  Host              OS         Driver      OS Move    Reboot
       Mode       Name              Name       Installed?  Required?  Required?
    admin         lin32             Linux      no          no         no
Oracle Secure Backup is now ready for your use.
```

The OSB administrative server, media server, and client are now installed. The OSB Web tool is used to configure the tape library and tape drives. Let's add the oracle user and a Database Backup Storage Selector to enable backup of an Oracle database.

Step 14. Connect and log into the OSB Web tool using the https://<administrative server> link as the admin user. Go to the Configure page, click the Users link, click the Add button, and add the oracle user, as shown next:

Step 15. After the oracle user is added, click the Edit button, and change Preauthorized Access:

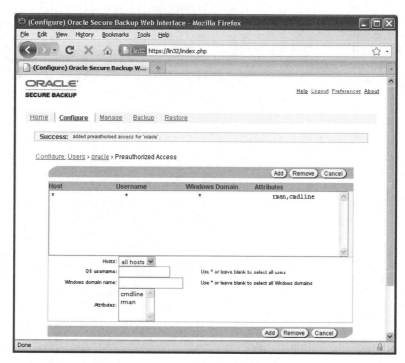

Step 16.   As a result, you will have the admin and oracle users:

Step 17. Go to Configure: Hosts, and make sure that the server has the mediaserver role, as shown here.

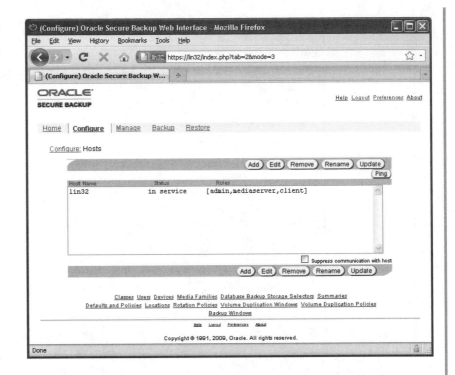

Step 18. To add a storage selector, click the Database Backup Storage Selectors link at the bottom of the Configure page, click Add, and fill in the fields, as shown in the illustration.

Step 19. Click OK and the storage will be created, as shown at right.

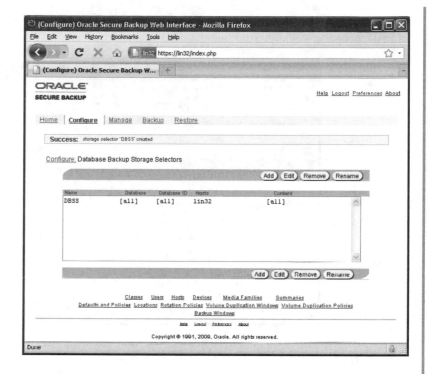

Step 20. Now, let's configure OEM for OSB usage. Connect to the database and go to the Availability tab in OEM. Click Backup Settings and go to the end of the page shown in this illustration.

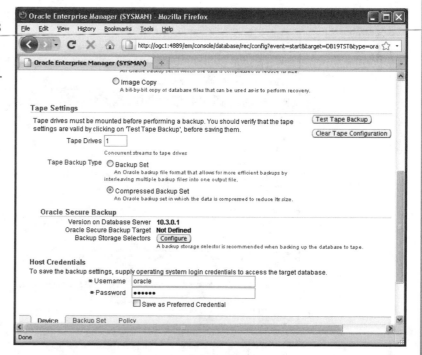

Step 21. Click Configure to specify your OSB target, and on the Specify Oracle Secure Backup Target page, click the Add button and then enter the host:

Step 22. Click Continue and enter the values shown here:

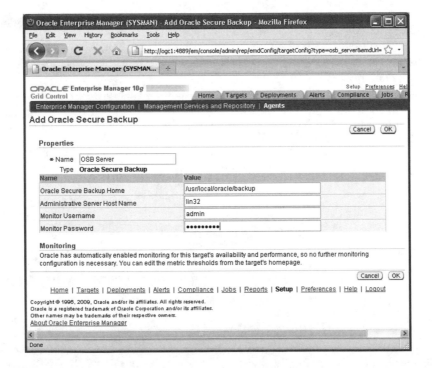

Step 23.   After clicking two OK buttons, you will see the Backup Storage Selectors page, shown at right.

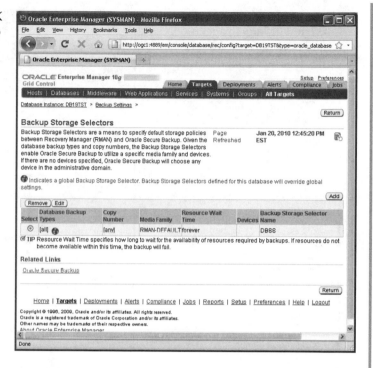

Step 24.   Click Return, and the OSB Server target is ready for backing up Oracle databases to tape, as shown here in the illustration.

The OSB administrative server is configured as an OEM target and can be managed by OEM.

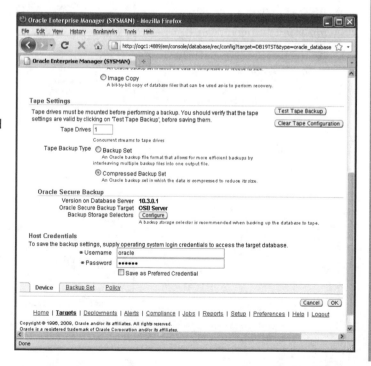

Step 25. Find the OSB server on the All Target page in OEM, and click it to see what is shown here.

Step 26. Click the Setup tab to configure the OSB server. The OSB devices can be configured on the Devices page, as shown in the illustration.

If you click the Manage tab, file system data backup and restore jobs can be scheduled.

Oracle Database and File System Data Backup Using Oracle Secure Backup

It is not possible to perform Oracle database backup and restore using the OSB Web tool. Therefore, we recommend using OEM as a centralized interface to schedule backup and restore jobs for Oracle database and file system data.

RMAN Workshop: *Schedule Oracle Database and File System Data Backups*

Workshop Notes

This workshop schedules OSB Oracle database and file system data backups. First, let's take a full Oracle database backup.

Step 1.   Connect to the database, go to the Availability tab in OEM, and click Schedule Backup. Then, choose Whole Database and click Schedule Customized Backup. On this page, you can choose different backup options. Click Next, and on the Settings page, choose Tape, and click Next:

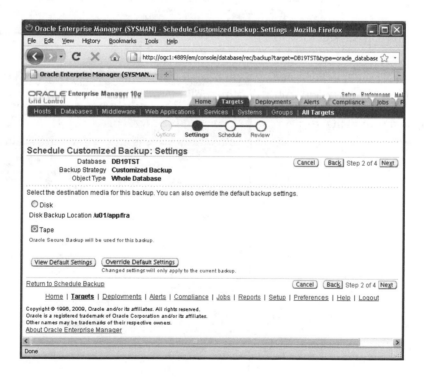

Step 2.   Choose the job as a one-time job and review the scheduled job. Click Submit Job, as shown here.

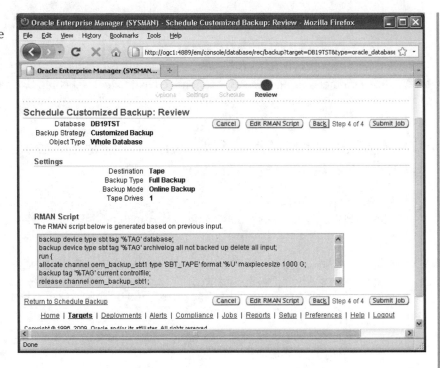

Step 3.   OEM will indicate that the job has been submitted. You can click View Job to see the status, as shown in the illustration.

Step 4. The executed job can be found on the Jobs tab:

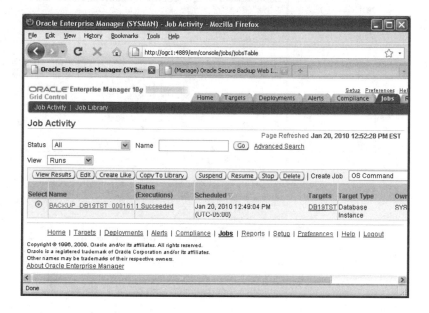

Now, let's take a backup of listener.ora file.

Step 5. On the Manage page of OEM OSB Server, click Schedule Backup, and then choose Specify Hosts, Directories and Files:

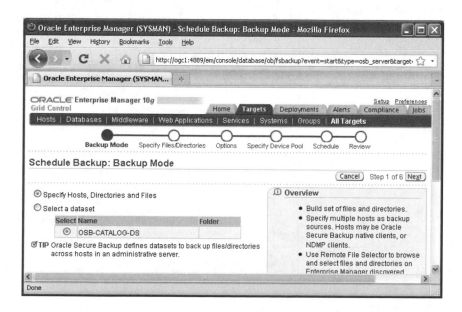

Step 6. Add the listener
.ora file to be included in
the backup, as shown at
right.

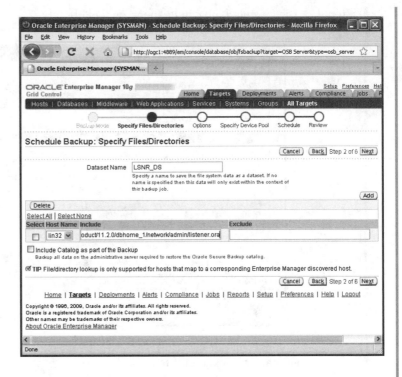

Step 7. Click Next, check
Privileged user to have the
job run by the root user, and
click Next again. On the
Specify Device Pool page,
the tape device can be
specified for the backup,
as the illustration shows.

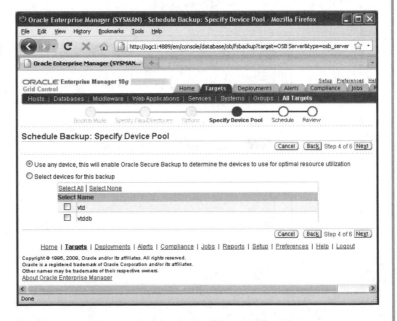

Step 8. Click Next, select the job schedule, and click Next again. Review the backup job:

Step 9. After the job is submitted, you can see the OEM confirmation. The job execution status can be seen on the Jobs page:

Oracle Database Backup Using Oracle Secure Backup Cloud Module

OSB provides the ability to use storage clouds, such as Amazon S3, as offsite backup storage destinations. To utilize Amazon S3 as backup storage, you need to sign up for Amazon S3 service and get the Access Key ID and the Secret Access Key. After the access identifiers are collected, they can be used to configure OSB during the OSB Cloud Module installation. The OSB Cloud Module install tool can be downloaded from OTN at the following address: http://www.oracle .com/technology/software/tech/cloud/index.html.

RMAN Workshop: *Installing OSB Cloud Module and Using It for OSB Backups*

Workshop Notes
This workshop installs OSB Cloud Module and schedules an OSB Oracle database backup.

Step 1. Download and install OSB Cloud Module:

```
[oracle@lin32 distrib]$ ls -l
total 2428
-rw-r--r-- 1 oracle oinstall 2480195 Jan 19 18:13 osbws_installer.zip
[oracle@lin32 distrib]$ unzip osbws_installer.zip
Archive:  osbws_installer.zip
  inflating: osbws_readme.txt
  inflating: osbws_install.jar
[oracle@lin32 distrib]$ vi osbws_install.sh
[oracle@lin32 distrib]$ cat osbws_install.sh
java -jar osbws_install.jar -AWSID <Access Key ID> -AWSKey <Secret Access Key> -
otnUser alisher.yuldashev@<mail_server>.com -otnPass <OTN password> -walletDir
$ORACLE_HOME/dbs/osbws_wallet
[oracle@lin32 distrib]$ chmod u+x osbws_install.sh
[oracle@lin32 distrib]$ ./osbws_install.sh
Oracle Secure Backup Database Web-Service Install Tool
OTN userid is valid.
AWS credentials are valid.
Creating new registration for this S3 user.
Created new log bucket.
Registration ID: <Registration ID>
S3 Logging Bucket: oracle-log-alisher-1
Validating log bucket location ...
Validating license file ...
Create credential oracle.security.client.connect_string1
OSB web-services wallet created in directory /u01/app/oracle/product/11.2.0/dbhome_1/dbs/
osbws_wallet.
OSB web-services initialization file /u01/app/oracle/product/11.2.0/dbhome_1/dbs/osbwsDB19TST
.ora created.
```

Step 2. Connect to the database, go to the Availability tab in OEM, and click Schedule Backup. Then, choose Whole Database and click Schedule Customized Backup. We recommend you encrypt the backup to store it on offsite storage:

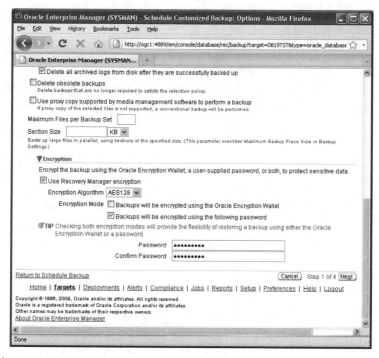

Step 3. On the Settings page, choose Tape and click Next:

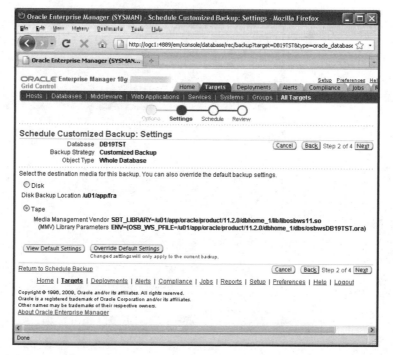

Step 4. Choose the job as a one-time job, review the scheduled job, and click Submit Job.

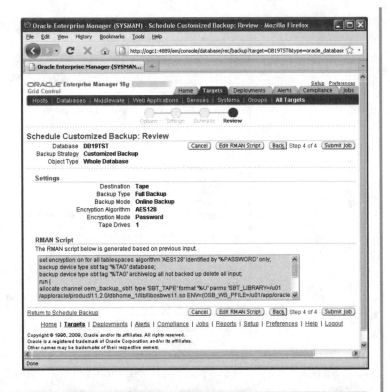

Step 5. OEM will show that the job has been submitted. The executed job can be found on the Jobs tab, as seen here.

Summary

Oracle Secure Backup delivers high performance and secure data protection crucial for both offsite and local storage of mission-critical data. Complete product support from Oracle Support Services, integration with Oracle Enterprise Manager, ability to use the Cloud as a next-generation offsite backup storage, and excellent pricing are only a few of the many reasons for employing OSB to meet your file system and Oracle database backup requirements. For centralized backup tape management in mixed, distributed environments that provides a complete backup solution for the enterprise, OSB is a strong contender.

CHAPTER
6

Backing Up to Amazon Web Services Using the Oracle Secure Backup Cloud Module

racle and Amazon.com have provided a media management library for RMAN that allows Oracle databases to be backed up directly to the Amazon Web Services cloud. This chapter provides an overview of cloud computing and how Amazon's cloud works, how Oracle can be used in a cloud computing context, and why backing up using the OSB Cloud Module and Amazon S3 may be a good idea for some sites. Additionally, we provide detailed instructions on installing and deploying the OSB Cloud Module and Amazon S3 as a backup solution.

Conventional Backups: Assumptions and Limitations

Two key requirements for robust Oracle backup and recovery are scalable high-capacity on-site backup infrastructure and regular off-site storage of backups in a location separate from the database.

Traditionally, onsite backup infrastructure has consisted of large tape libraries or disk arrays. Offsite storage has been accomplished by physically moving tapes to a secure remote facility. Offsite tape storage companies provide transport and remote facilities for a fee.

These traditional approaches have a number of disadvantages:

- High cost of enterprise backup infrastructure

- Limited capacity of enterprise backup infrastructure

- High cost of offsite media transport and storage

- Long time to recovery (TTR) for offsite backups

- Reliance on physical security for offsite backups

The Oracle Secure Backup Cloud Module

The OSB Cloud Module is a media management library (MML) for Recovery Manager (RMAN) that allows backups to be written directly to Amazon.com's Simple Storage Service (S3) over the Internet as if it were a tape library. S3 is a component of Amazon Web Services, Amazon's *cloud computing* platform.

Cloud computing, an emerging infrastructure model being pioneered by Amazon.com and others, offers a viable alternative to both physical hosting infrastructure and offsite data storage. The cloud backup model addresses many of the drawbacks of traditional backups. Additionally, storing backups in a cloud storage service offers several potential advantages.

What Is Cloud Computing?

The term *cloud computing* suffers from having been appropriated for use by numerous technology vendors to apply in various ways to their own products or services. This diffusion of the term's meaning has led to confusion among many in the technology field.

Generally, cloud computing refers to a remote pool of storage and computing resources available to the public over the Internet at as small or as large a scale as users require. The cloud resources of one user are discrete and secure from those of other users. Users manage cloud resources using a uniform, published software API (application program interface). A computing cloud conforms to set availability and performance service levels published by the provider.

More simply, from a user's perspective, a computing cloud is an Internet service on which users can deploy applications and services on professionally managed enterprise-class infrastructure.

In the case of Google, software such as visualization and mapping tools are available to be integrated into a user's web pages or applications as a component.

In the case of Amazon, users can deploy virtual server hosts and virtual storage. From the perspective of the users and applications, cloud services look and behave similarly to stand-alone server and storage equipment.

Oracle and the Amazon Cloud

Oracle and Amazon.com have worked together to provide a way to deploy several components of Oracle technology on *Amazon Web Services* (AWS), Amazon.com's cloud computing platform. Currently, Oracle supports two classes of services on AWS:

- Running Oracle software on AWS Elastic Compute Cloud (EC2)

- Backing up Oracle databases to AWS Simple Storage Service (S3)

Elastic Compute Cloud (EC2) and Elastic Block Store (EBS)

Amazon EC2 and EBS allow users to deploy virtual hosts running Windows or Linux and highly available volume storage to support virtually any application that runs on those operating systems. EC2 provides virtual hosts, and EBS provides storage volumes.

Simple Storage Service (S3)—Oracle's Cloud Backup Solution

Yet another component of Amazon's cloud is S3, a low-cost, reliable, redundant mass-storage service. Popular software packages such as Jungle Disk use S3 as an inexpensive way to back up your personal computer or just to get some extra storage space. Oracle has followed suit, providing the Oracle Secure Backup (OSB) Cloud Module, an RMAN media management library (MML) for S3. The OSB Cloud Module allows Oracle databases on the Amazon Cloud *and at customer sites,* to back up directly to S3 on the Amazon cloud from RMAN.

RMAN Backup to S3: The Oracle Secure Backup Cloud Module

The OSB Cloud Module is essentially a media management library (MML) that provides access to Amazon S3 storage via the SBT channel interface of RMAN. Just as with tape MMLs, the OSB Cloud Module is implemented as a shared library for Linux/Unix and as a DLL for Windows.

The OSB Cloud Module is available for Oracle versions 9*i* and higher on 32- and 64-bit Linux, 32-bit Windows, and Solaris (SPARC 64-bit). Oracle has offered to port it to any other Unix upon customer request.

S3 Backup over the Internet or from Amazon EC2

A database hosted elsewhere than on Amazon Web Services can back up over the public Internet to S3. As such, performance may be variable. In contrast, a database hosted on AWS can back up to S3 over Amazon's internal network, where performance will be predictably good.

For Amazon cloud-hosted databases, the decision to use the OSB Cloud Module is easy. It is a cheap, reliable way to store backups. It is also among the only options for cloud-hosted databases.

For databases hosted elsewhere than AWS, such as in the customer's own datacenter, it is necessary to determine first whether acceptable speed and performance can be achieved. This is discussed later in this chapter.

Oracle Cloud Backup Advantages

There are several benefits to using cloud backup instead of local or offsite disk or tape storage. Chief among these are

- **No up-front equipment costs**   Tape libraries and mass storage arrays are major capital expenses and require ongoing maintenance and upkeep. When physical storage capacity is exceeded, new equipment must be purchased and deployed. In contrast, deploying backups on cloud storage is affordable and requires no additional equipment, even as scale increases.

- **Low ongoing storage costs**   As of Q3 2009, Amazon S3 costs 15¢ per GB per month for storage and 1¢/GB for data transfer into the service. So daily backup of a 100GB database plus 20GB of archive logs would cost about $162 per month.

- **Elasticity**   With cloud computing, you can use as few or as many resources as you need. As requirements grow, there is no need to replace equipment such as tape libraries with new equipment of larger capacity.

- **Reliability**   Amazon provides redundancy and availability within their internal architecture and meets a published SLA (service-level agreement) of 99.99 percent availability for S3. One of the key features of S3 is geographic replication. S3 replicates data to three availability zones within an Amazon Web Services region. Availability zones are analogous to separate datacenters. Similar redundancy and availability within a customer's own datacenter would have to be architected as part of an enterprise backup infrastructure at significant expense and effort.

- **Time to recovery**   Unlike offsited tapes, which must be ordered and loaded into libraries, RMAN backups to Amazon S3 are always online and available for recoveries.

- **No third-party MML license costs**   The Oracle Secure Backup Cloud Module is licensed through Oracle and is priced per channel. That means that customers can leverage their preexisting license relationship with Oracle.

RMAN Workshop: *Deploying RMAN Backups to Amazon S3*

Workshop Notes

A few prerequisites and credentials are required to use the OSB Cloud Module:

- An oracle.com single sign-on account (the same one used to log into the Oracle Technology Network)

- An Amazon Web Services account

Step 1. Establish an Oracle single sign-on account, if needed. If you already have an Oracle.com or Oracle Technology Network account, you can skip this step. Otherwise:

   a. In a browser, navigate to http://www.oracle.com/admin/account.

   b. Click **Create your Oracle account now**.

Step 2. Establish an Amazon Web Services account:

   a. In a browser, navigate to http://aws.amazon.com.

   b. Click **Sign Up Now**. You will be prompted to sign into Amazon.com. Your AWS account is accessed via your Amazon.com retail account. If you do not have an existing account at Amazon.com, select **I am a new customer**.

   c. Once you are logged in, you must check a box and click **Continue** to accept the terms of the AWS Customer Agreement.

Step 3. When you successfully establish an account with AWS, you still need to sign up for Amazon's Simple Storage Service (S3):

   a. In a browser, navigate to http://aws.amazon.com/s3.

   b. Click **Sign up for Amazon s3**.

   c. On subsequent web pages, Amazon will prompt you to provide a credit card for payment and a billing address. Finally, you will be prompted to review your selections and to click **Complete Sign Up**.

Step 4. To store and retrieve data on S3, you will need your private access identifiers. The link to obtain these values should be sent to you in an e-mail from Amazon.com upon signing up for Amazon S3. If you do not have the URL handy, you can do the following:

   a. In a browser, navigate to http://aws.amazon.com.

   b. Hover your cursor over **Your Account**.

   c. Click **Security Credentials**.

   d. Note the values for **Access Key ID** and **Secret Access Key**. Keep these values in a safe place. They are the keys for charging AWS services to your account.

Step 5. Download and Install the Oracle Secure Backup Cloud Module installer.

> **NOTE**
> *If you are performing backups for an Oracle database running on Amazon EC2 using one of Oracle's Amazon Machine Images (AMIs), you do not need to install the OSB Cloud Module. It has already been installed for you under /home/oracle/scripts/.*

The OSB Cloud Module installer can be downloaded from the Oracle Technology Network Cloud Computing Center:

   a. In a browser, navigate to http://www.oracle.com/technology/software/tech/cloud.

   b. Review the license agreement, and click **All Supported Platforms**.

c. The download is a .zip file containing a .jar file and a readme. Place the .zip file on the database server that you will be backing up under the user that runs the Oracle software (usually oracle).

d. Verify that you have java 1.5 installed on the server. If you do not have java 1.5 installed, you will have to download and install it. Note that Oracle 11*g* includes java 1.5 under $ORACLE_HOME/jdk/bin/.

```
$ java -version
java version "1.5.0_16"
```

e. Install the OSB Cloud Module by running the installer and providing the appropriate arguments for your environment. You must pass these arguments to the installer:

Argument	Description
-awsid	Your Amazon Web Services Access Key ID
-awskey	Your Amazon Web Services Secret Access Key
-otnuser	Your Oracle.com Single Sign-on Account Login
-otnpass	Your Oracle.com Single Sign-on Password
-walletdir	Where to store the preceding login credentials

Linux Example

```
$ java -jar osbws_install.jar \
> -awsid 3HKFEHKTI6JW4R88GB72 -awskey  KjsopcHzhVMAoXpPs8d0jPCa4hspbrHbssRbspbq \
> -otnuser larry_e@gmail.com -otnpass iluvb0at$ \
> -walletdir $ORACLE_HOME/dbs/osbws_wallet -libdir $ORACLE_HOME/lib
OTN userid is valid.
AWS credentials are valid.
Creating new registration for this S3 user.
Created new log bucket.
Registration ID: 0f0a8aac-dad0-6254-7d70-be4ac4f112c4
S3 Logging Bucket: oracle-log-jane-doe-1
Create credential oracle.security.client.connect_string1
OSB web-services wallet created in directory /u01/oracle/product/11.1/db_1/dbs/osbws_wallet.
OSB web-services initialization file /u01/oracle/product/11.1/db_1/dbs/osbwst1.ora created.
Downloading OSB Web Services Software Library.
Downloaded 13165919 bytes in 204 seconds. Transfer rate was 64538 bytes/second.
Download complete.
Extracted file /u01/oracle/product/11.1/db_1/lib/libosbws11.so
```

Performing Backups by Using the OSB Cloud Module

RMAN backups to Amazon S3 work like backups to traditional MML products. From within RMAN:

■ Allocate one or more channels of type SBT.

■ Issue backup commands to the SBT channels.

RMAN must specify the location of the S3 SBT library and OSB Cloud Module parameter file (both created during install) when allocating the SBT channel to S3. You can specify this information persistently for the database by using the RMAN **configure** command, or each time you allocate a channel. If you also use other media management libraries such as NetWorker, NetBackup, or Oracle Secure Backup, you should not configure S3 persistently to be the default MML unless you really mean to do that.

To Persistently Store S3 as the Default SBT Channel

The following RMAN code snippet demonstrates how to persistently configure the default settings for RMAN's SBT I/O channels to use Amazon S3 using the OSB Cloud Module. Using this method, the default destination for SBT I/O will be Amazon S3. If other RMAN backup jobs need to write to or read from local tape, for instance, they will have to specify their local tape MML libraries in the **allocate channel** command.

```
RMAN> configure channel device type sbt
2>   parms 'ENV=(OSB_WS_PFILE=/u01/oracle/product/11.1/db_1/dbs/osbwst1.ora),
3>   SBT_LIBRARY=/u01/oracle/product/11.1/db_1/lib/libosbws11.so';
```

To Specify the OSB Cloud Module Each Time You Allocate a Channel

The following RMAN code snippet demonstrates how to manually configure each channel to use the OSB Cloud Module at script runtime. The default SBT channel configuration will remain unchanged. If there is a local tape MML in place, jobs that use that service will continue to function normally without modification.

```
RMAN> allocate channel t1 type sbt
2>   parms='ENV=(OSB_WS_PFILE=/u01/oracle/product/11.1/db_1/dbs/osbwst1.ora),
3>   SBT_LIBRARY=/u01/oracle/product/11.1/db_1/lib/libosbws11.so';
```

The following RMAN script demonstrates how to manually allocate an SBT I/O channel to S3 using the OSB Cloud Module, then perform a full backup of the database including the archived redologs.

```
RMAN> run {
2>   allocate channel t1 type sbt
3>   parms='ENV=(OSB_WS_PFILE=/u01/oracle/product/11.1/db_1/dbs/osbwst1.ora),
4>   SBT_LIBRARY=/u01/oracle/product/11.1/db_1/lib/libosbws11.so';
5>   backup database plus archivelog;
6>   }
allocated channel: t1
channel t1: SID=133 device type=SBT_TAPE
channel t1: Oracle Secure Backup Web Services Library
Starting backup at 27-OCT-09
channel t1: starting full datafile backup set
channel t1: specifying datafile(s) in backup set
input datafile file number=00002 name=+DG1/t1/datafile/sysaux.257.700422031
input datafile file number=00001 name=+DG1/t1/datafile/system.256.700422031
input datafile file number=00003 name=+DG1/t1/datafile/undotbs1.258.700422031
input datafile file number=00004 name=+DG1/t1/datafile/users.259.700422031
channel t1: starting piece 1 at 27-OCT-09
channel t1: finished piece 1 at 27-OCT-09
piece handle=03ksrndv_1_1 tag=TAG20091027T133142 comment=API Version 2.0,MMS Version 2.0.0.0
channel t1: backup set complete, elapsed time: 00:02:35
...
Finished backup at 27-OCT-09
released channel: t1
```

The exact syntax for allocating the SBT channel to S3 varies between Oracle versions. For instance, Oracle 11gR2 does not accept the ENV keyword. Instead you must use an alternate channel allocation syntax using the SBT_PARMS keyword. On some versions, you may also have to create a symbolic link in ORACLE_HOME/lib called libobk.so pointing to libosbws11.so:

```
$ ln -s $ORACLE_HOME/lib/libosbws11.so $ORACLE_HOME/lib/libobk.so
```

Listing RMAN Backups and Backup Sets Stored on S3

As with all RMAN backups, all management of stored backups must be performed with RMAN. If you manually delete backup sets, future RMAN recoveries will continue to assume that they exist. RMAN must be used to mark as obsolete and to purge all RMAN backups.

Similarly, listing and reporting existing backups is best performed via RMAN. For example, the following command lists all backups stored on an SBT device (such as S3 via the OSB Cloud Module) in the past 24 hours:

```
RMAN> list backup device type sbt completed after 'sysdate-1';
List of Backup Sets
===================
BS Key  Type LV Size        Device Type Elapsed Time Completion Time
1       Full   1.17G        SBT_TAPE    00:02:34     27-OCT-09
        BP Key: 2   Status: AVAILABLE   Compressed: NO  Tag: TAG20091027T133142
        Handle: 03ksrndv_1_1   Media:
  List of Datafiles in backup set 2
  File LV Type Ckp SCN    Ckp Time   Name
  1       Full 1515937    27-OCT-09  +DG1/t1/datafile/system.256.700422031
  2       Full 1515937    27-OCT-09  +DG1/t1/datafile/sysaux.257.700422031
  3       Full 1515937    27-OCT-09  +DG1/t1/datafile/undotbs1.258.700422031
  4       Full 1515937    27-OCT-09  +DG1/t1/datafile/users.259.700422031
```

Several third-party tools exist for browsing the contents of your S3 buckets, where the OSB Cloud Module stores RMAN backups. One popular such tool is a Firefox browser add-on called S3fox. Using S3fox, you can browse the backup pieces RMAN stores in S3.

Optimizing Backups and Recoveries over the Internet Using the OSB Cloud Module and Amazon S3

The effectiveness of backing up and restoring Oracle database backups over the Internet to Amazon S3 depends on a number of factors:

- Size of database
- Redo generation rate
- Internet bandwidth between the Oracle server and Amazon S3
- Backup strategy
- RMAN options
- Requirements for time-to-recovery

Very large databases not hosted in the Amazon cloud may be poor candidates for backup to Amazon S3 over the Internet in Q1 2010 given typical observed network speeds and performance. It could simply take too long to complete a backup and too long to restore in the event of a recovery. For the same reason, databases that generate very large amounts of redo per day may be poor candidates for this backup strategy. Amazon Web Services has reliable fast connectivity to S3, so databases hosted on Amazon EC2 can use the OSB Cloud Module without as much tuning and optimization.

For example, a level 0 backup of a database of 500GB that generates 50GB of redo per day might compress to 250GB. With a single T1, it might take over 50 hours to back up to S3, using most of the available network capacity. For this reason, you must carefully consider and test network throughput and compressed backup size when contemplating moving to an S3-based backup strategy over the Internet. The longest backup window in the backup cycle must be able to accommodate a level 0 backup, while using a percentage of the network resources that is acceptable to the enterprise. *Additionally, organizations must determine if the amount of time to perform a complete restore from S3 is acceptable to the enterprise.*

Because of the many caveats associated with deploying backups over the Internet to S3, any organization contemplating it should rigorously test both backup and recovery performance before embarking on a large-scale migration to this architecture.

Regardless of database size, customers using the OSB Cloud Module can optimize backup capacity and performance using a variety of means. By improving backup efficiency, larger databases can be backed up to S3 over the Internet than would otherwise have been possible. The main approaches are

- Using multiple SBT channels

- Backing up during times of minimal Internet use

- Using compressed backup sets

- Using an incremental backup strategy

- Backing up archive logs frequently

Sites contemplating an Oracle backup strategy over the Internet to Amazon S3 must have sufficient Internet bandwidth to back up the databases in question within an acceptable backup window. If sufficient bandwidth is available, the challenge becomes configuring RMAN to consume those resources. An effective way to maximize the use of network resources is opening multiple SBT channels. In testing, the goal should be to use sufficient network resources to complete the backup within the required timeframe, while leaving resources available for other services and purposes.

To minimize the impact to other users and services, Oracle backups to Amazon S3 should be scheduled for periods of minimal network use. The quantity of data transferred can be further reduced with compressed backup sets.

An incremental backup strategy can additionally reduce the daily backup size that must be written to Amazon S3. In most databases, only a small portion of the data changes on a daily, weekly, or even monthly basis. Therefore, full or level 0 backups can conceivably be taken very infrequently and can even be spread over the period of a whole night or a whole weekend. On a nightly or weekly basis, differential and incremental backups can be used to maintain recoverability while keeping the backup size small.

Example with Multiple Channels and Compressed Backup Sets

The following RMAN script demonstrates typical syntax for opening multiple channels to Amazon S3 using the OSB Cloud Module, then performing a full (level 0) compressed backup including archived redo logs over those channels.

```
RMAN> run {
2>   allocate channel t1 type sbt
3>   parms='ENV=(OSB_WS_PFILE=/u01/oracle/product/11.1/db_1/dbs/osbwst1.ora),
4>   SBT_LIBRARY=/u01/oracle/product/11.1/db_1/lib/libosbws11.so';
5>   allocate channel t2 type sbt
6>   parms='ENV=(OSB_WS_PFILE=/u01/oracle/product/11.1/db_1/dbs/osbwst1.ora),
7>   SBT_LIBRARY=/u01/oracle/product/11.1/db_1/lib/libosbws11.so';
8>   allocate channel t3 type sbt
9>   parms='ENV=(OSB_WS_PFILE=/u01/oracle/product/11.1/db_1/dbs/osbwst1.ora),
10> SBT_LIBRARY=/u01/oracle/product/11.1/db_1/lib/libosbws11.so';
11> backup as compressed backupset incremental level 0 database plus archivelog;}
```

Because archive log generation is periodic, it is possible to distribute the impact of archive log backup throughout the day and night. Frequently backing up archive logs reduces the amount of data to be backed up during the nightly database backup window. This approach has the added benefit of improving point-in-time recoverability, since more recent archive logs are available offsite for more recent points in time.

Licensing Considerations

Most media management library (MML) software packages for Oracle RMAN require licensing with a third party, such as EMC or Symantec. In the case of the OSB Cloud Module, the Oracle Secure Backup Licensing Information documentation (P/N E10310-02) states that customers must obtain a license "for each RMAN channel simultaneously used by the backup domain to an Amazon S3 destination."

Customers should thoroughly consult the documentation, any written license agreements, and their own legal counsel in order to determine the correct number of licenses to obtain for the OSB Cloud Module.

Summary

The OSB Cloud Module provides a compelling solution for secure offsite backup storage and vaulting, especially for Oracle databases hosted on Amazon's cloud. Cloud storage has the potential for lower cost, better time to recovery (TTR), and more geographically distributed disaster recovery properties, when compared to traditional magnetic tape vaulting.

Careful testing for performance of both backup and restore functions in a range of scenarios is a prerequisite before deploying backups to S3. In addition, those considering using the OSB Cloud Module must carefully review their licensing obligations with Oracle for the package.

CHAPTER
7

Enhancing RMAN with
VERITAS NetBackup™
for Oracle

ERITAS NetBackup Server software and Database Agent software work in collaboration with RMAN to manage enterprise backup, recovery, and storage administration. The products run on many operating systems, support popular databases, and integrate easily with an assortment of storage devices. NetBackup's tantalizing features, coupled with the vendor's close partnership with Oracle, make it a desirable choice. The information and downloads in this chapter are available on Symnatec's web site, as Veritas is now part of Symantec.

In this chapter, we will focus on VERITAS NetBackup Version 5.1 running on Unix, unless stated otherwise.

Key Features

NetBackup *for Oracle* has many features and benefits that augment the functionality of RMAN. A summary of the key features is listed in Table 7-1.

Some specialty add-ons worth looking into are NetBackup Advanced Client, NetBackup Vault, and NetBackup Bare Metal Restore.

Feature	Benefit
Backup to disk staging area	Provides faster backups and restores by avoiding the overhead of tape latency
Synthetic backups	Conserves network bandwidth by allowing incremental backups
Inline copy	Provides data redundancy by writing multiple copies of the data at the same time
Tape multiplexing	Improves performance by writing parallel streams of data from one or more clients to a single tape drive
Automatic tape device configuration	Reduces the time and effort that would otherwise be required to manually configure tape drives
Data encryption	Secures data as it is written to tape by offering multiple levels of data protection
Backup templates	Simplifies the effort of writing RMAN backup and recovery scripts by providing a graphical tool to assist with script generation and sample scripts preconfigured to run with NetBackup
Proxy copy	Offloads processing power from the database server to a separate media server when doing backups and restores
Checkpoint restart	Allows backups to resume where they left off in the case of a failure

TABLE 7-1 *NetBackup* for Oracle *Key Features*

Necessary Components

The following elements enable successful communication exchanges between RMAN, the NetBackup servers, and the storage devices:

- NetBackup Server software

- NetBackup *for Oracle* agent software—includes a required interface library file (libobk.*)

- Oracle database software—includes the RMAN utility and the Oracle Call Interface (OCI)

- NetBackup licenses—needed for all software, options, and agents being used

Storage/Media Device Configuration

Setting up tape drives, host bus adapters, SCSI IDs, and tape robots (see *NetBackup Media Manager Device Configuration Guide*) is usually left up to Unix or storage administrators. We will not discuss those vendor-specific steps here, but will instead provide a few commands to verify proper configuration of tape media devices.

NOTE
Hardware devices should be set up and tested for proper working order prior to installing the NetBackup for Oracle *agent software.*

Use the following command to query the master server from the client server to verify communications:

```
/<install_path>/netbackup/bin/bpclntcmd  ph
```

Next, query the master server from the client server to verify the version:

```
/<install_path>/netbackup/bin/bpclntcmd -sv
```

View which storage server will be servicing the client server by issuing the following:

```
cat /<install_path>/netbackup/bp.conf
```

Finally, verify that the NetBackup communication daemons are listening for requests:

```
netstat -a |grep bpcd
netstat -a |grep vnetd
```

NetBackup Installation

Multiple tiers make up a networked backup environment. Every layer needs some amount of software configuration to enable component interoperability. The installations are straightforward and should take less than 20 minutes each. Besides doing local installations, you can run remote installs, installs from the Administration Console, and software propagation to the clients from a central master server.

NOTE
NetBackup software should not be installed on a network file system (NFS)–mounted directory. Doing so could cause interference with its file-locking mechanisms.

NetBackup Server software gets installed on the following servers:

- Master server
- Media server (optional)
- Client (database) server

The NetBackup *for Oracle* agent software gets installed on the client (database) server. The following list defines the server types just mentioned:

- **Master server**   Orchestrates the NetBackup environment. It is placed in a layer referred to as Tier 1 (top server tier). *Tiers* are labels for each of the different architectural layers or groupings of architectural components. The role of the master server is to schedule backups, track job progress, manage tape devices, and store backup metadata in a repository. Since the master server plays such a critical role, it is a good idea to cluster this server for high availability (and greater peace of mind).

- **Media servers**   Occupy Tier 2 (middle tier) and are used to back up a group of files locally while other files are being backed up across the network. Media servers are introduced into the environment to boost performance, but they are not required.

- **Client servers**   Reside in Tier 3 (client tier) and are usually the database servers that house the databases to be backed up.

Pre-Installation Tasks for NetBackup *for Oracle* Agent

Before you install NetBackup *for Oracle,* you need to complete the following tasks:

1. Verify that the system administrator has installed and properly configured the NetBackup software on the master server, media servers (optional), and the client database servers.

2. Ensure that the proper license keys for all NetBackup servers, clients, agents, and options have been purchased and are registered on the master server. You can do this from either the Administration Console or the command line. From the Administration Console, launch the following and then choose Help | License Keys:

   ```
   /<install_path>/netbackup/bin/jnbSA &
   ```

   From the command line, run

   ```
   /<install_path>/netbackup/bin/admincmd/get_license_key
   ```

3. Obtain the NetBackup *for Oracle* agent software CD, or ask a Unix system administrator to push the software to the client database machine from the master server.

NOTE
On the database server, both the NetBackup Server software and NetBackup for Oracle *agent software need to be the same version. The software on the master server needs to be the same or a higher version as that on the database server.*

NetBackup *for Oracle* Agent Installation Steps

To install the NetBackup *for Oracle* agent, follow these steps:

1. Insert and mount the installation CD.
2. Log in as **root** to the client (database) server.
3. Change to the directory where the CD is mounted.
4. Run the ./install script.
5. Choose NetBackup Database Agent.
6. You are asked whether you want to do a local installation. Enter **y**.
7. Choose NetBackup for Oracle.
8. Enter **q** (Done Selecting Agents).
9. Enter **y** to verify your selection.
10. Installation proceeds as follows:

    a. A script called /<install_path>/netbackup/dbext/install_dbext is generated.
    b. The file /<install_path>/netbackup/bp.conf is updated with server names.
    c. Entries are added to /etc/services.
    d. Entries are added to the NIS services map if NIS is running on the server.
    e. Entries are added to the server /etc/initd.conf file for bpcd, vopied, and bpjava-msvc.
    f. Startup and shutdown scripts are copied to the /etc/init.d directory.
    g. Installation output is written to /<install_path>/netbackup/ext.

NOTE
In most cases, look for NetBackup to be installed in the /usr/openv/ netbackup directory.

How to Link Oracle to NetBackup Media Manager

After installing the NetBackup *for Oracle* agent, you need to link Oracle database software with the NetBackup Media Management Library. The link allows RMAN to write files to the media devices or to pull files from them. The NetBackup Media Management Library or API often is found in /<install_path>/netbackup/bin, while the Oracle library is located in $ORACLE_HOME/ lib. Both files are named libobk*.

Linking can be done either automatically or manually, as described next.

Automatic Link Method

NetBackup *for Oracle* includes a script to automate the library link process. Since all steps are automated, using the script is preferred over a manual method. The oracle_link script performs the following actions:

- Retrieves the database version

- Retrieves the operating system version

- Warns if the database is not shut down

- Checks environment variable settings

- Applies the appropriate library based on its assessment

The steps to automatically link Oracle9*i* Database, Oracle Database 10*g*, and Oracle Database 11g with NetBackup *for Oracle* follow:

1. Log into the Unix server as the Oracle Database owner account, usually *oracle*.

2. Set the variables $ORACLE_SID and $ORACLE_HOME.

3. Shut down each Oracle database instance:

```
sqlplus "/ as sysdba"
shutdown immediate
exit
```

4. Run the <install_path>/netbackup/bin/oracle_link script.

5. View the output that is written to /tmp/make_trace.pid for errors.

Manual Link Method

If you prefer more control over the link process, you may opt for the manual method. The following are the steps to manually link Oracle9*i* Database and Oracle Database 10*g* with NetBackup *for Oracle*:

1. Log into the Unix server as the oracle account.

2. Set the variables $ORACLE_SID and $ORACLE_HOME.

3. Shut down each Oracle database instance:

```
sqlplus "/ as sysdba"
shutdown immediate
exit
```

4. Perform the applicable linking steps in Table 7-2.

NOTE
*Starting with Oracle 9*i*, making a new Oracle executable is no longer required.*

For OS version...	...do these steps	If this file exists in ${ORACLE_HOME}/lib...	...then create a symbolic link from the Oracle library to the new NetBackup library

AIX 64-bit using 64-bit Oracle9*i* Release 9.0.1 and 9.2, Oracle 10*g* Release 10.1	n/a	libobk.a	`mv libobk.a libobk.a.orig`
			`ln -s /<install_path>/netbackup/bin/`
			`libobk.a64 libobk.a`

Compaq Tru64/ Digital UNIX (OSFI)	Put ${ORACLE_HOME}/lib in search path
	On Digital UNIX, set LD_LIBRARY_PATH
		libobk.so
		libobk.a
			`mv libobk.so libobk.so.orig`
			`mv libobk.a libobk.a.orig`
			`ln -s /<install_path>/netbackup/bin/`
			`libobk.so.1 libobk.so.1`
			`ln -s libobk.so.1 libobk.so`

HP-UX 64-bit using 64-bit Oracle9*i* Release 9.0.1 and 9.2, Oracle 10*g* Release 10.1	n/a	libobk.sl
		libobk.a
			`mv libobk.sl libobk.sl.orig`
			`mv libobk.a libobk.a.orig`
			`ln -s /<install_path>/netbackup/bin/`
			`libobk.sl64 libobk.sl`

Linux	Put ${ORACLE_HOME}/lib in search path On Digital UNIX, set LD_LIBRARY_PATH	libobk.so	`ln -s /<install_path>/netbackup/bin/` `libobk.so libobk.so`

Solaris (32-bit or 64-bit) using 32-bit Oracle9*i* Release 9.0.1 and 9.2, Oracle 10*g* Release 10.1	n/a	libobk.so	`mv libobk.so libobk.so.orig`
			`ln -s /<install_path>/netbackup/bin/`
			`libobk.so.1 libobk.so`

TABLE 7-2   *Manual Link Process*

Architecture

Now that the hardware is configured, the server and agent programs are installed, the daemons are running, and the libraries are linked, we've built a solid foundation (see Figure 7-1) upon which to run RMAN.

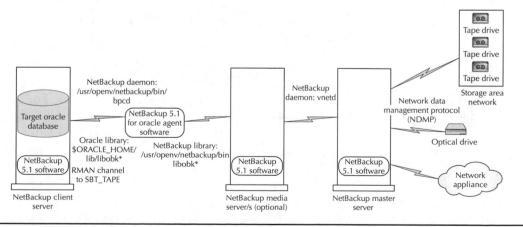

FIGURE 7-1   *NetBackup architecture*

Configuring NetBackup Policies

You need to give NetBackup instructions on how and when to execute the backups. These instructions are organized into special groupings called *policies.* Some points to be aware of when configuring policies are

- An RMAN job must be associated with at least one policy in order for it to execute.

- A default policy is provided with the agent software.

- Multiple policies can be created for a single database server.

The NetBackup Administration Console provides a nice and easy interface for configuring the following policy information:

- Attributes

- Schedule

- Clients on which the policy is implemented

- Backup selection

Adding New Policies

Here's how to add a new policy:

1. Start the NetBackup program on the storage server where the policy will be created.

2. Click the Policies tab. Expand NetBackup Management | Policies, as shown in Figure 7-2.

FIGURE 7-2 *Adding new policies*

3. In the All Policies pane, right-click Master Server, and then choose New.

4. Type a unique name in the Add a New Policy dialog box, shown in Figure 7-2. Once you add the name of the new policy in the dialog box, the Change Policy dialog box will appear.

As part of the policy definition, choose the policy attributes, shown on the Attributes tab in Figure 7-3, as follows:

FIGURE 7-3   *NetBackup policy configuration*

■ **Policy Type** This drop-down list contains many options; for Oracle RMAN backups, you can choose the Oracle policy type. The following are the various policy options with the intended use of each option:

Oracle	Use when the policy will contain only clients with the NetBackup for Oracle option.
DB2	Use when the policy will have only clients with the NetBackup for DB2 option.
DataStore	A policy type reserved for use by VERITAS or its partners to provide agents for new applications or databases.
Lotus-Notes	Use when the policy will contain only clients with the NetBackup for Lotus Notes option.
MS-Windows-NT	Use when the policy will contain only Windows 2000, NT, XP, or Windows Server 2003 clients.
MS-Exchange-Server	Use when the policy will contain only clients with the NetBackup for MS-Exchange-Server option.
MS-SQL-Server	Use when the policy will contain only clients with the NetBackup for MS-SQL Server option.
NCR-Teradata	Use when the policy will contain only clients with the NetBackup for Teradata option.
NetWare	Use when the policy will contain only NonTarget NetBackup Novell NetWare clients.
NDMP	Use when the policy will contain only clients with the NetBackup for NDMP option.
AFS	Use when the policy will be backing up only AFS file systems on clients.
DataTools-SQL-BackTrack	Use when the policy will contain only clients with the NetBackup for DataTools-SQL-BackTrack option.
FlashBackup-Windows	Applies only to NetBackup Enterprise Server; use when the policy will contain only NetBackup FlashBackup-Windows clients on Windows. This policy is available only when the NetBackup Advanced Client is installed.
FlashBackup	Use when the policy will contain only NetBackup FlashBackup clients on Unix.
Informix-On-BAR	Use when the policy will contain only clients that are running the NetBackup for Informix option.
MS-SharePoint	Use to configure a policy for NetBackup for SharePoint Portal Server.
Split-Mirror	Use when the policy will contain only clients with the NetBackup for EMC option.
SAP	Use when the policy will contain only clients with the NetBackup for SAP option.

| Sybase | Use when the policy will contain only clients with the NetBackup for Sybase option. |
| Standard | Use when the policy will contain any combination of the following:
■ NetBackup Novell NetWare clients that have the target version of NetBackup software.
■ Unix clients (including Mac OS X clients), except those covered by a specific policy such as Oracle. |

■ **Destination**   Choose settings for Policy Storage Unit and Policy Volume Pool.

■ **Limit Jobs Per Policy**   Check this box to restrict the number of jobs that can be run in parallel.

■ **Active. Go into Effect At**   Check this box and specify a date and time to turn on, at a later date and time, a policy that you create in advance.

Defining Schedules

If you are using the NetBackup scheduler, you must define when the jobs should run. A single policy can contain more than one job schedule and can be shared by multiple database servers (clients).

The *Oracle* policy type has options for Application Backup Schedule and Automatic Backup Schedule, as described next. One or more automatic backup schedules will be required depending on the job frequency.

Configure an Application Backup Schedule

Whenever the policy type is "Oracle," NetBackup creates an *Application Backup* schedule. This schedule defines the overall timeframe when any backup job can occur. Unscheduled Oracle backups will default to using this schedule. Special processes, needed for the execution of RMAN jobs, are initiated as part of the Application Backup schedule.

To configure an Application Backup schedule:

1. In the Change Policy dialog box, click the Schedules tab.

2. Double-click Default Application Backup Schedule.

3. Click the Attributes tab, shown in Figure 7-4, and make sure that the Retention option is set.

4. Click the Start Window tab. The Start Window defines the time limits during which a backup job can begin. It is a more granular subschedule within the overall Application Backup schedule. A backup job must start within the time limits of the Start Window, but will continue to run until it finishes.

NOTE
Set the backup window for the Application Backup schedule to 24 hours a day, seven days a week, in order to perform any unscheduled or schedule backup at any time and for any duration.

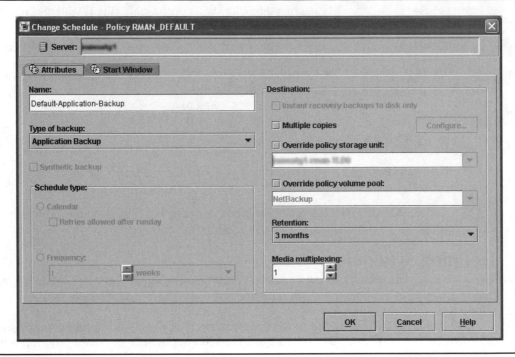

FIGURE 7-4 *Application Backup schedule*

Configure an Automatic Backup Schedule

To configure an Automatic Backup schedule:

1. In the Change Policy dialog box, click the Schedules tab.

2. Click the New button to open the Add Schedule window.

3. On the Attributes tab (refer to Figure 7-5), enter a unique name for the schedule.

4. Select from four different backup types in the Type of Backup drop-down list:

   ■ **Application Backup** Runs when an Oracle backup is started manually. Each Oracle policy must be configured with one Application Backup schedule.

   ■ **Automatic Full Backup** Backs up all the database blocks that have been allocated or that are in use by Oracle.

   ■ **Automatic Differential Incremental Backup** Backs up database blocks that have changed since the most recent full or incremental backup at level *n* or lower.

   ■ **Automatic Cumulative Incremental Backup** Backs up database blocks that have changed since the most recent full or incremental backup at level *n* – 1 or lower.

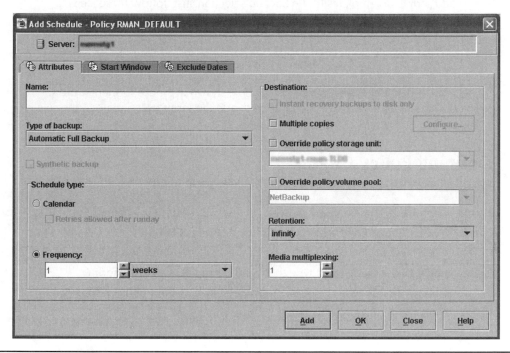

FIGURE 7-5 *Automatic Backup schedule*

5. Select from two different schedule types:

    ■ **Calendar** Specifies exact dates, recurring days of the week, or recurring days of the month.

    ■ **Frequency** Specifies the period that will elapse until the next backup operation can begin on this schedule. Options are hourly, daily, or weekly.

6. Select an appropriate retention period from the Retention drop-down list, which controls how long NetBackup retains the records for scheduled backups.

To add other schedules, repeat Steps 1 through 6.

Defining a Backup Selection

When running backup jobs, NetBackup will call any custom scripts or templates that are placed in the *backup selection list.* These files will be executed in the order they are listed. In NetBackup, two options can be used to define commands for Oracle RMAN backup or recovery:

■ **Templates** Stored in a known location on the central master server so that they do not need to be put on each database server. The filename is entered without a path.

■ **Scripts** Located on each database server listed and must be entered with a full pathname.

To add scripts or templates to the backup selections list, follow these steps:

1. From the Administration Console, double-click the policy name in the Policies list.

2. In the Change Policy dialog box, click the Backup Selections tab.

3. Click New.

4. In the Add Backup Selection dialog box, shown in Figure 7-6, enter the shell script or template name. Use the Add button to add the script or template to the selection list.

5. Click OK.

Defining Policy Clients

To add a database server (client) to a policy, follow these steps:

1. From the Administration Console, double-click the policy name in the Policies list.

2. In the Change Policy dialog box, click the Clients tab.

3. Click New to open the Add Client dialog box, shown in Figure 7-7.

4. In the Client Name box, type the name of the client you are adding.

5. Choose the hardware and operating system type from the drop-down list.

6. Click OK or click Add to set up another client.

FIGURE 7-6 *Backup selection*

FIGURE 7-7 *Define policy clients*

Managing Expired Backup Images

The NetBackup Media Manager and RMAN both have the ability to manage backup retention periods. This can be a problem if their retention settings don't match. Automatic expiration of backup images from both repositories is not supported. A work-around is to use the Retention setting in the Application Backup schedule and then to synchronize the NetBackup and RMAN repositories.

Delete Expired Backups Using NetBackup Repository

NetBackup controls the expiration of the Oracle backup images from its repository by using the Retention setting in an Application Backup schedule. The setting specifies the length of time before the backup image expires and is deleted. When you use NetBackup retention to delete backup images, you must do regular Oracle repository maintenance to remove references to expired backup files.

Delete Expired Backups Using RMAN

RMAN has a manual command to remove all database and archive log backups that have reached their retention limits. You can use this command to delete database backups from both the RMAN catalog and the NetBackup repository. When a request is issued to delete a backup file from the RMAN repository, RMAN sends the request to NetBackup to delete the corresponding images from its repository, regardless of the retention level. The code for deleting expired backups is shown next:

```
RMAN> allocate channel for maintenance type 'SBT_TAPE';
RMAN> crosscheck backup;
RMAN> delete expired backup;
```

The **crosscheck** command should be used only in cases where files marked with the status "Available" that no longer exist can be expired and marked deleted. RMAN should control the retention using the following command. If you configure the channel with the tape parameters, there is no need to allocate channels. This feature is available in Oracle 9*i* Database and newer versions.

```
RMAN> allocate channel for maintenance type 'SBT_TAPE';
RMAN> delete noprompt obsolete;
```

RMAN Sample Scripts

Something particularly clever about the NetBackup *for Oracle* agent installation is that it includes RMAN backup and recovery sample scripts that are pre-instrumented (that is, they already include code snippets or templates) with code for using NetBackup. Look for the sample scripts in /<install_path>/netbackup/ext/db_ext/oracle/samples/rman.

These sample scripts will be included:

```
cold_database_backup.sh
hot_database_backup_proxy.sh
cold_duplex_database_backup_full.sh
hot_tablespace_backup.sh
database_restore.sh
hot_tablespace_backup_proxy.sh
hot_database_backup.sh
pit_database_restore.sh
```

New scripts can be generated from the Administration Console. For anyone who has suffered through the time-consuming effort of trying to locate elusive punctuation errors, these scripts come as a pleasant surprise.

The following is an RMAN code snippet for calling NetBackup:

```
rman target / catalog <user>/<password>@rman_cat_db log=<my_output.log>
run
{
allocate channel t1 type 'SBT_TAPE'
parms="ENV=(NB_ORA_SERV=<storage_server>,
NB_ORA_POLICY=RMAN_DEFAULT, NB_ORA_CLIENT=<db_server>)";
backup database format 'db_%d%U%t'
}
```

The *NetBackup Administrator's Guide* recommends adding a %t at the end of the format string, since NetBackup uses a timestamp as part of its search criteria for catalog images. You can also do this by using **configure**.

The following is an RMAN code snippet for calling NetBackup that uses **configure** commands:

```
rman target / catalog <user>/<password>@rman_cat_db log=<my_output.log>
rman> CONFIGURE CHANNEL DEVICE TYPE 'SBT_TAPE' PARMS
'SBT_LIBRARY=/<install_path>/netbackup/bin/libobk.so64.1,
ENV=(NB_ORA_SERV=<storage_server>, NB_ORA_POLICY=<policy_name>,
NB_ORA_CLIENT=<db_server>)';
rman> CONFIGURE DEVICE TYPE 'SBT_TAPE' FORMAT 'db_%d%U%t'
rman> backup database;
```

Troubleshooting

Inevitably, something will break in the environment. Knowing how to prioritize problems in advance helps to resolve them more smoothly. This section highlights steps to help troubleshoot issues.

The following are general troubleshooting steps to take:

1. Verify Oracle agent installation by making sure that the proper libraries exist in /<install_path>/netbackup/bin. Refer to Table 7-2 earlier in the chapter to determine which library (for example, libobk.a) corresponds to your operating system.

2. Check the database server (client) to ensure that the bphdb executable exists. This is used by both the NetBackup scheduler and the GUI to start backups.

3. Check that the following executables exist:

    ■ /<install_path>/netbackup/bin/bpdbsbora

    ■ /<install_path>/netbackup/bin/bpubsora

    ■ /<install_path>/lib/libdbsbrman.so

    ■ /<install_path>/lib/libnbberman.so

4. Check that the following /<install_path>/netbackup/logs directories exist with 777 permissions:

    ■ On the database server (client): bpdbsbora, dbclient, bphdb, and bpcd

    ■ On the master server: bprd and bpdbm

    ■ On the media server: bpbrm and bptm

Use NetBackup Logs

NetBackup generates logs for backup and restore operations. These logs can be used to investigate media manager problems, but RMAN errors will be written to the RMAN logs. There are two types of NetBackup logs:

■ **Progress logs**   Located in /<install_path>/netbackup/logs/user_ops/username/logs, these logs are generated for any backup or restore operations. These files can sometimes be large and cumbersome. They contain sizable amounts of data. The key here is knowing how to extract the data you need. There are basically two error types, numbers 16 and 32; 16 is an error failure and 32 is a critical failure. The best way to find them is to search the log files for <16> and <32>.

- **Debug logs** Each debug log corresponds to a NetBackup process and executable. When debugging is turned on, the logs are written to /<install_path>/netbackup/logs. These logs can grow quickly in size, so use debugging only when necessary.

To enable logging on the database server (client), modify the /<install_path>/netbackup/bp.conf file with this line:

```
VERBOSE = #
```

is a value of 1 to 5 to indicate the level of logging. Keep in mind that a higher value generates a lot of information and could cause the directory to run out of space.

NOTE
Make sure that the debug file permissions are set to 777. Verify that libobk is linked properly if log files are not being created.

Determine Which Library Is in Use

Find out which NetBackup library is interfacing with Oracle:

```
ls -l $( echo $LD_LIBRARY_PATH | sed -e "s/:/ /g")/libobk* | grep libobk
```

Security Best Practices

Since the NetBackup software runs in a networked environment, it is susceptible to vulnerabilities such as denial of service attacks. To prevent these situations from happening, the following best practices are recommended by Veritas, which is now Symantec:

- Allow administrative access to privileged users only.

- Allow remote access only from trusted servers.

- Apply the latest patches.

- Install NetBackup behind a firewall.

- Ensure virus protection is running on the servers.

- Monitor network traffic for malicious activity.

- Block external access to the default ports used by NetBackup.

- NetBackup server and clients should face toward the internal network.

Cost Justification

It's not always easy to justify the costs of purchasing expensive software and licenses for an information technology department, which is traditionally considered to be a non-revenue generating part of an organization. This section provides some ideas for demonstrating to management the value of purchasing VERITAS NetBackup *for Oracle*.

The NetBackup *for Oracle* software extends the capabilities of RMAN. Since the software allows RMAN to speak directly to storage servers, it automates processes that would otherwise be done by people. It shortens backup and recovery time by eliminating some steps altogether and by cutting out process variation. Essentially, this translates into better overall application performance (since backups take less time), reduced business outages during recovery events, more error-free recoveries, and greater productivity of database and storage administrators.

The NetBackup software could easily pay for itself during just one significant business outage where productivity and revenue are negatively impacted.

Summary

We have explored how NetBackup software is used to facilitate a networked backup and recovery environment. We outlined the ways in which it extends existing RMAN functionality. We described how to configure each layer for direct component communication, which eliminates the need for manual intervention. We discovered that using NetBackup to enhance RMAN results in faster backup and recovery, reduced process variation, and shorter business outages during recovery events. NetBackup *for Oracle* software has been thoughtfully developed for those of us who are excited about easily deployed and feature-rich backup and recovery solutions.

CHAPTER
8

Configuring HP Data Protector for Oracle

I n large environments, it's hard for database administrators to schedule, manage, monitor, and report all database backups centrally. Another challenge for DBAs is managing the backup media: setting the protection, monitoring the usage, and checking on the backup history. For HP customers, using a backup user interface with RMAN such as HP Data Protector overcomes all these issues.

This chapter begins with a discussion of the integration between Oracle RMAN and HP Data Protector. It then describes the configuration of Oracle backups with Data Protector. You will learn how to back up and restore an Oracle database with Data Protector. Finally, you will learn how to set up synchronization between Oracle RMAN Metadata and Data Protector Media Management Database.

Integration of Oracle and Data Protector

You must properly integrate Oracle and Data Protector in order to run successful backup/restore operations. To integrate them, therefore, you'll now learn about the support matrix and the integration components, and do a workshop on integration configuration.

Support Matrix

HP Data Protector A.06.00 supports Oracle 11*g* Recovery Manager on the following operating systems:

Oracle 11*g* 64-bit	**Oracle 11*g* 32-bit**
HP-UX 11.23 (64-bit) (Itanium and PA-RISC)	SuSE Linux Enterprise Server 9 and 10
HP-UX 11.31 (64-bit) (Itanium and PA-RISC)	Red Hat Enterprise Linux 3.0, 4.*x*, 5.*x*
Solaris (Sparc) 9, 10 (64-bit) (x86 and x64)	Oracle Enterprise Linux 4.0, 5.*x* (32-bit)
Oracle Enterprise Linux 4.0, 5.0 (64-bit) (x64)	Windows Server 2003 (32-bit)
Oracle Enterprise Linux 5.3 (64-bit)	
Red Hat Enterprise Linux 3.0, 4.*x*, 5.*x* (x64)	
SuSE Linux Enterprise Server 9, 10 (x64)	
Windows Server 2003 (x64)	
Windows Server 2008 (32-bit) (64-bit)	
AIX 5.*x*, 6.1	

Integration Components

For Oracle and Data Protector integration, RMAN and the Data Protector Oracle Integration software work together to accomplish backup, copy, restore, recovery, and duplication operations.

The Data Protector Oracle Integration agent uses the information in the recovery catalog or in the control file to determine how to execute the requested backup and restore operations. By using this integration, you can perform Oracle full and incremental (up to incremental level 4) backups. Oracle incremental backups can be differential or cumulative. By default, Data Protector performs Oracle differential incremental backups. By changing the default RMAN script created by Data Protector, you can specify a cumulative backup.

NOTE
*Even if you configure an Oracle incremental backup, you won't
see the backup definition as "incremental" in Data Protector. Data
Protector will mark it "full," because Data Protector incremental
backup is a different concept, used on file system backups.*

With Data Protector, both online and offline database backups can be performed. However, successful backups require proper configurations. For an *online* database backup, the database instance must be in ARCHIVELOG mode, and for an *offline* database backup, the database needs to be prepared for backup with the Pre-exec and Post-exec options in the backup specification. You can use these options for shutting down the database or making a tablespace offline before backup, and then reverse operations after backup.

Figure 8-1 shows the general architecture of Oracle and Data Protector integration.

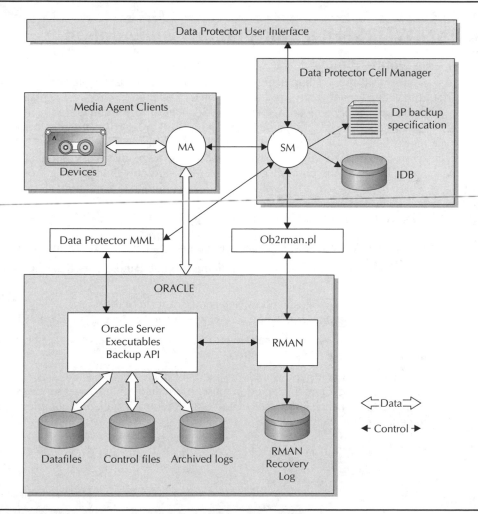

FIGURE 8-1 *Integration architecture of Oracle and Data Protector*

The components of this integration, as shown in Figure 8-1, are

SM   The Data Protector Session Manager, which manages the backup and restore sessions.

MA   The Data Protector General Media Agent, which reads and writes data from and to media devices.

Data Protector MML   The Data Protector Oracle Integration Media Management Library, which is a set of routines that enables data transfer between the Oracle server and Data Protector. The Data Protector MML links Data Protector and Oracle server software.

Ob2rman.pl   The Data Protector Oracle Integration agent, which works with RMAN to manage all aspects of the backup/recovery operations on the Oracle target database.

Backup API   The Oracle-defined application programming interface.

IDB   The Internal Database, where all the information about Data Protector sessions, including session messages, objects, data, used devices, and media, is written.

RMAN   The Oracle Recovery Manager.

RMAN WORKSHOP: *Integration Configuration*

Workshop Notes

To run a successful RMAN backup of an Oracle Database using Data Protector Integration, you should have the Oracle target database mounted or opened, the recovery catalog database configured and opened if being used, Oracle Net Services properly configured, and Data Protector Disk Agent, Media Agent, and Oracle Integration installed on the server the target database resides on.

In this workshop, it is assumed that devices and media are ready for use, and that Data Protector Cell Manager is installed and properly configured. HP OpenView Storage Data Protector Manager software, which may reside in a PC, will be used to configure the integration.

Step 1.   First you must install the Data Protector agent to target server.

a. Run HP OpenView Storage Data Protector Manager software and connect the Cell Manager.

b. In the Context List, select Clients, and in the Scoping Pane, right-click Clients and click Add Clients.

c. In the Add Client Systems window, select the platform of the target server (Windows or Unix), and choose the installation server, which can be the Cell Manager. Click Next.

d. Type the IP or host name (if it can be resolved) of the target server in the Name box and click Add. Click Next (see Figure 8-2).

e. Select the components you want to install. For Oracle Database backups, Disk Agent, Media Agent, and Oracle Integration must be installed on the target server. Select the components and click Finish (see Figure 8-3). After the installation completes, continue the configuration with Step 2.

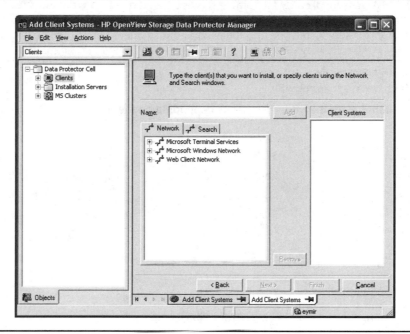

FIGURE 8-2 *Defining client IP/host name*

FIGURE 8-3 *Component selection*

Step 2.   MML is invoked by the Oracle server when it needs to write to or read from devices using Data Protector. For this integration to work properly, a manual link needs to be created between Oracle server software and the Media Management Library on the target system. MML is located in the following directory:

HP-UX and Solaris   /opt/omni/lib
Other Unix   /usr/omni/lib

The filename for the MML also differs depending on the platform, as shown in the following table:

Platforms	32-bit	64-bit
HP-UX	libob2oracle8.sl	libob2oracle8_64bit.sl
HP-UX on IA-64	libob2oracle8.so	libob2oracle8_64bit.so
Solaris	libob2oracle8.so	libob2oracle8_64bit.so
AIX	libob2oracle8.a	libob2oracle8_64bit.a
Other Unix	libob2oracle8.so	libob2oracle8_64bit.so

Now, proceed as follows:

a.   Change to the <ORACLE_HOME>/lib directory.

b.   Run:

   HP-UX   mv libobk.sl libobk.sl.orig

   Other Unix   mv libobk.so libobk.so.orig

NOTE
Perform the preceding step only if the libobk.sl (HP-UX) or libobk
.so (other Unix) file is already created in the <ORACLE_HOME>/lib
directory. Otherwise, skip this step.

c.   Run:

   HP-UX

■   **32-bit**   ln -s /opt/omni/lib/libob2oracle8.sl libobk.sl

■   **64-bit**   ln -s /opt/omni/lib/libob2oracle8_64bit.sl libobk.sl

   Solaris

■   **32-bit**   ln -s /optS/omni/lib/libob2oracle8.so libobk.so

■   **64-bit**   ln -s /opt/omni/lib/libob2oracle8_64bit.so libobk.so

Other Unix

- **32-bit**   ln -s /opt/omni/lib/libob2oracle8.so libobk.so

- **64-bit**   ln -s /opt/omni/lib/libob2oracle8_64bit.so libobk.so

If you start a backup without manually linking Oracle server software and MML as just shown, you will probably see this error message:

```
RMAN-00571: ===========================================================
RMAN-00569: ====== ERROR MESSAGE STACK FOLLOWS =======
RMAN-00571: ===========================================================
RMAN-03009: failure of allocate command on DP_TEST channel at 01/22/2010 08:54:22
ORA-19554: error allocating device, device type: SBT_TAPE, device name:
ORA-27211: Failed to load Media Management Library
Recovery Manager complete.
```

RMAN Backup Configuration on Data Protector

To configure an Oracle RMAN backup configuration on Data Protector, decide which devices, media pool, and media will be used for that backup operation. Then you can create the Data Protector Oracle backup specification.

Data Protector offers database backup templates that can be used when creating the backup specification. You can also create templates tailored to your needs.

RMAN WORKSHOP: *Backup Configuration*

Workshop Notes

Now that you have added the target host to Data Protector successfully, you can define a backup specification. Using this specification, you will be able to start the backup immediately or to schedule it to run within a specific period.

Step 1.   Run HP OpenView Storage Data Protector Manager and connect the Cell Manager.

Step 2.   In the Context List, select Backup; in the Scoping Pane, expand Backup Specifications; then, right-click Oracle Server and click Add Backup.

Step 3.   In the Create New Backup window, you can select one of the predefined backup templates, or select Blank Backup to specify backup operation details later (see Figure 8-4). Click OK.

Step 4.   In the next window, Data Protector asks for Client, Application Database, Username, and Group Name information. Specify the client the target database resides in, the SID of the target database, the username, and the name of the group that owns the Oracle instance (see Figure 8-5). Click Next.

FIGURE 8-4 *Template selection*

FIGURE 8-5 *Target selection*

Step 5.   In the Configure Oracle window, specify information about the target database. On the General tab, specify the Oracle Server Home Directory (see Figure 8-6). On the Primary tab, specify username, password, and service information. Don't forget that this user must have been granted Oracle SYSDBA or SYSOPER rights. Service is the name used to identify an SQL*Net server process for the target database. The Catalog tab requires the username, password, and service information for the Catalog database if it's being used. The last tab, Standby, is necessary to fill if the Oracle Data Guard environment is in use and will be backed up. Click OK.

Step 6.   This step asks you to specify which components of the database you want to back up. If you selected Blank Backup in Step 3, you will see all components unchecked (see Figure 8-7). Select the components you want to back up and then click Next.

Step 7.   Now, Data Protector asks you which hardware will be used for this backup. Select the drive that you want to use (see Figure 8-8). If you defined it earlier, you can also specify the Media Pool that will be used for the backup. Select the drive and click Properties. You'll see a drop-down menu to select a Media Pool. Make your choice and click Next.

FIGURE 8-6   *Oracle configuration*

FIGURE 8-7 *Database component selection*

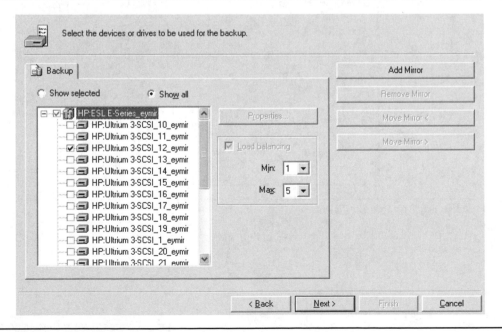

FIGURE 8-8 *Device/drive selection*

Step 8.   This step allows you to specify detailed configuration. As you can see in Figure 8-9, the three categories each have an Advanced button. You can define pre- and post-execution scripts under Backup Specification Options. You can define backup objects' protection and report level under Common Application Options. Lastly, you can see an overview of the prepared RMAN script and disable/enable Data Protector managed control file backup under Application Specific Options. Make your selections and click Next.

Step 9.   You can schedule the configured backup in this step. Specify the dates and times that you want backups performed. Select the Holiday box if you want to indicate that you do not want scheduled backups to run on holidays.

Step 10.   This last step gives you three options:

- ■ **Save as**   Save the newly created backup/template.

- ■ **Start Backup**   Begin an interactive backup with the current backup specification.

- ■ **Start Preview**   Begin an interactive preview (test) of backup with the current backup specification.

If you choose to save the backup specification, you can also preview or start the backup later.

FIGURE 8-9   *Advanced configuration*

Editing the Oracle RMAN Script

You can edit the RMAN script section only after the Data Protector Oracle backup specification has been saved.

To manually edit the RMAN script, in the Context List, select Backup; in the Scoping Pane, expand Backup Specifications; expand Oracle Server; and click the backup specification that you will edit. On the Options tab, click Advanced in the Application Specific Options box. The RMAN script appears with an Edit button. When you click Edit a warning will appear as:

"This operation will save the backup specification now and reopen the editor after the RMAN Script is saved. Would you like to continue?"

Click Yes and manually configure the script. You can save the configuration by clicking Save.

If the RMAN script contains additional manually entered backup commands—for example, a second backup command for backing up a database that is already listed in the first backup command—the object selection is disabled, and it is only possible to browse the Source tab.

RMAN Backup

Now that you've integrated Oracle with Data Protector and configured an RMAN backup on Data Protector, you'll learn how to run an RMAN backup of a Data Protector integrated Oracle database.

Backup Methods

To start an RMAN backup of a Data Protector integrated Oracle database, you can choose from these three methods:

- Use either Data Protector GUI or the Data Protector CLI to start an interactive backup of a predefined Oracle backup specification.

- Use Data Protector Scheduler to schedule a backup of a predefined Oracle backup specification.

- Use either Oracle Recovery Manager or Oracle Enterprise Manager to start a backup on the Oracle server.

Running an Interactive Backup

To start an interactive backup of an Oracle database using the Data Protector GUI:

1. In the HP OpenView Storage Data Protector Manager (Data Protector GUI), select Backup in the drop-down menu.

2. In the left pane, choose Backup | Backup Specifications | Oracle Server.

3. Right-click the backup specification you want to start and select Start Backup.

Scheduling a Backup

To schedule an Oracle backup specification:

1. In the HP OpenView Storage Data Protector Manager, select Backup in the drop-down menu.

2. In the left pane, choose Backup | Backup Specifications | Oracle Server.

3. Double-click the backup specification you want to schedule and click the Schedule tab.

4. In the Schedule page, select a date in the calendar, and click Add to open the Schedule Backup dialog box.

5. Specify necessary scheduling options.

Starting Oracle Database Backup Using RMAN or Enterprise Manager

You can also use RMAN CLI or Enterprise Manager to perform backups of Data Protector integrated databases. To use Data Protector backup media in Oracle database backups, you must specify the channel type SBT_TAPE.

Backup Procedure

When a backup is started with Data Protector, the following happens in the background:

1. Data Protector executes ob2rman.pl, which starts RMAN on the client and sends the preconfigured RMAN script.

2. RMAN contacts the Oracle server, which contacts Data Protector via the MML interface and initiates the backup.

3. During the backup session, the Oracle server reads data from the disk and sends it to Data Protector for writing to the backup device.

4. Messages from the Data Protector backup session and messages generated by Oracle are logged to the Data Protector database.

Restoring Oracle Using the Data Protector GUI

You can restore the following database objects by using both the Data Protector GUI and RMAN:

■ Control files

■ Datafiles

■ Tablespaces

■ Databases

■ Recovery catalog databases

You can also duplicate a database by using the Data Protector GUI. You need to create an Oracle instance in order to restore or duplicate a database.

Before you restore any database item or you duplicate a database, ensure that the database is in the correct state:

Item to Restore	Database State
Control file, duplicating a database	Nomount (started)
All other items	Mount

NOTE
When restoring only a few tablespaces or datafiles, the database can be open with the tablespaces or datafiles to be restored offline.

For restore, RMAN scripts are generated with necessary commands, depending on selections made in the GUI. If you want to perform additional actions, you cannot edit the RMAN restore script, but you can perform the actions manually from RMAN itself.

Restoring the Control File

Depending on the type of the control file backup, three types of restore are possible when restoring the control file:

Restoring from Data Protector Managed Control File Backup (CONTROLFILE FROM DP MANAGED BACKUP)

The control file was backed up automatically by ob2rman.pl at the end of a backup session, unless the option "Disable Data Protector managed control file backup" was selected.

The recovery catalog is not required for this restore option.

The control files are restored to the following locations:

Windows   <Data_Protector_home>\tmp\ctrl<DB_NAME>.dbf
HP-UX and Solaris   /var/opt/omni/tmp/ctrl<DB_NAME>.dbf
Other UNIX   /usr/opt/omni/tmp/ctrl<DB_NAME>.dbf

After the restore session finishes, you must run the following script:

```
run {
allocate channel 'dev0' type disk;
restore controlfile from '<TMP_FILENAME>';
release channel 'dev0';
}
```

where <TMP_FILENAME> is the location to which the file was restored.

Restoring from RMAN Autobackup (CONTROLFILE FROM RMANAUTOBACKUP)

The control file was automatically backed up by RMAN, and the recovery catalog is not available.

Restoring from RMAN Backup Set (CONTROLFILE FROM RMANBACKUPSET)

The recovery catalog is required.

Restoring Oracle Database Objects

To restore Oracle database objects:

1. Put the database in the mount state.

2. In the Data Protector GUI, switch to the Restore context.

3. Under Restore Objects, expand Oracle Server, expand the client on which the database whose objects you're restoring resides, and then click the database.

4. In the Restore Action drop-down list, select the type of restore you wish to perform.

5. In the Results Area, select objects for restore. If you are restoring datafiles, you can restore the files to a new location. Right-click the database object, click Restore As, and in the Restore As dialog box, specify the new datafile location.

NOTE
When restoring to a new location, current datafiles will be switched to the restored datafile copies only if you have selected Perform Restore and Recovery from the Restore Action drop-down list.

6. On the Options page, from the Client drop-down list, select the client on which the Data Protector Oracle Integration agent will be started. To restore the database objects to a different database than the agent has selected, click Settings and specify the login information for the target database.

7. In the Devices page, select the devices to be used for the restore. You can restore using a device other than that used for backup, although Data Protector defaults to the original device on which the backup was made. To change the device from which an item is restored, select your desired device and click Change.

8. Click Restore.

Oracle RMAN Metadata and Data Protector Media Management Database Synchronization

The RMAN metadata, which can be stored either in the recovery catalog database or in the control files, contains information about the target database. RMAN uses this information for all backup, restore, and maintenance operations.

Data Protector has its own data protection policy that is not automatically synchronized with Oracle RMAN metadata. To have both catalogs synchronized, run the following command using RMAN:

```
allocate channel for maintenance type 'sbt_tape' parms 'ENV=(OB2MAINTENANCE=1)';
crosscheck backup completed after "TO_DATE('01/13/10 12:00:00','MM/DD/YY HH24:MI:SS')";
release channel;
```

RMAN will check all backup information in its repository and query the Data Protector Internal Database for the availability of the backup pieces. RMAN then marks the backup piece as expired or available, depending on media availability. RMAN will not delete the backup information in its repository if it is expired in the Data Protector Internal Database, but instead also marks them as expired in the RMAN repository.

To delete expired backup objects from the recovery catalog database, run the following command using RMAN:

```
delete expired backup;
```

Summary

This chapter has given an overview of using HP Data Protector software for Oracle RMAN backups. After you configure the integration properly, preparing and scheduling backup configurations that meet your backup needs, it will be easy to manage the backup/restore operations.

CHAPTER
9

RMAN and Tivoli
Storage Manager

f you already use Tivoli Storage Manager (TSM) for backing up files in your enterprise, taking the next step and using TSM to back up your Oracle database makes a lot of sense: you not only can leverage an existing data protection asset, but also get a seamless connection from Oracle's RMAN utility to TSM. With only a few minor modifications to your RMAN scripts and a straightforward one-time TSM client installation, you won't even know that the tape or disk drive you're using for backup is on a different server. In your DBA role, you may never even have to run a TSM console command.

In this chapter, we'll cover a number of topics related to TSM, the TSM client in general, and the add-on module known as *Tivoli Data Protection for Oracle* (TDPO). First, we'll give you a brief overview of the TSM architecture and how an Oracle client connects to it. Your in-depth involvement with TSM begins when you must test and configure TDPO on the server where you will perform the RMAN backup commands.

Throughout this chapter, we'll briefly cover a couple of TSM and Oracle client utilities that you will use to perform initial and routine configuration and monitoring tasks.

We'll next perform a couple of backups using RMAN and see the effect of this backup in the storage pool assigned to your TSM Oracle client.

At the end of the chapter, we will cover a couple of common problems you might encounter in backing up Oracle databases with TSM and TDPO and how to resolve them.

Overview of Tivoli Storage Manager

TSM is a multitiered architecture: when you use it to back up an Oracle database, you may have as many as four tiers. In contrast, you could host all tiers on a single server, but this is not recommended in a distributed environment where you want to keep your backup server separate from the server whose data you want to back up.

Figure 9-1 is a diagram of a typical TSM environment. In the next few sections, we'll drill down into a few of the components shown in Figure 9-1 and explain some TSM concepts along the way.

Table 9-1 outlines the nodes shown in Figure 9-1. These nodes are used in the examples throughout this chapter to show you how you can distribute the TSM components across your network.

Table 9-2 lists and briefly describes the disk devices you will use on server tsm01 for your Oracle RMAN backups.

TSM Server System Objects

The multilevel structure of system objects in a TSM server makes it easy to optimally configure your backups for each of the wide variety of data sources in your environment. For the same reason, this flexible hierarchy also makes it easy to assign a specific configuration to unrelated data sources! Figure 9-2 shows the relationship between TSM system objects as well as the types and number of objects that a client uses on any given TSM server.

FIGURE 9-1 *TSM architecture*

Node Name	Operating System	Role
tsm01	Linux	TSM server
tsmadmin	Linux	Integrated Solutions Console, Administration Center server
oc1	Linux	Oracle database, Tivoli Data Protection for Oracle; TSM client
winxp07	Windows XP	Integrated Solutions Console/Administration Center web client

TABLE 9-1 *TSM Node Names and Roles*

Physical Device Name	Linux Mount Point	Capacity	Purpose
/dev/sda1	/tsm01	3.5GB	Disk 1 for Oracle backup pool
/dev/sdb1	/tsm02	3.5GB	Disk 2 for Oracle backup pool
/dev/sdc1	/tsm03	3.5GB	Disk 3 for Oracle backup pool
/dev/sdd1	/tsm04	3.5GB	Disk 4 for Oracle backup pool

TABLE 9-2 *Raw Disks for TSM Storage Devices*

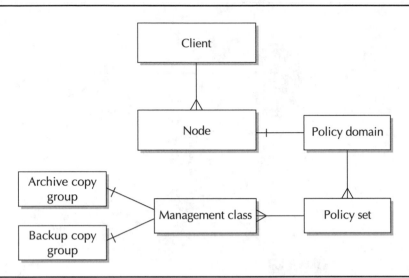

FIGURE 9-2 *Client/TSM relationship and TSM system objects*

At the highest level is the policy domain: a policy domain consists of one or more policy sets, and each policy set consists of one or more management classes. Each management class can have one archive copy group and one backup copy group. We'll tell you more about each of these objects in the following sections.

Policy Domain

A *policy domain* is a group of clients with similar requirements for backing up and archiving data. You might use a policy domain for everyone in a particular department, a particular building or floor, or all users of a specific file server.

A default TSM installation includes one default policy domain called **standard**. For the examples later in this chapter, we will use the **standard** policy domain. You assign backup clients to a policy domain.

Policy Set

A *policy set* is a group of management classes. Each policy domain can contain one or more policy sets, but only one policy set in a policy domain can be active at any given time. You use policy sets to easily switch between available management classes.

Management Class

A *management class* is a collection of zero, one, or two copy groups. You designate one management class within a policy set as the default management class. You typically use management classes to partition client data based on its criticality to the business, how frequently it changes, or whether the data must be retained indefinitely. A management class can have at most one backup copy group and at most one archive copy group.

Backup Copy Groups and Archive Copy Groups

A *copy group* specifies the common attributes that control these characteristics of a backup or archive file:

- **Generation**   How many copies of each file are retained

- **Destination**   Which storage pool will contain the backup

- **Expiration**   When a file will be deleted because the expiration date or retention period has passed

A *backup copy group* contains attributes that control whether a file that has changed since the last backup is backed up again, how many days must elapse before a file is backed up again, and how a file is processed if it is in use during a backup. In contrast, an *archive copy group* contains attributes that control whether a file is archived if it is in use, where the server stores archived copies of the files, and how long the server keeps archived copies of the files. TDPO only uses backup copy groups for Oracle backups.

TSM Client

You install the client piece of TSM, which includes the TSM API, on any server that needs to use a TSM server for backup or recovery. Also included in an installation on an Oracle server is the RMAN library interface to TSM: Tivoli Data Protection for Oracle (TDPO).

Real World Example

Suppose you are working for a web site development and hosting company. The company has several production Oracle databases that are backed up using TDPO and TSM by using a common management class. The backups are stored on tape for 30 days before the backups are deleted. Also, backups are copied to an offsite storage location the next day. Also, several nonproduction databases are used by developers for development web sites.

When you arrive Monday morning, you find that a hardware failure has occurred that hosts a nonproduction database. A disk failure has resulted in several online redo logs and all control files being lost. Since there are no backups, you spend several days re-creating the database, and the developers spend several more days redoing their changes. Afterward, management would like to start backing up development databases as well. But to keep the cost of tape storage down, the backups will only be kept for seven days, and backups will not be stored offsite.

You decide the best way to meet both requirements without impacting your production backups would be to create a second management class. You ask your TSM administrator to create a new management class that has a seven-day retention period and won't be copied offsite. When backing up nonproduction databases, you reference this new management class. Nonproduction databases can be backed up and retained for seven days and will not be copied offsite, and the production backups will not be affected.

Using TDPO, RMAN can back up these database objects to TSM:

- Databases

- Tablespaces

- Datafiles

- Archive log files

- Control files

- Pfiles and Spfiles

Plus, you can perform a full database restoration while the database is offline; you can perform tablespace or datafile restores while the database is either online or offline.

The server oc1 is a client node in an Oracle Real Application Clusters (RAC) database in Figure 9-1 and is a client of TSM on server tsm01.

TSM Administration Center and Web Client

The Administration Center is a web-based interface that you use to centrally configure and manage IBM TSM version 5.3 servers. You install it as an IBM Integrated Solutions Console (ISC) component—as a result, you can use ISC to manage a number of heterogeneous systems and applications using a common management interface.

In Figure 9-1, the server tsmadmin hosts ISC and the Administration Center plug-in. TSM administrators use a web browser on the workstation winxp07 to connect to ISC on tsmadmin, which in turn sends console commands and receives status information from the TSM server tsm01. You can administer TSM using this method from any web browser that has a network connection to server tsmadmin.

RMAN Workshop: *Configuring TDPO for Oracle*

Workshop Notes
For this workshop you will need an operational TSM server and client environment and Oracle database home installed.

Step 1. To install TDPO on your Oracle server, you need to install the following RPM packages:

- **TIVguid.i386.rpm**   Creates a globally unique identifier (GUID) to uniquely distinguish this server from other servers that will access TSM

- **TIVsm-API.i386.rpm**   Installs the application program interface (API) libraries to support TDPO or any other application that will programmatically access TSM

- **TDP-Oracle.i386.rpm**   Contains the libraries and link definitions that Oracle RMAN will use to connect to TSM

Here is what you see when you install TDP-Oracle:

```
[root@oc1 DPO]# rpm -i TDP-Oracle.i386.rpm
Post Installation of IBM Tivoli Storage Manager for Databases - Oracle.
Checking Tivoli Signature File.
Created Tivoli Signature File.
Creating symbolic links
created link /opt/tivoli/tsm/client/oracle/bin/libobk.so
      /usr/lib/libobk.so
created link /opt/tivoli/tsm/client/oracle/bin/tdpoconf /usr/bin/tdpoconf

Post Installation of IBM Tivoli Storage Manager
for Databases - Oracle Complete.
Be sure to set up the system configuration file
before starting the client!
[root@oc1 DPO]#
```

Step 2. The next step is to register the client oc1 on the TSM server:

```
TSM:SERVER1> reg node oc1_oracle orabakpw maxnummp=2 passexp=0
ANR2017I Administrator SERVER_CONSOLE issued command:
      REGISTER NODE oc1_oracle ?***? maxnummp=2 passexp=0
ANR2060I Node OC1_ORACLE registered in policy domain STANDARD.
ANR2099I Administrative userid OC1_ORACLE defined
      for OWNER access to node OC1.
TSM:SERVER1>
```

Note that we're setting **maxnummp=2**: this specifies the maximum number of parallel sessions that the client can use when backing up to tape. Even though we're using disk drives for backup in these examples, it's a good idea to define the parallelism you need on those occasions when you do back up to tape.

Registering a client node also creates an administrative account that you can use to connect to the TSM server; however, creating individual server accounts for each administrator gives you more control over privileges assigned to each administrator as well as more precise auditing information when an administrator changes the TSM server's configuration.

Next steps are to connect the Oracle database on server oc1 to the TSM server on tsm01. You do this by:

1. Defining the TDPO options in the configuration file tdpo.opt
2. Creating dsm.opt
3. Creating dsm.sys
4. Registering the TDPO node with the TSM server and defining other policy requirements
5. Configuring TSM copy group options
6. Generating the password file for the TSM server
7. Creating symbolic links in the Oracle library directory
8. Testing TDPO connectivity

Step 3. Define TDPO options. On the Oracle client node oc1, change to the directory /opt/tivoli/tsm/client/oracle/bin, and copy tdpo.opt.smp (the sample file) to tdpo.opt. The file tdpo.opt, as you might expect, defines the TDPO-specific options, such as how TDPO will connect to the TSM server. Uncomment the line beginning with TDPO_NODE and replace <hostname> with the name of the TSM client node. In this example, we will use oc1_oracle. In addition, uncomment the lines beginning with DSMI_ORC_CONFIG and DSMI_LOG if you installed TDPO in a directory different from the default location. Your tdpo.opt file should now look like this:

```
*****************************************************************
* IBM Tivoli Storage Manager for Databases
*    Data Protection for Oracle
*
* Sample tdpo.opt for the Linux86 Data Protection for Oracle
*****************************************************************

*DSMI_ORC_CONFIG     /opt/tivoli/tsm/client/oracle/bin/dsm.opt
*DSMI_LOG            /opt/tivoli/tsm/client/oracle/bin

*TDPO_FS             /adsmorc
TDPO_NODE            oc1_oracle
*TDPO_OWNER          <username>
*TDPO_PSWDPATH       /opt/tivoli/tsm/client/oracle/bin

*TDPO_DATE_FMT       1
*TDPO_NUM_FMT        1
*TDPO_TIME_FMT       1

*TDPO_MGMT_CLASS_2   mgmtclass2
*TDPO_MGMT_CLASS_3   mgmtclass3
*TDPO_MGMT_CLASS_4   mgmtclass4
```

Step 4. Create dsm.sys. The file dsm.sys defines how to connect to each TSM server, specifying the port number, TCP/IP address, and so forth. Copy the file /opt/tivoli/tsm/client/api/bin/dsm.sys.smp to /opt/tivoli/tsm/client/oracle/bin/dsm.sys and change the values as follows:

```
*****************************************************************
* Tivoli Storage Manager                                       *
*                                                              *
* Sample Client System Options file for UNIX (dsm.sys.smp)     *
*****************************************************************

*  This file contains the minimum options required to get started
*  using TSM.  Copy dsm.sys.smp to dsm.sys.  In the dsm.sys file,
*  enter the appropriate values for each option listed below and
*  remove the leading asterisk (*) for each one.

*  If your client node communicates with multiple TSM servers, be
*  sure to add a stanza, beginning with the SERVERNAME option, for
*  each additional server.
*****************************************************************
```

```
SErvername        SERVER1
COMMmethod        TCPip
TCPPort           1500
TCPServeraddress  192.168.2.69
Passwordaccess    prompt
```

The IP address 192.168.2.69 is the address of the server tsm01. To avoid manually entering a password for every backup, you will use the **tdpoconf** utility later in this chapter to create a password file that TDPO will use to authenticate with the TSM server.

Step 5.   Create dsm.opt. The file dsm.opt defines the TSM server name you will use for backups on this node. In the directory /opt/tivoli/tsm/client/oracle/bin, create a file with one line, as follows:

```
SERVERNAME SERVER1
```

Step 6.   Register the TDPO node. To register the Oracle server with TSM, use this command on the TSM console:

```
reg node oc1_oracle orabakpw maxnummp=2 passexp=0
```

To enable the RMAN catalog's archiving and expiration settings to control backup retention on the TSM server, update the configuration for node oc1_oracle on the TSM node by using this console command:

```
update node oc1_oracle backdelete=yes
```

Step 7.   Configure TSM copy group options. Since RMAN creates different backup filenames for each backup file it creates, all backup objects saved to the TSM backup storage pool have unique filenames, and therefore they will never expire. As a result, you must set the copy group attribute **verdeleted** to **0** so that TDPO can remove unwanted backup objects from the TSM backup storage pool when an RMAN command or policy sets the backup object to an inactive or expired state. The parameter **verdeleted** specifies the maximum number of backup versions to retain for files that have been deleted from the client; therefore, setting this value to **0** ensures that the expired backup files on the TSM server are deleted the next time expiration processing occurs.

In this example, you are using the default copy group for your TDPO backups, so you set the option **verdeleted** as follows:

```
TSM:SERVER1> update copygroup standard standard standard verdeleted=0
ANR2017I Administrator SERVER_CONSOLE issued command:
    UPDATE COPYGROUP standard standard standard verdeleted=0
ANR1532I Backup copy group STANDARD updated in policy domain
    STANDARD, set STANDARD, management class STANDARD.
TSM:SERVER1>
```

Step 8.   Generate the tdpo password file. To ensure that you do not have to interactively specify a password for every RMAN backup to the TSM server, use the **tdpoconf** utility as follows:

```
[root@oc1 bin]# tdpoconf password
```

```
IBM Tivoli Storage Manager for Databases:
Data Protection for Oracle
Version 5, Release 2, Level 0.0
(C) Copyright IBM Corporation 1997, 2003. All rights reserved.

*************************************************************
*      IBM Tivoli Storage Manager for Databases Utility *
*  Password file initialization/update program         *
*      ROOT privilege needed to update value            *
*************************************************************

Please enter current password:
Please enter new password:
Please reenter new password for verification:

ANU0260I Password successfully changed.
[root@oc1 bin]#
```

The **tdpoconf** utility creates or updates an encrypted password file called /opt/tivoli/tsm/client/oracle/bin/TDPO.oc1_oracle.

Step 9. In addition to the links created during the installation of the package TDP-Oracle.i386.rpm, you need to create a symbolic link to the TSM library functions in Oracle's default library directory, as follows:

```
ln /opt/Tivoli/tsm/client/oracle/bin/libobk.so
     $ORACLE_HOME/lib/libobk.so
```

The RPM utility has no way of knowing where your Oracle executables and libraries are stored, thus you must define this link manually. If you have multiple Oracle homes, you need to create the link in each home that you want to be able to use TDPO in.

Libobk is the generic name for the library file. Each backup vendor that wants to interface with RMAN will provide a library file that is linked to the libobk file.

Step 10. Test TDPO connectivity. To ensure that you can establish a connection to the TSM server, use the sbttest utility. You can find sbttest in the directory $ORACLE_HOME/bin. To run sbttest, set the environment variable TDPO_OPTFILE to point to the tdpo.opt configuration file you created earlier, and then run the **sbttest test** command, as in this example:

```
[oracle@oc1 bin]$ export
     TDPO_OPTFILE=/opt/tivoli/tsm/client/oracle/bin/tdpo.opt
[oracle@oc1 bin]$ sbttest test
The sbt function pointers are loaded from libobk.so library.
-- sbtinit succeeded
Return code -1 from sbtinit, bsercoer = 0, bsercerrno = 0
Message 0 not found;  product=RDBMS; facility=SBT
[oracle@oc1 bin]$
```

The output—sbtinit—succeeded and a return code of –1 from the command indicates that the test ran successfully.

Performing an RMAN Backup Using TDPO

Now that the TDPO setup is complete, you're ready to perform your first RMAN backup. You'll use the **allocate channel** command in an RMAN session to define the backup location; even though your channel type is always **sbt_tape**, the actual backup device on the TSM server could be a disk, a writable DVD, or a physical tape drive; RMAN doesn't know and you don't care what physical device will contain the backup, as long as you can recover the database when disaster strikes!

In this first example, you back up just the USERS tablespace to TSM:

```
[oracle@oc1 ~]$ rman target /

Recovery Manager: Release 11.2.0.1.0 - Production on Tue Jan 26 11:17:01 2010

Copyright (c) 1982, 2009, Oracle and/or its affiliates.  All rights reserved.


connected to target database: RAC (DBID=2170964680)

RMAN> run
2> { allocate channel tdpo type 'sbt_tape' parms
3>      'ENV=(TDPO_OPTFILE=
4>        /opt/tivoli/tsm/client/oracle/bin/tdpo.opt)';
5>   backup tablespace users;
6>   release channel tdpo;
7> }

using target database control file instead of recovery catalog
allocated channel: tdpo
channel tdpo: sid=293 instance=rac1 devtype=SBT_TAPE
channel tdpo: Tivoli Data Protection for
     Oracle: version 5.5.1.0

Starting backup at 22-JUL-06
channel tdpo: starting full datafile backupset
channel tdpo: specifying datafile(s) in backupset
input datafile fno=00004
     name=+DATA/rac/datafile/users.259.582982545
channel tdpo: starting piece 1 at 26-JAN-2010
channel tdpo: finished piece 1 at 26-JAN-2010
piece handle=02horjvc_1_1 tag=TAG20060722T212604
     comment=API Version 2.0,MMS Version 5.2.0.0
channel tdpo: backup set complete, elapsed time: 00:00:03
Finished backup at 25-JAN-2010

released channel: tdpo
RMAN>
```

The only bit of extra work you need to do to back up to TSM is to specify the location of the TDPO options file in the RMAN **env** parameter. In this second example, you back up the entire database:

```
RMAN> run
2> { allocate channel tdpo type 'sbt_tape' parms
3>     'ENV=(TDPO_OPTFILE=
4>            /opt/tivoli/tsm/client/oracle/bin/tdpo.opt)';
5>   backup database;
6>   release channel tdpo;
7> }

allocated channel: tdpo
channel tdpo: sid=293 instance=rac1 devtype=SBT_TAPE
channel tdpo: Tivoli Data Protection for Oracle: version 5.5.1.0

Starting backup at 26-JAN-2010
channel tdpo: starting full datafile backupset
channel tdpo: specifying datafile(s) in backupset
input datafile fno=00003 name=+DATA/rac/datafile/sysaux.257.582982545
input datafile fno=00001 name=+DATA/rac/datafile/system.256.582982545
input datafile fno=00002 name=+DATA/rac/datafile/undotbs1.258.582982545
input datafile fno=00005 name=+DATA/rac/datafile/example.264.582982703
input datafile fno=00006 name=+DATA/rac/datafile/undotbs2.265.582982943
input datafile fno=00007 name=+DATA/rac/datafile/undotbs3.266.582983003
input datafile fno=00004 name=+DATA/rac/datafile/users.259.582982545
channel tdpo: starting piece 1 at 26-JAN-2010
channel tdpo: finished piece 1 at 26-JAN-2010
piece handle=03hork9s_1_1 tag=TAG20060722T213140 comment=API
    Version 2.0,MMS Version 5.5.1.0
channel tdpo: backup set complete, elapsed time: 00:03:26
channel tdpo: starting full datafile backupset
channel tdpo: specifying datafile(s) in backupset
including current control file in backupset
including current SPFILE in backupset
channel tdpo: starting piece 1 at 26-JAN-2010
channel tdpo: finished piece 1 at 26-JAN-2010
piece handle=04horkga_1_1 tag=TAG20060722T213140 comment=API
    Version 2.0,MMS Version 5.5.1.0
channel tdpo: backup set complete, elapsed time: 00:00:06
Finished backup at 26-JAN-2010

released channel: tdpo

RMAN>
```

Note that you do not have to specify where the backup goes or what disk device to use. TSM automatically puts the backup files into one or more of the storage pool's volumes.

By querying the RMAN catalog, you can see both of the backups you just created:

```
RMAN> list backup;

using target database control file instead of recovery catalog
```

```
List of Backup Sets
===================


BS Key   Type LV Size         Device Type Elapsed Time Completion Time
-------  ---- -- ----------   ----------- ------------ ---------------
1        Full   2.00M         SBT_TAPE    00:00:02     26-JAN-2010
         BP Key: 1   Status: AVAILABLE  Compressed: NO  Tag:
                                              TAG20060722T212604

         Handle: 02horjvc_1_1   Media:
  List of Datafiles in backup set 1
  File LV Type Ckp SCN    Ckp Time   Name
  ---- -- ---- ---------- --------- ----
   4      Full 8772169    26-JAN-2010
                          +DATA/rac/datafile/users.259.582982545


BS Key   Type LV Size         Device Type Elapsed Time Completion Time
-------  ---- -- ----------   ----------- ------------ ---------------
2        Full   1.24G         SBT_TAPE    00:03:24     26-JAN-2010
         BP Key: 2   Status: AVAILABLE  Compressed: NO  Tag:
                                              TAG20060722T213140

         Handle: 03hork9s_1_1   Media:
  List of Datafiles in backup set 2
  File LV Type Ckp SCN    Ckp Time   Name
  ---- -- ---- ---------- --------- ----
   1      Full 8772449    26-JAN-2010
                          +DATA/rac/datafile/system.256.582982545
   2      Full 8772449    26-JAN-2010
                          +DATA/rac/datafile/undotbs1.258.582982545
   3      Full 8772449    26-JAN-2010
                          +DATA/rac/datafile/sysaux.257.582982545
   4      Full 8772449    26-JAN-2010
                          +DATA/rac/datafile/users.259.582982545
   5      Full 8772449    26-JAN-2010
                          +DATA/rac/datafile/example.264.582982703
   6      Full 8772449    26-JAN-2010
                          +DATA/rac/datafile/undotbs2.265.582982943
   7      Full 8772449    26-JAN-2010
                          +DATA/rac/datafile/undotbs3.266.582983003


BS Key   Type LV Size         Device Type Elapsed Time Completion Time
-------  ---- -- ----------   ----------- ------------ ---------------
3        Full   14.75M        SBT_TAPE    00:00:05     26-JAN-2010
         BP Key: 3   Status: AVAILABLE  Compressed: NO  Tag:
                                              TAG20060722T213140

         Handle: 04horkga_1_1   Media:
  Control File Included: Ckp SCN: 8772600       Ckp time: 26-JAN-2010
  SPFILE Included: Modification time: 26-JAN-2010


RMAN>
```

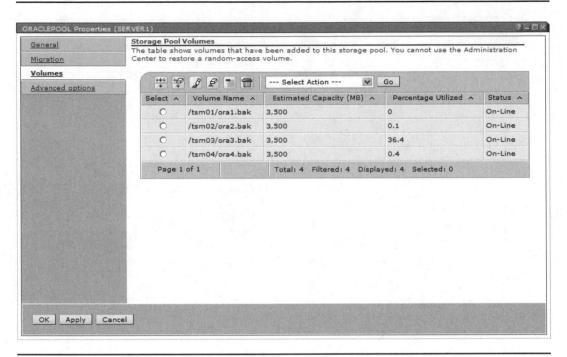

FIGURE 9-3 *Querying storage pool volumes*

And finally, you can see how much disk space the backups are using in the storage pool by looking at the properties of the storage pool volumes, as shown in Figure 9-3. You access this page by clicking the ORACLEPOOL storage pool link in Figure 9-4, then clicking the Volumes link in Figure 9-5.

FIGURE 9-4 *Displaying storage pools and capacity*

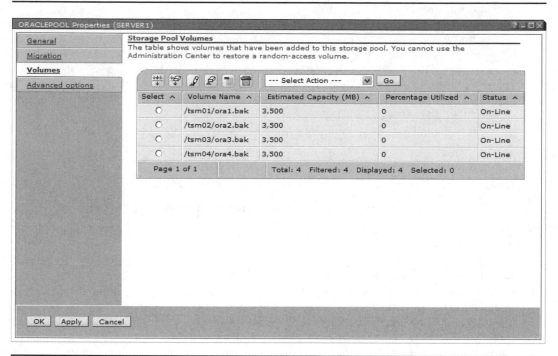

FIGURE 9-5 *Client displaying storage pool volumes*

What's in a Name?

TDPO_NODE can be called almost anything. In environments with many Oracle databases that are using TSM and TDPO for backups, TDPO_NAME could be the root of why backups and restores aren't working. If backups were done with a TDPO_NODE of oc1_oracle and then a new TDPO_NODE, oc2_oracle, were created, and if the tdpo file were changed to use the new TDPO_NAME, RMAN would be unable to access any backups taken under oc1_oracle until the TDPO_NODE were changed in the tdpo file to oc1_oracle. Another common problem is that the password file for the TDPO_NODE that is being used isn't on the database server. This will cause both backups and restore operations to fail.

Default Channels

While every DBA should know how to manually allocate channels, it can be a lot of error-prone typing, and if you have many databases, you may not know which tdpo file to use. By setting one parameter, you can back up a database with a simple backup database command with no manual channel allocation. Running a **show all** command from the RMAN> prompt will show the various RMAN options that are configured. To back up to TSM with automatic channel allocation, we are interested in only two options: CONFIGURE DEFAULT DEVICE TYPE TO 'SBT_TAPE' and CONFIGURE CHANNEL DEVICE TYPE 'SBT_TAPE' PARMS.

By running the following commands from the RMAN prompt, we can set default channels:

```
RMAN> CONFIGURE DEFAULT DEVICE TYPE TO 'SBT_TAPE';
RMAN> CONFIGURE CHANNEL DEVICE TYPE 'SBT_TAPE' PARMS
ENV=(TDPO_OPTFILE=/opt/tivoli/tsm/client/oracle/bin/tdpo.opt)' FORMAT %U';
```

After the configuration commands have been run, backups are even easier:

```
RMAN> backup database;
```

Deleting Database Backups

One of the main advantages of using RMAN is a common interface in deleting backups. It doesn't matter if the backups are a disk or tape, the same commands are used to delete expired backups. Even though the commands to delete backups are the same when using TSM and TDPO, there are times when additional cleanup may be needed. When you delete backups, you will notice the backups are deleted very quickly regardless of the size of the backup. When RMAN tells TSM to delete backup files, TSM does not immediately delete the files since the tape may not be available at the moment, or all the tape drives could be busy. So TSM marks the files to be deleted and returns a success code to RMAN. The TSM administrator will run a purge process that actually deletes the files. If you are using a catalog with the tdposync tool provided by TSM, it is possible to compare what the RMAN catalog shows as deleted and what TSM has actually deleted. To launch tdposync from the default location, using the example tdpo file run /opt/tivoli/tsm/client/oracle/bin/ tdposync SYNCDB -TDPOfile=/opt/tivoli/tsm/client/oracle/bin/tdpo.opt. You must have the tdpo file that was used to take the backups for the comparison to work. After launching, tdposync will ask for a username, password, and a connection string to the RMAN catalog. If more than one RMAN catalog holds backup records, add the parameter -NUMCATALOGS=number. If any discrepancies are found after the comparison, tdposync will provide a list and ask for confirmation before deleting the files from TSM.

Troubleshooting Common Backup Scenarios

Backing up an Oracle database using TSM involves four parts: RMAN, Oracle, O/S, and TSM—each of which can fail and report errors. When you use the RMAN console at first, it can be difficult to know which of the four parts is reporting the error, since errors from all sources are returned to the RMAN console. In the next example, an O/S, Oracle, and RMAN error returned after a simple backup database was issued.

```
RMAN> backup database;

RMAN-00571: ===========================================================
RMAN-00569: =============== ERROR MESSAGE STACK FOLLOWS ===============
```

```
RMAN-00571: ================================================================
RMAN-03002: failure of backup command at 07/17/2009 10:34:31
RMAN-03014: implicit resync of recovery catalog failed
RMAN-06403: could not obtain a fully authorized session
ORA-01034: ORACLE not available
ORA-27101: shared memory realm does not exist
Linux-x86_64 Error: 2: No such file or directory
RMAN>
```

It is usually best to take a bottom-up approach when reading the error messages.

6. RMAN-03002: failure of backup command

5. RMAN-03014: implicit resync of recovery catalog failed

4. RMAN-06403: could not obtain a fully authorized session

3. ORA-01034: ORACLE not available

2. ORA-27101: shared memory realm does not exist

1. Linux-x86_64 Error: 2: No such file or directory

Line 1 is an O/S error that was returned to Oracle. In this case, it doesn't prove too helpful in resolving the problem. Lines 2 and 3 provide the answer and should be recognizable to Oracle DBAs. "ORA-27101: shared memory realm does not exist" means the database instance was not running, and therefore RMAN could not connect to the database.

The first example could happen whether or not you are using TSM. The next scenario will introduce an error only if you are using TSM. We begin with an RMAN run block that allocates a channel, backs up the archive logs, deletes them, and then releases the channel.

```
RMAN> RMAN> run
2> { allocate channel tdpo type 'sbt_tape' parms
3>      'ENV=(TDPO_OPTFILE=
4>          /opt/tivoli/tsm/client/oracle/bin/tdpo.opt)';
5>    backup database;
6>    release channel tdpo;
7> }


RMAN-00571: ================================================================
RMAN-00569: =============== ERROR MESSAGE STACK FOLLOWS ===============
RMAN-00571: ================================================================
ORA-19506: failed to create sequential file, name="rac_9ikk7ac3_1_1", parms=""
ORA-27028: skgfqcre: sbtbackup returned error
ORA-19511: Error received from media manager layer, error text:
ANS1353E (RC53) Session rejected: Unknown or incorrect ID entered

RMAN>
```

Again, starting with the bottom-up approach, we read the error messages starting with 1.

4. ORA-19506: failed to create sequential file, name="a400_9ikk7ac3_1_1", parms=""

3. ORA-27028: skgfqcre: sbtbackup returned error

2. ORA-19511: Error received from media manager layer, error text:

1. ANS1353E (RC53) Session rejected: Unknown or incorrect ID entered

ANS and ANU are errors returned by the TDPO library. Line 3 indicates RMAN received an error from the media management layer (TDPO library). Lines 2 and 1 are again RMAN saying that it failed to create the backup file of the archive logs. ANU and ANS errors can be time-consuming to troubleshoot because many configuration and parameter files and settings have to be checked as well as many different TSM errors that can be returned. From the error message returned in step 1, "Session rejected," we can assume a connection was made from RMAN to TSM and TSM rejected the session. Many different causes may result in a session being rejected; in this case, it is a lack of a password file for the tdpo node. As mentioned earlier in the chapter, to back up or restore a RMAN backup, a tdpo node name and password are supplied to TSM. To quickly troubleshoot this error, check the tdpo options file for the tdpo name that RMAN is using, and then also check to ensure RMAN can access the password file for the tdpo name. Also look in the dsm.sys for the parameter ERRORLOGNAME. This will tell you the path to the file where TDPO will save error information and may provide more details. Your storage administrator may also be able to see if the session rejection message in the TSM logs fails and may be able to provide additional details.

Additional Troubleshooting

To turn on or off debug is a simple **debug on;** or **debug off;** command. Once debug is on, we need to inform RMAN what additional debug information is to be collected. On the **allocate channel** command, trace=1 is used to create trace files in the user_dump_destination directory. Also on the **allocate channel** command, the debug=2 instructs RMAN to send additional information to the sbtio.log file.

Summary

Once you perform the initial installation and setup of TSM and TDPO in a few easy steps, it's a case mostly of "set it and forget it," allowing you, the DBA, to focus more on the RMAN scripts themselves than on managing where and how TSM stores the backups. When problems do arise, by properly reading out an error, you will quickly be able to diagnose backup failures and whether the problem lies with the database or with TSM.

TSM and TDPO not only make it easy to back up your Oracle database using the familiar RMAN interface, but also reduce your enterprise's storage management administrative costs because you can use a single storage manager—Tivoli Storage Manager—for all of your backup, recovery, and archival needs.

CHAPTER
10

Using the Recovery Catalog

racle maintains all of the metadata related to RMAN operations in the *RMAN repository*. The RMAN repository is *always* stored in the control file of the target databases. In some cases, you might want to store the RMAN repository for your database in another location. This location is called the RMAN *recovery catalog*.

RMAN does not require the recovery catalog for most operations, so often it is truly an optional component. Because the recovery catalog is largely optional, RMAN actually defaults to a configuration with no recovery catalog. In this section, first we look at what the recovery catalog is and when you need to use it. Then, we look at how you create a recovery catalog and discuss backup and recovery of the recovery catalog.

What Is the Recovery Catalog?

The *recovery catalog* is an optional component of RMAN that stores historical backup information from RMAN backups. Unlike the database control file's RMAN information, the recovery catalog data is not purged on a regular basis. Thus, the historical information in the recovery catalog tends to be more comprehensive and to date further back than the historical information in the control file. Using a recovery catalog does have a few additional benefits over just using the database control file:

■ You must use a recovery catalog if you wish to use stored RMAN scripts.

■ A recovery catalog offers a single, enterprise-wide repository of RMAN information. This provides an easier and more flexible central repository of enterprise backup information.

■ A recovery catalog allows more flexibility when doing reporting, since you can report on the target database at a time other than the current time.

■ With a recovery catalog, certain default database RMAN channel configuration information will still be maintained.

If you are an old hand at RMAN, you may have noticed some bulleted items missing here. First, since version 10*g*, Oracle Database has easily supported recovery through **resetlogs** without a recovery catalog. Also, if you are using control file autobackups (which we strongly suggest), the need for a recovery catalog for control file recoveries is pretty much removed.

NOTE
If you are not going to use a recovery catalog, keep a record of your database DBIDs. While this is not required, and you can work around it, having the DBIDs for your databases will make recovery operations much easier.

Should you use a recovery catalog? If you have just a few databases, then the recovery catalog is probably not worth the extra effort and hassle. If you have a database environment with many databases in it, you should consider using a recovery catalog. Generally, the added flexibility and centralized enterprise-wide reporting benefits of the recovery catalog outweigh the maintenance and administrative requirements that are added with the use of a recovery catalog. One downside to using a recovery catalog, though, is that if the catalog database is down, *your backups will all fail* unless you have coded your backup scripts to perform a backup without the recovery catalog in cases where the first backup with the recovery catalog fails.

Additionally, a recovery catalog is an essential part of a Data Guard backup environment and split mirror backups. In these configurations, when you back up the database from the backup host, the recovery catalog is considered the most current information, so it is the brains behind the strategy and becomes a single point of failure if not maintained properly. The bottom line is that you need to decide for yourself whether your environment calls for a recovery catalog.

When connecting to RMAN, you must use the **catalog** command-line parameter to indicate that you want RMAN to connect to a recovery catalog. By default, RMAN uses the **nocatalog** option, which indicates that a recovery catalog will not be used. After using the **catalog** parameter, indicate the userid and password of the recovery catalog schema that contains the recovery catalog objects. Here is an example of connecting to the recovery catalog by using the RMAN command line:

```
RMAN target='sys/robert as sysdba@robt'
catalog='cataloguser/password@bcatalog'
```

Creating the Recovery Catalog

As you might expect, some setup is required before we can actually connect to the recovery catalog. First, we need to create the recovery catalog user and grant it the appropriate privileges. Then, we need to connect to it and create the recovery catalog schema objects. Let's look at each of these steps next.

Configuring the Database for the Recovery Catalog

The recovery catalog database should, if possible, exist on its own database. However, in our experience, many sites use an active database as the recovery catalog database, which is fine as long as you take precautions when backing up that database.

Oracle makes the following suggestions with regard to space allocations for a recovery catalog database that would maintain recovery catalog records for one year:

Tablespace Name	Size Requirement
SYSTEM	90MB
TEMP	5MB
UNDO	5MB
RECOVERY CATALOG SCHEMA	15MB per registered database
ONLINE REDO LOGS	1MB per online redo log file

Creating the Recovery Catalog User

Generally, the recovery catalog should reside in its own database, because the recovery catalog is pretty useless if it is in the same database that you are trying to recover. The next RMAN Workshop provides a set of detailed instructions on creating the recovery catalog user account.

RMAN Workshop: *Create the Recovery Catalog User Account*

Workshop Notes

For this workshop, you need an installation of the Oracle software. You also need to identify a database to create the recovery catalog schema in. You need administrative privileges in this database to create the recovery catalog user account. Finally, determine the name and password you will assign to the recovery catalog user account.

You should create a tablespace for the recovery catalog schema objects. We suggest that you size the tablespace at about 15MB to start.

Step 1. Create the recovery catalog user. Make sure you do not use the SYSTEM tablespace as the temporary tablespace (check out the Oracle Database 11*g* default temporary tablespace feature!). Assign the recovery catalog tablespace that you have created (as suggested in the "Workshop Notes") to this schema as its default tablespace. Also, assign the recovery catalog user to an *unlimited quota* on the recovery catalog tablespace. Here is an example of this operation:

```
CREATE USER rcat_user IDENTIFIED BY rcat_password
DEFAULT TABLESPACE catalog;
```

Step 2. Grant the following roles to the recovery catalog user:

- connect
- resource
- recovery_catalog_owner

Here is an example of granting the RCAT_USER user we created earlier the roles it requires:

```
GRANT connect, resource, recovery_catalog_owner TO rcat_user;
```

NOTE
The recovery catalog user account is somewhat of a privileged database account. Secure it as you would sys or system.

Creating the Recovery Catalog Schema Objects

Now that you have created the recovery catalog database and user, it's time to actually create the recovery catalog. This is a pretty simple process in Oracle Database 11*g*. All you need to do is use RMAN. When you start RMAN, use the **target** parameter to connect to the target database, and use the **catalog** parameter to connect to the recovery catalog database schema (which you just created).

At the RMAN prompt, you then issue the **create catalog** command. Optionally, you can use the **tablespace** parameter to define a tablespace in which to create the RMAN schema objects. The next RMAN Workshop provides an example of using the **create catalog** command to create the recovery catalog schema.

RMAN Workshop: *Create the Recovery Catalog*

Workshop Notes

For this workshop, you should have completed the previous RMAN Workshop ("Create the Recovery Catalog User Account"). Also, we assume that you have created a tablespace called CATALOG_TBS, and we will be creating the RMAN schema objects in that tablespace.

Step 1. Connect to the recovery catalog with RMAN:

```
RMAN catalog=rcat_user/rcat_password
```

Step 2. Issue the **create catalog** command from the RMAN prompt:

```
create catalog tablespace catalog_tbs;
```

Register the Database with the Recovery Catalog

Now that you have prepared the recovery catalog for use, you need to register databases with it. This is required before you can perform an RMAN backup of a database by using the recovery catalog. This is a rather simple process, as you can see in the associated RMAN Workshop.

RMAN Workshop: *Register Your Database in the Recovery Catalog*

Workshop Notes

For this workshop, you should have completed the previous RMAN Workshop ("Create the Recovery Catalog").

Step 1. Using RMAN, sign into the database and the recovery catalog at the same time:

```
set ORACLE_SID=main_db
RMAN target=backup_admin/backupuserpassword
CATALOG=rcat_user/rcat_password@recover
```

Step 2. Register the database with the recovery catalog:

```
RMAN> Register database;
```

Step 3. (optional) Verify that the registration of the database was successful by issuing the **report schema** command from the RMAN prompt when connected to the target database:

```
RMAN> Report Schema;
```

Dropping the Recovery Catalog

Just as you can create the recovery catalog schema, you may wish to drop it. Use the **drop catalog** command to drop the recovery catalog schema. Of course, you should understand that all the information contained in the schema is going to be lost, so you should consider backing up the recovery catalog database before you drop the catalog schema.

Adding RMAN Backups to the Recovery Catalog

If you have already executed RMAN backups without a recovery catalog and you wish to add them to the recovery catalog later, you can use the **catalog** command. You can catalog datafile copies, back up set pieces, archive log backups, and even archive whole directories of backups, as shown in the following examples:

```
RMAN> CATALOG DATAFILECOPY 'D:\ORACLE\ORA102\DATABASE\system01.dbf';
RMAN> CATALOG ARCHIVELOG 'D:\ORACLE\ORA102\DATABASE\arch_988.arc',
      'D:\ORACLE\ORA102\DATABASE\arch_988.arc';
RMAN> CATALOG BACKUPPIECE 'D:\ORACLE\ORA102\DATABASE\backup_820.bkp';
RMAN> CATALOG START WITH 'D:\ORACLE\ORA102\DATABASE\';
```

NOTE
Beware of the **catalog start with** *command. You must have the trailing backslash at the end of the directory path. If you were to use D:\ORACLE\ORA102\DATABASE instead, Oracle would traverse all possible directory combinations of DATABASE that are available in C:\ORACLE\ORA102. This might include directories such as C:\ ORACLE\ORA102\DATABASE, C:\ORACLE\ORA102\DATABASE-123, and C:\ORACLE\ORA102\DATABASE-OLD. Use the trailing backslash to indicate that you just want C:\ORACLE\ORA102\ DATABASE\.*

Unregistering a Database from the Recovery Catalog

You can use the **unregister database** command in RMAN to unregister a database. If you wish to unregister an existing database, simply connect to that database and to the recovery catalog, and issue the **unregister database** command:

```
RMAN>unregister database;
```

If the database has been removed and you wish to remove it from the recovery catalog, you simply need to know the name of the database you wish to unregister, in most cases. If you wish to unregister the OLDROB database, you would issue this command after connecting to the recovery catalog:

```
RMAN>unregister database OLDROB;
```

In cases where multiple databases with the same name are registered in the recovery catalog, you need to know the DBID for the database that you wish to unregister. You then need to run the **unregister database** command in a **run** block, while also using the **set dbid** command, as shown in this example:

```
rman CATALOG rman/rman@catdb
RMAN> RUN
{  SET DBID 2414555533;   # specifies the database by DBID
   UNREGISTER DATABASE ROBOLD NOPROMPT;
}
```

Utilizing a Virtual Private Catalog

In 11*g*, you can extend your catalog to be utilized by multiple users who can all independently log in create/view records in the catalog. Prior to this version, everyone was required to use the same RMAN user and would have access to information about all databases in the environment that were registered in this particular catalog. This led to security issues in a single catalog, or to catalog sprawl as all users created and maintained their own catalogs.

Now, a single recovery catalog can be utilized by multiple users through the implementation of a virtual private catalog (VPC). A virtual private catalog allows you to grant access to the catalog to a database user, but to allow access just to particular databases within that environment.

To build virtual private catalogs for users, you will need to perform actions in SQL*Plus on the recovery catalog database, as well as actions from within RMAN. First, you must log into the database and grant the role recovery_catalog_owner to the database user that will have a VPC. Then, you log into RMAN as your catalog owner and grant privileges—either CATALOG privileges for existing databases that are already registered, or REGISTER privileges so the user can register new databases.

In addition to creating the VPC, you can also revoke privileges and delete the VPC.

RMAN Workshop: *Create a Virtual Private Catalog*

Workshop Notes

In this catalog, we will create a VPC for user farouka in the database. The catalog is owned by rcat_user. The user farouka will need to manage 10*g* and 11*g* databases.

Step 1.   Grant access to the catalog from within the database.

```
Sqlplus system/password
SQL> Create user farouka identified by password
Default tablespace catalog_tbs
Quota unlimited on catalog_tbs;
SQL> Grant recovery_catalog_owner to farouka;
```

Step 2.   Log into RMAN and grant access to the database PROD, as well as the ability to register any new databases.

```
Rman CATALOG=rcat_user/rcat_password@recover
RMAN> Grant catalog for database PROD to farouka;
RMAN> Grant register database to farouka;
```

Step 3.   Exit RMAN, log back in as farouka, and create the VPC.

```
Rman CATALOG=farouka/password@recover
RMAN> create virtual catalog;
```

Step 4.   Log back into the database, and explicitly enable management of 10.2 and earlier database versions.

```
Sqlplus rcat_user/rcat_password
SQL> execute rcat_user.DBMS_RCVCAT.create_virtual_catalog;
```

Merging Multiple Recovery Catalogs

The other primary headache, once we overcome the inability to adequately share the recovery catalog via virtual private catalogs, is to vanquish catalog sprawl. For whatever reason, sometimes you end up with multiple catalogs, and there has historically been no way to import records from one catalog to the next in a way that didn't make matters worse.

In 11*g*, RMAN introduced a cleaner merge experience through the use of the new **import catalog** command. You can utilize this functionality to import one catalog into another. This import can include all databases in the source catalog, or only a subset that you specify at the time of import. This functionality provides the mechanism of sorting through the records and ensuring the correct records are brought in without creating dependency issues or duplicate rows.

The **import** command in RMAN can merge two catalogs; it cannot be used as an upgrade mechanism. Before you can import a lower version of the catalog into a newer version, you will have to use the **upgrade** command first against the source catalog, and then import it. While we are on the matter of versions, it should be noted that the source catalog, destination catalog, and RMAN executable version must all be the same version for the import to work.

The **import** command can also be used to move an exiting catalog to a new database or to a new schema. In such a case, you would create the new catalog in the new location, then use that new catalog as the destination catalog in an import operation.

RMAN Workshop: *Merge Two Recovery Catalogs*

Workshop Notes

In this workshop, we will import a subset of databases from the catalog RCAT1 into the destination catalog RCAT2.

Step 1. Connect to the destination catalog in RMAN.

```
Rman catalog=rcvcat_user/password@RCAT2
```

Step 2. Run the **import** command by specifying a connect string to the source catalog.

```
RMAN> import catalog rcvcat_user@RCAT1 DB_NAME=TEST, DEV, PROD;
```

Step 3. Confirm that the metadata for the databases was imported.

```
RMAN> CONNECT TARGET SYS/PASSWORD@TEST
RMAN>list backup of database;
```

Recovery Catalog Maintenance

Use of the recovery catalog involves some additional maintenance activities, which include upgrading the catalog during a database upgrade or migration, manually resetting the database incarnation, and resynchronizing the recovery catalog after certain database operations. This section describes those activities, as well as other maintenance considerations, including removing a database from the recovery catalog and using the Oracle EXP/IMP utilities to back up the recovery catalog. Finally, this section reviews the different recovery catalog views and what they are used for.

Unregistering a Database in RMAN

Prior to Oracle Database 10*g*, unregistering a database from the recovery catalog was a manual process. Now, Oracle makes removing a database from the recovery catalog as easy as issuing the command **unregister database**. Here is an example:

```
RMAN> Unregister database mydb;
```

Note that the backup files for this database are not deleted by this command; only the recovery catalog references to those backup files are deleted. Also note that you only need to be connected to the recovery catalog to issue this command.

Database Migration/Upgrade Issues

As you upgrade your Oracle databases, you need to upgrade your recovery catalog as well. As you saw in Chapter 9, some strict rules apply with regard to the version of the database you are using, the version of RMAN, and the version of the recovery catalog.

You can determine what version your recovery catalog is by querying the VERSION column of the RCVER view in the recovery catalog–owning schema:

```
% sqlplus rman/rman @catdb
SQL > SELECT * FROM rcver;
VERSION
------------
11.01.00
```

If the table displays multiple rows, then the highest version in the RCVER table is the current catalog schema version. For example, assume that the RCVER table displays the following rows:

```
VERSION
------------
08.01.07
09.02.00
10.02.00
```

As long as the version of the recovery catalog is at the same level or higher than your database, you will be in good shape. Thus, if you are storing multiple databases in the same recovery catalog, it's okay to upgrade the catalog to a higher version, even if only one of the databases stored in the recovery catalog is being upgraded.

To upgrade your recovery catalog, simply issue the command **upgrade catalog** from RMAN. RMAN will prompt you to enter the **upgrade catalog** command again. RMAN will then upgrade the recovery catalog for you.

Manually Resetting the Database Incarnation (reset catalog)

As we have already covered in earlier chapters, each time the **resetlogs** parameter is used when you open an Oracle database, a new incarnation of the database is created. If this is done during an RMAN operation, then the recovery catalog will be correctly updated. However, if you manually issue a **resetlogs** command (through SQL*Plus, for example), you need to reset the database incarnation in the recovery catalog. This is done with the **reset database** command:

```
reset database to incarnation 5;
```

Manually Resynchronizing the Recovery Catalog (resync catalog)

When RMAN uses a recovery catalog, it uses a resynchronization process to ensure that the recovery catalog is consistent with the target database control file. Generally, Oracle performs database resynchronization itself after RMAN operations such as backups and recoveries, so you really don't need to resync the recovery catalog often. One example of the need to resync the recovery catalog is if you are running backups sometimes with and sometimes without a recovery catalog. To manually get Oracle to resync the recovery catalog, use the **resync catalog** command:

```
resync catalog;
```

When Oracle synchronizes the recovery catalog, it first creates a snapshot control file and compares it with the recovery catalog. Once that comparison is complete, Oracle will update the recovery catalog so it is in sync with the database control file.

Purging Recovery Catalog Records

You might have noticed that very few records get removed from the recovery catalog. Unmaintained, old backups will sit forever in the recovery catalog with a DELETED status flag associated with them. We have seen this cause significant delays in processing a backup operation, often putting the backup window in jeopardy and leading to high-pressure late-night calls to Oracle Support.

So, how do you fix this problem? Oracle provides the solution with the $ORACLE_HOME/rdbms/admin/prgrmanc.sql script, which will remove all records in your recovery catalog with a DELETED status. We recommend that you run this script periodically to control the size of your recovery catalog.

If you want to remove old incarnation records from the recovery catalog, then you will want to remove these incarnations from the DBINC table. Use the RC_DATABASE_INCARNATION view to determine which incarnations you wish to remove. Record the DBINC_KEY value for each incarnation you wish to remove. Then, to remove the incarnation, use SQL*Plus and issue a **delete** command to remove the incarnation from the DBINC table using the DBINC_KEY values you previously recorded. Here is an example of the **delete** SQL command that you would use:

```
DELETE FROM dbinc WHERE dbinc_key=2;
```

Backing Up the Recovery Catalog

The procedure for using RMAN to back up a database can be found in Chapter 9, and it just so happens that it is perfectly okay to use RMAN to back up your recovery catalog database. Just make sure you have a sound recovery strategy, so you can restore your recovery catalog as quickly as possible. Also, remember that losing the recovery catalog is not the end of the world. Even if you are using a recovery catalog, you can still recover your databases later without it. All you really need is a backup of the database control file (or, in a really bad situation, some fancy work with DBMS_BACKUP_RESTORE!). The really important thing to note is that you need to test your entire recovery strategy. Only then can you know, and be comfortable with, your ability to recover your databases.

Recovery Catalog Views

The recovery catalog provides a series of views that can be used to explore the metadata being produced by your RMAN backup strategy. These views have base tables that are populated when you register your database, and then populated on any subsequent **resync** command from the catalog. The naming convention for these views is RC_*; for example, RC_BACKUP_SET or RC_BACKUP_REDOLOG.

As RMAN operations have grown increasingly independent of the recovery catalog, many of the views that previously were unique to it have been incorporated into tables in the target database control file. This means that there is now a corresponding v$view for most RC_* views in the catalog. For instance, if the recovery catalog view is RC_BACKUP_SET, the v$view would be V$BACKUP_SET. The only difference would be a primary key column in the recovery catalog that does not exist in the v$view.

Next, we provide a list of the critical RC_* (and corresponding V$) views in the catalog, along with brief explanations. It is beyond the scope of this book to give a complete rundown of each column in each view; the Oracle-provided documentation does this excellently. Instead, we give a brief explanation of what the view might mean to you and how you might use it. We've left out all views that deal with proxy copies, because they are not covered in this book, and have left out all views that deal with stored scripts.

Having access to these key views is a critical tool when setting up and refining a backup strategy; no doubt you will also want to access them prior to any restore and recovery operation. It is extremely useful to put together a series of scripts that you can run on demand, or even to schedule a report output on a regular basis. We provide an example of a few catalog queries that can prove useful to you during backup and recovery operations.

It is worth noting that some of the examples in this chapter select against the v$view of the target database, while others refer to the RC_* views in the catalog. If you are making selections against the catalog and have more than one database registered, you always need to limit your query based on the DBID or the DB_NAME (if it's unique within the catalog). Otherwise, you will get information for more than one database, which won't be that useful unless you are trying to gather enterprise-wide information.

RC_ARCHIVED_LOG (V$ARCHIVED_LOG)

The archive log history in V$ARCHIVED_LOG will be one of the most heavily utilized views you have at your disposal. Due to the confusing nature of backing up archive logs and restoring them for recovery purposes, having access to their metadata is critical. Bear in mind that RC_ARCHIVED_LOG does not hold information about any backups you have of your archive logs (see RC_BACKUP_REDOLOG for that); it holds only information about all archive logs that have been generated by the target. Because archive logs are constantly being generated, whereas catalog resyncs are relatively less frequent, you will find yourself most often at the V$ARCHIVED_LOG version of this view, instead of at RC_ARCHIVED_LOG. The kind of code that would give you the most out of this view would look something like this:

```
column name format a50
column completion_time format a25
alter session set nls_date_format= 'DD-MON-YYYY:HH24:MI:SS';
select name, sequence#, status, completion_time
from rc_archived_log;
```

RC_BACKUP_CONTROLFILE (V$BACKUP_DATAFILE)

This view provides information about backups you have taken of your control file. This does not include control file copies; there is a different view for copies that have been made with the **copy** command or cataloged with the **catalog** command. This view is an excellent source to reference if control file restore operations are behaving strangely, particularly if you are trying to duplicate for standby database creation.

To review control file copies in V$BACKUP_DATAFILE, you would look at records with a file number of 0—this represents the control file:

```
select file#, creation_time, resetlogs_time,
blocks, block_size, controlfile_type
from v$backup_datafile where file#=0;
```

The following query would give you information about all the control file backups for the database V102, with the completion time, the status, the type of control file (B for a normal backup and S for a standby control file backup), and the date of the autobackup (this will be null if you do not have the control file autobackup configured):

```
column completion_time format a25
column autobackup_date format a25
alter session set nls_date_format= 'DD-MON-YYYY:HH24:MI:SS';
select db_name, status, completion_time, controlfile_type,
autobackup_date from rc_backup_controlfile
where db_name= 'V102';
```

RC_BACKUP_CORRUPTION (V$BACKUP_CORRUPTION)

This view lists the corruption that exists in datafile backups. To tolerate corruption, the value of MAXCORRUPT must be set to a non-zero value, which indicates how many corrupt blocks RMAN will back up before it throws an error and aborts. The corrupt blocks are not discarded, but rather are backed up as is.

Do not confuse this view with RC_DATABASE_BLOCK_CORRUPTION (described later in this chapter), which lists blocks that are corrupt in the database based on the last backup operation (or **backup validate**). RC_BACKUP_CORRUPTION lists blocks that are corrupt in the backup, not in the database itself.

The following code provides a list of corrupt blocks, with block number, file number, backup piece in which the corruption exists, and the type of corruption for the database V102:

```
select db_name, piece#, file#, block#, blocks, corruption_type
from rc_backup_corruption where db_name='V102';
```

RC_BACKUP_DATAFILE (V$BACKUP_DATAFILE)

This view has extensive information about datafiles that exist in backup sets. If you are interested in viewing specific information about datafiles that have been backed up, use this view.

RC_BACKUP_FILES (V$BACKUP_FILES)

This view most completely corresponds to the information provided by the commands **list backup** and **list copy** from the RMAN command-line interface. This view provides details about all backup files known to the recovery catalog, regardless of whether the file is a backup set, datafile copy, or proxy copy.

To use this view, you must first call DBMS_RCVMAN.SETDATABASE to indicate which database you are looking for:

```
CALL DBMS_RCVMAN.SETDATABASE(null,null,null,2283997583,null);
select backup_type, file_type, status, bytes from rc_backup_files;
```

RC_BACKUP_PIECE (V$BACKUP_PIECE)

Reference this view for information about specific backup pieces that have been created during normal backup operations. Remember that a backup set contains more than one backup piece, and that the backup piece is the physical file that corresponds to the logical unit of the backup set.

RC_BACKUP_REDOLOG (V$BACKUP_REDOLOG)

The name of this view is something of a misnomer: RMAN cannot back up online redo logs; it can back up only archived redo logs, which most often are simply referred to as archive logs. This view lists archive logs that exist in backup sets. It has a record for each archive log that has been backed up; if the same archive log is backed up twice, there will be two records.

The following query provides information for a particular range of archive logs, with backup set information, the status of the backup set, and the completion time:

```
alter session set nls_date_format= 'DD-MON-YYYY:HH24:MI:SS';
select db_name, bs_key, sequence#, thread#, first_change#, status
from rc_backup_redolog;
```

RC_BACKUP_SET (V$BACKUP_SET)

Information in this view refers to each logical backup set. You have to specify what type of backup set you would like to review: full backups, incremental backups, or archive log backups.

RC_BACKUP_SPFILE (V$BACKUP_SPFILE)

In this view, you will find information on SPFILE backups that exist in backup sets.

RC_CONTROLFILE_COPY (V$DATAFILE_COPY)

Like RC_BACKUP_CONTROLFILE, the corresponding view here, V$DATAFILE_COPY, also includes information about control files, encoded as file number 0. In the catalog, this view contains control file copy information for control files created with the **copy** command or cataloged with the **catalog** command.

RC_COPY_CORRUPTION (V$COPY_CORRUPTION)

This view is the same as RC_BACKUP_CORRUPTION, except that it reports blocks that are corrupt in copies instead of in backup sets. The **select** statement, then, would omit a **piece#**, but would otherwise be identical:

```
select db_name, file#, block#, blocks, corruption_type
from rc_COPY_corruption where db_name='V102';
```

RC_DATABASE (V$DATABASE)

This view contains basic information about each database registered in the catalog: the database name, DBID, current incarnation number, and last RESETLOGS time and SCN.

RC_DATABASE_BLOCK_CORRUPTION (V$DATABASE_ BLOCK_CORRUPTION)

This view provides the corruption list that is populated when a **backup** or **backup validate** operation discovers corrupt blocks. Remember that these are the actual corrupt blocks in the database, and not in the backups or copies themselves. This view is refreshed on each backup operation to reflect current corruption (if any). V$DATABASE_BLOCK_CORRUPTION is the view used during block media recovery when you specify **blockrecover corruption list** and is therefore the one that you will most often be referencing. The following code is an example **select** statement against this view:

```
select file#, block#, corruption_type
from v$database_block_corruption;
```

DATABASE_INCARNATION (V$DATABASE_INCARNATION)

This view contains a record for each incarnation of each database registered in the catalog. The most important information here is the RESETLOGS information, which by definition defines each incarnation. The following code is an example **select** statement against this view:

```
select dbid, name, dbinc_key, resetlogs_time, current_incarnation
from rc_database_incarnation
where db_key = <database key>
and dbinc_key = <current incarnation key number>;
```

RC_DATAFILE (V$DATAFILE)

This view exists so that the catalog has access to the same schematic information as does the control file about the location and specifics of each datafile in the database. You are much more likely to use V$DATAFILE when you want to look at your datafile information; however, in a recovery situation, this view can be extremely helpful if a current control file is not available. It also contains tablespace information in addition to datafile information, and in that way resembles the fixed view DBA_DATA_FILES. In addition, this view contains permanent configuration information for the commands **configure exclude** and **configure auxname**. The following code is an example **select** statement against this view:

```
select db_name, ts#, tablespace_name, file#, name,
bytes, included_in_database_backup, aux_name
from rc_datafile
where db_name='V102';
```

RC_DATAFILE_COPY (V$DATAFILE_COPY)

This view provides metadata about datafile copies created by the **copy** command or OS copies that have been registered with the **catalog** command.

RC_LOG_HISTORY (V$LOG_HISTORY)

V$LOG_HISTORY is the view that contains historical information about online redo logs, such as when they switched and what the SCN was at the time of the switch. This is a little redundant with V$ARCHIVED_LOG, but V$LOG_HISTORY does not concern itself with any current files, just the historical log switching information.

RC_OFFLINE_RANGE (V$OFFLINE_RANGE)

Offline ranges set the parameters for when a datafile went offline or read-only, and when it came back to read/write mode (if ever). It is important for RMAN to know this about a file when doing backups and restores. From a recoverability standpoint, it is critical to know the entire time range when a file was offline. If a backup of a datafile exists from before a transition from online to offline (or read-only), archive logs will be required from the moment the file was taken offline or read-only until the current point in time.

RC_REDO_LOG (VLOG, VLOGFILE)

From a schematic point of view, this is the same for RMAN as knowing the information in V$DATAFILE on rebuilds, it needs to know where the online redo log files are located. This view is a combination of both V$LOG and V$LOGFILE, so that thread and group membership is available alongside the name of each log.

RC_REDO_THREAD (V$THREAD)

Thread information is really only important in RAC environments, where there is more than a single thread of redo being generated at once. This view lists a record for each separate thread in the current database incarnation, along with the status of the thread and its redo stream. The following code is an example **select** statement against this view:

```
select db_name, thread#, status, sequence# from rc_redo_thread
where db_name='V102';
```

RC_RESYNC

This view provides information for each catalog resync operation that occurs. Obviously, there is no corresponding v$view for this one. You can use this view to determine if any of your enterprise databases need a resync, or to troubleshoot possible resynchronization problems. The following code is an example **select** statement against this view:

```
select db_name, controlfile_time, controlfile_sequence#,
resync_type, resync_time
from rc_resync where db_name='V102';
```

RC_RMAN_CONFIGURATION (V$RMAN_ CONFIGURATION)

This view is equivalent to a **show all** command, giving the name and value for each configuration parameter that is set for each of your target databases. It is worth noting that three configuration parameters are not stored here: **configure exclude** information is found in RC_TABLESPACE

(V$TABLESPACE), **configure auxname** information is found in RC_DATAFILE (V$DATAFILE), and **configure snapshot controlfile** information is found only in the target database control file (there is no catalog equivalent).

It is also important to point out that RC_RMAN_CONFIGURATION does not have a DB_NAME column, so you have to use the primary key DB_KEY value from RC_DATABASE to get the values for the appropriate database registered in your catalog.

Furthermore, no values are listed in either V$RMAN_CONFIGURATION or RC_RMAN_CONFIGURATION for default values. Only values that have been manually changed will appear in this list. The following code is an example **select** statement against this view:

```
select name, value from rc_rman_configuration where db_key=1;
```

RC_TABLESPACE (V$TABLESPACE)

Tablespace information is included in this view. The real benefit of this view over V$TABLESPACE is that historical information about dropped tablespaces is kept in the catalog. Therefore, you can use this view to look back and see when a tablespace was dropped. In addition, this view contains the information recorded for any **configure exclude** commands.

RC_TEMPFILE (V$TEMPFILE)

RMAN, since version 10*g*, is tempfile aware and can rebuild tempfiles upon restore so that you do not have to do it manually, as in the past. RC_TEMPFILE provides the bridge for this functionality, and a window into the existing tempfiles for a database.

Catalog Views Intended for Use by Oracle Enterprise Manager

A series of new views in the recovery catalog were created specifically to provide performance and functionality enhancements to the OEM Console and thus have limited functionality for end users. Most of these views do not have corresponding v$views in the target database control file. It is worth taking a look at these views and identifying their parts, to avoid any misunderstanding. If you are looking for a way to leverage the information in these views, you can find the same information in them in OEM's backup and recovery functionality. The following table lists and briefly describes the RC_* views that are built primarily for use by OEM.

RC_* View	Note
RC_BACKUP_ARCHIVELOG_DETAILS	Detailed information about backed up archive logs.
RC_BACKUP_ARCHIVELOG_SUMMARY	Summarized archive log backup information.
RC_BACKUP_CONTROLFILE_DETAILS	Detailed control file backup information.
RC_BACKUP_CONTROLFILE_SUMMARY	Summarized information about all control file backups known to RMAN.
RC_BACKUP_COPY_DETAILS	Detailed information regarding all control file and datafile copies.
RC_BACKUP_COPY_SUMMARY	Summarized control file and datafile copy information.

RC_BACKUP_DATAFILE_DETAILS	Detailed information about all datafile backups—in backup sets as well as image copies.
RC_BACKUP_DATAFILE_SUMMARY	Summary information about datafile backups.
RC_BACKUP_PIECE_DETAILS	Detailed information about available backup pieces in the catalog.
RC_BACKUP_SET_DETAILS	Detailed information regarding available backup sets in the catalog. This includes backups created with the **backup backupset** command.
RC_BACKUP_SET_SUMMARY	Aggregated information about available backup sets.
RC_BACKUP_SPFILE_DETAILS	Detailed information about available SPFILE backups.
RC_BACKUP_SPFILE_SUMMARY	Summarized information about available SPFILE backups.
RC_RMAN_OUTPUT	Assists OEM with job status tracking. The corresponding v$view is V$RMAN_OUTPUT.
RC_RMAN_BACKUP_JOB_DETAILS	Detailed information on individual backup job sessions, combining all operations in the same session.
RC_RMAN_BACKUP_SUBJOB_DETAILS	Details concerning groups of similar operations within an RMAN session.
RC_RMAN_STATUS	A historical view of RMAN sessions for all databases in the recovery catalog. It does not contain current session information, as does its corresponding v$view, V$RMAN_STATUS.
RC_UNUSABLE_BACKUPFILE_DETAILS	A list of all backup files of any type that have been marked as UNAVAILABLE or EXPIRED.
RC_RMAN_BACKUP_TYPE	Provides filtering information to OEM during its report building.

Summary

In this chapter, we detailed what a recovery catalog is and how it can help you to manage your backups—and save you during a recovery. We discussed how to build the catalog, add managed databases to it, and how to drop it. Oracle Database 11*g* provides the option for generating virtual private catalogs to maintain privacy and security. In addition, 11*g* offers the capability to merge multiple catalogs as you work to centralize and simplify your ecosystem management. Finally, we provided an overview of the critical recovery catalog views that can be utilized to understand the metadata surrounding your backups and to help guide the backup maintenance and recovery operation planning.

CHAPTER
11

RMAN Backups

ow that we have covered all the startup essentials, we are actually ready to use RMAN to back up something. In this chapter, we are going to talk all about doing backups with RMAN. From offline backups to online backups, backups of archived redo logs to incremental backups, we will cover it all. We will look at how to back up entire databases and individual database datafiles. So, let's move on!

Benefits of RMAN Backups vs. Scripted Backups

Why use RMAN to back up your databases? You may already be doing online backups with some wonderfully crafted, homegrown scripts, and you may be asking yourself, "Why should I start using RMAN when my scripts work so reliably?" In this section, we hope to answer that question.

Although your scripts may never fail, some scripts out there that others have crafted do break. This raises two problems. First, when the script breaks, the database backup fails. Second, when the script fails, someone has to fix it. You might be a wizzo Unix scripter. Unfortunately, after you take that DBA job on the international space station, there is no guarantee that the person following you will be an equally gifted Unix scripter. That poor person is going to be sitting there looking at your marvelous code and cussing you up one side and down the other. His or her boss isn't going to be happy, and, most importantly, the database will be at risk. Of course, the other possibility is that you will be the one having to debug the "Code from the Netherworld" since it was your predecessor, the shell scripter from nether regions, who went to work on the space station. Therein lies one big plus for RMAN—it is supported by Oracle, so, you can go to Oracle with your RMAN woes.

Of course, there are a number of other positives to using RMAN:

- RMAN will detect corrupted blocks and report them to you.

- RMAN can back up your database online without having to put the tablespaces in hot backup mode. Thus, the additional (sometimes quite significant) redo generated during a hot backup is reduced.

- RMAN will automatically track new datafiles and tablespaces for you, which means you no longer have to add new tablespaces or datafiles to scripts.

- RMAN will only back up used data blocks (up to the high-water mark [HWM]). Thus, RMAN backup images typically are smaller than those of online backup scripts.

- RMAN offers true compression of backup images.

- RMAN provides easy, automated backup, restore, and recovery operations. RMAN tracks all the backups that you need to recover the database if a restore is required and will restore only those objects that are needed.

- RMAN can work fairly seamlessly with third-party media management products.

- RMAN supports incremental backup strategies.

- With RMAN, you can actually test your backups without restoring them. Try that with your backup scripts!

- If you use the repository, then RMAN provides a nice, centralized reporting facility.

- If you are running Oracle Database 11*g*, the new Data Recovery Advisor (DRA) can simplify diagnosing difficult database recovery issues quickly. It can then provide restore and recovery recommendations and can automate restores via RMAN.

- RMAN with DRA can simplify diagnosing difficult issues quickly and can implement the solutions to problems found using the 11*g* RMAN DRA commands.

If you used RMAN in versions prior to Oracle Database 10*g*, you will find that your earlier RMAN backup commands still work. RMAN is very backward compatible. However, if you don't take the time to review the features that RMAN offers and to implement those that might benefit you, you will not be getting the most out of RMAN.

RMAN Compatibility Issues

Before you haul off and start doing backups, you need to consider some compatibility issues. Your enterprise probably has differing versions of Oracle running, and you need to consider RMAN compatibility issues as you plan your backup strategy. Not all databases are compatible with all RMAN versions, and when you add the recovery catalog into the mix, things get even more complex. Table 11-1 provides a quick reference to the compatibility issues related to RMAN.

In Table 11-1, you can see the RMAN target database version (say your database is version 10.2.0) and the RMAN client that supports backups of that database version (in our example, a 10.2.0 database can be backed up by RMAN versions >=9.0.1.3 and up to version 10.2.0 of RMAN). Also, you will find the version of the RMAN catalog database that must be in place to support the backup of that database (in our 10.2.0 example, the catalog that is required is a 9.0.1 version of the catalog). Finally, the version of the catalog schema that is required is listed (>= the version of the RMAN client being used in our example).

As you can see from Table 11-1, you need to know what version your recovery catalog schema is. The RCVER view in the recovery catalog schema will give you this information. Here is an example:

```
SQL> select * from rcver;
VERSION
------------
10.02.00.00
```

Finally, if you are faced with having to create more than one recovery catalog, there is no reason that all recovery catalogs cannot be maintained in the same database, as long as the database is version 9.0.1 or later. This still makes for a single recovery catalog database, which facilitates easy enterprise-wide reporting from that database.

RMAN Target Database Version (with applied patches)	RMAN Client Version (with applied patches)	RMAN Catalog Database Version (with applied patches)	RMAN Catalog Schema (with applied patches)
8.0.6	8.0.6	>=8.1.7	>=8.0.6
8.1.7	8.0.6.1	>=8.1.7	>=8.1.7
8.1.7	8.1.7	8.1.7	>=RMAN client
8.1.7.4	8.1.7.4	>=8.1.7	8.1.7.4
8.1.7.4	8.1.7.4	>=8.1.7	>=9.0.1.4
9.0.1	9.0.1	>=8.1.7	>=RMAN client
9.2.0	>=9.0.1.3 and <=the target database executable version	>=8.1.7	>=RMAN client
10.1.0	>=9.0.1.3 and <=the target database executable version	>=9.0.1	>=RMAN client
10.2.0	>=9.0.1.3 and <=the target database executable version	>=9.0.1	>=RMAN client
11.1.0	>=9.0.1.3 and <=the target database executable version	>=9.0.1	>=RMAN client
11.2.0	>=9.0.1.3 and <=the target database executable version	>=9.0.1	>=RMAN client

TABLE 11-1   *RMAN Compatibility Matrix*

Monitoring RMAN Backup Status

RMAN produces output during the backup process. If you enable logging when you start RMAN, that output is suppressed. You can monitor RMAN operations by keeping an eye on the log file being generated, or you can use the V$ view V$RMAN_OUTPUT, as shown in this example:

```
SQL> select output from v$rman_output order by stamp;
OUTPUT
-----------------------------------------------------------------Starting
backup at 12-NOV-05
using target database control file instead of recovery catalog
allocated channel: ORA_DISK_1
channel ORA_DISK_1: sid=138 devtype=DISK
allocated channel: ORA_DISK_2
```

```
channel ORA_DISK_2: sid=154 devtype=DISK
channel ORA_DISK_1: starting compressed full datafile backupset
channel ORA_DISK_1: specifying datafile(s) in backupset
input datafile fno=00001
name=C:\ORACLE\PRODUCT\10.2.0\ORADATA\ROB10R2\SYSTEM01.DBF
input datafile fno=00004
name=C:\ORACLE\PRODUCT\10.2.0\ORADATA\ROB10R2\USERS01.DBF
channel ORA_DISK_1: starting piece 1 at 12-NOV-05
input datafile fno=00003
name=C:\ORACLE\PRODUCT\10.2.0\ORADATA\ROB10R2\SYSAUX01.DBF
channel ORA_DISK_2: specifying datafile(s) in backupset
channel ORA_DISK_2: starting compressed full datafile backupset
input datafile fno=00005name=C:\ORACLE\PRODUCT\10.2.0\ORADATA\ROB10R2\EXAMPLE01.DBF
input datafile fno=00002name=C:\ORACLE\PRODUCT\10.2.0\ORADATA\ROB10R2\UNDOTBS01.DBF
channel ORA_DISK_2: starting piece 1 at 12-NOV-05
```

Offline RMAN Database Backups

Okay, so you think this RMAN thing sounds good, and the first few chapters were sure interesting. Time to really put the beast to work! The first backup topic we will discuss is performing offline (or cold) backups of the Oracle database. An offline RMAN backup is taken with the database mounted, but not open (obviously). If you have set up your default configuration settings for RMAN (as discussed in Chapter 3), then an offline RMAN backup is fairly straightforward.

Offline Backups Using Default Settings

To do an offline backup, first sign into RMAN (in the example we provide for this backup, we are not using a recovery catalog). Next, use the RMAN commands **shutdown** and **startup mount** to mount the database, which is the condition that the database must be in to perform an offline backup. Once the database has been mounted, simply issue a **backup database** command and the backup will occur. Here is an example of the commands you would issue to perform an offline backup via RMAN:

```
shutdown
startup mount
backup database;
startup
```

If you prefer, you could do this as a compressed backup set:

```
shutdown
startup mount
backup as compressed backupset database;
startup
```

RMAN Workshop: *Do an Offline Backup*

Workshop Notes

This workshop assumes that your database has been configured with automatic channels, as shown in Chapter 3. It also assumes that you have configured a database account called backup_admin for backups (as described in Chapter 3). In addition, it assumes that if you are using the Media Management Library (MML) layer, it has been configured.

Step 1. Start up RMAN:

```
C:\>rman target=backup_admin/robert
```

Step 2. Shut down the database with the **shutdown immediate** command:

```
RMAN> shutdown immediate
```

Step 3. Mount the database with the **startup mount** command:

```
RMAN> startup mount
```

Step 4. Back up the database with the **backup database** command. In this case, to save disk space, we will compress our backup set (since we have not configured compression as a default setting):

```
RMAN> backup as compressed backupset database;
```

Step 5. Use the **alter database open** command to open the database:

```
RMAN> alter database open;
```

Here is an example of a complete offline RMAN backup following these steps:

```
C:\>rman target=backup_admin/Robert
RMAN> shutdown
using target database control file instead of recovery catalog
database closed
database dismounted
Oracle instance shut down
RMAN> startup mount
connected to target database (not started)
Oracle instance started
database mounted
Total System Global Area      272629760 bytes
Fixed Size                      1248504 bytes
Variable Size                  83886856 bytes
Database Buffers              184549376 bytes
Redo Buffers                    2945024 bytes
RMAN> backup as compressed backupset database;
Starting backup at 04-NOV-05
allocated channel: ORA_DISK_1
channel ORA_DISK_1: sid=157 devtype=DISK
allocated channel: ORA_DISK_2
```

```
channel ORA_DISK_2: sid=155 devtype=DISK
channel ORA_DISK_1: starting compressed full datafile backupset
channel ORA_DISK_1: specifying datafile(s) in backupset
input datafile fno=00001
name=C:\ORACLE\PRODUCT\10.2.0\ORADATA\ROB10R2\SYSTEM01.DBF
input datafile fno=00004
name=C:\ORACLE\PRODUCT\10.2.0\ORADATA\ROB10R2\USERS01.DBF
channel ORA_DISK_1: starting piece 1 at 04-NOV-05
channel ORA_DISK_2: starting compressed full datafile backupset
channel ORA_DISK_2: specifying datafile(s) in backupset
input datafile fno=00003
name=C:\ORACLE\PRODUCT\10.2.0\ORADATA\ROB10R2\SYSAUX01.DBF
input datafile fno=00005name=C:\ORACLE\PRODUCT\10.2.0\ORADATA\ROB10R2\EXAMPLE01.DBF
input datafile fno=00002name=C:\ORACLE\PRODUCT\10.2.0\ORADATA\ROB10R2\UNDOTBS01.DBF
channel ORA_DISK_2: starting piece 1 at 04-NOV-05
channel ORA_DISK_1: finished piece 1 at 04-NOV-05
piece handle=
C:\ORACLE\PRODUCT\10.2.0\FLASH_RECOVERY_AREA\ROB10R2\BACKUPSET\2005_11_04\
O1_MF_NNNDF_TAG20051104T102913_1PQ32XLB_.BKP
tag=TAG20051104T102913 comment=NONE
channel ORA_DISK_1: backup set complete, elapsed time: 00:01:12
channel ORA_DISK_2: finished piece 1 at 04-NOV-05
piece handle=
C:\ORACLE\PRODUCT\10.2.0\FLASH_RECOVERY_AREA\ROB10R2\BACKUPSET\2005_11_04\
O1_MF_NNNDF_TAG20051104T102913_1PQ33J52_.BKP
tag=TAG20051104T102913 comment=NONE
channel ORA_DISK_2: backup set complete, elapsed time: 00:01:11
Finished backup at 04-NOV-05

Starting Control File and SPFILE Autobackup at 04-NOV-05
piece handle=
C:\ORACLE\PRODUCT\10.2.0\FLASH_RECOVERY_AREA\ROB10R2\AUTOBACKUP\2005_11_04\
O1_MF_S_573474457_1PQ357T0_.BKP comment=NONE
Finished Control File and SPFILE Autobackup at 04-NOV-05
Finished Control File and SPFILE Autobackup at 04-NOV-05
RMAN> alter database open;
```

Note that in the preceding example and the RMAN Workshop, we used very few commands. RMAN will automatically use the default configuration settings that we have defined (refer to Chapter 3). We really didn't have to do anything but issue the **shutdown** and **startup mount** commands to shut down and restart the database. We then issued the **backup as compressed backupset database** command and sat back to watch our backup take off. Pretty easy, huh? RMAN has backed up our database datafiles, our control file, and our SPFILE (assuming we have configured it to do so). Once it's done, all we need to do is issue the **alter database open** command, and our backup is complete.

In this example, Oracle created two backup sets, each of which contains a single backup piece. As you can see from the output, these backup pieces will be created in the flash recovery area (FRA) of this database, which is C:\ORACLE\PRODUCT\10.2.0\FLASH_RECOVERY_AREA:

```
piece handle=
C:\ORACLE\PRODUCT\10.2.0\FLASH_RECOVERY_AREA\ROB10R2\BACKUPSET\2005_11_04\
O1_MF_NNNDF_TAG20051104T102913_1PQ33J52_.BKP
tag=TAG20051104T102913 comment=NONE
```

NOTE
Oracle only supports backups of SPFILEs. You cannot back up your
database text-based init.ora parameter file with RMAN.

Finally, we might have opted to connect to the recovery catalog when we did this backup
(and this applies to all backups that we do in this chapter). To connect to the recovery catalog,
all you need to do is add the **catalog** parameter when starting RMAN:

```
C:\>set oracle_sid=recover
C:\>rman target=backup_admin/Robert catalog=rcat_owner/password@robt
```

One interesting thing to note here is that when we connected to our recovery catalog owner,
we did so using Oracle Net because we had our ORACLE_SID set to the SID of our database
rather than the SID of the recovery catalog. When you do a backup with a recovery catalog, you
need to use a service name and Oracle Net to connect either to the database you are backing up
or to the catalog. We generally recommend using the networking connection to connect to the
catalog and connecting directly to the database if possible.

Also, note that if we had not configured automated backups of our control file, RMAN would
still back up the control file as long as we were backing up datafile 1. The control file would be
backed up into the backup set that contains datafile 1. You would also want to do a separate
control file backup after your database backup was complete, so you would have the most
current control file backed up (because the control file backed up with the backup set will not
have the complete information on the current backup in it). Note that this control file, if it must be
recovered, is a bit more complicated to recover if you have not configured control file autobackups.
Because of this, we strongly suggest that you configure control file autobackups on your system.

Offline Backups Without Using Configured Defaults

What if we had not configured default settings (see Chapter 3)? Or what if the defaults were not
what we wanted to use (maybe we don't want to back up to the FRA)? In this case, we have a few
more things that we need to do. Let's look at an example of such a backup and determine what it
is doing:

```
shutdown
startup mount
run
{
allocate channel c1 device type disk format 'd:\backup\robt\robt_%U';
allocate channel c2 device type disk format 'c:\backup\robt\robt_%U';
backup as compressed backupset database;
backup current controlfile;
}
```

The next few sections look at this example in a bit more detail.

In the Beginning, Shut Down and Mount the Database

This example looks a bit more complicated than the earlier example. First, we have the **shutdown**
and **startup mount** commands that we had in the previous example. These are required for any
offline backup. We will discuss online backups later in this chapter.

Run, Oracle, Run!

Next, we have a **run** block, which is a set of one or more statements, contained within the confines of braces of a **run** command, that are executed together as a block. Oracle will not run any of the statements until the entire block of statements has been entered. After you have entered all the statements, you complete the **run** block with the closing brace (followed, of course, by pressing ENTER). The **run** block is then compiled and executed.

NOTE
*This book was written using Oracle Database 11g Release 2. In this release of RMAN (and 9i and 10g, in general), many commands that previously had to run within the confines of a **run** block no longer need to. We deliberately do not use **run** blocks unless required by this release. Many of the backup and restore/recover commands you will see in this and the next chapter will work in previous versions, but need to be run within a **run** block.*

Allocate Channels

In the preceding code example, we have several different RMAN commands in the **run** block. First, the **allocate channel** commands each allocate a channel to RMAN for the database backup. We have discussed channels already (in Chapter 3, for example), but let's look into their use a bit more for a moment.

First, a word on backup sets and backup set pieces. Each time we create a channel, this implies that we are going to create one or more backup sets. There are some exceptions to this statement, but generally this is true, so for the sake of this discussion, assume this is a true statement. Let's quickly define some terms:

- **Backup sets** Logical entities, one or more of which will be created for each channel you define (generally, it's one backup set per channel).

- **Backup pieces** The actual physical files that the backed up data resides in. One or more backup pieces may be associated with each backup set.

You can control the overall backup set size with the **backup** command (or, alternatively, you can configure a default value for it), or you can control the overall backup piece size with the **allocate channel** command (again, this can be configured when you configure default channels). We will further discuss limiting backup set sizes later in this chapter.

The **allocate channel** command defines to which device a given channel (and thus, an individual backup set) is to be allocated. This device might be a disk (type **disk**) or a tape drive (type **sbt**). If we were allocating a channel to a tape system, we might also include certain parameter settings required by the MML vendor that we were using. An example of an **allocate channel** command to tape using an MML vendor, VERITAS NetBackup, might look like this:

```
allocate channel t1 type sbt parms='ENV=(NB_ORA_CLASS=RMAN_db01)';
```

This particular channel is being allocated to a tape device. Refer to Chapters 4 through 10, which discuss topics related to non-disk backup location, for more on allocating RMAN channels to MML devices, Amazon S3, and Oracle Secure Backup. Having allocated two channels to the backup, RMAN will automatically try to parallelize the backup stream among those channels.

Thus, since we have allocated two channels, two different backup sets will be created, and each backup set will have one backup piece. The size is defined in bytes, but you can use the *k, m,* or *g* specifications to indicate kilobytes, megabytes, or gigabytes, respectively, as required. Here is another example of the **allocate channel** command:

```
allocate channel t1 type disk maxpiecesize=100m;
```

In this example, we have limited to 100MB the maximum size of each individual piece of a backup set (remember that each channel will create a single backup set) created through that channel. This is a great way to ensure that you do not create an individual backup piece that is larger than your tape or file system can handle.

Here is another example:

```
allocate channel t1 type disk maxpiecesize=100m
format='d:\backup\robt\robt_%U.bak'
```

In this example, we have used the **format** parameter to define where the backup pieces will be put on the disk and what the naming convention will be for the backup pieces. Since we use the **format** parameter, we are essentially telling RMAN not to use the default location for the backup set pieces (which is typically the FRA).

Note the %U format placeholder in the **format** command. Since we are not backing up to the FRA, we need to define the file naming convention associated with the backup pieces that will be created; in this case we use the %U format indicator. The resulting name will include the database name (robt) followed by an underscore and then an eight-character mnemonic that consists of the following:

■ The backup set identifier. Each backup set is assigned a unique identifying number by RMAN when it is created.

■ The time the backup set piece was created.

Following the eight-character mnemonic will be an underscore, followed by the backup set piece number. Because the backup set piece number uniquely identifies each piece of the backup set, it is unique to that backup set. Finally, another underscore will be followed by the copy number of the backup set piece. Each multiplexed backup set piece copy has its own unique number assigned to it. If you are not multiplexing, the copy number will be 1.

An example of the resulting backup set piece name might look like this:

```
Rob1_16E112V9_1_1
```

Note in this filename that the time component of the eight-character mnemonic is not readily discernable, but that's not really a problem. The important thing about the use of the %U placeholder is that it guarantees that the name of each backup set piece is unique. Of course, several different mnemonics are available for use with the **format** command, but generally %U will suffice. We added the instance name to the name and the extension just out of habit and good practice. Finally, there are a number of other options with the **allocate channel** command. Check out Appendix A for the entire syntax of the **allocate channel** command.

If you are using the FRA, Oracle will create backup set filenames based on the Oracle Managed Files naming standard. See the Oracle Database 11*g* Release 2 Database Administrators Guide for more details on the Oracle OMF naming standard.

NOTE
You might have noticed that we are using SBT instead of SBT_TAPE.
Earlier versions of RMAN used SBT_TAPE, but this is now just SBT.
SBT_TAPE is still usable for backward compatibility.

Channels can fail. Perhaps the hardware might fail, or some other failure might occur. Many RMAN backups consist of more than one channel going to a different location. If RMAN is using multiple channels and one channel should fail, the remaining channels will attempt to complete the work of the failed channel.

Backup Is the Name of the Game

Moving on now with our example code, after we have allocated the channels, it's time to back up the database with the **backup** command (using the **database** option). The sum result of the **backup database** command is that RMAN will proceed to use the two channels we created and back up the database. The command is a bit different from the **backup database** command we issued earlier, as this **backup database** command is issued within the confines of a **run** command block. We had to perform this backup using a **run** block because we manually allocated the channels with the **allocate channel** command.

The **backup** command also takes care of the control file and server parameter file (SPFILE) for us if datafile 1 is getting backed up (which it always will during an offline backup or any full backup, which is the default). Where this control file backup is stored depends on the setting of the **controlfile autobackup** parameter. If this parameter is set to **off**, then the control file is included in the database backup set along with the server parameter file (if an SPFILE is being used). If the parameter is set to **on**, the control file and SPFILE backup will be made to a separate control file backup piece. You can force RMAN to put the control file in the database backup set by including the **include current controlfile** clause in the **backup database** command (assuming you are not backing up datafile 1). Better yet, as we have done in our example, a separate backup of the control file is a good idea, to ensure that you have a control file backup that is current, including the most recent database backup.

NOTE
RMAN will only back up a server parameter file (SPFILE). It will not
back up text-based init.ora files.

The **backup database** command comes with a number of different options (and is, in fact, a subset of the larger **backup** command). Let's look at the use of some of the options of the **backup** command.

NOTE
A new feature in Oracle Database 11g RMAN backups is the
elimination of the backup of most UNDO within the database. Since
a great deal of UNDO is not needed during a database recovery
(for transactions that are already committed), it does not need to be
backed up. This can reduce the size of the backups of the UNDO
tablespaces a great deal! Note that this is a feature that cannot be
disabled.

Backup Command Options

Now that we have introduced you to the **backup** command, let's look at the number of different options you can use with it. These **backup** command options can be used with many of the various **backup** command flavors, such as **backup database** (which we just covered), **backup tablespace**, **backup datafile**, and other backup options, which we will cover later in this chapter. A number of different options available for use with the **backup** command allow you to do such things as provide a naming format for individual backup pieces, or limit the size of those backup pieces. The **backup** command even allows you to manually decide which channels will be used to back up what, should you wish to override the choices that RMAN makes otherwise. Let's look at some of the options that you can use with the **backup** command.

Multisection Backups

A new feature in Oracle Database 11*g* is the ability to split out backups of large datafiles into multiple sections of a fixed size. These sections can be backed up over different channels, thus parallelizing the backup of a large datafile. This is very helpful if you are using bigfile tablespaces, which were first available in Oracle Database 10*g*. A backup that takes advantage of this new feature is called a multisection backup.

To enable multisection backups, you specify the section size parameter within RMAN. RMAN will divide the files being backed up into file sections, which are just logically divided, contiguous blocks in a file. RMAN will create a backup set with one backupset piece for each file section. Here is an example of backing up a bigfile tablespace called USER_DATA, chunking the backup into 1GB sections:

```
backup section size 1g tablespace USER_DATA;
```

Multisection backups are a great way to spread the load of a backup over a number of different I/O devices.

Compression

As you saw in previous examples, you can actually compress backup sets. By default, RMAN does NULL data block compression. RMAN also offers true compression of backup sets, which can reduce the overall storage space consumed by backup images. We discuss these two different types of compression next.

NULL Data Block Compression

With this form of compression, Oracle does not back up unused data blocks. NULL data block compression occurs in two different ways:

- Data blocks that have never been used will not be backed up.

- RMAN will also skip backing up blocks that were once used given specific criteria.

In the first case, any block that has never had data in it will simply not be backed up. In the second case, if the database and the associated block meet certain criteria, then an empty block will not be backed up even if it contained data at one time. The following are the conditions that must be met to allow RMAN to skip backing up these blocks:

- The compatible parameter is set to 10.2.

- No guaranteed restore points are defined for the database.

- The datafile is locally managed.

- The backup is a backup set and is a full backup or a level zero incremental backup.

- The backup set has been created on disk.

If these conditions are met, Oracle will not back up any unused block, and your backups will therefore take up less space on your disks or tape.

RMAN Backup Compression

We provided an example earlier in this chapter of a database backup using RMAN compression. RMAN has the ability to apply compression algorithms to your backup sets. The end result is that backup sets are often much smaller. RMAN compression can significantly reduce the size of backup sets. Compression can be significant; for example, in one of our test databases, we saw a 70 percent difference in the size of the backup set images when using compression. If you don't have the database configured to automatically compress backup sets, you can use the **as compressed backupset** parameter to create the backup set as a compressed backup set. If you have compression configured and you do not wish to use it in a given **backup** command, simply use the **as backupset** parameter (without the **compressed** keyword) of the **backup** command.

RMAN in Oracle Database 11*g* Release 2 offers several different compression options to choose from:

- DEFAULT

- LOW

- MEDIUM

- HIGH

The DEFAULT compression type is the same compression that was available starting with Oracle Database 10*g* Release 1 and does not require a license. The LOW, MEDIUM, and HIGH levels of compression offer you the ability to control the overall impact of compression on the system. LOW offers some compression with minimal CPU impact, whereas MEDIUM and HIGH offer incrementally better compression with incrementally higher performance impacts. If you use any compression other than DEFAULT, you must purchase a separate license from Oracle.

You can configure compression as a default value by using the RMAN **configure** command (discussed in Chapter 3). Here is an example of configuring default compression in an Oracle 11*g* Release 2 Database:

```
Configure compression algorithm 'DEFAULT';
Configure compression algorithm 'HIGH';
Configure compression algorithm 'MEDIUM';
Configure compression algorithm 'LOW';
Configure compression algorithm clear;
```

You could configure compression as a default in earlier Oracle Database 10*g* and 11*g* Release 1. Each is done in a slightly different way. Please reference the Oracle documentation for more information on how to enable compression for the version of the database that you are running.

Tags and Restore Points

Tags and restore points provide similar functionality in Oracle Database 11*g* and earlier versions. Both can be used to recover a database to a given point in time. Point-in-time (or incomplete) recovery is discussed in more detail in Chapter 14. In this section we will look at tags and restore points in more detail.

Tags

Each backup in Oracle can be assigned a tag. A tag is a name of no more than 30 characters that is associated with a specific backup and can be referenced during restore operations to indicate a specific backup to be used. This applies to full backups, tablespace backups, datafile backups, incremental backups, and even backup copies (all of which will be discussed in this chapter). Here is an example of assigning a tag to a full backup:

```
backup database tag='test backup';
```

In this example, we used the **tag** parameter to identify this backup. Each tag should be unique, and RMAN will allocate a tag to each backup set by using a default naming convention if one is not assigned. The same tag can be applied to multiple backups, and the latest backup will be restored by default.

Restore Points

While a tag is associated with a specific backup, a restore point is associated with a specific point-in-time. RMAN does not provide a command to create a restore point. You can use the RMAN **sql** command to issue the SQL **create restore point** command as seen here:

```
SQL "Create restore point Charlie_one";
```

You can also create a restore point from the SQL*Plus point with the **create restore point** command as seen in this example:

```
SQL>Create restore point Charlie_one;
```

If you create backups using the **keep** option, you can also create a restore point during that backup. See the section on the **keep** option later in this chapter for more information on creating restore points when using the **keep** option.

Restore points can be referenced during RMAN restores in lieu of other point-in-time restore methods (such as time-based restores). We will discuss using restore points for recovery in more detail in Chapter 14.

Limiting Backup Impacts

To assist you in reducing the overall I/O impact of an RMAN backup on other processes, RMAN offers the **duration** parameter of the **backup** command. The **duration** parameter is like an alarm clock; if the backup runs longer than the duration specified, RMAN will cancel the backup. Here is an example of using the **backup duration** command:

```
backup duration 00:30 database;
```

One thing that makes the **duration** parameter a bit less usable is that you cannot use the **backup database plus archivelog** command. The **duration** parameter also helps you to throttle your backups. When defining a duration, you can indicate that RMAN should try to minimize either of the following:

- The time that the backup takes to run

- The I/O load that the backup consumes

If you try to minimize the time that the backup runs, RMAN will back up at full speed. This is the default setting. Another feature when you use the default **minimize time** parameter is that RMAN will prioritize the datafiles that are backed up. Those that were backed up recently will have a lower priority than those that have not been backed up recently.

You can also tell RMAN to try to spread out the backup I/O over the duration window that you have established, thus eliminating the overall impact that the backup has on the system:

```
backup duration 00:30 minimize time database;
backup duration 00:30 minimize load database;
```

Finally, with the **duration** parameter, you can indicate how RMAN should treat backups that fail the **backup duration** time restriction. When you use the **partial** parameter, if the backup is terminated because it has exceeded the **duration** parameter, RMAN will not treat it as a failed backup. Thus, remaining commands in any **run** block will continue to be executed. This is handy if you have subsequent **backup** commands like archived redo log backups. Regardless of the setting of **partial**, Oracle will consider any backup set that has been completed successfully to be usable even if the entire backup process did not complete.

Limiting the Size of a Backup Set

The following example builds on our previous example by adding a new parameter, **maxsetsize**:

```
backup database maxsetsize=50m tag='test backup';
```

Using this parameter, we have limited the maximum size of the backup set to 50MB. This is handy if your tape has a size limit or if your disks can only handle datafiles that are a certain size. Oracle will split the backup into multiple backup sets, each no larger than the **maxsetsize** parameter that you defined.

The **maxsetsize** parameter can also lead to a problem in that it limits the overall size of an individual backup set. Thus, if you have a datafile in your backup set that is larger than the defined limit, the backup will fail, as shown in the next example (some output has been removed for brevity):

```
RMAN> set maxcorrupt for datafile 1 to 10;
RMAN> run
2> {
3> allocate channel c1 device type disk format 'd:\backup\robt\robt_%U';
4> allocate channel c2 device type disk format 'd:\backup\robt\robt_%U';
5> backup maxsetsize=50m tag='test backup' database;
6> }
allocated channel: c1
allocated channel: c2
Starting backup at 13-JUN-02
RMAN-00571: ===========================================================
```

```
RMAN-00569: =============== ERROR MESSAGE STACK FOLLOWS ==============
RMAN-00571: =========================================================
RMAN-03002: failure of backup command at 06/13/2002 22:07:47
RMAN-06183: datafile or datafilecopy larger than SETSIZE: file# 1
D:\ORACLE\ORADATA\ROBT\SYSTEM01.DBF
```

So, be careful using this restriction, and see whether you instead can use the **maxpiecesize** parameter of the **allocate channel** command.

Also, you can use the **configure** command to create default limits on the size of backup sets and limits on the backup piece size, if that is your preference. Refer to Chapter 3 for more information on this command.

Backing Up to a Specific Device Type

Perhaps you have configured different default channels, one to disk and one to tape. You can use the **device type** parameter to define which automatic channel device you wish to use when the backup begins. Here is an example:

```
backup database device type disk;
backup database device type sbt;
```

Modifying the Retention Policy for a Backup Set

Starting in Oracle Database 11*g*, the **keep** parameter of the RMAN **backup** command is used to override default retention criteria and creates what is called an archival backup. An archival backup is a self-contained backup (meaning it includes the archived redo logs needed to create a consistent backup). Note that starting in Oracle Database 11*g*, the **logs** and **nologs** options are no longer available, since the logs are always backed up. The **keep** parameter has the following options:

- **forever** Indicates that the archival backup should be maintained until it is manually removed. Using the **keep forever** option requires the use of a recovery catalog since control file records can be aged out. Here is an example of the use of the **keep forever** parameter during a backup:

  ```
  backup database keep forever;
  ```

- **until time** string This option defines an alternate retention criterion for the backup. Note that if the time exceeds 365 days, it is possible that the records will be aged out of the control file. Regardless, RMAN does not require that you use a recovery catalog as it does when you use the **keep forever** parameter.

  ```
  backup database format 'c:\oracle\backup\%U' keep untiltime='sysdate+180' tag Keep_backup;
  ```

This can be used to easily identify the backup for restore purposes. Here is an example where we create an archival backup and assign it a restore point called gold_copy:

```
backup database format 'c:\oracle\backup\%U'
keep until time='sysdate+180'
restore point gold_copy;
```

One restriction on archival backups is that they cannot be kept in the flash recovery area (FRA). If you attempt to use the FRA to store archival backups, RMAN will generate an error and the backup will fail.

The **keep** option is also available in Oracle Database 10*g* and earlier versions, but its implementation is slightly different. With the older version of the **keep** option, you need to back up your archived redo logs in a separate RMAN command because the **plus archivelog** option is not valid when using the **keep** option. Since the archived redo logs are not automatically backed up, you can potentially have an unrecoverable backup, so exercise caution. The older method gives you an option to mark all archived redo log backup sets with the same retention criteria by using the **logs** option, or to skip marking the archived redo log backup sets with the **nologs** option. The **logs** and **nologs** options are no longer available with archival backups in Oracle Database 11*g*.

If you are using the **keep** option with Oracle Database 10*g* and earlier, then you will want to know about the following options:

- **logs**   The backup sets that contain the archived redo log backed up during the backup would have the same retention criteria assigned to them as the backup. This would, in effect, keep the log backup sets for the same period as the backup itself, ensuring a consistent recovery was possible.

- **nologs**   This indicates that any archived redo logs will not have a different retention criterion established. Essentially, this makes your ARCHIVELOG mode backup useless if the archived redo logs are aged out, while the backup is not aged out. This parameter is useful for NOARCHIVELOG mode backups since there are no archived redo logs to back up.

Here is an example of a backup using the **keep** parameter in Oracle Database 10*g*. Note that we use the **plus archivelog** parameter to ensure that we back up the archived redo logs. Note in this example that we have two format clauses. The first is for the backup set pieces associated with the backup itself, and the second is for the backup set pieces associated with the archive log backups. This is required since we are using the FRA by default, and since both the archive log–backup backup set pieces and the database-backup backup set pieces cannot exist in the FRA if the **keep** parameter is used. This is not required in Oracle Database 11*g*.

```
backup database tag='keep_full' format='c:\oracle\backup\%U'
keep until time 'sysdate+180' logs plus archivelog
format='c:\oracle\backup\%U';
```

Regardless of which version of Oracle you are running, you may wish to see how long specific backups were set to be kept for. The **list backup of database** command will provide this information. We discuss the **list** command in more detail in Chapter 18, but here is an example of the output you might expect to see. Note in the output that there is a line that says "Keep: LOGS" and followed by "Until" and a date. This indicates that this is an archival backup in Oracle Database 11*g* and is a backup using the **keep logs** option in Oracle Database 10*g* and earlier versions. This backup will be kept up to the date listed in the Until section of the report.

```
BP Key: 36   Status: AVAILABLE  Compressed: NO  Tag: KEEP_FULL
        Piece Name: C:\ORACLE\BACKUP\1FKJVSSA_1_1
Keep: LOGS             Until: 08-JAN-10
  List of Datafiles in backup set 36
```

```
File LV Type Ckp SCN    Ckp Time   Name
---- -- ---- ---------- ---------- ----
1       Full 4358741    12-JUL-09  C:\ORACLE\ORADATA\MY\SYSTEM01.DBF
2       Full 4358741    12-JUL-09  C:\ORACLE\ORADATA\MY\SYSAUX01.DBF
3       Full 4358741    12-JUL-09  C:\ORACLE\ORADATA\MY\UNDOTBS01.DBF
4       Full 4358741    12-JUL-09  C:\ORACLE\ORADATA\MY\USERS01.DBF
5       Full 4358741    12-JUL-09  C:\ORACLE\ORADATA\MY\EXAMPLE01.DBF
6       Full 4358741    12-JUL-09  C:\ORACLE\ORADATA\MY\UNDO_NEW_01.DBF
7       Full 4358741    12-JUL-09  C:\ORACLE\ORADATA\MY\SMALL01.DBF
8       Full 4358741    12-JUL-09  C:\ORACLE\ORADATA\MY\SMALLTWO.DBF
9       Full 4358741    12-JUL-09  C:\ORACLE\ORADATA\MY\SMALL_THREE01.DBF
```

Also, you can query the V$BACKUP_SET and V$BACKUP_PIECE views as seen in the example query that follows. You can also substitute the RC* views to retrieve this same information from the recovery catalog schema.

```
select a.set_stamp, a.set_count, a.backup_type, a.pieces, b.piece#, a.keep_until,
a.keep_options
from v$backup_set a, v$backup_piece b
where a.set_stamp=b.set_stamp
and a.set_count=b.set_count
and a.keep='YES';
SET_STAMP  SET_COUNT B  PIECES     PIECE# KEEP_UNTIL          KEEP_OPTION
---------- ---------- -- ---------- ---------- ------------------- -----------
 691981428         26 D           1      1 01/08/2010 01:03:48 BACKUP_LOGS
 691982114         27 D           1      1 01/08/2010 01:15:13 BACKUP_LOGS
 691982117         28 L           1      1 01/08/2010 01:15:17 BACKUP_LOGS
 691982121         29 D           1      1 01/08/2010 01:15:20 BACKUP_LOGS
 691982247         30 D           1      1 01/08/2010 01:17:26 BACKUP_LOGS
 691983183         31 D           1      1 01/08/2010 01:33:02 BACKUP_LOGS
 691983206         32 L           1      1 01/08/2010 01:33:25 BACKUP_LOGS
 691983252         33 D           1      1 01/08/2010 01:34:11 BACKUP_LOGS
 692023212         36 D           1      1 10/20/2009 12:40:12 LOGS
 692024018         37 D           1      1 10/20/2009 12:40:12 LOGS
 692056970         47 D           1      1 01/08/2010 22:02:50 LOGS
 692057685         48 D           1      1 01/08/2010 22:02:50 LOGS
```

Archive Log Deletion Policies

Starting in Oracle Database 11g Release 1, you can configure a retention policy for archived redo logs beyond just Oracle Standby Databases (see Chapter 21 for more on RMAN and Oracle Standby Databases). Starting with Oracle Database 11g Release 1, you can configure retention policies that apply to normal archived redo logs.

You use the **configure** command to configure an archive log deletion policy. The retention policy exists for all archived redo logs, including those in the FRA. RMAN will automatically delete archived redo logs in the FRA, but you will need to manually remove obsolete archived redo logs from other directories with the **delete obsolete** command if you are not using the FRA.

The archived redo log deletion policy is determined based on how many times an archived redo log is actually backed up by RMAN. By default, the archive log deletion policy is set to a value of none, which means you will need to handle the removal of archived redo logs yourself (for example, during a backup using the RMAN **delete input** command). If you wanted to ensure that at least two backups of an archived redo log occur and that the archived redo log would be marked obsolete, you could issue the following **configure** command:

```
Configure archivelog deletion policy to backed up 2 times to device type disk;
```

Note that logs subject to standby database–related retention policies are not subject to this retention policy. Also note that Oracle will not immediately remove archived redo logs when they become obsolete. Instead, the obsolete archived redo logs will be removed as space in the FRA is exhausted. As a result, archived redo logs will remain in the FRA as long as possible.

Overriding the configure exclude Command

You can configure RMAN to exclude from your backups any datafiles that have not changed since the last backup, by issuing the **configure exclude** command (discussed in Chapter 3). If you want to ensure that RMAN backs up these datafiles, you can include the **noexclude** parameter in the **backup** command as follows:

```
backup database noexclude keep forever tag='test backup';
```

Checking the Database for Errors with the backup Command

Another handy RMAN feature is the ability to use RMAN to actually scan the database for physical and logical errors without actually doing a backup. This is facilitated through the use of the **validate** parameter of the **backup** command along with the use of the **check logical** option. Here is an example of the use of this option:

```
backup validate check logical database;
```

NOTE
Even though some of the text generated during an RMAN **validate** *run will make it look like a backup set is being created, this is not the case. No RMAN backup file pieces will be generated during the* **validate** *run.*

Skipping Offline, Inaccessible, or Read-Only Datafiles

Sometimes, you will have a datafile in your database that has a status other than ONLINE. In the case of read-only datafiles, you may not want to back them up every time you do a backup of the database. In the case of offline or inaccessible datafiles, RMAN backups will fail if you don't do something to indicate to RMAN to skip the missing datafiles. This is what the **skip** parameter is used for. You can skip offline, read-only, or inaccessible datafiles (or all three) as required. Here are some examples of how to do this:

```
backup database skip readonly;
backup database skip offline;
backup database skip inaccessible;
backup database skip readonly skip offline skip inaccessible;
```

The **inaccessible** parameter causes Oracle to skip files that cannot be read at all. These files are not physically on the disk (for example, if the datafiles have been deleted from the disk or moved to another location). Datafiles that are offline but physically still in place are skipped using the **offline** parameter. Finally, the **skip readonly** parameter is used to cause Oracle to skip backing up a read-only datafile. Of course, you can use the **configure** command to indicate that Oracle should not back up read-only tablespaces at all, which leads us to our next section.

NOTE
In previous versions of Oracle Database, RMAN could not back up a transportable tablespace that was still read-only. Starting in Oracle Database 11g, this is no longer the case, and you can use RMAN to back up a transportable tablespace when it's still in read-only mode.

Forcing a Backup of Read-Only Datafiles

In the preceding section, we showed you how to cause a backup to skip read-only datafiles, but this can be a bit tedious. Oracle offers backup optimization to make life a bit easier. We talked about backup optimization in Chapter 3 in association with the **configure** command. Backup optimization causes RMAN to not back up unchanged tablespaces (for example, read-only tablespaces) by default. If you want a specific backup to be forced to ignore that configuration setting, you can use the **force** parameter to ensure that all datafiles are backed up. Here is an example:

```
backup database force;
```

Backing Up Datafiles Based on Their Last Backup Time

Oracle allows you to indicate in your backup process if you prefer to only back up database datafiles that have not been backed up since a given time. This is handy if you have added new datafiles (as we discuss first in this section), or if you only want to back up datafiles that have changed in a given number of days. Let's look at each of these choices in a bit more detail.

Backing Up Only Newly Added Datafiles

Here is a neat option you can use. Suppose you have just added four or five new datafiles to the database, and you want to back them up without having to back up the entire database. You could just back up the individual datafiles (as we will show you later in this chapter), but there is an easier way. You can use the **not backed up** option of the **backup** command, and RMAN will only back up datafiles that have not been backed up. Here is an example:

```
backup database not backed up;
```

Backing Up Files Not Backed Up in a Specific Time Period

Perhaps you have a backup strategy in which you back up only specific datafiles on specific nights. The **since time** option is also really handy if you need to restart a failed backup. If the backup fails, you can use this option, after you have corrected the cause of the failure, to restart the backup. For example, let's assume that your tape system died two days ago in the middle of a backup. You finally got the tape system fixed, so how would you restart the backup? Simply issue this command:

```
backup database not backed up since time='sysdate - 2';
```

In this case, RMAN only backs up those datafiles that have not been backed up within the last two days. Note that you can express the time in the format of the database NLS_DATE format, or you can use a SQL date expression such as the one in our example. An additional parameter to the **since time** option applies to archive log backups to ensure that each archive log is backed up a certain number of times before it is removed. We will cover that option later in this chapter.

Some backup strategies include backing up the archived redo logs once, shortly after they are created, and then perhaps later during the nightly backup. Once they are backed up for the nightly backup, they are to be removed. The configured retention defaults don't really allow you to configure the database to meet this requirement, but we can manually define retention criteria in our **backup** commands. As an example, we can perform this kind of backup using the **backup archivelog** command and the **backup database** command, as shown here:

```
-- This command backs up archived redo logs not already backed up.
Backup archivelog all not backed up 1 times;
-- Later in the day, back up the database and archived redo logs, and
-- remove the archived redo logs
backup as compressed backupset database plus archivelog
not backed up 1 times delete input;
```

Checking for Logical Corruption During a Backup

By default, RMAN checks for physical corruption of database blocks. If any corruption is discovered, the backup will fail. If you want even more error checking, you can configure a backup to check for logical corruption by using the **check logical** option of the **backup** command. Here are a couple of examples of the use of this option:

```
backup check logical database;
backup validate check logical database;
```

NOTE
If you are running your database in a standby database configuration, Oracle Database 11g Release 2 offers automatic repair of corrupt blocks. If a corrupt block is identified on the standby or primary database, it will be corrected by using a block from the unaffected database. See Chapter 15 for more information on this new feature!

The first example physically backs up the database as it is checking for logical corruption. The second example just validates the database blocks performing a logical database verification without performing an actual physical backup of the database. If you wish the backup to continue through a given number of errors, you need to set the **maxcorrupt** parameter first. This requires using a **run** block, as shown in this example:

```
run {
set maxcorrupt for datafile 1,2,3,4,5,6,7 to 10;
backup validate check logical database;
}
```

Making Copies of Backups on Your RMAN Copier

Perhaps you wish to create multiple copies of the backup pieces of a backup set. While this can be configured by default, you can also use the **copies** parameter to configure a specific backup to create multiple copies of the backup pieces. (You could also use the **set backup copies** parameter.) Here is an example of this option in use:

```
backup database copies=2;
```

Capturing the Elusive Control File

The **include current controlfile** option creates a snapshot of the current control file and places it into each backup set produced by the **backup** command. Here is an example of the use of this command:

```
backup database device type disk include current controlfile;
```

By default, if you do a backup of datafile 1, the control file will get backed up anyway. So this parameter comes in much more handy if you are doing tablespace or datafile backups. Furthermore, if automated backup of control files is configured, then this command can cause the current control file to be stored in the backup set also (so you have two copies of the control file, though they might be slightly different if you are running in ARCHIVELOG mode).

Introducing the set Command

We have covered a great deal of material about offline backups. Now that you have some idea of how RMAN commands work when backing up—and before we move on to discuss online backups—we should take a quick detour and look at the RMAN **set** command.

The **set** command is used to define settings that apply only to the current RMAN session. In other words, the **set** command is a lot like the **configure** command (refer to Chapter 3), but the settings are not persistent. You can use the **set** command one of two ways, depending on the **set** command you need to use. You can use it outside a **run** block for these operations:

- To display RMAN commands in the message log, use the **set echo** command.

- To specify a database's database identifier (DBID), use the **set dbid** command.

Certain **set** commands can only be used within the confines of a **run** block. The most common are the following:

- The **set newname** command is useful if you are performing tablespace point-in-time recovery (TSPITR) or database duplication. The **set newname** command allows you to specify new database datafile names. This is useful if you are moving the database to a new system and the file system names are different. You need to use the **switch** command in combination with the **set newname** command. You will see examples of this in later chapters.

- Using the **set maxcorrupt for datafile** command enables you to define a maximum number of data block corruptions allowed before the RMAN operation will fail.

- Using the **set archivelog destination** command allows you to modify the archive_log_dest_1 destination for archived redo logs.

- Using **set** with the **until** clause enables you to define a specific point in time, an SCN, or a log sequence number, to be used during database point-in-time recovery.

- Using the **set backup copies** command enables you to define how many copies of the backup files should be created for each backup piece in the backup set.

- Using the **set command id** setting enables you to associate a given server session to a given channel.

- Using the **set controlfile autobackup format for device type** command enables you to modify the default format for control file autobackups.

When doing backups, you may well need to use some of these commands. For example, if you wish to do a backup that creates two copies of each backup piece that is created and you want to allow for ten corruptions in datafile 3, you would craft a backup script that looks like this:

```
run
{
set maxcorrupt for datafile 3 to 10;
set backup copies = 2;
backup database;
}
```

Online RMAN Database Backups

We have spent the first half of this chapter on offline backups and the **set** command. If you are interested in online backups, then this section (and the following one) is for you. Still, don't skip the previous sections, because they present a great deal of foundational information that won't be repeated here. If you are jumping into the chapter at this point, first go back and read the previous sections. If you have read the first half of the chapter already and you find that you are a bit punchy, then take a short break before you forge on.

In this section, we first discuss several different kinds of online backups: backups of the entire database, tablespace backups, and datafile backups. We then look at archive log file backups and, finally, backups of the control file and parameter files.

Online Database Backups

As described in Chapters 1 and 3 in detail, to perform online backups with RMAN, our database must be in ARCHIVELOG mode. If your database is not in ARCHIVELOG mode, RMAN will generate an error if you try to perform an online backup. So, having ensured that we are in ARCHIVELOG mode, we are ready to do our first RMAN online backup.

NOTE
From this point on in this chapter, we assume that you have configured default channels (refer to Chapter 3), unless we need to point out something specifically. This saves you typing and allows us to leave out commands such as **allocate channel***, giving us more space to give you important information.*

You will find that online backups are not all that different from offline backups. In fact, they are a bit simpler because you don't have to mess with shutting down and then mounting the database. When you have your defaults configured (refer to Chapter 3), an online backup is as simple as this:

```
backup database plus archivelog;
```

This command does it all. First, the process does a log switch (using the **alter system archivelog current** command). Next, it backs up any existing archived redo logs. Then, the actual database backup occurs. At this point, another log switch occurs (using the **alter system archivelog current** command), and RMAN backs up the remaining archived redo logs (using the **backup archivelog all** command). Finally, the autobackup of the control file and SPFILE occurs. Because a full database backup will always include datafile 1, which belongs to the SYSTEM tablespace, there will always be a backup of the control file and SPFILE.

RMAN Workshop: *Do an Online Backup*

Workshop Notes
This workshop assumes that your database has been configured with automatic channels (as shown in Chapter 3). It also assumes that you have configured a database account called backup_admin for backups (as described in Chapter 3). In addition, it assumes that if you are using the MML layer, it has been configured. Finally, your database must be configured for and operating in ARCHIVELOG mode.

Step 1. Start up RMAN:

```
C:\>rman target=backup_admin/robert
```

Step 2. Start the backup:

```
RMAN> backup database plus archivelog;
```

Here is an example of a complete online RMAN backup following these steps:

```
C:\>rman target=backup_admin/robert
RMAN> backup database plus archivelog;
Starting backup at 15-JUN-02
current log archived
using target database controlfile instead of recovery catalog
configuration for DISK channel 3 is ignored
allocated channel: ORA_DISK_1
channel ORA_DISK_1: sid=13 devtype=DISK
channel ORA_DISK_1: starting archive log backupset
channel ORA_DISK_1: specifying archive log(s) in backup set
input archive log thread=1 sequence=351 recid=13 stamp=464457020
channel ORA_DISK_1: starting piece 1 at 15-JUN-02
input archive log thread=1 sequence=352 recid=14 stamp=464609012
input archive log thread=1 sequence=353 recid=15 stamp=464609115
channel ORA_DISK_1: finished piece 1 at 15-JUN-02
piece handle=D:\BACKUP\ROBT\BACKUP_20DR2QJ8_1_1 comment=NONE
channel ORA_DISK_1: backup set complete, elapsed time: 00:00:11
channel ORA_DISK_1: starting archive log backupset
channel ORA_DISK_1: specifying archive log(s) in backup set
input archive log thread=1 sequence=357 recid=19 stamp=464610450
input archive log thread=1 sequence=358 recid=20 stamp=464611007
input archive log thread=1 sequence=359 recid=21 stamp=464611921
channel ORA_DISK_1: starting piece 1 at 15-JUN-02
channel ORA_DISK_1: finished piece 1 at 15-JUN-02
piece handle=D:\BACKUP\ROBT\BACKUP_22DR2QJK_1_1 comment=NONE
channel ORA_DISK_1: backup set complete, elapsed time: 00:00:03
```

```
Finished backup at 15-JUN-02
Starting backup at 15-JUN-02
using channel ORA_DISK_1
channel ORA_DISK_1: starting full datafile backupset
input datafile fno=00001 name=D:\ORACLE\ORADATA\ROBT\SYSTEM01.DBF
input datafile fno=00005 name=D:\ORACLE\ORADATA\ROBT\USERS01.DBF
input datafile fno=00004 name=D:\ORACLE\ORADATA\ROBT\TOOLS01.DBF
input datafile fno=00003 name=D:\ORACLE\ORADATA\ROBT\INDX01.DBF
input datafile fno=00002
name=D:\ORACLE\ORADATA\ROBT\ROBT_TEST_RECOVER_02.DBF
input datafile fno=00010 name=D:\ORACLE\ORADATA\ROBT\ROBT_RBS_01.DBF
input datafile fno=00011
name=D:\ORACLE\ORADATA\ROBT\ROBT_TEST_TBS_01.DBF
input datafile fno=00007
name=D:\ORACLE\ORADATA\ROBT\ROBT_TEST_RECOVER_01.DBF
input datafile fno=00006
name=D:\ORACLE\ORADATA\ROBT\ROBT_TEST_RECOVER_03.DBF
channel ORA_DISK_1: starting piece 1 at 15-JUN-02
channel ORA_DISK_1: finished piece 1 at 15-JUN-02
piece handle=D:\BACKUP\ROBT\BACKUP_23DR2QJU_1_1 comment=NONE
channel ORA_DISK_1: backup set complete, elapsed time: 00:04:56
Finished backup at 15-JUN-02
Starting backup at 15-JUN-02
current log archived
using channel ORA_DISK_1
channel ORA_DISK_1: starting archive log backupset
channel ORA_DISK_1: specifying archive log(s) in backup set
input archive log thread=1 sequence=360 recid=22 stamp=464612416
channel ORA_DISK_1: starting piece 1 at 15-JUN-02
channel ORA_DISK_1: finished piece 1 at 15-JUN-02
piece handle=D:\BACKUP\ROBT\BACKUP_25DR2R2K_1_1 comment=NONE
channel ORA_DISK_1: backup set complete, elapsed time: 00:00:04
Finished backup at 15-JUN-02
Starting Control File and spfile Autobackup at 15-JUN-02
piece handle=D:\BACKUP\ROBT_C-3395799962-20020615-02 comment=NONE
Finished Control File and spfile Autobackup at 15-JUN-02
```

We have now completed an entire online database backup! Next, we will look at tablespace backups.

NOTE
As we will discuss later in this chapter, a full database backup cannot be used as a base for application of incremental backups.

Tablespace Backups

Occasionally, you will wish to do tablespace-level backups instead of backups of the entire database. This might be before you drop a partition that is specific to that tablespace, or perhaps just after you have made the tablespace read-only. To do a tablespace-level backup, simply use the **backup** command with the **tablespace** parameter:

```
backup tablespace users;
```

If you want to back up any archived redo logs at the same time, you could issue the command like this:

```
backup tablespace users plus archivelog;
```

Or perhaps you want to also make sure your current control file is backed up:

```
backup tablespace users include current controlfile plus archivelog;
```

Of course, you are not really backing up a tablespace, but rather the datafiles associated with that tablespace. Oracle just converts the tablespace name into a list of datafiles that are associated with that tablespace. Normally, a control file backup will not occur during these backups unless you have configured automatic control file backups (refer to Chapter 3) to occur (and you are not backing up datafile 1). If you use the **include current controlfile** parameter, then the control file will be backed up.

> **NOTE**
> *RMAN will not prevent you from doing a tablespace or datafile backup in NOARCHIVELOG mode (as long as the database is not open). However, these backups are not really all that usable when the database is in NOARCHIVELOG mode (unless you back up all the tablespaces and datafiles at the same time).*

Datafile Backups

You might want to back up specific database datafiles. Perhaps you are getting ready to move them to a new device, and you wish to back them up before you move them. RMAN allows you to back up a datafile by using the **backup** command with the **datafile** parameter followed by the filename or number of the datafiles you wish to back up. The following are examples of some **backup datafile** commands:

```
backup datafile 2;
backup datafile 'd:\oracle\oradata\robt\users01.dbf';
backup datafile 'd:\oracle\oradata\robt\users01.dbf' plus archivelog;
```

Again, the control file and the SPFILE will get backed up if datafile 1 is backed up or if automated control file backups are configured. In the last example, the archived redo logs will get backed up as well.

Archived Redo Log Backups

For a number of reasons, you might well want to back up your archived redo logs but not the database. In this event, you use the **backup archivelog** command. To back up all of the archived redo logs, simply issue the command **backup archivelog all**. Optionally, you might want to back up a specific range of archived redo logs, for which you have several options available, including time, SCN, or redo log sequence number (or a selected range of those values). Specific options are **from SCN**, **from sequence**, and **from time**. Keep in mind that using the **from** option may result in some archived redo logs being left on disk and not being backed up. Here are some examples of backing up the archived redo logs:

```
backup archivelog all;
backup archivelog from time 'sysdate - 1';
backup archivelog from sequence 353;
```

NOTE
A new feature in Oracle Database 11g Release 2 is that if the archived redo logs in the FRA are corrupted, Oracle will "fail over" to any other defined archived redo log destination. If the archived redo log is in that destination directory and it is not corrupted, RMAN will back up the archived redo log from that source destination.

Once you have backed up archived redo logs, you may want to have RMAN remove them for you. The **delete input** option allows you to perform this operation. The **delete input** option can also be used with datafile copies (which we will discuss later in this chapter) or with backup set copies. Here are a couple of examples of using the **delete input** parameter on an archived redo log backup:

```
backup archivelog all delete input;
backup archivelog from sequence 353 delete input;
```

You can also instruct RMAN to make redundant copies of your archived redo logs. In the following example, we use the **not backed up** *n* **times** parameter of the **backup** command to make sure that we have backed up our archived redo logs at least three times. Any archived redo logs that have already been backed up three times will not be backed up again.

```
backup archivelog not backed up 3 times;
```

Also, you can use the **until time** parameter with the **backup** command to ensure that a certain number of days' worth of archived redo logs remain on disk:

```
backup archivelog until time 'sysdate - 2' delete all input;
```

NOTE
Use of the **not backed up** *parameter and use of the* **delete input** *parameter are somewhat mutually exclusive. The* **delete input** *parameter will remove the archived redo log regardless of how many times it has been backed up.*

Control File and Parameter File Backups

Just as with archived redo logs, sometimes you may just want to back up the control file or the server parameter files. RMAN provides specific commands for these functions as well. Use the **backup spfile** command to back up the server parameter file. This is handy if you have made a configuration change to the database, for example. To back up the control file, you can use the **current controlfile** parameter of the **backup** command to generate a copy of the current control file. The **current controlfile** parameter also comes with a **for standby** clause that will create a backup control file for use with a standby database.

You can use the **controlfilecopy** parameter of the **backup** command to create a backup set that contains an externally created backup of the control file. This control file backup might be the result of the **alter database backup controlfile to 'file_name'** SQL command or the use of the RMAN **copy** command (covered later in this chapter) to create a control file backup. Also, you can back up a standby database control file that was created with the **alter database create standby controlfile** command. The benefit of this feature is that you can take external control file backup files and register them with RMAN, and create a backup set that contains the control file backup. Here are some examples of the use of this parameter:

```
backup current controlfile;
sql "alter database backup controlfile
to ''d:\backup\robt\contf_back.ctl''";
backup controlfilecopy 'd:\backup\robt\contf_back.ctl';
```

Backup Set Backups

Perhaps you like to back up to disk first, and then to back up your backup sets to tape. RMAN supports this operation through the use of the **backup** command. For example, suppose we issued a **backup database** command, and the entire backup set went to disk because that is our configured default device. Now, we wish to move that backup set to tape. We could issue the **backup** command with the **backupset** parameter, and Oracle would back up all of our backup sets to the channel that is allocated for the backup.

You can choose to back up all backup sets with the **backup backupset** command, or you can choose to back up specific backup sets. Further, you can only back up from disk to disk or from disk to tape. There is no support for tape-to-tape or tape-to-disk backups. The **delete input** option, which we previously discussed in regard to archive log backups, is also available with backup set backups. When used, the **delete input** option will cause the files of the source backup set to get deleted after a successful backup. Here are some examples of this command:

```
backup backupset all;
backup backupset all
format='d:\backup\newbackups\backup_%U.bak'
tag='Backup of backupsets on 6/15'  channel 'ORA_DISK_1';
backup backupset completed before 'sysdate - 2';
backup backupset completed before 'sysdate - 2' delete input;
backup backupset completed after 'sysdate - 2' delete input;
```

An example of a backup strategy here might be to perform RMAN backups to disk, and then to back up the backup sets to tape with the **backup backupset** command. Perhaps you want to keep two days' worth of your backup sets on disk. You could then issue two commands. First, issue the **backup backupset completed before 'sysdate - 2'** command to back up the last two days of backups. Next, to back up and then remove any backup sets older than two days, issue the **backup backupset completed after 'sysdate - 2' delete input** command, which would cause one final backup of the old backup sets and then remove them.

NOTE
Backup set backups are very handy if you want to back up your control file automated backups elsewhere and to still have the catalog track the location of the backup set.

Flash Recovery Area Backups

RMAN offers the ability to back up the entire FRA to tape via the **backup recovery area** command. Not all files in the FRA are backed up. Files that are backed up include full and incremental backup sets, control file autobackups, archived logs, and datafile copies. If your backup FRA contains flashback logs, the current control file, and/or online redo logs, these files will not be backed up. Note that files must be backed up to tape.

Copies

Okay, all this newfangled talk of backup sets and pieces is just blowing your mind. You ask, "Can't I just make a copy of these database datafiles?" We're here to make you feel better. With RMAN, you can just make copies of your different database structures, and that's what we are going to talk about in this section. First, we will review the upside, and downside, to creating copies instead of backup sets. Then, we will look at how we create datafile copies, control file copies, and archived redo log file copies.

Introducing Image Copies

RMAN can create an exact duplicate of your database datafiles, archived redo logs, or your control file. An RMAN image copy is just that—it is simply a copy of the file with the name and/or location changed. There are no backup pieces or anything else to worry about. Image copies can only be made to disk, and you cannot make incremental copies. The database must be either mounted or open to make image copies. A history of the copies made is kept in the database control file, so you can track when copies have been made and where they reside.

You can make image copies of the entire database, tablespaces, or datafiles, just like a regular backup (this is very different from earlier versions of RMAN). The RMAN copy process provides some of the same protections as normal RMAN backup sets, such as checking for corrupted blocks and, optionally, logical corruption. Also, image copies can be combined with normal backup sets such as incremental backups and archived redo log backups to facilitate a complete database recovery.

Database, Tablespace, and Datafile Image Copies

The **backup** command supports the creation of database image copies. Simply use the **backup as copy** command to do image copies, and the process is much like performing backup sets. Here is an example of making a database image copy with RMAN:

```
RMAN> backup as copy database;
```

RMAN will use the FRA to store backup copies, if it is configured. If you are using the FRA, the datafile images will be stored in a directory called datafile, as shown in this partial example output from a datafile image copy:

```
RMAN> backup as copy database;
Starting backup at 12-NOV-05
using channel ORA_DISK_1
using channel ORA_DISK_2
channel ORA_DISK_1: starting datafile copyinput datafile fno=00001
name=C:\ORACLE\PRODUCT\10.2.0\ORADATA\ROB10R2\SYSTEM01.DBF
```

```
channel ORA_DISK_2: starting datafile copy
input datafile fno=00003
name=C:\ORACLE\PRODUCT\10.2.0\ORADATA\ROB10R2\SYSAUX01.DBF
output Filename=C:\ORACLE\PRODUCT\10.2.0\FLASH_RECOVERY_AREA\ROB10R2
\DATAFILE\O1_MF_SYSAUX_1QFBPPON_.DBF tag=TAG20051112T205403 recid=
2stamp=574203351
channel ORA_DISK_2: datafile copy complete, elapsed time: 00:01:55
channel ORA_DISK_2: starting datafile copy
```

Image copies of tablespaces work pretty much the same way; just use the **backup as copy** command and the **tablespace** keyword:

```
backup as copy tablespace users;
```

Finally, you can create image copies of datafiles:

```
backup as copy datafile 1;
backup as copy datafile
'C:\ORACLE\PRODUCT\10.2.0\ORADATA\ROB10R2\SYSTEM01.DBF';
```

NOTE
An image copy can be made with the database mounted or, if the database is in ARCHIVELOG mode, with the database open.

Control File Copies

Control file copies can also be made with the **backup controlfile** command. These backups can occur with the database either mounted or open. Generally, it is a best practice to enable control file autobackups and allow RMAN to back up the control file automatically after a backup.

If you need to manually create an RMAN backup set that contains a control file, here is an example of such a backup:

```
backup current controlfile;
```

Note that this is not the same as a control file autobackup, and an attempt to restore from a control file autobackup will not result in the recovery of a control file backed up using this method.

You can also create control file copies. These copies are just like backup control files created with the **alter database backup controlfile to trace** command; thus, they are usable for recovery purposes. Here is an example of the creation of a control file copy from RMAN:

```
backup as copy current controlfile
format 'c:\controlback\control01.ctl' reuse;
```

Note that the **backup as copy** command will not overwrite an existing backup control file unless you use the **reuse** keyword as we did in our example. Also note that the **backup as copy** command does not create an RMAN backup set, only a physical file that is a backup control file.

If you wish to create a control file for use with a standby database that you are creating, then you use the **for standby** clause. Again this will create an RMAN backup set:

```
backup as copy standby controlfile;
```

As you did with regular backup control files, you can indicate a specific filename/location when you create a control file backup, which would result in the physical file being created in that location and not in the creation of an RMAN backup set:

```
backup as copy current controlfile format 'c:\oracle\controlfilecopy.ctl';
```

ARCHIVELOG Image Copies

Having copies of archived redo logs can be helpful. It's certainly easier to mine a copy of an archived redo log with Oracle's LogMiner product than to have to first extract that archived redo log from a backup set. The **copy** command allows you to create copies of archived redo logs by using the **archivelog** parameter of the **copy** command. Unfortunately, as we mentioned earlier, the use of **copy archivelog** requires us to list each archived redo log by name, rather than to specify some temporal range when we make copies of the archived redo logs. Here is an example of making an ARCHIVELOG file copy:

```
backup as copy archivelog all;
```

Incremental RMAN Backups

We hope you have made it this far through the book without much difficulty and have been able to get at least one good backup of your database done. Now, we are going to move on to incremental backups in RMAN. Through incremental backups, RMAN allows you to back up just the data blocks that have changed since the last incremental backup. The following are the benefits of incremental backups:

- Less overall tape or disk usage

- Less network bandwidth required

- Quicker backup times

You can do incremental backups either online or offline and in either ARCHIVELOG mode or NOARCHIVELOG mode, which is pretty handy. Keep in mind that if you choose an incremental backup strategy, a give and take exists in terms of the benefits. While you are deriving a benefit in the reduction of overall backup times (and this may be significant), the cost comes on the recovery side. Because Oracle will need to use several backup sets to recover the database if an incremental strategy is used, the time required to recover your database can significantly increase.

NOTE
If you choose to do incremental backups on a NOARCHIVELOG mode database, make sure you shut down the database in a consistent manner each time you back up the database.

The Block Change Tracking File

By default, when doing an incremental backup, any datafile that has changed in any way will be backed up. This can make incremental backups take longer and will make them larger. RMAN offers the ability to just back up changed database blocks. This can make your incremental database backups much smaller and shorter. To enable block change tracking, issue the command **alter database enable block change tracking**. The result of this command will be the creation of a file called the block change tracking file (BCTF).

When enabling block change tracking, you can choose to allow Oracle to name the related block change tracking file for you. Oracle will use the Oracle Managed Files (OMF) naming standard when naming the BCTF. You can also choose to define the location and name of the block change tracking file yourself, as shown in this example:

```
alter database enable block change tracking using file
'/u01/app/oracle/block_change/rob10gr2_block_change.fil';
```

If a previous block change tracking file already exists, you need to use the **reuse** parameter:

```
alter database enable block change tracking using file
'/u01/app/oracle/block_change/rob10gr2_block_change.fil' reuse;
```

You disable block change tracking by using the **alter database disable block change tracking** command. The block change tracking file size is pre-allocated and is related to the size of the database and the number of redo log threads. The typical size of the block change tracking file is quite small and is proportional to the size of the database. Its size is roughly 1/250,000 the size of the database.

If you are running an Oracle Real Application Clusters (RAC) database configuration, each node will need to have access to the BCTF. In these configurations, you may want to consider storing the BCTF in ASM for ease of file sharing.

The BCTF size also depends on the number of incremental backups that occur between each level 0 backup. The more incremental backups, the more changed block-related metadata has to be stored in the BCTF.

The BCTF can hold a maximum of eight backups' worth of information (for example, one base and seven level-1 incremental backups). After this, the next backup will remove the information of a previous backup, making the BCTF useless. The BCTF file will grow automatically in 10MB increments. A minimum of 320KB of space is allocated to each datafile in the BCTF regardless of the size of the datafile.

The Oracle Database defaults to not using block change tracking, and you can determine if block change tracking is enabled by checking the V$BLOCK_CHANGE_TRACKING view. The STATUS column indicates if block change tracking is enabled, and the FILENAME column contains the filename of the block change tracking file. You can move the block change tracking file by using the **alter database rename file** command just as you would any other database file.

```
SQL> select status from v$block_change_tracking;

STATUS
----------
DISABLED
```

The Base Backup

When doing an incremental backup, the first thing you need is an *incremental base backup*. This backup is the backup that all future incremental backups will be based on. Each time you perform a backup of the database, you assign that backup an incremental level identifier through the use of the **incremental** parameter of the **backup** command. Incremental backups have levels assigned to them. A *base* backup will always have a level value of 0, and you must have a base backup to be able to perform any type of incremental backup. An incremental backup will always have a level value of 1 (more on level 1 incrementals in a moment). If you do not have a base backup and you try to perform an incremental backup (using a backup level 1), then RMAN will perform a base backup for you automatically. Here is an example of performing a base incremental backup:

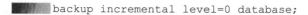
```
backup incremental level=0 database;
```

NOTE
Earlier versions of RMAN used to support more than level 0 and level 1 backups. Starting in Oracle Database 10g Release 1, any incremental level backup other than 0 or 1 was deprecated by Oracle.

Differential vs. Cumulative Incremental Backups

Now, we need to decide how we want to perform our incremental backups. We can use one of two methods:

- Differential
- Cumulative

Each is a different method of performing an incremental backup. Let's look at these two different types of incremental backup in a bit more detail.

Differential Backups

This is the default type of incremental backup that RMAN generates. With a differential backup, RMAN backs up all blocks that have changed since the last level 1 backup or since the last level 0 backup if the differential backup is the first incremental backup after a level 0 backup. Understanding how this all works can get a bit confusing. Figure 11-1 should help you better understand the impacts of using different levels.

In this example, we have a level 0 differential backup being taken on Sunday. This backup will back up the entire database. Following the level 0 backup, we perform a level 1 differential backup on Monday. This backup will back up all changed blocks since the level 0 backup on Sunday. On Tuesday, the level 1 incremental backup will back up all blocks changed since the level 1 backup on Monday. On Wednesday, another level 0 backup is performed, which backs up all database blocks. On Thursday and Friday, we have level 1 backups again, which back up only the changed blocks, just as the Monday and Tuesday backups did. Finally, on Sunday, we start all over again with a level 0 backup.

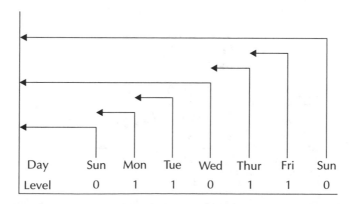

FIGURE 11-1 *Differential backups*

Here is an example of a level 1 differential backup being executed. Remember, if a level 0 has not already occurred, this will result in a level 0 backup instead of a level 1 backup.

```
backup incremental level=1 database;
```

Cumulative Backups

RMAN provides another incremental backup option, the cumulative backup. Using this option causes backup sets to back up changed blocks since the last level 0 backup, ignoring any previous level 1 backups. This is an optional backup method and requires the use of the **cumulative** keyword in the **backup** command. Again, this can all be somewhat confusing, so let's look at an example. Figure 11-2 is an example of the impacts of cumulative backups using different levels.

In Figure 11-2, just as in Figure 11-1, we start with a level 0 differential backup being taken on Sunday. This backup backs up the entire database. Following that, on Monday, we perform a level 1 backup. This backup is not unlike the differential backup. Now things change a little bit. On Tuesday, we perform another level 1 differential backup. This time, the backup will contain not only changed blocks since Monday's backup, but also the blocks that were contained in Monday's backup. Thus, a cumulative backup accumulates all changed blocks for any backup level equal to or less than the level of the backup. As a result, for recovery purposes, we need only Tuesday's backup along with Sunday's base backup. We continue to take level 0 and level 1 backups over the remainder of the week to complete our backup strategy.

Here is an example of the creation of a level 1 cumulative backup:

```
backup incremental level=1 cumulative database;
```

Incremental Backup Options

Oracle allows you to perform incremental backups of not only the database, but also tablespaces, datafiles, and datafile copies. Control files, archived redo logs, and backup sets cannot be made

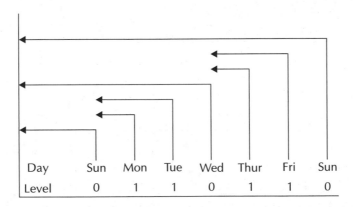

Day	Sun	Mon	Tue	Wed	Thur	Fri	Sun
Level	0	1	1	0	1	1	0

FIGURE 11-2 *Incremental backups*

as incremental backups. Additionally, you can choose to back up the archived redo logs at the same time. Here are some examples:

```
backup incremental level=0 tablespace users;
backup incremental level=1 tablespace users;
backup incremental level=0 datafile 4;
backup incremental level=1 datafile 4;
backup incremental level=1 database plus archivelog;
```

Incrementally Updated Backups

RMAN offers incrementally updated backups (also called merged incremental backups), which let you avoid the overhead of taking full image copy backups of datafiles, yet provide the same recovery advantages as image copy backups.

Merged incremental backups are cumulative incremental backups by default. Older versions of Oracle will generate an error if you try to do them as differential incremental backups. With a merged incremental backup, you create a level 0 (full) backup. Subsequent backups will be level 1 incremental backups. As these incremental backups are made, they are merged into the previous level 0 backup. Thus, there is no need to re-create the level 0 backup, which can save time. Use a block change tracking file in combination with a merged incremental backup to further reduce the time it takes to back up a database.

Let's look at an example of a merged incremental backup:

```
RUN {
    RECOVER COPY OF DATABASE WITH TAG 'incr_update';
    BACKUP INCREMENTAL LEVEL 1 FOR RECOVER OF COPY WITH TAG 'incr_update'
    DATABASE;
    }
```

The **recover copy of database** command does not actually recover your database, but it causes RMAN to apply any incremental backups to the datafile copies associated with the tag listed (incr_update). The previous commands will create the backup in three stages:

1. The first backup using these commands will result in the creation of a level 0 backup (assuming a level 0 incremental backup does not already exist). Note that some errors will appear during this backup, starting with "no copy of datafile 1 found to recover." This is expected, since there is no level 1 incremental backup.

2. The second time you run this set of commands, a level 1 incremental backup will occur. Nothing else will occur during this run. Again, you will see the same error as seen on execution number 1.

3. On the third and subsequent iterations of this backup, the previous level 1 incremental backup will be applied to the level 0 backup. As a result, the level 0 backup will be up to date as of the applied level 1 incremental backup. A new level 1 incremental backup will then occur. This means that any recovery/restore effort only requires the recovery of the level 0 backup, followed by only one level 1 incremental backup (and any required archived redo logs). This can significantly reduce the time required to restore your database.

Note that we use tags for these backups. It is important that the tags are named the same in both the **recover** and **backup** commands.

You can also change the order of the command, performing the **backup incremental** first and then the **recover copy of database** command second, as seen in this example:

```
RUN {
    BACKUP INCREMENTAL LEVEL 1 FOR RECOVER OF COPY WITH TAG 'incr_update'
    DATABASE;
    RECOVER COPY OF DATABASE WITH TAG 'incr_update';
    }
```

Changing the order in this way will result in the incremental level 1 backups being applied to the level 0 base backups immediately; thus, there is no delay in the application of the incrementals to the base backup. This keeps the base backup as current as possible.

Note that this strategy assumes a retention policy of redundancy 1. If you need a more complex retention policy, you will need to use the **until** clause to ensure that you can meet your recovery window. For example, if your retention policy is 7 days, you will set your retention policy to redundancy of 1, and you will adjust your script to use the **until** clause as seen here:

```
RUN {
    BACKUP INCREMENTAL LEVEL 1 FOR RECOVER OF COPY WITH TAG 'incr_update'
    DATABASE;
    RECOVER COPY OF DATABASE WITH TAG 'incr_update' until time "sysdate-8";
    }
```

Metalink note 7457989.1 provides a more in-depth discussion on the issue of retention. It is important if your retention is time based that you still set redundancy to 1, and that you use the **until** clause to properly ensure your recovery window. Using a recovery window or a redundancy > 1 will result in files never being removed from the FRA, and thus, you will quickly run out of space.

Metalink note 7457989.1 also provides some insight into the block change tracking file and an inherent limit in that file. By default, Oracle's block change tracking file can only track bitmap changes of up to 8 days between **recover** commands. If you need a recovery window of > 7 days or if you want to perform additional level 1 incrementals, you will need to modify the parameter **_bct_bitmaps_per_file** to allow for additional bitmaps.

RMAN Workshop: *Do an Incremental Backup*

Workshop Notes

This workshop assumes that your database has been configured with automatic channels (as shown in Chapter 3). It also assumes that you have configured a database account called backup_admin for backups (as described in Chapter 3). In addition, it assumes that if you are using the MML layer, it has been configured. Finally, your database must be configured for and operating in ARCHIVELOG mode.

Step 1.   Start up RMAN:

```
C:\>rman target=backup_admin/robert
```

Step 2. Perform a level 0 incremental backup. Include the archived redo logs in the backup set, and then remove them after the backup:

```
backup incremental level=0 database plus archivelog delete input;
```

Step 3. The next day, perform a level 1 incremental backup. Again, include the archived redo logs in the backup, and remove them after they are backed up:

```
backup incremental level=1 database plus archivelog delete input;
```

That about covers RMAN backups. The next chapter will be even more fun, because in it we discuss how to restore these backups and recover our databases.

Getting Started

We have covered a number of different backup options, and you may be left wondering where you should start. Let us make a suggestion or two. We recommend that you start with a test database, one that is very unimportant (better yet, one you have created for just this process). Here is an RMAN Workshop to get you started!

RMAN Workshop: *Get Your Database Backed Up!*

Workshop Notes

This workshop is more of an overall list of things that you need to accomplish to get your database backed up. We have covered a great deal of ground in the last few chapters, and we felt it would be a good idea to summarize everything important up to this point.

Step 1. Set up a special account in your test database that will be responsible for backup operations. Configure the account as described in Chapter 3. Note that you can opt to use the SYS account, but we prefer to use a separate account.

Step 2. Set up your MML layer, and be clear on what it requires you to do when performing backup and recovery commands.

Step 3. As we describe in Chapter 3, use the **configure** command to configure a separate default channel for each device that you are backing up to, unless your specific device supports multiple channels (as some do). Set the default degree of parallelism, as shown in Chapter 3, such that each of the channels will be used during the backup. If you need to configure maximum set sizes, do so; otherwise, don't bother with that now.

Step 4. Use the **configure** command to configure automated backups of your control file and SPFILE (if you are using one). For now, let them be created in the default location. You will want to change this later, but for now, just leave it there.

Step 5. Make sure your operating system backup backs up your Oracle RDBMS software (this also makes sure your control file backups will be backed up!).

Step 6.   At first, we suggest that you not use a recovery catalog. Once you have the RMAN basics down pat and are ready to deploy RMAN to the enterprise, then you can consider a recovery catalog.

Step 7.   For the first few trials, run your database in NOARCHIVELOG mode if you can. Shut down and mount your database, and execute a few **backup database** commands. Make sure the backup sets are getting created where you expect them to.

Step 8.   Go to Chapter 13 and recover the database. We suggest you make cold backups of the entire database, control file, and online redo logs (using the **cp** or **copy** command) first, just in case you run into some learning curves.

Step 9.   Once you are good at recovering databases in NOARCHIVELOG mode, put the database in ARCHIVELOG mode, and do the same thing again. Back up the database using the **backup database plus archivelog** command.

Step 10.   Go to Chapter 13 and Chapter 15 and do some recoveries. Become an RMAN recovery expert before you go any further.

Step 11.   Play around with the **crosscheck** command, the **list** command, and the **report** commands (see Chapters 17 and 18 for more details on these commands). Become really comfortable with these commands and their purpose.

Step 12.   If you have a large enterprise environment (say, over ten databases), go ahead and add a recovery catalog to the mix, and connect to it and back up your database with it. We strongly encourage you to use a separate recovery catalog for development/test and production databases. Again, we suggest that you run through the gamut of backup and restore situations while using a recovery catalog before you move on.

Step 13.   Once you are very comfortable with RMAN, create scripts to automate and schedule the process. For example, if you are running on Unix, a script such as the following could be scheduled through **cron** (we include an offline and online script here):

```
# For offline backups, use this script
#!/bin/ksh
# for offline backups, avoid shutdown aborts at all costs!
rman target rman_backup/password<<EOF
shutdown immediate
startup mount
backup database;
alter database open;
quit
EOF
```

If you are doing online backups, use this script:

```
#!/bin/ksh
rman target rman_backup/password<<EOF
backup database plus archivelog;
quit
EOF
```

These are korn shell scripts, which is one of the more commonly used shell scripting languages in Unix. Of course, RMAN works on a number of different platforms, so you can use the scripting language you are most comfortable with. In this script, we use what is known as a *here* document. That's what the EOF is in the fourth line of the first script and in the second line of the second script. A here document acts like the user is "here" and typing the input that you see listed from the EOF on the top line, until the closing EOF several lines later. Optionally, you could just use a command script created by a text editor, and call it from the RMAN command line, like this:

```
rman target rman_backup/password @backup.cmd
```

In this case, your backup.cmd script would look like this for an offline backup:

```
shutdown immediate
startup mount
backup database;
alter database open;
quit
```

For a hot backup, it would look like this:

```
backup database plus archivelog;
quit
```

You can also store scripts in RMAN by using the RMAN **create script** command. We will discuss stored RMAN scripts in Chapter 11, since storing scripts in RMAN requires a recovery catalog.

Step 14. Before you move your backups into production, test restores of the backups you have set up in your test environments. Make sure you are comfortable that everything works as it should. We suggest that you use your old backup strategy in dual until you have successfully tested several restores.

Step 15. Move your RMAN backup strategy into production carefully. Do it one system at a time. Choose your least "visible" systems to convert first. We suggest that you do several test recoveries as you move out into production, and continue (if possible) to do dual backups on each database until you have recovered that production database on a test box with an RMAN backup successfully. Also, you might want to consider separate archived redo log backups, if that is required.

Step 16. Perform disaster recovery and test backups often. We also suggest that, at least once a week, you execute a **restore database validate check logical** command on each database to make sure that the database is recoverable.

You will note that with each of these steps, we err on the side of caution. We leave it up to you to decide when you feel comfortable with your RMAN setup. There is just nothing more disheartening than trying to restore your database and getting the following error message from RMAN:

```
RMAN-00571: ===========================================================
RMAN-00569: =============== ERROR MESSAGE STACK FOLLOWS ===============
RMAN-00571: ===========================================================
RMAN-03002: failure of restore command at 07/07/2006 17:14:55
RMAN-06026: some targets not found - aborting restore
```

Summary

In this chapter, we have covered RMAN backups galore. We looked at how to do offline backups and online backups using RMAN. We also looked at RMAN incremental backups. We discussed the impact of configured defaults on backups, and how much easier they make the backup process. We also introduced the numerous options you can use with backups, such as using tags, overriding the default retention policy, and forcing backups of read-only datafiles. We looked at methods of detecting database corruption with RMAN. All in all, it's been a full chapter, but we hope you have found it to be a worthwhile one. You are now a step closer to being an RMAN expert, but the real fun is yet to come, and that's recovery. Hang on, because that's coming up next.

CHAPTER
12

RMAN Restore and Recovery

ll of your planning and backing up is about to pay off. This chapter is about restoring your backups and then recovering your database. We will first address some basic issues regarding the overall recovery process. Then, we will look at the different methods that you might need to use to restore your RMAN backups to disk and to recover your Oracle database in the event of an outage. We strongly suggest that you test these different types of recoveries on a test database, because you never quite know when you will need to recover your database, and under what conditions.

This chapter is an introduction to foundational restores in RMAN. The number of situational recovery permutations that might exist for a given database is pretty large (we tried to figure it out, but we blew our budget on designing a computer to calculate the answer, and it ended up just giving us plans for a bigger computer to do the job), so it's important that you understand not only the mechanics of recovery (as we will discuss here), but also how it works in concert with Oracle's architecture. In this chapter, you will find some rather straightforward recovery situations. In Chapter 15, we will address some of the more advanced recovery techniques. In Chapter 21, we will plow through a number of different recovery case studies. We suggest you read this chapter and test each of the recoveries documented here. Then, look at the more advanced situations in Chapter 15. Once you are really good at recoveries, look at Chapter 21 and try out some of those restores.

RMAN Restore and Recovery Basics

In this chapter, we will be discussing the concepts of restores and recoveries. In RMAN parlance, "restore" and "recovery" have different meanings. A *restore* implies that we are accessing a previously made backup set to get one or more objects from it and to restore them to some location on disk. A restore is separate from a recovery, then, in that a *recovery* is the actual process of making a database consistent to a given point in time so that it can be opened, generally through the application of redo (contained in online redo logs or archived redo logs).

If the Oracle RDBMS is anything, it is particular. The database is particular about the state of the data within the database, and it demands that the data be consistent to a given state in time when the database is started. If the database is consistent, then it will open; if it isn't consistent, then it will not open. Through the use of rollback segments, this consistency is maintained while the database is up and running. When the database is shut down normally, the datafiles are made consistent again. As you've likely noticed, the ongoing theme here is consistency.

Unfortunately, inconsistency can creep into the database through myriad causes. An abnormal shutdown of the database (as happens with a **shutdown abort**, or due to power loss on the server) will leave it in an inconsistent state. Oracle hates inconsistency, and it refuses to just start the database in the face of this demon.

Of course, other problems can plague your database. You can lose database datafiles through the loss of a disk, or perhaps lose the entire database. It is because these kinds of losses occur that you back up your database datafiles with RMAN. The problem is that when you restore those datafiles, they are likely to be inconsistent. Worse yet, those restored datafiles are likely to be anywhere from a few hours old to several days old—which safely qualifies as really inconsistent.

As we said, Oracle is a stickler about consistency. When you try to restart the database after recovering datafiles, Oracle is going to detect that those datafiles are in an inconsistent state. How does it do this? Recall from Chapter 1 our discussion of the SCN. Oracle tracks the current SCN in the datafile headers of each database datafile and in the database control file. Oracle goes through three stages when opening the database: nomount, mount, and open. When the database startup enters the open stage, Oracle begins attempting to open the database. As it opens the database, it checks the SCN in the control file against the SCNs in each of the database datafiles. If the SCNs don't match, Oracle knows that something is amiss with the database and that it is inconsistent.

Other checks occur during startup, as well, and some of these are not consistency checks. For example, Oracle checks each datafile for a bit that indicates the datafile is in hot backup mode. If this bit is set, Oracle will not open the database. In this event, a simple **alter database datafile end backup** command will suffice to restart the database. Oracle might also determine, while trying to open the database, that a given datafile is missing. The solution to this problem might be as easy as mounting the file system the datafile is on, or perhaps a restore of the datafile will be required.

If Oracle discovers that the database is inconsistent, it needs to determine whether it can recover the database based on the online redo logs, or whether it's going to require archived redo logs to do the trick. If it can perform the recovery with the online redo logs, then Oracle will perform crash recovery (or instance recovery in the case of Real Application Clusters). If Oracle cannot make the database consistent with the online redo logs, it will stop the startup process and report that media recovery is required.

Media recovery is a condition where Oracle will require archived redo logs to recover the database and to make it consistent if the database is in ARCHIVELOG mode. If the database is in NOARCHIVELOG mode, then a restore/recovery of a consistent backup of the database will likely be required. This chapter is all about recovery of your database. You can do all kinds of recoveries. Sometimes you will need to recover the entire database, and sometimes you will just need to recover a few datafiles. We will discuss all of these different possibilities in this chapter.

We have highlighted the issues that revolve around restore and recovery of your database. Now it's time to hit the road and see how this all works in practice.

Before You Can Restore the Database

In this chapter, we are going to approach the restore and recovery process from the beginning, assuming you have nothing left of your database except a backup somewhere. First, we are going to look at restoring the SPFILE, if you are using one, and then we will look at restoring the control file. Once we have those preliminaries out of the way, we will move on to the bigger topic of restoring and recovering the database. Of course, your specific recovery situation may not require recovery to this depth. You might have lost just a few datafiles, or perhaps you want to perform a point-in-time recovery. Some restores will need to use these preliminary steps and others will not. We think that between the layout of this chapter and the case studies later in this book, you will be quite confident as to what you need to restore and when.

Finally, you will note that in most of the examples we use, we do not connect to a recovery catalog unless the operation is different when using the recovery catalog. This lends some consistency to our examples and saves a few pages with duplicate results. So, keep an eye out for any notes that we might include about recovery catalog issues.

Before RMAN Can Get Going

Before RMAN can do its thing, you need to do a few things first. Preparation is the mother of success, someone once said, and this is so true when it comes to restoring your database. You need to work with your system administrator to make sure the following are done before you attempt your restore/recovery:

- The OS parameters are configured for Oracle.

- Your disks are configured correctly and are the correct sizes.

- The tape drives are installed, and the tape software is installed and configured.

- Your network is operational.

- The Oracle RDBMS software is installed.

- The MML is configured.

- Ancillary items are recovered from backups that RMAN does not back up, which include

    - The database networking files (for example, sqlnet.ora and listener.ora)

    - The oratab file, if one is used

    - The database parameter files, if they are not SPFILEs and are not backed up by RMAN

    - Any RMAN control file backups that were made to disk if you have enabled autobackup of control files

Once these items have been restored, you are ready to begin restoring your Oracle database. If you are using a recovery catalog, you will want to recover it first, of course. Then, you can recover the remaining databases.

When you start recovering databases, you need to start by recovering the SPFILE (if you are using one and it was backed up), followed by the control file. The next two sections cover those topics for you.

A Note about Recoveries, the Recovery Catalog, and the MML Layer

In our travels around the world to talk about RMAN, and in our own experiences, we've learned a thing or two that really strike us as important. One of these lessons learned is that when you are using one of the MML API interfaces, it is almost a requirement to use a recovery catalog. Why is the recovery catalog so important, you might ask?

Remember that all of the important RMAN metadata is stored in the control file. If you lose the control file, then all of this important metadata is lost. If you are doing automated control file backups (**set controlfile autobackup on**), then this is one way of making sure that you protect the control file from loss. We have had some cases, however, where restoring the control file from the MML backups was quite complex and time-consuming. For example, we have had a case where the backup was successful, but the control file autobackup was not. In this case, you really want to have a recovery catalog available!

Having a recovery catalog would have made the job much easier, and when we are talking about restores, time is a precious component. Many of the MML vendors do not support taking RMAN files directly off of their backup media and restoring them without using the RMAN client.

Also, getting a list of all the RMAN backup set pieces contained on backup media along with the time/date they were created can be difficult. Finally, you cannot use the **catalog** command to catalog backup set pieces backed up to an MML device. Thus, if you lose your control file and have to recover it manually, the recovery of backup set pieces is much more complex (possible, but complex). Overall, you have several pretty good reasons to use a recovery catalog. We discuss the recovery catalog in great detail in Chapter 10.

Restoring the SPFILE

If you are not using Oracle9*i* Release 2 or later and are not using an SPFILE, then this section really does not apply to you. As a result, you need to restore your SPFILE (or your database parameter file) from an operating system backup. On the other hand, if you have started using SPFILEs and you have backed them up using RMAN's control file autobackup abilities, then you are in good shape!

Recall from Chapter 9 that we suggested that if you are performing RMAN database backups without a recovery catalog, you might want to note the DBID of your database for restore and recovery purposes. This is one of those times that such an action comes in handy, though it is not 100 percent critical.

SPFILE recoveries come in several flavors, including recoveries that do not use the flash recovery area (FRA) and those that do use the FRA. RMAN offers other ways to recover the SPFILE, as we will find in the following sections.

Recovering the SPFILE from an Autobackup Using RMAN, No FRA

If you have lost your SPFILE, you will want to recover it from the control file autobackup set if you are using this feature. As we have already described, Oracle will by default back up the SPFILE (along with the control file) to the $ORACLE_HOME/dbs or to the ORACLE_HOME%\database directory (depending on the operating system). If you choose to use the default location (or if you back up to an alternate disk location), you will probably want to back up these backup sets to another backup medium such as tape (which RMAN can do for you).

The general procedure to restore the SPFILE is to first set your ORACLE_SID and then log into RMAN. Then, you need to set the DBID, so that RMAN will know which database SPFILE it is looking for. We have to start the database instance at this point in the operation. The instance of an Oracle Database 10*g* database will not start on its own without a basic parameter file being present.

Having started the instance, if you are using the default location to back up your control file autobackup to, you can simply issue the **restore spfile from autobackup** command, and RMAN will look for the control file backup set that contains the most current SPFILE backup. Once the SPFILE is recovered, you need to shut down the instance and restart it to allow your new SPFILE parameters to take effect. If you are using a nondefault location, then you will need to allocate a channel pointing to that location, and then you can restore the SPFILE using the same method.

When you issue the **restore spfile from autobackup** command, Oracle looks in the default location for automated control file backup sets (or in the location you defined with the **allocate channel** command). Since you used the **set dbid** command, RMAN knows your database's DBID. It uses the DBID to search through the defined directory to look specifically for the most current control file backup sets for your database. When RMAN creates the control file autobackup pieces, it uses a default naming convention. The following graphic shows an example of an automated control file backup set piece and how the naming convention is used. Note that this naming convention does not apply to the FRA.

Keep in mind that if we are not using a recovery catalog (and if we are not using a control file, which is likely), Oracle doesn't know for sure what the name of the most current control file backup piece is. Thus, Oracle constructs the name of the control file backup piece based on the default naming standard that is used for those backup sets (which we will document later in this chapter). Oracle will traverse the directory, looking backward in time for a control file backup set for your database. By default, Oracle looks for one created within the last ten days. If it cannot find a backup set created within that period, it generates an error. If Oracle finds a valid backup set, it proceeds to restore the SPFILE for you.

You can modify how far back RMAN looks for a control file autobackup by using the **maxseq** and **maxdays** parameters of the **restore** command. Here are a couple of examples of recovering control files. First, we use the default settings of the **restore** command:

```
set oracle_sid=recover
rman target sys/robert
set DBID = 2539725638;
startup nomount;
restore spfile from autobackup;
shutdown immediate;
```

We are not that likely to be using the defaults, of course, so let's assume we need to define a specific location for the autobackups in the **restore** command. Here is an example of this type of operation:

```
set oracle_sid=recover
rman target sys/robert
set DBID = 206232339;
startup nomount;
run
{
set controlfile autobackup format for device type disk
to 'c:\oracle\backup\%F';
allocate channel c1 device type disk;
restore spfile from autobackup;
}
shutdown immediate;
```

Next, we use the **maxseq** and **maxdays** parameters to look back beyond the default ten days:

```
set oracle_sid=recover
rman target sys/robert
set DBID = 2539725638;
startup nomount;
run
{
set controlfile autobackup format for device type disk
to 'c:\oracle\backup\%F';
allocate channel c1 device type disk;
restore spfile from autobackup maxseq 200 maxdays 100;
}
shutdown immediate;
```

Restoring an SPFILE to a different location and filename is not terribly complex. In this example, we assume that the database is up and running, so we don't need to indicate the location of the autobackup file sets:

```
set oracle_sid=recover
rman target sys/robert
set DBID = 2539725638;
startup nomount;
restore spfile to 'c:\oracle\spfile.restore' from autobackup;
shutdown immediate;
```

Recovering the SPFILE from an Autobackup Using RMAN and the FRA

The process to recover the SPFILE when using the FRA is actually much easier than the process if you don't use the FRA. First, you don't need to worry about all the DBID nonsense or allocating channels, which saves time and headaches. All you need to do to recover the SPFILE is to configure your temporary parameter file correctly (make sure the FRA destination directory is properly set), start the Oracle instance, and issue the **restore spfile** command. Here is an example:

```
set oracle_sid=recover
rman target sys/robert
startup nomount;
restore spfile from autobackup;
shutdown immediate;
```

You can still recover the SPFILE by using the **maxseq** and **maxdays** parameters, as shown in this snippet:

```
restore spfile from autobackup maxseq 200 maxdays 100;
```

Recovering the SPFILE from a Specific Backup Set

If you used RMAN before Oracle Database 10g, you know that recovery of the SPFILE could be difficult if you did not have autobackups configured. In such cases, you needed to write a nasty bit of PL/SQL in order to restore the SPFILE from the RMAN backups.

Oracle Database 10g makes this process much easier. Now the **restore** command includes a **from backup** clause that allows you to simply indicate the backup set piece that contains the SPFILE backup in it. Thus, all you need to know is the backup set piece name and where it is, and you can restore your SPFILE. In some cases, it might take a bit of trial and error to find the backup set piece with the SPFILE backup in it, but once you do, the restore should be a snap (of course, it would be best to restore the most current control file backup!).

Thus, to restore the SPFILE, start the database instance and identify the backup set piece that contains the SPFILE (or guess at it). Fire up RMAN. You need to set the DBID of the database also (as we have already discussed). Once you have set the DBID, you also need to allocate a channel to the device you are going to restore from. Having allocated the channel, you issue the **restore spfile from** command, and pass the backup set piece name in at the end of the command. RMAN will then restore the SPFILE to the correct location. Here is an example of this type of restore in action:

```
set oracle_sid=recover
rman target sys/robert
set DBID = 2539725638;
startup nomount;
run
{
 allocate channel c1 device type disk;
 restore spfile
 from 'd:\backup\recover\C-2539725638-20060629-00';
}
shutdown immediate;
```

You can now perform any additional recovery activities that might be required.

Recovering the SPFILE When Using a Recovery Catalog

If you are using a recovery catalog, restoring the most current SPFILE is as simple as issuing the **restore spfile** command after starting (nomount) the Oracle instance. RMAN will use the recovery catalog to locate the most current control file backup and will extract that backup for your use. Here is an example:

```
set oracle_sid=recover
rman target sys/robert catalog rcat_manager/password@robt
startup nomount;
restore spfile from autobackup;
shutdown immediate;
```

Note that we shut down the database after the restore. Again, this is to make sure that the database will be restarted using the correct parameter value settings.

Restoring the Backed Up SPFILE with an Operational Database Online

Extracting a copy of your SPFILE from a database backup with the database up is really easy regardless of whether you are using a control file or a recovery catalog. You should note that this operation will result in a text parameter file, and not an SPFILE, so you will need to convert it if you wish it to be an SPFILE.

If you are not using a recovery catalog and you have enabled automatic backups of control files, just issue the following command:

```
RMAN> restore spfile to pfile 'd:\backup\test.ora' from autobackup;
```

This command restores the SPFILE to a file called test.ora in a directory called d:\backup. Again, with any autobackup restore, RMAN looks only for the past seven days to find a control file autobackup piece unless you supply **maxseq** and **maxdays** parameter values.

If you are not using a recovery catalog and are not using control file autobackups, or if you are using a recovery catalog, then this is the command you would use:

```
RMAN> restore spfile to pfile 'd:\backup\test.ora';
```

In this case, Oracle uses the control file of the database to locate the most current backup set to restore the SPFILE from. So, now that you have your SPFILE back, you are ready to go out and recover your control file.

Restoring the Control File

Restoring the control file is not much different from restoring your SPFILE. First, the database needs to be mounted; so to restore the control file, you should have already restored your SPFILE, or have created one, and mounted your database. Once that occurs, you are ready to proceed to recover the control file for your database.

Control file recoveries come in several flavors, including recoveries that do not use the FRA and those that do use the FRA. In the following sections, we deal with additional control file recovery situations.

Recovering the Control File from an Autobackup Using RMAN, No FRA

If you have lost your control file and you are not using the FRA, you will want to recover the file from the control file autobackup set (if you are using this feature, which we strongly recommend). As we have already described, Oracle will by default back up the control file (along with the SPFILE) to the $ORACLE_HOME/dbs or $ORACLE_HOME/database directory (depending on the operating system). If you choose to use the default location (or if you back up to an alternate disk location), you will probably want to back up these backup sets to another backup medium such as tape (which RMAN can do for you).

When restoring the control file, it is assumed that the instance parameter file has been restored and that the instance can be started (for example, by using **startup nomount**). Once the instance is up and running, the general procedure to restore the control file when not using the FRA is to first set your ORACLE_SID and then log into RMAN (if you have not done so already). As with SPFILE restores, you need to set the DBID so that RMAN will know which database control file it is looking for.

We are now ready to restore the control file. As with the SPFILE restore, if you are using the default location (not likely) to back up your control file autobackup to, you can simply issue the **restore control file from autobackup** command, and RMAN will look for the control file backup set that contains the most current control file backup. Once the control file is recovered, you need to shut down the instance and restart it to allow your new control file parameters to take effect. If you are using a nondefault location, then you need to use the **allocate channel** command to allocate a channel pointing to that location, and then you can restore the control file using the same method.

When you issue the **restore controlfile from autobackup** command, Oracle looks in the default location for automated control file backup sets (or in the location you defined with the **allocate channel** command). Since you used the **set dbid** command, RMAN knows your database's DBID. It uses the DBID to search through the defined directory to look specifically for the most current control file backup sets for your database. See the previous section on SPFILE recoveries for more information about the format of the naming convention that RMAN uses for control file autobackup backup sets. As with SPFILE recoveries, you can modify how far back RMAN looks for a control file autobackup by using the **maxseq** and **maxdays** parameters of the **restore** command.

Let's look at some examples of recovering control files. First, we use the default settings of the **restore** command:

```
set oracle_sid=recover
rman target sys/robert
set DBID = 2539725638;
startup nomount;
restore controlfile from autobackup;
shutdown immediate;
```

Next, we use the **maxseq** and **maxdays** parameters to look back beyond the default ten days. This time we assume that we are not backing up to a default location:

```
set oracle_sid=recover
rman target sys/robert
set DBID = 2539725638;
startup nomount;
run
{
set controlfile autobackup format for device type disk
to 'c:\oracle\backup\%F';
allocate channel c1 device type disk;
restore controlfile from autobackup maxseq 200 maxdays 100;
}
shutdown immediate;
```

Restoring a control file to a different location and filename is not terribly complex. In this example, we assume the database is up and running, so we don't need to define the location of the control file autobackups:

```
set oracle_sid=recover
rman target sys/robert
set DBID = 2539725638;
startup nomount;
run
{
 restore controlfile to 'c:\oracle\control file.restore' from autobackup;
}
shutdown immediate;
```

Recovering the Control File from an Autobackup Using RMAN and the FRA

As was the case with SPFILE recoveries, the process to recover the control file when using the FRA is very easy. First, ensure that the parameters defining the location of the FRA are set correctly. Then, start the database instance; issue the **restore controlfile from autobackup** command, and the control file will be recovered. Here is an example:

```
set oracle_sid=recover
rman target sys/robert
startup nomount;
```

```
restore controlfile from autobackup;
shutdown immediate;
```

You can still recover using the **maxseq** and **maxdays** parameters, as shown in this snippet:

```
restore controlfile from autobackup maxseq 200 maxdays 100;
```

Recovering Older Control File Backups

You may wish to restore a control file backup that was taken some time ago, such that it's not the most current backup (this is often the case if you issued a **resetlogs** command). The **restore controlfile from autobackup** command allows you to do this when coupled with the **until time** parameter. For example, we can find and restore the control file backup created on or before 12/09/2005 at 04:11 A.M. by issuing this command:

```
restore controlfile from autobackup until time
"to_date('12/09/2005 13:00:00','MM/DD/YYYY HH24:MI:SS')";
```

You will want to know which control file backups are available to restore if you are going to use this command. We discuss the **list** command in more detail in Chapter 18, but for now, you should know that you use the **list backup of controlfile** command to determine which control file backups are available for you to restore. Here is an example:

```
RMAN> list backup of controlfile;
List of Backup Sets
===================
BS Key  Type LV Size       Device Type Elapsed Time Completion Time
------- ---- -- ---------- ----------- ------------ ---------------
38      Full    6.80M      DISK        00:00:05     01-JAN-06
  BP Key: 39    Status: EXPIRED  Compressed: NO  Tag: TAG20060108T183828
        Piece Name: C:\ORACLE\PRODUCT\10.2.0\FLASH_RECOVERY_AREA\TESTOEM
\AUTOBACKUP\2006_01_08\O1_MF_S_579206308_1W3D485F_.BKP
  Control File Included: Ckp SCN: 3568285    Ckp time: 08-JAN-06

BS Key  Type LV Size       Device Type Elapsed Time Completion Time
------- ---- -- ---------- ----------- ------------ ---------------
40      Full    6.80M      DISK        00:00:06     08-JAN-06
  BP Key: 41    Status: AVAILABLE  Compressed: NO  Tag: TAG20060108T183857
        Piece Name: C:\ORACLE\PRODUCT\10.2.0\FLASH_RECOVERY_AREA\TESTOEM
\AUTOBACKUP\2006_01_08\O1_MF_S_579206337_1W3D5495_.BKP
  Control File Included: Ckp SCN: 3568311    Ckp time: 08-JAN-06
```

In the preceding example, we used the **list** command to discover that we have two different control file backups. The first control file backup (BS Key 38) has a status of EXPIRED because of the current backup retention policy. Since it is expired, RMAN will not try to use it during a restore operation (if the backup set piece is still available, we can change the status with the **change** command and be able to use it). The second control file backup (BS Key 40) is available. RMAN will be able to restore this backup.

Note that the **list** command is only available if you have the database mounted with a current control file. If you do not have a control file available, then the **list** command will not work. Also, if you do not have a control file available, then the retention criteria will not be an issue, and you could restore any control file by using the **autobackup** command.

Recover the Control File from a Backup Set

If you used RMAN before Oracle Database 10g, you know that recovery of the control file could be difficult if you did not have autobackups configured. In such cases, you needed to write a nasty bit of PL/SQL in order to restore the control file.

Since Oracle Database version 10g control file recovery is much easier. Now the **restore** command includes a **from backup** clause that allows you to simply indicate the backup set piece that contains the control file backup in it. Thus, all you need to know is the backup set piece name, and where it is, and you can restore your control file. In some cases, it might take a bit of trial and error to find the backup set piece with the control file backup in it, but once you do, the restore should be a snap (of course, it would be best to restore the most current control file backup!).

To restore the control file, start the database instance and identify the backup set piece that contains the control file (or guess at it). Fire up RMAN. You will need to set the DBID of the database also (as we have already discussed). Once you have set the DBID, you will also need to allocate a channel to the device you are going to restore from. Having allocated the channel, you issue the **restore controlfile from** command, and pass the backup set piece name in the end of the command. RMAN will then restore the control file and replicate it to the different CONTROL_FILE parameter locations. Here is an example of this type of restore in action:

```
set oracle_sid=recover
rman target sys/robert
set DBID = 2539725638;
startup nomount;
run
{
 allocate channel c1 device type disk;
 restore controlfile
 from 'd:\backup\recover\C-2539725638-20020629-00';
}
shutdown immediate;
```

You can now perform any additional recovery activities that might be required.

Recovering a Control File Using a Recovery Catalog

If you are using a recovery catalog, restoring the most current control file backup is as simple as issuing the **restore controlfile** command. RMAN will use the recovery catalog to locate the most current control file backup and will extract that backup for your use. Here is an example:

```
set oracle_sid=recover
rman target sys/robert catalog rcat_manager/password@robt
# Note - We would issue a startup nomount
# and restore control file from autobackup here if we needed to.
# shutdown immediate here if we recovered the control file.
startup nomount;
restore controlfile;
# mount the database in preparation for a restore.
alter database mount;
```

Database Recovery after Restoring a Control File

When you restore a control file with RMAN (and there are no datafiles or online redo logs lost), you have two different things to consider. First, you need to consider how to actually get your database up and running after restoring the control file. Second, you need to recover information related to RMAN, such as registering archived redo logs and backup sets in the newly created control file with RMAN. Let's look at each of these topics in a bit more detail.

Opening the Database after a Control File Recovery   In the event that only your control file was lost, recovery of the control file and your database is generally pretty straightforward (if any kind of Oracle recovery can be thought of as straightforward). The commands to recover the control file are the same; you just need to simulate incomplete recovery in order to open the database. Note that in some cases, you may need to register archived redo logs or even register backup sets before you can complete recovery. We discuss this process in the next section.

If you are running in NOARCHIVELOG mode, you would use the following method (in this example, we assume you are not using the FRA, so we set the DBID):

```
set oracle_sid=recover
rman target sys/robert
set DBID = 2539725638;
startup nomount;
restore controlfile from autobackup;
alter database mount;
recover database noredo;
alter database open resetlogs;
```

If you are running in ARCHIVELOG mode, recovery is only slightly different (note in this example, we are assuming you are using the FRA, so we do not set the DBID):

```
set oracle_sid=recover
rman target sys/robert
startup nomount;
restore controlfile from autobackup;
alter database mount;
recover database;
alter database open resetlogs;
```

Of course, loss of other database physical files can make this complex. Also, if you don't have a recent control file backup, then things can get quite complicated, and you may end up having to manually re-create the control file with the **create control file** command. This is a horror we hope you never have to face, and you should not need to face it if your backup and recovery strategy is sound.

Restoring RMAN-Related Records to the Control File   Once you have restored the control file, you need to consider the distinct possibility that you have lost RMAN-related data. Since RMAN stores all of its data in the control file, there is a good possibility that you have at least lost some records that relate to archived redo logs (which Oracle needs for a full recovery).

RMAN makes this problem easier to deal with, because you can register various RMAN-related backup files after the restore of a control file just to ensure that you have everything you need for a recovery in the control file. To re-create RMAN-related archived redo log records, you can use the RMAN **catalog** command to register archived redo logs in your control file. The **catalog** command can be used to register a specific backup set piece, as shown in this example:

```
RMAN>Catalog backuppiece 'c:\oracle\product\10.2.0\flash_recovery_area
\testoem\backupset\2005_12_09\O1_MF_ANNNN_TAG20051209T041150_
1SLP386H_.BKP';
```

You can also catalog archived redo logs, as in this example:

```
RMAN>Catalog archivelog
'c:\oracle\product\10.2.0\flash_recovery_area\testoem\archivelog\
2005_12_15\O1_MF_1_2_1T3SVF05_.ARC';
```

Now, if you are thinking ahead, you might sigh and say to yourself, "Who wants to manually catalog the 1,000 archived redo logs that I have generated throughout the day?" Fortunately, the RMAN developers had the same thought! With RMAN, you can catalog a whole directory without having to list individual files. Simply use the **catalog** command again, but use one of the following keywords:

- **recovery area** or **db_recovery_file_dest**

- **start with**

The **recovery area** and **db_recovery_file_dest** keywords have the same function: they cause the entire FRA to be cataloged by RMAN. If RMAN finds files that are already cataloged, it simply skips over them and continues to catalog any remaining files that are not found in the control file. Here is an example of cataloging all files in the FRA:

```
RMAN> catalog recovery area;
```

If you are not using the FRA, then you will want to use the **start with** syntax instead. The **start with** syntax allows you to traverse a non-FRA backup directory and to catalog any RMAN-related files contained in that directory and any subdirectories under that directory. Here is an example of the use of the **catalog start with** command:

```
catalog start with 'c:\oracle\backups\testoem';
```

NOTE
RMAN in Oracle Database 10g R2 automatically catalogs the FRA for you if you perform a restore operation with a backup control file.

Restoring a Control File Online

Extracting a copy of your control file from a database backup while the database is up is really easy regardless of whether you are using a control file or a recovery catalog.

If you are not using a recovery catalog and you have enabled automatic backups of control files, just issue the following command:

```
RMAN> restore controlfile to 'd:\backup' from autobackup;
```

This command restores the SPFILE to a file called test.ora in a directory called d:\backup. Again, with any autobackup restore, RMAN looks only for the past seven days by default to find a control file autobackup piece. Use **maxseq** and **maxdays** to modify this default.

If you are not using a recovery catalog and are not using control file autobackups, or if you are using a recovery catalog, then this is the command you would use:

```
RMAN> restore controlfile to 'd:\backup';
```

In this case, Oracle uses the control file of the database to locate the most current backup set to restore the control file from. Of course, you could use the manual restore process by using the **dbms_backup_restore** procedure, which we discussed earlier in this section.

RMAN Workshop: *Recover Your Control File*

Workshop Notes

For this workshop, you need an installation of the Oracle software and an operational test Oracle database. We also assume that you have the FRA configured and that your backups are being done to that area.

> **NOTE**
> *For this workshop, the database is in ARCHIVELOG mode.*

Step 1. Ensure that you have configured automated backups of your control files:

```
configure controlfile autobackup on;
```

In this case, we are accepting that the control file backup set pieces will be created in the default location.

Step 2. Complete a backup of your system (in this case, we assume this is a hot backup). In this workshop, we assume that the backup is to a configured default device:

```
set oracle_sid=recover
rman target rman_backup/password
backup database plus archivelog;
```

Step 3. Shut down your database by using the **shutdown immediate** command. Do not use the **shutdown abort** command in this workshop.

```
shutdown immediate;
```

Step 4. Rename all copies of your database control file. Do not remove them, just in case your backups cannot be recovered.

Step 5. Start your database. It should complain that the control file cannot be found and it will not open.

```
startup;
```

Step 6. Recover your control file with RMAN by using your autobackup of the control file:

```
restore controlfile from autobackup;
```

Step 7. Mount the database and then simulate incomplete recovery to complete the recovery process:

```
Alter database mount;
recover database;
alter database open resetlogs;
```

The restore and recover Commands

The basic process of recovering a database is a two-step process. The first step is to use the **restore** command to restore the database backups. The second step is to use the **recover** command to recover the database, including the application of archived redo logs. Let's look at each of these commands in a bit more detail before we move on to the details of how to recover your database using them.

The restore Command

While the **restore** command has several ancillary purposes, its main function is to restore files from RMAN backups in preparation for recovery. RMAN and the **restore** command are quite intelligent, and they will choose the most recent backup to restore, in an effort to reduce recovery time. As a result, the **restore** command might restore your datafiles from a backup set, or it might restore them from an image copy, or it might choose to do a little of both, if that will help speed up the restore process.

The **restore** command is used to restore SPFILEs and control files from automated backups. The **restore** command can also be used to create a standby control file for a standby database. You also use the **restore** command to restore the database to any point in time, and in that case, it will find the closest backups to that given point in time to restore. Without a recovery catalog, RMAN can restore the database to any point in time within that database's incarnation (assuming that a backup is available). The **restore** command can also be used to restore databases from previous incarnations, but a control file backed up during that incarnation is required. If you are using a recovery catalog, you can restore the database back to any incarnation.

The **restore** command can also be used to restore a specific backup based on a given tag assigned to that backup. This might be useful in development environments where you might have a "golden" backup that you want to restore to on a regular basis. The **restore** command can also be used to restore archived redo logs, if that is required for operations like LogMiner (but the **recover** command will do this during database recoveries).

Want more? The **restore** command can be used to validate the ability to actually recover the database. It will make sure that backups are available to restore the database, and it will validate the integrity of those backups. You can also use the **restore preview** command to identify the backups that will be needed to restore the database (much like the **list** command that we discuss in Chapter 18).

NOTE
*The **restore preview** command can be quite handy if you are moving backup sets from a storage device that RMAN is not aware of. For example, if you back up to disk with RMAN and then later use an OS backup to move those files to tape, RMAN will not be aware of this move. You can use the **restore preview** to determine which files need to be restored from the OS backup, simplifying the restore process.*

When using the **restore** command, if you are using encryption for your backups, you need to ensure that the encryption method in use is properly configured. Thus, if you are using transparent-mode encryption, the required wallet must be available.

When you use the **restore** command, it overwrites any files that already exist without notice, unless you use the **set newname** command (which we document later in this chapter). Because of this, be very careful when restoring files, and make sure that you don't mind overwriting what is already out there.

The **restore** command also has a failover feature. If, during a recovery, RMAN finds that a given backup file is not available or is corrupted, it automatically tries to use previous backups to complete the recovery process. In cases where failover happens, RMAN puts a message in the database alert log.

The recover Command

The **recover** command is used to recover the database. It can perform a complete recovery, or it can perform a point-in-time recovery of the database. The **recover** command determines which archived redo logs are required and extracts and applies them. Once the application of the redo is complete, all you need to do is open the database with the **alter database open** command.

The **recover** command also determines if any incremental backup images are available to apply. These images can be applied to base incremental backups or to datafile image copies. The **recover** command always tries to use incremental backups first, if they are available, because that will be the quickest way to restore your database (as opposed to applying archived redo logs).

When restoring the archived redo logs, the **recover** command attempts to use any redo logs that are already present on disk. If they are not available on disk, the **recover** command then tries to restore them from the various archived redo log backup sets. Note that you can use the **noredo** parameter in the **recover** command to indicate that RMAN should not try to apply redo to the database. As you will see in an example later in this chapter, the **noredo** parameter is used for recovery of NOARCHIVELOG databases.

Restore and Recover the Database in NOARCHIVELOG Mode

If your database is in NOARCHIVELOG mode, you will be recovering from a full, offline backup, and point-in-time recovery won't be possible. If your database is in ARCHIVELOG mode, read the "Database Recoveries in ARCHIVELOG Mode" section later in this chapter. If you are doing incremental backups of your NOARCHIVELOG database, then you will also want to read "What If I Use Incremental Backups?" later in this chapter.

Preparing for the Restore

If you are running in NOARCHIVELOG mode, and assuming you actually have a backup of your database, performing a full recovery of your database is very easy. First, it's a good idea to clean everything out. You don't have to do this, but we have found that in cases of NOARCHIVELOG recoveries, cleaning out old datafiles, online redo logs, and control files is a good idea. You don't want any of those files lying around. Since you are in NOARCHIVELOG mode, you will want to start afresh (of course, it's also a very good idea to make sure that those files are backed up somewhere just in case you need to get them back!).

Having cleaned out your datafiles, control files, and redo logs, you are ready to start the recovery process. First, recover the control file from your last backup, as we demonstrated earlier in this chapter. Alternatively, you can use a backup control file that you created at some point after the backup you wish to restore from. If you use the **create control file** command, you need to catalog the RMAN backup-related files before you can restore the database.

For this example, we assume that you are not using a recovery catalog. We also assume you want to recover from the most current backup, which is the default setting for RMAN. If you want to recover from an older backup, you need to use the **set time** command, which we will discuss later in this section.

The differences in recovery with and without a recovery catalog are pretty much negligible once you are past the recovery of the SPFILE and the control file. So, we will only demonstrate recoveries without a recovery catalog. Also, at this point, there is little difference in how you perform a recovery if you are using the FRA or not. In the upcoming examples, we use the FRA and highlight any issues that arise from this fact in the text.

First, let's look at the RMAN commands you use to perform this recovery:

```
startup mount;
restore database;
recover database noredo;
alter database open resetlogs;
```

Looks pretty simple. Of course, these steps assume that you have recovered your SPFILE and your database control files. The first command, **startup mount**, mounts the database. So, Oracle reads the control file in preparation for the database restore. The **restore database** command causes RMAN to actually start the database datafile restores. Following this command, **recover database noredo** instructs RMAN to perform final recovery operations in preparation for opening the database. Since the database is in NOARCHIVELOG mode, and there are no archived redo logs to apply and the online redo logs are missing, the **noredo** parameter is required. If the online redo logs were intact, the **noredo** parameter would not be needed. Finally, we open the database with the **alter database open resetlogs** command. Since we have restored the control file and we need the online redo logs rebuilt, we need to use the **resetlogs** command. In fact, you will probably use **resetlogs** with about every NOARCHIVELOG recovery you do.

So, let's look at this recovery in action:

```
d:>set oracle_sid=testoem
d:>rman target sys/robert
RMAN> startup mount
connected to target database (not started)
Oracle instance started
database mounted
Total System Global Area      209715200 bytes
Fixed Size                      1248164 bytes
Variable Size                 100664412 bytes
Database Buffers              104857600 bytes
Redo Buffers                    2945024 bytes
RMAN> restore database;
Starting restore at 26-DEC-05
channel ORA_DISK_1: starting datafile backupset restore
channel ORA_DISK_1: specifying datafile(s) to restore from backup set
restoring datafile 00001 to
C:\ORACLE\DATAFILE\TESTOEM\TESTOEM\SYSTEM01.DBF
restoring datafile 00002 to
C:\ORACLE\DATAFILE\TESTOEM\TESTOEM\UNDOTBS01.DBF
restoring datafile 00003 to
C:\ORACLE\DATAFILE\TESTOEM\TESTOEM\SYSAUX01.DBF
```

```
restoring datafile 00004 to C:\ORACLE\DATAFILE\TESTOEM\TESTOEM\USERS01.DBF
restoring datafile 00005 to
C:\ORACLE\DATAFILE\TESTOEM\TESTOEM\CATALOG01.DBF
channel ORA_DISK_1: reading from backup piece
C:\ORACLE\PRODUCT\10.2.0\FLASH_RECOVERY_AREA\TESTOEM\BACKUPSET
\2005_12_26\O1_MF_NNNDF_TAG20051226T085336_1V00ZL3Y_.BKP
channel ORA_DISK_1: restored backup piece 1
piece handle=C:\ORACLE\PRODUCT\10.2.0\FLASH_RECOVERY_AREA\TESTOEM\
BACKUPSET\2005_12_26\O1_MF_NNNDF_TAG20051226T085336_1V00ZL3Y_.BKP
tag=TAG20051226T085336
channel ORA_DISK_1: restore complete, elapsed time: 00:03:26
Finished restore at 26-DEC-05
RMAN> recover database;
Starting recover at 26-DEC-05
using channel ORA_DISK_1
Finished recover at 26-DEC-05
RMAN> alter database open;
```

Well, we now have a happy bouncing baby database back again! Woo hoo!

NOTE
Use the **restore database noredo** *command when your online redo logs are not available. Use the* **restore database** *command without the* **redo** *parameter when your online redo logs are available during the recovery.*

Restoring to a Different Location

Of course, we don't always have the luxury of restoring back to the original file system names that the Oracle files resided on. For example, during a disaster recovery drill, you might have one big file system to recover to, rather than six smaller-sized file systems. That can be a bit of a problem, because, by default, RMAN is going to try to restore your datafiles to the same location that they came from when they were backed up. So, how do we fix this problem?

Enter the **set newname for datafile** and **switch** commands. These commands, when used in concert with **restore** and **recover** commands, allow you to tell RMAN where the datafiles need to be placed.

The **set newname** command offers several options with respect to relocation of database datafiles. In Oracle Database 10*g* and earlier, you can set the new name for individual datafiles. In Oracle Database 11*g*, new features include the ability to change the location for all datafiles in a tablespace or in the entire database.

In our first example, we have datafiles originally backed up to d:\oracle\data\recover, and we want to recover them to a different directory: e:\oracle\data\recover. To do this, we would first issue the **set newname for datafile** command for each datafile, indicating its old location and its new location. Here is an example of this command's use:

```
set newname for datafile 'd:\oracle\data\recover\system01.dbf'
to 'e:\oracle\data\recover\system01.dbf';
```

This example would work for all versions of the Oracle Database when using RMAN. Note that we define both the original location of the file and the new location that RMAN should copy the file to. Once we have issued **set newname for datafile** commands for all of the datafiles that we want to restore to a different location, we proceed as before with the **restore database** and **recover database** commands. Finally, before we actually open the database, we need to indicate to Oracle that we really want to have it use the relocated datafiles that we have restored. We do this by using the **switch** command.

The **switch** command causes the datafile locations in the database control file to be changed so that they reflect the new location of the Oracle database datafiles. Typically, you use the **switch datafile all** command to indicate to Oracle that you wish to switch all datafile locations in the control file. Alternatively, you can use the **switch datafile** command to switch only specific datafiles.

If you use the **set newname for datafile** command and do not switch all restored datafiles, then any nonswitched datafile will be considered a datafile copy by RMAN, and RMAN will not try to use that nonswitched datafile when recovering the database. Here is an example of the commands that you might use for a restore using the **set newname for datafile** command:

```
startup nomount
restore controlfile from autobackup;
alter database mount;
run
{
set newname for datafile 'd:\oracle\oradata\recover\system01.dbf' to
'e:\oracle\oradata\recover\system01.dbf';
set newname for datafile
'd:\oracle\oradata\recover\recover_undotbs_01.dbf' to
'e:\oracle\oradata\recover\recover_undotbs_01.dbf';
set newname for datafile 'd:\oracle\oradata\recover\users01.dbf' to
'e:\oracle\oradata\recover\users01.dbf';
set newname for datafile 'd:\oracle\oradata\recover\tools01.dbf' to
'e:\oracle\oradata\recover\tools01.dbf';
set newname for datafile 'd:\oracle\oradata\recover\indx01.dbf' to
'e:\oracle\oradata\recover\indx01.dbf';
restore database;
recover database noredo;
switch datafile all;
alter database open resetlogs;
}
```

Note that if the recovery is not successful but the files were restored successfully, the datafiles restored will become datafile copies and will not be removed.

In Oracle Database 11g, we can make this restore even easier by using the **set newname** command with the **for database** command to rename all database files in one command. You can also use the **set newname for tablespace** command if you wish to just rename datafiles associated with a given tablespace.

In conjunction with these new **set newname** commands, you must use substitution variables to avoid any collisions with filenames that might occur during the movement of the datafiles. The substitution variables are seen in Table 12-1.

Here is an example of using the **set newname for database** command that will result in the renaming of all datafiles of that database:

```
RUN
{
shutdown abort;
startup mount;
SET NEWNAME FOR DATABASE TO 'C:\oradata1\%b';
Restore database;
Recover database;
switch datafile all;
Alter database open;
}
```

If you just wanted to rename the files for a specific tablespace, you would change the **set newname** command slightly, as seen in this example:

```
RUN
{
shutdown immediate;
startup mount;
SET NEWNAME FOR TABLESPACE user_data TO 'c:\oradatanew\users\user_data%b.dbf';
Restore database;
switch datafile all;
Recover database;
Alter database open;
}
```

Variable	Meaning
%b	This will result in the full filename without any directory path information.
%f	This will result in the absolute file number for the datafile.
%U	This will result in a system-generated filename guaranteed to be unique.
%I	This will result in the DBID of the database.
%N	This will result in the tablespace name.

TABLE 12-1   *set newname Substitution Variables*

RMAN Workshop: *Recover Your NOARCHIVELOG Mode Database*

Workshop Notes

For this workshop, you need an installation of the Oracle software and an operational test Oracle database.

> **NOTE**
> *For this workshop, the database is in NOARCHIVELOG mode.*

Step 1. Set the ORACLE_SID and then log into RMAN. Ensure that you have configured automated backups of your control files. Because this is an offline backup, you need to shut down and mount the database:

```
set oracle_sid=recover
rman target rman_backup/password
configure controlfile autobackup on;
shutdown immediate;
startup mount;
```

Note that in this case, we are accepting that the control file backup set pieces will be created in the default location.

Step 2. Complete a cold backup of your system. In this workshop, we assume that the backup is to a configured default device:

```
backup database;
```

Step 3. Shut down your database:

```
shutdown immediate;
```

Step 4. Rename all database datafiles. Also rename the online redo logs and control files. (Optionally, you can remove these files if you don't have the space to rename them and if you really can afford to lose your database, should something go wrong.)

Step 5. Startup nomount your database and restore your control file:

```
startup nomount;
set DBID = <enter the DBID of the database here>;
restore controlfile from autobackup;
alter database mount;
```

Step 6. Recover your database with RMAN using the backup you took in Step 2:

```
restore database;
recover database noredo;
alter database open resetlogs;
```

Step 7. Complete the recovery by backing up the database again:

```
shutdown immediate;
startup mount;
backup database;
```

NOTE
*If your online redo logs had not been removed, you would have used
the* **recover database** *command instead of* **recover database noredo***.*

Database Recoveries in ARCHIVELOG Mode

Typically, you will find production databases in ARCHIVELOG mode because of one or more
requirements, such as the following:

■   Point-in-time recovery

■   Minimal recovery time service-level agreements (SLAs) with customers

■   The ability to do online database backups

■   The ability to recover specific datafiles while the database is available to users

When the database is in ARCHIVELOG mode, you have a number of recovery options that
you can choose from:

■   Full database recovery

■   Tablespace recoveries

■   Datafile recoveries

■   Incomplete database recovery

■   Online block media recovery

We cover the first three items in this section. Later in this chapter, we look at incomplete
database recoveries. In Chapter 15, we will look at online block media recovery in more detail.
With each of these types of recoveries, you will find that the biggest difference compared with
NOARCHIVELOG mode recovery is the application of the archived redo logs, as well as some
issues with regard to defining when you wish to recover to if you are doing incomplete recovery.
For now, let's start by looking at a full database recovery in ARCHIVELOG mode.

NOTE
*Recoveries of SPFILEs and control files are the same regardless of
whether you are running in ARCHIVELOG mode.*

Point-of-Failure Database Recoveries

With a point-of-failure database recovery (also known as a full database recovery), you hope that
you have your online redo logs intact; in fact, any unarchived online redo log must be intact. If
you lose your online redo logs, you are looking at an incomplete recovery of your database.
Reference Chapter 15 for more information on incomplete recoveries. Finally, we are going to
assume that at least one control file is intact. If no control file is intact, you need to recover a
control file backup, and again you are looking at an incomplete recovery (unless your online
redo logs are intact).

In this first example, we have lost all of our database datafiles. Our online redo logs and control files are safe, and we just want our database back. In this case, we opt for a full recovery of our database to the point of the failure. Here is the command set we use to perform this restore operation:

```
shutdown;
startup mount;
restore database;
recover database;
alter database open;
```

And here is an actual restore operation:

```
RMAN> restore database;
Starting restore at 09-JAN-06
using target database control file instead of recovery catalog
allocated channel: ORA_DISK_1
channel ORA_DISK_1: sid=156 devtype=DISK
channel ORA_DISK_1: starting datafile backupset restore
channel ORA_DISK_1: specifying datafile(s) to restore from backup set
restoring datafile 00001 to
C:\ORACLE\DATAFILE\TESTOEM\TESTOEM\SYSTEM01.DBF
restoring datafile 00002 to
C:\ORACLE\DATAFILE\TESTOEM\TESTOEM\UNDOTBS01.DBF
restoring datafile 00003 to
C:\ORACLE\DATAFILE\TESTOEM\TESTOEM\SYSAUX01.DBF
restoring datafile 00004 to C:\ORACLE\DATAFILE\TESTOEM\TESTOEM\USERS01.DBF
restoring datafile 00005 to
C:\ORACLE\DATAFILE\TESTOEM\TESTOEM\CATALOG01.DBF
restoring datafile 00009 to C:\ORACLE\TESTDBF\TABLESPACE_NOASSM_01.DBF
restoring datafile 00010 to C:\ORACLE\TESTDBF\TABLESPACE_YESASSM_01.DBF
channel ORA_DISK_1: reading from backup piece
C:\ORACLE\PRODUCT\10.2.0\FLASH_RECOVERY_AREA\TESTOEM
\BACKUPSET\2006_01_08\O1_MF_NNNDF_TAG20060108T224324_1W3THND6_.BKP

channel ORA_DISK_1: restored backup piece 1
piece handle=C:\ORACLE\PRODUCT\10.2.0\FLASH_RECOVERY_AREA\TESTOEM
\BACKUPSET\2006_01_08\O1_MF_NNNDF_TAG20060108T224324_1W3THND6_.BKP
tag=TAG20060108T224324

channel ORA_DISK_1: restore complete, elapsed time: 00:07:46
channel ORA_DISK_1: starting datafile backupset restore
channel ORA_DISK_1: specifying datafile(s) to restore from backup set
restoring datafile 00006 to C:\ORACLE\TESTDBF\TABLESPACE_2K.DBF

channel ORA_DISK_1: reading from backup piece
C:\ORACLE\PRODUCT\10.2.0\FLASH_RECOVERY_AREA\TESTOEM
\BACKUPSET\2006_01_08\O1_MF_NNNDF_TAG20060108T224324_1W3TTCT2_.BKP

channel ORA_DISK_1: restored backup piece 1
piece handle=C:\ORACLE\PRODUCT\10.2.0\FLASH_RECOVERY_AREA\TESTOEM\
BACKUPSET\2006_01_08\O1_MF_NNNDF_TAG20060108T224324_1W3TTCT2_.BKP
```

```
tag=TAG20060108T224324
channel ORA_DISK_1: restore complete, elapsed time: 00:00:07
channel ORA_DISK_1: starting datafile backupset restore
channel ORA_DISK_1: specifying datafile(s) to restore from backup set
restoring datafile 00007 to C:\ORACLE\TESTDBF\TABLESPACE_4K.DBF
channel ORA_DISK_1: reading from backup piece
C:\ORACLE\PRODUCT\10.2.0\FLASH_RECOVERY_AREA\TESTOEM
\BACKUPSET\2006_01_08\O1_MF_NNNDF_TAG20060108T224324_1W3TTNWO_.BKP

channel ORA_DISK_1: restored backup piece 1
piece handle=C:\ORACLE\PRODUCT\10.2.0\FLASH_RECOVERY_AREA\TESTOEM
\BACKUPSET\2006_01_08\O1_MF_NNNDF_TAG20060108T224324_1W3TTNWO_.BKP
tag=TAG20060108T224324

channel ORA_DISK_1: restore complete, elapsed time: 00:00:03
channel ORA_DISK_1: starting datafile backupset restore
channel ORA_DISK_1: specifying datafile(s) to restore from backup set

restoring datafile 00008 to C:\ORACLE\TESTDBF\TABLESPACE_16K.DBF
channel ORA_DISK_1: reading from backup piece
C:\ORACLE\PRODUCT\10.2.0\FLASH_RECOVERY_AREA\TESTOEM
\BACKUPSET\2006_01_08\O1_MF_NNNDF_TAG20060108T224324_1W3TTYJM_.BKP

channel ORA_DISK_1: restored backup piece 1
piece handle=C:\ORACLE\PRODUCT\10.2.0\FLASH_RECOVERY_AREA\TESTOEM
\BACKUPSET\2006_01_08\O1_MF_NNNDF_TAG20060108T224324_1W3TTYJM_.BKP
tag=TAG20060108T224324
channel ORA_DISK_1: restore complete, elapsed time: 00:00:03
Finished restore at 09-JAN-06
RMAN> recover database;
Starting recover at 09-JAN-06
using channel ORA_DISK_1
starting media recovery
media recovery complete, elapsed time: 00:00:12
Finished recover at 09-JAN-06

RMAN> alter database open;
database opened
```

Looks pretty easy, and it is. However, there are a few things to realize about restore operations like this. First, Oracle touts that if the file is there already and it doesn't need to be recovered, Oracle will not recover it. After reading the Oracle documentation, you might think that if you lose a single datafile, all you need to do is run the **restore database** command, and Oracle will recover only the datafile you lost.

What really happens is that Oracle determines whether the file it's going to restore already exists. If so, and the file that exists is the same as the file it's preparing to restore, then RMAN will not restore that file again. If the file on the backup image is different in any respect from the existing datafile, then RMAN will recover that file. So, if you lose a datafile or two, you will want to do a datafile or tablespace recovery instead of a full database recovery (since the datafile recoveries will be faster), which we will talk about shortly.

Let's take a moment now and look at what's happening during each step of the restore/recovery process. Each of these steps is quite similar for any type of ARCHIVELOG restore. After we have recovered our SPFILE and control files, if that was required, we have the **restore database** command, which causes RMAN to begin restoring all database datafiles. Note that, in this case, the database has to be down because we are restoring critical tablespaces, namely the SYSTEM tablespace. While many ARCHIVELOG recoveries can be done online, a full database point-in-time restore cannot.

Once the datafiles have been restored, Oracle will move on to the next command, the **recover database** command. This command is much like the **recover database** command that you would issue from inside SQL*Plus in that it will cause the Oracle RDBMS to start recovering the database to the point of failure by applying the archived redo logs needed to perform a full point-in-time recovery. An additional benefit that you get from RMAN is that it restores the needed archived redo logs from disk so that they can be applied during the recovery process. Once Oracle has recovered the database, it's as simple as issuing an **alter database open** command to get Oracle to finish the process of opening the database for use.

In Chapter 11, we talked about how using multiple channels can make a backup go faster, and the same is true with respect to a database recovery. If you have backed up to two different devices with two different channels, make sure that during your restores you also allocate two channels (assuming the hardware being used for the restore is the same). You can benefit from parallelism when restoring both normal backups and backups that occurred using multiple section sizes.

NOTE
If you attempt a full database restore and it fails, all recovered datafiles will be removed. This can be most frustrating if the restore has taken a very long time to complete. We suggest that you test different recovery strategies, such as recovering tablespaces (say four to five tablespaces at a time), and see which works best for you and which method best meets your recovery SLA and your disaster recovery needs.

RMAN Workshop: *Complete Recovery of Your ARCHIVELOG Mode Database*

Workshop Notes
For this workshop, you need an installation of the Oracle software and an operational test Oracle database.

NOTE
For this workshop, the database must be configured for and running in ARCHIVELOG mode.

Step 1. Ensure that you have configured automated backups of your control files:

```
set oracle_sid=recover
rman target rman_backup/password
configure controlfile autobackup on;
```

Note that in this case, we are accepting that the control file backup set pieces will be created in the default location.

Step 2.   Because this is an online backup, there is no need to shut down and then mount the database. Complete an online backup of your system. In this case, we will back up the database and the archived redo logs. Once the archived redo logs are backed up, we will remove them. In this workshop, we will assume that the backup is to a configured default device.

```
backup database plus archivelog delete input;
```

Step 3.   Shut down your database:

```
shutdown immediate;
```

Step 4.   Rename all database datafiles. Also rename the control files. Do not rename your online redo logs for this exercise. (Optionally, you can remove these files if you don't have the space to rename them and if you really can afford to lose your database, should something go wrong.)

Step 5.   Startup nomount your database and restore your control file:

```
startup nomount;
set DBID = <enter the DBID of the database here>;
restore controlfile from autobackup;
alter database mount;
```

Step 6.   Recover your database with RMAN using the backup you took in Step 2:

```
restore database;
recover database;
alter database open resetlogs;
```

Step 7.   Complete the recovery by backing up the database again:

```
shutdown immediate;
startup mount;
backup database;
```

Tablespace Recoveries

Perhaps you have just lost datafiles specific to a given tablespace. In this event, you can opt to recover just a tablespace rather than the entire database. One nice thing about tablespace recoveries is that they can occur while the rest of the database is humming along. For example, suppose you lose your accounts payable tablespace, but your accounts receivable tablespace is just fine. As long as your application doesn't need to access the accounts payable tablespace, you can be recovering that tablespace while the accounts receivable tablespace remains accessible. Here is an example of the code required to recover a tablespace:

```
sql "alter tablespace users offline";
restore tablespace users;
recover tablespace users;
sql "alter tablespace users online";
```

As you can see, the recovery process is pretty simple. First, we need to take the tablespace offline. We use a new command, **sql**, to perform this action. Enclosed in quotes after the **sql** command is specific SQL that we want the database to execute; in this case, we are taking the USERS tablespace offline with the command **alter tablespace users offline**. Next, we restore the datafiles associated with the tablespace, and then we recover the tablespace. Finally, we use the **sql** command again to issue the **alter tablespace users online** command, and the recovery of the USERS tablespace is complete.

NOTE
You cannot recover an individual tablespace or datafile to a point in time different from that of the rest of the database.

You can also recover multiple tablespaces in the same command set, as shown in this code snippet:

```
sql "alter tablespace users offline";
sql "alter tablespace data offline";
restore tablespace users, data;
recover tablespace users, data;
sql "alter tablespace users online";
sql "alter tablespace data online";
```

Datafile Recoveries

Second cousin to a tablespace recovery is a datafile recovery, which is a very granular approach to database recovery. Here, we can replace lost database datafiles individually, while the rest of the tablespace remains online. Datafile recovery allows the DBA to recover specific datafiles while allowing the rest of the tablespace to remain online for users to access. This feature is particularly nice if the datafile was empty or sparsely populated, as opposed to recovering the entire tablespace. Here is some sample code required to recover a datafile:

```
sql "alter database datafile 3 offline ";
sql "alter database datafile 'd:\oracle\oradata\users01.dbf' offline ";
restore datafile 3;
restore datafile 'd:\oracle\oradata\users01.dbf';
recover datafile 3;
recover datafile 'd:\oracle\oradata\users01.dbf';
sql "alter database datafile 3 online";
sql "alter database datafile 'd:\oracle\oradata\users01.dbf' online ";
```

We recovered a couple of datafiles in this example, by using two methods of defining which datafile we were recovering. First, we used the **sql** command again and took the offending datafiles offline with an **alter database datafile offline** command (they may be already offline in some cases, but we want to make sure). We then restore the datafiles with the **restore datafile** command. The first command restores the datafile by number, and the second restores the datafile by name.

Next we recover the datafiles. Again we recover the first datafile by number and then we recover the datafile by name. Finally we use the SQL command to bring the datafiles back online. Again we used the datafile number in the first SQL command, and the datafile name on the second.

Before we move on, let's look more closely at one component of the **alter database** command: how we reference datafiles. There are two different ways to reference datafiles. The first is to reference the datafile by number, and that's what we did with datafile 3 in the preceding example. The second is to reference a datafile by name, `'d:\oracle\oradata\ users01.dbf'`. Either method is acceptable, but we often find using the datafile number is easier. Generally, when a datafile is missing or corrupt, Oracle gives you both the datafile name and number in the associated error message, as shown in this example:

```
ORA-01157: cannot identify/lock data file 4 - see DBWR trace file
ORA-01110: data file 4: 'D:\ORACLE\ORADATA\RECOVER\TOOLS01.DBF'
```

Notice in this listing that datafile 4 is associated with the tools01.dbf datafile. Often, it's much easier to just indicate that you want to restore datafile 4 than to indicate you want to restore d:\oracle\oradata\recover\tools01.dbf.

Once we have taken our datafiles offline, we will restore them (again using either the file number or the filename) and then recover them. Finally, we will bring the datafiles online again, which will complete the recovery process.

What If I Use Incremental Backups?

Oracle will determine automatically if you are using an incremental backup strategy when you restore your datafiles and will automatically apply the required incremental backup sets as required. You do not need to do anything different to recover in these cases.

During a restore using an incremental backup, the **restore** command restores only the base backup. Once that restore is complete, you issue the **recover** command, which causes the incremental backups to be applied to the database, and then the archived redo logs will be applied. Once that is complete, then you can open the database as usual. In all cases, Oracle attempts to restore the base backup and incremental backup that is the most recent. This reduces the amount of redo that has to be applied to fully recover the database and thus reduces the overall restore time.

Note that since the database will likely be applying multiple backup sets during the recover process, your recovery will likely take longer than you might expect. However, depending on a number of factors (data change velocity being a large factor), applying incremental backup sets can be faster than the application of a generous amount of redo, and thus, the incremental backup solution can be a faster one. Therefore, the ultimate benefit of incremental backups is a quicker backup strategy (and a smaller overall space requirement for the backup set pieces) at the expense of a potentially slower recovery timeline.

Recovering from Online Redo Log Loss

One recovery situation you might experience is the loss of the database online redo logs. You will need to contend with four different situations if you lose the online redo logs:

- Loss of a redo log file group member

- Loss of an inactive online redo log group

- Loss of an active but not current online redo log group

- Loss of the current online redo log group

The first two types of online redo log loss are an annoyance at best. The last two categories can be catastrophic with respect to data loss.

Recall that the redo logs are written to as soon as there is a commit or as soon as the online redo log buffer is filled to a certain size (and other events can cause writes, too). As a result, uncommitted undo, along with committed changes, can be written to the online redo logs. Because the database datafiles are written to later, sometimes much later, the database datafiles are often way out of synchronization with the actual current state of the database. Due to this lack of synchronization between the actual state of the database data and the data contained in the database datafiles, Oracle will have to apply redo from the online redo logs during database recoveries.

Since database datafiles are often out of synch with the actual state of the database, loss of an *active online redo log* can result in loss of data. Loss of the current online redo log can also result in data loss. Obviously, redo logs are quite important. The current, active, and inactive redo logs differ as follows:

- **Active** This is a online redo log that is not currently in use. However, it contains redo that still needs to be written to the datafiles, and the group may (or may not) still need to be archived.

- **Current** This is the current online redo log group. Oracle is actively writing to this online redo log group.

- **Inactive** This online redo log is not currently in use, and redo has been written to datafiles by DBWR.

You can see the status of an online redo log group by querying the STATUS column of the V$LOG view. Let's look at what to do when it comes to recovering from loss of our redo log groups.

Loss of an Inactive Online Redo Log Group Member

To recover from the loss of one or more members of an online redo log group (but not the entire group), the response is pretty easy. You can simply re-create the member by using the **alter database add logfile member** command. You might discover that you have lost a member via an alert in OEM or in the alert log that might look something like this:

```
ORA-00313: open failed for members of log group 2 of thread 1
ORA-00312: online log 2 thread 1: 'C:\ORACLE\ORADATA\DANCE\REDO01a.LOG'
```

As a best practice, we'd recommend that if the database has not shut down and the member is part of an active or current redo log group, you immediately attempt to checkpoint the database by using the **alter system checkpoint** command. The **alter system checkpoint** command will force the database to write any dirty blocks from the database buffer cache to the database datafiles in an urgent manner. This can help protect your database against data loss should the database crash because of this missing online redo log.

Once the checkpoint has completed, we would issue the **alter database add logfile** command to re-create the redo log group member redo02a.log:

```
SQL>Alter database add logfile 'C:\ORACLE\ORADATA\DANCE\REDO02a.LOG' reuse to group 2;
```

If the database happened to crash before you could add the logfile, you would mount the database, and then issue the **alter database add logfile** command. You should then be able to open the database.

Another option that is available is that you could shut down the database in a consistent manner (**shutdown normal**) and then copy another member of the redo log group to the missing member. You can then restart the database normally.

NOTE
We strongly advise against using a **shutdown abort** *anytime you are dealing with the loss of an online redo log group or a member of such a group.*

Loss of an Inactive Online Redo Log Group

Loss of an *inactive online redo log group* is a very survivable event and is easy to recover from. You will need to understand two different situations that might occur. First is loss of an inactive online redo log group during database startup. Second is loss of an inactive online redo log group during database operations. In the next two sections, we will address these situations.

Loss of an Inactive Online Redo Log Group on Startup

If you start up the database and the inactive online redo log group cannot be opened, you will get the following error message:

```
ORA-00313: open failed for members of log group 2 of thread 1
ORA-00312: online log 2 thread 1: 'C:\ORACLE\ORADATA\DANCE\REDO02a.LOG'
```

First, determine if one of the online redo log group members has survived. If so, follow the steps listed in the previous section on recovering from the loss of an online redo log member. If none of the members survived, then you will need to drop the logfile group by using the **alter database** command as seen here:

```
SQL> alter database drop logfile group 2;
```

Once the online redo log group is dropped, you simply re-create the online redo log group by using the **alter database add logfile** command:

```
SQL> Alter database add logfile
2  group 2 'c:\oracle\oradata\dance\redo02a.log' size 50m;
```

Loss of an Inactive Online Redo Log Group When the Database Is Running

If you have lost an inactive online redo log group (or it becomes corrupted) while the database is running, it is possible that the database will continue to operate. Oracle Database will sometimes skip the online redo log group that went missing and continue to operate normally. If this occurs, you can issue an **alter system checkpoint** command, and then clear the logfile group with the **alter database clear logfile group** command, as seen here:

```
SQL>alter system checkpoint;
SQL>alter database clear logfile group 1;
```

If the logfile you are trying to clear has not been archived, you may get the following error:

```
SQL> alter database clear logfile group 1;
alter database clear logfile group 1
*
ERROR at line 1:
ORA-00350: log 1 of instance orcl (thread 1) needs to be archived
ORA-00312: online log 1 thread 1: '/oracle01/oradata/dance/redo01.log'
```

Of course, since the logfile is not there, it cannot be archived. In this case, we use the **alter database clear unarchived logfile** command to clear the unarchived log file and rebuild the log file in its current location, as seen here:

```
SQL> alter database clear unarchived logfile '/oracle01/oradata/dance/redo01.log';
```

You will need to back up your database in this case, since an archived redo log will have been lost.

In some cases, the database will not crash, but will freeze. If this occurs, open another SQL*Plus session and connect to the database. Then issue the **alter database checkpoint** command followed by either the **alter database clear logfile** or the **alter database clear unarchived logfile** command, depending on the type of recovery required. After you issue these commands, the database should operate as usual.

Loss of an Active but Not Current Online Redo Log Group

If you suffer the loss of an *active online redo log group,* you will need to use the **alter database clear unarchived logfile** command as shown in the previous section. This is because the active online redo log will not have been archived, and you need to indicate to Oracle that this is okay. This command will rebuild the online redo log and allow Oracle to proceed with normal operations. You should always back up the database after this operation.

Loss of the Current Online Redo Log Group

If you want to have a bad day, losing the *current online redo log group* probably would do it for you. If you have lost the current online redo log group, you probably will experience some loss of data. When you lose the current online redo log group, you can expect that the database will shut down, and not in the normal, pleasant kind of way that you would like.

If you are lucky and the database has not yet shut down, you should immediately attempt to reduce the overall loss of data by checkpointing the database using the **alter system checkpoint** command, and then shut down the database afterward as soon as practical. The **alter system checkpoint** command forces the database to write any dirty blocks from the database buffer cache to the database datafiles.

You may be able to open the database without any recovery being required. To try to restart the database:

1. Issue the **startup mount** command.
2. Issue the **alter database clear unarchived logfile** command for the redo log group that was lost. Examples of this command can be seen in earlier sections of this chapter.
3. Issue the **alter database open** command.

If the database opens successfully, you are in luck and a celebration is warranted.

If the database fails to open, you are in a bad way. You will need to perform incomplete recovery of the database. Incomplete recovery with RMAN is covered in Chapter 14 of this book.

The Data Recovery Advisor

In Oracle Database 11*g*, Oracle introduced a new feature called Automatic Diagnostic Repository (ADR). The ADR provides a great deal of new information and many new tools that ease database administration. In this section, we want to discuss one of these new tools, the Data Recovery Advisor.

The Data Recovery Advisor has both an OEM interface and a command-line interface. In this section, we will cover the command-line interface. If you wish to use the OEM interface, please refer to Chapter 13, which contains much more information about using OEM and RMAN.

Using the Data Recovery Advisor Through RMAN

To use the manual interface into the Data Recovery Advisor, you simply use the RMAN command-line interface. Oracle has added new RMAN commands to allow you to execute the Data Recovery Advisor from the command line. These commands are

- **list failure**
- **advise failure**
- **repair failure**
- **change failure**

All of the Data Recovery Advisor (DRA) commands will work when the database instance is started. If the failure is new and the database has been shut down, you will often not get any results until you have tried to open the database and a failure has been detected. Once a failure has been detected, though, the DRA will remember the failures, and you can access those failures with the **advice failure** command with the database in nomount, mount, or open stage.

The state that the database needs to be in when repairing failures depends on the nature of the failure. For example, for a control file recovery, the database will be in nomount stage. If you are repairing missing data files, the **repair failure** command will require the database to be mounted or open.

We have also found cases where the **repair failure** command does not quite complete the job. The most common case seems to be where control file recoveries occur. Often, the **repair failure** command has to be followed up with a **recover database** command and then with an **alter database open resetlogs** command for the restore to complete. Still, the DRA is a good start to helping the Junior DBA figure out how to deal with a database in trouble.

Typically, when dealing with a data corruption error, the workflow will be to use the **list failure** command, then the **advise failure** command, and finally, the **repair failure** command, in that order. Let's look at the use of these commands in a bit more detail.

The list failure Command   The RMAN **list** command now has a new **failure** parameter that will list detected failures and their priorities (Critical, High, or Low), status (Open or Closed), when they occurred, and a summary of the failure. In this context, a failure is any persistent data corruption that currently exists on your system. Here is an example of the **list failure** command:

```
RMAN> list failure;
using target database control file instead of recovery catalog
```

```
List of Database Failures
=========================
Failure ID Priority Status      Time Detected Summary
---------- -------- ---------   ------------- -------
187        HIGH     OPEN        05-JUN-09     One or more non-system
                                              datafiles are missing
```

Note that in the preceding sample output, the datafiles that are missing are not listed. You can use the **list failure detail** command to generate additional details on the failure. Additionally, the **list failure exclude failure** *n* command allows you to exclude specific failure numbers from the report output. Other options include listing only closed failures, only critical failures, only failures with high or low priorities, and listing or excluding failures by failure ID. Here are some examples of the use of these options:

```
RMAN> list failure detail;
List of Database Failures
=========================
Failure ID Priority Status      Time Detected Summary
---------- -------- ---------   ------------- -------
187        HIGH     OPEN        09-JUN-09     One or more non-system
                                              datafiles are missing
   List of child failures for parent failure ID 187
   Failure ID Priority Status      Time Detected Summary
   ---------- -------- ---------   ------------- -------
   2075       HIGH     OPEN        09-JUN-09     Datafile 6:
'C:\ORACLE\ORADATA\ROB11GR4\ROB11GR4\BOOGLE01.DBF' is missing
      Impact: Some objects in tablespace BOOGLE might be unavailable

-- Let's exclude failure_id 187...
RMAN> list failure exclude failure 187;
no failures found that match specification
```

The following table gives a complete list of all the options available on the **list failure** command:

Option	Description
ALL	List all failures.
CRITICAL	List only failures with a priority of critical.
HIGH	List only failures with a priority of high.
LOW	List only failures with a priority of low.
CLOSED	List only failures that are closed.
EXCLUDE FAILURE	From the list, remove the failure numbers listed. This option is followed by a comma-delimited list of failure IDs that you want to exclude.
DETAIL	Provide additional detail for the failure listed.
#	This is the actual failure number to be listed.

Here are some additional examples (note that some unimportant output was removed for brevity's sake...we do like trees, after all!):

```
RMAN> list failure closed 254;
List of Database Failures
=========================
Failure ID Priority Status    Time Detected Summary
---------- -------- --------- ------------- -------
254        HIGH     CLOSED    04-JUN-09     Redo log file
C:\ORACLE\ORADATA\DOODLE\REDO03.LOG is corrupt

RMAN> list failure closed exclude failure 242,248;
List of Database Failures
=========================
Failure ID Priority Status    Time Detected Summary
---------- -------- --------- ------------- -------
8298       CRITICAL CLOSED    03-AUG-09     System datafile 1:
'C:\ORACLE\ORADATA\DOODLE\SYSTEM01.DBF' needs media recovery
8295       CRITICAL CLOSED    03-AUG-09     Control file needs media recovery
8104       CRITICAL CLOSED    03-AUG-09     Control file
C:\ORACLE\ORADATA\DOODLE\CONTROL03.CTL is missing
8101       CRITICAL CLOSED    03-AUG-09     Control file
C:\ORACLE\ORADATA\DOODLE\CONTROL02.CTL is missing
8098       CRITICAL CLOSED    03-AUG-09     Control file
C:\ORACLE\ORADATA\DOODLE\CONTROL01.CTL is missing
```

NOTE
The **list failure** *command can only be run on a single instance database (thus, the RAC cluster must now be brought to single instance mode). You also cannot use this command with a physical standby database.*

The **list failure** command does not check for database errors itself. The database is constantly checking for corruption issues, and those issues regularly are recorded in the data dictionary (and in the physical ADR repository, which is on disk and not in the database).

If the failure occurred while the database was shut down, a failure will not be detected until that missing component is needed. For example, if the control file is missing, that will not be detected until an attempt to mount the database occurs. If a datafile is missing, then that event will not be detected until you try to open the database. If the database was open when the event occurred, it is likely that the event will be detected while the database is open.

If a failure with an OPEN status appears in the list, this means you have a current problem that you will need to deal with. This problem will be linked to one or more repair actions that you can view via the new **advise failure** command. These options will help you to determine what repair options are available to correct the situation. Let's look at that command next.

NOTE
If you just have a datafile offline, then that datafile will not be reported as a failure. If the offline datafile is physically missing, then it will be reported as a failure.

The advise failure Command   Once the **list failure** command displays an open failure, the **advise failure** command can be used to provide recommended actions that you can take to correct the failure. Here is an example of the use of the **advise failure** command:

```
RMAN> advise failure;
List of Database Failures
=========================

Failure ID Priority Status    Time Detected Summary
---------- -------- --------- ------------- -------
187        HIGH     OPEN      05-JUN-09     One or more non-system
                                            datafiles are missing
analyzing automatic repair options; this may take some time
allocated channel: ORA_DISK_1
channel ORA_DISK_1: SID=129 device type=DISK
analyzing automatic repair options complete


Manual Checklist
================
1. If file C:\ORACLE\ORADATA\ROB11GR4\ROB11GR4\DOOGLE01.DBF was
unintentionally renamed or moved, restore it


Automated Repair Options
========================
Option Repair Description
------ ------------------
1      Restore and recover datafile 6
  Strategy: The repair includes complete media recovery with
            no data loss
Repair script:
C:\ORACLE\PRODUCT\diag\rdbms\rob11gr4\rob11gr4\hm\reco_1214740950.hm
```

NOTE
*As with the **list failure** command, the **advise failure** command can only be run on a single instance database (thus, the RAC cluster must be brought now to single instance mode). You also cannot use this command with a physical standby database.*

You will notice from the output that RMAN provides both manual and automated repair options. The automated repair option contains RMAN commands that can be used to correct the problem. These automated repair options may differ based on the state the database is in (say, nomount versus mount). We recommend then that you open the database as much as possible. For example, if you can successfully mount the database, do so rather than leave it in nomount mode.

Also note that repair options may involve data loss, and that the Data Recovery Advisor will indicate if data loss will occur if a given recovery option is used. These commands are contained in a file within the ADR structure. Here is an example of the recovery file:

```
# restore and recover datafile
restore datafile 6;
recover datafile 6;
sql 'alter database datafile 6 online';
```

You can choose to run the recovery file manually, or you can use the **repair failure** command, which is our next topic.

The repair failure Command   Now that we have detected a failure and determined the recovery actions recommended by Oracle, we can manually repair the failure, or allow Oracle to repair the failure automatically with the **repair failure** command. To run the **repair failure** command, the target database instance must be started. If multiple repairs are required, Oracle will try to consolidate them into one repair operation. Also, RMAN will double-check that the failures still exist and will not perform a recovery operation if the failure has been corrected. Here is an example of using the **repair failure** command from RMAN (we have removed some RMAN output for brevity's sake):

```
RMAN> repair failure;
Strategy: The repair includes complete media recovery with no data loss
Repair script:
C:\ORACLE\PRODUCT\diag\rdbms\rob11gr4\rob11gr4\hm\reco_110341808.hm
contents of repair script:
   # restore and recover datafile
   restore datafile 6;
   recover datafile 6;
   sql 'alter database datafile 6 online';
Do you really want to execute the above repair (enter YES or NO)? yes
executing repair script
Starting restore at 05-JUN-09
using channel ORA_DISK_1
... Typical RMAN restore output is removed for brevity...
Starting recover at 05-JUN-00
using channel ORA DISK 1
... Typical RMAN recover output is removed for brevity...
media recovery complete, elapsed time: 00:00:03
Finished recover at 05-JUN-09
sql statement: alter database datafile 6 online
repair failure complete
```

NOTE
Again, the **repair failure** *command can only be run on a single instance database (thus, the RAC cluster must be brought now to single instance mode). Note that this command will not repair failures such as datafiles that cannot be accessed by a specific node in a RAC cluster.*

If you wish to preview a failure action, you can use the **repair failure preview** command. This command will display the repair actions to be applied, but not execute the repair itself.

The change failure Command   The RMAN **change** command now has a new **failure** keyword that allows you to change the status of failures detected by the Oracle Database. For example, you can change the priority of a specific failure, or change all failures from high to low. You can also opt to close one or more failures. By default, RMAN will prompt you to ensure that you wish to make the change. You can use the **noprompt** clause of the **change** command to force the change to occur without prompting. Here is an example where we change the priority of failure 187 to LOW:

```
RMAN> Change failure 187 priority low;
List of Database Failures
=========================
Failure ID Priority Status     Time Detected Summary
---------- -------- ---------- ------------- -------
187        HIGH     OPEN       09-JUN-09     One or more non-system
                                             datafiles are missing
Do you really want to change the above failures (enter YES or NO)? yes
changed 1 failures to LOW priority
```

NOTE
You cannot switch the status of a CLOSED failure to OPEN.

Data Recovery Advisor Data Dictionary Views

Several new views have been added to Oracle Database 11*g* to support the Data Recovery Advisor. These views start with V$IR as seen in this table:

View Name	Description
V$IR_FAILURE	Provides information on the failure. Note that records in this view can have parent records within this view.
V$IR_FAILURE_SET	This table provides a list of the various advice records associated with the failure. This allows you to join the view V$IR_FAILURE to the V$IR_MANUAL_CHECKLIST view.
V$IR_ MANUAL_CHECKLIST	This view provides detailed informational messages related to the failure. These messages provide information on how to manually correct the problem.
V$IR_REPAIR	This view, when joined with V$IR_FAILURE and V$IR_FAILURE_SET, provides a pointer to the physical file created by Oracle that contains the repair steps required to correct a detected error.

Here is an example of a query against the DRA views:

```
-- Do we have an open error reported?
select failure_id, time_detected, description from v$ir_failure
Where status='OPEN';

FAILURE_ID TIME_DETE DESCRIPTION
---------- --------- ----------------------------------------
       242 19-SEP-07 One or more non-system datafiles are missing
       605 19-SEP-07 Datafile 4: '/oracle01/oradata/orcl/user
                     s01.dbf' is missing
```

Summary

In this chapter, we have looked at the basics of recovering your database with RMAN. We have looked at the many different ways that you can recover your control files and SPFILEs. We have also looked at restoring and recovering your databases from RMAN backups with the **restore** and **recover** commands. We have discussed the different recovery options available, from full database recovery to recovery of specific tablespaces or datafiles. Finally, we have provided some workshops for you to practice your newly learned recovery skills.

We want to leave you with one big piece of advice at the end of this chapter. Practice recoveries, over and over and over. Know how RMAN works and how to recover your database without having to use this book. Become the RMAN expert in your place of work. Then you are poised to be the hero!

PART

III

Using RMAN Effectively

CHAPTER
13

Using Oracle Enterprise Manager for Backup and Recovery

p to this point, we have provided guidance on interacting with RMAN strictly from the RMAN client utility. Hopefully, this has enabled you to build some confidence using the RMAN command-line syntax. It is critical to become comfortable with this syntax because you will encounter situations in which the command-line syntax of RMAN is the only thing available to get you through a painful downtime.

Oracle does provide a toolset for monitoring all the databases throughout your business, and this toolset includes a graphical user interface for taking backups and performing recoveries. This product, collectively referred to as Oracle Enterprise Manager (OEM), has existed in one form or another since 1998. For most of its history, it has been available as a Java application that could be installed on a client system and used to monitor and administer remote databases.

However, starting in 10g, Enterprise Manager (EM) underwent a radical transformation that moved it from primarily a desktop application to a fully functional web application. From the early 10g Release 1 (10gR1) days, this new EM has been consistently upgraded so that nearly all functionality that is available at the command line is now also available from any Internet browser. To put it mildly, this changes the game.

Oracle Enterprise Manager: The New Paradigm

Oracle engineered OEM specifically to embrace the new paradigm of enterprise computing, often referred to as the grid. Oracle built OEM to tame the management chaos unleashed by grid computing. Grid computing enables many compelling business advances, providing an always-up, highly redundant, commodity-based, service-oriented environment in which to deploy enterprise computing resources (enough buzzwords for you?). We have already seen its principles deployed at customer sites, and grid computing is powerful. But it is also complicated.

To contrast traditional enterprise computing and grid computing, it helps to look at some example environments. First, consider the simplified scenario of a traditional enterprise environment shown in Figure 13-1. Configuring this database environment includes the following:

- Requisition as powerful a computer as can be found.

- Manage as small a list of computers as can be reasonably grouped.

- Manage multiple databases on a single computer.

- Segregate data by division and function.

- Assign a highly ritualized set of responsibilities to each professional segment (network admin, system admin, database admin, etc.).

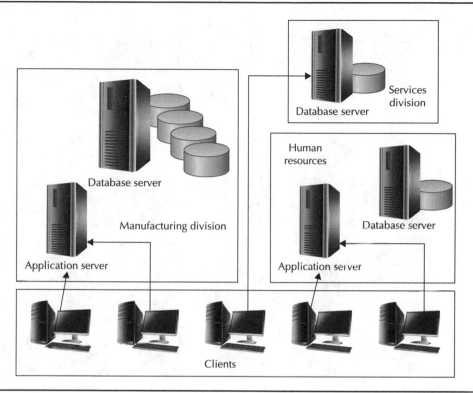

FIGURE 13-1   *Traditional enterprise computing*

If you take the same business needs and deploy them into a grid computing environment, such as that shown in Figure 13-2, configuring the environment includes the following:

- Requisition as many commoditized computers as can be found.

- Manage a single database running on many computers.

- Segregate data as an abstraction (service).

- Take on new professional responsibilities rapidly.

- Manage enterprise computing as a single resource, distributed to divisions and functions based on usage requirements.

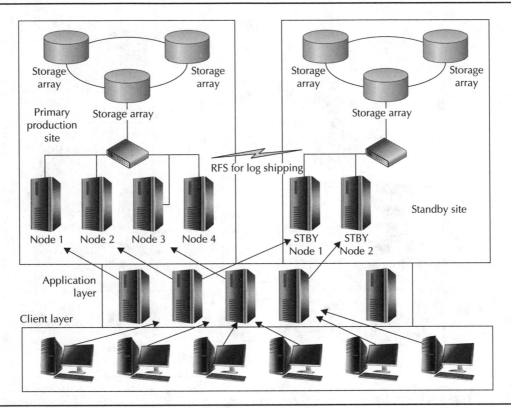

FIGURE 13-2 *The enterprise grid*

The ability of a grid to add and subtract resources without downtime leads to an ever-increasing level of complexity. DBAs find themselves every day doing more operational architecture work, more network administration work, and more system administration.

Oracle Enterprise Manager 10*g* was designed to handle this new world order. It was built around the principles of the service-oriented architecture, and its function is far wider than that envisioned for its predecessor, Oracle9*i* Enterprise Manager. Now, OEM is capable of monitoring and administering the entire Oracle ecosystem: the host servers, the disk storage, the databases, the application servers, and the applications.

Coverage of everything that OEM can do is beyond the scope of this book (we recommend *Oracle Enterprise Manager Grid Control 10g Handbook* from Oracle Press). This book is about RMAN, so the coverage of OEM is limited to how it employs RMAN to provide a backup and recovery interface from its console. However, OEM is worth a high-level overview to familiarize yourself with the architecture and overall function of EM prior to any discussion of its backup and recovery functions.

One more thing to note before we jump in: OEM 10*g* takes two forms: Grid Control and Database Control. *OEM 10g Grid Control* is the fully functioning enterprise-wide tool for managing the Oracle ecosystem. *OEM 11g Database Control* is the version of OEM that can be deployed as just a database management utility.

What's the Difference Between Grid Control and Database Control?
Enterprise Manager Grid Control has the ability to monitor the entire Oracle ecosystem. It has a centralized repository that collects data about multiple targets that exist on multiple computers and that provides an interface that displays collective information for all discovered targets.

Enterprise Manager Database Control is a subset of Grid Control functionality. It does not monitor anything but a single database and cannot be used to monitor more than one database. It runs local to the database itself.

From a database administration perspective, the functionality is mostly the same between the two utilities, with Grid Control providing more functionality for operations that involve more than one computer and more than one database. But the interface is the same, the underlying code is the same, and there is little to differentiate the two. From a backup and recovery perspective, the two utilities are nearly identical—the only primary difference being the ability to share RMAN scripts across your ecosystem and to utilize Grid Control's knowledge of multiple servers for duplication and restore.

Grid Control

Let's get a few things straight. First, OEM is a web application, with all the power and limitations that come with a web application. The OEM console is a web page that runs on an HTTP server that will be installed and configured as part of the Grid Control install. There is no client install.

Second, Grid Control is deployed on Oracle Application Server (OAS). When you install Grid Control, you are installing OAS, and then the Grid Control application is deployed as an Oracle Containers for J2EE (OC4J) application on top of OAS. We point this out so that you realize that a commitment to Grid Control necessitates that you familiarize yourself, to some degree, with the OAS architecture. A discussion of OAS is well beyond the scope of this book, but we will refer to it occasionally. Grid Control can monitor many different types of *targets* (as it calls them): databases, application servers, the hosts themselves, even storage devices. In this book, we stick to databases…and mostly to backups of databases only.

Grid Control performs a task that is simple to outline but complicated to realize: it gathers information about computing systems throughout the enterprise, consolidates that information into a central repository, and then displays that information to the DBA from its web console. Based on the information, the DBA can then ask Grid Control to perform tasks on behalf of the DBA at those computing systems.

Whatever Happened to the OEM Client Install on the Oracle Client CD?
There used to be a "thick" Java client that could be installed as a stand-alone product. This was the old, Oracle9*i* Enterprise Manager client software, which could be found on the Oracle Client CD. This lingered in the 10*g* space because certain functionality had not yet been migrated from the desktop application to the Database Control web application. In 11*g*, you will find all functionality for all database options has been integrated into the web application, and there is no longer a desktop-installable OEM.

The Grid Control Architecture

The Grid Control architecture (see Figure 13-3) starts with the Oracle Management Service (OMS), which is the application that is deployed on the application server. The OMS collects data from registered target servers via the central agent. The agent is installed on a target server, collects information, and pushes the data to the OMS. The OMS loads the data into the repository database. The OMS then builds web pages based on the information in the repository, which can be retrieved from any browser that can hit the OMS server's URL.

The Central Agent

The central agent is installed at each computer that you will be monitoring with Grid Control. The agent is a "dummy" software piece, meaning it cannot make any decisions on its own. It gathers data using Perl scripts and pushes that data over HTTPS to the OMS. The OMS performs any intelligence that is required and then sends an action to the agent to perform.

The agent has a relatively small footprint, from a memory perspective. However, it can be a visible player on the CPU, depending on what you are asking it to do.

The Oracle Management Service

The OMS is a deployed web application on the middle tier of the Grid Control architecture. It is constantly receiving information from agents, in the form of .xml files, that it then loads into the tables of the repository. It is responsible for building web content for the HTTP server that

FIGURE 13-3   *Grid Control architecture*

provides the console web pages, and as such may ask the agent for specific information. However, the typical data is pushed from the agent, rather than the OMS pulling it.

The Repository Database
The OMS uses an Oracle database for its data source. The repository database is used to store information about the managed targets, as well as Grid Control operations (such as jobs or notifications).

Advanced RDBMS features are put to good use within the repository; Advanced Queuing (AQ) gets a workaround, partitioning is employed heavily, and even the internal DBMS_JOB is used.

Installing and Configuring Grid Control
In the previous version of this book, we spent a few pages going through the Grid Control installation. Because other books have caught up to Grid Control and cover this topic better, and because we will be showing you examples from here on that have to do with utilizing Enterprise Manager Database Control, we are forgoing that conversation here. The best place for comprehensive coverage of Grid Control is the Oracle Press title, *Oracle Enterprise Manager Grid Control 10g Handbook.* That being said, we do want to make one final point about Grid Control. Grid Control is not something you casually install somewhere. Be very careful when you are testing it, because you can easily overwhelm resources at your disposal (especially in extremely low-cost testing environments such as the ones we've been known to discuss in the RMAN books).

NOTE
*If you do have both the Grid Control centralized agent and Database Control running on the same server, you must go to great lengths to keep yourself oriented as to which $ORACLE_HOME directory you are in at each step. This is because an **emctl** executable will exist in the bin directory of every ORACLE_HOME (including the ORACLE_HOME that houses the agent), but bad things happen if you start running the wrong **emctl** command in the wrong ORACLE_HOME. We suggest running a nice set of environment-changing scripts before any operation.*

Database Control
As we stated previously, Database Control is a subset of Grid Control functionality, limited to the management and monitoring of a single database. As such, the functionality is database-centric but not exactly limited to just the database. There are host statistics gathered for the server on which the database resides, so the host, while not a separate "target," does have some information reported. In addition, Database Control can be configured to monitor and administer an Automatic Storage Management (ASM) instance that the target database uses for storage.

Database Control can also be configured to monitor a RAC database, and thus to monitor multiple hosts, multiple instances, and multiple ASM instances. Still, it can monitor only a single database—so the limitation of Database Control is still the same.

The Database Control Architecture
The Database Control architecture is very similar to that of Grid Control, but the scale is much smaller. The central agent and the OMS are rolled into the same OC4J application, and the repository is housed in the target database itself. Figure 13-4 shows how this architecture looks.

FIGURE 13-4 *Database Control architecture*

Of importance in this diagram is that the Database Control repository is located in the target database that it monitors. So, if the target database is down, Database Control cannot function except to start and stop the database and perform recovery. On a Windows system, the Database Control process is monolithic, and starts and stops as a single service from the Services control panel. On Linux and Unix, you stop and start dbconsole as a single application, but it still spawns separate agent and Java processes.

Database Control is not a separate install from the RDBMS installation. It runs from the same ORACLE_HOME that its target database runs from. Specifically, when dbconsole has been configured for a database, a new subdirectory in the ORACLE_HOME is created with the name *host_sid,* where *host* is the computer name and *sid* is the SID of the instance being monitored. For instance, if the server is named horatio.hadba.com, and we are monitoring the database that is named v112, then the configuration files would all be located in $ORACLE_HOMEhoratio.hadba.com_v112.

In a RAC environment, there are always multiple directories named for every node in the cluster, suffixed by the globalname for the RAC database. So, if you have a two-node RAC cluster on nodes dex and horatio, and the database is v112c, then there would be two directories on each node's RDBMS home: ORACLE_HOME/dex_v112c and $ORACLE_HOME/horatio_v112c. On each node, only the directory that corresponds in name to that node would actually have any files in it. The other would be empty. This convention is used in cases where the RAC cluster shares the same $ORACLE_HOME software tree on a shared drive.

Stopping and starting Database Control requires a simple command from the target database $ORACLE_HOME/bin directory:

```
emctl start dbconsole
emctl stop dbconsole
```

Installing and Configuring Database Control

There is no specific installation of Database Control software required. It is installed by default with every version 10.2 (and higher) RDBMS installation that you already have. In fact, you may already have Database Control up and running on your computer right now, if you had the Universal Installer provide you with a starter database at the time of install. At that time, you would have been asked by the Installer how you wanted to manage your database, and one of the choices is Database Control.

Using the Database Configuration Assistant to Configure Database Control

Oracle provides a GUI utility to help you build databases, long referred to as the Database Configuration Assistant (DBCA). This is started by using the executable **dbca** out of the $ORACLE_HOME/bin directory; thus, we refer to it hereafter as lowercase **dbca.**

You can put **dbca** to good use for all kinds of purposes—for example, building a new database, deleting an old database, and installing database options. You can also use it to add Database Control functionality to your database. You can use **dbca** to add Database Control to a new database at the time you build it, or you can use **dbca** to modify an existing database. This is by far the simplest and most straightforward of all ways to get Database Control up and running.

The **dbca** executable cannot be used to remove or modify Database Control after it has been added. It is an addition tool only; for subtraction, you have to use the command-line tool **emca** (described next).

Notice in the next illustration the option to specify whether a backup will be scheduled automatically, with the Enable Daily Disk Backup to Recovery Area check box. This option enables the Oracle-suggested backup strategy, which we describe later in the chapter in the section "Oracle-Suggested Backup Strategy." This is an out-of-the box backup strategy. You can also configure this with **emca**.

Using Enterprise Manager Configuration Assistant to Configure Database Control

Sometimes, as with all things Oracle, the GUI will simply prove to be too obtuse, too rigid, or too mystifying to serve your purposes when configuring Database Control. In these cases, you can use the command-line utility called Enterprise Manager Configuration Assistant (EMCA), run using the **emca** executable in the $ORACLE_HOME/bin directory of the RDBMS installation (again, we use the lowercase convention **emca** for this utility).

Unlike **dbca**, **emca** is not what you would call intuitive to use. But it offers all kinds of tweaks and switches that make it powerful and more easily debugged than the GUI **dbca**. Besides which, it's always nice to avoid an X window when you don't really need one. Because of this, **emca** is a valuable tool to look at. All the switches and controls are best described in the Oracle documentation; from our perspective, only a few are worth noting. These are the switches we use to identify the database we want to configure Database Control for, and to specify whether we want a default backup strategy put into place:

```
emca -config dbcontrol db -repos create -backup
emca -deconfig dbcontrol db -repos drop
```

When you fire off a command, **emca** prompts you in an interactive mode for information about what database SID you will be configuring (or deconfiguring), the listener port for the listener that will connect **emca** to the database, and for the required user passwords. Note that if you use the **–backup** switch, **emca** will prompt for backup configuration settings.

RMAN Workshop: *Configure Database Control Using emca*

Workshop Notes
This workshop assumes an operational 10.2.0.1.0 database, named v102, running on Linux. This workshop details how to configure a default Database Control application for this database by using the command-line utility **emca**.

Step 1. Use **emca** to drop an existing dbcontrol configuration and the dbcontrol repository:

```
[oracle@localhost dbhome_1]$ emca -deconfig dbcontrol db -repos drop

STARTED EMCA at Jun 11, 2009 3:03:30 PM
EM Configuration Assistant, Version 11.2.0.0.2 Production
Copyright (c) 2003, 2005, Oracle.  All rights reserved.

Enter the following information:
Database SID: dev1
Listener port number: 1521
Password for SYS user:
Password for SYSMAN user:
Password for SYSMAN user:
Do you wish to continue? [yes(Y)/no(N)]: Y
Jun 11, 2009 3:03:52 PM oracle.sysman.emcp.EMConfig perform
INFO: This operation is being logged at
/home/oracle/app/oracle/cfgtoollogs/emca/dev1/emca_2009_06_11_15_03_30.log.
Jun 11, 2009 3:03:52 PM oracle.sysman.emcp.EMDBPreConfig performDeconfiguration
WARNING: EM is not configured for this database. No EM-specific actions can be performed.
```

```
Jun 11, 2009 3:03:52 PM oracle.sysman.emcp.ParamsManager
checkListenerStatusForDBControl
WARNING: Error initializing SQL connection. SQL operations cannot be
performed
Jun 11, 2009 3:03:52 PM oracle.sysman.emcp.EMReposConfig invoke
INFO: Dropping the EM repository (this may take a while) ...

Jun 11, 2009 3:09:23 PM oracle.sysman.emcp.EMReposConfig invoke
INFO: Repository successfully dropped
Enterprise Manager configuration completed successfully
FINISHED EMCA at Jun 11, 2009 3:09:23 PM
```

Step 2.   Use **emca** to create a new dbcontrol configuration for this database. (Note that the following output is truncated in the middle; there are more steps executed by **emca** than shown here.)

```
$ emca -config dbcontrol db -repos create
STARTED EMCA at Jun 11, 2009 3:16:23 PM
EM Configuration Assistant, Version 11.2.0.0.2 Production
Copyright (c) 2003, 2005, Oracle.  All rights reserved.
Enter the following information:
Database SID: dev1
Listener port number: 1521
Listener ORACLE_HOME [ /home/oracle/app/oracle/product/11.2.0/dbhome_1 ]:
Password for SYS user:
Password for DBSNMP user:
Password for SYSMAN user:
Email address for notifications (optional):
Outgoing Mail (SMTP) server for notifications (optional):
-----------------------------------------------------------------
You have specified the following settings

Database ORACLE_HOME ...............
/home/oracle/app/oracle/product/11.2.0/dbhome_1
Local hostname ............... horatio.hadba.com
Listener ORACLE_HOME ...............
/home/oracle/app/oracle/product/11.2.0/dbhome_1
Listener port number ............... 1521
Database SID ............... dev1
Email address for notifications ..............
Outgoing Mail (SMTP) server for notifications ..............
-----------------------------------------------------------------
Do you wish to continue? [yes(Y)/no(N)]: Y
Jun 11, 2009 3:16:58 PM oracle.sysman.emcp.EMConfig perform
INFO: This operation is being logged at
/home/oracle/app/oracle/cfgtoollogs/emca/dev1/emca_2009_06_11_15_16_23.log.
Jun 11, 2009 3:17:00 PM oracle.sysman.emcp.EMReposConfig createRepository
INFO: Creating the EM repository (this may take a while) ...
Jun 11, 2009 3:24:54 PM oracle.sysman.emcp.EMReposConfig invoke
INFO: Repository successfully created
...
Jun 11, 2009 3:37:09 PM oracle.sysman.emcp.EMDBPostConfig performConfiguration
INFO: Database Control started successfully
```

```
Jun 11, 2009 3:37:09 PM oracle.sysman.emcp.EMDBPostConfig performConfiguration
INFO: >\>\>\>\>\>\>\> The Database Control URL is
https://horatio.hadba.com:1158/em <<<<<<<<<<

Jun 11, 2009 3:45:27 PM oracle.sysman.emcp.EMDBPostConfig invoke
WARNING:
************************  WARNING  ************************
Management Repository has been placed in secure mode wherein Enterprise Manager
data will be encrypted.  The encryption key has been placed in the file:
/home/oracle/app/oracle/product/11.2.0/dbhome_1/localhost.localdomain_dev1/sysman/
config/emkey.ora.   Please ensure this file is backed up as the encrypted data
will become unusable if this file is lost.
**************************************************************
Enterprise Manager configuration completed successfully
FINISHED EMCA at Jun 11, 2009 3:45:27 PM
```

Configuring Backup Settings in Enterprise Manager

It has taken us a bit of extra time to come to terms with Enterprise Manager, but now we can use our recently configured OEM Grid or Database Control to take database backups. Hopefully, you have navigated yourself to the point where you are excited about OEM's possibilities, and you are ready to begin scheduling your backups so you can get back to the rest of your day. As we get started on this section, bear in mind that we are utilizing EM Database Control, not Grid Control, for this conversation. Thus, we will not be orienting ourselves to a database first—we assume there is only one database available in the console.

First, we need to get our backup settings dialed in. That means a few page clicks in the OEM console. All backup- and recovery-related operations will come from the Availability tab, shown next.

From the Availability tab, the first thing that you need to do is configure backup settings, so click the link called Backup Settings. The Backup Settings page has three tabs, Device, Backup Set, and Policy, which are described in the following sections.

Device Configuration

From the Device tab, shown next, you can set up both disk and tape settings. These settings are not for setting which is the default device, but rather are individual settings for all channels on these devices. For disk backups, you set parallelism, the backup location, and the type of backup (backup set or image copy). This is also where you would turn compression on, if you want to use it. For tape backups, you tell OEM how many tape devices will be employed, and the tape backup type (compressed or noncompressed). In addition, for tapes, you can provide any environment settings that are required for the tape backup software to operate (for more on tape backup settings, see Chapters 4 through 8).

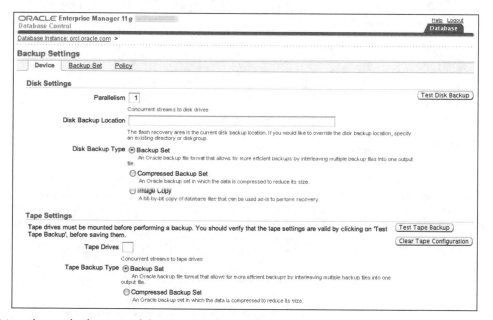

Note that at the bottom of the Device tab is a place (not shown in the screen shot) for host credentials. These are required in order for OEM to submit a job to make the desired changes on the target database. This same requirement appears at the bottom of each tab of the Configure Backup Settings page.

Backup Set Configuration

After making device configuration decisions, click the Backup Set tab, which allows you to make permanent configuration settings for how the backup sets will be generated. Remember, this only applies to those backups that use backup sets instead of image copies (disk backups can be either; tape backups are always backup sets).

If you are using disk backups, you have two things to configure here: the maximum size of your backup pieces, and the compression algorithm. The compression choice is between BZIP2 and ZLIB—with the former optimizing for maximum compression (at the cost of CPU cycles), and the latter optimizing for low CPU utilization (at the cost of less compression). If you will be backing up to tape, you can set up how many copies of each datafile backup set you will create on the tape devices and the number of copies of each archive log backup to create.

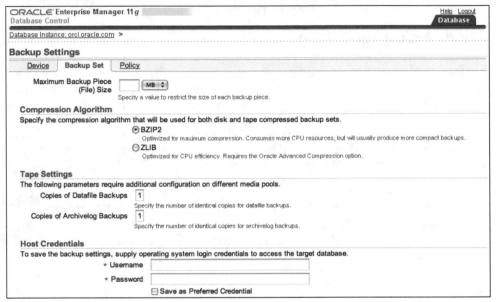

Policy Settings

The Policy tab allows for configuration of those settings that relate to your business backup policy. This includes turning on autobackups of the control file and SPFILE, and specifying where the autobackups will be (if disk backups are used). On the Policy tab, you can turn on backup optimization (see Chapter 3 for details on backup optimization). This is also where you turn on block change tracking (see Chapter 16) and configure tablespace exclusions (see Chapter 3).

You also use the Policy tab to configure your retention policy. OEM provides three options: retain all backups (ack!), set a policy based on a recovery window, or set a policy based on redundancy. If you choose a recovery window or redundancy, you are required to specify how many days or how many copies, respectively. After this, you again provide host credentials and click OK to submit the changes. OEM connects to the target database host and issues the RMAN **configure** commands to make these changes.

What Is Missing from OEM's Backup Configuration?

Not all things that RMAN can configure are configured in OEM. Some changes can be made only from the RMAN command line:

- **Backup encryption**   Encryption is enabled when you schedule a specific backup, not in the overall backup settings. When you go to schedule an Oracle-Suggested or Customized Backup, you can specify the Encryption level.

- **Default device type**   It could be argued that because you schedule backups within OEM to repeat, the default device type is not required. Regardless, you will not find it in the OEM interface.

- **Archive deletion policy**   From RMAN, you can set a specific archive log retention policy that is different from the backup set retention policy. No such option exists in OEM.

- **Snapshot control file location**   RMAN allows you to modify the snapshot control file location, which is handy for RAC configurations. OEM has no way of accomplishing this.

- **Backup throttling**   There is no **rate** command available in any OEM backups, so there is no way to throttle back the RMAN backup speed. This also holds true for the **duration** command that allows you to specify a backup window with the **minimize time** or **minimize load** options.

RMAN Workshop: *Configure Backup Settings in OEM*

Workshop Notes

This workshop assumes that you have the v102 database and want to configure it to back up to a disk location other than the FRA with two channels, that you want **filesperset** to be 2, and that you want a recovery window of seven days.

Step 1.   Set up the disk backup settings. Click the Availability tab and then click the Backup Settings link. The default page that appears is the Device tab. Change Parallelism to **2** and Disk Backup Location to **/u01/backup**. Click the Test Disk Backup button to the right to confirm that the location you have specified exists.

Step 2.   Click the Backup Set tab. Change Maximum Backup Piece (File) Size to **500MB**. Change the Compression Algorithm to ZLIB.

Step 3.   Click the Policy tab. Click the Automatically Backup the Control File and Server Parameter File check box. Set the Autobackup Disk Location to **u01/backup** (the same location as the backups in Step 1).

Step 4. Under the Retention Policy heading, change the policy to the second option, *Retain backups that are necessary for a recovery to any time,* and set the value to **7 days.**

Step 5. Under Host Credentials, set the host server username and password to the user that installed your database software. Then click OK.

Step 6. Confirm that the changes have taken effect for this database. Connect to the host server where this database resides:

```
Export ORACLE_SID=v112
rman target /
RMAN> show all;
using target database control file instead of recovery catalog
RMAN configuration parameters are:
CONFIGURE RETENTION POLICY TO RECOVERY WINDOW OF 7 DAYS;
CONFIGURE CONTROLFILE AUTOBACKUP ON;
...
CONFIGURE CONTROLFILE AUTOBACKUP FORMAT FOR DEVICE TYPE DISK TO
'/u01/backup/%F';
...
CONFIGURE DEVICE TYPE DISK PARALLELISM 2 BACKUP TYPE TO BACKUPSET;
CONFIGURE CHANNEL DEVICE TYPE DISK FORMAT   '/u01/backup/%U'
MAXPIECESIZE 500 M;
...
CONFIGURE CHANNEL DEVICE TYPE 'SBT_TAPE' MAXPIECESIZE 500 M;
...
```

Configuring Recovery Settings

After configuring the backup settings, you will need to configure the database recovery settings. You can access this page from the main Availability tab of the database target by clicking the Recovery Settings link. Configuring the recovery settings actually covers a wide scope of options. On the Recovery Settings page, OEM further divides the recovery settings into three types of recovery: Instance Recovery, Media Recovery, and Flash Recovery, as described in the following sections.

Instance Recovery

Only one setting refers to instance recovery, FAST_START_MTTR_TARGET, as shown next. This is an initialization parameter that determines a target value, in seconds, which you are interested in hitting when instance recovery is initiated on the database. MTTR is an acronym for *mean time to recover* and is a common name for exactly how long it takes for a database to be operational again after it has crashed for some reason.

Recovery Settings   Show SQL   Revert   Apply

Instance Recovery

The fast-start checkpointing feature is enabled by specifying a non-zero desired mean-time to recover (MTTR) value, which will be used to set the FAST_START_MTTR_TARGET initialization parameter. This parameter controls the amount of time the database takes to perform crash recovery for a single instance. When fast-start checkpointing is enabled, Oracle automatically maintains the speed of checkpointing so that the requested MTTR is achieved. Setting the value to 0 will disable this functionality.

Current Estimated Mean Time To Recover (seconds) **7**

Desired Mean Time To Recover 0   Minutes ⬍

Instance recovery is initiated automatically by Oracle when a database is started after a hard crash (or a shutdown abort). Instance recovery uses online redo logs and undo segments to remove any transactions that were uncommitted at the time of the crash and to set the database to a clean, synchronized state for further activity. Instance recovery must complete before the database can be started, so minimizing how long this takes affects how fast your database comes back to life after a crash.

FAST_START_MTTR_TARGET is a combination of a number of changes that are made internally to facilitate the speedy recovery of your instance (also referred to as *automatic checkpoint tuning*). This parameter makes the LOG_CHECKPOINT_TIMEOUT and LOG_CHECKPOINT_INTERVAL parameters obsolete. From OEM, you can specify this value in seconds. The valid range is 0 to 3600 seconds (or 0 to 60 minutes).

Media Recovery

The ARCHIVELOG mode/NOARCHIVELOG mode switch appears in the Media Recovery section of the Recovery Settings page. It's hard to find if no one has told you to look there—you might mistakenly start looking in, say, the Archive Logs link from the Server page of the database target. But here it is, halfway down the Recovery Settings page. It shows up here as a simple check box, but do not think that OEM has fired some magic bullet at the Oracle RDBMS: you still must reboot before this will take effect. In fact, OEM will submit a job to the OS to restart the database and perform the change.

In addition to enabling ARCHIVELOG mode, you can specify your LOG_ARCHIVE_FORMAT and LOG_ARCHIVE_DEST parameters here. By default in 11*g*, the parameter USE_DB_RECOVERY_FILE_DEST, also referred to as the flash recovery area (FRA), is set.

In 11*g*, a new check box (shown next) has been added to Enable Minimal Supplemental Logging. This configures the database for additional logging required for using the LogMiner utility.

Media Recovery

The database is currently in NOARCHIVELOG mode. In ARCHIVELOG mode, hot backups and recovery to the latest time are possible, but you must provide space for archived redo log files. If you change the database to ARCHIVELOG mode, you should perform a backup immediately. In NOARCHIVELOG mode, only cold backups are possible and data may be lost in the event of database corruption.

☑ ARCHIVELOG Mode*

Log Archive Filename Format* %t_%s_%r.dbf

Number	Archived Redo Log Destination	Status	Type
1	USE_DB_RECOVERY_FILE_DEST	VALID	Local

Add Another Row

☑ TIP It is recommended that archived redo log files be written to multiple locations spread across the different disks.
☑ TIP You can specify up to 10 archived redo log destinations.

☐ Enable Minimal Supplemental Logging
Minimal supplemental logging logs the minimal amount of information needed for LogMiner (and any product building on LogMiner technology) to identify, group, and merge the redo operations associated with DML changes.

Flash Recovery

Under the heading Flash Recovery, you can configure your FRA, providing both an FRA destination and size. More useful, and unfortunately buried here in a configuration page, is an excellent pie graph displaying current used space in the FRA, broken down by file type. This is an excellent quick view of the FRA that is hard to find anywhere else. Remember it is here under the Flash Recovery configuration settings; it can save you valuable time down the road.

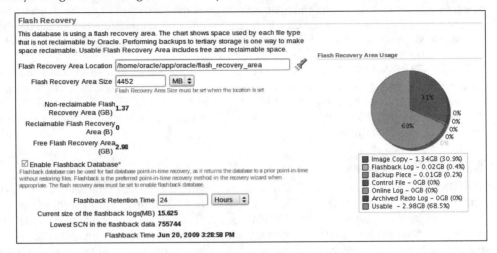

In addition to being where you configure the FRA, the flash recovery area is where you can turn on Flashback Database, functionality introduced in 10*g* that can radically reduce point-in-time recovery by rewinding the database (literally). Flashback Database, and all of the different configuration requirements and resource needs thereof, are discussed in Chapter 15.

As with ARCHIVELOG mode, turning on Flashback Database requires a database reboot; we suggest that you do them both at the same time to save yourself a bit of hassle. Along with turning on Flashback Database, you can set your flashback retention time target, in hours.

Note, finally, the Apply Changes to SPFILE Only check box. Checking this option is the same as changing parameters like this:

```
alter database set db_recovery_file_dest='/u01/fra' scope=spfile;
```

Note, of course, that checking this box will not "save" the ARCHIVELOG mode and Flashback Database changes. Either you restart the database and change them, or you wait and restart the database and change them later.

Why Are My Archive Log and Flash Recovery Options Grayed Out?

If you arrived at the Recovery Settings page only to find the options to turn on ARCHIVELOG mode and to modify the LOG_ARCHIVE_DEST locations grayed out in OEM (disallowing you from making changes to the mode or the flash recovery options), you have logged in as a user that does not have SYSDBA privileges. You must log out of Grid or Database Control, and log back in as user SYS with the role SYSDBA, to make changes on the Recovery Settings page.

RMAN Workshop: *Configure Recovery Settings in OEM*

Workshop Notes

This workshop makes changes that set a second archive destination in addition to the FRA, add more space to the FRA, and enable Flashback Database. This workshop assumes you are already in ARCHIVELOG mode (see Chapter 3 if you are not, or just choose the ARCHIVE Log check box on the Recovery Settings page).

Step 1. Log into OEM as user SYS with role SYSDBA. If you are not logged in as SYS, the options on the Recovery Settings page will be grayed out.

Step 2. Navigate to the Database | Availability | Recovery Settings page.

Step 3. Set a new archive log destination to **/u01/backup**. Click Add Another Row and then specify the location (here, we use /home/oracle/backup).

Step 4. Change the Flash Recovery Area Size to **4GB**.

Step 5. Check the Enable Flashback Database check box. Set the Flashback Retention Time to **24 Hours**.

Step 6. Click the Apply button. This prompts you to restart the database. Click Yes. You then need to provide host and database credentials for the shutdown.

Step 7. After the database is restarted, navigate back to the Recovery Settings page to confirm the changes.

Configuring Recovery Catalogs in OEM

Enterprise Manager cannot actually create a recovery catalog. You still need to manually create the catalog user, grant the user the RECOVERY_CATALOG_OWNER role, and then connect RMAN to this user and issue the command **create catalog**. There is no wizard or anything for these steps in OEM. This can be a bit confusing, as there is an Add Recovery Catalog button on the Recovery Catalog Settings page. However, this button only adds an existing recovery catalog to the Enterprise Manager repository; that is, we make EM aware of the existence of a recovery catalog, so that it can then add this particular database to the specified catalog.

Once the catalog is created, you can inform OEM that you wish to use the recovery catalog. After you have registered the recovery catalog with OEM, you can register targets in the catalog. If you have registered more than one recovery catalog, you can specify that a particular one be put in use during different backup and recovery operations.

RMAN Workshop: *Register the Recovery Catalog with OEM*

Workshop Notes

This workshop creates a catalog in the database emrep manually and then registers it for use in OEM.

Step 1.   Connect to the repository database as user SYS and create the user for the catalog:

```
SQL> create tablespace reco_cat datafile
'/u01/app/oracle/oradata/emrep/reco_cat1.dbf' size 100m;
Tablespace created.
SQL> create user rman identified by rman
  2   default tablespace reco_cat
  3   quota unlimited on reco_cat;
User created.
SQL> grant connect, resource, recovery_catalog_owner to rman;
Grant succeeded.
SQL> connect rman/rman
Connected.
```

Step 2.   Make sure that you have the 11.2 $ORACLE_HOME/bin in your path before this step so that the RMAN executable is 11.2. Otherwise, OEM will not be able to register your catalog!

```
$ echo $PATH
/u01/app/oracle/product/10.2.0/bin
[oracle@dex oracle]$ rman catalog rman/rman@v112
Recovery Manager: Release 11.2.0.0.2 on Wed Dec 21
Copyright (c) 1982, 2009, Oracle.  All rights reserved.
connected to recovery catalog database
RMAN> create catalog;
recovery catalog created
```

Step 3.   Now that the catalog is created, go to OEM | Database | Availability | Recovery Catalog Settings. Select Use Recovery Catalog, and then click the Add Recovery Catalog button. From Grid Control, you can choose an already discovered database or provide the host, the port, the SID, and the RMAN username and password. From Database Control, you cannot choose from a list and must provide the host:port:sid combination. In addition, you need to provide the recovery catalog credentials (the RMAN user created in Step 2).

Database Instance: v112 > Recovery Catalogs >

Cancel   Next

Add Recovery Catalog: Database

Specify the host, port, and SID of a database with an existing recovery catalog along with the recovery catalog username and password. The recovery catalog should be stored in a dedicated database that is on a different disk than the target database. Protect the recovery catalog by backing it up.

* Host	horatio
* Port	1521
* SID	v112
* Recovery Catalog Username	rman2
* Recovery Catalog Password	•••••

Cancel   Next

Step 4. After the Add Recovery Catalog action returns you to Recovery Catalog Settings, you need to provide the Recovery Catalog user and password again, along with host credentials to run the job. When this is complete, you can click OK, and the register database action will complete.

Database Instance: v112 >
Recovery Catalog Settings

ⓘ **Information**
The target database has been registered in the recovery catalog.

The Recovery Manager (RMAN) repository is a collection of metadata about the target database that is used by backup and recovery operations. The information can be stored in the control file or in a recovery catalog - a schema in a separate database that can hold information for one or more databases.

If you select a recovery catalog for which this database is not registered, the database will automatically be registered when you click OK.

○ Use Control File

    Keep RMAN Records (days)   [7]
    Specify how long to keep RMAN records in the control file before they can be reused.

◉ Use Recovery Catalog

    Recovery Catalog [horatio:1521:v112-rman2 ▲▼]   (Add Recovery Catalog)
  * Recovery Catalog Username [rman2]
  * Recovery Catalog Password [•••••]

Host username and password is required if your database is not registered with the selected catalog.
    * Username [oracle]
    * Password [•••••]
    □ Save as Preferred Credential

Related Links for Recovery Catalog Settings

Three "related links" that provide additional functionality are at the bottom of the Recovery Catalog Settings page:

- **Resynchronize Catalog** Manually do a sync operation to bring the database control file and the recovery catalog into a synchronized state.

- **Recovery Catalogs** View and manage all recovery catalogs that EM has been made aware of.

- **Unregister Database** Remove this database from the selected recovery catalog permanently.

Database Backups from Enterprise Manager

Now that you have configured your database for backups from the OEM interface, you can get to the nitty-gritty of actually taking a backup. From the OEM Console, after you have selected your database and clicked the Availability tab, click the Schedule Backup link. On the Schedule Backup page, you are given two options: the Oracle-Suggested Backup or Schedule a Customized Backup.

Oracle-Suggested Backup Strategy

Starting with Oracle Database 10*g*, Oracle has put together a full backup strategy that is "ready to wear" straight from the rack. This is available only via OEM (in both Grid Control and Database Control) and requires the existence of the FRA. The Oracle-suggested strategy checks the backup and recovery settings you've configured for your database and draws conclusions about whether you want a disk-only backup, a tape-only backup, or a combined disk and tape backup.

Disk-Only Oracle-Suggested Backup Strategy

The disk-only backup strategy is the most straightforward. It uses the "incremental apply to database copy" functionality to create a backup strategy that is self-cleaning. Here's an example of how it works. In this example, we start the Oracle-suggested strategy on a Monday evening at 10 P.M. The database is running in ARCHIVELOG mode, has automatic control file and SPFILE backups enabled, and uses the FRA.

- **Monday night**   A full image copy of every datafile is taken for the database. This backup is stored in the FRA.

- **Tuesday night**   A level 1 incremental backup set is created. All blocks that have changed since Monday night at 10 P.M. are backed up.

- **Wednesday night**   First, RMAN applies the Tuesday night incremental backup to the Monday night image copy, which makes the full image copy backup a current copy of the database as it looked Tuesday night at 10 P.M. After that is complete, RMAN takes a new level 1 backup.

- **Thursday night**   RMAN applies the Wednesday night incremental backup to the image copy, which makes our database backup current as of Wednesday night at 10 P.M. Then, a new incremental level 1 backup is taken, with all changes since Wednesday night.

- **Friday night**   RMAN does the exact same thing it did on Thursday night. On Saturday, it does the same thing. Same with Sunday. This action repeats every day until you tell it to stop.

Notice a few things about this backup strategy. First, a full database backup is taken only once. After that, RMAN takes only level 1 incremental backups. Then, nightly, the previous night's incremental backup is applied. This strategy ensures that the database backup is at least 24 hours behind the current point in time. This allows for a point-in-time recovery to any point in the previous 24 hours, but nothing earlier than that. At most, the database backup is 48 hours behind the current time, so recovery is never that far behind.

There are limitations to this strategy, but that's one of the drawbacks to a "one-size-fits-all" approach to backups.

Tape-Only Oracle-Suggested Backup Strategy

The tape-only suggested strategy differs in many ways from the disk-only suggested strategy. First, no backup will ever be created in the FRA. Sure, archive logs will accumulate there, but all backups will go directly to the tape device. In addition, the tape-only strategy cannot take advantage of the incremental apply feature. Remember, an image copy backup cannot be taken to tape. All backups to tape will be of the backup set type.

When you schedule an Oracle-suggested tape-only backup, two RMAN scripts are generated: a daily backup and a weekly backup. First, the weekly script is run. This creates a full database backup, including all archive logs. Then, the daily script is run. The daily backup does an incremental backup of only changed blocks, along with all archive logs not already backed up. Then, once a week, the full database backup runs again.

During the tape-only backup wizard, if you have not specified a retention policy, OEM asks you to specify one. Then, as part of the daily backup, your retention policy is enforced on the tape channel.

After generating a tape-only suggested strategy, you will find that the scripts might look something like this:

```
Daily Script:
run {
allocate channel oem_sbt_backup1 type 'SBT_TAPE' format '%U' parms
'nb_ora_server=(horatio.hadba.com)';
allocate channel oem_sbt_backup2 type 'SBT_TAPE' format '%U' parms
'nb_ora_server=(horatio.hadba.com)';
backup incremental level 1 cumulative database;
backup archivelog all not backed up;
}
allocate channel for maintenance device type 'SBT_TAPE' parms
'nb_ora_server=(horatio.hadba.com)';
delete noprompt obsolete recovery window of 7 days device type 'SBT_TAPE';

Weekly Script:
run {allocate channel oem_sbt_backup1 type 'SBT_TAPE' format '%U' parms
'nb_ora_server=(horatio.hadba.com)';
allocate channel oem_sbt_backup2 type 'SBT_TAPE' format '%U' parms
'nb_ora_server=(horatio.hadba.com)';
backup incremental level 0 database;
backup archivelog all not backed up;
```

Combined Disk and Tape Oracle-Suggested Backup Strategy

When you combine disk backups with tape backups, the hybrid solution demands more input from you than either of the previous Oracle-suggested strategies. And, for the first time, you must make a configuration decision.

First, consider the disk part of the strategy. Backups to disk are identical in the combined disk and tape strategy and in the disk-only strategy: a full image copy in the FRA, and then incremental backups each night that are then applied to the image copy.

As far as the tape part of the strategy, you must decide how much you want backed up to tape on a daily basis. On a weekly basis, the suggested strategy backs up all recovery-related files (with the **backup recovery files** command in RMAN). But, you must choose how much to back up daily: nothing, archive logs only, archive logs and incrementals, or archive logs and the full database copy.

If you decide to back up archive logs and incrementals to tape daily, this would be the resulting daily and weekly script that OEM builds:

```
Daily Script:
run {
allocate channel oem_disk_backup device type disk;
recover copy of database with tag 'ORA$OEM_LEVEL_0';
backup incremental level 1 cumulative
copies=1 for recover of copy with tag
'ORA$OEM_LEVEL_0' database;
release channel oem_disk_backup;
allocate channel oem_sbt_backup1 type 'SBT_TAPE' format '%U' parms
```

```
'nb_ora_server=(horatio.hadba.com)';
backup archivelog all not backed up;
backup backupset all not backed up since time 'SYSDATE-1';
}
allocate channel for maintenance device type 'SBT_TAPE' parms
 'nb_ora_server=(horatio.hadba.com)';
delete noprompt obsolete recovery window of 7 days device type
'SBT_TAPE';

Weekly Script:
run {
allocate channel oem_disk_backup device type disk;
recover copy of database with tag 'ORA$OEM_LEVEL_0';
backup incremental level 1 cumulative  copies=1 for recover of copy with tag
 'ORA$OEM_LEVEL_0' database;
release channel oem_disk_backup;
allocate channel oem_sbt_backup1 type 'SBT_TAPE' format '%U' parms
'nb_ora_server=(horatio.hadba.com)';
backup recovery area;
}
allocate channel for maintenance device type 'SBT_TAPE' parms
'nb_ora_server=(horatio.hadba.com)';
delete noprompt obsolete recovery window of 7 days device type 'SBT_TAPE';
```

Final Note on Oracle-Suggested Strategies

Taking a default backup strategy "off the shelf" has its benefits and its drawbacks. The benefits come from being able to "set and forget" the backups—they will run forever and clean themselves up. There is some assurance in having this option, particularly for low-priority development databases that typically are operated by someone other than you. If they come to you in a panic, you can always use these backups to fix the problem and save everyone a lot of headaches.

But there is (almost) no customization, and sometimes the default strategy will not match your SLA. The most glaring example of this is in the ability to do point-in-time recoveries to some point in the past (a limitation of the disk-based strategy only). Remember, these strategies are merely Oracle suggestions. You don't have to use them, and if they are giving you any heartburn, there is a simple answer: drop the suggested strategy and build your own.

Scheduling a Customized Backup

From the same Availability page where you can choose to schedule an Oracle-suggested backup strategy, you can also choose to build your own customized backup job. This is a wizard-driven process that steps you through the different choices to be made about the backup. When the wizard is finished, you can run the backup as a one-time backup immediately, schedule it for later, or set it up to repeat continually on a schedule.

It is important that you take the time to develop a full backup strategy ahead of time, but OEM will provide some guidance about how to develop that strategy. These tips appear as small-font hints under some of the choices you will be asked to make in the Backup Scheduling Wizard.

The Backup Scheduling Wizard is divided into four steps:

1. Choose backup options (what do you want to back up?).
2. Choose backup settings (how do you want to back up?).
3. Schedule the backup (when do you want to back up?).
4. Perform a final review (is everything to your liking?).

On the final review page, you will be presented with the RMAN script that the wizard has created, as shown in the following example. At this stage, you can either submit the job for execution or edit the RMAN script from there. This allows you to make any minor tweaks in the script. Note that if you decide to modify the script manually, OEM warns you that you will not be able to go back and make any changes in the backup wizard pages. After you make any of your own changes, you can either cancel them or submit the job.

RMAN Script Job vs. Scheduled Backup Wizard

There is another way to use OEM to schedule and run RMAN backups of a target database. If you go to the Jobs tab in Grid Control (or the Jobs link under Related Links in Database Control) and look at the drop-down list of possible job types to create, you will see RMAN Script. This is a specific type of job specification that allows you to use OEM to execute an RMAN script that already exists at the target server.

So what is the difference between an RMAN script job and a host command job? Both require a script to exist prior to scheduling the job. But if you choose an RMAN script job, OEM uses its built-in mechanisms to ensure that the environment is properly configured for your target database before running the script. This is a very nice feature, which you know if you have ever run into the dreaded "compatibility matrix" of RMAN executables versus target databases.

Why Does OEM Always Try to Allocate a Tape Channel for Maintenance?

You may notice that when you review your RMAN script after using the OEM wizard to schedule a backup, OEM has the following lines:

```
allocate channel for maintenance type 'SBT_TAPE';
delete noprompt obsolete device type disk;
```

What gives? OEM has this little quirk. If you have, at any point, gone into the Configure Backup Settings page and set the number of tape drives to some value, then OEM has gone to your target database and configured a tape channel in the permanent configuration parameters. Thus, it assumes that any maintenance operation should always check tape and disk. From within OEM, there is no way to change this. You have to go to the RMAN command line and enter the following:

```
configure channel device type 'sbt_tape' clear;
```

RMAN Workshop: *Create an RMAN Script Job in OEM*

Workshop Notes

This workshop uses OEM to schedule an RMAN backup. However, the backup will be specified by an RMAN script that already exists as a file on the Linux machine where database v112 exists. In this example, this script, named rmanback.rcv, already exists in /home/oracle/scripts and contains the following code:

```
backup incremental level 1 cumulative device type disk
 filesperset = 2 database;
backup device type disk filesperset = 2 archivelog all not backed up
 delete all input;
delete noprompt obsolete device type disk;
```

Step 1.   Go to the Jobs page of OEM. In Grid Control, there is a Jobs tab along the upper-right side. In Database Control, go to the bottom under Related Links to find the Jobs link.

Step 2.   Create a new job of type RMAN Script by using the drop-down list (that defaults to OS Command) to specify RMAN Script and then clicking Go. This will take you to a page with multiple tabs.

Step 3.   On the General tab, give the job the name **RMAN_BACK_INC_1_ARCH_DELETE_OBS**, as shown next. On this tab, you also need to add the target you want to back up. Click the Add button and select your desired database.

Step 4. Click the Parameters tab. In the text box, provide the full path and name to the backup script you created on the target server.

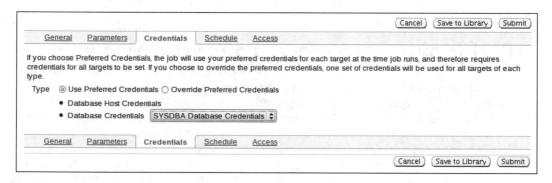

Step 5. On the Credentials tab, ensure that you have selected SYSDBA Database Credentials, as this is required by RMAN.

Step 6. On the Schedule tab, set a schedule for the job. Your choice is One Time (Immediately), One Time (Later), or Repeating. New in 11*g*, you can also specify a Grace Period for the backup job: by specifying Indefinite, you are telling EM to let the job run until it signals that it is finished.

By choosing End After, you are indicating to EM that you want the job killed if it hasn't completed in the specified time.

Step 7. Click the Submit button at the top of the page to send the job to the active jobs page. This submits the job as a one-time event. You can, alternatively, save the job to the library without submitting it immediately, or both submit the job now and save it to the library.

Performing Recovery in Enterprise Manager

After seeing all the backing up that can be done from OEM, it should come as no surprise that you can also perform recovery from OEM. That being said, there are not many situations where we've seen OEM's recovery options being used—even when OEM is used for backups. The decision to use OEM for recovery boils down to your ability to mitigate the overwhelming sensation typically felt when you realize your database is hosed: panic.

OEM does not help you manage your panic very well. You'd think that a GUI would be the best defense against panic—easy to use, quickly implemented, and all that. But this is actually quite the opposite of all DBAs' reactions we've seen in a recovery situation. During the most solemn and distressing recovery situations we've been a part of, the one overwhelming DBA desire that we've noticed is not ease of use, built-in intelligence, or anything like that. What every DBA wants at that time is control. They want complete, total control over everything that they can possibly get control over. Database recovery is no time to be hitting the big red button and hoping for the best.

The Recovery Wizard in OEM is primarily useful in all those databases you deployed in development for people who assured you that they would take care of it themselves. In other words, OEM Recovery is for databases that have Oracle-suggested backup strategies.

There is one notable exception: if you have made yourself aware of how OEM Recovery works, you have noticed that it has the capabilities to lead you to the Oracle Flashback Technology, outlined in Chapter 15. Flashback Technology provides a whole new arsenal against downtime, particularly when it comes to user-induced trauma. So, if it is control you seek, understand that you are not in complete control of your recovery situation until you have explored your Flashback Technology options.

While the Recovery Wizard may not help you manage panic after an unknown failure, there is a new feature in 11gR2 that will help you know about failures proactively, thereby saving you from the panic altogether. This new utility is built into each 11.2 database, and it is collectively referred to as the Data Recovery Advisor.

Data Recovery Advisor and the OEM Checkers

The Data Recovery Advisor (DRA) is an advisory function built into the core RDBMS of the database. It utilizes the same Diagnostic Repository that has been established in 11g for consolidating all diagnostic and fault information, so that remediation can occur more programmatically (for more on the Automatic Diagnostic Repository, see the discussion in Chapter 3). The DRA mines the data in the diagnostic repository to determine if there is a recovery action that the DBA should take in order to rectify the database and keep it available.

To be able to provide intelligence on recovery situations, the DRA must have access to additional data in the diagnostic repository. Some of that information, such as the known state of datafiles, will end up in the repository no matter what, and if RMAN has discovered any corrupt blocks during its last backup. However, some of it will get there only if you run one of the newly integrated health checkers against the database. These checkers perform diagnostic data gathering operations on different aspects of the database and then store that data in the Diagnostic Repository for action by different actors (such as the DRA).

The health checkers and the DRA are native components of the RDBMS in 11.2, so you don't need Enterprise Manager to utilize the functionality. There is a fuller discussion on the command-line DRA in Chapter 3. Here, we are going to focus on the EM interface for the tools. This is one of those places where the GUI interface really earns its keep—in scheduling health check operations and in giving you a one-stop location to rectify any outages.

The Checkers in EM

There are seven checkers available in 11.2. Each of these performs actions against different database objects, or with different architectural needs. Each of these is described next. What they all have in common is that you get to them in EM from the main database home page, by scrolling down to Related Links and clicking Advisor Central. Advisor Central offers two pages—

Advisors and Checkers. Advisors is the default view; you will need to click the Checkers tab to see the health check utilities.

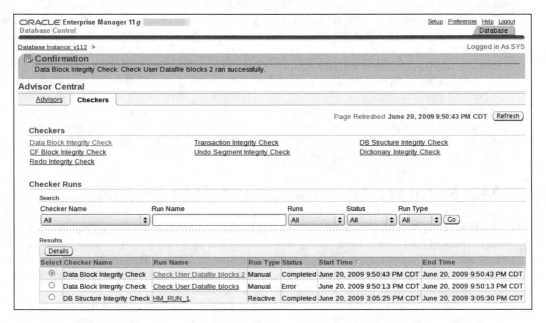

From the Checkers page, you can see the most recent runs of the checkers and the results. By clicking on the Run Name, you can move to the Findings page to see if any alerts have been raised that require action. Each of the checkers may require unique inputs to run, but they all require at least two items in common: you must name the run you are asking to start (and it must be unique), and you must provide a time-out after which EM aborts the checker if it has not completed.

- **Data Block Integrity Check**   Checks a single block for corruption. You need to know the suspected file and block number (such as reported by an ORA-1578 error) to run this checker.

- **CF Block Integrity Check**   This is the Control File checker. Again, the expectation in the tool is that you know the suspected back block number that requires an integrity check.

- **Redo Integrity Check**   This checks for online or archive redo corruption and accessibility. You specify the SCN that you want to start moving forward from, and EM performs the check from there.

- **Transaction Integrity Check**   This is the same as the Undo Segment Integrity Check, in that it checks for logical undo corruptions, except that it does so for a single transaction. The required input is the transaction ID.

- **Undo Segment Integrity Check**   This checks for logical undo corruptions for an entire Undo segment. The Undo segment number is the required input.

- **DB Structure Integrity Check**   This checker provides a proactive mechanism for checking all database files for accessibility, header corruption, and SCN synchronicity across the files and the control file. There is no input required.

- **Dictionary Integrity Check**   This examines core data dictionary items to ensure consistency and integrity. You must provide the name of the data dictionary table you are checking, and the check mask.

Data Recovery Advisor

As with the health check utilities, you get to the Data Recovery Advisor through the Advisor Central link from Related Links on the database home page. If there are no current recovery-related findings in the database, the DRA will simply have a search field to search previous cataloged failures. If a new failure exists that hasn't been rectified yet, you will see the option to *Select failures and...* take an action.

If you click the Advise button, EM will take a few moments to examine the information and then will provide advice on what to do about the particular failure at hand. If there is an action it can take automatically, it will ask permission and then do so. Otherwise, it will recommend a manual action to take, as shown next.

The recovery action that is advised will be technically accurate, but what you cannot ensure is that it will be the absolute best path. As we stated, you are not in 100 percent control, because Oracle cannot know all the details. For instance, in the example being worked in the illustrations, a file has been renamed. Before we fire up a restore operation for a file, it would probably behoove us to do some manual investigation on the server and see if we can rectify the problem in a more straightforward fashion. Otherwise, we are going to go with the recommended action, restore the file and then recover it, shown next.

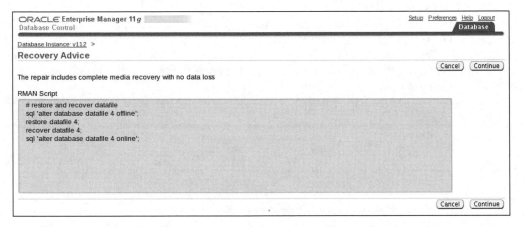

Finally, after showing the possible action, the Data Recovery Advisor is prepared to submit a recovery job to act on the recommendation it has made to you. You get a chance to see, shown next, the possible impacts (at least the ones programmatically feasible and safe to tell you), the RMAN script that will be run, and then to click the Submit Recovery Job button and let the actions go forward. After this, you will be tracking this like any other job in EM, and can go to the Jobs page to see how things are progressing.

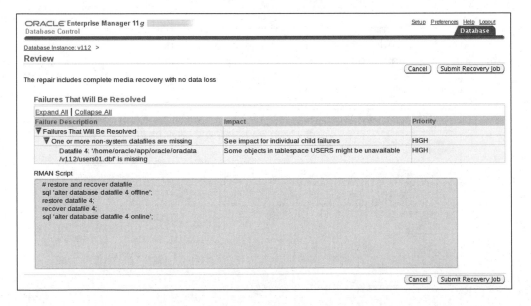

The Perform Recovery Page and Data Recovery Advisor

If the Data Recovery Advisor has detected a failure, when you click the Perform Recovery page, you will see a section entitled "Oracle Advised Recovery." This will briefly describe the failures detected and will provide an Advise and Recover button. This will take you to the ADR page and guide you through the wizard outlined in the preceding DRA conversation. If DRA has not currently detected failures, the Advise and Recover button will be grayed out.

User Directed Recovery

If you are not taking the advice of the RDBMS on how exactly to perform database recovery, Enterprise Manager still provides the mechanisms by which you can select different types of recovery and perform them using a guided set of steps. From the Perform Recovery link on the Availability page, you first see the Oracle Advised Recovery (discussed earlier), then the section on User Directed Recovery.

Whole Database Recovery

The first type of recovery is Whole Database Recovery. When you select Whole Database Recovery, you have several options: Recover to the Current Time or Previous Point-in-Time; Restore All Datafiles; and Recover from Previously Restored Datafiles.

Recover to Current or Previous Point in Time   The first option is the one that will do what you would expect: restore datafiles and recover them using archive logs. The only variable that you decide is the time at which you want the database to be opened. In fact, if you walk through this wizard, you will find that the generated RMAN script is as follows (click the Edit RMAN Script button to see the output):

```
run {
restore database;
recover database;
}
```

Not exactly rocket science.

The other option is to perform point-in-time-recovery (PITR). You can specify the point in time that you want to recover to as a point in time, but also as a log sequence number, an SCN, or as a restore point. Note that when you do a PITR and you have Flashback Database turned on, you see a blue-font TIP telling you to consider Flashback Database (which you can choose from the next screen). When you specify your time (or SCN or log), OEM evaluates whether this point falls within the timeframe that is available for Flashback Database and offers you the choice: Flashback or Traditional PITR? Choosing Flashback takes you to the Flashback Wizard; choosing Traditional PITR carries you through the present wizard. For more on Flashback Database, see Chapter 15.

Whenever you do any kind of file restore in OEM, you are always allowed to change the location of the restored files to a new location. From the OEM wizard, for a full database recovery, the options are limited to a single new location for all datafiles. You cannot pick and choose different file locations for individual files. However, when you get to the end of the wizard, you can always choose to Edit RMAN Script and make filename changes there.

Restore All Datafiles   From the main Perform Recovery page, the second option is Restore All Datafiles. Choosing this option initiates a datafile restore that does not also perform a recovery. As you may have guessed, following this through to the end of the wizard and selecting Edit RMAN Script yields:

```
run {
restore database;
}
```

If you choose to rename the datafiles upon restore, you are asked for the single location for all files and are given a check box option to Update the Control File to Use the Renamed Files. Selecting this check box will modify your current control file to point to the datafiles at the new location. This is the same as executing the RMAN command **switch datafile all**. Do this only if you are actually restoring the database, and not just making another set of datafiles in a second location. You can check your script at the end if you want to modify individual filenames.

If you choose to restore datafiles to a new location without recovery, OEM still shuts down the target database and then puts it into mount mode. This actually is not required by RMAN, but OEM's intelligence only goes so far, and it sees a database restore as the first step to recovery. Anyway, OEM leaves the database mounted after the file restore. You have to go to the database home page and click Startup to start the database.

A final note about the option Restore All Datafiles. OEM has buried the **backup validate** command at the bottom of the first page of this wizard, under Backup Validation. If you want to simply validate whether a certain type of restore is possible (current point in time or previous point in time), select this option and then follow the wizard as you otherwise would. Note, then, that if you select Edit RMAN Script, it has a slight difference:

```
run {
restore database validate;
}
```

Recovery from Previously Restored Datafiles   Finally, you can choose to recover the database from previously restored datafiles. This simply means that if you choose this option, only a **recover** command will be issued in RMAN. This does *not* mean that if you choose to restore datafiles to a different location, you can then specify those files in this wizard. This is a recovery only. It relies completely on the control file's V$DATAFILE list to determine which files to restore.

A check box at the bottom lets OEM open the database in READ ONLY mode after the recovery so that you can validate the database. This option allows you to confirm that the point in time you specified was correct.

RMAN Workshop: *Perform Database Recovery from OEM*

Workshop Notes
In this workshop, we perform a PITR to a point in the past, using the backups taken previously in this chapter with OEM.

Step 1.   Go to the Database | Availability | Perform Recovery page. Choose Recover to the Current Time or a Previous Point-in-Time, and then click the Perform Whole Database Recovery button. You will be asked to confirm that EM will bring the database down and then into a mount state for the action.

Step 2. Select the Recover to a Prior Point-in-Time option. We choose to set this with a date in this example. Click Next.

Step 3. If you have turned on Flashback Database and your point in time falls within the Flashback window, you get a screen asking if you would like to use Flashback Database. Choose No, Use Traditional Point-in-Time Recovery. Click Next.

Step 4. Choose to restore the files to the default location. Click Next. This takes you to the Schedule page, but all recovery jobs run immediately. Click Next.

Step 5. Click the Edit RMAN Script button to look at what RMAN will be running. Click Cancel after your review. Then click Submit Job.

Step 6. OEM presents a screen saying, "The job has been successfully submitted." Click the View Job button. The job page shows the history of each job step, known as an *execution*. You can refresh your browser to get up-to-date step and elapsed time values.

Step 7. Click the Step: Recovery link in the Name column. This allows you to monitor the progress of the RMAN job.

Recovery Scope Less Than the Entire Database

On the Perform Recovery page, under User Directed Recovery, you can change the scope of recovery from Whole Database to a smaller subset of recoverable items in the database. This is anything that is not the whole database. Tablespaces, datafiles, archive logs, tables, and transactions—for anything below the entire database in granularity, you perform recovery from this section.

From here, then, you can recover both logical objects and physical objects. Some logical objects, such as tablespaces, still require a physical media restore/recovery operation. Selecting other logical objects, such as tables, actually takes you into the Oracle Flashback Technology world, which is completely different from media recovery. Physical objects are straightforward: want to recover a single datafile? That would be a restore and recover. You also can perform block media recovery from this location. Note that when you make a selection from the drop-down list, the web page refreshes and displays suboptions related to your choice.

Oracle has done a good job of providing for a complete set of recovery options within OEM, so it would be impossible in this single chapter to review the wizard steps that you walk through based on each type of object level recovery. This chapter would be as long as the rest of this book. We encourage you to go through each of the different types of OEM recovery, to familiarize yourself with the language Oracle uses within OEM for each type of recovery. Often, this language is not the same as that used within RMAN itself.

Backup Management and Reporting

It is perhaps in the area of managing your backups that OEM really proves its worth. Running backups and recoveries from the command line is one thing; reading the output of report and list commands from a terminal is something else completely. From OEM, managing existing backups is considerably more user friendly. The management is divided into three types: managing current backups, managing restore points, and creating backup reports.

Managing Current Backups

On the database Availability tab, click the Manage Current Backups link to access the page where you can perform common management activities: run crosschecks, delete obsolete backups, delete expired backups, and so forth.

Across the top of the Manage Current Backups page, you will see some quick link buttons for common tasks: Catalog Additional Files, Crosscheck All, Delete All Obsolete, and Delete All Expired. These buttons do exactly what they say they do, and you can read about these options in Chapter 14.

The two tabs below these buttons, Backup Sets and Image Copies, enable you to manage backups in subsets or individually. The Search area allows you to find a backup based on certain search vectors. The default is to list all backups. In the Results area, you can select one or more backups by clicking the corresponding check box, and then select one of the management options: Crosscheck, Change to Unavailable, Delete, or Validate.

When you choose one of these options, the Job Creation Wizard helps you to schedule the maintenance job. This allows you to schedule a particular job, such as a crosscheck, to occur at a regular interval. You can also click Show RMAN Script to see what RMAN is doing.

Managing Restore Points

Click Manage Restore Points on the Maintenance tab to open the page on which you can create new restore points, view existing restore point information, or delete existing restore points. From OEM, you can look at the restore point creation time, the amount of storage required, and the creation SCN. If you notice that Guaranteed Restore Point is grayed out, this is because you are logged into the target database with NORMAL privileges, and SYSDBA privileges are required for creation of guaranteed restore points. In addition, the Recover Whole Database To button is functional only if you are logged in as SYSDBA user. Clicking this button asks you for confirmation, and then takes you to the Perform Whole Database Recovery page.

Creating Backup Reports

Clicking the Backup Reports link on the Maintenance tab takes you to the Backup Reports page, which shows all backup jobs known to the database. These are not just those backups taken by an OEM job—OEM is actually querying the recovery catalog (or control file) to find all backups. The Backup Reports page enables you to search based on status, start time, and type.

You can click the name of the backup to retrieve specific details about that particular backup, as shown next. This includes a nice summary of the input (what was backed up) and the output (the backup pieces that were created). Then, there is a detailed listing of each input file, its checkpoint information, compression ratio, and so forth. There is enough data here to put anyone to sleep. But this is valuable stuff, and it's far easier to read and comprehend than the report and list options from the RMAN command line.

Database Cloning from Enterprise Manager

OEM has a subsystem in place to perform database cloning. The database cloning process that OEM uses employs RMAN functionality, but do not confuse the database cloning with the RMAN **duplicate** command (covered in Chapter 19). OEM cloning has its own logic and its own restrictions that differentiate it from RMAN duplication. As opposed to OEM in 10g, in the 11.2 model, the database cloning is far more similar to RMAN than before.

OEM may use RMAN behind the curtain, but the database cloning functionality is logically organized in a completely different area of the vast OEM landscape. You need to navigate to the Data Movement tab from the main EM pages, and then look under Move Database Files for the link Clone Database. Cloning to a different server than the target database is only possible in Grid Control. Database Control can clone only to the same server as the target.

The first decision to be made reflects the newer flexibility of cloning from EM: you can choose to take a new RMAN backup for cloning, use a staging area (10g-type cloning), or use an existing RMAN backup. This last option, the most straightforward and logical, was not available on 10g, so let us be the first to rejoice and use it as the working example in this book.

After choosing to use an existing RMAN backup, you need to provide the source host credentials and click Continue. Then, because you've registered the source database with a known recovery catalog, you don't need to enter any further source database specifications. Just specify the point in time to which you want to clone.

After ironing out the source database information, you need to sort out how things will look at the destination: the Destination Oracle Home, Destination Host Credentials, the Destination Database specifics, and the degree of parallelism (number of RMAN channels to use—this is not shown in the illustration below). If you are using Database Control, you can change the Oracle Home but not the host. You can change the database name, but it will default to a different name from the existing source database. This is also where you can change the storage type for the new database from File System to ASM, or vice versa.

On the third step of the wizard, you specify destination database elements that are internal to its operation, such as the Memory Confirmation. You can make Listener changes, and run any Post Cloning scripts that are particular to your environment. On the next page, you can specify file locations, FRA specifications, archive log destinations, and where to put diagnostic and audit files (where to put the ADR). After this, you schedule the job, review the specifications, and then execute.

After the cloning is finished, you will have a clone database on your destination server, open and available, and OEM will have discovered it, meaning that you can now manage it from within OEM—If you are using Grid Control. If you are using Database Control, you will need to utilize **emca** to drop and re-create the EM repository in the new clone. This is not automated in the cloning process.

Summary

In this chapter, we discussed the architecture and configuration of Oracle Enterprise Manager 11*g* Grid Control and Oracle Enterprise Manager 11*g* Database Control. We provided examples of configuring these utilities to take RMAN backups and of configuring a database for recovery in OEM. We discussed the Oracle-suggested backup strategy and showed how to schedule a customized backup. We touched on how to perform recovery. Finally, we showed how OEM can be used to clone a database using RMAN as the underlying technology.

CHAPTER
14

RMAN Advanced
Recovery Topics

his chapter introduces you to some advanced recovery topics. We start with a topic that tends to cause the most trouble and confusion when it comes to recovery topics, incomplete recoveries. Next, we look at some miscellaneous recovery topics. We will then look at tablespace point-in-time recovery, followed by a look at how you can verify your backups. Finally, we will look at the DBMS_BACKUP_RESTORE package that is associated with RMAN.

Incomplete Recoveries

An incomplete recovery is just what it sounds like—a recovery of the database that is incomplete. It is similar to a complete recovery in many respects; the basic command set is the same, but with a few added wrinkles. The possible causes of an incomplete recovery are numerous, such as the loss of online or archived redo logs or a major user error that has seriously compromised the database. Incomplete recoveries impact the entire database; in other words, you cannot perform an incomplete recovery on just one part of the database, because it would result in that part of the database having a different System Change Number (SCN, or point in time if you prefer) than the remainder of the database.

Many junior DBAs fail to recognize the important impact incomplete recovery has on the entire database. Oracle demands that a database be consistent at startup, and if it is not consistent, Oracle will complain bitterly. To illustrate the point, consider an example in which a user who has his own tablespace has just mistakenly truncated a table in that tablespace, for which he has no backup. He calls a junior DBA in a panic and asks her to recover just that tablespace to the point in time before he issued the truncate operation.

At first thought, the junior DBA might think that she can just restore the datafiles of the offending tablespace and recover them to a time before the truncate operation was executed. Seems somewhat logical, doesn't it? (In fact, that's what a logical backup is for.) So, the junior DBA restores the datafiles and recovers the tablespace to a point in time before the truncate operation. Now, she's feeling pretty good about herself. Unfortunately, her euphoria is short lived, because when she tries to open the database, RMAN slaps her with this message:

```
ERROR at line 1:
ORA-01113: file 3 needs media recovery
ORA-01110: data file 3: 'D:\ORACLE\ORADATA\RECOVER\INDX01.DBF'
```

Oracle is basically saying (in this case), "You recovered the datafile all right, but you didn't do enough recovery on it, and it's not consistent with the rest of the database!" So, as you can see, incomplete recovery is not the solution to all of your woes, but it can be the solution to some of them. If you need a form of inconsistent recovery (a fancy way of saying you need to restore some database data to a point in time different from the rest of the database), then look at tablespace point-in-time recovery, discussed later in this chapter, or Oracle's Flashback Technology, discussed in Chapter 16.

However, if you want to restore the entire database to some point in time in the past that Flashback Database can't touch, then incomplete recovery is the way you need to go. When you perform a database incomplete recovery, you need to use the **resetlogs** command, because it is common to just about every incomplete recovery situation there is. We discuss **resetlogs** next, and then we discuss actual incomplete recovery methods, including time-, SCN-, log sequence–, and cancel-based recoveries.

Using the resetlogs Command

During incomplete recoveries, you pretty much always need to use the **resetlogs** command when opening the database, because you are deviating from an already established stream of redo, and you need to indicate this to Oracle. The **resetlogs** command really represents the end of one logical life of your database and the beginning of the next logical life of your database. This logical lifespan of a database is known as an *incarnation*. Each time you use **resetlogs**, you are creating a new incarnation of the database. This can be critical with regard to recovery, as we will discuss later in this section.

With each use of the **resetlogs** command, the SCN counter is not reset. However, Oracle does reset other counters, such as the log sequence number, and resets (and re-creates if required) the contents of the online redo logs.

Starting with Oracle Database 10*g*, Oracle has made recovery through the **resetlogs** command much easier. A new substitution string has been added for the archived redo log names (**%r**), which represents the *resetlog ID number*. When **%r** is included in the **log_archive_dest_format** parameter string, the archived redo log names will remain unique through each **resetlogs** command. This, and other internal Oracle database changes, allows Oracle to easily recover a database through a given **resetlogs** operation. Therefore, the requirement to back up the database immediately after a **resetlogs** operation is relaxed. However, we still think that backing up your database after any incomplete recovery is probably a good idea.

NOTE
*In previous versions of RMAN, you needed to re-create any temporary tablespace temp files. This is not required in Oracle Database 10*g* and later versions. RMAN creates these datafiles for you during the recover database process, even during incomplete recoveries!*

Establishing a Point to Recover To

One of the things you need to do when performing incomplete recovery with RMAN is to establish a recovery target. The recovery target is the point at which you wish to terminate the recovery process and can be identified based on a point in time, a specific SCN, or a log sequence number. The recovery target can be established in a number of different ways. First, you can use the **set** command along with the **until time**, **until SCN**, or **until sequence** parameter within a **run** block, as shown in this example, which uses the **set until time** command to establish the recovery target as 3 P.M. on July 1, 2006:

```
run
{
set until time "to_date('07/01/06 15:00:00','mm/dd/yy hh24:mi:ss')";
restore database;
recover database
alter database open resetlogs;
}
```

When this command is issued, RMAN looks for the backup set closest to, but not including or after, this period and restores the database from that backup set. If the database is in NOARCHIVELOG mode, then recovery will stop at that point; otherwise, during the execution of the **recover** command, Oracle will apply the archived redo logs (and any incremental backups that need to be applied) up to, but not including, the defined recovery target.

NOTE
*If you are trying to recover to the point of completion of a specific backup, you must recover to the CKP SCN or CKP TIME of the files in the backup set as listed in the RMAN **list** command for the different backup sets (for example, **list backupset**). Using the CKP TIME of the backup is not sufficient and can lead to ORA-1152 errors.*

You can also opt to use the **until time**, **until SCN**, or **until sequence** commands directly in the **restore** and **recover** commands, which eliminates the need for the **run** block entirely (which we prefer). Here is an example of the use of the **until time** command when restoring and recovering a database:

```
-- We assume that your control file is intact
startup mount;
restore database UNTIL TIME
"TO_DATE('06/28/06 13:00:00','MM/DD/YY HH24:MI:SS')";
recover database UNTIL TIME
"TO_DATE('06/28/06 13:00:00','MM/DD/YY HH24:MI:SS')";
alter database open resetlogs;
```

Time-Based Recovery

In the previous section, we provided some examples of time-based recovery. This type of recovery allows you to recover the database as it looked consistently at a specific time. Of course, if you don't have backups or archived redo logs available to restore the database to the time you are requesting, then Oracle will generate an error somewhat like this one:

```
RMAN-00571: ===========================================================
RMAN-00569: =============== ERROR MESSAGE STACK FOLLOWS ===============
RMAN-00571: ===========================================================
RMAN-03002: failure of restore command at 07/02/2006 21:33:02
RMAN-20207: UNTIL TIME or RECOVERY WINDOW is before RESETLOGS time
```

The bottom line is that you need to make sure you have a backup of your database that was taken before the time you wish to recover to. You also need all of your archived redo logs. In Chapter 15, we discuss the **list** and **report** commands that allow you to determine what backups are available for RMAN to restore from.

SCN-Based Recovery

We talked about the SCN in detail in Chapter 1. Oracle allows you to recover the database to a specific SCN. In practice, this is not a frequently used recovery method, but it's nice to know it's available. We will use it later in this chapter to recover to a previous database incarnation. Here is an example of a recovery to a specific SCN:

```
-- We assume that your control file is intact
startup mount;
```

```
restore database UNTIL SCN 10000;
recover database UNTIL SCN 10000;
alter database open resetlogs;
```

In this case, we restore up to, but not including, SCN 10000.

Log Sequence–Based Recovery

RMAN allows you to perform a recovery up to a specific archived redo log sequence number. This is handy if there is a gap in your archived redo logs, which generally means that you can recover only up to the point where the gap begins. Here is the command to perform this recovery in RMAN:

```
-- We assume that your control file is intact
startup mount;
restore database UNTIL SEQUENCE 100 thread 1;
recover database UNTIL SEQUENCE 100 thread 1;
alter database open resetlogs;
```

In this case, we restore up to, but not including, log sequence 100 of thread 1.

Cancel-Based Recovery

RMAN doesn't support cancel-based recovery like SQL*Plus does (though, in a way, cancel-based recovery is much like log sequence–based recovery). RMAN expects you to know what time, SCN, or log sequence number you want to recover to, and that makes sense. If you have some need to perform cancel-based recovery, you need to restore the datafiles from RMAN to some time before the point in time you are going to recover to. You need to manually extract the archived redo logs that you will need for the cancel-based recovery, and then you need to perform cancel-based recovery of the database from the SQL*Plus client. Chapter 1 describes the process of performing manual cancel-based database recovery.

Recovery Using Restore Points

You can use restore points to define the point in time that you want to restore your database to. To restore a database based on a restore point, simply include the **to restore point** clause of the **restore** and **recover** commands, as seen in this example:

```
Startup mount;
Restore database until restore point TANGO_ONE;
Recover database until restore point TANGO_ONE;
Alter database open resetlogs;
```

You can also use a **run** block and use the **set until restore point** command to establish the target restore point, for example:

```
Startup mount;
run {
set restore point TANGO_ONE;
Restore database TANGO_ONE;
Recover database TANGO_ONE;   }
Alter database open resetlogs;
```

Other RMAN Recovery Topics

We have covered a number of restore operations that you can do with RMAN, but a few more topics remain. In this section, we discuss more of the restore operations that are available. First, we look at how to restore archived redo logs from your backup sets. Next, we look at restoring control file copies from backup. Then, we move on to discuss restoring datafile copies and backup set backups. Finally, we discuss validating your backups, an important feature in RMAN.

Read-Only Tablespace Recovery Considerations

By default, RMAN will not restore read-only datafiles when you do a full database restore, even if the read-only datafile is not there. To restore a read-only datafile during a full recovery, you need to include the **check readonly** parameter in the **restore** command:

```
restore database check readonly;
```

Note that the RMAN behavior is different if you issue a **recover tablespace** or **recover datafile** command. When you use either of these two **recover** commands, recovery occurs regardless of the read-only nature of the tablespace.

Archived Redo Log Restores

During the normal course of recovery with RMAN, there is no real need to recover the archived redo logs. However, restoring one or more archived redo logs may be required occasionally. For example, you might want to use LogMiner to mine some information from the archived redo log files stored in your backups. In this event, RMAN allows you to restore specific archived redo logs by using the **restore archivelog** command, as shown in these examples:

```
restore archivelog all;
restore archivelog from logseq=20 thread=1;
restore archivelog from logseq=20 until logseq=30 thread=1;
```

You might want to have Oracle restore the archived redo logs to a location other than the default location. To do this, use the **set** command with the **archivelog destination to** parameter:

```
run
{
set archivelog destination to "d:\oracle\newarch";
restore archivelog all;
}
```

Note that there is no alternative to the **set** command, so a **run** block is required. Finally, be aware that RMAN will not restore an archived redo log to disk if it determines that the archived redo log already exists. Even if you change the destination to a destination other than the default archive log destination, Oracle will not recover an archived redo log to that new destination.

Datafile Copy Restores

You can restore your database datafiles from a datafile copy (as opposed to a backup set). To do this, use the **restore from datafilecopy** command, and then use the **recover** command as you normally would to recover the database (or tablespace or datafile), as shown in this example:

```
restore (datafile 5) from datafilecopy;
recover datafile 5;
sql "alter database datafile 5 online;"
```

Note that when you issue a **restore** command, it will identify the most current copy of the datafiles that needs to be restored and then restore those datafiles from that copy. The most current copy of a datafile might be within a datafile copy rather than a backup set. In that case, Oracle will recover the datafile copy. Also note that the use of parentheses is important; if they are not used, this command will fail.

Recovering Corrupted Data Blocks

RMAN offers *block media recovery* (BMR), which allows you to do block-level recoveries to repair logically or physically corrupted blocks in your Oracle database, even while the associated datafile is online and churning away the whole time.

So, just how do you do a block media recovery? It's easy, as demonstrated in the following example. Suppose you receive the following error message when querying an Oracle table:

```
ORA-01578: ORACLE data block corrupted (file # 19, block # 44)
ORA-01110: data file 19: 'd:\oracle\oradata\data\mydb_maintbs_01.dbf'
```

This message is telling you that a block in the MAINTBS tablespace is corrupted. Of course, you need to do something about that. Without BMR, you would have had to recover the datafile from a backup. During this recovery, all data within that datafile would be unavailable to the users.

Instead, you can use BMR to recover just the corrupted blocks. This is facilitated through the **blockrecover** command. In the preceding example, the **blockrecover** command would look like this:

```
blockrecover datafile 19 block 44;
```

You can recover multiple blocks in multiple datafiles at the same time, if you like. Here are two examples of using **blockrecover** for such an operation:

```
BLOCKRECOVER DATAFILE 19 BLOCK 44,66,127;
BLOCKRECOVER DATAFILE 19 BLOCK 44 DATAFILE 22 BLOCK 203;
```

Of course, Oracle tracks block corruption that occurs during backups and copies. If a backup or copy operation has detected corruption, the operation will fail by default because Oracle will allow zero corruption in a backup. You can configure RMAN to allow a set amount of corruption, but this is not a recommended practice.

If you want to see all database corruption that might be detected by RMAN, you can use the **backup validate database** command, which populates the views V$BACKUP_CORRUPTION and V$DATABASE_BLOCK_CORRUPTION with the results of all corrupted blocks. Here is some partial output of an execution of the **backup validate database** command:

```
RMAN> backup validate database;
Starting backup at 18-JUL-09
using target database control file instead of recovery catalog
allocated channel: ORA_DISK_1
channel ORA_DISK_1: SID=117 device type=DISK
channel ORA_DISK_1: starting full datafile backup set
```

```
channel ORA_DISK_1: specifying datafile(s) in backup set
input datafile file number=00002 name=C:\ORACLE\ORADATA\BORG\SYSAUX01.DBF
input datafile file number=00003 name=C:\ORACLE\ORADATA\BORG\UNDOTBS01.DBF
input datafile file number=00001 name=C:\ORACLE\ORADATA\BORG\SYSTEM01.DBF
input datafile file number=00005 name=C:\ORACLE\ORADATA\BORG\EXAMPLE01.DBF
input datafile file number=00006 name=C:\ORACLE\ORADATA\BORG\UNDO_NEW_01.DBF
input datafile file number=00009 name=C:\ORACLE\ORADATA\BORG\SMALL_THREE01.DBF
input datafile file number=00004 name=C:\ORACLE\ORADATA\BORG\USERS01.DBF
input datafile file number=00007 name=C:\ORACLE\ORADATA\BORG\SMALL01.DBF
input datafile file number=00008 name=C:\ORACLE\ORADATA\BORG\SMALLTWO.DBF
channel ORA_DISK_1: backup set complete, elapsed time: 00:10:45
List of Datafiles
=================
File Status Marked Corrupt Empty Blocks Blocks Examined High SCN
---- ------ -------------- ------------ --------------- ----------
1    OK     0              12166        93440           4480511
   File Name: C:\ORACLE\ORADATA\BETA1\SYSTEM01.DBF
   Block Type Blocks Failing Blocks Processed
   ---------- -------------- ----------------
   Data       0              66011
   Index      0              12036
   Other      0              3227
channel ORA_DISK_1: starting full datafile backup set
channel ORA_DISK_1: specifying datafile(s) in backup set
including current control file in backup set
including current SPFILE in backup set
channel ORA_DISK_1: backup set complete, elapsed time: 00:00:03
List of Control File and SPFILE
===============================
File Type    Status Blocks Failing Blocks Examined
------------ ------ -------------- ---------------
SPFILE       OK     0              2
Control File OK     0              1426
Finished backup at 18-JUL-09
```

Note in the sample output that all of the datafiles are checked. Once the check for corruption has completed, a report specific for each individual datafile is displayed (we only showed you the report for datafile system01.dbf in our example). Note also that the current control file and the current SPFILE are checked during the operation.

If corruption occurs during a copy operation, the V$COPY_CORRUPTION view indicates which backup sets contain corruption. Note that V$BACKUP_CORRUPTION is a historical view of past corruption. V$DATABASE_BLOCK_CORRUPTION is a view of current block corruption. Once you have corrected the database block corruption, rerun the **backup validate database** command, and then query V$DATABASE_BLOCK_CORRUPTION to ensure that no further corruption exists.

As we mentioned already, you can query the view V$DATABASE_BLOCK_CORRUPTION for details on corrupted blocks. To make it easy to correct corrupted blocks in V$DATABASE_BLOCK_CORRUPTION, you can use the **blockrecover** command with the **corruption list restore** parameter:

```
BLOCKRECOVER CORRUPTION LIST RESTORE UNTIL TIME 'SYSDATE - 5';
```

If you are restoring from an older level 0 and you want to validate that the block and redo stream will have problems during **blockrecover**, use NOFILEUPDATE to make a test run before you apply and redo:

```
BLOCKRECOVER CORRUPTION LIST RESTORE UNTIL TIME 'SYSDATE - 5' NOFILEUPDATE;
```

In this case, we restore all corrupted blocks on our corrupt block list that are no older than five days. You can also use the **until time** and **until sequence** keywords with this command.

Recovering to a Previous Incarnation

Recall from our earlier discussion about the **resetlogs** command that an incarnation of a database is a representation of a specific logical lifetime for that database. As a hotshot DBA, you may find yourself in an odd restore situation in which you need to restore your database using a backup that took place from before the last time you opened the database using the **resetlogs** command, and/or you may wish to restore to a point in time before you issued the last **resetlogs** command. In this section, we discuss how to recover your database from a previous incarnation both with a recovery catalog (a rather easy task) and without a recovery catalog (plan for time and frustration). Finally, we will cover a rather unique recovery situation in which you need to recover through the **resetlogs** command.

Recovering to a Previous Incarnation with a Recovery Catalog

Let's look at an example of recovering from a previous incarnation. In this example, we assume we have done backups using a recovery catalog and that we have recently done a point-in-time recovery using **resetlogs**. Now, we need to recover our database using a backup taken from a point in time before we issued our **resetlogs** command. First, we need to list the database incarnations by using the **list incarnation** command (covered in detail in the next chapter):

```
RMAN> list incarnation;
List of Database Incarnations
DB Key  Inc Key DB Name  DB ID            CUR Reset SCN  Reset Time
------- ------- -------- ---------------- --- ---------- ----------
1       2       RECOVER  2539725638       NO  763059     08-JUL-02
1       123     RECOVER  2539725638       YES 764905     09-JUL-02
```

In this list, we discover that there have been two different incarnations of our database, incarnation key 2 and incarnation key 123. The CUR column indicates that we are on incarnation key 123 right now (since it says YES). So, we need to switch back to incarnation 2 of the database.

Now that we know which incarnation we want to recover, we proceed to do the recovery (we removed some of the output here to make this example clearer):

```
RMAN> startup force nomount
Oracle instance started
RMAN> reset database to incarnation 2;
database reset to incarnation 2 in recovery catalog
RMAN> restore controlfile;
Finished restore at 10-JUL-02
RMAN> restore database until scn 764904;
 Finished restore at 10-JUL-02
RMAN> recover database until scn 764904;
starting media recovery
media recovery complete
```

```
Finished recover at 10-JUL-02
RMAN> alter database open resetlogs;
database opened
new incarnation of database registered in recovery catalog
starting full resync of recovery catalog
full resync complete
```

The following steps describe what we have done in this example:

1. Start the instance. We don't mount it, though, because we first want to get a control file that is associated with the incarnation of the database we wish to recover.

2. Use the **reset database to incarnation** command to indicate to RMAN which incarnation's backup sets we wish to be considered for the recovery.

3. Issue the **restore controlfile** command, prompting RMAN to restore the most current control file for us.

4. Mount the database.

5. Restore the database, doing an SCN-based restore (discussed earlier in this chapter). We have decided to restore the database to the SCN just before the last **resetlogs** (which was at SCN 764905), so we issue the **restore database** command, limiting the restore to SCN 764904.

6. Issue the **recover** command, again limiting the recovery of the database to SCN 764904, and wait for the recovery to complete.

7. Open the database, resetting the online redo logs.

Now, when we run the **list incarnation** command, the results are as follows:

```
RMAN> list incarnation;
List of Database Incarnations
DB Key  Inc Key DB Name  DB ID              CUR Reset SCN  Reset Time
------- ------- -------- ---------------- --- ---------- ----------
1       2       RECOVER  2539725638         NO  763059     08-JUL-02
1       123     RECOVER  2539725638         NO  764905     09-JUL-02
1       245     RECOVER  2539725638         YES 764905     10-JUL-02
```

Note the new incarnation of the database that has been created (with incarnation key 245). Also note that the reset SCN for this new incarnation is the same as that of incarnation 123 (which was the active incarnation). The reset time, however, reflects the actual time that this incarnation was created.

Recovering to a Previous Incarnation Without a Recovery Catalog

Oracle has made recovery to a previous incarnation without a recovery catalog so much easier in Oracle Database 10*g*. No longer are you required to jump through hoops, ask Oracle developers for favors, and send them cookies! No, it's simple!

To recover through a previous incarnation, you have a control file that is aware of the previous incarnation. This can be the current control file in most cases. If the current control file is not aware of the incarnation that you need to restore to, you need to restore a control file that is aware of this information to use this method of recovering your database. You can determine which incarnations your control file is aware of by using the **list incarnation of database** command, as shown in this example:

```
RMAN> list incarnation;
List of Database Incarnations
DB Key  Inc Key DB Name  DB ID            STATUS  Reset SCN  Reset Time
------- ------- -------- ---------------- --- ---------- ----------
4       4       ROB10R2  3753137102       PARENT  3599781    05-FEB-06
5       5       ROB10R2  3753137102       PARENT  3715262    08-FEB-06
6       6       ROB10R2  3753137102       CURRENT 4296046    20-FEB-06
```

In this example, we find that the control file contains information on incarnations (Inc Key) 4, 5, and 6. The current incarnation is incarnation 6. If we needed to restore incarnation 3, we could not use this control file, because incarnation 3 does not exist in this control file.

Note that the **list incarnation** output when not connected to a recovery catalog looks slightly different from the **list incarnation** output when connected to a recovery catalog. This is because you are getting your information from the control file, so certain keys (Inc Key, for example) will be different. This is perfectly normal.

If we wish to reset to incarnation 5 and then recover our database, we need to do the following:

1. Run the **list incarnation** command from RMAN, and determine which incarnation we wish to reset to.

2. Shut down the database.

3. Startup mount the database.

4. Issue the **reset database to incarnation** command to reset the incarnation.

5. Restore the database using the **restore** command (e.g., **restore until sequence 100 thread 1**).

6. Recover the database (**recover until sequence 100 thread 1**).

7. Open the database using the **resetlogs** command.

Like we said, so much easier! Here is some sample output of a recovery that resets the incarnation. Notice what happens in the **list incarnation** command as we complete the recovery. Also note that if Oracle needed to recover through the **resetlogs** command of incarnation 6, it would have done so automatically without our having to tell it to. We have removed some unneeded output to protect the innocent (trees, that is!).

```
RMAN> list incarnation of database;
List of Database Incarnations
DB Key  Inc Key DB Name  DB ID            STATUS  Reset SCN  Reset Time
------- ------- -------- ---------------- --- ---------- ----------
1       1       ROB10R2  3753137102       PARENT  1          30-AUG-05
2       2       ROB10R2  3753137102       PARENT  534907     03-OCT-05
3       3       ROB10R2  3753137102       PARENT  3586765    04-FEB-06
4       4       ROB10R2  3753137102       PARENT  3599781    05-FEB-06
5       5       ROB10R2  3753137102       PARENT  3715262    08-FEB-06
6       6       ROB10R2  3753137102       CURRENT 4296046    20-FEB-06
RMAN> shutdown immediate
database closed
database dismounted
Oracle instance shut down
RMAN> startup mount
connected to target database (not started)
Oracle instance started
```

```
database mounted
RMAN> reset database to incarnation 5;
database reset to incarnation 5
-- Note the reset SCN on the current incarnation is greater than
-- the SCN we wish to restore to. This is why we had to do a
-- restore to the previous incarnation.
RMAN> restore database until scn 4296041;
Starting restore at 20-FEB-06
allocated channel: ORA_DISK_1
channel ORA_DISK_1: sid=156 devtype=DISK
allocated channel: ORA_DISK_2
channel ORA_DISK_2: sid=155 devtype=DISK
... blah blah blah… more stuff here we don't really need to see...
RMAN> recover database until scn 4296041;
Starting recover at 20-FEB-06
using channel ORA_DISK_1
using channel ORA_DISK_2
... blah blah blah… more stuff here we don't really need to see...
RMAN> list incarnation;
List of Database Incarnations
DB Key  Inc Key DB Name  DB ID             STATUS  Reset SCN  Reset Time
------- ------- -------- ----------------- ------  ---------  ----------
1       1       ROB10R2  3753137102        PARENT  1          30-AUG-05
2       2       ROB10R2  3753137102        PARENT  534907     03-OCT-05
3       3       ROB10R2  3753137102        PARENT  3586765    04-FEB-06
4       4       ROB10R2  3753137102        PARENT  3599781    05-FEB-06
5       5       ROB10R2  3753137102        CURRENT 3715262    08-FEB-06
6       6       ROB10R2  3753137102        ORPHAN  4296046    20-FEB-06
RMAN> alter database open resetlogs;
database opened
RMAN> list incarnation;
List of Database Incarnations
DB Key  Inc Key DB Name  DB ID             STATUS  Reset SCN  Reset Time
------- ------- -------- ----------------- ------  ---------  ----------
1       1       ROB10R2  3753137102        PARENT  1          30-AUG-05
2       2       ROB10R2  3753137102        PARENT  534907     03-OCT-05
3       3       ROB10R2  3753137102        PARENT  3586765    04-FEB-06
4       4       ROB10R2  3753137102        PARENT  3599781    05-FEB-06
5       5       ROB10R2  3753137102        PARENT  3715262    08-FEB-06
6       6       ROB10R2  3753137102        ORPHAN  4296046    20-FEB-06
7       7       ROB10R2  3753137102        CURRENT 4296046    20-FEB-06
```

Tablespace Point-In-Time Recovery

Tablespace point-in-time recovery (TSPITR) is yet another feature of RMAN that was made easier in Oracle Database 10*g*. Much of the previous hassle with the creation of the auxiliary instance has now been done away with, although you can still manually create the auxiliary instance if you choose to. Why use tablespace point-in-time recovery? Consider a case where your user has dropped a table in error…in fact, the user has dropped three tables, truncated two more tables, and then called you asking for your help in getting it all back. Fortunately for you, RMAN allows you to do TSPITR. TSPITR might come in handy in a number of cases. Such situations might include accidentally dropping a table, as in our first example of the chapter, or perhaps a big bulk data load program ended up logically corrupting data.

Before you begin performing TSPITR, you need to be aware of some terms related to TSPITR since Oracle Database 10*g*:

- **Auxiliary destination**   An optional location where Oracle will create the auxiliary set.

- **Auxiliary instance**   A temporary instance that you create. RMAN uses this instance to perform TSPITR. After you complete your TSPITR, you can remove the auxiliary instance.

- **Auxiliary set**   The set of remaining target database files that you need to perform TSPITR. This set includes a backup control file, rollback and undo segment tablespace datafiles, the SYSTEM tablespace datafiles, online redo logs of the auxiliary database, and, optionally, a temporary tablespace in the auxiliary database.

- **Recovery set**   The set of tablespaces/datafiles that you wish to perform TSPITR on.

- **Target instance**   Contains the tablespace(s) to be recovered.

In the next section, we will look at an example of performing automated tablespace point-in-time recovery using RMAN. We will also address manual tablespace point-in-time recovery with RMAN.

Performing Automated TSPITR

In this example, we will have Oracle create the auxiliary instance for us. The basic steps of successful TSPITR are as follows:

1. Prepare for a TSPITR.

2. Perform the actual TSPITR.

Let's look at each of these steps in more detail next. We will also look at performing automated tablespace point-in-time recovery with the auxiliary instance already prepared.

Prepare for a TSPITR

Before you can begin TSPITR, you need to complete some steps that we discuss in this section:

- Determine what point in time to restore to.

- Make sure the objects are fully contained within the tablespace(s) you wish to restore.

- Preserve objects or data that will otherwise be lost.

Determine the Point in Time to Restore To   The most critical factor here is to determine what point in time you wish to restore your tablespace to. Be cautious here, because recovery of the tablespace is a one-shot deal if you are not using a recovery catalog. If you misidentify the point in time to recover to, you will not be able to retry the recovery. If you are using a recovery catalog, then this restriction does not exist.

Make Sure the Objects in the Transport Set Are Self-Contained   You should also use the TS_ PITR_CHECK view to make sure your recovery set is complete, and identify any other tablespaces that might need to be included. For example, assume that you have a tablespace TEST_RECOVER and need to restore it using TSPITR. You first need to check the TS_PITR_CHECK view to make sure that there are no other dependent tablespaces. Here is an example of a query to check if the TEST_RECOVER tablespace can be transported alone:

```
Set lines 132
Column obj1_owner format a20
column obj1_name format a20
column obj1_type format a20
column reason format a60
SELECT obj1_owner, obj1_name, obj1_type, reason
FROM SYS.TS_PITR_CHECK
WHERE ( TS1_NAME IN ('TEST_RECOVER')
       AND TS2_NAME NOT IN ('TEST_RECOVER') )
OR    ( TS1_NAME NOT IN ('TEST_RECOVER')
        AND TS2_NAME IN ('TEST_RECOVER') );
```

This would return no rows if there were no conflicts. If there were conflicts, you would see a row describing each conflict, as shown here:

```
OBJ1_OWNER    OBJ1_NAME         OBJ1_TYPE     REASON
------------  ----------------  ----------    ------------------------------
SCOTT         TEST_TSPITR       TABLE         Tables and associated indexes
                                              not fully contained in the
                                              recovery set
```

In this case, we have an index that appears to be created in another tablespace. This index is associated with the TEST_TSPITR object. We need to find out what tablespace that index is in and restore that tablespace, too.

Preserve Objects or Data that Might Be Lost in the Recovery   Obviously, if you are going to restore the TEST tablespace to 2 P.M., any changes to that tablespace (new objects, update/insert or delete operations) will be lost after that point. Losing those objects may be fine, but suppose that you need to preserve that data. If this is the case, you need to export the data to be preserved (or, alternatively, copy it to somewhere else in the database). Oracle provides a view, TS_PITR_OBJECTS_TO_BE_DROPPED, that lists all objects that will be lost during the recovery operation. Use this view to determine what the status of the objects in the tablespace will be after the recovery.

For example, if you were going to restore the TEST_TSPITR tablespace to a point in time of 02/20/2006 at 23:40:00, you would lose the TEST_TSPITR_TWO object, as shown in this sample output:

```
SQL>select * from TS_PITR_OBJECTS_TO_BE_DROPPED where
2> tablespace_name='TEST_RECOVER';

OWNER        NAME                   CREATION_TIME         TABLESPACE_NAME
----------   --------------------   -------------------   ----------------
SCOTT        TEST_TSPITR_TWO        02/20/2006 23:42:46   TEST_RECOVER
SCOTT        TEST_TSPITR            02/20/2006 23:26:26   TEST_RECOVER
SCOTT        TEST_TSPITR_THREE      02/21/2006 00:18:29   TEST_RECOVER
```

Perform the Actual TSPITR
RMAN will perform automated TSPITR for you, which means that it will create the auxiliary instance for you. In this case, all you need to do is connect to the target database and the optional

recovery catalog (if you use one) and issue the **recover tablespace** command. RMAN will do the rest of the work for you.

In the following code snippet, we provide an example of using the **recover tablespace** command to recover the TEST_RECOVER tablespace. In this example, we use the optional parameter **auxiliary destination** to indicate where RMAN and Oracle should create the files associated with the auxiliary database. Using this parameter makes this recovery a *customized TSPITR with an automatic instance.* If you do not use this parameter, the TSPITR is known as a *fully automated TSPITR recovery.*

Note that if you use the **auxiliary destination** parameter, the destination directory should already be created, and Oracle must be able to write to that destination. Also note that there is no trailing slash (\ or /, depending on your OS) in the destination pathname. Including a slash will cause TSPITR to fail (and the message you get isn't exactly all that descriptive). Here is an example of the **recover tablespace** command that we used to successfully perform TSPITR in Oracle Database 10*g* Release 2:

```
recover tablespace test_recover
until time "to_date('02/21/2006 00:18:00','mm/dd/yyyy hh24:mi:ss')"
auxiliary destination 'c:\oracle\auxdest';
```

NOTE
To do automatic TSPITR, you must have configured channels on the target. That way, channels used in the auxiliary instance will be the same as those on the target.

Once the TSPITR has been completed, you should be able to look at the objects in the recovered tablespace and find that they have been recovered to the point in time you requested. You need to bring the tablespaces recovered back online to use them. From RMAN, you can issue the command

```
Sql 'alter tablespace test_recover online';
```

If an error occurs, Oracle leaves the auxiliary instance and its related datafiles intact. You can try to correct the problem and restart the recovery. In this case, you would restart RMAN using the **auxiliary** parameter, connecting to the auxiliary instance (as we demonstrate later, in the section "Manual TSPITR").

If the auxiliary instance creation is not entirely successful, it may be easier to just remove the auxiliary instance and its service than to restart the recovery using the manual TSPITR process. First, figure out what failed, and then remove the auxiliary instance/service and restart the automated TSPITR process. You can remove the auxiliary instance/service by issuing the following command from SQL*Plus when logged in as SYSDBA:

```
exec dbms_backup_restore.manageauxinstance('auxiliary_sid_name',1);
```

Note that you need to put the SID that Oracle assigned to the auxiliary instance in the place of the **auxiliary_sid_name** placeholder. The name of the SID will be listed in the RMAN output. This will clean up any old auxiliary instances before you start your TSPITR recovery. You will want to go to the auxiliary destination directory after you execute this command and remove any files that are in that directory.

Customized Automated TSPITR with an Automatic Instance

We already mentioned that you can customize some aspects of the automatic instance creation when performing TSPITR. We demonstrated the use of the **auxiliary destination** parameter to indicate where the recovery set should be created. Other ways of customizing the creation of the TSPITR, and still allowing Oracle to create the instance for you, include the following:

- Using the **set newname** command to indicate the location of the individual datafiles of the recovery set.

- Using the **configure auxname** command to define the name of the auxiliary instance.

- Creating your own parameter file for the auxiliary instance and supplying parameters such as **db_file_name_convert** in that parameter file. This can be done by creating a file called parms_auxint.ora in $ORACLE_HOME/rdbms/admin (this filename and location are OS dependent). Optionally, you can use the RMAN command **set auxiliary instance parameter file** to indicate the path on the client where the auxiliary instance parameter file resides. See the next section for more information on parameters that apply when configuring an instance for TSPITR.

Once you have customized your auxiliary instance, you can have RMAN create it for you by issuing the **recover tablespace** command, as shown earlier in the section "Performing Automated TSPITR."

Manual TSPITR

Oracle supports the creation of your own auxiliary instance for TSPITR. You can also use manual TSPITR to complete a failed automatic TSPITR. The steps listed earlier in the preparation phase still apply. You then must prepare the auxiliary instance and execute the TSPITR process. We discuss these steps in the next few sections.

Prepare the Auxiliary Instance

The first thing we need to do is get an auxiliary instance up and running. As already defined, an auxiliary instance is just a temporary instance that RMAN uses to perform TSPITR. The auxiliary instance must reside on the same box as the target database, and you will never be able to execute any type of DML on the auxiliary instance.

Before we can start TSPITR, we need to get the auxiliary instance ready. This is a manual process that RMAN has no part in, but it's not unlike creating a normal database instance. To create the auxiliary instance, perform these actions:

1. Create the password file.
2. Create the database parameter file if you are running the restore from OEM.
3. If you are running Oracle on Windows NT, add the database service with the **oradim** program (for example, **oradim –new –sid recover**).
4. Start the auxiliary instance and check to make sure that you have network connectivity.

You should be familiar in general with each of these steps, as these are typical DBA tasks. Basically, it's a lot like creating an instance in preparation for issuing the **create database** command. We need to note a few issues specific to TSPITR, however, so let's do that quickly.

Configure the Auxiliary Parameter File   The parameter file of the auxiliary database is a separate parameter file from the one used on the target database. You configure the parameter file for the auxiliary instance in much the same way you configure a normal database parameter file. You need to include a few additional parameters in this parameter file, which are listed in Table 14-1.

Parameter Name	Optional/Required	Comment
db_name	Optional	The same name as the target database.
lock_name_space	Required	Should be a name that is unique among all other databases on the system that you are creating your auxiliary database on. In our examples, we will use aux1.
db_file_name_convert	Optional	Can be used to define a set of file-naming conversion patterns for datafiles in the auxiliary database as they are restored by RMAN. This is an alternative to using the **configure auxname** RMAN command.
log_file_name_convert	Optional	Can be used to define a set of file-naming conversion patterns for redo log files in the auxiliary database as they are restored by RMAN. This is an alternative to using the **set newname** RMAN command.
control_files	Required	The control file parameter defines the names and locations of the auxiliary instance control files. The control files should be unique in name from any existing control file in the location(s) you intend on creating the control files in.
remote_login_ passwordfile	Optional/ Required	Used to allow RMAN to connect to the auxiliary database via Oracle Networking services. Requires the presence of a current password file. If you will be connecting to the auxiliary database locally, then this doesn't need to be set.
Compatible	Required	Must be the same as the target database's setting.
db_block_size	Optional/ Required	If set on the target database, must be set in the auxiliary database to the same value.

TABLE 14-1   *Auxiliary Instance Parameter File Parameters of Interest*

Each of these parameters is further defined in the Oracle reference manual, if you need further information on how to configure them. For our example, we simply copied the target instance parameter file and made a few changes to it. Here is a copy of the resulting auxiliary database instance parameter file:

```
# These parameters already exist in the target database parameter file and
# require no changes.
db_name=rob10r2
db_block_size=8192
db_cache_size=8388608
timed_statistics=TRUE
shared_pool_size=110M
large_pool_size=1M


# Note that remote_login_passwordfile must be set to exclusive
# if we want to connect to the aux database through RMAN via Oracle Net.
# remote_login_passwordfile=EXCLUSIVE
compatible=10.2.0.1


# These parameters required changes to directory locations
# to reflect the new database instance.
background_dump_dest= c:\oracle\auxdest
core_dump_dest= c:\oracle\auxdest
user_dump_dest= c:\oracle\auxdest
control_files=c:\oracle\auxdest\control01.ctl


# These are new parameters that are exclusive to the aux database
db_unique_name=recover
db_create_file_dest=c:\oracle\auxdest
log_file_name_convert=
('C:\ORACLE\PRODUCT\10.2.0\ORADATA\ROB10R2','d:\oracle\auxdest')
```

NOTE
We dump everything into c:\oracle\auxdest in the parameter file here. This kind of goes with the very temporary nature of the auxiliary database. You can, of course, create more sophisticated directory structures if you like.

Start the Auxiliary Instance and Check Network Connectivity   Now that we have everything in place, we can start our auxiliary instance. To do so, we simply use the **startup nomount** command, as shown in this example:

```
sqlplus "sys as sysdba"
startup nomount pfile=c:\oracle\auxdest\initrecover.ora
```

Once you have started the instance, connect to it using Oracle Net to ensure your network connectivity is correct.

Perform TSPITR with a Manual Auxiliary Instance   To perform the actual recovery, we need to connect to RMAN. The connection string we are going to use is a bit different because we need to connect to the target database, the auxiliary database, and the recovery catalog (if we are using one) all at the same time. To connect to the auxiliary database, we use the **auxiliary** command-line parameter, along with the **target** and **catalog** parameters, as shown in these examples:

```
C:\Oracle\auxdest>rman target=sys/robert@rob10r2 auxiliary=/
Recovery Manager:Release 10.2.0.1.0 Production on Thu Feb 23 10:25:49 2006
Copyright (c) 1982, 2005, Oracle.  All rights reserved.
connected to target database: ROB10R2 (DBID=3753137102)
connected to auxiliary database: RECOVER (not mounted)
```

Now that we have connected to RMAN, we need to be able to mount the auxiliary (clone) database. To do this, we restore a clone control file and then open the auxiliary database. Note that the **alter system archive log current** command is important here to make sure that we have all the redo we need available for recovery of the clone database. The following is an example of using the **restore clone controlfile** command to restore the control file, and then an example of mounting the clone database. Note that these commands are contained inside of a **run** block. Also note the use of the **sql clone** command to indicate that the SQL commands executed should be on the clone database, as opposed to using the **sql** command without the **clone** parameter, which implies that the command is executed on the target database.

```
Run {
Set until time "to_date(' 02/23/2006 11:42:55','mm/dd/yyyy hh24:mi:ss')";
Restore clone controlfile;
sql clone 'alter database mount clone database';
sql 'alter system archive log current';
}
```

Now, we need to prepare for our TSPITR. First, we need to know which datafiles we need to restore. We need the following tablespace-related datafiles:

- The SYSTEM tablespace datafiles. The SYSTEM tablespace datafile is always at least datafile number 1. (There may be others if you added datafiles to SYSTEM, of course.)

- The UNDO tablespace datafiles.

- The temporary tablespace (TEMP) tempfiles. These can also be manually created if they are not available.

- The datafiles of the tablespace to be restored (in our case, TEST_RESTORE).

NOTE
We don't have to restore the SYSAUX tablespace in this case.

So, let's look up these locations in our database using SQL*Plus. We use the DBA_DATA_FILE view to find the FILE_IDs associated with these tablespace datafiles. We also need the filename for the tablespace (or tablespaces) that we will be actually performing the TSPITR on. In our case, here is what the output looks like (yours might be a bit different, of course):

```
SQL> select tablespace_name, file_id
2> from dba_data_files
3> where tablespace_name in
4> ('SYSTEM','UNDOTBS1','TEST_RECOVER');
```

```
TABLESPACE_NAME                       FILE_ID
------------------------------ ----------
UNDOTBS1                                    2
SYSTEM                                      1
TEST_RECOVER                                7

SQL> select file_name from dba_data_files where file_id=7;

FILE_NAME
--------------------------------------------------------------
C:\ORACLE\PRODUCT\10.2.0\ORADATA\ROB10R2\TEST_RECOVER_01.DBF


SQL> select tablespace_name, file_id
2> from dba_data_files
TABLESPACE_NAME                       FILE_ID
------------------------------ ----------
TEMP                                        1
```

Before we start creating the auxiliary database, we need to offline the tablespaces we are going to perform recovery on. For each tablespace, issue the SQL command **alter tablespace tablespace_name offline for recover;** as shown in this example:

```
Sql 'Alter tablespace test_recover offline for recover';
```

We are ready to actually create the auxiliary (clone) database that will be used for the recovery. First, we use the **until time** parameter again, since this is a new **run** block. This way, we are sure to get the correct datafiles. Next, we use the **set newname for clone** command to make sure these files are correctly named during the restore. In this example, we are using OMF, so it's easy to do using the **new** parameter. We also issue a **set newname** command for datafile 7, in preparation for its restore. We then issue the **switch clone tempfile all** command to rename the temp files. Finally, we restore the datafiles and get the clone database running.

```
Run {
Set until time "to_date('02/23/2006 11:42:55','mm/dd/yyyy hh24:mi:ss')";
Set newname for clone datafile 1 to new;
Set newname for clone datafile 2 to new;
set newname for clone tempfile 1 to new;
Set newname for datafile 7 to
"C:\ORACLE\PRODUCT\10.2.0\ORADATA\ROB10R2\TEST_RECOVER_01.DBF";
Switch clone tempfile all;
restore clone datafile  1, 2, 7;
switch clone datafile all;
sql clone "alter database datafile  1 online";
sql clone "alter database datafile  2 online";
sql clone "alter database datafile  7 online";
sql clone "alter database mount clone database";
}
```

Now, open the clone database in preparation to do the TSPITR:

```
Run {
Set until time "to_date('02/23/2006 11:42:55','mm/dd/yyyy hh24:mi:ss')";
recover clone database
tablespace  "TEST_RECOVER", "SYSTEM", "UNDOTBS1" delete archivelog;
alter clone database open resetlogs;
}
```

We are now ready to perform the final step in the recovery process. We need to export the metadata from the clone database to the host database. Here is that process:

```
C:\Oracle\auxdest>exp 'sys/robert as sysdba' point_in_time_recover=y
tablespaces=test_recover file=tspitr_a.dmp

Export: Release 10.2.0.1.0 - Production on Thu Feb 23 12:44:30 2006
Copyright (c) 1982, 2005, Oracle.  All rights reserved.
Connected to: Oracle Database 10g Enterprise Edition
Release 10.2.0.1.0 - Production
With the Partitioning, OLAP and Data Mining options
Export done in WE8MSWIN1252 character set and AL16UTF16 NCHAR character set
Note: table data (rows) will not be exported

About to export Tablespace Point-in-time Recovery objects...
For tablespace TEST_RECOVER ...
. exporting cluster definitions
. exporting table definitions
. . exporting table                      TEST_TSPITR
. . exporting table                  TEST_TSPITR_TWO
. . exporting table                TEST_TSPITR_THREE
. exporting referential integrity constraints
. exporting triggers
. end point-in-time recovery
Export terminated successfully without warnings.
```

Now we shut down the clone:

```
C:\Oracle\auxdest>sqlplus "/ as sysdba"
SQL*Plus: Release 10.2.0.1.0 - Production on Thu Feb 23 12:47:05 2006
Copyright (c) 1982, 2005, Oracle.  All rights reserved.
Connected to:
Oracle Database 10g Enterprise Edition Release 10.2.0.1.0 - Production
With the Partitioning, OLAP and Data Mining options
SQL> shutdown immediate
Database closed.
Database dismounted.
ORACLE instance shut down.
```

Finally, we import the metadata into the source database. Note that we already recovered the datafile to the source database earlier, so we don't have to physically move the file.

```
C:\Oracle\auxdest>imp 'sys/robert as sysdba'
point_in_time_recover=y file=tspitr_a.dmp
```

Now, all that remains to be done is to online the tablespace:

```
Alter tablespace test_recover online;
```

Perform Post-TSPITR Activities After a Manual TSPITR

There are a few actions that you need to perform once your TSPITR is complete. First, you should reconnect RMAN to just the target database (and the recovery catalog if you are using one), and back up the tablespaces you just recovered. You will also want to remove the remnants of the auxiliary/clone instance.

TSPITR Restrictions

TSPITR has a number of restrictions, a quick summary of which follows:

- You can't restore tablespaces with objects owned by SYS.

- Any tablespace with replicated master tables cannot be recovered with TSPITR.

- Tablespaces with snapshot logs are not supported.

- You can't restore tablespaces that contain rollback segments.

- If an object within the tablespace to be recovered has one of the following types, then TSPITR is not supported:

  - VARRAY

  - Nested tables

  - External files

Additionally, TSPITR cannot be used to recover a dropped tablespace. You also will not be able to recover older object statistics.

Finally, there are some restrictions with regard to TSPITR if you are using RMAN without a recovery catalog:

- The current physical structure of the undo and rollback segments in the target database must be unchanged between the point you wish to recover to and the current point. In other words, the rollback segments can't change during the recovery.

- Once you have completed TSPITR on a given tablespace, all previous backups of that tablespace are no longer usable for future TSPITR recoveries of that tablespace. This is why a backup of the tablespace after TSPITR is very important, in case you need to run another TSPITR.

Verifying Your Backups Are Recoverable

Of course, backups are not useful if they are not recoverable. RMAN provides a method of checking the restorability of your database without actually restoring it. In fact, RMAN offers you a couple of options. In this section, we look at some different ways to verify that your database backups, and thus your database, are recoverable. First, we will look at the **verify** and **check logical** options of the **restore** command. Then, we will look at the **validate backupset** command.

The restore preview Command

If you want to see which backup sets RMAN will use to perform a particular recovery, you can use the **restore preview** command. This command will detail the backup sets that will be required to perform the restore you indicate on the command line. For example, you can determine which backup set a full restore will apply by using the command **restore database preview**. In the following example, we see the results of the **restore database preview** command. In the output, we find that RMAN will apply an incremental level 0 backup and then an incremental level 1 backup (as shown in the LV column under the individual List of Backup Sets reports). It then also displays the archived redo logs that will be applied. At the end, we also get information that will help us with incomplete recovery if that is what we wanted.

```
RMAN> restore database preview;
Starting restore at 23-FEB-06
using channel ORA_DISK_1
using channel ORA_DISK_2

List of Backup Sets
===================
BS Key  Type LV Size       Device Type Elapsed Time Completion Time
------- ---- -- ---------- ----------- ------------ ---------------
210     Incr 0  66.36M      DISK        00:01:23     23-FEB-06
        BP Key: 210   Status: AVAILABLE  Compressed: YES
Tag: AG20060223T142518
        Piece Name:
C:\ORACLE\PRODUCT\10.2.0\FLASH_RECOVERY_AREA\ROB10R2\BACKUPSET\2006_02_23
\O1_MF_NNND0_TAG20060223T142518_1ZW6KK4H_.BKP
  List of Datafiles in backup set 210
  File LV Type Ckp SCN    Ckp Time  Name
  ---- -- ---- ---------- --------- ----
  2    0  Incr 4471679    23-FEB-06
C:\ORACLE\PRODUCT\10.2.0\ORADATA\ROB10R2\UNDOTBS01.DBF
  3    0  Incr 4471679    23-FEB-06
C:\ORACLE\PRODUCT\10.2.0\ORADATA\ROB10R2\SYSAUX01.DBF
  4    0  Incr 4471679    23-FEB-06
C:\ORACLE\PRODUCT\10.2.0\ORADATA\ROB10R2\USERS01.DBF
  5    0  Incr 4471679    23-FEB-06
C:\ORACLE\PRODUCT\10.2.0\ORADATA\ROB10R2\EXAMPLE01.DBF

BS Key  Type LV Size       Device Type Elapsed Time Completion Time
------- ---- -- ---------- ----------- ------------ ---------------
211     Incr 0  83.30M      DISK        00:01:45     23-FEB-06
        BP Key: 211   Status: AVAILABLE  Compressed: YES
Tag: TAG20060223T142518
        Piece Name:
C:\ORACLE\PRODUCT\10.2.0\FLASH_RECOVERY_AREA\ROB10R2\BACKUPSET\2006_02_23
\O1_MF_NNND0_TAG20060223T142518_1ZW6KYN2_.BKP
```

```
  List of Datafiles in backup set 211
  File LV Type Ckp SCN    Ckp Time  Name
  ---- -- ---- ---------- --------- ----
  1    0  Incr 4471684    23-FEB-06
C:\ORACLE\PRODUCT\10.2.0\ORADATA\ROB10R2\SYSTEM01.DBF
  6    0  Incr 4471684    23-FEB-06
C:\ORACLE\PRODUCT\10.2.0\ORADATA\ROB10R2\NEWTBS01.DBF
  7    0  Incr 4471684    23-FEB-06
C:\ORACLE\PRODUCT\10.2.0\ORADATA\ROB10R2\TEST_RECOVER_01.DBF
  8    0  Incr 4471684    23-FEB-06
C:\ORACLE\PRODUCT\10.2.0\ORADATA\ROB10R2\TEST_RECOVER_TWO_01.DBF


BS Key  Type LV Size       Device Type Elapsed Time Completion Time
------- ---- -- ---------- ----------- ------------ ---------------
216     Incr 1  728.00K    DISK        00:00:38     23-FEB-06
        BP Key: 216   Status: AVAILABLE  Compressed: YES
Tag: TAG20060223T144904
        Piece Name:
C:\ORACLE\PRODUCT\10.2.0\FLASH_RECOVERY_AREA\ROB10R2\BACKUPSET\2006_02_23
\O1_MF_NNND1_TAG20060223T144904_1ZW7Y40G_.BKP
  List of Datafiles in backup set 216
  File LV Type Ckp SCN    Ckp Time  Name
  ---- -- ---- ---------- --------- ----
  2    1  Incr 4472638    23-FEB-06
C:\ORACLE\PRODUCT\10.2.0\ORADATA\ROB10R2\UNDOTBS01.DBF
  3    1  Incr 4472638    23-FEB-06
C:\ORACLE\PRODUCT\10.2.0\ORADATA\ROB10R2\SYSAUX01.DBF
  4    1  Incr 4472638    23-FEB-06
C:\ORACLE\PRODUCT\10.2.0\ORADATA\ROB10R2\USERS01.DBF
  5    1  Incr 4472638    23-FEB-06
C:\ORACLE\PRODUCT\10.2.0\ORADATA\ROB10R2\EXAMPLE01.DBF


BS Key  Type LV Size       Device Type Elapsed Time Completion Time
------- ---- -- ---------- ----------- ------------ ---------------
217     Incr 1  328.00K    DISK        00:01:10     23-FEB-06
        BP Key: 217   Status: AVAILABLE  Compressed: YES
Tag: TAG20060223T144904
        Piece Name:
C:\ORACLE\PRODUCT\10.2.0\FLASH_RECOVERY_AREA\ROB10R2\BACKUPSET\2006_02_23
\O1_MF_NNND1_TAG20060223T144904_1ZW7Z98D_.BKP
  List of Datafiles in backup set 217
  File LV Type Ckp SCN    Ckp Time  Name
  ---- -- ---- ---------- --------- ----
  1    1  Incr 4472653    23-FEB-06
C:\ORACLE\PRODUCT\10.2.0\ORADATA\ROB10R2\SYSTEM01.DBF
  6    1  Incr 4472653    23-FEB-06
C:\ORACLE\PRODUCT\10.2.0\ORADATA\ROB10R2\NEWTBS01.DBF
  7    1  Incr 4472653    23-FEB-06
C:\ORACLE\PRODUCT\10.2.0\ORADATA\ROB10R2\TEST_RECOVER_01.DBF
  8    1  Incr 4472653    23-FEB-06
C:\ORACLE\PRODUCT\10.2.0\ORADATA\ROB10R2\TEST_RECOVER_TWO_01.DBF
```

```
List of Archived Log Copies
Key      Thrd Seq     S Low Time  Name
-------  ---- -------  - --------- ----
300      1    23       A 23-FEB-06 C:\ARCHIVE\ROB10R2ARC00023_0582936761.001

Media recovery start SCN is 4472638
Recovery must be done beyond SCN 4472653 to clear data files fuzziness

Finished restore at 23-FEB-06
```

Some vendors support "recalling" media from a DR site to use for a local restore. The **restore database preview recall** supports this functionality, allowing you to initiate a recall of the required backup files from a remote disaster recovery site in order to perform the restore preview.

Restoring with the validate and check logical Commands

The **restore** command comes with some great options that allow you to verify that your database is recoverable and that the backup itself is valid. First, you can use the **validate** parameter of the **backup** command to cause RMAN to check the backup sets and to make sure your database is recoverable. When you use the **validate** option, Oracle checks the most current backup set that will be needed to recover your database, ensuring that it is complete. This option also checks any datafile copies and archived redo log backup sets that will be required for recovery and ensures that they are all complete. Additionally, the **validate** option does a general validation of the backup sets to ensure that they are intact. Validation doesn't take very long and is one way to ensure that your database is recoverable. Here is an example of a **validate** operation on our database:

```
RMAN> restore database validate;
Starting restore at 05-JUL-02
using channel ORA_DISK_1
using channel ORA_DISK_2
channel ORA_DISK_1: starting validation of datafile backupset
channel ORA_DISK_2: starting validation of datafile backupset
channel ORA_DISK_1: restored backup piece 1
piece handle=D:\BACKUP\RECOVER\BACKUP_4QDSM5IB_1_1
tag=TAG20020703T221224 params=NULL
channel ORA_DISK_1: validation complete
channel ORA_DISK_2: restored backup piece 1
piece handle=D:\BACKUP\RECOVER\BACKUP_4RDSM5IC_1_1
tag=TAG20020703T221224 params=NULL
channel ORA_DISK_2: validation complete
Finished restore at 05-JUL-02
```

Another, more complete check of the most current backup set is the **check logical** parameter of the **restore** command. This command causes RMAN to check the backups of the database, if they pass a physical corruption check, for logical corruption within the data and index segments backed up. If logical errors are found, Oracle responds in one of two ways:

- If the **maxcorrupt** parameter has been set and this count is not exceeded during the restore check logical operation, RMAN populates the Oracle V$ table V$DATABASE_BLOCK_CORRUPTION with a list of corrupted block ranges.

- If **maxcorrupt** is exceeded during the operation, then the operation will terminate.

By default, **maxcorrupt** is set to 0, so any logical corruption will cause the operation to fail. The **maxcorrupt** parameter default is modified via the **set** command and can only be established within the confines of a **run** block. Additionally, **maxcorrupt** is set for each datafile individually, not collectively. The following is an example of setting **maxcorrupt** to allow for some corruption to appear, and then logically validating backups of our database. In this example, we have set **maxcorrupt** for all the datafiles in our database (1 through 5), and we not only are checking that the latest backup sets are present and recoverable, but also are looking for logical corruption within the backup sets.

```
RMAN> run {
2> set maxcorrupt for datafile 1,2,3,4,5,6 to 5;
3> restore database check logical validate;
4> }
executing command: SET MAX CORRUPT
Starting restore at 05-JUL-02
using channel ORA_DISK_1
using channel ORA_DISK_2
channel ORA_DISK_1: starting validation of datafile backupset
channel ORA_DISK_2: starting validation of datafile backupset
channel ORA_DISK_1: restored backup piece 1
piece handle=D:\BACKUP\RECOVER\BACKUP_4QDSM5IB_1_1
tag=TAG20020703T221224 params=NULL
channel ORA_DISK_1: validation complete
channel ORA_DISK_2: restored backup piece 1
piece handle=D:\BACKUP\RECOVER\BACKUP_4RDSM5IC_1_1
tag=TAG20020703T221224 params=NULL
channel ORA_DISK_2: validation complete
Finished restore at 05-JUL-02
```

Using the validate backupset Command

Using the **restore** command with the **validate** and/or **check logical** parameters only checks the most current backup set. There may well be times that you want to check a specific backup set. To do this, you use the **validate backupset** command. To use this command, you first need to determine the backup set key that you want to back up. Each backup set, when it is made, is assigned a unique identifier called the *backup set key.* To determine the key assigned to the backup set you are interested in, you can use the **list backupset** command, as shown in the following example:

```
RMAN> list backupset;
List of Backup Sets
===================
BS Key  Type LV Size       Device Type Elapsed Time Completion Time
------- ---- -- ---------- ----------- ------------ ---------------
141     Full    320K        DISK         00:02:09     03-JUL-02
        BP Key: 141   Status: AVAILABLE   Tag: TAG20020703T221224
        Piece Name: D:\BACKUP\RECOVER\BACKUP_4QDSM5IB_1_1
  List of Datafiles in backup set 141
  File LV Type Ckp SCN    Ckp Time  Name
  ---- -- ---- ---------- --------- ----
    2     Full 647435     03-JUL-02 D:\ORACLE\ORADATA\RECOVER\REVDATA.DBF
```

```
    4         Full 647435    03-JUL-02 D:\ORACLE\ORADATA\RECOVER\TOOLS01.DBF
    6         Full 647435    03-JUL-02 D:\ORACLE\ORADATA\RECOVER\REVINDEX.DBF

BS Key  Type LV Size         Device Type Elapsed Time Completion Time
------- ---- -- ----------   ----------- ------------ ----------------
142     Full    113M         DISK           00:03:28     03-JUL-02
        BP Key: 142    Status: AVAILABLE    Tag: TAG20020703T221224
        Piece Name: D:\BACKUP\RECOVER\BACKUP_4RDSM5IC_1_1
  List of Datafiles in backup set 142
  File LV Type Ckp SCN    Ckp Time  Name
  ---- -- ---- ---------- --------- ----
    1      Full 647439    03-JUL-02 D:\ORACLE\ORADATA\RECOVER\SYSTEM01.DBF
    3      Full 647439    03-JUL-02 D:\ORACLE\ORADATA\RECOVER\INDX01.DBF
    5      Full 647439    03-JUL-02 D:\ORACLE\ORADATA\RECOVER\USERS01.DBF
```

Here, we are interested in the report's BS Key column, which lists the backup set key number. Notice that the files in the backup set also are listed, as are the date and time of the backup. All of this information should make it easy to identify the backup set you wish to validate. Once you have determined the set you need to check, then validating the backup set is as easy as running the **validate backupset** command, as shown in the next two examples:

```
RMAN> validate backupset 141;
using channel ORA_DISK_1
using channel ORA_DISK_2
channel ORA_DISK_1: starting validation of datafile backupset
channel ORA_DISK_1: restored backup piece 1
piece handle=D:\BACKUP\RECOVER\BACKUP_4QDSM5IB_1_1
tag=TAG20020703T221224 params=NULL
channel ORA_DISK_1: validation complete

RMAN> validate backupset 141 check logical;
using channel ORA_DISK_1
using channel ORA_DISK_2
channel ORA_DISK_1: starting validation of datafile backupset
channel ORA_DISK_1: restored backup piece 1
piece handle=D:\BACKUP\RECOVER\BACKUP_4QDSM5IB_1_1
tag=TAG20020703T221224 params=NULL
channel ORA_DISK_1: validation complete
```

Call the Movers! Cross-Platform Database Movement and RMAN

Oracle Database supports manually moving databases across different platforms, even those of different *endian* formats. The endian formats relate to byte ordering, and there are two different formats, big endian and little endian. If you want to move a database between databases of different endian byte formats, then you have to do so manually, using the RMAN **convert datafile** or **convert tablespace** command along the way to convert the datafiles being transported to the correct endian format.

In this section, we quickly cover cross-platform transportable tablespaces. We then discuss the different endian byte-ordering formats. Next, we discuss converting tablespaces for transport to platforms with different endian byte formats. We finish with a discussion of using RMAN to move databases between different platforms with the same endian byte format.

Introduction to Cross-Platform Transportable Tablespaces

On several occasions, we, as DBAs, really wanted to be able to move our tablespaces between our development NT Oracle database and our production Sun Oracle database. We have had cases where we really wanted to move them between a Sun platform and an AIX platform. Until Oracle Database 10g, this was just a dream.

Now, Oracle supports transporting tablespaces across almost all platforms of the Oracle database family. This has a number of benefits, including:

■ Efficient publication of data between different content providers

■ Easy movement of data between data warehouses, data marts, and OLTP systems

■ Easy migration of databases across platforms

NOTE
Not all platforms are currently supported for this functionality. Check your platform-specific documentation to determine if your platform is eligible.

There are a few other issues to mention. To move a tablespace between platforms, **compatible** must be set to 10.0.0 or higher. When this occurs, tablespace datafiles will be made platform-aware upon the next startup operation. Note that read-only and offline datafiles become cross-platform compatible only after they have been made read-write or brought online.

Byte Ordering and Datafile Conversion

In this section, first, we introduce you to the concept of byte ordering in Oracle database datafiles and how this impacts transporting your tablespace between different platforms. Then, we will look at how to convert these datafiles, if that is required.

Datafile Byte Ordering

Oracle platforms generally use two different byte-ordering schemes (known as the endian formats). If the platforms use the same byte-ordering scheme, then you can transport tablespaces as you always have in the past, no problem…. Go ahead and try it. We will wait for you!

If the byte-ordering scheme is different, then you will need to use the **convert** command in RMAN to convert the tablespace to the format that it will need to be in on the target platform. You can determine the endian format via a join of the dynamic view V$DATABASE and the new V$TRANSPORTABLE_PLATFORM view, as shown in this example:

```
SQL> Select endian_format
  2  From v$transportable_platform tp, v$database d
  3  Where tp.platform_name=d.platform_name;

ENDIAN_FORMAT
-------------
Little
```

In this case, the system we are on is using the little endian format. Thus, if the query returns the same result on both systems, you have a compatible datafile format; if it does not, you need to use RMAN and the **compatible** parameter to transport the tablespaces.

Converting the Tablespace Endian Format with RMAN

If you need to convert a tablespace for another platform, RMAN is the tool you use. First, create the directory that the converted file will be copied to. In our example, we will use the directory path c:\oracle\oradata\betatwo. Next, make the tablespace that you wish to convert read-only. Then, simply start RMAN and use the new **convert tablespace** command, as shown in this example:

```
Rman target=/
RMAN> convert tablespace users
to platform = ' AIX-Based Systems (64-bit)'
db_file_name_convert='c:\oracle\oradata\betatwo',
'c:\oracle\admin\transport_aix';
```

You can also convert datafiles at the destination site:

```
Rman target=/
RMAN> convert datafile =  c:\oracle\oradata\betatwo\*'
from platform = ' AIX-Based Systems (64-bit)'
db_file_name_convert='c:\oracle\oradata\betatwo',
'c:\oracle\admin\transport_aix';
```

The platform name that we use comes from the PLATFORM_NAME column of the V$TRANSPORTABLE_PLATFORM view. Oracle is very picky about putting the name in just right.

Once you have completed the conversion, you may complete the move by manually moving the datafiles/tablespaces using transportable tablespaces. Note that in cases where the endian format is different, RMAN will not be able to help you. If the endian format is the same, read the next section to see if you can use RMAN's new feature that moves your database across platforms for you!

We Like to Move It! Move It!

RMAN in Oracle Database 10*g* offers a brand-new feature to assist you in moving your databases across platforms of the same endian byte format. The **convert database** command, in combination with the DBMS_TDP package, can help reduce the overall workload of moving your database between platforms. The process consists of the following steps:

1. Open the database as read only:

   ```
   startup mount;
   alter database open read only;
   ```

2. Use the **dbms_tdb.check_db** procedure to check the database state. You should have already determined your platform name (from the PLATFORM_NAME column of the V$TRANSPORTABLE_PLATFORM view). This program should be run with **serveroutput** turned on, as in this example:

   ```
   set serveroutput on
   declare
        db_ready boolean;
       begin
        db_ready := dbms_tdb.check_db
   ```

```
            ('Microsoft Windows IA (32-bit)',dbms_tdb.skip_readonly);
        end;
        /
```

3. Use the **dbms_tdb.check_external** procedure to identify external objects:

```
set serveroutput on
Declare
    external boolean;
begin
    external := dbms_tdb.check_external;
end;
/
```

4. When the database is ready for transport, use the RMAN **convert database** command. RMAN creates scripts that are required for the database move. RMAN does not actually do the move, but creates only the files that are used for the move.

```
CONVERT DATABASE NEW DATABASE 'copydb'
        transport script 'c:\oracle\copydb\copyscripts'
        to platform 'Microsoft Windows IA (32-bit)';
```

The optional **db_file_name_convert** parameter allows you to define the directory filenames for datafiles that need to be converted. Here is an example:

```
CONVERT DATABASE NEW DATABASE 'copydb'
        transport script 'c:\oracle\copydb\copyscripts'
        to platform 'Microsoft Windows IA (32-bit)'
        db_file_name_convert
        'C:\ORACLE\PRODUCT\10.2.0\ORADATA\ROB10R2','C:\ORACLE\NEWDBDEST';
```

Once the command completes, simply follow the directions that RMAN will give you to complete the conversion process on the target database.

Sometimes Things Just Go Wrong

Sometimes you just cannot get a break. On some rare occasions, RMAN just will not work like it's supposed to. So, what do you do? Here are some suggestions we suggest you try if your RMAN restore/recover is not quite going the way you want it to.

If the restore is not working successfully, execute the **crosscheck** command, and make sure that all the backup sets that RMAN thinks are available are actually available. The **crosscheck** command is used to make sure that the RMAN catalog and control file are in synch with what is actually on disk. We discuss the **crosscheck** command in detail in Chapter 17. In the case where a **restore** command is not working, or is picking up a wrong backup set, run these commands:

```
crosscheck backup of database;
crosscheck backup of archivelog all;
crosscheck archivelog all;
```

If any of the backup sets show up with a status of EXPIRED, then you may be missing backup sets that are needed to perform the restore. This can be due to many reasons—loss of a disk drive, or perhaps a well-meaning system administrator has backed them up to tape for you.

If the backup sets are all okay, and the restore is still not running correctly, then make sure you check things such as how you have set the UNTIL TIME parameter if you are doing a point-in-time restore. True story: In one case, we had a DBA (a really smart one, by the way) who was trying to restore from a backup taken on 04/01/09. Unfortunately, it took something like four hours for him to realize that his restore string read 03/01/09 instead. It is small syntax errors like this that can drive you mad.

Oftentimes the error messages can give you some clue as to the problem. For example, they may indicate that the media management layer is not properly configured. This is a common problem, particularly if you are restoring a backup to a database server other than the one where the backup originally occurred.

If the **restore** command works great but the **recover** command is failing, check for syntax errors again. This is another place where you can get your dates wrong. Also make sure that all the needed archived redo logs are available. One problem we see from time to time is that some of the needed redo ends up not having been archived. Sometimes we have to go to the online redo logs to replay that redo. In cases like this, we will actually need to go into SQL*Plus and complete the recover process manually.

To recover manually using the SQL*Plus prompt, do the following:

1. Perform the normal RMAN **restore** command. It's fine to use the **until time** clause.

2. Perform the normal RMAN **recover** command.

3. If Step 2 fails, start SQL*Plus from a separate terminal window.

4. Determine which archived redo logs are required for your restore. You can use the V$ARCHIVED_LOG and V$LOG views to determine the location of the archived redo logs, the time they were created, and their associated log sequence number. Here is an example of queries against the V$ARCHIVED_LOG, V$LOG, and V$LOGFILE views that give us some important information that we will need to complete our recovery:

```
-- This tells us the last archived redo log file sequence number.
select max(sequence#), max(resetlogs_time), max(resetlogs_change#)
from v$log_history
where resetlogs_time=(select max(resetlogs_time) from v$log_history);

-- This tells us the online redo log sequence numbers.
select a.sequence#, a.first_time, b.member
from v$log a, v$logfile b
where a.group#=b.group#
order by a.sequence#;
```

5. The **recover database** command will indicate which archived redo log it wishes to recover. In some cases, you may need to enter the name of the online redo log to recover the database, because the redo contained in it had not been archived yet. In this case, we will apply the redo from online redo log C:\ORACLE\ORADATA\BETA1\REDO02.LOG:

```
SQL> recover database
ORA-00279: change 5071334 generated at 08/17/2008 15:35:51 needed for
thread 1
ORA-00289: suggestion :
/oracle01/flash_recovery_area/ORCL/archivelog/2008_08_17/
o1_mf_1_5_4bk6onh8_.arcORA-00280:
```

```
change 5071334 for thread 1 is in sequence #5
Specify log: {<RET>=suggested | filename | AUTO | CANCEL}
C:\ORACLE\ORADATA\BETA1\REDO02.LOG
Log applied.
Media recovery complete.
```

6. Then simply open the database:

```
SQL> alter database open;
Database altered.
```

Summary

In this chapter, we have explored point-in-time recoveries that are available in RMAN. Time-based, SCN-based, and cancel-based recoveries are all supported by RMAN. This chapter also touched on RMAN's ability to recover through the **resetlogs** command, a welcome feature to us old-time DBAs who have struggled with this issue.

This chapter also covered some miscellaneous recovery topics. We touched on things like archived redo log recoveries, read-only tablespace recovery considerations, and block-level recovery. In short, we covered the wide gamut of RMAN's recovery toolbox.

Finally, in this chapter, we explored tablespace point-in-time recoveries. Specifically with tablespace point-in-time recovery, you can run into complexities for various reasons, and thus, it might well be that you will need to reference the Oracle documentation for implementation details that relate to your case.

CHAPTER
15

Surviving User Errors:
Flashback Technologies

edia recovery with RMAN provides critical safeguards against all kinds of unforeseeable problems—block corruption, hardware failure, even complete database loss. But so far, this book has ignored the largest cause of media recovery operations: user error.

User errors can be roughly defined as errors caused by a human mistake (rather than a software or hardware malfunction), such as a table updated with wrong values, a table dropped, or a table truncated. Such errors are far more common than hardware failures (although, let's face it, human errors get *called* hardware errors all the time). In general, user errors are classified as logical errors—the error is logical, within the data itself, and a correction that is done using media recovery options will typically be very expensive.

In this chapter, we will discuss the new means in Oracle Database 11*g* to programmatically prepare for and recover from logical errors. This includes some functionality that existed already in the Oracle10*g* Database, but has been extended (and made less painful). This also includes brand-new functionality that can radically change the time it takes to recover from user-induced disasters.

Prepared for the Inevitable: Flashback Technology

When it comes to logical errors, media recovery should not be our first line of attack. It frequently is the line of attack, but this leads to massive outages. Typically, user error is not something that we can recover from, because the action is not interpreted as an error by the database. "Delete * from scott.emp" is not an error; it's a perfectly legitimate DML statement that is duly recorded in the redo stream. So if you restore the datafile and then perform recovery, all you will do is, well, delete * from scott.emp again. Point-in-time recovery can be a solution, but not for the DBA who is committed to avoiding full restore of the database—way too much outage. Tablespace point-in-time recovery (TSPITR) offers a toned-down version of media recovery for user error, but it still requires a full outage on the tablespace, has huge space demands for a temporary clone instance, and has object-level limitations (think advanced queuing tables).

To assist with user error recovery, and to complement RMAN's media recovery excellence, Oracle introduced in Oracle Database 10*g* the concept of Flashback Technology. Flashback Technology refers to a suite of features that give you a multitude of different ways to survive user errors. These features have as a unifying concept only the simple idea that user errors occur and recovering from them should be simple and fast. The Flashback features are

- Flashback Query

- Flashback Table

- Flashback Transaction—*new* in 11*g*

- Flashback Drop

- Flashback Database

- Flashback Data Archive—*new* in 11*g*

Flashback Query

If you think you recognize Flashback Query from earlier versions of the RDBMS, you're right: there was some Flashback Query functionality that existed as early as 9*i*. Since version 10.2, that functionality has been expanded and simplified to allow you better access. By better access, we mean you don't rely on the PL/SQL interface. Now, it's all built into SQL (and sometimes RMAN!), so you don't have to program a PL/SQL block to look at historical versions of a row.

Flashback and the Undo Segment: A Love Story

The first two types of flashback—Flashback Query and Flashback Table—have their functionality based entirely on technology that has existed in the Oracle Database for years: the undo segments (the segments formerly known as rollback). Undo segments exist to undo transactions that have not been committed. In the past, a committed transaction could not be undone because the associated "before" image of the row in the rollback segment was immediately freed up to be overwritten—so the before images could not be reliably found later on.

This is still true: when you commit a transaction, the extent in the undo segment that contains the before image of the row is freed up to be overwritten. However, changes in the way undo space was used in 9*i* mean that all new transactions look for unused space in the undo tablespace before overwriting previously used segments. Even then, the transaction always goes to the oldest remaining extents first. This means that "before" images of rows in the database last far longer than they ever have in the past—we can reliably find undo segments from past transactions.

This is all very good news, and in 9*i* and later, Oracle put it to use with the flashback query. Now, we can actually control how long we want the undo extents to remain before they are overwritten. After doing so, we can put undo to good use—to help us undo committed transactions that were mistakes.

The ability to query or change objects back to a certain time in the past is predicated on how long our undo extents can remain in the undo tablespace before they are overwritten. Undo extents are used by new transactions based on space pressure in the undo tablespace. Basically, Oracle will not overwrite undo extents until it has exhausted all other possibilities first—that is, until every extent in the undo tablespace has been utilized. Then, it finds the oldest extent and overwrites it. The threshold for how far back you can use a flashback query/table is set by how long Oracle can go from the time a transaction is committed until the time that undo extents for that transaction get overwritten. The period from committed transaction to undo extent being overwritten is the *flashback window*.

Plenty of factors go into determining the flashback window, but the most important is your transaction load. You can view statistics for undo usage with the view V$UNDOSTAT. Each row in this view represents the number of undo blocks utilized for a ten-minute period. Running a few analyses of this view through peak usage should provide a decent template to guide your settings for undo.

Setting Undo Parameters for Flashback Query and Flashback Table

The guidelines for using Flashback Query demand that you first have automatic undo enabled—no rollback segments are allowed. (Okay, that's a lie. It is feasible to use flashback operations with old-school rollback segments, but Oracle discourages it and so do we. There is no reason to try to set up rollback segments manually anymore.) Oracle is best left to control undo management by using new algorithms that emphasize retention of transactional history—algorithms that do not exist in rollback segments. Therefore, you need to set UNDO_MANAGEMENT = AUTO in the PFILE or SPFILE. Second, set your UNDO_TABLESPACE parameter to point to which tablespace will handle undo duties. Finally, set UNDO_RETENTION = *value in seconds.* This sets the desired length of time to keep undo segments around.

Performing Flashback Query

Performing a flashback query of a table is simple, now that it has been integrated into SQL. All you need to know is the point in time in the past for which you would like to view the contents of a table, and then you plug it into your query:

```
select scr_id, head_config from ws_app.woodscrew as of timestamp
 to_timestamp('2009-06-27 04:27:00','YYYY-MM-DD HH:MI:SS')
 where scr_id=1001;

    SCR_ID HEAD_CONFIG
---------- --------------------
      1001 Phillips
      1001 Phillips
```

You can also use an SCN qualifier, if you know the System Change Number (SCN) of the change you are looking for:

```
select scr_id, head_config from ws_app.woodscrew
as of scn 751652 where scr_id=1001;

    SCR_ID HEAD_CONFIG
---------- --------------------
      1001 Slot
      1001 Slot
```

Flashback Versions Query with Oracle Enterprise Manager

Implementing Flashback Query—and its relatives, Flashback Transaction Query and Flashback Versions Query—is far simpler when you use Oracle Enterprise Manager (OEM). OEM allows you to quickly turn a flashback query into an operation that can undo a user-induced error, whether through a flashback table or by applying the undo SQL for the bad transaction.

OEM combines the best features of multiple technologies to provide a user interface that helps you get answers quickly. Underneath the covers, it uses transaction queries to build a more complete investigation into what logical errors have occurred. The first of these is Flashback Versions Query, which also is referred to as row history. Flashback Versions Query provides the ability to look at every version of a row that existed within a specified timeframe. So, you provide a query to look at a row, and a timeframe that you want to review, and Oracle returns a list of every iteration that row has been through. This allows you to see a row morph over time, to determine what may be at the root of the problem.

RMAN Workshop: *Explore Flashback Versions Query*

Workshop Notes

This workshop has you build a few tables and populate them with a few dummy rows so that you can watch Flashback Versions Query in action. The following is the DDL and DML for the WOODSCREW table and indices. This code also builds a secondary table with rows for future use in Flashback Drop and Flashback Database. You are obviously not compelled to use our simplistic little test here and could easily test with existing dummy tables in your system.

```
create table woodscrew (
 scr_id           number not null,
 manufactr_id     varchar2(20) not null,
 scr_type         varchar2(20),
 thread_cnt       number,
 length           number,
 head_config      varchar2(20));

alter table woodscrew add primary key
 (scr_id, manufactr_id) using index;

create index woodscrew_identity on woodscrew
(scr_type, thread_cnt, length, head_config);

create table woodscrew_inventory (
 scr_id           number not null,
 manufactr_id     varchar2(20) not null,
 warehouse_id     number not null,
 locale           varchar2(20),
 count            number,
 lot_price     number);

insert into woodscrew values
(1000, 'Tommy Hardware', 'Finish', 30, 1.5, 'Phillips');
insert into woodscrew values
(1000, 'Balaji Parts, Inc.', 'Finish', 30, 1.5, 'Phillips');
insert into woodscrew values
(1001, 'Tommy Hardware', 'Finish', 30, 1, 'Phillips');
insert into woodscrew values
(1001, 'Balaji Parts, Inc.', 'Finish', 30, 1, 'Phillips');
insert into woodscrew values
(1002, 'Tommy Hardware', 'Finish', 20, 1.5, 'Phillips');
insert into woodscrew values
(1002, 'Balaji Parts, Inc.', 'Finish', 20, 1.5, 'Phillips');
insert into woodscrew values
(1003, 'Tommy Hardware', 'Finish', 20, 1, 'Phillips');
insert into woodscrew values
(1003, 'Balaji Parts, Inc.', 'Finish', 20, 1, 'Phillips');
```

```
insert into woodscrew_inventory values (
1000, 'Tommy Hardware', 200, 'NORTHEAST', 3000000, .01);
insert into woodscrew_inventory values (
1000, 'Tommy Hardware', 350, 'SOUTHWEST', 1000000, .01);
insert into woodscrew_inventory values (
1000, 'Balaji Parts, Inc.', 450, 'NORTHWEST', 1500000, .015);
insert into woodscrew_inventory values (
1005, 'Balaji Parts, Inc.', 450, 'NORTHWEST', 1700000, .017);
commit;
```

Step 1.   Open the OEM console's database home page and go to Schema | Tables. This opens a view of all tables in the schema of the user you have logged in as. You can change this to the owner of the WOODSCREW table by changing the Schema to the user and then clicking Go. Then, you can select the WOODSCREW table, and choose View Data from the Actions drop-down list. After you click View Data, OEM will display the view shown in the following illustration. Note that the value for column HEAD_CONFIG is Phillips for all rows.

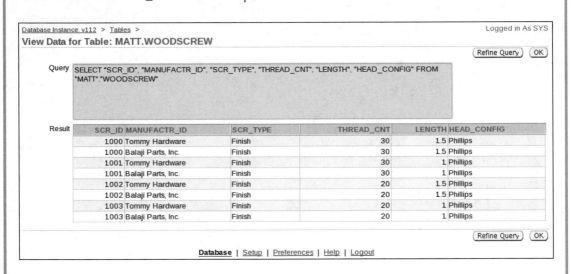

Step 2.   Change rows in the table to reflect a different head configuration for the woodscrews:

```
update woodscrew set head_config= 'Slot'
where scr_id=1001;
commit;
```

Step 3.   View the new data in the table. From Tables, select the WOODSCREW table, choose View Data from the Actions drop-down list, and then click Go. Note in the following illustration that two rows now have Slot instead of Phillips.

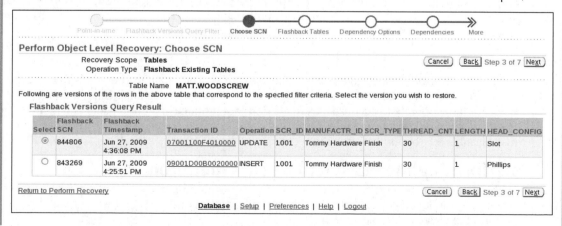

Database Instance: v112 > Tables >   Logged in As SYS
View Data for Table: MATT.WOODSCREW

| | Refine Query | OK |

Query SELECT "SCR_ID", "MANUFACTR_ID", "SCR_TYPE", "THREAD_CNT", "LENGTH", "HEAD_CONFIG" FROM
"MATT"."WOODSCREW"

Result

SCR_ID	MANUFACTR_ID	SCR_TYPE	THREAD_CNT	LENGTH	HEAD_CONFIG
1000	Tommy Hardware	Finish	30	1.5	Phillips
1000	Balaji Parts, Inc.	Finish	30	1.5	Phillips
1001	Tommy Hardware	Finish	30	1	Slot
1001	Balaji Parts, Inc.	Finish	30	1	Slot
1002	Tommy Hardware	Finish	20	1.5	Phillips
1002	Balaji Parts, Inc.	Finish	20	1.5	Phillips
1003	Tommy Hardware	Finish	20	1	Phillips
1003	Balaji Parts, Inc.	Finish	20	1	Phillips

| | Refine Query | OK |

Step 4. Within the woodscrew business organization, it was determined that the screws with scr_id 1001 are *not* slot-headed, but rather Phillips. There has been a logical corruption introduced into the database. Let's review a single row and see what versions the row has been through. From the Tables view, select the WOODSCREW table, choose Flashback Versions Query from the Actions list, and then click Go. This takes you to the Perform Object Level Recovery Wizard.

Step 5. In the wizard, we need to provide the parameters of our flashback query. First, choose all columns by selecting Move All under Step 1 of the wizard. Click the Next button from the right side of the page. Under Step 2, specify a clause that isolates a single row. We will use the following WHERE clause:

```
where scr_id=1001 and manufactr_id='Tommy Hardware'
```

After specifying the clause and clicking the Next button, we see the different versions of the row, along with the option to select which SCN to recover back in time to (should we so decide). Here, we see the insert and the update as two transactions. We can click the Transaction ID to view the specific transactions (we'll discuss the function Flashback Transaction later in this chapter).

Point-in-time   Flashback Versions Query Filter   **Choose SCN**   Flashback Tables   Dependency Options   Dependencies   More

Perform Object Level Recovery: Choose SCN

Recovery Scope **Tables**   Cancel | Back | Step 3 of 7 | Next
Operation Type **Flashback Existing Tables**

Table Name **MATT.WOODSCREW**

Following are versions of the rows in the above table that correspond to the specfied filter criteria. Select the version you wish to restore.

Flashback Versions Query Result

Select	Flashback SCN	Flashback Timestamp	Transaction ID	Operation	SCR_ID	MANUFACTR_ID	SCR_TYPE	THREAD_CNT	LENGTH	HEAD_CONFIG
⦿	844806	Jun 27, 2009 4:36:08 PM	07001100F4010000	UPDATE	1001	Tommy Hardware	Finish	30	1	Slot
○	843269	Jun 27, 2009 4:25:51 PM	09001D00B0020000	INSERT	1001	Tommy Hardware	Finish	30	1	Phillips

Return to Perform Recovery   Cancel | Back | Step 3 of 7 | Next

Database | Setup | Preferences | Help | Logout

Step 6. Review the different operations that have occurred against this row in the database, and determine which row may be in error. From this view, we can continue with the wizard and perform a flashback of the table.

Step 7. If you want proof that OEM is working hard for you, click Back to go to the Recovery: Row History Filter page. At the bottom is a button for Show Flashback Versions Query SQL; after clicking this, you will see the SQL you are blissfully ignoring, as shown next.

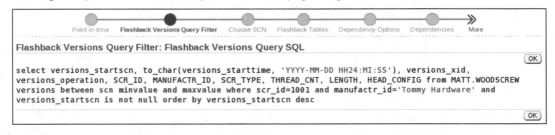

Flashback Table

Perhaps the most compelling function of the Flashback Technology is the ability to simply revert a table to a previous point in time in a simple and straightforward fashion. The ability to perform point-in-time recovery on a table or group of tables has often been the grounds by which entire clone databases are built—just so that a single table could be extracted and then imported back into production. With Flashback Table, unnecessary cloning operations can be put to pasture.

Flashback Table employs the same mechanisms as Flashback Query—with information stored in the undo segments, Oracle can rewind a database one transaction at a time to put the table back the way it was at a specified time in the past. Because the Flashback Table operation depends on undo, the same restrictions apply here as they do to Flashback Versions Query: you can only flashback a table as far back as the undo segments allow you.

In addition to undo, the ability to flashback a table requires you to enable row movement for the table. Row movement was initially put in place as a function of partitioned tables, which allowed an updated row to move to the appropriate partition if the update changed the partition key value. Flashback Table employs row movement to assist in the rewind operations. To enable row movement, use the following **alter table** command:

```
alter table woodscrew enable row movement;
```

Flashback Table cannot save you from all user errors. Certain DDL operations that occur against a table cannot be undone. Most importantly, you cannot flashback a table to before a **truncate table** operation, because a **truncate** does not produce any undo—that is why **truncate** exists, versus a **delete * from table**. Also, Flashback Table cannot be used for a dropped table (use Flashback Drop for that—see the section "Flashback Drop").

Performing the Flashback Table Operation from SQL

With row movement enabled, you can move forward with normal operations on the table. Then, when a user-induced corruption occurs in the table, you can use SQL at the command line to perform the Flashback Table operation:

```
flashback table matt.woodscrew to timestamp
to_timestamp('2009-06-29 13:30:00','YYYY-MM-DD HH24:MI:SS')
```

Alternatively, you can use the SCN if you have been able to determine the SCN (through investigation via Flashback Query, for example):

```
flashback table matt.woodscrew to scn 751652;
```

Like Flashback Query, the performance of a Flashback Table operation depends on the amount of data that has to be rewound, and how far back you are rewinding. The more data that has to be undone, the longer the operation will take. But this will always be faster than trying to perform a point-in-time recovery of the table by other methods: you can try TSPITR, or you can try to restore the tablespaces to a different instance and then export the table from the clone instance and import back into production. Nothing can come close to Flashback Table in terms of performance.

Flashback Table with Oracle Enterprise Manager

The added strength of OEM for Flashback Table is the ability to first explore the table via Flashback Versions Query to determine exactly what time you want to flashback to. If you already know the exact time for flashback, using SQL at the command line would be just as simple as using the Flashback Table Wizard in OEM. OEM does, however, provide a way to determine what dependencies are at play, as described in the following RMAN Workshop.

Enabling Row Movement and Flashback Table

It is critical that you foresee possible Flashback Table candidates and enable row movement as soon as possible. You cannot enable row movement and then flashback the table to a point prior to enabling row movement. Such an operation will result in the following error:

```
ORA-08189: cannot flashback the table because row movement is not enabled.
```

In other words, you cannot wait until you need to flashback a table, and then enable row movement as part of the flashback operation.

RMAN Workshop: *Explore Flashback Table*

Workshop Notes

In this workshop, we will "accidentally" delete all the rows from the WOODSCREW table, and then flashback the entire table to the point in time right before the delete transaction took place.

Step 1. View the data in WOODSCREW. Because of previous exercises, it might be worthwhile to truncate the table and then to reinsert the records manually using the original population script (as shown earlier in the "Explore Flashback Versions Query" RMAN Workshop). Make sure you have all eight rows. Also, make sure you enable row movement prior to inserting the fault:

```
alter table woodscrew enable row movement;
```

Step 2. Insert the fault. We will delete all the rows in the table by using a SQL*Plus DELETE statement. Afterward, select View Data from the Actions drop-down list in OEM to view the empty table.

```
delete from woodscrew;
commit;
```

Step 3. From the OEM database home page, go to Schema | Tables, select the schema that owns the WOODSCREW table, and then choose the WOODSCREW table. From the Actions drop-down list, choose Flashback Table, and then click Go. This takes you into a Perform Object Level Recovery: Point-in-Time Wizard, which first asks you to specify the point in time to recover to. We will pretend not to know when the delete took place, so choose to evaluate row changes and transactions—the first choice. Click Next.

Step 4. You will now see a familiar screen for the RMAN Workshops in this chapter—the Flashback Versions Query interface. Here, we have to set our columns (MOVE ALL) and a WHERE clause to narrow down our search. Because the delete affected all rows, we can choose a single row to review here. We will use the same row as in previous workshops:

```
where scr_id=1001 and manufactr_id='Tommy Hardware'
```

Now we can see the information about the DELETE operation that whacked our poor WOODSCREW table.

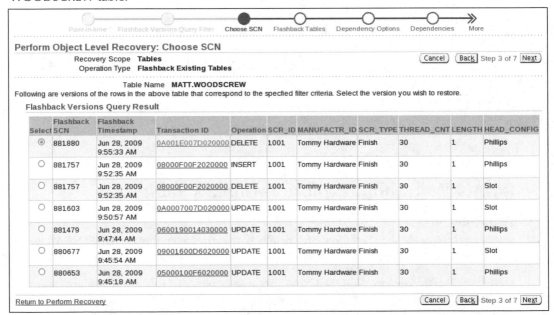

Step 5. You can click the Transaction ID to review the entire delete. However, of more importance to us is the Flashback SCN column, which shows us the SCN to set to undo the DELETE operation. With the appropriate DELETE transaction checked from the list, simply click Next to automatically choose the flashback SCN specified on this screen.

Step 6.   In Step 4 of 7 in the Flashback Table Wizard, Oracle allows you to specify any logically related objects that should be rewound to the same SCN as this table. Oracle automatically honors all constraints that exist for the table, but you may have logically related tables that should be flashed back. If so, this is your opportunity to specify them. In our example, we do not have any related tables, so click Next.

Step 7.   Voilà! We are magically transported to Step 7 of 7, where we see the summary of the action that will take place. Of most use here are the Show Row Changes and Show SQL buttons, which will show, respectively, what rows will be changed and what SQL will be executed by OEM on your behalf. Click Submit. If there is any problem, or if you just feel better about it, you can cut the OEM-generated SQL into a SQL*Plus session to run the Flashback Table operation:

```
FLASHBACK TABLE MATT.WOODSCREW TO SCN 804109;
```

Flashback Transaction

There's always more than one way to organize a hunt for bad data in the database. Flashback Transaction allows you to look at all changes made by a specific transaction, or all transactions in a certain timeframe. Then you can go in and undo an error at the transaction level, instead of rolling back the entire table. This focused level of flashback allows you to keep all other changes that have occurred since the error—that is, you are removing the smallest possible error and leaving the good data. You can also flashback a subset of the transaction, instead of undoing the entire transaction as an atomic unit.

Unlike Flashback Versions Query, Flashback Transaction does not use the undo segment to understand what needs to be done to back out of an error. It utilizes the Redo instead and takes advantage of the LogMiner capabilities to dig out the transaction change vectors and then determine the best way to roll back the changes.

Again, the best way to use Flashback Transaction is through OEM. Save yourself the grief and log into the OEM Console for the database, and use the same set of operations described in the RMAN Workshop "Explore Flashback Versions Query" to get yourself back to the WOODSCREW table, where you can see one of the available actions is Flashback Transaction.

Before you can utilize Flashback Transaction, you will need to have turned on supplemental log data for the table in question. As with enabling row movement for Flashback Table, if you don't turn on supplemental log data before you need Flashback Transaction, it's too late. The undo segment won't have the necessary information required to perform the flashback. From within OEM, if you try to utilize Flashback Transaction, you will see an error informing you of the actions you need to take.

Flashback Transaction Query is compelling because it allows you to review a bad transaction in its entirety, even though the window into the error may be only a single row. For instance, if we found that a row of our WOODSCREW table had been deleted, we could look up that row in Flashback Versions Query. Then, we could get the Transaction ID for the delete operation and see how many other rows were deleted at the same time. This provides a look at the full scope of the problem.

RMAN Workshop: *Utilize Flashback Transaction from Enterprise Manager*

Workshop Notes
This workshop will introduce a fault and then utilize Flashback Transaction to undo the fault. The same WOODSCREW table is used as in previous workshops in this chapter.

Step 1. Enable supplemental log data for the WOODSCREW table:

```
SQL> alter database add supplemental log data;
SQL> alter database add supplemental log data (primary key) columns;
```

Step 2. Introduce a fault into the WOODSCREW table:

```
SQL> delete from woodscrew where scr_id='1001';
commit;
```

Step 3. Someone querying for a one-inch finish woodscrew manufactured by Tommy notices that the screw has been deleted from the database, even though these are still offered by the company to customers. What happened? We turn to the OEM Database Home | Schema | Tables page. Choose the owner of the WOODSCREW table and click Go.

Step 4. Select the WOODSCREW table, choose Flashback Transaction from the Actions list, and click Go. Select a time range from the Query Time Range that matches when the possible deletion may have taken place. Click Go and watch as OEM briefly mines the logfiles for information on all transactions for the table in question. Then, the available transactions for flashback are displayed.

Step 5. Click the linked Transaction ID from the available table of transactions, and you can view the details of each change vector associated with this transaction. This provides you with the specific SQL statement that was used to perform each of the undesirable actions and provides a roadmap for undoing just a specific subset of the whole transaction. Click OK to go back to the Flashback Transaction Wizard.

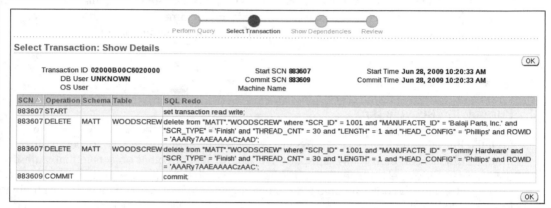

Step 6. Click Next, and the Flashback Transaction will finalize the operations that will be required to complete the rollback. This may take a few moments to complete. When it's completed, you will get a final review page of the operations, as well as a box in which to run any follow-up SQL that may be required to confirm the changes, prior to a commit. Then, click Finish.

Step 7. OEM provides a confirmation that the selected transaction has been backed out completely. Click OK and then you are put back in the Tables page, where you can View Data on WOODSCREW again to confirm that the delete has been backed out.

Flashback Drop

Flashback Drop allows you to "undrop" database objects. No longer will you have users desperate for the entire database to be restored to a point in the past because they thought they were on the DEV instance instead of PROD.

There's nothing all that dramatic about how Flashback Drop has been implemented. In Oracle Database 10g, when you drop a table, it merely gets renamed to a system-identifiable string, but the segment remains in the tablespace it was dropped from. It will remain there until you undrop the object or purge it manually, or until the tablespace runs out of space for regular objects. If space pressure exists in the tablespace, Oracle will begin to age out dropped objects from oldest to newest.

When you drop an object, Oracle doesn't just rename that object. All dependent objects move to the Recycle Bin as well: indices, triggers, and constraints. Therefore, when you undrop the table, its entire dependent chain comes back with it.

The Recycle Bin

The Recycle Bin is a virtual directory of all dropped objects in the database—simply a list of objects that have been dropped but not purged. The Recycle Bin is a logical container and does not require a specific storage location; actual storage for all dropped objects is in the tablespace the object was in prior to being dropped. Consider an example. User matt drops the table WS_APP.WOODSCREWS. The WOODSCREWS table is in the tablespace WS_APP_DATA, but its two indices are in the WS_APP_IDX tablespace. When WOODSCREWS is dropped, the table is renamed to an internal name, and so are the two indices that existed on the table. Both appear in the DBA_RECYCLEBIN view. However, the actual WOODSCREWS table segment still exists in the WS_APP_DATA tablespace, and the indices still exist in the WS_APP_IDX tablespace. They are logically part of the Recycle Bin, but physically exist in the same place they always have.

The Recycle Bin is quickly viewed via the following two data dictionary views:

- USER_RECYCLEBIN

- DBA_RECYCLEBIN

Purging the Recycle Bin

Manually eliminating dropped objects from the Recycle Bin is not necessary. Objects are purged from the Recycle Bin as the space is required by other segments in the tablespace. In other words, dropped objects continue to take up space in a tablespace until other objects in that tablespace run out of free space elsewhere. Then, the first dropped object is the first object to be purged. Oracle automatically looks to purge indices before tables so that actual data is the last thing to be lost. Recycle Bin objects will also be dropped before a tablespace autoextends, if autoextend is on.

The new **purge** command exists to purge the Recycle Bin. You can purge by user, by object, by tablespace, or purge the entire Recycle Bin:

```
purge table matt.woodscrews;
purge index matt.woodscrews_pk_idx;
purge tablespace sales;
purge recyclebin;
```

How Long Do Objects Live in the Recycle Bin?

A valid question, but the answer, of course, is: it depends. No, really. It depends. The real question you probably want to ask is, "Can I control how long an object lives in the Recycle Bin?" The answer to this question is no.

You cannot force an object to remain in the Recycle Bin if space pressure exists in the tablespace of the dropped object. Even with autoextend on, the dropped object is purged before the tablespace extends. So, if you want to determine a certain lifespan on objects in the Recycle Bin, you are left with two choices: either make the tablespace overly large to accommodate drops, or manually manage the Recycle Bin and purge those objects you don't want to keep, to leave space for those you do want to keep.

You can, therefore, shorten the stay of an object in the Recycle Bin. But you cannot force something to remain, given a shortage of tablespace room.

Undropping Objects in the Recycle Bin

Getting objects back from the Recycle Bin is pretty simple—a simple SQL command renames the object back to its original name, along with any dependent objects:

```
flashback table ws_app.woodscrews to before drop;
```

Of course, sometimes it's not that simple. For instance, if you have multiple dropped objects with the same name, then you would have to refer to the object by its new and improved Recycle Bin name:

```
SQL> select object_name, original_name, droptime,
dropscn from user_recyclebin;
OBJECT_NAME                           ORIGINAL_NAME
------------------------------------  ---------------

DROPTIME               DROPSCN
-------------------   ----------
RB$$48623$INDEX$0                     PK_WOODSCREW
2004-01-12:15:21:26     1241651
RB$$48622$TABLE$0                     WOODSCREW
2004-01-12:15:21:26     1241652
SQL> flashback table " RB$$48622$TABLE$0" to before drop;
```

Note the quotes around the Recycle Bin object name. These are required due to special symbols in the name.

If you have dropped an object and then created a new object with the same name, you can still flashback the first object. There is syntax in the flashback SQL to rename the object when you pull it from the Recycle Bin:

```
flashback table ws_app.woodscrews to before drop rename to woodscrews_history;
```

RMAN Workshop: *Explore Flashback Drop and the Recycle Bin*

Workshop Notes

It's time to drop our WOODSCREW table and review the Recycle Bin contents. Although you can do this at the command line, this workshop shows you how to undrop a table by using OEM.

Step 1.   Drop the WOODSCREW table. From OEM, choose Schema | Tables and change the schema to the owner of the WOODSCREW table. Select the WOODSCREW table from the list of tables, and then click the Delete with Options button. A screen offers multiple delete options— drop the table, delete the rows, or truncate. Choose the first option (DROP) and click Yes.

Step 2. View the list of tables. Note that WOODSCREW is no longer in the list. Click the Recycle Bin link in the lower-right corner of the screen to access the Recycle Bin, shown in the following screen shot. First, under Search, enter the Schema Name of the owner of the WOODSCREW table and click Go.

Database Instance: v112 > Tables >
Recycle Bin

When you drop a table from a non-system, locally managed tablespace, Oracle does not immediately reclaim the space associated with the table. Oracle places the table and any associated objects in the Recycle Bin, where, in case the table was dropped in error, it can be recovered (Flashback Drop) at a later time.

Search

Schema Name		Table	
MATT	🔦		(Go)

Results

(Purge) (Flashback Drop)
Select All | Select None | Expand All | Collapse All

Select	Object Name	Schema	Recovery Scope	Tablespace	Drop Time	Create Time	Size	Operation
☐	▼ Recycle Bin							(View Content)
☐	▼ WOODSCREW	MATT	TABLE	USERS	2009-06-28:10:41:32	2009-06-27:16:16:58	8	(View Content)
☐	▷ SYS_C0010415	MATT	INDEX	USERS	2009-06-28:10:41:32	2009-06-27:16:17:14	8	(View Content)
☐	▷ WOODSCREW_IDENTITY	MATT	INDEX	USERS	2009-06-28:10:41:32	2009-06-27:16:17:14	8	(View Content)

Note in the screen shot that the table WOODSCREW is in the Recycle Bin, along with the primary key index and the WOODSCREW_IDENTITY index. Also worth noting is the View Content button on the right, which allows you to look at the rows in the dropped table to determine if it is the correct object to be flashback dropped.

Step 3. Check the box next to the WOODSCREW table, and then click the Flashback Drop button.

Step 4. The next page enables you to rename the undropped object. After you click Next, you get the Impact Analysis from OEM explaining what exactly will be flashback dropped, as shown next.

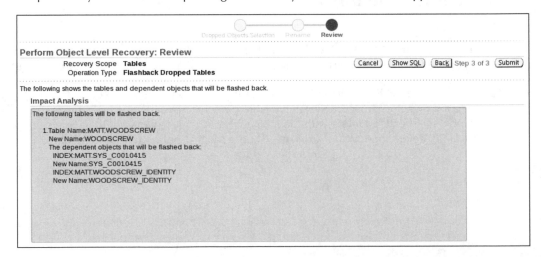

Dropped Objects Selection — Rename — **Review**

Perform Object Level Recovery: Review

Recovery Scope **Tables**   (Cancel) (Show SQL) (Back) Step 3 of 3 (Submit)
Operation Type **Flashback Dropped Tables**

The following shows the tables and dependent objects that will be flashed back.

Impact Analysis

The following tables will be flashed back.

1. Table Name:MATT.WOODSCREW
   New Name:WOODSCREW
   The dependent objects that will be flashed back:
   INDEX:MATT.SYS_C0010415
   New Name:SYS_C0010415
   INDEX:MATT.WOODSCREW_IDENTITY
   New Name:WOODSCREW_IDENTITY

Step 5.   Click Submit. A confirmation screen tells you the selected tables have been restored from the Recycle Bin. You can confirm this by navigating back to OEM and choosing Administration | Schema | Tables and choosing the schema of the WOODSCREW owner. The WOODSCREW table will be back in place.

Step 6.   Delete the WOODSCREW table again. Click Recycle Bin and find the dropped table again, as outlined in Step 2. Check the box next to WOODSCREW, and then click Purge (next to Flashback Drop).

Step 7.   A confirmation screen asks you if you want to purge the selected objects and their dependents. Click Continue. The Recycle Bin of the WOOD user is now empty of the WOODSCREW table and its indices. They have been permanently removed from the database.

Flashback Database

The most revolutionary Flashback Technology may also be the one that gets used the least often. Flashback Database provides the ability to quickly rewind the entire database to a previous point in time. This operation has the same end result as you would get from doing point-in-time recovery using RMAN or user-managed recovery. However, Flashback Database does not require the restore of all of the database's datafiles from the most recent backup, followed by a roll-forward using all the archive logs that have accumulated since that backup. By avoiding these costly operations, Flashback Database can perform a point-in-time recovery in a fraction of the time typically required for such an operation.

Flashback Database works by incrementally recording all blocks that have changed at a timed interval. These flashback "checkpoints" then provide the points to which the database can be "rewound." After rolling back to the flashback checkpoint, you can use archive logs to then roll forward to the exact time or SCN specified by the **flashback database** command. So, the operation uses new technology as well as that old standby, the archive logs, to provide a fast way to perform point-in-time recovery.

Typically, there are fewer archive logs to be applied after a flashback checkpoint than must be applied to the last backup (typically taken every night, versus every few minutes for flashback logs), so the recovery stage of flashback is very quick.

Flashback Logs

Flashback Database implements a new type of log, called the *flashback log*. Flashback logs are generated by the database at regular intervals and accumulate in the flash recovery area (FRA). You must have an FRA for Flashback Database; the logs cannot be created anywhere else. The flashback log contains a copied image of every block that has been changed since the last flashback log was generated. These blocks can then be reinstated into the database when a **flashback database** command is issued to rewind the database back to its state at the time specified in the **flashback** command.

Because entire blocks are being dumped to the flashback logs, they can accumulate very quickly in extremely active databases. Setting an appropriately sized FRA is crucial to the success of meeting your Flashback Database needs. In addition, you can manually turn off flashback logging, as follows, for certain tablespaces that could be manually re-created after a Flashback Database operation, and thereby decrease the amount of logging that occurs:

```
alter tablespace ws_app_idx flashback off;
```

You can turn flashback logging back on at any time, as follows, but it is worth noting that you cannot rewind backward through a flashback logging gap for the tablespace you turned off:

```
alter tablespace sales_idx flashback on;
```

Any tablespace that has flashback logging turned off for any period within the **flashback database** command would need to be offlined prior to performing the Flashback Database operation.

Flashback Retention Target

The lifespan of flashback logs correlates directly to how far back in time you would like to have the Flashback Database option. By default, the flashback logs are kept long enough so that you can always flashback 24 hours from the current time. If this is too long or too short a time, you can change it with an initialization parameter:

```
alter system set db_flashback_retention_target=720;
```

The value is specified in minutes (720 would be 12 hours).

RMAN Workshop: *Configure for Flashback Database*

Workshop Notes

This workshop walks you through the primary steps required to configure the database initially for using flashback logging for Flashback Database operations.

Step 1. Shut down the database and startup mount. The database must be mounted but not open.

```
SQL> select status from v$instance;
```

In addition, check to make sure the database is in ARCHIVELOG mode, which is required for Flashback Database:

```
SQL> archive log list;
Database log mode              Archive Mode
Automatic archival             Enabled
Archive destination            USE_DB_RECOVERY_FILE_DEST
Oldest online log sequence     62
Next log sequence to archive   64
Current log sequence           64
```

Step 2. Set the flashback retention target to your desired value. We will use 12 hours as the window.

```
alter system set db_flashback_retention_target=720
SCOPE=BOTH SID='*';
```

Step 3. Set the values for DB_RECOVERY_FILE_DEST and DB_RECOVERY_FILE_DEST_SIZE (FRA parameters). Note that if you have already set these for your RMAN backup strategy, you should review the parameters now. Flashback logs increase FRA usage significantly. It would behoove you to at least double the given size of the FRA.

```
SQL> ALTER SYSTEM SET DB_RECOVERY_FILE_DEST_SIZE = 2335825920
SCOPE=BOTH SID='*';
SQL> ALTER SYSTEM SET DB_RECOVERY_FILE_DEST = '/u02/fra/'
SCOPE=BOTH SID='*';
```

Step 4.   Turn flashback logging on. This is done in the same fashion as turning ARCHIVELOG mode on—with an **alter database** command when the database is mounted but not open:

```
alter database flashback on;
```

Step 5.   Turn flashback logging off for any tablespaces that you deem do not require it:

```
alter tablespace sales_idx flashback off;
```

Step 6.   Open the database:

```
alter database open;
```

Flashback Database: Tuning and Tweaking

So, you've determined that Flashback Database provides you with a fallback position you desire for your database, and you have determined how far back you want your fallback position to be. You've set your DB_FLASHBACK_RETENTION_TARGET. Now, the questions come up: "How do I know if I have enough space in my FRA to handle the volume of flashback logs being generated? And, for that matter, how much flashback logging is occurring?" The following sections answer those questions.

Using V$FLASHBACK_DATABASE_LOG

One thing at a time. First, Oracle provides built-in analysis for you to use in determining if you need to increase the size of your FRA. After you enable flashback logging, Oracle begins to keep track of the amount of flashback logging that is occurring, and stores it in the view V$FLASHBACK_DATABASE_LOG. This view actually provides an estimate for the total flashback size:

```
select estimated_flashback_size from v$flashback_database_log;
```

Note that this view gives the size for flashback logs, not for all users in the FRA, so you need to add this value to whatever size you need for archive logs and RMAN backups. This estimated value only gets better with age, meaning that as the database runs through its day-to-day (and then month-to-month) operations, Oracle can provide a better estimate of the size. So, it is a good idea to check back in with this estimator to find out if you still have the right specifications in place.

V$FLASHBACK_DATABASE_LOG also provides you with the actual oldest time that you can flashback the database to, given the current size of the FRA and the currently available flashback logs. You can use this as another indicator of space issues in the FRA. The following **select** statement will provide you with a basic understanding of the state of the flashback logs:

```
select oldest_flashback_scn, oldest_flashback_time
from v$flashback_database_log;
```

Using V$FLASHBACK_DATABASE_STAT

Oracle has built a monitoring view so that you can keep your eye on flashback logging activity. V$FLASHBACK_DATABASE_STAT provides you with information on flashback data generated over the course of a period of time (typically, a one-hour window extending back from sysdate). In addition to showing how much flashback logging occurred, this view posts the redo generated and the actual database data generated over the same period. The following **select** shows a sample output of this view:

```
select * from v$flashback_database_stat;
BEGIN_TIM END_TIME  FLASHBACK_DATA   DB_DATA  REDO_DATA
--------- --------- --------------- ---------- ----------
ESTIMATED_FLASHBACK_SIZE
-----------------------
19-SEP-05 19-SEP-05       9003008   15294464    3986944
 210247680
19-SEP-05 19-SEP-05      15884288   21225472    5766144
 210247680
19-SEP-05 19-SEP-05      10248192   25772032    5162496
 210075648
```

RMAN Workshop: *Perform Flashback Database*

Workshop Notes

It's time to give it a test-drive. We are going to introduce a fault that cannot be handled by any of the other, less-intrusive forms of flashback: the table truncate. Because the truncate does not produce any redo, we cannot do a Flashback Table operation. So, we are forced to do a flashback of the entire database.

Here, we are using the WOOD.WOODSCREW_INVENTORY table that we built earlier, during the "Explore Flashback Versions Query" RMAN Workshop. If you did not build the table yet, do so now.

Step 1.   First, get the current SCN from the database. Because we are simply testing, we can prepare for the test by getting the current SCN prior to putting the fault into the database:

```
SQL> select current_scn from v$database;
CURRENT_SCN
----------------
885524
```

Step 2.   Introduce the fault:

```
SQL> truncate table wood.woodscrew_inventory;
Table truncated.
```

Step 3.   Shut down the database, and then remount. The database must be mounted and not open for flashback.

```
SQL> connect / as sysdba
Connected.
SQL> shutdown immediate;
Database closed.
Database dismounted.
ORACLE instance shut down.
SQL> startup mount;
```

Step 4. Issue the **flashback** command:

```
SQL> flashback database to scn 885524;
Flashback complete.
```

Step 5. Open the database in READ-ONLY mode to confirm that the table has been flashed back to the appropriate SCN:

```
SQL> alter database open read only;
Database altered.
SQL> connect wood/wood;
Connected.
SQL> select count(*) from woodscrew_inventory;
  COUNT(*)
----------
        4
```

Step 6. Open the database by using the **resetlogs** operation:

```
SQL> connect / as sysdba
SQL> shutdown immediate;
SQL> startup mount;
SQL> alter database open resetlogs;
```

Flashback Data Archive (Total Recall)

New in Oracle 11g, Flashback Data Archive (sometimes referred to as Oracle Total Recall) is a set of functions that allow you to permanently archive all changes to a table so that you can go back to any point in time and look at the data as it was in the past. Unlike Flashback Query, which is dependent on the transitory nature of undo, Flashback Data Archive requires a specific type of tablespace to be built so that it can house the version information required to look back in time at a particular table.

Flashback Data Archive is useful for auditing and archival purposes on tables that have legal or regulatory sensitivities. You can configure the data archive to be of a set retention period that matches either the business or regulatory need, and then you assign the table to that archive. Once this is complete, you can utilize a straightforward flashback query in SQL to look back in time at the table as of months or even years ago.

You should be mindful of two architectural restrictions based on how the archive data is generated and accessed. If you put a table in a data archive mode, you cannot:

■ Perform an **alter table** command with an UPGRADE clause

■ Perform a drop table

Either of these actions will result in an error:

```
ORA-55610: Invalid DDL statement on history-tracked table
```

> ## RMAN Workshop: *Create a Flashback Data Archive*
>
> ### Workshop Notes
> In this workshop, we will create a Flashback Data Archive, and then add our WOODSCREW_
> INVENTORY table to the archive. This archive will have a Quota of 500MB and a retention
> period of one year.
>
> **Step 1.** Create a tablespace to house the Flashback Data Archive:
>
> ```
> SQL> create tablespace FBS datafile'/home/oracle/app/oracle/oradata/v112/fbs01.dbf' size 1024M;
> ```
>
> **Step 2.** Create the Data Archive in the FBS tablespace:
>
> ```
> SQL> create flashback archive default FDA01 tablespace FBS quota 500M retention 1 year;
> ```
>
> **Step 3.** Add the matt.woodscrew_inventory table to the Flashback Data Archive FDA01. This is
> straightforward because we made FDA01 the default data archive for any table added without a
> specification.
>
> ```
> SQL> alter table matt.woodscrew_inventory flashback archive;
> ```

Summary

In this chapter, we introduced the new means of recovering from user-induced errors, known
collectively in the Oracle Database as Flashback Technology. The new Flashback Technology
allows you to recover from logical errors in a faster, less-intrusive way than running a full-bore
media recovery. We discussed using Flashback Versions Query to determine the full scope of the
logical corruption. We illustrated using the Flashback Table command to recover from a bad DML
statement, as well as from a table drop. We discussed the new Flashback Transaction option in
11*g* that utilizes the redo logs to undo an erroneous action at the transaction level instead of at the
table level. We discussed the Flashback Database functionality, which allows for a point-in-time
recovery of an entire database without requiring a full restore of the datafiles from backup. We
ended the chapter by reviewing the new 11*g* functionality for creating a Flashback Data Archive,
which allows a historical point of view on a table as far back as you have space to hold the records.

CHAPTER
16

Maintaining RMAN

ntropy is a nasty result of the second law of thermodynamics. Basically, *entropy* describes the tendency of an ordered system to become disordered, the result of which is the requirement to maintain that system. RMAN is no different. When using RMAN, you have to maintain a number of things to keep it running smoothly.

In this chapter, we talk all about maintaining RMAN. From the **crosscheck** command to retention policies to redundancy policies, everything you need to know about keeping RMAN from falling apart is provided here. After we have talked about RMAN maintenance issues, we will discuss some issues specific to the recovery catalog, including an introduction to the recovery catalog schema itself.

RMAN Maintenance

You didn't think you could just continue using RMAN without having to maintain it, did you? The truth is, RMAN is fairly maintenance free, but you need to be aware of a few maintenance-related things, which we address in this section. First, we are going to talk about the **crosscheck** command, followed by a discussion of retention policies. Next, we discuss the **change** command, and then, the **delete** command. Finally, we end this section with a discussion of cataloging your existing database backups in RMAN.

Cross-Checking RMAN Backups

You may encounter situations in which backup set pieces or copies are listed in the control file or recovery catalog but do not physically exist on the backup media (disk or tape). The physical files constituting the backup or copy might have been deleted, either by some process (for example, a separate retention policy for the tape management system that you are using or a damaged tape), or perhaps by the loss of a physical device that had backup set pieces on it.

In cases where the RMAN catalog and the physical backup destinations are out of synchronization, the **crosscheck** command is used to validate the contents of the RMAN information in the control file or in the recovery catalog against the actual physical backup set pieces that are on the backup media.

When using the **crosscheck** command, we are interested in the status of each backup set or copy. Each backup set or copy has status codes that are listed in the STATUS column of the views: V$BACKUP_SET for backup set pieces and V$DATAFILE_COPY for copies if you are using a control file, and RC_BACKUP_SET for backup set pieces and RC_DATAFILE_COPY for copies if you want to look in the recovery catalog. There are several different backup status codes, but for now we are interested primarily in two:

- **A**   AVAILABLE; RMAN assumes the item is available on the backup media.

- **X**   EXPIRED; the backup set piece or the copy is stored in the RMAN catalog (meaning the control file or the recovery catalog), but is not physically on the backup media.

When the **crosscheck** command is executed, RMAN checks each backup set or copy listed in the catalog and determines if it is on the backup media. If it is not, that piece will be marked as EXPIRED and will not be a candidate for any restore operation. If the piece exists, then it will maintain its AVAILABLE status. If a backup piece or copy was previously marked EXPIRED and it becomes available again (for example, after the recovery of a failed disk drive), then the **crosscheck** command will return that piece's status to AVAILABLE.

You must be connected to a target database to run the **crosscheck** command. There is no requirement to be connected to a recovery catalog. If your backups are on disk, you will not need to allocate a channel before issuing the **crosscheck** command. If you are backing up to a tape device (via MML, for example), then you will need to allocate a maintenance channel before you can issue the **crosscheck** command. This is not required if you have configured predefined channels. If you use mixed channels (some to disk and some to SBT, for example), then the **crosscheck** command will only check the backups that were made using the channel used during the backup.

In the following example of the execution of the **crosscheck** command, we are checking the status of all backup sets and determining whether they exist on the backup medium:

```
RMAN> crosscheck backup;
using channel ORA_DISK_1
crosschecked backup piece: found to be 'AVAILABLE'
backup piece
handle=/oracle/app/oracle/flash_recovery_area/ROB1/backupset/2009_09_08
/o1_mf_annnn_TAG20090908T025101_5bd6qydw_.bkp RECID=2 STAMP=696999070
crosschecked backup piece: found to be 'AVAILABLE'
backup piece
handle=/oracle/app/oracle/flash_recovery_area/ROB1/backupset/2009_09_08
/o1_mf_nnndf_TAG20090908T025112_5bd6r0mz_.bkp RECID=3 STAMP=696999072
crosschecked backup piece: found to be 'EXPIRED'
backup piece
handle=/oracle/app/oracle/flash_recovery_area/ROB1/backupset/2009_09_08
/o1_mf_annnn_TAG20090908T031112_5bd7xjo7_.bkp RECID=9 STAMP=697000272
Crosschecked 3 objects
```

In this example, we have crosschecked a total of four backup set pieces. Notice that the **crosscheck** command lists all the backup set pieces that were found to be available. It also lists those backup set pieces that were not found on the backup media, shows them to be EXPIRED, and sets their status to EXPIRED at the same time. Note that the **crosscheck** command will not change a backup set piece with a status of DELETE to AVAILABLE. Any backup marked with a status of DELETE cannot be changed.

You can also crosscheck datafile backups, tablespace backups, control file backups, and SPFILE backups. Additionally, you can be selective in the specific backup you want to crosscheck by identifying the tag associated with that backup. You can even crosscheck all backups taken based on the device used or based on a time period. The following are several examples of crosschecking backups:

```
crosscheck backup of datafile 1;
crosscheck backup of tablespace users;
crosscheck backup of controlfile;
crosscheck backup of spfile;
crosscheck backup tag='SAT_BACKUP';
crosscheck backup completed after 'sysdate - 2';
crosscheck backup completed between 'sysdate - 5' and 'sysdate - 2;
crosscheck backup device type sbt;
```

The first example is a crosscheck of backups. As you might expect, you also can crosscheck archive log backups:

```
RMAN> crosscheck archivelog all;
released channel: ORA_DISK_1
allocated channel: ORA_DISK_1
channel ORA_DISK_1: SID=36 device type=DISK
validation succeeded for archived log
archived log file
name=/oracle/app/oracle/flash_recovery_area/ROB1/archivelog/2009_09_08
/o1_mf_1_7_5bd8qq6g_.arc RECID=10 STAMP=697001111
validation succeeded for archived log
archived log file
name=/oracle/app/oracle/flash_recovery_area/ROB1/archivelog/2009_09_08
/o1_mf_1_8_5bd8qr29_.arc RECID=11 STAMP=697001112
validation failed for archived log
archived log file
name=/oracle/app/oracle/flash_recovery_area/ROB1/archivelog/2009_09_08
/o1_mf_1_9_5bd8qv45_.arc RECID=12 STAMP=697001115
validation succeeded for archived log
archived log file name=/oracle/app/oracle/flash_recovery_area/ROB1/archivelog/2009_09_08
/o1_mf_1_10_5bd8rco9_.arc RECID=13 STAMP=697001131
Crosschecked 4 objects
```

You can crosscheck archived redo log backups based on a number of criteria, including time, SCN (specific or high/low range), or log sequence number. You can even use the **like** parameter, along with wildcards, to crosscheck specific archive log backups. Here are some variations in the **crosscheck** command:

```
crosscheck archivelog like 'ARC001.log';
crosscheck archivelog 'D:\ORACLE\ADMIN\RECOVER\ARCH\ARC00012.001';
crosscheck archivelog like '%ARC00012.001';
crosscheck archivelog from time "to_date('01-10-2006', 'mm-dd-yyyy')";
crosscheck archivelog until time "to_date('01-10-2006', 'mm-dd-yyyy')";
crosscheck archivelog from sequence 12;
crosscheck archivelog until sequence 522;
```

To crosscheck copies, use the **crosscheck copy** command. You can crosscheck datafile copies, control file copies, archived redo log copies, and archived redo logs (on disk). Here are two examples of crosschecking these kinds of objects:

```
crosscheck copy of datafile 5;
crosscheck datafilecopy 'd:\oracle\oradata\recover\recover_users_01.dbf';
```

RMAN Workshop: *Using the crosscheck Command*

Workshop Notes

This workshop assumes that you have a functional Oracle database running in ARCHIVELOG mode. Additionally, this workshop assumes that you are backing up your database to disk, that you have a tablespace called USERS in your database, and that one datafile is associated with the USERS tablespace. Note that our sample output might look different than your output does.

Step 1. Using RMAN, back up the USERS tablespace:

```
RMAN> backup tablespace users;
```

```
Starting backup at 08-SEP-09
using channel ORA_DISK_1
channel ORA_DISK_1: starting full datafile backup set
channel ORA_DISK_1: specifying datafile(s) in backup set
input datafile file number=00004 name=/ora01/oracle/rob1/rob1/users01.dbf
channel ORA_DISK_1: starting piece 1 at 08-SEP-09
channel ORA_DISK_1: finished piece 1 at 08-SEP-09
```
piece handle=/oracle/app/oracle/flash_recovery_area/ROB1/backupset/2009_09_08
/o1_mf_nnndf_TAG20090908T032848_5bd8yjmq_ .bkp tag=TAG20090908T032848
comment=NONE
```
channel ORA_DISK_1: backup set complete, elapsed time: 00:00:01
Finished backup at 08-SEP-09
Starting Control File and SPFILE Autobackup at 08-SEP-09
piece handle=/oracle/app/oracle/flash_recovery_area/ROB1/autobackup/2009_09_08
/o1_mf_s_697001330_5bd8ylgv .bkp comment=NONE
Finished Control File and SPFILE Autobackup at 08-SEP-09
```

Step 2.   Look at the output of the backup, and determine the backup set piece that has just been created. The backup set piece is highlighted in the output in Step 1. Note that we are not removing the control file autobackup set piece.

Step 3.   Remove the backup piece from the disk.

Step 4.   Issue the **crosscheck** command to determine the status of the backup set piece. RMAN will detect that the backup set piece has been removed and mark it EXPIRED. Note that the control file autobackup piece is still available.

```
RMAN> crosscheck backup;
using channel ORA_DISK_1
crosschecked backup piece: found to be 'AVAILABLE'
backup piece
handle=/oracle/app/oracle/flash_recovery_area/ROB1/backupset/2009_09_08
/o1_mf_annnn_TAG20090908T025101_5bd6qydw_.bkp RECID=2 STAMP=696999070
crosschecked backup piece: found to be 'AVAILABLE'
backup piece
handle=/oracle/app/oracle/flash_recovery_area/ROB1/backupset/2009_09_08
/o1_mf_nnndf_TAG20090908T025112_5bd6r0mz_.bkp RECID=3 STAMP=696999072
crosschecked backup piece: found to be 'EXPIRED'
backup piece
handle=/oracle/app/oracle/flash_recovery_area/ROB1/backupset/2009_09_08
/o1_mf_annnn_TAG20090908T031112_5bd7xjo7_.bkp RECID=9 STAMP=697000272
crosschecked backup piece: found to be 'EXPIRED'
backup piece
handle=/oracle/app/oracle/flash_recovery_area/ROB1/backupset/2009_09_08
/o1_mf_nnndf_TAG20090908T032848_5bd8yjmq_.bkp RECID=14 STAMP=697001328
crosschecked backup piece: found to be 'AVAILABLE'
backup piece
handle=/oracle/app/oracle/flash_recovery_area/ROB1/autobackup/2009_09_08
/o1_mf_s_697001330_5bd8ylgv_.bkp RECID=15 STAMP=697001330
Crosschecked 5 objects
```

Validation of RMAN Backups

RMAN provides the **validate** command, which allows you to examine a given backup set and verify that it can be restored. This command is similar to the **backup validate** command, with a few extra bells and whistles. With this command, you can choose which backup sets to verify, whereas the **validate** parameter of the **backup** or **restore** command allows RMAN to determine which backup set to validate. Typically, in a production environment, you would use the **backup validate check logical** command after you have completed a backup to perform database validation. Thus, the **validate** command is most often used for specific occasions where you want to check specific backup sets, or perhaps you want to check all backup sets in the flash recovery area.

The **validate** command does not check all database blocks. Those blocks that have never been used will not be checked. If you are running with compatibility set to 10.2 or greater, then blocks contained in locally managed tablespaces that were once used but are now unused will not be checked.

The **validate** command, by default, will only check for physical corruption, and logical corruption is not considered. If you wish to also check for logical corruption of the block, use the **check logical** option of the **validate** command. When the **validate** command has completed its checks, it will populate the V$DATABASE_BLOCK_CORRUPTION view. It might be a good idea, if you have configured monitoring of your databases, to include the count of the number of rows in this view in that monitoring. This way, you can tell if you have corruption issues you need to deal with.

The **validate** command will not discover certain types of corruption. Thus, it's possible to run this command and still experience problems with your database. These situations are rare, but they do happen. One example of this is interblock corruption. This is corruption that occurs between two blocks, as might be the case in a block chaining situation. The **validate** command will not detect interblock corruption.

Here is an example of the use of the **validate** command to get the primary key of the backup set and validate that backup set. Note that you must pass the primary key ID of the backup set that you wish to validate. This primary key can be determined by running the **list backupset summary** command.

```
RMAN> list backup summary;
List of Backups
===============
Key     TY LV S Device Type Completion Time #Pieces #Copies Compressed Tag
------- -- -- - ----------- --------------- ------- ------- ---------- ---
2       B  A  A DISK        08-SEP-09       1       1       YES        TAG20090908T025101
3       B  F  A DISK        08-SEP-09       1       1       YES        TAG20090908T025112
4       B  F  A DISK        08-SEP-09       1       1       YES        TAG20090908T025112
5       B  A  A DISK        08-SEP-09       1       1       YES        TAG20090908T025311
6       B  A  A DISK        08-SEP-09       1       1       NO         TAG20090908T025326
7       B  F  A DISK        08-SEP-09       1       1       NO         TAG20090908T025328
8       B  A  A DISK        08-SEP-09       1       1       NO         TAG20090908T025355
9       B  A  X DISK        08-SEP-09       1       1       YES        TAG20090908T031112
10      B  F  X DISK        08-SEP-09       1       1       YES        TAG20090908T031114
11      B  A  X DISK        08-SEP-09       1       1       YES        TAG20090908T031116
12      B  A  A DISK        08-SEP-09       1       1       NO         TAG20090908T032531
13      B  F  A DISK        08-SEP-09       1       1       NO         TAG20090908T032815
14      B  F  X DISK        08-SEP-09       1       1       NO         TAG20090908T032848
15      B  F  A DISK        08-SEP-09       1       1       NO         TAG20090908T032850
```

Note the different columns. These columns are defined in the Oracle Database Backup and Recovery Reference Guide (and there are a number of them). In this case, most of the columns are pretty self-explanatory except, perhaps, these:

- **Key** This is a unique identifier for each backup.

- **TY** This is the backup, either a backup set (B) or a proxy copy (P).

- **LV** This indicates the type of backup. A full database backup set is denoted with an F. An archived redo log backup is denoted by an A. If the backup is an incremental backup, the LV column will contain a 0 for a base backup or a 1 for an incremental backup.

- **S** This indicates the status of the backup. This value can include A for available, U for unavailable, and X if all the backup set pieces have expired.

To make sure the backup is usable (not corrupted, as opposed to physically present), we can validate the backup set. In this case, it's an archive log backup:

```
RMAN> validate backupset 2;
```

We can also validate all backups in the flash recovery area:

```
RMAN> validate recovery area;
```

Backup Retention Policies

In Chapter 3, we mentioned configuration of a retention policy for RMAN backups and copies. A *retention policy* is a method of managing backups and copies and specifying how long you want to keep them on your backup media. You can define two basic types of retention policies: the *recovery window backup retention policy* and the *backup redundancy backup retention policy*. We will talk more about those shortly.

Each redundancy policy is persistent until changed or removed (or until the control file is rebuilt using the **create controlfile** command). Additionally, the two redundancy policies are mutually exclusive. Finally, even with a redundancy policy, physical backup pieces are not removed until you use the **delete** command with the **obsolete** parameter to remove them.

Now, let's look at each of these retention policies in more detail. After that, we will look at how we manage RMAN backups and copies that are made obsolete as a result of the retention policies.

Recovery Window Backup Retention Policy

The use of this type of retention policy is based on the latest possible date that you want to be able to recover your database to. With a recovery window backup retention policy, you can direct Oracle to make sure that if you want to be able to recover your database to a point in time two weeks ago, you will be able to do so.

For example, assume that today is Monday and you have three backups. The first backup was taken the day before, on Sunday; the second backup was taken on the previous Thursday; and the last backup was taken ten days ago, last Saturday. If the recovery window is set to seven days, then the first two backups (Sunday's and Thursday's) would be considered current. However, the backup taken ten days ago, on the previous Saturday, would be considered obsolete. If we wanted to establish this seven-day redundancy policy for RMAN, we would use the **configure** command with the **retention policy to recovery window** parameter:

```
configure retention policy to recovery window of 7 days;
```

Backup Redundancy Backup Retention Policy

When the backup redundancy backup retention policy is used, RMAN will maintain *x* number of database backups, starting with the most current backup. For example, suppose you have configured a backup redundancy of 3 and you did backups on Monday, Tuesday, Wednesday, and Thursday. Because the retention policy is set to 3, Oracle will obsolete the Monday backup as soon as the Thursday backup is successfully completed.

The backup window backup retention policy is enabled using the **configure** command with the **retention policy to redundancy** parameter. If you wanted to set the backup window backup retention policy to 3, you would use the following command:

```
configure retention policy to redundancy 3;
```

Retention Policy Maintenance

When a given backup or copy meets the criteria of a backup retention policy and becomes obsolete, what happens depends on whether you are using the flash recovery area (FRA) or a manual backup location. You may also want to change a backup so that its retention policy is different than the default retention policy. Let's look at these options next.

Retention Policy Maintenance When Using the Flash Recovery Area   If you are using the flash recovery area, RMAN will eventually remove the backup set pieces, image copies, or archived redo logs (we will just call these backups for now) from the FRA based on space demands. This means that the backups will remain in place potentially for some time, until the space is needed by another backup or archive log. As a result, you might look at FRA space utilization and be concerned because it's growing when you feel it should be steady state. You can determine the amount of FRA space that is consumed by obsolete backups by querying the V$RECOVER_FILE_DEST view column SPACE_RECLAIMABLE. By using this view, you can determine if you have allocated sufficient space to the FRA. Here is an example of a query against V$RECOVER_FILE_DEST:

```
SQL> select * from v$recovery_file_dest;
NAME                               SPACE         SPACE       SPACE            NUM
                                   LIMIT          USED  RECLAIMABLE          FILES
-------------------------------- ------------- ----------- ----------- -------------
c:\oracle\flash_recovery_area  3,221,225,472 934,699,008  23,445,504            17
```

In this case, we find that about 23MB of space is reclaimable. RMAN will clear these files once there is a need for the free space. If we were to find that the amount of used space is quite high and the amount of reclaimable space is low, we may have underallocated the amount of space to the FRA. If you find the amount of reclaimable space is quite high, then you might want to review your retention criteria and make sure they are set correctly. You will also want to make sure you have not overallocated space to the FRA.

If you see that you have space being allocated to obsolete backup sets, you can use the RMAN **report obsolete** command to see details of the obsolete backups, as seen here:

```
RMAN> report obsolete;
```

```
using target database control file instead of recovery catalog
RMAN retention policy will be applied to the command
RMAN retention policy is set to redundancy 2
Report of obsolete backups and copies
Type                    Key     Completion Time     Filename/Handle
------------------- ------  ------------------  --------------------
Backup Set              61      08-SEP-09
   Backup Piece         71      08-SEP-09
/oracle/app/oracle/flash_recovery_area/ROB1/autobackup/2009_09_08
/o1_mf_s_697001330_5bd8ylgv_.bkp
```

Retention Policy Maintenance When Using a Manual Backup Location   If you are not using the FRA, you are backing up to a manual backup location. In this case, you will need to manage the expired backups a little differently. As with the FRA, once a backup is no longer needed, RMAN will mark the backup or copy as OBSOLETE. You can determine which backups RMAN has marked as OBSOLETE with the **report obsolete** command (we will look at the **report** command in the next chapter):

```
report obsolete;
```

In the case of a manual backup area, you will need to perform one more step to get RMAN to remove the obsolete backups. This extra step is the execution of the **delete obsolete** command. This command tells RMAN to physically delete the backup on physical disk. It will also mark the metadata related to the backup in the control file as deleted, and it will remove all records associated with the backup in the recovery catalog.

Retention Policy Maintenance When Using the Flash Recovery Area   Of course, you might take a backup and decide that you want to change its retention policy. In this event, you would use the RMAN **change** command with the **keep** parameter to change the retention policy of the backup you want to retain. When you use this command, the backups or copies impacted are considered to be *long-term backups* and are not subject to the chosen retention policy.

In Oracle Database 11*g*, the **change** command modifies a backup so that it becomes an archival backup (discussed first in Chapter 11). The resulting archival backup can be retained forever (this requires a recovery catalog), or you can define a new date where the archival backup should later be made obsolete by RMAN (if the retention date is greater than 365 days from now, you will need a recovery catalog). With an archival backup, the related archived redo log backups are also preserved and will be marked obsolete at the time indicated (assuming they are not needed for another archival backup). Here is an example of using the **change** command in Oracle Database 11*g* to create an archival backup:

> **NOTE**
> *If you are using a flash recovery area, you cannot use the* **keep forever** *clause of the* **keep** *command.*

```
-- Run the list backup command to get the backup key we need
-- This is just a partial listing of the list backup output
-- We bolded the backup set key values that we will be using.
RMAN> list backup;
```

```
List of Backup Sets
===================
BS Key  Type LV Size       Device Type Elapsed Time Completion Time
------- ---- -- ---------- ----------- ------------ ---------------
267     Full    1.09G      DISK        00:06:50     12-FEB-10
        BP Key: 200  Status: AVAILABLE  Compressed: NO  Tag:
TAG20100212T121310
        Piece Name: C:\ORACLE\FLASH_RECOVERY_AREA\CLASS\BACKUPSET\2010_02_12\
O1_MF_NNNDF_TAG20100212T1
21310_5QCB274D_.BKP
  List of Datafiles in backup set 3
-- change a backup so it will be retained forever. 267 is the backup key
-- that we get from the list backup RMAN command
-- Change backup 267 from an obsolete status to a keep status.
-- Note that this command requires a recovery catalog
change backupset 267 keep forever;

-- change a backup so it will be kept for 7 more days
change backupset 267 keep until time 'sysdate + 7' logs;

-- Obsolete a backup
change backupset 33 nokeep;
```

In versions of Oracle before Oracle Database 11*g*, the **change** command will change the retention criteria as stated previously. These are not considered archival backups, though, and as a result, the archived redo logs are not automatically preserved. To ensure the backup will always be recoverable to the current point in time (but consider the impact that this might have on storage), you will need to use the **keep logs** parameter to make sure the retention criteria of archived redo log backups is also modified, as seen in this example:

```
change backupset 267 keep forever logs;
```

When you change a backup or copy, you have to reference the key that is associated with that backup. As you can see from the previous example, you find this key by using the **list backup** or **list copy** command (in our case, we use backup set key 267), each of which is described in the next chapter. Note that the **keep forever** option has some restrictions. First, it's only available if you are using a recovery catalog in any versions. Second, in any version prior to Oracle Database 11*g*, the **keep forever** option is not available if you are using the FRA.

Once you have reviewed the report, you can direct RMAN to actually remove the backups with the RMAN **delete** command with the **obsolete** parameter:

```
delete obsolete;
```

The change Command

We introduced the **change** command earlier in this chapter and explained how it can be used to modify the retention window assigned to a specific backup. The **change** command allows you to change the status of a backup. You might have a case where one of your backup media devices becomes unavailable for a period of time (perhaps someone spilled a drink down the power supply). In this event, you can use the **change** command to indicate that the backups on that device are unavailable.

Once you have properly scolded the employee for fiddling around in your hardware area with a drink and have fixed the device, you can change the status of that backup set with the **change** command again so that it will take on an AVAILABLE status. You can also change a backup status to UNAVAILABLE, indicating that the backup is not currently available. This effectively disqualifies the backup from consideration during restore and recovery operations, but protects the backup record from being removed during the execution of the **delete expired** command. Here are some examples of the use of the **change** command:

```
change backup of database tag = 'GOLD' unavailable;
change backup of database like '%GOLD%' unavailable;
change backupset 33 unavailable;
change backupset 33 available;
change archivelog 'd:\oracle\mydb\arch\arch_001.arc' unavailable;
```

Using the **change** command, you can modify the status of archived redo log backups. For example, you can modify the status to UNAVAILABLE for all archived redo logs that have been backed up at least a given number of times. You can also change the status of all backups that occurred using a given device. Examples of these operations are shown next:

```
change archivelog all backed up 5 times to device type disk unavailable;
change backup of database device type disk unavailable;
```

You can also use the **change** command to delete backup sets (physically on the backup media and from the control file and recovery catalog). The **delete** parameter is used for this operation. First, you need to identify the RMAN backup IDs of the backups that you wish to remove. Use either the **list backup** or **list copy** command (each of which is covered in detail in the next chapter) to perform this operation. Here is an example of how to get the backup ID using the **list backup** command (we have modified the output somewhat to save space):

```
RMAN> list backup;
List of Backup Sets
===================

BS Key  Size
------- ----------
56      18.88M
  List of Archived Logs in backup set 56
  Thrd Seq      Low SCN    Low Time  Next SCN  Next Time
  ---- ------- ---------- --------- ---------- ---------
  1    69      593930     07-SEP-09 612201     07-SEP-09
  1    70      612201     07-SEP-09 635114     08-SEP-09
  1    71      635114     08-SEP-09 635383     08-SEP-09
  Backup Set Copy #1 of backup set 56
  Device Type Elapsed Time Completion Time Compressed Tag
  ----------- ------------ --------------- ---------- ---
  DISK        00:00:05     08-SEP-09       YES        TAG20090908T025101

    List of Backup Pieces for backup set 56 Copy #1
    BP Key  Pc# Status      Piece Name
    ------- --- ----------- ----------
    72      1   AVAILABLE
/oracle/app/oracle/flash_recovery_area/ROB1/backupset/2009_09_08
/o1_mf_annnn_TAG20090908T025101_5bd6qplq_.bkp
```

```
    Backup Set Copy #2 of backup set 56
    Device Type Elapsed Time Completion Time Compressed Tag
    ----------- ------------ --------------- ---------- ---
    DISK        00:00:05     08-SEP-09          YES       TAG20090908T025101

      List of Backup Pieces for backup set 56 Copy #2
      BP Key  Pc# Status      Piece Name
      ------- --- ----------- ----------
      87       1   AVAILABLE
/oracle/app/oracle/flash_recovery_area/ROB1/backupset/2009_09_08
/o1_mf_annnn_TAG20090908T025101_5bd9od5x_.bkp


BS Key  Size
------- ----------
57      57.50K

  List of Archived Logs in backup set 57
  Thrd Seq     Low SCN     Low Time  Next SCN   Next Time
  ---- ------- ----------- --------- ---------- ---------
  1    1       635384      08-SEP-09 635574     08-SEP-09

  Backup Set Copy #1 of backup set 57
  Device Type Elapsed Time Completion Time Compressed Tag
  ----------- ------------ --------------- ---------- ---
  DISK        00:00:00     08-SEP-09          YES       TAG20090908T025101

    List of Backup Pieces for backup set 57 Copy #1
    BP Key  Pc# Status      Piece Name
    ------- --- ----------- ----------
    73       1   AVAILABLE
/oracle/app/oracle/flash_recovery_area/ROB1/backupset/2009_09_08
/o1_mf_annnn_TAG20090908T025101_5bd6qydw_.bkp

  Backup Set Copy #2 of backup set 57
  Device Type Elapsed Time Completion Time Compressed Tag
XX
  ----------- ------------ --------------- ---------- ---
  DISK        00:00:00     08-SEP-09          YES       TAG20090908T025101

    List of Backup Pieces for backup set 57 Copy #2
    BP Key  Pc# Status      Piece Name
    ------- --- ----------- ----------
    88       1   AVAILABLE
/oracle/app/oracle/flash_recovery_area/ROB1/backupset/2009_09_08
/o1_mf_annnn_TAG20090908T025101_5bd9ohdb_.bkp


BS Key  Type LV Size
------- ---- -- ----------
58      Full    243.80M
  List of Datafiles in backup set 58
```

```
File LV Type Ckp SCN    Ckp Time  Name
---- -- ---- ---------- --------- ----
1       Full 635590     08-SEP-09 /ora01/oracle/rob1/rob1/system01.dbf
2       Full 635590     08-SEP-09 /ora01/oracle/rob1/rob1/sysaux01.dbf
3       Full 635590     08-SEP-09 /ora01/oracle/rob1/rob1/undotbs01.dbf
4       Full 635590     08-SEP-09 /ora01/oracle/rob1/rob1/users01.dbf
Backup Set Copy #1 of backup set 58
Device Type Elapsed Time Completion Time Compressed Tag
----------- ------------ --------------- ---------- ---
DISK        00:01:53     08-SEP-09       YES        TAG20090908T025112

   List of Backup Pieces for backup set 58 Copy #1
   BP Key  Pc# Status      Piece Name
   ------- --- ----------- ----------
   74      1   AVAILABLE
/oracle/app/oracle/flash_recovery_area/ROB1/backupset/2009_09_08
/o1_mf_nnndf_TAG20090908T025112_5bd6r0mz_.bkp

  Backup Set Copy #2 of backup set 58
  Device Type Elapsed Time Completion Time Compressed Tag
  ----------- ------------ --------------- ---------- ---
  DISK        00:01:53     08-SEP-09       YES        TAG20090908T025112

   List of Backup Pieces for backup set 58 Copy #2
   BP Key  Pc# Status      Piece Name
   ------- --- ----------- ----------
   89      1   AVAILABLE
/oracle/app/oracle/flash_recovery_area/ROB1/backupset/2009_09_08
/o1_mf_nnndf_TAG20090908T025112_5bd9ojln_.bkp

BS Key  Type LV Size
------- ---- -- ----------
59      Full    1.03M
  SPFILE Included: Modification time: 08-SEP-09
  SPFILE db_unique_name: ROB1
  Control File Included: Ckp SCN: 635636     Ckp time: 08-SEP-09

  Backup Set Copy #1 of backup set 59
  Device Type Elapsed Time Completion Time Compressed Tag
  ----------- ------------ --------------- ---------- ---
  DISK        00:00:02     08-SEP-09       YES        TAG20090908T025112

   List of Backup Pieces for backup set 59 Copy #1
   BP Key  Pc# Status      Piece Name
   ------- --- ----------- ----------
   75      1   AVAILABLE
/oracle/app/oracle/flash_recovery_area/ROB1/backupset/2009_09_08
/o1_mf_ncsnf_TAG20090908T025112_5bd6vpb1_.bkp
  Backup Set Copy #2 of backup set 59
```

```
Device Type Elapsed Time Completion Time Compressed Tag
----------- ------------ --------------- ---------- ---
DISK         00:00:02     08-SEP-09       YES        TAG20090908T025112

  List of Backup Pieces for backup set 59 Copy #2
  BP Key  Pc# Status       Piece Name
  ------- --- ----------- ----------
    90     1   AVAILABLE
/oracle/app/oracle/flash_recovery_area/ROB1/backupset/2009_09_08
/o1_mf_ncsnf_TAG20090908T025112_5bd9ozwy_.bkp
```

The results of this report provide us with a detailed list of all database backups and the backup piece identifiers. We can then remove either the entire backup set, by using the BS Key identifier, or individual backup pieces, by using the BP Key identifier. Let's assume we want to remove both backup sets. The BP Key IDs for these sets are 117 and 118. Once we have this information, we simply need to use the **change** command with the **delete** parameter, and our backup will be gone. If you are not using the FRA, then the physical piece will be removed. If you are using an FRA, then the physical file will be removed as any other file in the FRA is removed. Here is what we would do to remove these backup sets:

```
RMAN> change backupset 56, 57, 58, 59 delete;
using channel ORA_DISK_1
List of Backup Pieces
BP Key  BS Key  Pc# Cp# Status       Device Type Piece Name
------- ------- --- --- ----------- ----------- ----------
87      56      1   2   AVAILABLE    DISK
/oracle/app/oracle/flash_recovery_area/ROB1/backupset/2009_09_08
/o1_mf_annnn_TAG20090908T025101_5bd9od5x_.bkp
72      56      1   1   AVAILABLE    DISK
/oracle/app/oracle/flash_recovery_area/ROB1/backupset/2009_09_08
/o1_mf_annnn_TAG20090908T025101_5bd6qplq_.bkp
88      57      1   2   AVAILABLE    DISK
/oracle/app/oracle/flash_recovery_area/ROB1/backupset/2009_09_08
/o1_mf_annnn_TAG20090908T025101_5bd9ohdb_.bkp
73      57      1   1   AVAILABLE    DISK
/oracle/app/oracle/flash_recovery_area/ROB1/backupset/2009_09_08
/o1_mf_annnn_TAG20090908T025101_5bd6qydw_.bkp
89      58      1   2   AVAILABLE    DISK
/oracle/app/oracle/flash_recovery_area/ROB1/backupset/2009_09_08
/o1_mf_nnndf_TAG20090908T025112_5bd9ojln_.bkp
74      58      1   1   AVAILABLE    DISK
/oracle/app/oracle/flash_recovery_area/ROB1/backupset/2009_09_08
/o1_mf_nnndf_TAG20090908T025112_5bd6r0mz_.bkp
75      59      1   1   AVAILABLE    DISK
/oracle/app/oracle/flash_recovery_area/ROB1/backupset/2009_09_08
/o1_mf_ncsnf_TAG20090908T025112_5bd6vpb1_.bkp
90      59      1   2   AVAILABLE    DISK
/oracle/app/oracle/flash_recovery_area/ROB1/backupset/2009_09_08
/o1_mf_ncsnf_TAG20090908T025112_5bd9ozwy_.bkp
```

```
Do you really want to delete the above objects (enter YES or NO)? yes
deleted backup piece
backup piece
handle=/oracle/app/oracle/flash_recovery_area/ROB1/backupset/2009_09_08
/o1_mf_annnn_TAG20090908T025101_5bd9od5x_.bkp RECID=16 STAMP=697002060
deleted backup piece
backup piece
handle=/oracle/app/oracle/flash_recovery_area/ROB1/backupset/2009_09_08
/o1_mf_annnn_TAG20090908T025101_5bd6qplq_.bkp RECID=1 STAMP=696999062
deleted backup piece
backup piece
handle=/oracle/app/oracle/flash_recovery_area/ROB1/backupset/2009_09_08
/o1_mf_annnn_TAG20090908T025101_5bd9ohdb_.bkp RECID=17 STAMP=697002063
deleted backup piece
backup piece
handle=/oracle/app/oracle/flash_recovery_area/ROB1/backupset/2009_09_08
/o1_mf_annnn_TAG20090908T025101_5bd6qydw_.bkp RECID=2 STAMP=696999070
deleted backup piece
backup piece
handle=/oracle/app/oracle/flash_recovery_area/ROB1/backupset/2009_09_08
/o1_mf_nnndf_TAG20090908T025112_5bd9ojln_.bkp RECID=18 STAMP=697002064
deleted backup piece
backup piece
handle=/oracle/app/oracle/flash_recovery_area/ROB1/backupset/2009_09_08
/o1_mf_nnndf_TAG20090908T025112_5bd6r0mz_.bkp RECID=3 STAMP=696999072
deleted backup piece
backup piece
handle=/oracle/app/oracle/flash_recovery_area/ROB1/backupset/2009_09_08
/o1_mf_ncsnf_TAG20090908T025112_5bd6vpb1_.bkp RECID=4 STAMP=696999190
deleted backup piece
backup piece
handle=/oracle/app/oracle/flash_recovery_area/ROB1/backupset/2009_09_08
/o1_mf_ncsnf_TAG20090908T025112_5bd9ozwy_.bkp RECID=19 STAMP=697002079
Deleted 8 objects
```

In this example, backup sets 56, 57, 58, and 59, as well as all the associated backup pieces, will be removed. Here are some additional examples of other options for the **change** command that will result in the removal of backup set pieces:

```
change backuppiece 1304 delete;
change archivelog until logseq = 544 delete;
```

Finally, you can use the **change backuppiece uncatalog** command to remove backup set pieces from the catalog. If the **change backuppiece uncatalog** command removes the last remaining backup set piece, then it will also remove the backup set record. Here is an example of using the **change backuppiece uncatalog** command:

```
RMAN> Change backuppiece
'/u01/oracle/RMAN/mydb/mydb_user01_01.bak' uncatalog;
```

RMAN Workshop: *Using the change Command*

Workshop Notes

This workshop assumes that you have a functional Oracle database running in ARCHIVELOG mode, that you are backing up your database to disk, that you have a tablespace called USERS in your database, and that one datafile is associated with the USERS tablespace.

Step 1. Using RMAN, back up the USERS tablespace:

```
RMAN> backup tablespace users;
Starting backup at 08-SEP-09
using channel ORA_DISK_1
channel ORA_DISK_1: starting full datafile backup set
channel ORA_DISK_1: specifying datafile(s) in backup set
input datafile file number=00004 name=/ora01/oracle/rob1/rob1/users01.dbf
channel ORA_DISK_1: starting piece 1 at 08-SEP-09
channel ORA_DISK_1: finished piece 1 at 08-SEP-09
piece handle=/oracle/app/oracle/flash_recovery_area/ROB1/backupset/2009_09_08
/o1_mf_nnndf_TAG20090908T051140_5bdgzfc9_.bkp tag=TAG20090908T051140 comment=NONE
channel ORA_DISK_1: backup set complete, elapsed time: 00:00:01
Finished backup at 08-SEP-09
```

Step 2. Look at the output of the backup, and determine the backup set piece that has just been created. The backup set piece is highlighted in the output in Step 1.

Step 3. Use the **list backup of tablespace users** command to determine the backup key of the backup set piece that you need to mark as DELETED in the control file or recovery catalog. Note in the following output that we have highlighted the backup set key and the related backup set piece:

```
RMAN> list backup of tablespace users;
List of Backup Sets
===================
BS Key  Type LV Size
------- ---- -- ----------
68      Full    1.03M
  List of Datafiles in backup set 68
  File LV Type Ckp SCN    Ckp Time   Name
  ---- -- ---- ---------- --------- ----
  4       Full 637442     08-SEP-09 /ora01/oracle/rob1/rob1/users01.dbf

  Backup Set Copy #2 of backup set 68
  Device Type Elapsed Time Completion Time Compressed Tag
  ----------- ------------ --------------- ---------- ---
  DISK        00:00:01     08-SEP-09       NO         TAG20090908T032815

    List of Backup Pieces for backup set 68 Copy #2
    BP Key  Pc# Status      Piece Name
    ------- --- ----------- ----------
    96      1   AVAILABLE
/oracle/app/oracle/flash_recovery_area/ROB1/backupset/2009_09_08
/o1_mf_nnndf_TAG20090908T032815_5bd9pon1_.bkp
```

```
   Backup Set Copy #1 of backup set 68
   Device Type Elapsed Time Completion Time Compressed Tag
   ----------- ------------ --------------- ---------- ---
   DISK        00:00:01     08-SEP-09       NO         TAG20090908T032815

     List of Backup Pieces for backup set 68 Copy #1
     BP Key  Pc# Status      Piece Name
     ------- --- ----------- ----------
      84      1   AVAILABLE
/oracle/app/oracle/flash_recovery_area/ROB1/backupset/2009_09_08
/o1_mf_nnndf_TAG20090908T032815_5bd8xhxm_.bkp


BS Key  Type LV Size        Device Type Elapsed Time Completion Time
------- ---- -- ----------   ----------- ------------ ---------------
176     Full 5.07M          DISK        00:00:01     08-SEP-09
        BP Key: 179   Status: AVAILABLE  Compressed: NO  Tag: TAG20090908T040309
        Piece Name: /oracle/backup/0hkomrbt_1_1
  List of Datafiles in backup set 176
  File LV Type Ckp SCN    Ckp Time  Name
  ---- -- ---- ---------- --------- ----
   4      Full 642222     08-SEP-09 /ora01/oracle/rob1/rob1/users01.dbf

BS Key  Type LV Size        Device Type Elapsed Time Completion Time
------- ---- -- ----------   ----------- ------------ ---------------
421     Full 5.52M          DISK        00:00:00     08-SEP-09
        BP Key: 424   Status: AVAILABLE  Compressed: NO  Tag: TAG20090908T051140
        Piece Name:
oracle/app/oracle/flash_recovery_area/ROB1/backupset/2009_09_08
/o1_mf_nnndf_TAG20090908T051140_5bdgzfc9_.bkp
  List of Datafiles in backup set 421
  File LV Type Ckp SCN    Ckp Time  Name
  ---- -- ---- ---------- --------- ----
   4      Full 644956     08-SEP-09 /ora01/oracle/rob1/rob1/users01.dbf
```

Step 4.   Exit to the operating system, and do a directory listing on the backup set piece. You should see it.

Step 5.   Use the **change backuppiece** command to change the status flag of this backup set piece from AVAILABLE to DELETED:

```
RMAN> change backuppiece 96 delete;
using channel ORA_DISK_1
List of Backup Pieces
BP Key  BS Key  Pc# Cp# Status      Device Type Piece Name
------- ------- --- --- ----------- ----------- ----------
96      68       1   2   AVAILABLE   DISK
/oracle/app/oracle/flash_recovery_area/ROB1/backupset/2009_09_08
/o1_mf_nnndf_TAG20090908T032815_5bd9pon1_.bkp
Do you really want to delete the above objects (enter YES or NO)? yes
deleted backup piece
backup piece
handle=/oracle/app/oracle/flash_recovery_area/ROB1/backupset/2009_09_08
/o1_mf_nnndf_TAG20090908T032815_5bd9pon1_.bkp RECID=25 STAMP-697002101
Deleted 1 objects
```

Step 6. Use the **list backup of tablespace users** command to determine that the backup set piece is no longer available for use during a recovery:

```
RMAN> list backup of tablespace users;
```

Step 7. Exit to the operating system, and do a directory listing on the backup set piece. You should no longer see the backup set piece. Oracle removed it, if it existed.

The delete Command

All good things must come to an end, and the same is true about the life of a given backup set. With a retention policy, we can mark backups whose usefulness and lifetime are at an end. As we mentioned already, enforcement of a redundancy policy does not remove the backups from the catalog, but rather just marks the backups with a status of OBSOLETE. The same is true with the **crosscheck** command, which we discussed earlier in this chapter. The **crosscheck** command marks obsolete backups and copies as EXPIRED, but does not remove them.

Enter the **delete** command, the grim reaper of RMAN. It is the raven that swoops down and puts the kibosh on your backups and copies. With the **delete** command, you can remove any backups that have been made obsolete based on a retention criterion, and you can change the status of any expired backups in the recovery catalog or control file to a status of DELETED. Here are a couple of examples of the **delete** command in use:

```
delete expired;
delete obsolete;
```

When you issue a **delete** command, the associated RMAN backup records will be removed from the recovery catalog. You can see this by looking at the recovery catalog view WR_BACKUP_ PIECE. Records contained in the database control file will be kept in the control file until overwritten. These records will appear in the V$BACKUP_PIECE view with a status of D. These deleted records will not appear in RMAN command output, such as **list backup of database summary**.

When you issue a **delete** command, RMAN will request that you confirm your instructions. Once you have confirmed your instructions, RMAN will complete the **delete** operation. You can use the **noprompt** option of the **delete** command to avoid the requirement to verify the execution of the **delete** command. This is handy if you are writing scripts to work with RMAN. Here is an example of using the **delete** command with the **noprompt** option:

```
delete noprompt obsolete;
```

> **NOTE**
> *Once a backup has been marked with a DELETED status, you cannot get it back. You can still recover the backup, if it's physically available, by using the* **catalog** *command to register the backup sets in the control file/recovery catalog.*

RMAN Workshop: *Using the delete Command*

Workshop Notes

This workshop builds on the previous RMAN Workshop, "Using the **change** Command," which deals with using the **crosscheck** command.

Step 1. Having determined that the backup set piece is missing, we want to mark it as permanently missing. From the RMAN prompt, issue the **delete expired backup** command:

```
RMAN> delete expired backup;
using channel ORA_DISK_1
using channel ORA_DISK_2
List of Backup Pieces
BP Key  BS Key  Pc# Cp# Status       Device Type Piece Name
------- ------- --- --- ----------- ----------- ----------
53      53      1   1   EXPIRED      DISK
D:\BACKUP\RECOVER\BACKUP_1VE25VC0_1_1
Do you really want to delete the above objects (enter YES or NO)?
```

Step 2. Review the objects listed to be marked with a DELETED status. If they can all be marked as DELETED, reply to the prompt with a YES and press ENTER. Review the output for a successful operation:

```
deleted backup piece
backup piece handle=D:\BACKUP\RECOVER\BACKUP_1VE25VC0_1_1 recid=53
stamp=472055171
Deleted 1 EXPIRED objects
```

Cataloging Other Backups in RMAN

The **catalog** command enables you to record datafile backups, archive log backups, and control file backups in RMAN, and these backups can later be used to restore and recover the database. Oracle Database allows you to also use the **catalog** command to catalog existing backup set pieces in the control file. This is a nice feature if you have to restore the database with an old backup control file that might not have the most current RMAN information in it.

Here are some examples of the use of the **catalog** command to catalog old datafile backups:

```
-- first, backup the users tablespace
sqlplus sys/robert as sysdba
alter tablespace users begin backup;
host copy d:\oracle\oradata\recover\users01.dbf
d:\backup\recover\users01.dbf.backup
alter tablespace users end backup;
alter system archive log current;
host copy d:\oracle\admin\recover\arch\*.* d:\backup\recover
-- get a list of archivelog files that were created
host dir d:\backup\recover
alter database backup control file to 'd:\backup\recover.ctl'
quit
```

```
-- Now, catalog the backup in rman
rman target sys/robert
catalog datafilecopy 'd:\backup\recover\users01.dbf.backup';
-- Replace arc001.log with the list of archive logs you generated earlier
catalog archivelog 'd:\backup\recover\arc001.log';
-- Now catalog the control file.
catalog controlfilecopy 'd:\backup\recover.ctl';
```

The **catalog** command allows you to enter new backup set–related information into the control file or recovery catalog. RMAN overwrites any pre-existing catalog information that conflicts with the information being cataloged. This command can be handy if you need to move the location of your backup set pieces. In this example, we have moved all our backup set pieces to a new directory. We use the **catalog** command to load the correct directory location for each of the moved pieces in the control file:

```
RMAN> catalog backuppiece '/opt/oracle/oracle-10.0.0/dbs/backup';
```

You can also use the **catalog** command with the **start with** option, which allows you to define the directory that contains the RMAN backup set pieces to be cataloged. RMAN will then catalog all backup set pieces in that directory. Here is an example of using the **catalog** command in this way:

```
RMAN> catalog start with '/u01/oracle/RMAN/mydb';
```

Once you press ENTER, this command prompts you with a list of files to catalog and asks if you wish to catalog the files listed. If you respond in the affirmative, RMAN catalogs all the backup set pieces listed (which will be contained in the /u01/oracle/RMAN/mydb directory). This command also allows you to catalog several like-named backup set pieces. For example, if you want to catalog several backup set pieces that start with the name "backup" (e.g., backupset01, backupset02, and so forth), then you could issue the following command:

```
RMAN> catalog start with '/u01/oracle/RMAN/mydb/backup';
```

When you use the **catalog start with** command, it is indiscriminate about which files it tries to catalog; it will try to catalog everything that matches the argument list. However, as the **catalog** process proceeds, files that are not backup set pieces will fail the catalog process and an error will occur. Files that are backup set pieces will be cataloged successfully, in spite of other errors.

RMAN Stored Scripts

If you find that you are often doing the same RMAN operations over and over, then you would probably like to be able to store those operations somewhere and execute them when needed. Of course, you could create a command file, which is just a text file physically located on disk somewhere, with the RMAN commands, and then execute the command file from the RMAN command-line interface using the **cmdfile** parameter, as shown in this example:

```
rman target robert/password cmdfile=run_backup.cmd
```

Or, you can run a command file from within RMAN itself, using the @ command:

```
@@run_backup.cmd
```

RMAN offers another option, which is to store scripts in the recovery catalog. As you might guess, this requires that you use a recovery catalog, so if you are not using one, you will not be able to store RMAN scripts. This section shows you how to store scripts in the recovery catalog and how to manage those scripts.

Creating Stored Scripts

To store a script in the recovery catalog, you use the **create script** RMAN command. Each stored script is assigned a name when you create it. You can create scripts that do backups, recoveries, and maintenance of your databases. To create a script, you must be connected to the recovery catalog. Here is an example of using the **create script** command to create a backup script. RMAN also allows you to store comments related to your stored scripts by using the **comment** parameter:

```
create script my_backup_script
comment 'This script backs up the database'
{ backup database plus archivelog;}
```

Oracle Database 11*g* supports the use of substitution variables. Each substitution variable is denoted with an ampersand and a number that makes each variable unique. For example, you could rewrite this script as follows:

```
create script my_backup_script
comment 'This script backs up the database'
{ backup database tag '&1' plus archivelog;}
```

When you execute this command, RMAN will prompt you for initial values for the substitution variables.

Querying the Recovery Catalog for Stored Script Information

You can use the recovery catalog views to determine the name of scripts stored in the recovery catalog by querying the RC_STORED_SCRIPT view. You can see the contents of a given script by querying the RC_STORED_SCRIPT_LINE view.

Changing Stored Scripts

You use the **replace script** command to replace stored scripts in the recovery catalog. Here is an example of using the **replace script** command. Note that we also add a comment to the script.

```
replace script my_backup_script
comment 'This script backs up the database'
{ backup database plus archivelog delete input;}
```

Deleting Stored Scripts

To drop a script, you use the **delete script** command. You must be connected to the recovery catalog to successfully drop a stored script. Here is an example of using the **delete script** command:

```
delete script my_backup_script;
```

Using Stored Scripts

Now that you have created some stored scripts, you probably want to use them. This is what the **execute script** command is for. Simply connect to the recovery catalog and use the **execute script** command within the confines of a **run** block, as shown in this example:

```
run {execute script my_backup_script;}
```

If you are using substitution variables, you can use the **using** parameter to include the values of those parameters in the **execute script** command, as seen in this example:

```
Run {execute script my_backup_script using TEST_BACKUP;}
```

Printing Stored Scripts

If you want to print a copy of your stored script, you can use the **print script** command. Connect to the recovery catalog, and run the **print script** command, as shown in this example:

```
RMAN> print script my_backup_script;

printing stored script: my_backup_script
{ backup database plus archivelog;}
```

You can also use the RC_STORED_SCRIPT_LINE recovery catalog view to display the contents of a stored script, as shown in this example:

```
select script_name, text from rc_stored_script_line
order by script_name, line;
SCRIPT_NAME        TEXT
---------------    ---------------------------------------
my_backup_script  { backup database plus archivelog;}
```

RMAN Workshop: *Using RMAN Stored Scripts*

Workshop Notes

This workshop expects that you have an operational Oracle database (called recover) and that you are also using a separate Oracle database to store the recovery catalog in (called catalog).

Step 1. Connect to the target database and to the recovery catalog:

```
rman target rman_account/rman_password catalog rcat_user/rcat_password@catalog
```

Step 2. Create a stored script to back up the target database:

```
RMAN> create script my_backup_script
2> {backup database plus archivelog;}
created script my_backup_script
```

Step 3. Print the stored script:

```
RMAN> print script my_backup_script;
printing stored script: my_backup_script
{backup database plus archivelog;}
```

Step 4. Execute the stored script to back up your database:

```
RMAN> run {execute script my_backup_script;}
```

Step 5. Delete the stored script:

```
RMAN> delete script my_backup_script;
```

When You Just Can't Take It Anymore

If you are sick and tired of your database and you just can't take it anymore, RMAN offers the perfect response, the **drop database** command. If only terrorists were as easy to get rid of. Simply put the database in restricted session mode, connect to the target database with RMAN, issue the **drop database** command, and watch your database quietly go away. You can add the **including backups** parameter, and all RMAN-related backups will be removed, too. When you issue this command, RMAN will confirm the action first and then proceed to remove the database. If you wish to not be prompted, you can use the **noprompt** parameter. Here is an example of the use of the **drop database** command:

```
SQL> alter system enable restricted session;
SQL> quit;
.. log into RMAN ..
RMAN>drop database including backups;
```

Summary

In this chapter, we discussed the various maintenance operations that RMAN may require. We discussed the **crosscheck** command and validating RMAN backups, both very important operations. We also talked about retention policies and how RMAN uses them to control how long your backups will remain available to you for recovery purposes.

We also talked about the **change** and **delete** commands and how they can be used to modify the status of RMAN records in the control file or recovery catalog. We also covered adding backups to the control file or recovery catalog. Finally, we discussed maintenance of the recovery catalog and the use of stored scripts for RMAN operations.

CHAPTER
17

Monitoring and
Reporting on RMAN

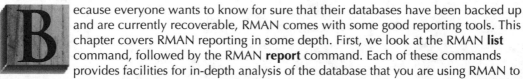 ecause everyone wants to know for sure that their databases have been backed up and are currently recoverable, RMAN comes with some good reporting tools. This chapter covers RMAN reporting in some depth. First, we look at the RMAN **list** command, followed by the RMAN **report** command. Each of these commands provides facilities for in-depth analysis of the database that you are using RMAN to back up and its backups. These commands are the primary ways of extracting information from RMAN. You will find that lists and reports come in handy not only during recovery, but also when you want to see how RMAN is configured and when you need to perform other administrative tasks (such as determining if a tablespace has been backed up).

The RMAN list Command

The RMAN **list** command is a method of querying either the database control file or the recovery catalog for historical information on backups. Lists provide an array of information, from lists of database incarnations, to lists of backup sets and archive log backups. The bottom line is that if you want to know whether the database was backed up and when, then you want to generate a list. The format of lists initially tends to appear not very reader friendly. Once you have looked at a few lists, though, they seem a little easier to read. So, let's look at the **list** commands and how they can be interpreted.

Listing Incarnations

The **list incarnation** command provides you a list of each database incarnation for the target database. This list can be used to recover your database to a point in time before your last **resetlogs** command was issued, if this is required (refer to Chapter 14 for more details on this operation). Here is an example of the **list incarnation** command output:

```
RMAN> list incarnation of database;
using target database control file instead of recovery catalog
List of Database Incarnations
DB Key  Inc Key DB Name  DB ID            STATUS  Reset SCN  Reset Time
------- ------- -------- ---------------- --- ---------- ----------
1       1       ROB1     1854903786       PARENT  1          07-SEP-09
2       2       ROB1     1854903786       CURRENT 635384     08-SEP-09
```

In this listing, we find that our database has had two different incarnations, with each incarnation represented in each row of the report. Each individual incarnation has its own key (Inc Key), which we would use if we wanted to reset the database incarnation (refer to Chapter 14). We also get our database name and ID in this report.

The STATUS column displays the status of the incarnation listed. It indicates whether the incarnation is an older incarnation (PARENT), the current incarnation, or, if a recovery past **resetlogs** has occurred, an orphan incarnation. Finally, the Reset SCN and Reset Time columns basically indicate when the database incarnation was created (which is why the Reset SCN for the first entry is 1). This column helps support recovery through **resetlogs** and also helps support easier recovery to a previous incarnation.

An important point to note is that output generated with a recovery catalog and output generated without a recovery catalog generally look somewhat different. For example, this is the output of the **list incarnation** command while attached to a recovery catalog:

```
RMAN> list incarnation of database;
List of Database Incarnations
DB Key  Inc Key DB Name  DB ID             STATUS   Reset SCN  Reset Time
------- ------- -------- ----------------- ---      ---------- ----------
2       18      ROB1     1854903786        PARENT   1          07-SEP-09
2       4       ROB1     1854903786        CURRENT  635384     08-SEP-09
```

Note in this example that both the DB keys and the incarnation keys are different from those reported when using the control file. This leads to an important point: Many reports have keys that identify specific items in the reports. You will use these keys in other RMAN commands (such as in the **reset database** command). Since the values of the keys change depending on whether you are connected to the recovery catalog, you need to be careful about determining which keys you need.

Listing Backups

The **list** command comes with a number of different options that allow you to report on the status of database backups and copies. In this section, we are going to look at several of these reports.

Summarizing Available Backups

Let's first look at a few ways of getting summary backup information. The **list** command provides a couple of options. The first option is the **list backup summary** report:

```
RMAN> list backup summary;
List of Backups
===============
Key     TY LV S Device Type Completion Time #Pieces #Copies Compressed Tag
------- -- -- - ----------- --------------- ------- ------- ---------- ---
60      D  A  A DISK        08-SEP-09       1       2       YES        TAG20090908T025311
61      B  A  A DISK        08-SEP-09       1       2       NO         TAG20090908T025326
62      B  F  A DISK        08-SEP-09       1       2       NO         TAG20090908T025328
63      B  A  A DISK        08-SEP-09       1       2       NO         TAG20090908T025355
67      B  A  A DISK        08-SEP-09       1       2       NO         TAG20090908T032531
68      B  F  A DISK        08-SEP-09       1       1       NO         TAG20090908T032815
70      B  F  A DISK        08-SEP-09       1       1       NO         TAG20090908T032850
176     B  F  A DISK        08-SEP-09       1       1       NO         TAG20090908T040309
207     B  F  A DISK        08-SEP-09       1       1       NO         TAG20090908T040315
421     B  F  A DISK        08-SEP-09       1       1       NO         TAG20090908T051140
433     B  F  A DISK        08-SEP-09       1       1       NO         TAG20090908T051144
```

This report provides us with some nice summary information. The backup set key is listed in the Key column. The TY (type) and the LV (level) columns indicate the type of backup listed (B = backup, F = full, A = archive log, and 0 and 1 = incremental backups). The S column indicates the status of the backup (AVAILABLE, UNAVAILABLE, or EXPIRED). The Device Type column lets us know whether the backup is a tape or disk backup. We also have columns for the date of the backup (Completion Time), the number of pieces (#Pieces) or copies (#Copies) that the backup set consists of, if the backup was compressed, and any tag that was assigned to the backup set (Tag).

Most of the **list** commands will accept the **summary** parameter at the end. For example:

```
list backup of database summary;
list expired backup of archivelog all summary;
list backup of tablespace users summary;
```

Listing Backups by Datafile

Another way to summarize backups is to use the **list backup by file** command to list each backup set and backup set piece. Here is an example of this report (we have removed some output to save a few trees):

```
RMAN> list backup by file;
List of Datafile Backups
=========================

File Key      TY LV S Ckp SCN   Ckp Time    #Pieces #Copies Compressed Tag
---- -------  -- -- - ---------- ---------- ------- ------- ---------- ---
2    62       B  F  A 635676     08-SEP-09  1       2       NO         TAG20090908T025328
4    421      B  F  A 644956     08-SEP-09  1       1       NO         TAG20090908T051140
     176      B  F  A 642222     08-SEP-09  1       1       NO         TAG20090908T040309
     68       B  F  A 637442     08-SEP-09  1       1       NO         TAG20090908T032815


List of Archived Log Backups
=============================

Thrd Seq     Low SCN    Low Time   BS Key  S #Pieces #Copies Compressed Tag
---- ------- ---------- ---------- ------- - ------- ------- ---------- ---
1    2       635574     08-SEP-09  60      A 1       2       YES        TAG20090908T025311
1    3       635642     08-SEP-09  61      A 1       2       NO         TAG20090908T025326
1    4       635668     08-SEP-09  63      A 1       2       NO         TAG20090908T025355
1    7       636872     08-SEP-09  67      A 1       2       NO         TAG20090908T032531
1    8       637317     08-SEP-09  67      A 1       2       NO         TAG20090908T032531
1    9       637320     08-SEP-09  67      A 1       2       NO         TAG20090908T032531
1    10      637324     08-SEP-09  67      A 1       2       NO         TAG20090908T032531


List of Control File Backups
=============================

CF Ckp SCN Ckp Time  BS Key  S #Pieces #Copies Compressed Tag
---------- --------- ------- - ------- ------- ---------- ---
644990     08-SEP-09 433     A 1       1       NO         TAG20090908T051144
642268     08-SEP-09 207     A 1       1       NO         TAG20090908T040315
637490     08-SEP-09 70      A 1       1       NO         TAG20090908T032850


List of SPFILE Backups
=======================

Modification Time BS Key  S #Pieces #Copies Compressed Tag
----------------- ------- - ------- ------- ---------- ---
08-SEP-09         433     A 1       1       NO         TAG20090908T051144
08-SEP-09         207     A 1       1       NO         TAG20090908T040315
08-SEP-09         70      A 1       1       NO         TAG20090908T032850
```

This report summarizes each backup file that has been created by the type of backup (datafile backup, archived log backup, control file backup, and SPFILE backup) and then by datafile for the datafile backups. In this report, we get the date of the backup and the specific keys associated with the backup file. Depending on the type of backup, we get information that pertains to that type of backup.

Additional Backup Information

If you want as much information reported on your RMAN backups as you can get, then the **list backup** command is for you. It provides detailed information on the backups that you have taken, including backup sets, archived redo log backups, and control file/SPFILE backups. Let's look at an example of the results of the execution of the **list backup** command:

```
RMAN> list backup;
BS Key   Size        Device Type Elapsed Time Completion Time
-------  ----------  ----------- ------------ ---------------
509      12.43M      DISK          00:00:04     08-SEP-09
         BP Key: 513   Status: AVAILABLE   Compressed: YES   Tag: TAG20090908T192844
         Piece Name:
/oracle/app/oracle/flash_recovery_area/ROB1/backupset/2009_09_08
/o1_mf_annnn_TAG20090908T192844_5bg16fk5_.bkp

  List of Archived Logs in backup set 509
  Thrd Seq     Low SCN    Low Time  Next SCN   Next Time
  ---- ------- ---------- --------- ---------- ---------
  1    7       636872     08-SEP-09 637317     08-SEP-09
  1    8       637317     08-SEP-09 637320     08-SEP-09
  1    10      637324     08-SEP-09 637349     08-SEP-09
  1    11      637349     08-SEP-09 675660     08-SEP-09
  1    12      675660     08-SEP-09 676291     08-SEP-09
```

This first listing is an archive log backup. The backup set key (BS Key) is 509. The size of the backup is listed, and we see that it went to disk, instead of to SBT. The elapsed time of the backup is pretty short, at four seconds, and we see that it was completed on September 8. Later in the report, we see that the backup is available and that it is a compressed backup. We also find the backup set piece name, which tells us where the backup is physically located. Finally, a list of archived redo logs appears. These are the archived redo logs contained in this backup set. Here is an example of the listing of the rest of this backup:

```
BS Key   Type LV Size        Device Type Elapsed Time Completion Time
-------  ---- -- ----------  ----------- ------------ ---------------
510      Full    243.36M     DISK          00:01:16     08-SEP-09
         BP Key: 514   Status: AVAILABLE   Compressed: YES   Tag: TAG20090908T192853
         Piece Name: /oracle/app/oracle/flash_recovery_area/ROB1/backupset/2009_09_08
/o1_mf_nnndf_TAG20090908T192853_5bg16pwv_.bkp

  List of Datafiles in backup set 510
  File LV Type Ckp SCN    Ckp Time  Name
  ---- -- ---- ---------- --------- ----
  1       Full 676334     08-SEP-09 /ora01/oracle/rob1/rob1/system01.dbf
  2       Full 676334     08-SEP-09 /ora01/oracle/rob1/rob1/sysaux01.dbf
  3       Full 676334     08-SEP-09 /ora01/oracle/rob1/rob1/undotbs01.dbf
  4       Full 676334     08-SEP-09 /ora01/oracle/rob1/rob1/users01.dbf

BS Key   Size        Device Type Elapsed Time Completion Time
-------  ----------  ----------- ------------ ---------------
536      783.00K     DISK          00:00:01     08-SEP-09
         BP Key: 541   Status: AVAILABLE   Compressed: YES   Tag: TAG20090908T193014
         Piece Name:
/oracle/app/oracle/flash_recovery_area/ROB1/backupset/2009_09_08
/o1_mf_annnn_TAG20090908T193014_5bg196xr_.bkp

  List of Archived Logs in backup set 536
  Thrd Seq     Low SCN    Low Time  Next SCN   Next Time
  ---- ------- ---------- --------- ---------- ---------
  1    13      676291     08-SEP-09 676364     08-SEP-09
```

```
BS Key   Type LV Size        Device Type Elapsed Time Completion Time
-------  ---- -- ----------  ----------- ------------ ---------------
555      Full    9.67M        DISK         00:00:01     08-SEP-09
         BP Key: 557    Status: AVAILABLE  Compressed: NO  Tag: TAG20090908T193017
         Piece Name:
/oracle/app/oracle/flash_recovery_area/ROB1/autobackup/2009_09_08
/o1_mf_s_697059017_5bg19b6p_.bkp
    SPFILE Included: Modification time: 08-SEP-09
    SPFILE db_unique_name: ROB1
    Control File Included: Ckp SCN: 676443       Ckp time: 08-SEP-09
```

This is an actual database backup. The output looks much like the previous output, except that now we get a full list of all the datafiles contained in the backup. We see that the datafile backup consists of one backup set piece (BS Key 510). Of course, when we perform a recovery, RMAN will look for the most current backup. Once it knows that, it will pick the best backups to use to perform the recovery. Perhaps this is a small point, but it's an important one.

Also in this listing, we find that there is an archive log backup (backup set key 536) with a single archive log in it. On the final section of the report, we find an autobackup of the control file/SPFILE (backup set 555). We know this is an autobackup by virtue of the "SPFILE Included" and "Control File Included" wording in the output.

Let's look at the archive log backup output a bit more closely:

```
BS Key   Size        Device Type Elapsed Time Completion Time
-------  ----------  ----------- ------------ ---------------
536      783.00K      DISK         00:00:01     08-SEP-09
         BP Key: 541    Status: AVAILABLE  Compressed: YES  Tag: TAG20090908T193014
         Piece Name:
/oracle/app/oracle/flash_recovery_area/ROB1/backupset/2009_09_08
/o1_mf_annnn_TAG20090908T193014_5bg196xr_.bkp

    List of Archived Logs in backup set 536
    Thrd Seq     Low SCN    Low Time   Next SCN    Next Time
    ---- ------- ---------- ---------- ---------- ---------
    1    13      676291     08-SEP-09 676364      08-SEP-09
```

This backup set has a backup set key of 536. The header information looks the same as in the previous backup set. However, this backup is an archive log backup, so in subsequent lines, RMAN provides a list of the archived redo logs backed up in the backup set. The thread and sequence number of the archive log are listed, along with the low SCN and time, and the next SCN and time. The low time/SCN and high (or Next SCN as listed in the report) time/SCN ranges allow you to determine when the archive log was created.

Let's look at an incremental backup set report:

```
BS Key   Type LV Size        Device Type Elapsed Time Completion Time
-------  ---- -- ----------  ----------- ------------ ---------------
857      Incr 1  1000.00K     DISK         00:00:27     08-SEP-09
         BP Key: 861    Status: AVAILABLE  Compressed: YES  Tag: TAG20090908T202840
         Piece Name:
/oracle/app/oracle/flash_recovery_area/ROB1/backupset/2009_09_08
/o1_mf_nnnd1_TAG20090908T202840_5bg4psxw_.bkp
    List of Datafiles in backup set 857
```

```
File LV Type Ckp SCN    Ckp Time  Name
---- -- ---- ---------- --------- ----
  1   1  Incr 679212     08-SEP-09 /ora01/oracle/rob1/rob1/system01.dbf
  2   1  Incr 679212     08-SEP-09 /ora01/oracle/rob1/rob1/sysaux01.dbf
  3   1  Incr 679212     08-SEP-09 /ora01/oracle/rob1/rob1/undotbs01.dbf
  4   1  Incr 679212     08-SEP-09 /ora01/oracle/rob1/rob1/users01.dbf
```

Again, this report is very similar to the other reports. The only differences are that Incr is used in the Type field to indicate that the backup is an incremental backup, and the LV (level) column shows the level of the incremental backup. If the incremental backup were a level 0 backup, then the LV column would show the number 0, which corresponds to a level 0 base backup.

Listing Backups Eligible for Recovery

If you want to see all datafile backups or copies that are able to be used to restore and recover your database, then use the **list recoverable** command. This **list** command provides a list of all backups with a status of AVAILABLE that can be used to restore your database (this is only for the current incarnation). Backups, image copies, and incremental backups will all be included. If an incremental backup does not have a valid parent, it will not be included in this backup.

```
RMAN> list recoverable backup of database;
List of Backup Sets
===================
BS Key  Type LV Size       Device Type Elapsed Time Completion Time
------- ---- -- ---------- ----------- ------------ ---------------
713     Incr 0  243.27M     DISK        00:01:10     08-SEP-09
        BP Key: 715    Status: AVAILABLE  Compressed: YES  Tag: TAG20090908T202601
        Piece Name:
/oracle/app/oracle/flash_recovery_area/ROB1/backupset/2009_09_08
/o1_mf_nnnd0_TAG20090908T202601_5bg4ktk1_.bkp

  List of Datafiles in backup set 713
  File LV Type Ckp SCN    Ckp Time  Name
  ---- -- ---- ---------- --------- ----
    1   0  Incr 678900     08-SEP-09 /ora01/oracle/rob1/rob1/system01.dbf
    2   0  Incr 678900     08-SEP-09 /ora01/oracle/rob1/rob1/sysaux01.dbf
    3   0  Incr 678900     08-SEP-09 /ora01/oracle/rob1/rob1/undotbs01.dbf
    4   0  Incr 678900     08-SEP-09 /ora01/oracle/rob1/rob1/users01.dbf

BS Key  Type LV Size       Device Type Elapsed Time Completion Time
------- ---- -- ---------- ----------- ------------ ---------------
857     Incr 1  1000.00K    DISK        00:00:27     08-SEP-09
        BP Key: 861    Status: AVAILABLE  Compressed: YES  Tag: TAG20090908T202840
        Piece Name:
/oracle/app/oracle/flash_recovery_area/ROB1/backupset/2009_09_08
/o1_mf_nnnd1_TAG20090908T202840_5bg4psxw_.bkp

  List of Datafiles in backup set 857
  File LV Type Ckp SCN    Ckp Time  Name
  ---- -- ---- ---------- --------- ----
    1   1  Incr 679212     08-SEP-09 /ora01/oracle/rob1/rob1/system01.dbf
    2   1  Incr 679212     08-SEP-09 /ora01/oracle/rob1/rob1/sysaux01.dbf
    3   1  Incr 679212     08-SEP-09 /ora01/oracle/rob1/rob1/undotbs01.dbf
    4   1  Incr 679212     08-SEP-09 /ora01/oracle/rob1/rob1/users01.dbf
```

Listing Expired Backups

Using the **list backup** command shows you both available and expired backup sets. If you want to see only expired backups, then you can use the **expired** keyword, as shown in this example:

```
RMAN> list expired backup;


List of Backup Sets
===================


BS Key  Size       Device Type Elapsed Time Completion Time
------- ---------- ----------- ------------ ---------------
1025    489.00K    DISK        00:00:01     08-SEP-09
        BP Key: 1028   Status: EXPIRED  Compressed: NO  Tag: TAG20090908T203418
        Piece Name: /oracle/app/oracle/flash_recovery_area/ROB1/backupset/2009_09_08/
o1_mf_annnn_TAG20090908T203418_5bg51c2c_.bkp
List of Archived Logs in backup set 1025
  Thrd Seq     Low SCN    Low Time  Next SCN   Next Time
  ---- ------- ---------- --------- ---------- ---------
  1    18      679230     08-SEP-09 679716     08-SEP-09
```

This command will display all expired backup sets. With the **list expired backup** command, you can also get a list of expired tablespace and datafile backups and lists of expired archive log backups and control file/SPFILE autobackups by inserting the correct keyword, such as **list expired backup of datafile 3** or **list expired backup of archivelog all**.

Listing Backups by Tablespace Name and Datafile Number

The output of the **list backup of tablespace** or **list backup of datafile** command is very similar to the **list backup** output. These two **list backup** commands allow you to list output specific for a tablespace or a datafile, as shown in this example:

```
RMAN> list backup of tablespace users;
List of Backup Sets
===================
BS Key  Type LV Size       Device Type Elapsed Time Completion Time
------- ---- -- ---------- ----------- ------------ ---------------
713     Incr 0  243.27M    DISK        00:01:10     08-SEP-09
        BP Key: 715   Status: AVAILABLE  Compressed: YES  Tag: TAG20090908T202601
        Piece Name:
oracle/app/oracle/flash_recovery_area/ROB1/backupset/2009_09_08
/o1_mf_nnnd0_TAG20090908T202601_5bg4ktk1_.bkp

  List of Datafiles in backup set 713
  File LV Type Ckp SCN    Ckp Time  Name
  ---- -- ---- ---------- --------- ----
  4    0  Incr 678900     08-SEP-09 /ora01/oracle/rob1/rob1/users01.dbf
```

```
BS Key   Type LV Size        Device Type Elapsed Time Completion Time
-------  ---- -- ---------- ----------- ------------ ---------------
857      Incr 1  1000.00K    DISK        00:00:27     08-SEP-09
         BP Key: 861    Status: AVAILABLE  Compressed: YES  Tag: TAG20090908T202840
         Piece Name: /oracle/app/oracle/flash_recovery_area/ROB1/backupset/2009_09_08
/o1_mf_nnnd1_TAG20090908T202840_5bg4psxw_.bkp
  List of Datafiles in backup set 857
  File LV Type Ckp SCN    Ckp Time  Name
  ---- -- ---- ---------- --------- ----
   4    1  Incr 679212       08-SEP-09 /ora01/oracle/rob1/rob1/users01.dbf
```

Note in this example that this backup has expired, which might be of particular interest to us, especially if this were the only backup of the USERS tablespace available! Again, you can use the **expired** keyword to only list expired backups (**list expired backup of tablespace**).

In much the same way, you can list the backups of a specific datafile with the **list backup of datafile** command:

```
RMAN> list backup of datafile 3;
List of Backup Sets
===================

BS Key   Type LV Size        Device Type Elapsed Time Completion Time
-------  ---- -- ---------- ----------- ------------ ---------------
713      Incr 0  243.27M     DISK        00:01:10     08-SEP-09
         BP Key: 715    Status: AVAILABLE  Compressed: YES  Tag: TAG20090908T202601
         Piece Name:
/oracle/app/oracle/flash_recovery_area/ROB1/backupset/2009_09_08
/o1_mf_nnnd0_TAG20090908T202601_5bg4ktk1_.bkp

  List of Datafiles in backup set 713
  File LV Type Ckp SCN    Ckp Time  Name
  ---- -- ---- ---------- --------- ----
   3    0  Incr 678900       08-SEP-09 /ora01/oracle/rob1/rob1/undotbs01.dbf

BS Key   Type LV Size        Device Type Elapsed Time Completion Time
-------  ---- -- ---------- ----------- ------------ ---------------
857      Incr 1  1000.00K    DISK        00:00:27     08-SEP-09
         BP Key: 861    Status: AVAILABLE  Compressed: YES  Tag: TAG20090908T202840
         Piece Name:
/oracle/app/oracle/flash_recovery_area/ROB1/backupset/2009_09_08
/o1_mf_nnnd1_TAG20090908T202840_5bg4psxw_.bk

  List of Datafiles in backup set 857
  File LV Type Ckp SCN    Ckp Time  Name
  ---- -- ---- ---------- --------- ----
   3    1  Incr 679212       08-SEP-09 /ora01/oracle/rob1/rob1/undotbs01.dbf
```

One place where the **list** command can be helpful is if you are trying to do a point-in-time restore and you are getting errors that indicate no backup or copy is found. In this case, try a **list** command using the same **until** clause to see if it lists any available backups. Doing this can help reveal any problems with your **until** clause, and you can adjust the **until** clause to determine what point-in-time recovery is truly available from.

Listing Archive Log Backups

Several options exist for listing archive log backups in RMAN. To obtain a complete summary of archive logs currently on disk (this does not mean that they have been backed up), the **list archivelog all** command is perfect, as shown here:

```
RMAN> list archivelog all;
List of Archived Log Copies for database with db_unique_name ROB1
=====================================================================

Key     Thrd Seq     S Low Time
------- ---- ------- - ---------
54       1    9       X 08-SEP-09
         Name:
/oracle/app/oracle/flash_recovery_area/ROB1/archivelog/2009_09_08
/o1_mf_1_9_5bd8qv45_.arc

1170     1    19      A 08-SEP-09
         Name:
/oracle/app/oracle/flash_recovery_area/ROB1/archivelog/2009_09_08
/o1_mf_1_19_5bg611l1_.arc
```

Here, we find a list of each archived redo log that Oracle has created that is waiting to be backed up, along with the thread number and the sequence number of that archived redo log.

To get a report of those archive logs that we have backed up, we use the **list backup of archivelog all** report as seen here:

```
RMAN> list backup of archivelog all;

List of Backup Sets
===================
BS Key  Size        Device Type Elapsed Time Completion Time
------- ----------  ----------- ------------ ---------------
712     1.53M       DISK          00:00:00     08-SEP-09
         BP Key: 714   Status: AVAILABLE  Compressed: YES  Tag: TAG20090908T202600
         Piece Name:
/oracle/app/oracle/flash_recovery_area/ROB1/backupset/2009_09_08
/o1_mf_annnn_TAG20090908T202600_5bg4kr90_.bkp

  List of Archived Logs in backup set 712
  Thrd Seq     Low SCN    Low Time  Next SCN   Next Time
  ---- ------- ---------- --------- ---------- ---------
   1    14      676364     08-SEP-09 678853     08-SEP-09

BS Key  Size        Device Type Elapsed Time Completion Time
------- ----------  ----------- ------------ ---------------
744     61.50K      DISK          00:00:00     08-SEP-09
```

```
         BP Key: 749   Status: AVAILABLE  Compressed: YES  Tag: TAG20090908T202721
         Piece Name:
/oracle/app/oracle/flash_recovery_area/ROB1/backupset/2009_09_08
/o1_mf_annnn_TAG20090908T202721_5bg4n9qy_.bkp

  List of Archived Logs in backup set 744
  Thrd Seq     Low SCN    Low Time  Next SCN   Next Time
  ---- ------- ---------- --------- ---------- ---------
  1    15      678853     08-SEP-09 678935     08-SEP-09

BS Key  Size       Device Type Elapsed Time Completion Time
------- ---------- ----------- ------------ ---------------
856     370.50K    DISK        00:00:00     08-SEP-09
         BP Key: 860   Status: AVAILABLE  Compressed: YES  Tag: TAG20090908T202838
         Piece Name:
/oracle/app/oracle/flash_recovery_area/ROB1/backupset/2009_09_08
/o1_mf_annnn_TAG20090908T202838_5bg4pq6x_.bkp

  List of Archived Logs in backup set 856
  Thrd Seq     Low SCN    Low Time  Next SCN   Next Time
  ---- ------- ---------- --------- ---------- ---------
  1    16      678935     08-SEP-09 679163     08-SEP-09

BS Key  Size       Device Type Elapsed Time Completion Time
------- ---------- ----------- ------------ ---------------
894     63.00K     DISK        00:00:01     08-SEP-09
         BP Key: 899   Status: AVAILABLE  Compressed: YES  Tag: TAG20090908T202920
         Piece Name:
/oracle/app/oracle/flash_recovery_area/ROB1/backupset/2009_09_08
/o1_mf_annnn_TAG20090908T202920_5bg4r0y0_.bkp

  List of Archived Logs in backup set 894
  Thrd Seq     Low SCN    Low Time  Next SCN   Next Time
  ---- ------- ---------- --------- ---------- ---------
  1    17      679163     08-SEP-09 679230     08-SEP-09

BS Key  Size       Device Type Elapsed Time Completion Time
------- ---------- ----------- ------------ ---------------
1025    489.00K    DISK        00:00:01     08-SEP-09
         BP Key: 1028   Status: EXPIRED  Compressed: NO  Tag: TAG20090908T203418
         Piece Name:
/oracle/app/oracle/flash_recovery_area/ROB1/backupset/2009_09_08
/o1_mf_annnn_TAG20090908T203418_5bg51c2c_.bkp

  List of Archived Logs in backup set 1025
  Thrd Seq     Low SCN    Low Time  Next SCN   Next Time
  ---- ------- ---------- --------- ---------- ---------
  1    18      679230     08-SEP-09 679716     08-SEP-09
```

Note that the last archive log backup set in this report has an EXPIRED status, while the others have an AVAILABLE status. Thus, all the archived redo log backup sets are available for RMAN recoveries, while the last is not. If you want to look at expired backup sets only, add the **expired** keyword, as in **list expired backup of archivelog all**.

Listing Control File and SPFILE Backups

As you might expect, you can also list control file and SPFILE backups. The **list backup of controlfile** command provides you with a list of control file backups, and the **list backup of spfile** command provides output for SPFILE backups. Here is an example of each command and its results:

```
RMAN> list backup of controlfile;

List of Backup Sets
===================
BS Key  Type LV Size       Device Type Elapsed Time Completion Time
------- ---- -- ---------- ----------- ------------ ---------------
774     Full    9.67M       DISK         00:00:01     08-SEP-09
        BP Key: 776   Status: AVAILABLE  Compressed: NO  Tag: TAG20090908T202724
        Piece Name:
/oracle/app/oracle/flash_recovery_area/ROB1/autobackup/2009_09_08
/o1_mf_s_697062444_5bg4ndym_.bkp
  Control File Included: Ckp SCN: 679035      Ckp time: 08-SEP-09


BS Key  Type LV Size       Device Type Elapsed Time Completion Time
------- ---- -- ---------- ----------- ------------ ---------------
928     Full    9.67M       DISK         00:00:01     08-SEP-09
        BP Key: 930   Status: AVAILABLE  Compressed: NO  Tag: TAG20090908T202923
        Piece Name:
/oracle/app/oracle/flash_recovery_area/ROB1/autobackup/2009_09_08
/o1_mf_s_697062563_5bg4r47m_.bkp
  Control File Included: Ckp SCN: 679329      Ckp time: 08-SEP-09


BS Key  Type LV Size       Device Type Elapsed Time Completion Time
------- ---- -- ---------- ----------- ------------ ---------------
1062    Full    9.67M       DISK         00:00:01     08-SEP-09
        BP Key: 1064   Status: AVAILABLE  Compressed: NO  Tag: TAG20090908T203421
        Piece Name:
/oracle/app/oracle/flash_recovery_area/ROB1/autobackup/2009_09_08
/o1_mf_s_697062861_5bg51g1m_.bkp
  Control File Included: Ckp SCN: 679822      Ckp time: 08-SEP-09


RMAN> list backup of spfile;

List of Backup Sets
===================
BS Key  Type LV Size       Device Type Elapsed Time Completion Time
------- ---- -- ---------- ----------- ------------ ---------------
774     Full    9.67M       DISK         00:00:01     08-SEP-09
        BP Key: 776   Status: AVAILABLE  Compressed: NO  Tag: TAG20090908T202724
        Piece Name:
/oracle/app/oracle/flash_recovery_area/ROB1/autobackup/2009_09_08
/o1_mf_s_697062444_5bg4ndym_.bkp
  SPFILE Included: Modification time: 08-SEP-09
  SPFILE db_unique_name: ROB1

BS Key  Type LV Size       Device Type Elapsed Time Completion Time
------- ---- -- ---------- ----------- ------------ ---------------
928     Full    9.67M       DISK         00:00:01     08-SEP-09
```

```
         BP Key: 930   Status: AVAILABLE  Compressed: NO  Tag: TAG20090908T202923
         Piece Name:
/oracle/app/oracle/flash_recovery_area/ROB1/autobackup/2009_09_08
/o1_mf_s_697062563_5bg4r47m_.bkp
  SPFILE Included: Modification time: 08-SEP-09
  SPFILE db_unique_name: ROB1

BS Key  Type LV Size       Device Type Elapsed Time Completion Time
------- ---- -- ---------- ----------- ------------ ---------------
1062    Full    9.67M      DISK         00:00:01    08-SEP-09
         BP Key: 1064   Status: AVAILABLE  Compressed: NO  Tag: TAG20090908T203421
         Piece Name:
/oracle/app/oracle/flash_recovery_area/ROB1/autobackup/2009_09_08
/o1_mf_s_697062861_5bg51g1m_.bkp
  SPFILE Included: Modification time: 08-SEP-09
  SPFILE db_unique_name: ROB1
```

We'll bet you have already guessed that you can use the **list expired backup of archivelog all** command here, too. Also, you can limit the report by time or log sequence number. For example, to list expired archive log backups until a given sequence, you could use the command **list expired backup of archivelog until sequence**.

Listing Image Copies

Just as you can use the **list** command to determine the status of backup sets, you can also use the **list** command to determine the status of database image copies. You can generate a list of all copies with the **list copy** command:

```
RMAN> list copy;
starting full resync of recovery catalog
full resync complete
specification does not match any control file copy in the repository
List of Datafile Copies
=======================
Key     File S Completion Time Ckp SCN    Ckp Time
------- ---- - --------------- ---------- ---------------
1215    3    A 08-SEP-09       681024     08-SEP-09
        Name:
/oracle/app/oracle/flash_recovery_area/ROB1/datafile
/o1_mf_undotbs1_5bg6sw1s_.dbf
        Tag: TAG20090908T210427

List of Archived Log Copies for database with db_unique_name ROB1
=================================================================
Key     Thrd Seq     S Low Time
------- ---- ------- - ---------
54      1    9       X 08-SEP-09
        Name:
/oracle/app/oracle/flash_recovery_area/ROB1/archivelog/2009_09_08
/o1_mf_1_9_5bd8qv45_.arc
```

```
1170    1   19       A 08-SEP-09
        Name:
/oracle/app/oracle/flash_recovery_area/ROB1/archivelog/2009_09_08
/o1_mf_1_19_5bg6114l_.arc
```

In addition to this summary list, you can create lists of individual datafile copies, archived redo logs, and control file copies. Let's look at those options in more detail for a moment.

Listing Datafile Copies

Oracle allows you to generate a summary list of all datafile copies with the **list copy of database** command:

```
RMAN> list copy of database;

List of Datafile Copies
=======================
Key     File S Completion Time Ckp SCN    Ckp Time
------- ---- - --------------- ---------- ---------------
1215    3    A 08-SEP-09       681024     08-SEP-09
        Name:
/oracle/app/oracle/flash_recovery_area/ROB1/datafile
/o1_mf_undotbs1_5bg6sw1s_.dbf
        Tag: TAG20090908T210427
```

In this output, we have two copies of datafiles that belong to our database, datafile2.copy and datafile3.dbf. While the actual name of the datafile or its assigned tablespace name is not listed, the file number is listed in the second column of the report. We could relate this file number to the associated tablespace by running the **report schema** command, which we discuss later in this chapter.

If you want to know whether you have a datafile copy of a tablespace or a datafile, you can use the **list copy of tablespace** or **list copy of datafile** command, as shown here:

```
RMAN> list copy of tablespace undotbs1;

List of Datafile Copies
=======================

Key     File S Completion Time Ckp SCN    Ckp Time
------- ---- - --------------- ---------- ---------------
1215    3    A 08-SEP-09       681024     08-SEP-09
        Name:
/oracle/app/oracle/flash_recovery_area/ROB1/datafile
/o1_mf_undotbs1_5bg6sw1s_.dbf
        Tag: TAG20090908T210427
```

Listing Archived Redo Log Copies

If you want a list of archived redo log copies, you can use the **list copy of archivelog all** command:

```
RMAN> list copy of archivelog all;
List of Archived Log Copies for database with db_unique_name ROB1
=====================================================================
Key     Thrd Seq     S Low Time
```

```
------- ---- ------- - ---------
54      1    9          X 08-SEP-09
        Name:
/oracle/app/oracle/flash_recovery_area/ROB1/archivelog/
2009_09_08/o1_mf_1_9_5bd8qv45_.arc

1170    1    19         A 08-SEP-09
        Name:
/oracle/app/oracle/flash_recovery_area/ROB1/archivelog/2009_09_08
/o1_mf_1_19_5bg61141_.arc
```

You can also list copies of specific archived redo logs by time, sequence, or database SCN. Here are some examples of listing archived redo logs based on differing criteria:

```
RMAN> list copy of archivelog from sequence 9;

List of Archived Log Copies for database with db_unique_name ROB1
=================================================================================
Key     Thrd Seq    S Low Time
------- ---- ------- - ---------
54      1    9          X 08-SEP-09
        Name:
/oracle/app/oracle/flash_recovery_area/ROB1/archivelog/2009_09_08
/o1_mf_1_9_5bd8qv45_.arc

1170    1    19         A 08-SEP-09
        Name:
/oracle/app/oracle/flash_recovery_area/ROB1/archivelog/2009_09_08
/o1_mf_1_19_5bg61141_.arc

RMAN> list copy of archivelog from sequence 9 until sequence 19;
List of Archived Log Copies for database with db_unique_name ROB1
=================================================================================
Key     Thrd Seq    S Low Time
------- ---- ------- - ---------
54      1    9          X 08-SEP-09
        Name:
/oracle/app/oracle/flash_recovery_area/ROB1/archivelog/2009_09_08
/o1_mf_1_9_5bd8qv45_.arc

1170    1    19         A 08-SEP-09
        Name:
/oracle/app/oracle/flash_recovery_area/ROB1/archivelog/2009_09_08
/o1_mf_1_19_5bg61141_.arc
```

Listing Control File Copies

Finally, RMAN can report on control file copies with the **list copy of controlfile** command:

```
RMAN> list copy of controlfile;
List of Control File Copies
===========================
Key     S Completion Time Ckp SCN    Ckp Time
------- - --------------- ---------- ---------------
```

```
1795    A 08-SEP-09        682922      08-SEP-09
        Name:
/oracle/app/oracle/flash_recovery_area/ROB1/controlfile
/o1_mf_TAG20090908T213230_5bg8gh41_.ctl
        Tag: TAG20090908T213230
```

The RMAN report Command

The RMAN **report** command is used to determine the current recoverable state of your database and to provide certain information on database backups. In this section, we look at reports that tell you which datafiles have not been backed up in a specified period. We also look at reports that tell you when specific tablespaces need to be backed up because of UNRECOVERABLE operations on datafiles. Finally, we look at the use of the **report** command to report on database schemas and obsolete database backups.

Reporting on Datafiles That Have Not Been Backed Up Recently

A question DBAs frequently ask themselves is, "When was the last time I backed up this tablespace?" RMAN provides some answers to that question with the **report need backup** command. For example, if you want to know what tablespaces have not been backed up in the last three days, you could issue the **report need backup days=3** command and find out. Here is an example of the output of just such a report:

```
RMAN> report need backup days=3;

Report of files whose recovery needs more than 3 days of archived logs
File Days   Name
---- -----  -------------------------------------------------------
4    2      D:\ORACLE\ORADATA\RECOVER\TOOLS01.DBF
5    2      D:\ORACLE\ORADATA\RECOVER\USERS01.DBF
```

From this report, it appears that two datafiles require application of more than three days' worth of archived redo to be able to recover them (which implies that these datafiles have not been backed up in the last three days). In this event, we might well want to back up the datafiles or their associated tablespaces.

We can also generate reports based on a given number of incrementals that would need to be applied, as shown in this example:

```
RMAN> report need backup incremental = 3;

Report of files that need more than 3 incrementals during recovery
File Incrementals Name
---- ------------ -------------------------------------------------
1    4            D:\ORACLE\ORADATA\RECOVER\SYSTEM01.DBF
2    4            D:\ORACLE\ORADATA\RECOVER\RECOVER_UNDOTBS_01.DBF
3    4            D:\ORACLE\ORADATA\RECOVER\INDX01.DBF
4    4            D:\ORACLE\ORADATA\RECOVER\TOOLS01.DBF
5    4            D:\ORACLE\ORADATA\RECOVER\USERS01.DBF
```

In this example, several database datafiles require four incrementals to be applied. This may well indicate that we need to perform a new backup on these datafiles at a higher incremental level, or even perform a new incremental base backup.

Reporting on Backup Redundancy or Recovery Window

We can use the **report need backup redundancy** command to determine which, if any, datafiles need to be backed up to meet our established backup redundancy policy. The following is an example of the use of this report. In this case, we want a list of all datafiles that do not have at least two different backups that can be used for recovery. These may be backup set backups or datafile copies.

```
RMAN> report need backup redundancy = 2;

Report of files with less than 2 redundant backups
File #bkps Name
---- ----- --------------------------------------------
1    1     D:\ORACLE\ORADATA\RECOVER\SYSTEM01.DBF
4    1     D:\ORACLE\ORADATA\RECOVER\TOOLS01.DBF
5    1     D:\ORACLE\ORADATA\RECOVER\USERS01.DBF
```

Likewise, we can establish a minimum recovery window for our backups and report on any datafiles whose backups are older than that recovery window. This is done with the **report need backup recovery window days** command:

```
RMAN> report need backup recovery window of 2 days;

Report of files whose recovery needs more than 2 days of archived logs
File Days  Name
---- ----- -------------------------------------------------------
1    4     D:\ORACLE\ORADATA\RECOVER\SYSTEM01.DBF
2    4     D:\ORACLE\ORADATA\RECOVER\RECOVER_UNDOTBS_01.DBF
3    4     D:\ORACLE\ORADATA\RECOVER\INDX01.DBF
4    4     D:\ORACLE\ORADATA\RECOVER\TOOLS01.DBF
5    4     D:\ORACLE\ORADATA\RECOVER\USERS01.DBF
```

In this case, several of our datafiles require application of more than two days' worth of archived redo. So, if our recovery policy says we want backups where we only need to apply one day of redo, then we need to back up these datafiles.

Reporting on Unrecoverable Operations on Datafiles

Unrecoverable operations on objects within tablespaces, and the datafiles that make up those tablespaces, lead to certain recoverability issues. For example, if a table is created using the **Unrecoverable** option and is subsequently loaded using the direct load path, then the tablespace needs to be backed up, or else the data that was loaded will not be recoverable. It is for these circumstances that the **report unrecoverable** command is used, as shown here:

```
RMAN> report unrecoverable;
Report of files that need backup due to unrecoverable operations
```

```
File  Type of Backup Required  Name
----  -----------------------  ------------------------------------
5     full or incremental      D:\ORACLE\ORADATA\RECOVER\USERS01.DBF
```

Reporting on the Database Schema

We are using the word "schema" here to mean the physical structure of the database. The schema includes the datafile name and number, the tablespaces they are assigned to, the size of the datafiles, and whether the datafiles contain rollback segments. This can be the current schema, or you can generate a report on the database schema at some past point in time. Here is an example of the execution of the **report schema** command:

```
RMAN> report schema;

Report of database schema for database with db_unique_name ROB1
List of Permanent Datafiles
===========================
File Size(MB) Tablespace          RB segs Datafile Name
---- -------- ------------------- ------- ------------------------
1    700      SYSTEM              YES     /ora01/oracle/rob1/rob1/system01.dbf
2    600      SYSAUX              NO      /ora01/oracle/rob1/rob1/sysaux01.dbf
3    280      UNDOTBS1            YES     /ora01/oracle/rob1/rob1/undotbs01.dbf
4    8        USERS               NO      /ora01/oracle/rob1/rob1/users01.dbf
```

Reporting on Obsolete Backups

Backups are marked with an OBSOLETE status if you are using a retention policy (which we discussed in Chapter 14). Here is an example of the execution of **report obsolete** with a retention policy set to **redundancy 1**:

```
RMAN> report obsolete;
RMAN retention policy will be applied to the command
RMAN retention policy is set to redundancy 1
Report of obsolete backups and copies
Type                 Key    Completion Time    Filename/Handle
-------------------- ------ ------------------ --------------------
Archive Log          54     08-SEP-09
/oracle/app/oracle/flash_recovery_area/ROB1/archivelog/2009_09_08
/o1_mf_1_9_5bd8qv45_.arc
Backup Set           712    08-SEP-09
  Backup Piece       714    08-SEP-09
/oracle/app/oracle/flash_recovery_area/ROB1/backupset/2009_09_08
/o1_mf_annnn_TAG20090908T202600_5bg4kr90_.bkp
Backup Set           774    08-SEP-09
  Backup Piece       776    08-SEP-09
/oracle/app/oracle/flash_recovery_area/ROB1/autobackup/2009_09_08
/o1_mf_s_697062444_5bg4ndym_.bkp
Backup Set           928    08-SEP-09
  Backup Piece       930    08-SEP-09
/oracle/app/oracle/flash_recovery_area/ROB1/autobackup/2009_09_08
/o1_mf_s_697062563_5bg4r47m_.bkp
Backup Set           1062   08-SEP-09
  Backup Piece       1064   08-SEP-09
/oracle/app/oracle/flash_recovery_area/ROB1/autobackup/2009_09_08
/o1_mf_s_697062861_5bg51g1m_.bkp
```

```
Backup Set          1259   08-SEP-09
  Backup Piece      1262   08-SEP-09              /oracle/app/oracle/flash_recovery_area/ROB1/
autobackup/2009_09_08/o1_mf_s_697064685_5bg6tfxj_.bkp
Backup Set          1413   08-SEP-09
  Backup Piece      1416   08-SEP-09              /oracle/app/oracle/flash_recovery_area/ROB1/
backupset/2009_09_08
/o1_mf_ncnnf_TAG20090908T212707_5bg84dxo_.bkp
Backup Set          1475   08-SEP-09
  Backup Piece      1477   08-SEP-09
/oracle/app/oracle/flash_recovery_area/ROB1/autobackup/2009_09_08
/o1_mf_s_697066032_5bg84jf9_.bkp
Backup Set          1598   08-SEP-09
  Backup Piece      1601   08-SEP-09
/oracle/app/oracle/flash_recovery_area/ROB1/backupset/2009_09_08
/o1_mf_ncnnf_TAG20090908T213150_5bg8f7q1_.bkp
Control File Copy   1795   08-SEP-09
/oracle/app/oracle/flash_recovery_area/ROB1/controlfile
/o1_mf_TAG20090908T213230_5bg8gh41_.ctl
Backup Set          1664   08-SEP-09
  Backup Piece      1666   08-SEP-09
/oracle/app/oracle/flash_recovery_area/ROB1/autobackup/2009_09_08
/o1_mf_s_697066314_5bg8fbx9_.bkp
```

This report has several different backup sets, datafile copies, control file copies, and archive log copies that have been marked OBSOLETE by Oracle. If you want to mark these backups as DELETED, run the **delete obsolete** command, as shown in Chapter 14.

Data Dictionary Views for Reporting

Oracle provides a number of RMAN-related data dictionary views (v$views) that you can use to perform reporting from the SQL prompt. You can use these views to produce customized reports. You can then use these reports for a number of purposes, such as notifications when databases have not been backed up, or of databases that are not registered with the recovery catalog (you would use some form of configuration control that is reliable to compare against). All of the Oracle views related to RMAN are available in the Oracle Reference Guide, along with the purpose of the view and description of the columns. Many of the RMAN views begin with V$BACKUP*, V$RECOVERY*, and V$RMAN. Some of the more useful views are seen in the following table:

View Name	Description
V$BACKUP_ARCHIVELOG_DETAILS	Contains information about all restorable archive logs
V$BACKUP_ASYNC_IO	Provides performance information about ongoing and recently completed RMAN backups and restores
V$BACKUP_CONTROLFILE_DETAILS	Provides information about restorable control files
V$BACKUP_COPY_DETAILS	Provides information about all available control file and datafile copies
V$BACKUP_CORRUPTION	Provides information about corrupt block ranges in datafile backups from the control file
V$BACKUP_DATAFILE	Provides information about control files and datafiles in backup sets from the control file

View Name	Description
V$BACKUP_DATAFILE_DETAILS	Provides information about restorable datafiles
V$BACKUP_FILES	Provides information about all RMAN backups (both image copies and backup sets) and archived logs
V$BACKUP_PIECE	Provides information about backup pieces from the control file
V$BACKUP_PIECE_DETAILS	Provides information about all available backup pieces
V$BACKUP_REDOLOG	Provides information about archived logs in backup sets from the control file
V$BACKUP_SET	Provides information about backup sets from the control file
V$BACKUP_SET_DETAILS	Provides detailed information on backup sets from the control file
V$BACKUP_SPFILE	Provides information from the control file on SPFILEs contained in backup sets
V$BACKUP_SPFILE_DETAILS	Provides information from the control file on SPFILEs contained in backup sets
V$BACKUP_SYNC_IO	Provides performance information about ongoing and recently completed RMAN backups and restores
V$DATABASE_BLOCK_CORRUPTION	Provides information about database blocks that were corrupted after the last backup
V$RECOVER_FILE	Contains the status of files needing media recovery
V$RECOVER	Provides information about recovery areas
V$RMAN_BACKUP_JOB_DETAILS	Provides details about backup jobs
V$RMAN_BACKUP_TYPE	Provides information about RMAN backup types
V$RMAN_CONFIGURATION	Provides information about RMAN persistent configuration settings
V$RMAN_OUTPUT	Displays messages reported by RMAN
V$RMAN_STATUS	Contains information on the finished and ongoing RMAN jobs

Many of the RMAN control file views also have recovery catalog equivalents. Each of these views starts with an RC_ instead of a V$ prefix. The names are generally very similar. For example, V$ARCHIVED_LOG shows the archived redo logs listed in the control file. The RC_ARCHIVED_LOG provides the same view sourced from the recovery catalog. Finally, you will find that many of the performance-related views in Oracle can be used to help performance-tune RMAN operations. We will discuss the use of those views in more detail next in Chapter 18.

Summary

Information! We want information! This chapter provides you with the commands you can use to extract information from RMAN. The **list** and **report** commands provide a wealth of information that you can use to administer RMAN and make sure that you are getting good backups of your database. We think it's a good idea to sit down and determine what kinds of reporting you want to do for your databases, and to automate that reporting so that you always know the backup and recovery state of your database.

CHAPTER
18

Performance Tuning RMAN Backup and Recovery Operations

MAN actually works pretty well right out of the box, and you generally will find that it requires very little tuning. However, a number of other pieces fit into the RMAN architectural puzzle, and when all those pieces come together, you sometimes need to tweak a setting here or there to get the best performance out of your backup processes. Generally, then, the RMAN tuning you end up having to do involves dealing with inefficiencies in the logical or physical database design, tuning of the Media Management Library (MML), or tuning RMAN and the MML layer to coexist better with the physical device that you are backing up to.

If you have used RMAN before Oracle Database 10*g*, you will find some changes to the performance-related commands. In our estimation, these changes make the tuning process easier to understand overall. In this chapter, we look at what you need to tune before you begin to tune RMAN itself. We then provide some tuning options for RMAN.

Before You Tune RMAN

If your RMAN backups take hours and hours to run, it's probably not RMAN's fault. More likely, it's some issue with your database or with your MML. The last time you drove in rush-hour traffic, did you think the slow movement was a problem with your car? Of course not. The problem was one of too many cars trying to move on a highway that lacked enough lanes. This is an example of a bandwidth problem, or a bottleneck. Cities attempt to solve their rush-hour problem by expanding the highway system or perhaps by adding a subway, busses, or light rail.

The same kind of problem exists when it comes to tuning RMAN and your backup and recovery process. It's often not the fault of RMAN, although RMAN often gets blamed. More likely, the problem is insufficient bandwidth of the system as a whole, or some component in the infrastructure that is not configured correctly. RMAN often gets the initial blame, but in the end, it is just a victim.

Once you have the architecture working correctly, much of RMAN tuning really turns out to be an exercise in tuning your Oracle database. The better your database performs, the better your RMAN backups will perform. Very large books have already been written on the subject of tuning your Oracle database, so we will just give a quick look at these issues. If you need more detailed information on Oracle database performance tuning, we suggest another title from Oracle Press: *Oracle Wait Interface: A Practical Guide to Performance Tuning & Diagnostics,* by Richmond Shee, Kirtikumar Deshpande, and K. Gopalakrishnan (2004).

NOTE
We make some tuning recommendations in this chapter and in other places in this book. Make sure you test our recommendations on your system before you decide to "fire and forget" (meaning to make a change without checking that the change was positive). While certain configurations may work for us in our environments, you may find that they do not work as well for you.

RMAN Performance: What Can Be Achieved?

What level of RMAN performance can be achieved with the currently available technology? Oracle Corporation, in its white paper "Oracle Recovery Manager: Performance Testing at Sun Customer Benchmark Center" (October 2001), available at www.oracle.com/technology/index

.html, found that a backup or recovery rate of 1 terabyte (TB) per hour to tape was possible. As tape backup technology continues to improve, rates exceeding this will likely be possible.

Have the Right Hardware in Place

If you want high backup performance, the first thing to look at is the backup hardware at your disposal. This consists of items such as tape drives, the associated infrastructure such as cabling, robotic tape interfaces, and any MML-layer software that you might choose to employ.

Backup media hardware will provide you with a given speed at which the device will read and write. Of course, the faster the device writes, the faster your backups. Also, the more devices you can back up to, the better your backup timing tests will be. This was clearly pointed out in Oracle's RMAN performance white paper mentioned in the preceding section. The doubling of the number of drives that RMAN could write to causes an almost linear improvement in performance of both backup and restore operations. The ability to parallelize your backups across multiple channels (or backup devices) is critical to quickly backing up a large Oracle database.

RMAN will benefit from parallel CPU resources, but the return diminishes much quicker with the addition of CPUs, as opposed to the addition of physical backup devices. The bottom line, then, is that in most cases, having multiple backup devices will have a much greater positive impact on your backup and restore windows than adding CPUs will.

You will find that most backup devices are asynchronous rather than synchronous. An *asynchronous* device allows the backup server processes to issue I/O instructions without requiring the backup server processes to wait for the I/O to complete. An asynchronous operation, for example, allows the server process to issue a tape write instruction and, while that instruction is being performed, proceed to fill memory buffers in preparation for the next write operation. A *synchronous* device, on the other hand, would have to wait for the backup operation to complete before it could perform any other work. Thus, in our example, the synchronous process will have to wait for the tape I/O to complete before it can start filling memory buffers for the next operation. So, an asynchronous device is more efficient than a synchronous one.

Because asynchronous operations are preferred, you may want to know about a few of their parameters. First, the parameter BACKUP_TAPE_IO_SLAVES (which defaults to FALSE) will cause all tape I/O to be asynchronous in nature. We suggest you set this parameter to TRUE to enable asynchronous I/O to your tape devices (if that setting is supported). Once this parameter is established, you can define the size of the memory buffers that are used by using the **parms** parameter of the **allocate channel** command or **configure channel** command.

The tape buffer size is established when the channel is configured. The default value is OS specific, but is generally 64KB. You can configure this value to be higher or lower by using the **allocate channel** command. For the best performance, we suggest that you configure this value to 256KB or higher, as shown here:

```
allocate channel c1 device type
sbt parms="blksize=262144, ENV=(NB_ORA_CLASS=RMAN_db01)"
```

If you are backing up to disk, then you need to determine whether your OS supports asynchronous I/O (most do these days). If it does, then Oracle automatically uses that feature. If it does not, then Oracle provides the parameter DBWR_IO_SLAVES, which, when set to a non-zero value, causes Oracle to simulate asynchronous I/O to disks by starting multiple DBWR processes.

When either DBWR_IO_SLAVES or BACKUP_TAPE_IO_SLAVES is configured, you may also want to create a large pool. This will help eliminate shared-pool contention and memory allocation error issues that can accompany shared-pool use when BACKUP_TAPE_IO_SLAVES is enabled. If you are using Automatic Shared Memory Management (ASMM) Oracle will manage the memory allocation of the shared pool for you. If you want to manually set the large pool, the total size of disk buffers is limited to 16MB per channel. The formula for setting the LARGE_POOL_SIZE parameter for backup is as follows:

LARGE_POOL_SIZE = (number of allocated channels) * (16MB + (4 * size of tape buffer))

NOTE
If DBWR_IO_SLAVES or BACKUP_TAPE_IO_SLAVES is not configured, RMAN will not use the large pool. Generally, you do not need to configure these parameter settings to get good performance from RMAN, unless your OS does not natively support asynchronous I/O.

Tune the Database

A badly tuned database can have a significant negative impact on your backup times. Certain database tuning issues can also have significant impact on your restore times. In this section, we briefly look at what some of these tuning issues are, including I/O tuning, memory tuning, and SQL tuning.

Tune I/O

Most DBAs understand the impact of I/O on basic database operations. Contention on a given disk drive for database resources (say, for example, that the online redo log and a database datafile are on the same device) can cause significant system slowdowns. Just as poor I/O distribution can impact your database performance, it can also affect your backup and restore times. This makes sense, because RMAN is going to be just another process (or, more likely, many processes due to parallel streams) that contends for I/O time on your devices.

Backing up is a read-intensive operation. If you have poor I/O distribution, not only will RMAN performance suffer, but also other users will suffer, if not even worse, during the backup operation. Recovery may be somewhat easier if all of your recoveries are full database recoveries. However, if you are just recovering a datafile or a tablespace, while the database is open and in use, you may find that poor I/O distribution impacts your recovery window, and your users. The bottom line is that bad I/O distribution impacts not only your day-to-day database users, but also your backups and recoveries, causing them to take longer.

Much has been written on distribution of I/O on an Oracle database and how to do it properly. We suggest that you take a look at the Oracle white paper titled "Oracle Storage Configuration Made Easy" (Juan Loaiza, Oracle Corporation, available at www.oracle.com/technology/index.html). In this paper, Mr. Loaiza makes a compelling argument for using an I/O distribution known as Stripe and Mirror Everything (SAME), discusses current disk speeds and feeds, and then demonstrates the logic of his SAME methodology. This methodology recommends that you stripe your data among the largest number of disks possible and suggests this is a much better approach than striping across a few disks or using a parity disk approach, such as RAID-5 (mirroring is, of course, more expensive). Further, this paper recommends that a stripe size of about 1MB is generally optimal and demonstrates that such a configuration in Oracle's testing resulted in a 13 percent better read/write from the disk than nonstriped systems, with an associated loss in CPU overhead. This faster disk read/write will translate into faster backup timings.

Tune Memory Usage

Like any Oracle process, RMAN uses memory. When an RMAN operation is started, a buffer is allocated to the operation for RMAN to work out of. The size of the buffer allocated depends on a number of different factors, including the following:

- RMAN backup and recovery multiplexing effects

- The device type used

- The number of channels allocated during the operation

Each of these factors affects how much memory RMAN will require. RMAN allocates memory buffers for operations. How it allocates these buffers depends on the type of device you are going to use. Let's look at the different buffer allocation methods in a bit more detail next.

Allocating Memory Buffers for Disk Devices   When backing up to disk devices, RMAN will allocate up to 16MB of memory. This memory is allocated based on the level of multiplexing (based on the **filesperset** setting). If the level of multiplexing is 4 or less, then RMAN will allocate 16 buffers of 1MB each. These 1MB buffers are divided among the number of datafiles to be backed up. So, if **filesperset** is set to 2, then each datafile will be allocated eight 1MB buffers.

If **filesperset** is between 5 and 8, then 512MB buffers are allocated and distributed evenly between the different datafiles. This way, no more than 16MB of buffers will be allocated. Finally, if the level of multiplexing is greater than 8, four buffers of 128MB will be allocated to each datafile, which amounts to 512KB per datafile.

Allocating Memory Buffers for SBT Devices   When backing up to an SBT device, RMAN allocates four buffers for each channel that is allocated. These buffers are 256KB in size generally, and thus the total memory allocated per channel is 1MB. The buffer sizes can be managed using the PARMS and BLKSIZE parameters of the **allocate** and **send** commands.

This memory is generally allocated from the PGA, but if the BACKUP_TAPE_IO_SLAVES parameter is set to TRUE, then the SGA is used unless the large pool is allocated, in which case the large pool will be used. Thus, if you configure I/O slaves (and generally you should if you back up to SBT devices), then you should configure a large pool to reduce the overall memory requirements on the large pool.

Tune Your SQL

You might ask yourself what bad SQL running in your database has to do with performance tuning your backup and recovery times. It's really quite simple. The negative performance impact of poor SQL statement operations has an overall negative performance impact on your database and the system the database is on. Anything that has a negative impact on your database is likewise going to have a negative impact on your backup operations. Tune your SQL operations such that they reduce the overall number of I/Os required (logical and physical), and schedule your backups to occur during times of typical low system usage (if that is possible).

Tune Your Environment

Carefully consider your backup schedules, and ensure that they do not conflict with I/O-intensive database operations such as data loads or reports. Also, if you find your backups are taking too long, consider an incremental backup strategy, and analyze your database to determine whether certain tablespaces might be made read-only, so you don't have to continue to back them up often. Further, if you are running in ARCHIVELOG mode, you can consider staggering the backups of tablespaces on different days to reduce the overall timeframe of your backups (at the cost of somewhat longer recovery times, of course).

If you are running your database using Oracle Real Application Clusters, then RMAN can take advantage of the clustered environment to parallelize your RMAN operations.

Tune Your Backup and Recovery Strategy

We already talked about tuning when you do your backups, but we also want to discuss tuning how you do your backups. If you have a large database, rather than just issuing a **backup database** command to back up the whole kit and caboodle, consider a more partitioned backup strategy. Consider backing up related datafiles that you are likely to restore together using individual **backup tablespace** or **backup datafile** commands, and assign those backups to one specific channel. Why do this? This reduces the need to swap tapes during recoveries and allows the recovery of related datafiles to occur as quickly as possible. Here is an example of such an operation:

```
RMAN> backup (tablespace tools channel 'ORA_DISK_1')
             (tablespace system, undotbs, users, testrbs, indx);
```

We might want to do this if we are backing up a read-only tablespace that we might later want to recover, or perhaps we have a tablespace that we seem to do frequent tablespace point-in-time recoveries (TSPITRs) on. These would be good candidates for such backup strategies.

Oracle Database 11*g* offers a new feature that can be used to help tune your backup and recovery strategies. With normal RMAN backups, a given datafile can only be backed up via one channel. This means that if you have several smaller datafiles and one or two large datafiles, the single channel per backupset rule can cause the backup or restore to take longer. Using multisection backups, you can spread the I/O for the single datafile over more than one channel, which can significantly speed up the backup process.

Another issue to consider is the impact of your backup strategy on your recovery. One of the more painful problems with RMAN is that, depending on the platform (Unix is one example; the following three paragraphs do not apply to Oracle on Windows NT), if you restore an entire database with the **restore database** command, you must be careful to ensure that enough space is available for the restore. Everything is just fine as long as you have enough disk space, but consider for a moment a true disaster recovery situation where you do not have enough disk space in the right places. In this case, RMAN is going to spend perhaps an hour or more recovering your database. Once it runs out of disk space, you would assume that RMAN would just stop at that point, alert you to the lack-of-space problem, and then just stop the restore at that position. The truth, however, is a bit more painful.

If the datafile restore process fails, RMAN removes every incompletely restored file from that restore session. Thus, if you spend two hours restoring all but one database datafile and then you run out of space during that restore, you are in deep trouble, because RMAN is now going to remove that one datafile, and you will have to restore it again. This equates to a very unhappy DBA.

One solution to this problem is to restore specific tablespaces with different **restore** commands for each tablespace (or for a number of tablespaces). This allows you to restore your database datafiles in a bit more granular fashion, and the failure of one operation will not cause you to lose hours. Of course, if you use this type of operation, you will want to parallelize the restores and utilize multiple tape or disk devices to reduce contention and tape streaming issues. In this case, you need to run parallel RMAN sessions, each restoring its own set of tablespace data. Note that this type of restore operation is another reason why it's important to try to back up clusters of files that you will likely need to restore on the same channel. That way, you can stream the data off the tape quickly.

Note that some platforms, such as Windows NT, do check for available space before you actually start an RMAN database, datafile, or tablespace restore. In this case, the issue of running out of space, while still a problem, is not as much of a time waster.

Tuning RMAN

As we stated at the beginning of the chapter, RMAN out of the box really works pretty well. Still, you can do a few things to tune it so that you get better performance, which is what this section is all about. First, we discuss the tuning options in RMAN itself. Then, we discuss some MML tuning issues.

Tuning RMAN Settings

There are a few ways to tune RMAN, which we discuss in this section. Tuning RMAN itself can involve tuning parallel operations and also configuring RMAN to multiplex (or not to multiplex, that is the question). This section also covers some things that you can do to actually tune down RMAN.

Parallel Channel Operations

Perhaps the biggest impact you can make when tuning your database backups is to parallelize them by using multiple RMAN channels. Typically, you configure a channel for each device you are going to back up to. Thus, if you back up to three different disks, configure three different channels. You will see little or no benefit of paralleling backups on the same device, of course; so if you have a D: drive and an E: drive on your Windows NT system but both are just partitioned on the same disk, you will derive no benefit from paralleling backups to those two devices.

NOTE
The memory buffering on tape systems may well make the allocation of additional channels worthwhile, so you should always do some timing tests to decide exactly how many channels you need to use on your system.

Paralleling backups is accomplished by allocating channels to the backup. Channels can have default values configured for them (along with the default degree of parallelization that will determine how many of the channels are used) with the **configure** command, discussed in Chapter 3. For example, if we have two tape devices that we are going to back up to, we'd likely configure two default channels and a default level of parallelization, as shown here:

```
CONFIGURE DEVICE TYPE DISK PARALLELISM 2;
CONFIGURE CHANNEL 1 DEVICE TYPE sbt FORMAT PARMS
'ENV=(NB_ORA_CLASS=RMAN_rs100_tape)';
CONFIGURE CHANNEL 2 DEVICE TYPE sbt FORMAT PARMS
'ENV=(NB_ORA_CLASS=RMAN_rs100_tape)';
```

This would serve to ensure that each **backup** or **recover** command is automatically allocated two channels to parallelize the process.

Of course, depending on your device, you may well be able to run parallel streams to the device. The best thing to do is run several tests and determine from those tests the performance of a varying number of backup streams from both a backup and a recovery point of view. It may be that a different number of streams will be more efficient during your backup than during your recovery, and only testing will determine this.

We have already discussed the multiplexing of backups in RMAN and how to tune this feature. Tuning multiplexing can have significant performance impacts on your backups and recoveries. As we also discussed earlier, how you configure your multiplexing will impact the amount of memory that is allocated to the RMAN backup process. The more memory the better, as long as you do not start to induce swapping back and forth to disk.

Also, properly configuring multiplexing can make streaming to tape devices more efficient. The more memory you can allocate to RMAN, the more data that can be streamed to your I/O devices. Finally, tape streaming is rarely an issue with newer-generation tape drives. Generally, they have a great deal of onboard buffer memory that is used to ensure that the tape is written to at a constant rate.

RMAN Multiplexing

Before we dive headfirst into performance considerations, we should take a moment to discuss multiplexing in RMAN. *Multiplexing* allows a single RMAN channel to parallelize the reading of database datafiles during the backup process and to write the contents of those datafiles to the same backup set piece. Thus, one backup set piece may contain the contents of many different datafiles.

Note that the contents of a given datafile can reside in more than one backup set piece (which is evidenced by the fact that you can set **maxpiecesize** to a value smaller than that of any database datafile, but **maxsetsize** must be at least the size of the largest tablespace being backed up). However, in a given backup, a given datafile will only be backed up through one channel (or one backup set). Thus, if you allocate two channels (and, as a result, have two backup sets) and your database consists of one large datafile, the ability of RMAN to parallelize that datafile's backup will be greatly limited.

The level of RMAN's multiplexing is determined by the lesser of two RMAN parameters. The first is the **filesperset** parameter (established when you issue the **backup** command), and the second is the **maxopenfiles** parameter (established when the channel is allocated).

The **filesperset** parameter establishes how many datafiles should be included in each backup set. The number of datafiles in a given backup set will be some number less than or equivalent to **filesperset**. When you do a backup, RMAN will assign a default value for **filesperset** of either 64 or the number of input files divided by the number of allocated channels, whichever is less. You can use a nondefault value for **filesperset** by using the **filesperset** parameter of the **backup** command, as shown in this example:

```
backup database filesperset 4;
```

The **maxopenfiles** parameter establishes a limit on how many datafiles RMAN can read in parallel (the default is 8). You establish the **maxopenfiles** limit on a channel-by-channel basis. Here is an example of the use of **maxopenfiles**:

```
CONFIGURE CHANNEL 1 DEVICE TYPE DISK MAXOPENFILES 3 FORMAT
"d:\backup\recover\%U";
```

For example, if you created a backup set with **filesperset** set to 6 and **maxopenfiles** set to 3, RMAN would only be able to back up three datafiles in parallel at a time. The backup sets created would still contain at most six datafiles per backup set (assuming one channel is allocated and a degree of parallelism of 1), but only three datafiles would be written to the backup set at any time.

NOTE
If you have your data striped on a large number of disks, you will not need to multiplex your backups, and you can set **maxopenfiles** *to a value of 1. If you are striped across a smaller set of disks, consider setting* **maxopenfiles** *to a value between 4 and 8. If you do not stripe your data at all,* **maxopenfiles** *generally should be set to some value greater than 8.*

Multiplexing, and the establishment of the **filesperset** and **maxopenfiles** parameters, can have a significant impact (good and bad) on the performance of your backups. Tuning RMAN multiplexing can decrease the overall time of your backups, as long as your system is capable of the parallel operations that occur during multiplexing. As with most things, too much of a good thing is too much, and certainly you can overparallelize your backups such that the system is overworked. In this case, you will quickly see the performance of your system diminish and your backup times increase.

Multiplexing can also have an impact on tape operations. Since tape systems are streaming devices, it's important to keep the flow of data streaming to the device at a rate that allows it to continue to write without needing to pause. Generally, once a tape has a delay in the output data stream, the tape device will have to stop and reposition the write head before the next write can occur. This can result in significant delays in the overall performance of your backups. By setting **filesperset** high and **maxopenfiles** low, you can tune your backup so that it streams to your tape device as efficiently as possible. Beware, of course, of overdoing it and bogging down your system so much that the I/O channels or CPU can't keep up with the flow of data that RMAN is providing. As always, finding the proper balance takes some patient tuning and monitoring.

Controlling the Overall Impact of RMAN Operations

Sometimes you want to tune RMAN *down* rather than up. Prior to Oracle Database 10*g*, you would use the RMAN parameters **rate** and **readrate** to throttle RMAN down, freeing system resources for other operations. These parameters would be set when you allocated channels for RMAN operations. These parameters are still available in Oracle Database, but they have been replaced.

Oracle Database makes controlling RMAN backups much easier. Now, you simply use the **duration** parameter in the **backup** command to control the duration of the backup. The **duration** parameter has an additional keyword, **minimize load**, that allows you to indicate to RMAN that it should minimize the I/O load required to back up the database over the given duration. For example, if the backup typically takes five hours and consumes 90 percent of the available I/O, you can indicate to RMAN that it should use a duration of ten hours for the backup. When this is included with the **minimize load** parameter, you might well expect to see only 45 to 50 percent of available I/O consumed, rather than the 90 percent. The negative side of this is, of course, that your backup will take longer. Here is an example of using the **duration** parameter when starting a backup; in this case, we want the backup to run ten hours:

```
Backup as copy database duration 10:00 minimize load database;
```

Of course, one problem with the use of the **duration** parameter is that the backup could actually take longer than ten hours. Any completed backup set can be used for recovery, even if the overall backup process fails due to duration issues. You can use the **partial** keyword to suppress RMAN errors in the event that the duration limit is exceeded and the backup fails.

One final thing to note about the use of the **duration** parameter is that the database files with the oldest backups will be given priority over files that have newer RMAN backup dates. Thus, if the backup of a database with 20 datafiles fails after 10 are backed up, the next time the backup runs, the 10 that were not backed up would get first priority.

Tune the MML Layer

As you will recall from earlier chapters the MML is an API that Oracle provides that interfaces with the software of various vendors who provide external backup solutions (such as tape devices). Each component of RMAN may require some tuning effort, including the MML layer. You need to consider a number of things with regard to the MML backup devices. Most are going to be running in asynchronous mode, but if they do not, that may be a big cause of your problems. Also, sometimes DBAs will set the rate parameter when they allocate a channel for backups. This is generally something you do not want to do, because this will create an artificial performance bottleneck.

Also, some of the MML vendors provide various configurable parameters, such as a configurable buffer size, that you can configure in vendor-specific parameter files. Look into the tuning possibilities that these parameter files offer you.

There are other factors related to the MML layer, such as the supported transfer rate of the backup device you are using, compression, streaming, and the block size. You must analyze all of these factors in an overall effort to tune the performance of your RMAN backups.

Identifying Database–Related RMAN Issues

In many ways, RMAN tuning is a lot like SQL tuning. RMAN uses the Oracle Database in much the same way that SQL statements do, such as using the buffer cache, issuing dynamic SQL calls, and calling stored PL/SQL packages. These operations, such as timed wait events, show up in the Oracle Database–generated statistics. As a result, several views are available to help give you some idea as to the kinds of problems you might be encountering and the source of those problems.

A number of views are useful for RMAN performance tuning. This book isn't a tuning book, but we can provide a few RMAN-specific insights. Some views you might be interested in with respect to RMAN tuning would include

- V$RMAN_BACKUP_JOB_DETAILS

- V$ACTIVE_SESSION_HISTORY

- V$SESSION

- V$PROCESS

- V$SESSION_LONGOPS

- V$BACKUP_ASYNC_IO

- V$BACKUP_SYNC_IO

There are a number of different potential sources for performance problems. When you are performing read operations with RMAN, such as reading the control file, these components can be involved in the performance issues:

- **Control file**

    - RMAN frequently needs to read the control file for RMAN metadata. If the control file is experiencing slow I/O (perhaps due to slow disk response times), this can slow down RMAN operations. In the past, certain RMAN-related bugs have also caused performance problems related to the database control file, so it's important to get Oracle involved if you experience unexplainable performance problems involving the control file.

- **Recovery catalog**

    - If you are using the recovery catalog, RMAN will frequently access the catalog to read the RMAN metadata. If the recovery catalog is experiencing slow I/O, this can slow down RMAN operations. Keep in mind that the recovery catalog is often a separate database from the database you are backing up. Thus, performance problems can be a result of the recovery catalog database or of the database being backed up. When performance tuning RMAN problems, then, you will need to look at the statistics of both the database being backed up and the recovery catalog database. In the past, certain RMAN-related bugs have also caused performance problems related to the recovery catalog, so it's important to get Oracle involved if you experience unexplainable performance problems involving the control file.

- **Reading memory buffers**

    - As with any other database operation, memory is important. The SGA should be properly configured. Typically, memory issues on the target database will surface for problems beyond RMAN. Memory issues on the recovery catalog database can cause significant performance issues.

- **Reading database blocks**

    - RMAN must read database blocks either from memory or from disk. If the disks are not sufficiently responsive, then I/O rates will suffer. This can cause performance impacts on RMAN operations. Likewise, if the SGA is too small, you will end up reading blocks from disk more frequently, so this can have an impact on RMAN performance.

Write operations (such as a datafile restore) can also cause performance issues. Many of the same components can be involved in write operations as with read operations. Database components that can be involved in write-related performance issues include

- **Control file**

- **Recovery catalog**

- **Writing to tape/disk**

    - As with reading from tape or disk, the I/O rates that you can achieve can make a difference with respect to performance.

- **Writing to memory buffers**

We mentioned several views in this section that can be used to monitor and tune RMAN performance. Using these views, you can determine how well the database, RMAN, and the MML are performing. You can also use these views to determine how long a backup or recovery process has taken and how much longer you can expect it to take. Let's look at these views and how you can best use them.

V$RMAN_BACKUP_JOB_DETAILS

The V$RMAN_BACKUP_JOB_DETAILS view provides some insight into each backup that occurs in your database. The view provides details on the start time, stop time, elapsed time, and bytes associated with each RMAN backup operation. Here is an example of V$RMAN_BACKUP_JOB_DETAILS:

```
select /*+ RULE */ session_key, session_recid,
start_time, end_time, output_bytes, elapsed_seconds
from v$rman_backup_job_details
where start_time >= sysdate-180
and status='COMPLETED'
And input_type='DB FULL';

SESSION_KEY SESSION_RECID START_TIM END_TIME  OUTPUT_BYTES ELAPSED_SECONDS
----------- ------------- --------- --------- ------------ ---------------
        456           456 11-JAN-09 11-JAN-09    228353024             397
        461           461 12-JAN-09 12-JAN-09    229755904             422
```

In this example, we see that two backup operations have successfully executed. Over time, we would be very interested in how long the backups were taking and whether the trend is increasing. By looking at the trends with respect to backup execution times, we can address problems before they actually become problems.

V$SESSION_LONGOPS and V$SESSION

The V$SESSION_LONGOPS view is useful during a backup or restore operation to determine how long the operation has taken and how much longer it is expected to take to complete. Join this view to the V$SESSION view for additional information about your RMAN backup or recovery sessions. Here is an example of a join between V$SESSION_LONGOPS and V$SESSION during a database backup:

```
SQL> select a.sid, a.serial#, a.program, b.opname, b.time_remaining
from v$session a, v$session_longops b
where a.sid=b.sid
and a.serial#=b.serial#
and a.program like '%RMAN%'
and time_remaining > 0;
 SID SERIAL# PROGRAM  USERNAME  OPNAME               TIME_REMAINING
---- ------- -------- --------- -------------------- --------------------
  10       8 RMAN.EXE SYS RMAN: aggregate input                     1438
  14       3 RMAN.EXE SYS RMAN: full datafile backup                7390
```

In this example, we have an RMAN process running a backup. It has connected to the database as SID 14. The time remaining, 7390, is the expected time in seconds that this backup will take. You can thus determine how long your backup will take by looking at this report. Note that we also did a join to V$SESSION to get some additional information on our RMAN session, such as the username and the program name.

V$ACTIVE_SESSION_HISTORY

Oracle Database offers a feature called Active Session History (ASH) that provides historical session-related information on Oracle database operations. ASH is a very powerful tool that can be used to review historical runtime information, providing information that can be effective for use when tuning RMAN operations. One use of ASH is to look at wait times that various sessions have experienced, and what the associated waits are. Here is an example of such a query:

```
-- First we use V$SESSION to get the session
-- specific information if possible.
select sid, serial#, program
 from v$session
 where lower(program) like '%rman%';


   SID    SERIAL# PROGRAM
------ ---------- ----------
   125        149 rman.exe
   128        130 rman.exe
   134        164 rman.exe
-- Note that runtime session information may not always be available.
Set lines 132
Column session_id format 999 heading "SESS|ID"
Column session_serial# format 999 heading "SESS|SER|#"
Column event format a40
Column total_waits format 9,999,999,999 heading "TOTAL|TIME|WAITED|MICRO"
Select session_id, session_serial#, Event, sum(time_waited) total_waits
From v$active_session_history
Where sample_time > sysdate - 1
-- The next line can be remarked out if you don't know
-- the session information.
And session_id||session_serial# in (120102, 128102, 134129)
And program like '%rman%'
And session_state='WAITING' And time_waited > 0
Group by session_id, session_serial#, Event
Order by session_id, session_serial#, total_waits desc;
```

SESS ID	SESS SER #	EVENT	TOTAL TIME WAITED MICRO
125	149	control file single write	1,388,961
125	149	control file sequential read	45,964
125	149	control file parallel write	3,789
128	130	RMAN backup & recovery I/O	192,263,005
128	130	control file single write	1,095,253
128	130	control file parallel write	529,012

V$BACKUP_ASYNC_IO and V$BACKUP_SYNC_IO

The V$BACKUP_ASYNC_IO and V$BACKUP_SYNC_IO views contain detailed information on RMAN asynchronous and synchronous backup operations. These views are transitory in nature and are cleared each time the database is shut down. These views contain a row for each asynchronous or synchronous backup or recovery operation. Perhaps the biggest benefit from this view is the EFFECTIVE_BYTES_PER_SECOND column in rows where the TYPE column is set to AGGREGATE. This column represents the rate at which the objects are being backed up or recovered in bytes per second. This number should be close to the listed read/write rate of your backup hardware. If the EFFECTIVE_BYTES_PER_SECOND column value is much lower than the rated speed of your backup hardware, then you should be looking for some sort of problem with your backup process. The problem could be caused by any number of things, from an overburdened CPU to a saturated network, or perhaps a configuration issue with the MML interface to your vendor's backup solution.

NOTE
If you see data in V$BACKUP_SYNC_IO, this implies that you are not doing asynchronous backups. If this is the case, you need to investigate why your backups are occurring in synchronous fashion.

Here is an example of a query against V$BACKUP_ASYNC_IO and its results after a database backup has been completed:

```
select device_type "Device", type, filename,
to_char(open_time, 'mm/dd/yyyy hh24:mi:ss') open,
to_char(close_time, 'mm/dd/yyyy hh24:mi:ss') close,
elapsed_time ET, effective_bytes_per_second EPS
from v$backup_async_io
where close_time > sysdate - 30
order by close_time desc;

Device           TYPE
---------------- ---------
FILENAME
--------------------------------------------------------------------------------
OPEN                CLOSE                    ET          EPS
------------------- -------------------- ---------- ----------
DISK            INPUT
/oracle/app/oracle/flash_recovery_area/ROB1/backupset/2009_09_10
/o1_mf_nnndf_TAG20090910T110421_5b1ddpg9_.bkp
09/10/2009 11:15:35 09/10/2009 11:16:38     6300     4078836

DISK            OUTPUT
/ora01/oracle/rob1/rob1/system01.dbf
09/10/2009 11:15:35 09/10/2009 11:16:37     6200    11838761

DISK            AGGREGATE
09/10/2009 11:15:35 09/10/2009 11:16:37     6200    21986271

DISK            OUTPUT
/ora01/oracle/rob1/rob1/sysaux01.dbf
09/10/2009 11:15:36 09/10/2009 11:16:24     4800    13107200
```

```
DISK                AGGREGATE
09/10/2009 11:10:54 09/10/2009 11:11:06       1200   42269355

DISK                OUTPUT
/ora01/oracle/rob1/rob1/sysaux01.dbf
09/10/2009 11:10:55 09/10/2009 11:11:06       1100   9245789

DISK                INPUT
/oracle/app/oracle/flash_recovery_area/ROB1/backupset/2009_09_10
/o1_mf_nnndf_TAG20090910T110421_5blddpg9_.bkp
09/10/2009 11:10:54 09/10/2009 11:11:05       1100   1429132

DISK                OUTPUT
/ora01/oracle/rob1/rob1/system01.dbf
09/10/2009 11:10:54 09/10/2009 11:11:05       1100   9341114

DISK                OUTPUT
/ora01/oracle/rob1/rob1/undotbs01.dbf
09/10/2009 11:10:55 09/10/2009 11:11:00        500   58720256

DISK                OUTPUT
/ora01/oracle/rob1/rob1/users01.dbf
09/10/2009 11:10:55 09/10/2009 11:10:56        100   9175040

10 rows selected.
```

In this case, we can see the effective transfer rate from the database to the backup set by RMAN. Further, we can see the name of the datafile that was backed up and the actual start and stop time of the backup itself.

Another way to measure the efficiency of your backup process is to use the V$BACKUP_ASYNC_IO view. This view has several columns of interest, which are listed and described in Table 18-1.

Column Name	Represents
IO_COUNT	The total number of I/O counts
READY	The number of asynchronous I/O calls for which a buffer was available immediately
SHORT_WAITS	The number of times that a buffer was requested and not available but became available after a nonblocking poll for I/O completion
LONG_WAITS	The number of times that a buffer was requested and not available and Oracle had to wait for the I/O device

TABLE 18-1 *V$BACKUP_ASYNC_IO Column Descriptions*

To determine whether there is an I/O problem, we can look at the ratio of I/Os to long waits (LONG_WAITS/IO_COUNTS), as shown in the following code segment:

```
select b.io_count, b.ready, b.short_waits, b.long_waits,
b.long_waits/b.io_count, b.filename
from v$backup_async_io b;
IO_COUNT      READY SHORT_WAITS LONG_WAITS B.LONG_WAITS/B.IO_COUNT
---------- ---------- ----------- ---------- -----------------------
FILENAME
----------------------------------------
         2          1          0          1          .5
D:\ORACLE\ADMIN\RECOVER\ARCH\ARC00052.001
         2          1          0          1          .5
D:\ORACLE\ADMIN\RECOVER\ARCH\ARC00046.001
         2          1          0          1          .5
D:\ORACLE\ADMIN\RECOVER\ARCH\ARC00051.001
         2          1          0          1          .5
D:\ORACLE\ADMIN\RECOVER\ARCH\ARC00050.001
       171        107         12         52          .304093567
D:\ORACLE\ORADATA\RECOVER\SYSTEM01.DBF
        11          8          2          1          .090909091
D:\ORACLE\ORADATA\RECOVER\RECOVER_UNDOTBS_01.DBF
         6          4          0          2          .333333333
D:\ORACLE\ORADATA\RECOVER\TOOLS01.DBF
         6          3          0          3          .5
D:\ORACLE\ORADATA\RECOVER\USERS01.DBF
         6          4          1          1          .166666667
D:\ORACLE\ORADATA\RECOVER\RECOVER_TESTRBS_01.DBF
         3          1          0          2          .666666667
D:\ORACLE\ORADATA\RECOVER\INDX01.DBF
         2          1          0          1          .5
D:\ORACLE\ORADATA\RECOVER\TOOLS02.DBF
```

The numbers returned by this query clearly indicate some sort of I/O bottleneck is causing grief (in this case, it's an overly taxed, single CPU).

Tracing RMAN Sessions

Sometimes using views is not enough to track down problems. Sometimes you need to get down to the nitty and the gritty. This means tracing the Oracle sessions related to the RMAN operation. This can be somewhat complex, because RMAN will actually create a number of Oracle sessions in order to complete its work. In this section, we will introduce you to the notion of tracing, and how to start tracing. Tracing, like tuning, is a topic unto itself. If you find yourself needing to actually trace RMAN sessions, then you have a serious problem. In these cases, you will want to do some more research on Oracle tracing, and consult with Oracle.

Depending on the nature of the RMAN problem, you may need to trace one or all of those sessions. There are several ways to start tracing RMAN sessions. Generally, we try to start with the easiest method and then move to the more complicated method as required.

Tracing in Oracle is done by enabling an Oracle event. An Oracle event is something a DBA or developer "sets" in order to get Oracle to do something that it does not normally do. Each event is numbered and in our case the event we are interested in is the 10046 event. When you set the 10046 event, you are telling the Oracle database that you want it to create a trace file and start tracing. Tracing can be enabled at the database or session level. Because of the overhead involved, you want to be cautious about tracing, and only trace the sessions that need to be traced.

Reading the output of a trace file is beyond the scope of this book, and the need to do such a thing should be very rare, indeed. However, you may want to investigate such things, or Oracle might ask you to trace your RMAN sessions. So, we are going to show you how to do it! Depending on your needs, you might want to enable tracing in one of these ways:

- From the RMAN prompt, use the SQL command to enable 10046 tracing, as seen in this example. This will start tracing only on the sessions that the RMAN client is already connected to. As a result, some sessions will not be traced. Usually, this is the easiest way to trace a session, and it may produce some fruit.

  ```
  sql "alter session set events ''10046 trace name context forever, level 12''";
  RMAN> backup as compressed backupset database plus archivelog delete input;
  ```

- You may also want to start tracing on the recovery catalog database. You can trace the entire database, or you can use the logon trigger demonstrated in the following bullet. Here is an example of enabling tracing for the recovery catalog database. This example would enable tracing for the whole database. If you wish to be more tactical, you could use the trigger code in the next bullet to just trace RMAN connections.

  ```
  ALTER SESSION SET EVENTS='10046 trace name context off';
  ```

- If the trace files in the first session do not help identify the problems you might be dealing with, you can create a login trigger to start tracing when a session logon occurs. This example trigger will enable tracing for any RMAN session that connects to the database:

  ```
  Create or replace trigger tr_rman_logon
  After logon on database
  Declare
       v_program    varchar2(1000);
  Begin
       SELECT distinct program into v_program
       FROM v$session
       WHERE audsid = userenv('sessionid')
       and program like '%rman.exe%' and rownum < 2;
     if v_program='rman.exe'
       then
       execute immediate 'alter session set events ''10046 trace name context
       forever, level 12''';
       end if;
  Exception
       when NO_DATA_FOUND then
             NULL;
  End;
  /
  ```

In Oracle Database 11g, the resulting trace file can be found in the Automatic Diagnostic Destination directory structure pointed to by the DIAGNOSTIC_DEST parameter. You can use the

show parameter in 11*g* and to find the setting for DIAGNOSTIC_DEST, or you can also look for the default setting for USER_DUMP_DEST to find this directory (this parameter is deprecated in Oracle Database 11*g*, but is still handy to find the file paths for various files in the ADR). In Oracle Database versions previous to Oracle Database 11*g*, you will find the resulting trace files in the directory path pointed to by the USER_DUMP_DEST parameter.

You can find the location and name of a specific trace file if you can identify the session IDs by using the V$SESSION and V$PROCESS views. These views have a column called TRACEFILE that will give you the name and location of the trace file.

The 10046 trace files created as a result of the scripts in this book are long and complex beasts, well beyond the scope of this book. Most DBAs are aware of the tkprof tool that Oracle offers for reformatting these trace files, and many DBAs are also aware of generally how to read and interpret the resulting output. If you need more information on how to read trace files, several good sources of information are available including books, the Web, and Oracle Metalink.

Summary

RMAN will support very fast backup and recovery schemes given that the appropriate infrastructure is in place to support it. Often, we find the reason that RMAN does not perform well is not because of the database, or because of RMAN, but because of the underlying network or insufficient numbers of backup devices.

We also talked about the times that RMAN is too fast and takes up too much CPU, or floods the network. We discussed the **duration** parameter and its various options that allow you to reduce the overall runtime impact of RMAN operations.

PART
IV

RMAN in the Oracle Ecosystem

CHAPTER
19

Duplication: Cloning the Target Database

e've hinted at this chapter's content since the earliest part of the book: RMAN will help you leverage your backups beyond disaster recovery. We covered using RMAN for corruption checking and cross-platform database conversion in Chapter 14. But one of the most highly leveraged ways to use backups is to make copies of the production database for testing and development purposes. In the database world, we refer to this as *cloning*.

Database cloning can provide an excellent way to test version upgrades, new application rollouts, and even bug patches. Cloning can also be used to prepare reporting databases that are kept separate from transaction processing databases. In these ways, database backups can be put to work. They can be used to restore the database to another system, or even just to another disk on the same system. We can then do load testing for performance reasons, or try out a new hardware configuration. With clone databases at our disposal, we can leave little to chance and have an almost perfect grasp of what will happen if we change our production environment. RMAN can be also be used to create a standby database that can be kept up to date for disaster recovery. But we are getting ahead of ourselves.

RMAN helps you create clones via the **duplicate** command. This simple little command hides many levels of complexity that are worth knowing about before you begin to use it. In addition, there is a fair amount of prep work required so that duplication goes smoothly. But once understood, and after you've had a little time to practice, you'll find that database duplication is one of the real "killer apps" within the backup and recovery world. Or perhaps you already know this. But leveraging the RMAN interface will save you hours of scripting pain.

RMAN Duplication: A Primer

The RMAN **duplicate** command is a simple command that hides a high level of complexity. If you've ever been through the process of restoring image copy backups of your database to another system, you know the amount of information that you have to keep track of: filenames, file locations, backup locations, archive log information, ftp processes, moving tapes around... there's plenty to keep track of. RMAN, on the other hand, has a straightforward command:

```
duplicate target database to aux1;
```

This will perform the entire process of cloning your target database to another database. Granted, you have to do a little legwork first, but once you become familiar with the architecture, you'll see that the legwork is not too bad a trade-off.

Why Use RMAN Duplication?

Why is duplication necessary? Why can't we just copy the control file to a new location and run a restore and recovery? The answer is: you can! There is no reason that this won't work. The only problem is, you will have an exact copy—not just of the data in the database (the part you want to be the same), but also of the metadata about the database (this will cause headaches). If you use a recovery catalog, you will run into problems if you clone your database without using duplication. You see, RMAN registers databases in the catalog based on the database ID (DBID), which is a number that identifies your database as unique, even if it has the same DB_NAME as another database. If you don't use the **duplicate** command, you will have two databases with the same DBID. If you try to register your clone in the same catalog as your production system, you will get an error:

```
rman-20002: target database already registered in recovery catalog
```

This error can be a little misleading: you haven't registered the database! If you shrug your shoulders at this and go ahead and try to back up your database, it will give you an even stranger error:

```
rman-20011: target database incarnation is not current in recovery catalog
```

"Whoa," you say, "what does that mean?" So you go ahead and issue a **reset database**, as you think you should, and this works. You can now back up your database. Sweet. However, you have caused bigger problems. Now, you connect RMAN to your original production server and try to back it up. But when you do, you get a hauntingly similar error:

```
rman-20011: target database incarnation is not current in recovery catalog
```

The reason for this error is that RMAN considers your clone no more than a restored version of your production system, so it now thinks the clone is the current incarnation of your production server, and it has no idea what your production server is. You can reset the incarnation back to the one that actually matches your production database, but you've essentially corrupted your catalog and should unregister your database and reregister it in the catalog (see Chapter 3). It should be noted, of course, that the Oracle documentation clearly states in each release that you should never connect RMAN to a test database and the recovery catalog because of this very problem.

If you don't use a catalog, nonduplicated clones can wreak havoc, as well. Let's lay it out in an example. You clone your database to the same system as your primary database. You are using RMAN to back up both databases to tape, and because you aren't using a catalog, you have automatic control file backups turned on for both instances. One day, you lose a disk array, and your entire system goes belly up. Both databases, and all of their control files, are lost. "No problem," you think, "I've got control file autobackup turned on. I'll just use one of those to restore my systems."

But here's the stickler: the command **restore controlfile from autobackup** uses the DB_ID to track down the control file autobackup. Because both of your databases back up to the same tape, it may try to restore the control file from the wrong database, giving you the wrong files with the wrong data.

A third reason, new to environments where you are using Oracle Enterprise Manager Grid Control, also comes to the surface. Grid Control needs to understand all of its managed targets as unique snowflakes. If you clone a database, and you leave the metadata the same for both databases, and then try to use Grid Control to manage both databases, you give Grid Control brain damage. It will either refuse to discover one of the databases, or make you go through some gyrations to rectify how the new clone registers itself with the listener (note: this problem can occur even if your clone database is on a different server).

Obviously, any of these scenarios can be fixed, and they don't cause a loss of data. But they cause a loss of time. They can potentially extend your downtime past your agreement levels. In addition to these problems, using duplication in RMAN provides the power of the RMAN interface to keep things as simple as possible. And simple is good. Simple is wise.

Different Types of RMAN Duplication

Oracle 11*g* offers multiple ways to perform database cloning using RMAN. In the past, you always needed a few critical things to perform duplication: access to the target database (the one you want to copy) and access to existing backups. In different situations, both of these dependencies have been stripped, allowing for more flexibility in how you plan and execute a clone operation with RMAN.

Duplicate Using RMAN Backups and with Access to the Target Database

This is the "traditional" RMAN duplication from versions 9*i* and 10*g*: we leverage our existing RMAN backups to create a copy of an existing target database to a new location. To understand how far, and what, to duplicate, RMAN connects to the existing database's control file throughout the duplication operation.

Duplicate Using RMAN Backups and No Access to the Target

New to 11*g*, now you have the option of performing a duplication when the target is not available. This is useful in situations where the target database is in a different incarnation, is in an inaccessible network location, or is simply not at your disposal for the duplication. In this case, RMAN can pull what it needs from the recovery catalog, a few additional parameters you will pass to the **duplicate** command. We cover this near the end of the chapter, in the section "Target-Less Duplication in 11*g*."

Duplicate an Active Database Without Using Backups

Duplicating an active database sounds new, but this operation was actually introduced in Enterprise Manager in the 10*g* timeframe. At that time, Enterprise Manager would clone a database by calling the package dbms_backup_restore directly, instead of using the RMAN client command syntax, and it would make a live copy of each datafile in the database in real time, and then would move that datafile to the new location.

Now, in 11*g*, this is codified in the RMAN command syntax, but it's the same operation. Instead of relying on an existing RMAN backup, RMAN simply connects to the target database, runs a backup operation directly against the database in real time, and writes the file to the specified location. So, nothing all that special, other than a syntactic difference in what you call the operation.

All three of these duplication types rely on the same underlying architecture. We will walk through the operations for the backup-based, target database–connected duplication so that the underlying principles can be observed.

The Duplication Architecture

Here's how duplication works. RMAN connects to your target database or to the catalog, if you use one. This connection is necessary to gain access to the target database control file for details about where to locate backups. After you connect to the target or catalog, you must connect to your auxiliary instance (the instance that will house your cloned database). Before duplication starts, you must have already built an init.ora file for the auxiliary instance, and have started it in NOMOUNT mode. This way, the memory segment has been initialized, and therefore RMAN can make a SYSDBA connection to it. The auxiliary instance does not have a control file yet (duplication will take care of that), so you cannot mount the auxiliary instance, even if you want to.

With these connections made, you can issue your **duplicate** command. It can look as simple as this:

```
duplicate target database to aux1;
```

or it can be complicated, depending on where the auxiliary instance is

```
run {
set until time = '08-JUL-2002:16:30:00';
duplicate target database to aux1 pfile=/u02/oracle/admin/aux1/pfile/init.ora
nofilenamecheck
device type sbt parms "env=(nb_ora_serv=rmsrv)"
logfile
'/u04/oracle/oradata/aux1/redo01.log' size 100m,
'/u05/oracle/oradata/aux1/redo02.log' size 100m,
'/u06/oracle/oradata/aux1/redo03.log' size 100m;}
```

The duplication process can be broken down into its distinct phases:

1. RMAN determines the nature and location of the backups.
2. RMAN allocates an auxiliary channel at the auxiliary instance.
3. RMAN restores the datafiles to the auxiliary instance.
4. RMAN builds a new auxiliary control file.
5. RMAN restores archive logs from backup (if necessary) and performs any necessary recovery.
6. RMAN resets the DBID for the auxiliary instance and opens the auxiliary database with **open resetlogs**.

First, RMAN sets any runtime parameters, such as an **until time** clause on the **duplicate** command. Then, based on these parameters, it checks the target database control file (or recovery catalog) for the appropriate backups. It then builds the RPCs for how to access the backups, and which ones to access, but it does not execute the code at the target. Instead, RMAN creates a channel process at the auxiliary instance, referred to as the *auxiliary channel,* and to this channel, RMAN passes the call to DBMS_BACKUP_RESTORE. The auxiliary instance, then, accesses the backups and restores all necessary datafiles. Figure 19-1 illustrates how this takes place for both disk backups and tape backups.

Auxiliary Channel Configuration

For duplication to work, RMAN must allocate one or more channel processes at the auxiliary instance. From Oracle9*i* onward, you do not need to manually allocate an auxiliary channel at the time of duplication, because one will automatically be created using permanent configuration parameters stored in the target control file. The makeup of the auxiliary channel mainly comes from parameters you established for target channels: the default device type and the degree of parallelism both get set using the same persistent parameters that set the target channels. Therefore, if you are duplicating using backups taken to disk, you need not do anything to configure your auxiliary channels. However, if you are duplicating your database using backups

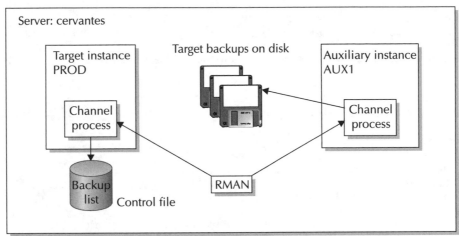

Duplication from Disk (same server)

Duplication from Tape (different server)

FIGURE 19-1 *A bird's-eye view of duplication*

taken to tape, you need to configure your auxiliary channels to contain any media manager environment parameters that your target channels have. For example, the following code sets the default device type to tape, sets the default level of parallelism to 2, and then configures two auxiliary channels with the correct parameters:

```
configure default device type to sbt;
configure device type sbt parallelism 2;
configure auxiliary channel 1 device type sbt parms
= "env=(nb_ora_serv=mgtserv, nb_ora_class=oracle)";
configure auxiliary channel 2 device type sbt parms
= "env=(nb_ora_serv=mgtserv, nb_ora_class=oracle)";
```

Restoring Datafiles to a Different File Location

After mounting the new control file, RMAN moves forward with the datafile restore. If you are duplicating your database to the same server that your target resides on, it is obviously necessary to change the location to which the files will be restored.

Even when restoring to a different server, differences in mount points and directory structures can require a new file location. The datafile restore step of the duplication process can be modified to point to a new file location in three ways.

First, you can use the **configure** command to configure the auxname for any (or all) datafiles that need a new location. These configurations are stored in the target database control file.

```
configure auxname for datafile 1 to '/u04/oradata/aux1/system01.dbf';
configure auxname for datafile 2 to '/u04/oradata/aux1/undo01.dbf';
...
```

Second, you can specify the new datafile names in a **run** command, as you would in previous versions:

```
run {allocate channel c1 type 'sbt_tape';
set newname for datafile 1 to '/u04/oradata/aux1/system01.dbf';
set newname for datafile 2 to '/u04/oradata/aux1/undo01.dbf';
duplicate target database to aux1;}
```

Finally, you can use a parameter in your auxiliary database's init.ora file to set a new location for the files. The parameter is DB_FILE_NAME_CONVERT, and you pass two strings to it: first, the old location of the file on the target, and second, the new location for the file in your auxiliary instance. You can do this in matched file pairs, like this:

```
db_file_name_convert=(
'/u02/oradata/prod/system01.dbf', '/u02/oradata/aux1/system01.dbf',
'/u03/oradata/prod/prd_data_01.dbf', '/u03/oradata/aux1/prd_data_01.dbf')
```

NOTE
In 11gR2, the SET NEWNAME function has been significantly improved to make scripting even simpler. Now you can do a SET NEWNAME for an entire tablespace, or for the entire database. For instance:

```
SET NEWNAME for tablespace USERS01 to '/u01/%U';
```

This will rename all datafiles to the new location, with unique naming as defined by the variable %U. This greatly simplifies the duplication scripting in situations where the new location will have a different, but consistent, file location.

In addition, there is a Metalink note for those with Oracle Support access that provides methods for dynamic SQL to generate the SET NEWNAME commands for user-managed files, or for converting files to Oracle's Automatic Storage Manager (ASM) and Oracle Managed Files (OMF) infrastructure. This is Note 549972.1, "RMAN: SET NEWNAME Command SQL."

This is a simple string conversion parameter, so you can simply pass a single directory name to be changed. For instance, let's say you have your files spread over four mount points, but they all have prod in the directory structure, so that a **select** from V$DATAFILE looks like this:

```
Select name from v$datafile;
------------------------------------------------------------
/u02/oradata/prod/system01.dbf
/u03/oradata/prod/prd_data_01.dbf
/u04/oradata/prod/indx_prd01.dbf
/u05/oradata/prod/temp01.dbf
```

Instead of pairing up each file, you can simply do the following:

```
db_file_name_convert=('prod' , 'aux1')
```

This works, so long as everything else about the file location is the same for your auxiliary database, such as the mount point.

Creating the New Control File

The new control file is created for the auxiliary instance after all the files have been restored. RMAN just issues a **create controlfile** command at the auxiliary instance, using the parameters you outlined in your **duplicate** command. After creating the control file, the auxiliary database is mounted. Now, RMAN performs a switch operation to switch to the new files. The switch is the means by which RMAN modifies the new control file at the auxiliary site to point to the new location of the datafiles.

Recovery and Archive Logs

After the files are restored and switched, it is time to perform recovery on the database, either to bring it to the current point in time or to bring it to the time specified in the **until time** clause. To perform recovery, RMAN needs access to the archive logs. If they have been backed up by RMAN, then RMAN can simply restore them from the backup location to the LOG_ARCHIVE_ DEST specified in the init.ora file of the auxiliary database. You can also manually move archive logs to the location required by the new instance so that they are found on disk by RMAN and no restore is required. If you are duplicating to the same server as the one that the target currently resides on, RMAN can find the archive logs in the LOG_ARCHIVE_DEST of the target.

Once the archive logs are restored, RMAN performs the required amount of recovery. If you did not specify a point in time to end the recovery, RMAN restores up to the last available archive log (as found in the view V$ARCHIVED_LOG) and then stops. During duplication, RMAN cannot check the online redo log files for further recovery information. After it hits the end of the archive logs, it stops recovery. After recovery has completed, if RMAN restored any archive logs from backup, they are deleted.

Changing the Database ID (DBID)

After media recovery is complete, the database is in a consistent state, and it is time for RMAN to change the database ID of the new clone. RMAN has to wait until all other activity in the database has completed, as all operations to this point required the clone database to have the same DBID as the target. The archive logs would not apply to the clone during media recovery if the control file had a different DBID.

The process of changing the DBID is simple. RMAN has at its disposal a little procedure called dbms_backup_restore.zerodbid(). With the database in a mounted state (not open), this package goes into the file headers and zeros out the DBID in each file header. Then, RMAN shuts down the database and re-creates the auxiliary control file again. When the control file is rebuilt, Oracle checks the file headers for the DBID. When it does not find one, Oracle generates a new one and broadcasts it to every file header.

Log File Creation at the Auxiliary Site

When RMAN issues the final **open resetlogs** command at the completion of the duplication process, it must build brand-new log files for the auxiliary database. This always happens when you issue a **resetlogs** command, but with a **duplicate** command, you need to take into consideration what you want the new redo log files to look like. If you are duplicating to the same system as your target, at a minimum you will have to rename your log files.

The zerodbid Procedure: Warning! Achtung!

As you can imagine, the following is a very vulnerable state for a database to be in: shut down without a DBID in the file headers and with a control file that is being rebuilt. In the RMAN duplication process, however, elements that could go wrong are tightly controlled, so you don't have to worry too much. We point this out because it is possible to execute this package against any database to generate a new DBID. You just mount the database and run the following code:

```
execute sys.dbms_backup_restore.zerodbid(0);
```

Then, you shut down the database and rebuild the control file using the **set** parameter:

```
create controlfile SET database <db_name> resetlogs…
```

And voilà! You have a new DBID. Seems simple enough, doesn't it?

However, a lot can go wrong if you are trying to do this without the complete control over the environment that RMAN has during duplication. For instance, if you did not get a clean shutdown and you need to perform media recovery before you can open reset logs, you are out of luck. The archive logs have a different DBID. There is no way you will be able to open the database—it is stuck in an inconsistent state, and you cannot fix it. The same thing can happen if a file was accidentally left offline—it won't get the new DBID when you do an **open resetlogs** command, and therefore you will not be able to bring it online. Ever. You will get the following error:

```
ORA-01190: control file or datafile <name> is from before the last RESETLOGS
```

The moral of the story is to be very careful if you decide to use this procedure manually. There is a better way. As of Oracle9*i* Release 2, Oracle has a utility called DBNEWID, which is a safe and secure way of generating a new ID for a database without making a manual call to the DBMS_BACKUP_RESTORE package. We talk about DBNEWID at the end of this chapter in the section "Incomplete Duplication: Using the DBNEWID Utility."

You can specify completely new redo log file definitions when you issue the **duplicate** command. Do this if you want to change the size, number, and/or location of the redo logs for the new database. This would look something like the following:

```
duplicate target database to aux1
pfile=/u02/oracle/admin/aux1/init.ora
logfile
'/u04/oracle/oradata/aux1/redo01.log' size 100m,
'/u05/oracle/oradata/aux1/redo02.log' size 100m,
'/u06/oracle/oradata/aux1/redo03.log' size 100m;
```

Alternatively, you can use the existing log file definitions from your target and simply move them to a new location using the init.ora parameter LOG_FILE_NAME_CONVERT. This parameter acts exactly like DB_FILE_NAME_CONVERT, so you can convert the log files in coupled pairs, or you can simply use string conversion to change a single directory name:

```
log_file_name_convert=('/u02/oracle/oradata/redo01a.dbf',
'/u03/auxiliary/redo01a.dbf',…)
```

Duplication: Location Considerations

So far, we've completely glossed over one of the biggest stumbling blocks to understanding duplication. You must account for the location of your auxiliary instance in relation to the location of your target instance. Duplicating to the same server is very different from duplicating to a remote server. There are elements unique to each that you must understand before you proceed with duplication.

Duplication to the Same Server: An Overview

You must tread lightly when duplicating to the same server, so that you don't walk all over your existing target database. If you were to simply make a copy of your target init.ora file and then run the following code:

```
duplicate target database to aux1;
```

you would run into a series of problems and errors. These errors would be related to the fact that you already have an instance running with the same name and have the same file locations for two databases.

Memory Considerations

The first memory consideration is the database name. Oracle references memory segments on the server based on the value of the init.ora parameter DB_NAME. Therefore, Oracle cannot allow two instances with the same DB_NAME to run on the same system. If you try to startup mount a second instance with the same name, you will get the following error:

```
ORA-01102: cannot mount database in EXCLUSIVE mode
```

Therefore, when duplicating to the same system, you need to change the DB_NAME parameter in the auxiliary init.ora file to be different from the database name of your target:

```
db_name='aux1'
instance_name='aux1'
```

File Location Considerations

Okay, you've squared away your memory problems, but you still have two databases that are trying to write to the same file locations. In fact, you have three different types of files that are all competing for the same name. If you don't account for file locations, duplication will fail at the step of trying to rebuild the control file:

```
RMAN-00571: ============================================================
RMAN-00569: =============== ERROR MESSAGE STACK FOLLOWS ============
RMAN-00571: ============================================================
RMAN-03002: failure of Duplicate Db command at 07/02/2009 13:52:14
RMAN-06136: ORACLE error from auxiliary database:
      ORA-01503: CREATE CONTROLFILE failed
ORA-00200: controlfile could not be created
ORA-00202: controlfile:
'/space/oracle_user/OraHome1/oradata/sun92/control01.ctl'
ORA-27086: skgfglk: unable to lock file - already in use
SVR4 Error: 11: Resource temporarily unavailable
```

This is good news for you, because otherwise you would have overwritten your production control file. You must change the auxiliary init.ora parameter CONTROL_FILES to point to a new location on disk, as this is the means by which RMAN determines where to restore the control files to.

After we change the location of the control files, we must change the location of the datafiles. We talked about this previously: your three choices are to use the **configure** command, use the DB_FILE_NAME_CONVERT parameter, or use a **run** block, Oracle8*i*-style. If you fail to change the datafile locations when duplicating to the same server, you will get an error very similar to the preceding control file error, telling you that the files are currently in use and cannot be overwritten.

Finally, you must change the redo log file location. We talked about this previously, when we discussed the different steps that duplication walks through. You can use the **logfile** keyword as part of the **duplicate** command to build completely different redo files, with different sizes, number of groups, and number of members. This option essentially rewrites the similar **logfile** parameter of the **create controlfile** stage of duplication. Alternatively, you can simply use the LOG_FILE_NAME_CONVERT parameter in the auxiliary init.ora file.

Duplication to the Same Server, Different ORACLE_HOME

It is common practice to clone the production database from its location to a different location on the same server but to have it be hosted by a different Oracle software installation. When you have a different ORACLE_HOME for the auxiliary instance, slightly different rules apply. All the rules about hosting on the same system apply as outlined previously. However, you must also consider the location of the backup pieces. If you are duplicating from disk backups, this won't be a problem—just make sure you have your OS permissions worked out ahead of time. If you are duplicating from tape backups, however, you need to make sure that you have your MML file appropriately linked with the auxiliary ORACLE_HOME in the same way as it is linked in your target's ORACLE_HOME. Otherwise, your tape backups will be inaccessible by the auxiliary instance, and duplication will fail because the media manager will be inaccessible.

Duplication to a Remote Server: An Overview

A successful duplication to an auxiliary instance on a different server from the target is no more or less complicated than duplication to the same server. It's just complicated in different ways.

Memory Considerations

Unlike duplication to the same server, you do not have to worry about the DB_NAME parameter in the init.ora file. Because we are on a different server, Oracle has no hang-ups about the LOCK_NAME used for memory.

Of course, it is good operational procedure to always be mindful of the DB_NAME parameter during a duplication process, and crosscheck all other instances running on the same server before beginning the duplication. That way you have no unexpected errors down the road. In addition, from a management perspective, it makes the most sense to always have every database in your ecosystem with a unique name.

File Location Considerations

Again, because we are on a new server, there is not quite the urgency to change any of the file location specifications for your auxiliary instance. No database already is running with the same files, so we can leave all file specifications the same as for the target instance, and thus avoid any possible errors in the configuration. Again, we can simplify much of this process when we are on a different system. If you do not change the location of the files, you must specify **nofilenamecheck** in the **duplicate** command. This tells duplication not to confirm that the filenames are different before performing the restore. If this is not specified, RMAN will give you an error.

The one caveat to this simplicity is if the auxiliary host does not have the same file structure and mount point setup that the target host has. If you have different mount points or drive configurations, you still need to change your file specifications for the auxiliary instance so that RMAN can restore to a location that actually exists.

The Backup Location: Disk

The complicating factor for restoring to a different server comes from providing the auxiliary channel process access to backups that were taken at a different server. You must account for whether you backed up to disk or to tape.

If you are duplicating from disk backups, your choices are limited. Remember that RMAN passes the calls to DBMS_BACKUP_RESTORE to a channel process at the auxiliary instance, but it cannot take into account any file system differences. It must look for the backup pieces in the exact location and format that was recorded in the target database control file. For example, suppose you took a full database backup at your target system using the following command:

```
backup database format= '/u04/backup/prod/%U.full.PROD';
```

This created your backup piece as a file called 01DSGVLT_1_1 in the directory /u04/backup/prod. This is recorded in the target control file. Then, during duplication, RMAN passes the **file restore** command to the auxiliary instance and tells it to restore from /u04/backup/prod/01DSGVLT_1_1. That means your auxiliary instance must have a mount point named /u04, and there must be a directory named backup/prod in which a file called 01DSGVLT_1_1 resides. If not, the duplication will fail with an error:

```
RMAN-03002: failure of Duplicate Db command at 07/02/2002 14:49:55
RMAN-03015: error occurred in stored script Memory Script
ORA-19505: failed to identify file "/u04/backup/prod/01dsgvlt_1_1"
ORA-27037: unable to obtain file status
SVR4 Error: 2: No such file or directory
Additional information: 3
```

You can make duplication from disk work in three ways. The first, and most straightforward, is to simply copy the backups from your target host to the auxiliary host, and place them in the same location. Obviously, this involves a huge transfer of files across your network.

The second way to proceed is to NFS mount the backup location on the target host from the auxiliary host. This works only if you can mount the target location with the same mount point name as RMAN will use (in the preceding example, you would have to NFS mount /u04/backup/ prod as /u04/backup/prod). For example, you would need to do the following from your auxiliary instance:

```
mount cervantes:/u04/backup/prod /u04/backup/prod
```

That way, from your auxiliary node, you should be able to do the following:

```
cd /u04/backup/prod
ls -l
touch testfile
ls -l
```

If you get an error when you try to change directories, or when you try to touch a file, you need to sort out your NFS and permissions issues before you proceed with duplication. Figure 19-2 illustrates the mounted file system approach to duplicating to a different server using disk backups.

If you are on a Windows platform instead of NFS, you will be mounting a network drive. The same rule applies: the drive specification must be the same on the auxiliary as it is on the target. So if the backup was written to F:\backup, then you must be able to use F: as a network drive, or duplication will fail. In addition, you will have to set up your auxiliary service (oracleserviceaux1) and your listener service (oracleOraHome92tnslistener) to log on as a domain administrator that

FIGURE 19-2 *Duplication to a different server using disk backups*

has read/write privileges at both the auxiliary host and the target host. Otherwise, you will not be able to access the backups over the networked drive.

As you may have already noticed, it could be difficult to make a network file system operation be successful. If you have the same file systems on both the target and the auxiliary servers, you would not be able to use a straight NFS mount from the auxiliary node to the target location of the backups on disk. Therefore, your only option would be to copy the backup pieces from one node to the other.

The source of these types of headaches, of course, is the fact that RMAN hard-codes the backup location when we back up to disk, and this location cannot be changed. In Oracle Database 10g, however, there are now two options for us to change the backup location: the **backup backupset** command and the **catalog backupset** command.

With the **backup backupset** command, we can back up a previous backup set that was on disk and move it to a different disk location. This gives us considerable flexibility. Now, we can move the backup pieces from /u04/backup/prod to, say, /u06/backup/prod, which could then be NFS mounted from our auxiliary system. Or, from the target host, we could NFS mount a drive at the auxiliary host and then use the **backup backupset** command to move the backups to the auxiliary host. For more information on this command, see Chapter 11.

The **catalog backupset** (and **catalog datafilecopy**) command offers another, simpler means of relocating backup sets on a new server. To make RMAN aware that a backup set exists in any location, you need only tell RMAN to catalog a certain file (or a certain directory), and it will look for any valid backups in that location and generate metadata for them. For more details on the **catalog** command, see Chapter 16.

The Backup Location: Tape

By all estimations, duplicating to a remote server using tape backups is far less complicated or demanding than using disk backups, because a tape backup does not have a location, per se, just a file handle. This file handle is all that RMAN knows or cares about; how that file handle relates to a location on a specific tape is completely controlled by the media manager. Therefore, all configuration steps that occur for duplication from tape come from the media management layer.

First, you must configure your MML file at the auxiliary site in the same way as at the target site. Because an auxiliary channel is doing the restore operations, it must be able to initialize the MML, as outlined in Chapter 4. So, make sure you've linked your MML at the auxiliary site.

Next, you need to make sure that your media management server is configured correctly. This means that your auxiliary node must be registered as a client in the same media management server that your target node is registered in, and it must have the necessary privileges to access the tapes for restore purposes. In particular, you must enable the auxiliary node to restore backups that were taken from a different server. This functionality is usually disabled by default in most media management software, because allowing files to be restored from one client to another is a potential security hole. The steps for enabling clients to restore files from a different client are outlined in each of our four media management chapters (Chapters 5, 6, 7, and 8), depending on your software vendor.

After configuring your media management server, your final configuration step is to set up your auxiliary channels. As mentioned earlier, RMAN allocates one or more channels at the auxiliary instance to perform the restore and recovery steps of duplication. You configure these channels via the **configure** command when you are connected to your target database from RMAN. The **parms** parameter for the auxiliary channels must contain the usual media management environment control variables. In particular, it needs to specify the client from which the backups were taken. For instance, let's say your target node is named cervantes, and your auxiliary node is named quixote. Because you have been backing up from cervantes, this client name is encoded with your RMAN backups at the media management server. So, to be able to access these backups from the client quixote, you must specify from within RMAN that the client name is cervantes. Your auxiliary channel configuration command, then, would look something like this (given a NetBackup media management system):

```
RMAN> configure auxiliary channel 1 device type sbt parms
2> = "env=(nb_ora_serv=mgtserv, nb_ora_client=cervantes)";
new RMAN configuration parameters:
CONFIGURE AUXILIARY CHANNEL 1 DEVICE TYPE 'SBT_TAPE' PARMS
"env=(nb_ora_serv=mgtserv, nb_ora_client=cervantes)";
new RMAN configuration parameters are successfully stored
```

Then, when the auxiliary channel makes its sbt() calls to the MML, it is telling the media management server to access backups that were taken using the client cervantes, instead of checking for backups made by quixote.

Duplication and the Network

Take a deep breath; we're almost through explaining all the intricacies of duplication and are about to walk you through the steps themselves. There's one more area that you need to prepare prior to running a **duplicate** command from RMAN: the network. By *network,* we mostly mean configuring your Oracle Net files—tnsnames.ora and listener.ora. However, take this opportunity to consider your overall network as well. Make sure that the target node, auxiliary node, and media management server can all access each other okay and that you have plenty of bandwidth.

From an Oracle perspective, we have to configure the Oracle Net files. As discussed in Chapter 2, RMAN must make a SYSDBA connection to the target database. If you are connecting remotely, you have to configure a password file for the target node. In addition, you need a tns alias that uses a dedicated server process instead of a shared server process. For duplication, this still holds true, but you must also be able to connect to the auxiliary instance as SYSDBA using only dedicated servers.

This means that, no matter what, you have to create a password file for either your target or your auxiliary machine. You may have been forgoing this step until now by always making a local connection to the target database. But you cannot simultaneously make a local connection to both the target and the auxiliary instance. So now, if you haven't done so already, it's time to build a password file.

RMAN Workshop: *Build a Password File*

Workshop Notes

On Unix platforms, the name of the password file must be orapw<sid>, where <sid> is the value of the ORACLE_SID to which the password is giving access. In this workshop, the ORACLE_SID = prod. On Windows, the filename must be in the format pwd<sid>.ora. The locations given in this workshop must be used; the password file cannot be created anywhere else or it will be unusable.

Step 1.   Edit the init.ora file and add the following parameter:

```
remote_login_passwordfile=exclusive
```

If you are using an SPFILE, you need to execute the following:

```
alter system set remote_login_passwordfile=exclusive scope=spfile;
```

Both operations require a database restart to take effect.

Step 2. Decide what your password will be, and then navigate to your ORACLE_HOME/dbs directory (ORACLE_HOME/database on Windows) and type the following:

```
orapwd file=orapwprod password=<OraclE4ever>
```

Step 3. Check that the file was created successfully, and then test it by making a remote connection as SYSDBA.

After your password file has been created for your auxiliary instance, you need to configure the listener to route incoming connections to the auxiliary instance. As you may have already noticed, there is no need in 10*g* or 11*g* for a listener.ora file if you will be connecting only to open databases. This is because the database PMON process automatically registers the database with a running listener daemon on the system. So, you will often see that after a default 11*g*R2 installation, a listener is running, and it is listening for your database, even though you've done no configuration.

While this is excellent news, it does nothing for us in a duplication environment, because we must be able to make a remote connection to an auxiliary instance that is started (in NOMOUNT mode) but not open. Because it is not open, there is no PMON process to register the auxiliary instance with the listener, so the listener has no idea the auxiliary instance exists. To get past this, you must set up an old-fashioned listener.ora file, with a manual entry for the auxiliary database. We recommend using the Oracle Net Manager utility, shown here, to build this entry:

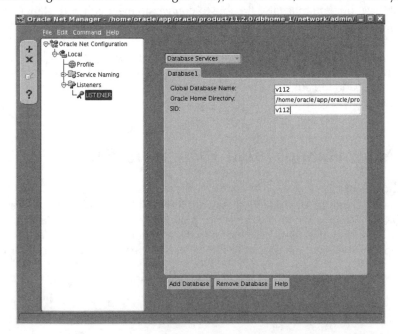

After you have configured the listener.ora at your auxiliary instance location, you must also build a tnsnames.ora entry at the site from which you will be running RMAN. This is the same as almost any other entry, except that when you build it, you must specify the auxiliary SID_NAME instead of the SERVICE_NAME. From the Net Manager, you fire up the Net Service Name Wizard by clicking Service Naming and then going to the menu and choosing Edit | Create. After you give the Net Service Name (Step 1), then provide the protocol (Step 2), provide the hostname and port number (Step 3), and finish with specifying the Service Name.

Duplication to the Same Server

Okay, so enough of the explanations, it's time to run through the duplication itself. First, we give a detailed step-by-step workshop for duplicating to the same server on which the target resides, using disk backups. Then, we briefly explain what you would need to do the same thing with tape backups.

Setting an until Clause When Duplicating

When performing duplication, you sometimes will encounter a situation that requires you to specify an **until** clause when duplicating. If you have ever used RMAN to restore your database using a backup control file, and you are now attempting to duplicate that database, you will be required to set an **until** clause. It is recommended to determine the most recent archive log available to duplication and then to use it as the ending point during duplication:

```
run { set until sequence n thread 1;
duplicate target database... }
```

Or, as a fix-all, you can set the SCN to an impossibly high value:

```
set until scn  281474976710655;
```

RMAN Workshop: *Duplication to the Same Server, Using Disk Backups*

Workshop Notes

Make sure that your OS has been configured to handle another Oracle instance and that adequate memory and disk space exists. In the following example, our target database, v112, has all of its datafiles, control files, and redo log files located at /u01/app/oracle/product/oradata/v112. All backups have been going to the local flash recovery area (FRA) at /u01/app/oracle/product/flash_recovery_area. We will set the ORACLE_SID for the auxiliary instance to be aux1.

Step 1. Build your auxiliary database directory structures:

```
$ pwd
/u01/app/oracle/product/oradata
$ mkdir aux1
$ mkdir aux1/arch
$ cd ../admin
$ mkdir aux1
$ cd aux1
$ mkdir pfile bdump udump cdump
$ ls
 bdump  cdump  pfile  udump
```

Step 2. Copy the target init.ora file to the auxiliary location. If your target database uses an SPFILE, you need to create a PFILE from the SPFILE to capture parameters to move over.
 If you use an SPFILE at your target, enter the following:

```
SQL> connect / as sysdba
Connected.
SQL> create pfile='/u01/app/oracle/product/admin/aux1/pfile/init.ora'
  from spfile;
```

 If you use an init.ora file at your target, enter the following:

```
cp u01/app/oracle/product/admin/v112/pfile/init.ora
   u01/app/oracle/product/admin/aux1/pfile/init.ora
```

Step 3. Make all necessary changes to your aux1 init.ora file:

```
audit_file_dest='/u01/app/oracle/product/admin/aux1/adump'
background_dump_dest='/u01/app/oracle/product/admin/aux1/bdump'
compatible='11.2.0.1.0'
control_files='/u01/app/oracle/product/oradata/aux1/control01.ctl',
     '/u01/app/oracle/product/oradata/aux1/control02.ctl',
     '/u01/app/oracle/product/oradata/aux1/control03.ctl'
core_dump_dest='/u01/app/oracle/product/admin/aux1/cdump'
db_block_size=8192
db_file_multiblock_read_count=16
db_name='aux1'
db_recovery_file_dest='/u01/app/oracle/product/flash_recovery_area'
```

```
db_recovery_file_dest_size=4294967296
dispatchers='(PROTOCOL=TCP) (SERVICE=aux1XDB)'
job_queue_processes=10
open_cursors=300
pga_aggregate_target=93323264
processes=150
remote_login_passwordfile='EXCLUSIVE'
sga_target=279969792
undo_management='AUTO'
undo_tablespace='UNDOTBS1'
user_dump_dest='/u01/app/oracle/product/admin/aux1/udump'
db_file_name_convert=('v112','aux1')
instance_name='aux1'
```

Step 4. Build your aux1 password file. See the "Build a Password File" RMAN Workshop earlier in this chapter.

Step 5. Start up the aux1 instance in NOMOUNT mode:

```
ORACLE_SID=aux1
export ORACLE_SID
sqlplus /nolog
sql>connect / as sysdba
SQL> startup nomount
pfile=/u01/app/oracle/product/admin/aux1/pfile/init.ora
```

Step 6. Configure your network files for connection to aux1. After making any changes to your listener.ora file, be sure that you bounce your listener, or the change will not take effect.

```
$ lsnrctl reload
```

The tnsnames.ora file should have an entry like this:

```
AUX1 =
  (DESCRIPTION =
    (ADDRESS_LIST =
(ADDRESS = (PROTOCOL = TCP)(HOST = horatio)(PORT = 1521))
    )
    (CONNECT_DATA =
      (SID = aux1)
      (SERVER = DEDICATED)
    )
  )
```

The listener.ora file should have an entry like this:

```
SID_LIST_LISTENER =
  (SID_LIST =
    (SID_DESC =
      (GLOBAL_DBNAME = aux1)
      (ORACLE_HOME = /u01/app/oracle/product/11.2.0/dbhome_1)
      (SID_NAME = aux1)
    )
  )
```

Step 7. From RMAN, connect to the target and auxiliary instance and run the **duplicate** command:

```
$ ORACLE_SID=aux1;export ORACLE_SID
$ rman target /
RMAN> connect auxiliary sys/ora10g@aux1
RMAN> duplicate target database to aux1
 pfile=/u01/app/oracle/product/admin/aux1/pfile/init.ora
 logfile
 '/u01/app/oracle/product/oradata/aux1/redo01.dbf' size 100m,
 '/u01/app/oracle/product/oradata/aux1/redo02.dbf' size 100m,
 '/u01/app/oracle/product/oradata/aux1/redo03.dbf' size 100m;
```

Using Tape Backups

If you were to perform the preceding exercises but with your backups on tape, little would change. In fact, none of the code itself would change; you would simply insert an additional step prior to running the **duplicate** command itself. That step would be to configure your auxiliary channel(s) to resemble the channels that the backups were taken with. In other words, do a **show** command:

```
RMAN> show channel;
RMAN configuration parameters are:
CONFIGURE CHANNEL 1 DEVICE TYPE 'SBT_TAPE' PARMS
"env=(nb_ora_serv=mgtserv)";
CONFIGURE CHANNEL 2 DEVICE TYPE 'SBT_TAPE' PARMS
"env=(nb_ora_serv=mgtserv)";
```

Then, simply create the auxiliary channels to match:

```
CONFIGURE AUXILIARY CHANNEL 1 DEVICE TYPE 'SBT_TAPE' PARMS
"env=(nb_ora_serv=mgtserv)";
CONFIGURE AUXILIARY CHANNEL 2 DEVICE TYPE 'SBT_TAPE' PARMS
"env=(nb_ora_serv=mgtserv)";
```

Duplication to a Remote Server

Duplication to a remote server has many of the same configuration steps as duplication to the same server. In particular, if you are duplicating remotely but will use disk backups, the steps would be identical, although you could forgo all file-renaming steps. In addition, you would have to either copy your backups to the remote server or use NFS to mount the backups at the remote site. Covering NFS is outside the scope of this book, so we assume in the following RMAN Workshop that you have the same file systems on both the target and auxiliary servers and have copied the backups to the auxiliary system.

RMAN Workshop: *Duplication to a Remote Server, Using Disk Backups*

Workshop Notes

This workshop assumes the use of two servers: dex, the target, and horatio, the auxiliary. It assumes that you have the same file system on both nodes and have copied your backups from dex to horatio. The most important thing to note here is that we maintain the v112 database SID throughout the process (instead of changing it to aux1, which we do when duplicating to the same server).

Step 1. At horatio (the auxiliary server), build your auxiliary database directory structures:

```
$> pwd
/u01/app/oracle/oradata
$> mkdir v112
$> cd ../admin
$> pwd
/u01/app/oracle/admin
$> mkdir v112
$> cd v112
$> mkdir pfile bdump udump cdump adump
$> ls
adump   bdump   cdump   pfile   udump
```

Step 2. At dex (the source server), make a copy of the target init.ora file so that it can be moved to the auxiliary server. If your target database uses an SPFILE, you need to create a PFILE from the SPFILE in order to capture parameters to move over.

   If you use an SPFILE at your target, enter the following:

```
SQL> connect / as sysdba
Connected.
SQL> create pfile='/home/oracle/scratchpad/init.ora'
  from spfile;
```

   If you use an init.ora file at your target, enter the following:

```
cp /u01/app/oracle/admin/v112/pfile/init.ora*
   /home/oracle/scratchpad/init.ora
```

Step 3. Move the target init.ora file to the auxiliary site:

```
cd /home/oracle/scratchpad/
ftp horatio.hadba.com
username: oracle
password:
cd /u01/app/oracle/admin/v112/pfile
put init.ora
exit
```

You also need a local copy of the init.ora file at the target server dex, for reference by RMAN in the **duplicate** command itself. We will reference the copy that we left in /home/oracle/ scratchpad/init.ora when we run the **duplicate** command in Step 9.

Step 4. Start the auxiliary instance in NOMOUNT mode at quixote:

```
ORACLE_SID=v112; export ORACLE_SID
sqlplus /nolog
SQL>connect / as sysdba
SQL>startup nomount
pfile=/u01/app/oracle/admin/v112/pfile/init.ora
```

Step 5. Configure the listener.ora at the auxiliary site (proto):

```
SID_LIST_LISTENER =
  (SID_LIST =
    (SID_DESC =
      (GLOBAL_DBNAME = v112)
(ORACLE_HOME = /u01/app/oracle/product/11.2.0/dbhome_1)
      (SID_NAME = v112)
    )
  )
```

Step 6. Configure the tnsnames.ora file at the target site (dex):

```
V112_HORATIO =
  (DESCRIPTION =
    (ADDRESS_LIST =
      (ADDRESS = (PROTOCOL = TCP)(HOST = horatio)(PORT = 1522))
    )
    (CONNECT_DATA =
      (SERVICE_NAME = v112)
    )
```

Step 7. Create a password file at the remote server (proto). Follow the instructions from the earlier RMAN Workshop, "Build a Password File."

Step 8. Move the FRA files from dex to horatio.

Step 9. From the target system (dex), run your **duplicate** command:

```
ORACLE_SID=v112; export ORACLE_SID
rman target /
RMAN> connect auxiliary sys/password@v112_horatio
duplicate target database to v112
pfile=/home/oracle/scratchpad/init.ora
logfile
'/u01/app/oracle/11.2.0/oradata/v102/redo01.dbf' size 100m,
'/u01/app/oracle/11.2.0/oradata/v102/redo02.dbf' size 100m,
'/u01/app/oracle/11.2.0/oradata/v102/redo03.dbf' size 100m;
```

Using Tape Backups for Remote Server Duplication

All the steps in the preceding RMAN Workshop apply if you are using tape backups instead of disk backups; again, the only difference is that you would also have to configure your auxiliary channels to reflect the needs of your media manager. In addition to specifying the media management server, and any classes or pools that you have for your regular channels, you also need to specify the target client name:

```
RMAN> configure auxiliary channel 1 device type sbt parms
2> = "env=(nb_ora_serv=mgtserv, nb_ora_client=dex)";
```

Target-Less Duplication in 11g

Starting in 11gR2, RMAN has been innovated to break some of the dependencies that made the duplication process complex in previous versions. Primarily, it is now possible to duplicate a database from RMAN backups without making a connection to the target database. While providing access to the active target database makes some aspects of duplication simpler, it sometimes simply isn't possible. In fact, we've been involved in "fake target database" operations where we have pulled a backup control file from an inaccessible target database, mounted the control file, and pointed RMAN at this "instance" long enough to kick off duplication. Perhaps Oracle heard our cries of anguish.

To duplicate without a target, the next best thing is a connection to your recovery catalog, where the requisite target database metadata can be extracted with little effort. The primary element to be concerned with in this situation is to care for the database ID (DBID) when performing the duplication. When you are connected to the target database, RMAN has no difficulty understanding what "prod" means. But if you have multiple "prod" databases in your catalog, you may run into ambiguity issues. Therefore, you should dig into the recovery catalog and get your DBID:

```
SQL> select dbid, name, resetlogs_time from rc_database;

     DBID NAME     RESETLOGS
---------- -------- ---------


2203908660 V112     20-JUN-09
```

Once the DBID is known, you can kick off your nontarget duplication in much the same way as our previous workshops:

```
RMAN> connect auxiliary sys/password@v112_horatio
Connect catalog rman2/rman2@rcv_cat
duplicate database v112 to aux1
dbid 2203908660
until time "to_date('2009-07-08', 'YYYY-MM-DD')"
pfile=/home/oracle/scratchpad/init.ora
logfile
'/u01/app/oracle/11.2.0/oradata/v102/redo01.dbf' size 100m,
'/u01/app/oracle/11.2.0/oradata/v102/redo02.dbf' size 100m,
'/u01/app/oracle/11.2.0/oradata/v102/redo03.dbf' size 100m;
```

Incomplete Duplication: Using the DBNEWID Utility

One of the most frustrating elements of performing duplication is that there is no "restartable duplication." What we mean by this is that if you make it through the step that restores all your files—arguably the longest step of the process—but a failure occurs, say, during the recovery, you must restart the duplication process from scratch and restore all the files again. There is no way to correct the recovery process (by making missing archive logs available, for instance) and then pick up where you left off.

With RESTORE OPTIMIZATION turned ON, RMAN will not restore files again that already exist in the restore location with the same datafile header SCN information. This applies to duplication as well: if duplication restores a file, and then duplication restarts, RMAN will not restore the file again. However, if you have applied even one archive log to the file, it will be restored again.

Starting in version 9*i* Release 2, Oracle Database includes the DBNEWID utility, which gives your clone database a new DBID in a safe and controlled manner. This allows you to do manual recovery against a duplicated database, prepare all the elements, and then run DBNEWID, which will complete the process started by duplication. This allows you to at least manually complete a duplication.

DBNEWID usage is simple. First, you must make sure you have a good backup taken prior to using DBNEWID. Although it has a verification process, DBNEWID can still encounter unrecoverable errors during the changing of the DBID. After confirming a good backup, you need to get the database shut down in a consistent state and then brought back up to a mounted state:

```
shutdown immediate;
startup mount
```

Then, run the DBNEWID utility from the command line:

```
nid target =/
DBNEWID: Release 10.2.0.1.0 - Production on Sat Sep 3 14:06:43 2005
Copyright (c) 1982, 2005, Oracle.  All rights reserved.
Connected to database AUX1 (DBID=366194736)
Connected to server version 10.2.0
Control Files in database:
 /u01/app/oracle/product/oradata/aux1/control01.ctl
 /u01/app/oracle/product/oradata/aux1/control02.ctl
/u01/app/oracle/product/oradata/aux1/control03.ctl
Change database ID of database AUX1? (Y/[N]) => Y
Proceeding with operation
Changing database ID from 366194736 to 366203699
    Control File /u01/app/oracle/product/oradata/aux1/control01.ctl
- modified
    Control File /u01/app/oracle/product/oradata/aux1/control02.ctl
- modified
    Control File /u01/app/oracle/product/oradata/aux1/control03.ctl
- modified
    Datafile /u01/app/oracle/product/oradata/aux1/system01.dbf
- dbid changed
    Datafile /u01/app/oracle/product/oradata/aux1/undotbs01.dbf
- dbid changed
```

```
     Datafile /u01/app/oracle/product/oradata/aux1/sysaux01.dbf
- dbid changed
     Datafile /u01/app/oracle/product/oradata/aux1/users01.dbf
- dbid changed
     Datafile /u01/app/oracle/product/oradata/aux1/temp01.dbf
- dbid changed
     Control File /u01/app/oracle/product/oradata/aux1/control01.ctl
- dbid changed
     Control File /u01/app/oracle/product/oradata/aux1/control02.ctl
- dbid changed
     Control File /u01/app/oracle/product/oradata/aux1/control03.ctl
- dbid changed
     Instance shut down
Database ID for database AUX1 changed to 366203699.
All previous backups and archived redo logs for this database are unusable.
Database is not aware of previous backups and archived logs in Recovery
Area.
Database has been shutdown, open database with RESETLOGS option.
Successfully changed database ID.
DBNEWID - Completed successfully.

[oracle@dex oracle]$ sqlplus "/ as sysdba"

SQL> alter database open resetlogs;
```

Summary

In this chapter, we discussed the architecture behind the RMAN duplication process. Using duplication, we can produce clone databases from our RMAN backups to either the local system or a remote server. There are different configuration steps, depending on whether you will be duplicating locally or remotely. In addition, you have specific guidelines to follow depending on whether your backups are on disk or on tape. Two RMAN Workshops gave step-by-step instructions for duplication. We wrapped everything up with a brief discussion of the DBNEWID utility that comes with Oracle Database 10g and later.

CHAPTER
20

RMAN and Data Guard

any DBAs are already familiar with the functionality known as Oracle Standby Database. It is an architectural feature that adds a little functionality to operations that already take place on your system: the archiving of every single change that happens on a database. The Standby Database started as a simple concept, and although the overall architecture is now referred to as Data Guard, the foundation is still simple: take the archive logs from your production database, move them to another computer that has a copy of that database, and apply the archive logs to the copy. In such a way, Data Guard is able to provide an efficient disaster recovery solution by maintaining transactionally consistent copies of the production database at a remote site. These copies, or standbys, can be one of two types, physical or logical. Which one you choose to include in your Data Guard configuration depends on what business needs you are trying to satisfy.

A *physical* standby database is kept in sync with the primary database by using media recovery to apply redo that was generated on the primary database. Because media recovery is used, we can be assured that a physical standby is a block-for-block identical copy of the primary database. Because of its nature, a physical standby database is an excellent choice for disaster recovery. In the event of a failure, we can rest assured that our data will be intact and consistent with data that existed on the primary database.

A *logical* standby database is kept in sync with the primary database by transforming redo data received from the primary database into logical SQL statements, and then executing those SQL statements against the standby database. Because we are applying SQL statements instead of performing media recovery, it is possible for the logical standby database to contain the same logical information as the primary database, but at the same time to have a different physical structure. Because a logical standby database is open for user access while applying changes, it is an ideal solution for a reporting database while maintaining its disaster recovery attributes.

RMAN and Data Guard are complementary technologies that together make a complete Oracle solution for disaster recovery and high availability. RMAN backups can be used to create the underlying standby database, along with providing the initial recovery phase. Then, after you have created the standby database and configured the Data Guard broker, RMAN can connect to the standby database and take backups that can be restored to the primary database. In this way, the resources used to perform a backup can be completely removed from your production environment.

Obviously, this book is about RMAN and not Data Guard. If you have more questions about standby databases or Data Guard, check out the Oracle Press titles on Data Guard (the latest from Larry Carpenter and company is excellent). From here on in this chapter, we assume that you are familiar with the basics of Data Guard standby databases and are ready to create one using RMAN.

RMAN and the Standby Database

Primarily, the relationship between RMAN and the standby database is a simple one: RMAN is used to create the standby database. If you are implementing a backup strategy that has RMAN doing all of your backups, you wouldn't really have any choice but to use RMAN, because the standby database must have primary database datafiles copied into place to begin with.

As of Oracle Database 10g, RMAN backups can be used to create both physical and logical standby databases. This was not the case in Oracle9i Database, because the primary database had to be quiesced prior to taking a backup to be used for a logical standby. Now, however, a hot backup can be used as the basis for a logical standby database, and that means RMAN backups can be used.

However, if you were a reader of our *Oracle10g RMAN Backup & Recovery* book, you may find that we have changed little in the instructions that follow. This is because RMAN does not discriminate between creating a physical and a logical standby database. RMAN does not discriminate because the first step to creating a logical standby database is to create a physical standby database. After you create a physical standby database, a conversion takes place to turn it into a logical standby database. And RMAN is involved only in the physical creation, leaving the logical standby conversion to you.

Requirements for Using RMAN for Standby Database Creation

Before RMAN can create the standby database, you have to walk through a few initial steps. These steps are identical to those outlined in the duplication process in Chapter 17:

1. Make all necessary changes in both the primary and standby database init.ora files.

2. Complete all necessary Oracle Net configuration.

3. Start the standby database in NOMOUNT mode.

The reason for these steps is that RMAN uses the **duplicate** command to create the standby database, so all rules that apply to duplication also apply to standby database creation. This means that any file-renaming issues are the same, the password file requirement is the same, and the way that you have to configure the listener.ora and tnsnames.ora files is the same. If you're not sure what we're talking about, review Chapter 19 prior to proceeding: everything from here on is in addition to the duplication requirements and restrictions laid out in Chapter 19.

In addition to reviewing Chapter 19, you must also have a specific kind of control file backup. A regular control file backup is not used when we create a standby database, because a standby database control file is different from a regular control file. It places more stringent conditions on applying archive logs during media recovery. A standby control file also does not allow a standby database to be opened with an **alter database open** command. Instead, you must activate a standby database (and thus make it the primary database) by using **alter database activate standby database**.

To create a standby control file, you can use a SQL command:

```
alter database create standby controlfile as
'/u04/backup/stby_cfile01.ctl';
```

If you create a standby control file in this fashion, you have to catalog it with RMAN before RMAN can use it in a **duplicate...for standby** operation:

```
RMAN>catalog controlfilecopy '/u04/backup/stby_cfile01.ctl';
```

Even simpler, you can use RMAN to create a standby control file. That way, you can create a copy on your tape device (if you use tape backups) using the **backup** command:

```
RMAN>  backup current controlfile for standby;
```

Once you've got a standby control file ready, you can move forward with your standby database creation using RMAN.

Finally, before we discuss the commands for creating your standby database, a little vocabulary lesson will come in handy. As you know from Chapter 19, the RMAN duplication process refers to two databases: the target database and the auxiliary database. The *target database* is where the backups came from, and the *auxiliary database* is the clone database being created from the target database backups.

In the language of the standby database architecture, you have two databases, as well: the *primary database,* which is your current production database, and the *standby database,* which is the unopened copy of the primary database that receives the archived redo logs from the primary database. When you are using RMAN to create a standby database, remember this: the target database is the primary database, and the auxiliary database is the standby database.

The duplicate...for standby Command

The **duplicate** command is used a bit differently when you are using it for standby database creation. As we stated previously, all duplication rules apply, but we must add a few caveats and restrictions.

Memory Considerations

First of all, the DB_NAME parameter in the init.ora file of the standby database must match the DB_NAME of the primary database. This is only marginally interesting news if you are creating your standby database on a different server, but it has important implications if you are building the standby database on the same server as the primary database. Oracle uses the DB_NAME to lock memory segments at the OS level, so if you try to mount two instances with the same DB_NAME, you will get an error:

```
<ORA-01102: cannot mount database in exclusive mode>
```

To get around this, you can modify the init.ora file of the standby database, and add the parameter LOCK_NAME_SPACE. You set this to a value different from the DB_NAME, and then Oracle uses this to lock memory segments without changing the DB_NAME:

```
lock_name_space='stby'
```

Because the DB_NAME must be the same, the **duplicate for standby** command does not use the format **duplicate target database to <aux_name>**. This format was necessary to reset the database name in the new control file during duplication, but during standby database creation, we don't create a new control file. Therefore, the command looks like this:

```
duplicate target database for standby;
```

Log File Considerations

In addition to not using the missing **to** clause of the **duplicate** command, you cannot use the **logfile** clause when creating a standby. The reason for this has everything to do with standby database options, such as the standby redo log file that is available as part of a Data Guard solution. None of these options applies to the duplication process, but because of them, RMAN disallows the **logfile** clause. Instead, if you are doing a straight standby database configuration and need to specify a different location for the log files, you need to use the LOG_FILE_NAME_ CONVERT parameter in your standby init.ora file. This parameter acts exactly like DB_FILE_ NAME_CONVERT in that it is a simple string conversion and can be used to change a single directory name, or can be used in pairs to make multiple changes.

Datafile Considerations

If you will be creating your standby database to a different server from the one that holds the primary database, you do not have to change anything about the datafile location, so long as the standby database server has the same mount point and directory structure as the primary database server. As with regular duplication, if you will be using the same datafile locations on the standby database that exist on the primary database, you will need to use the **nofilenamecheck** keyword in the **duplicate** command:

```
duplicate target database for standby nofilenamecheck;
```

If you are creating the standby database on the same server as the one that holds the primary database, you are required to change the file locations for the standby datafiles. You can do this in any of the same ways that you would with regular duplication: using the **configure auxname** command, using **set newname** in a **run** block, or using DB_FILE_NAME_CONVERT in the standby init.ora file.

Media Recovery Considerations

A physical standby database is never opened for read/write activity. It is mounted and placed in a state of media recovery, or it is opened in READ-ONLY mode, and users are allowed to perform **select** statements only. Because of this peculiarity, the RMAN duplication performs a little differently than it would if you wanted to clone the database. It doesn't re-create the control file; it restores a standby control file. It does not, by default, perform any media recovery on the datafiles after restoring them, and then it skips the steps that reset the DBID and open the database reset logs. So, when the **duplicate...for standby** completes, your standby database is mounted but not open, and you will need to decide how to proceed with media recovery.

If you would like RMAN to perform the initial media recovery and apply archive logs that have been backed up by RMAN, you can use the keyword **dorecover** in your **duplicate** command:

```
duplicate target database for standby dorecover;
```

Typically, you will want to provide an **until** clause along with your **duplicate** command if you will be doing recovery, particularly if you are creating the standby database at a remote site. If you are at a remote site, using **set until time** or **set until sequence** will enable you to make sure that the recovery attempts to use only archive logs that are available at the other site. Of course, because we aren't setting the DBID or opening the clone, a failed media recovery session out of the **duplicate** command is no big deal: you can just pick up manually where it left off.

RMAN Workshop: *Create a Standby Database Using RMAN*

Workshop Notes

This exercise creates a standby database on the same server as the primary database. The ORACLE_SID for the standby database is stby, but the DB_NAME will be the same as for the primary database: v112. We will use both the DB_FILE_NAME_CONVERT and LOG_FILE_NAME_CONVERT parameters, and we will perform media recovery.

Step 1. Use RMAN to create a standby control file:

```
ORACLE_SID=v112;export ORACLE_SID
rman target /
RMAN> backup current controlfile for standby;
```

You need to specify a point in time after you created this standby control file, so perform a few log switches, and then record the last log sequence number from V$ARCHIVED_LOG:

```
SQL> alter system switch logfile;
SQL> alter system switch logfile;
SQL> select sequence# from v$archived_log;
```

Step 2. Build your standby database directory structures:

```
$ cd $ORACLE_BASE
$ cd oradata
$ pwd
/u01/app/oracle/oradata
$ mkdir stby
$ cd ../admin
$ pwd
/u01/app/oracle/admin
$ mkdir stby
$ cd stby
$ mkdir pfile adump bdump cdump udump
```

Step 3. Copy the target init.ora file to the auxiliary location. If your target database uses an SPFILE, you need to create a PFILE from the SPFILE in order to capture parameters to move over.
   If you use an SPFILE at your target, enter the following:

```
SQL> create pfile='/u01/app/oracle/admin/stby/pfile/init.ora'
  2   from spfile;
```

If you use an init.ora file at your target, enter the following:

```
cp /u01/app/oracle/admin/v112/pfile/init.ora
/u01/app/oracle/product/admin/stby/pfile/init.ora
```

Step 4. Make all necessary changes to your stby init.ora file:

```
*.audit_file_dest='/u01/app/oracle/admin/stby/adump'
*.background_dump_dest='/u01/app/oracle/admin/stby/bdump'
*.compatible='11.2.0.1.0'
*.control_files='/u01/app/oracle/oradata/stby/control01.ctl',
     '/u01/app/oracle/oradata/stby/control02.ctl',
     '/u01/app/oracle/oradata/stby/control03.ctl'
*.core_dump_dest='/u01/app/oracle/admin/stby/cdump'
*.db_block_size=8192
*.db_domain=''
*.db_file_multiblock_read_count=16
*.db_name='v112'
*.db_recovery_file_dest='/u01/app/oracle/flash_recovery_area'
*.db_recovery_file_dest_size=4294967296
*.job_queue_processes=10
*.open_cursors=300
*.pga_aggregate_target=93323264
*.processes=150
*.remote_login_passwordfile='EXCLUSIVE'
```

```
*.sga_target=279969792
*.undo_management='AUTO'
*.undo_tablespace='UNDOTBS1'
*.user_dump_dest='/u01/app/oracle/admin/stby/udump'
lock_name_space='stby'
db_file_name_convert=('v112','stby')
log_file_name_convert=('v112','stby')
lock_name_space='stby'
```

Step 5. Build your stby password file. See the "Building a Password File" RMAN Workshop in Chapter 19.

Step 6. Start up the stby instance in NOMOUNT mode:

```
ORACLE_SID=stby; export ORACLE_SID
sqlplus "/ as sysdba"
sql>startup nomount
pfile=/u01/app/oracle/admin/stby/pfile/init.ora
```

Step 7. Configure your network files for connection to stby. After making any changes to your listener.ora file, be sure that you bounce your listener, or the change will not take effect:

```
Lsnrctl reload
```

The tnsnames.ora file should have an entry like this:

```
STBY =
  (DESCRIPTION =
    (ADDRESS_LIST =
      (ADDRESS = (PROTOCOL = TCP)(HOST = horatio)(PORT = 1521))
    )
    (CONNECT_DATA =
      (SERVICE_NAME = stby)
    )
  )
```

The listener.ora file should have an entry like this:

```
  (SID_DESC =
    (GLOBAL_DBNAME = stby)
    (ORACLE_HOME = /u01/app/oracle/product/11.2.0/dbhome_1)
    (SID_NAME = stby)
  )
```

Step 8. From RMAN, connect to the target and auxiliary instances and run the **duplicate** command:

```
ORACLE_SID=v112; export ORACLE_SID
rman target /
RMAN> connect auxiliary sys/password@stby
RMAN>run {
  set until sequence = 789 thread = 1;
  duplicate target database for standby
  dorecover;}
```

Taking Backups from the Standby Database

After creating your standby database, you can use it for a number of purposes. Its primary reason for existence, of course, is to provide a disaster recovery solution for your production database. However, you can also suspend media recovery against the standby database, open it as read-only, and perform any number of data-mining operations that would suck too many resources away from your production system.

From the RMAN perspective, there is another excellent way to put the standby database to work. As you know from Chapter 16, there is a price to pay for running RMAN against your production database in terms of resources used. You utilize precious memory, CPU, and disk I/O resources when the backup is running. So, we recommend running your backups during the off-peak hours of your database. Sometimes, though, there are no off-peak hours. You could be a 24-hour operation, with constant database updates, or your database could be so large that backups are pretty much running around the clock.

If you have a physical standby database, you can take your production backups from the standby database; these backups can then be restored to the primary database if the primary database has a failure. Because the standby database has the same DBID as the primary database and is always from the same incarnation, the RMAN datafile backups are interchangeable between the standby database and the primary database. The standby database is a true clone of the primary database.

The thing to understand about using a standby database to take production backups is that RMAN will connect to the standby database as the target database. Remember, up to this point, we've encouraged you to think of the standby database as the auxiliary database. But that only holds true for duplication operations. Once the standby database is established, you can connect to it as the target database and perform **backup** commands. These backups can then be used for restore operations at the primary database.

To use the standby database in this fashion, you must have a recovery catalog set up. Without a recovery catalog, there is no way to propagate the records of the backups from the standby control file to the primary control file. With a recovery catalog, you resync with the standby control file after a backup, so the records of the backup are put in the catalog. Then, you connect to the primary database as the target and make your catalog connection. To RMAN, the primary and standby databases are indistinguishable, so it accesses the same record set in the catalog when connected to either. Therefore, you can perform a resync operation while connected to the primary database, and it will refresh the primary control file with the records of backups taken while connected to the standby database.

Using the UR=A Parameter

If you are using instance registration, there will not be any entries in the listener.ora file by default for the database. You can manually configure the database entry in the listener. Or, you can update the tnsnames.ora file with the parameter UR=A. This is to allow administrative connections only; for example:

```
CONNECT_DATA=((SID=....)  (UR=A))
```

There is also the possibility of changing from using a pfile to an spfile in 11*g* that allows you to get past the blocked connection errors due to instance registration. This is effective for duplication from backups or from an active database.

Impact of the DB_UNIQUE_NAME Initialization Parameter

In 11*g*, the parameter DB_UNIQUE_NAME must be set for a database if that database will exist in a database ecosystem with other databases with the same DB_NAME parameter—for example, when a reporting database is in the same environment as the production database, or when a standby database exists for a primary database. The value of DB_UNIQUE_NAME must be unique for every database in the enterprise.

RMAN, as we stated, requires access to the recovery catalog in order to perform backups from the standby database. To assist in this, RMAN is aware of the setting of DB_UNIQUE_NAME in the recovery catalog, and when it is set, RMAN can track the exact location where a backup is taken, without limiting where it can be restored to (based on the DBID being the same).

For example, in some situations, you will use two standby databases as part of your overall solution: standby1 database has a lag of 5 minutes, and standby2 has a lag of 30 minutes to ensure no errors are propagated to standby2 in case standby1 is corrupted. In this environment, you would set each database's DB_UNIQUE_NAME to standby1 and standby2, respectively. Then, RMAN can connect to any of the databases to back up from, and RMAN will know exactly which database the backup came from. Keep in mind if you are backing up from the standby1 and it goes down for any amount of time, recovery is still running on standby2, and backups can continue without impacting production.

Datafile Backups from the Standby Database

Backing up the datafiles from the standby database is the most common activity. To back up the datafiles and then use them at the primary database, you would do something like this:

1. From RMAN, connect to the standby database as the target, and connect to the recovery catalog:

   ```
   RMAN> connect target sys/pswd@stby
   RMAN> connect catalog rman/rman@rcat
   ```

2. Take your database backup. The catalog is automatically resynchronized after any **backup** command.

   ```
   RMAN>backup database;
   ```

3. Exit RMAN and then start it again (this is the only way to disconnect from the target and catalog):

   ```
   RMAN> exit
   $ rman
   ```

4. Connect to your primary database as the target, and connect to the catalog:

   ```
   RMAN> connect target sys/pswd@sun92
   RMAN>resync catalog;
   ```

5. Perform a **restore** operation that utilizes backups taken from the standby database:

   ```
   RMAN> restore datafile 3;
   RMAN> recover datafile 3;
   ```

Archive Log Backups from the Standby Database

Backing up the archive logs from the standby database is a somewhat trickier affair because of how RMAN determines which archive logs need to be backed up: it checks the view V$ARCHIVED_LOG. On the primary database, this view is incremented with each new archive log after it has been successfully created in the LOG_ARCHIVE_DEST. However, on the standby database, this view is updated only if your standby database is in MANAGED RECOVERY mode (where the archive logs are automatically applied at the standby database). If your standby database is not in MANAGED RECOVERY mode, or if, due to your setup, you will get archive log gaps at the standby database on a regular basis, it may be hard to get all the required archive logs backed up successfully from the standby database. In this case, we recommend using your primary database for its own archive log backups and using the standby database just for datafile backups.

Using Flashback Database for Standby Database Reinstantiation

We weren't sure where to mention this neat little trick that crosses the boundaries of multiple distinct Oracle technologies. We decided that if you were reading this chapter, you were interested in Data Guard implementations, but if you read Chapter 13 on Flashback Technology, you may not be. So, here it is.

One of the toughest moments of a Data Guard implementation is failing over your production database to the standby database. Despite all the preparation and testing, failing over still leaves a knot in the belly. When (if!) it happens to you, we hope it all goes well.

The second toughest moment is coming to terms with how to put the Data Guard deployment back into operation. In other words, now that your standby database has become your primary database, what do you do next? This is truly a question for another book, but it's worth mentioning in this context because Oracle used some of its own tricks to help you out with the tough next step: rebuilding a new standby database after failover.

Here's how it went down in the old days: Suppose your production database is PROD, and your standby is PROD2. You lose PROD for some reason. You fail over to PROD2, which becomes your new primary database. Then, you take a full new backup of PROD2, move it over to the computer housing PROD, and lay it down over the top of PROD. Next, you start shipping logs from PROD2 to PROD. At some point, perhaps, you purposefully fail back over to PROD, and then this labor- and resource-intensive process repeats.

Fast forward to modern times, and a new way of rebuilding the standby database emerges: you can use Flashback Database for standby database reinstantiation. When a failover occurs from the primary database to the standby database, in the past you were forced to use backups to restore a copy of the new primary database back to the old primary database and make it a standby database, and then to fail back over. Now, you can instead use Flashback Database on the old primary database to move it back to the exact SCN where the standby database was prior to activation. Then, you set up the flow of archive logs from the new primary database to the old primary database, give it a new standby control file, and you are back in business in minutes.

Summary

In this chapter, we discussed the relationship that RMAN can have with the standby database architecture. Primarily, RMAN can be used to create the standby database using the **duplicate… for standby** command. We discussed the means by which you use the **duplicate** command to create the standby database and included an RMAN Workshop that walked through the steps of creating the standby database on the same server as the primary database. Then, we discussed how you could use an existing standby database to create backups using RMAN that could be restored to the primary database, as a means of offloading the work away from the production environment.

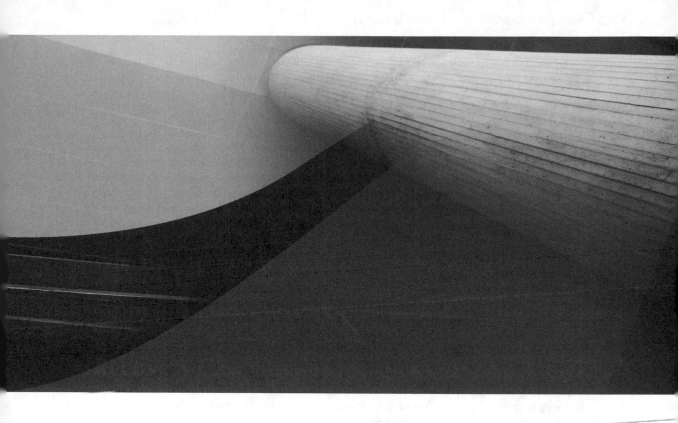

CHAPTER
21

RMAN and Real
Application Clusters

hile it is well beyond the scope of this book to guide you through the intricacies of Oracle Real Application Clusters (RAC), we can provide some guidance on preparing your RAC configuration for backup and recovery. As with Data Guard in Chapter 20, we assume that you have a working knowledge of RAC in Oracle Database 11*g*, and thus, our brief discussion of RAC architecture is intended more as a reminder than as an education.

Throughout this chapter, we will use an example cluster database that has only two nodes: winrac1 and winrac2. These nodes share a disk array, which is configured with Oracle ASM as its volume manager. Each node has an instance: prod1 on winrac1, and prod2 on winrac2. While we will limit our explanations to the simplest of RAC environments—a two-node cluster—nothing changes when you scale out to three, four, or more nodes. In our examples, you simply change the number of nodes from 2 to 3, and the number of channels from 2 to 3, and so on. The more nodes you have, the more complex your backup/recovery strategies and scripts, but the basic rules apply no matter the number of instances.

There are two basic ways to share a file system across multiple computers. The first, which was also available with Oracle9*i* Database, is to use a clustered file system. This is frequently provided by a third-party vendor, such as VERITAS. On Windows and Linux, Oracle provides its own Cluster File System (OCFS). A cluster file system is defined by its ability to properly handle and queue requests for files coming from multiple nodes simultaneously—which is a requirement if you are going to cluster your databases.

The second way to share a file system across multiple computers, introduced in Oracle Database 10*g*, is to use Automatic Storage Management (ASM). ASM is Oracle's first volume management product and can be used to manage raw disks that have no other formatting on them. Because of its architecture, ASM is built for cluster configurations and can easily handle the demands of RAC. You could say that ASM was built for RAC, because if you decide to deploy RAC on Oracle Standard Edition, ASM is the *only* file system allowed for the shared Oracle database files.

And that is all you're going to get from us on the subject, except to say this: you can still use manually built raw partitions on a shared disk array to arrange your RAC datafiles and log files. So, if you desire, you do not need a cluster file system or ASM. You just need raw, uncooked, shared disks. However, we do not recommend this, nor will we spend more than a fleeting moment explaining how to configure RMAN to back up a RAC database running on raw disks. This is because, given the opportunity to simplify your life with OCFS or ASM, manually maintaining raw disks is folly. There, we said it. In particular, when it comes to backup and recovery on RAC, OCFS and ASM will save your life. Using raw disks will only lead to blood, sweat, tears, and updated résumés.

Real Application Clusters: Unique Backup Challenges

Before we dig any deeper, it's helpful to consider the architectural nature of a RAC. Essentially, you have at least two different servers, each with its own memory and local disks, and each connected to a shared disk array. Oracle uses this hardware by creating two instances, one on each node, with their own SGA/PGA memory areas. Each instance has its own redo logs, but they exist on the shared disk and are accessible by the other nodes. All control files and datafiles are shared between the two instances, meaning there is only one database, with two threads accessing and updating the data simultaneously. Figure 21-1 provides an oversimplified look at RAC.

FIGURE 21-1 *RAC at its most basic*

From the RMAN perspective, this architecture creates interesting challenges for taking backups. First of all, multiple instances are running, but RMAN can connect to only a single node. This shouldn't pose any problems for backing up the datafiles, but we do have a problem when it comes to archive logs. Each instance is archiving its own redo logs to a local drive rather than to the shared disks, so the issue is how we get to those other archive logs. But let's start by considering the datafile backups.

Datafile Backups

Datafile backups in a RAC environment are pretty much the same as datafile backups in a single-node database: RMAN connects to a node and issues a **backup database** command. The memory that RMAN needs to perform the backup operation will be grabbed from that one node. If backing up to disk, the backups will be local to that node; if backing up to tape, that instance will have to be configured for integration with your MML.

The RMAN Snapshot Control File and RAC

You need to move the snapshot control file to a shared location if you plan to run backups from more than one node. If you do not move the snapshot control file to a shared file system such as OCFS or an ASM disk group, then you must make sure that the local destination is identical on all nodes. To see the snapshot control file location, use the **show** command:

```
rman> show snapshot controlfile name;
```

To change the value, use the **configure** command:

```
rman> configure snapshot controlfile name to
    '/u02/oradata/grid10/snap_grid10.scf';
```

The only problem with this scenario is that it puts quite a bit of load on a single node. This may be what you are after; if not, there is a better way. RMAN can connect to only a single node initially, but it can allocate channels at all of your nodes during an actual backup operation. The following shows an example of how this would be done:

```
configure default device type sbt;
configure device type sbt parallelism 2;
configure channel 1 device type sbt
connect 'sys/password@prod1';
configure channel 2 device type sbt
connect 'sys/password@prod2';
backup database;
```

Then, you can run your backup, and RMAN will spread the work between your two nodes. RAC datafiles sometimes have something known as *node affinity,* where a particular datafile is accessed faster from one node or the other. If this is the case for your cluster, RMAN knows about it and will back up the datafile from the node where it can be read the fastest. If there is no node affinity on your system, RMAN just distributes the work across the two channels as it would any two channels used to parallelize a backup. Obviously, you could allocate two channels at each node, or three, four, or more. How many channels each node utilizes should be based on the same performance parameters we explored in Chapter 16.

Automatic Distribution of Backup Work Across Nodes

Since Oracle Database 10*g* Release 2, RMAN can utilize information gleaned from Oracle's Cluster Ready Services (CRS) to provide better RAC integration. Of most importance, you no longer have to configure a channel to specifically connect at a particular node. If you have two nodes and you set parallelism to 2, RMAN will query CRS for the node information and automatically spread the two channels across the two nodes. In addition, CRS keeps track of node utilization and will spread RMAN backup jobs out to those nodes that are currently being least utilized, to avoid I/O traffic jams. This is a significant automation improvement, and the lesson to take away is simple: don't try to out-think CRS. Let it do the footwork of determining how to distribute work across your cluster. Just set your level of parallelism equal to the total number of nodes you want involved in your backup, and let CRS do the work.

Archive Log Backups

Archive log backups are far trickier than datafile backups, because each node is responsible for its own archiving, which means that each node has unshared files that only it can access. If we connect to only one node and issue a **backup archivelog all** command, RMAN will look in the control file and discover the listing for the archive logs from both nodes, but when it looks at the local node, it will find only the archive logs from that node and it will error out.

Of course, the question may be posed, "Why not write archive logs to a raw partition on the shared disk array?" The answer is that you could, if you don't mind the administrative nightmare. Think about it: with raw partitions, you can write only one file per partition, which means you would have to anticipate all of your archive log filenames and create symbolic links to a partition that exists for each archive log. Such a task is simply too labor intensive for even the most scheming Unix-scripting mind among us. It is better to use a shared disk volume that has a clustered file system or that is managed by Oracle ASM.

RMAN, RAC, and Net Connections

RAC comes with many extremely powerful load-balancing and failover features as part of the Net configuration, but this means changes in the listener.ora file and in the tnsnames.ora files for both the cluster nodes and the clients. RMAN is a little too picky for these features. RMAN can only connect to one node and cannot fail over or be load balanced. Therefore, the Net aliases you use for the target connection and for the **connect** clause of the channel allocation string must be configured to connect to a single node with a dedicated server. This means that you cannot use the same NET aliases configured for failover that you use for other connection purposes.

If you insist on leaving archive logs local to each node, a solution is available that allows RMAN to cope with the non-shared disk locations. First, make sure that each node is archiving to a unique file location. For example, prod1 archives to a directory called /u04/prod1/arch, and prod2 archives to /u04/prod2/arch. Then, you can allocate channels at each node, as you did to load balance the datafile backups earlier, and back up the archive logs:

```
configure default device type sbt;
configure device type sbt parallelism 2;
configure channel 1 device type sbt
connect 'sys/password@prod1';
configure channel 2 device type sbt
connect 'sys/password@prod2';
backup archivelog all delete input;
```

RMAN has a feature known as *autolocate* that identifies which archive logs belong to which node and that attempts to back them up only from that node. In this way, you don't have to specify in RMAN which logs you need backed up at which node—RMAN can figure it out for you.

Another option that would allow you to perform your archive log backup from a single node would be to NFS mount the archive log destination of the other node. For example, at the node winrac1, you have local archive logs located at /u04/prod1/arch. Then, on winrac1, you NFS mount the drive /u04/prod2/arch on winrac2 as /u04/prod2/arch. That way, when you run your archive log backups, RMAN checks the control file for the archive log locations, and it can find both locations while connected to only prod1. Figure 21-2 illustrates this methodology.

The only problem in the scenarios we've provided so far is that you are giving yourself a single point of failure for archive logs. If you archive your logs only to their respective nodes and you lose a node, you lose the archive logs from that node. That means you may have to perform point-in-time recovery of the entire database to the point right before the node was lost.

A better strategy is to set up each node with a LOG_ARCHIVE_DEST_2 parameter that writes to another node. One way to approach this task is to consider the NFS mount strategies already discussed in this chapter. Instead of just NFS mounting in READ ONLY mode the archive destination of the other node, consider NFS mounting a drive on the other node with write access, and then setting that NFS mount as a second archive destination. Take our two-node RAC database, for example. On winrac1, we could mount the shared directory /u04/prod2/arch from

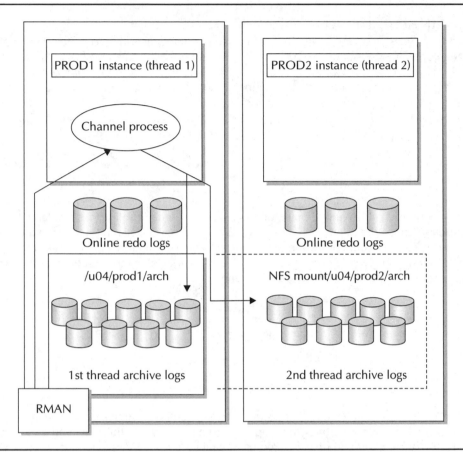

FIGURE 21-2 *Mounting the archive log destination*

winrac2, and on winrac2, we could mount winrac1's /u04/prod1/arch directory. Then, we could set up the init.ora files for each node, as shown next:

```
winrac1 init.ora file:
log_archive_dest_1='location=/u04/prod1/arch'
log_archive_dest_2='location=/u04/prod2/arch'
...
winrac2 init.ora file:
log_archive_dest_1='location=/u04/prod2/arch'
log_archive_dest_2='location=/u04/prod1/arch'
```

When set up like this, Oracle writes archive logs from each node to the archive destination of the other node. This gives us an elegant solution for backing up the archive logs from a single node and provides us with fault tolerance in case a node is lost.

Avoid Archive Log Backup Complexity with ASM and the Flash Recovery Area

All of these complications can be avoided by creating a location on the shared disk array that has a volume cooked with a cluster file system, such as OCFS. Even better, you can employ ASM as your volume manager for all your RAC files. Then, you can create a second disk group and deploy your flash recovery area (FRA) to the disk group. With an FRA on an ASM disk group, managing archive logs in RAC is essentially the same as managing them in a single-thread environment. If you configure the database to archive to the FRA, both nodes will deposit the logs in a single location where they are visible to both nodes at all times. Managing archive logs during cleanup operations is no different than managing them on a single-thread database.

RAC Recovery Challenges

Perhaps more confusing than getting backups done is getting restore and recovery tasks taken care of in a RAC environment. Again, this is due to the complex nature of a database that has multiple instances. The challenges can be roughly divided into three areas: restore operations, media management considerations, and recovery challenges.

Restore Operations

When performing a restore from RMAN, we must point out again that RMAN can connect to only one node, but then can allocate channels at each node. This should sound pretty familiar by now; but that's not the tricky part. The part that hangs people up is keeping track of where files were backed up from.

File accessibility is the key to restore success on an RAC node. If you have been backing up to disk using channels allocated at each node, you must allocate the same channels at each node during a restore operation. This is not a problem, unless you've lost a node. If the node is down, your disk backups on that node are inaccessible and restore operations will fail. The lesson is, if you're spending all this time and money on RAC so that you don't have a single point of failure, make sure you apply this philosophy to your backup and recovery strategy, as well. If you back up to disk, duplex the backup to more than one node. This might mean overriding the default autolocate feature so that you can specify where exactly you want your backups to be backed up from. You do this by specifying the channel for datafile sets:

```
configure default device type disk;
configure device type sbt parallelism 2;
configure channel 1 device type disk
connect 'sys/password@prod1';
configure channel 2 device type disk
connect 'sys/password@prod2';
backup (datafile 1,2,3,4,5 channel ORA_DISK_1)
       (datafile 6,7,8,9,10 channel ORA_DISK_2);
# then switch the channels for the datafiles
backup (datafile 1,2,3,4,5 channel ORA_DISK_2)
       (datafile 6,7,8,9,10 channel ORA_DISK_1);
```

Here, again, ASM will save you time and energy. More to the point, running an FRA on a shared ASM disk volume makes disk backups in a RAC environment simple and requires little configuration beyond what you normally do for a single-thread database. Using an FRA on ASM allows you to take advantage of job multiplexing across your nodes, yet still to have all the backups end up in a location that is always accessible by other nodes during restore. So you no longer need to fear that a disk backup might be left inaccessible on a downed node. Nor do you need to fear a single point of failure, because ASM comes with automatic redundancy, so you can mirror your FRA and have a duplexed copy of your backup without any additional work.

Media Management Considerations During a Restore

Another way to make your backups available to all nodes during a restore is to back up to tape and to use a centralized media management server to house your tape backups. If you have tape devices at each node and use them all for tape backup, you're increasing the degree of complexity unnecessarily. If you lose a node in your cluster, you then lose the media management catalog for all backups taken from that node. Chances are that your media management product has an automatic catalog backup, but then you have another restore to do, and where do you do it, and when? You need the catalogs at both of your other nodes for their backup information. So, you have a disaster that is fixable, but valuable minutes are racing by as you stick your nose in manuals, trying to figure it all out.

We prefer to use a centralized media management system, so that all nodes can back up to tape devices that are all managed by the same media manager server, so that there is a single media management catalog. That way, when a node is lost, you can simply specify the client name in your RMAN channel and do the restores to a different node. This brings us to the most important note to remember when you use RMAN to restore your backup from tape: you must consider the node from which RMAN made the backup when doing the restore.

As an example, suppose that in our two-node cluster, we have lost node winrac2, and the disaster that took it out also corrupted some of our datafiles. We've been employing a backup strategy that allocates channels at both nodes to perform the backup, so our restore is going to have to allocate channels from both nodes. Oops! No chance of that! Instead, we can allocate two kinds of channels at winrac1: normal tape channels and channels that specify the client as winrac2. It would look something like this:

```
configure default device type sbt;
configure device type sbt parallelism 2;
configure channel 1 device type sbt
parms="env=(nb_ora_serv=rmsrv)";
configure channel 2 device type disk
parms="env=(nb_ora_serv=rmsrv, nb_ora_client=winrac2)";
restore datafile 5,12,13,18;
```

This is obviously a very simple example of what can be a complex headache. We recommend a backup approach that takes datafile backups from only a single node in the cluster. If the size of your database prohibits such a simplistic approach, try to at least restrict RMAN to a small subset of your nodes. By doing so, you keep the complexity down when it comes time to perform restore operations.

Another option is to first stage your backups to a disk location using an FRA on an ASM disk volume. If you have the space on the disk array to stage your backups to disk first, your ultimate move to tape can happen from one or more nodes at a more controlled time. Using the **backup recovery area** command would allow you to take a consolidated set of backups from the FRA and move them all to tape in a separate operation. This tape operation could occur from any node or any combination of nodes. If you did the tape backup from a single node, then the SBT channel parameters would be simplified during the restore, even if a different node were responsible for the restore.

Recovery Considerations After a Restore

After you get your files restored, it's time to perform media recovery by applying archive logs. Media recovery in a RAC environment has one rule that you must never forget: *only one node can perform recovery.* Burn it into your brain. This means that one node must have access to all the archive logs on disk. So, if you have been using an archive log strategy that has each node holding its own archive logs in a local disk, you must make that local disk available to the recovery node. You can do this via NFS, if you followed the guidelines specified in "Archive Log Backups" earlier in this chapter. You simply mount the archive log destination of the other node and issue your recover statement from within RMAN. If you're using CFS, this is not a problem, and you can ignore all this. If you are using an FRA on ASM, again, access to all archive logs is not an issue.

If you have archive logs that you need to restore from RMAN backups, the same rules and guidelines apply to archive logs that apply to datafile restores. If you allocated channels at each node for the backup, then you need to do so for the restore as well. If you are missing a node, you have to allocate a channel that includes the client name so that the media manager can find the proper backups (see the preceding section, "Media Management Considerations During a Restore"). In addition, you may have to restore the archive logs to a directory that exists locally if the LOG_ARCHIVE_DEST parameter that existed on the missing node does not exist on the node doing the restore operation:

```
restore archivelog like '%prod2%' to '/u04/prod1/arch%';
```

While only one node can perform recovery with RMAN, RMAN does media recovery in parallel. You cannot control this level of parallelism, other than to turn it off:

```
rman> Recover database noparallel;
```

By default, though, RMAN automatically selects the degree of recovery parallelism based on the number of available CPUs on the node performing recovery.

Advanced RMAN/RAC Topics

Once you have determined what your backup and recovery strategies will be for your RAC database, you can consider many of the same benefits that RMAN offers you in a single-node database environment: block corruption checking, null compression, block media recovery—all of these benefits are yours in a RAC environment. Advanced functionality such as database duplication exists as well. RMAN backups of RAC databases work for duplication and standby database creation, just as they would for a single-node system. We have some caveats, however, which we discuss next.

Duplication to a Single-Node System

If you administer a RAC cluster and aren't convinced yet that RMAN is the right tool for you, here's a little something to seal the deal: you can use your RMAN backups of your RAC database to create a clone of your RAC database on a single-node database. This gives you a copy of your production database without having to purchase and administer a second RAC cluster. Instead, you have a single-node database running on a cooked file system.

In fact, RMAN cannot actually duplicate from one RAC cluster to another RAC cluster. It can duplicate only to a single-thread database. However, once the database is duplicated, you can easily turn the clone database into a RAC database. Just make sure that you duplicate to an ASM disk group on a node that already has CRS installed.

RMAN Workshop: *Duplicating a RAC Database to a Single-Node Database*

Workshop Notes

This workshop creates a single-node clone of a two-node database. You can do this either to a new server or to a cooked file system on one of the nodes of the RAC cluster. This example duplicates to a file system on one of the nodes in the RAC cluster. Because duplication must perform recovery, you must remember that a recovery session has access only to the node on which the recovery is being performed, so that node must have access to all the nodes' archive logs. This workshop assumes that you have NFS mounted the archive destination of each node on each other node so that a full copy of each archive log stream is available at every node.

The two nodes of our cluster are opcbs01 and opcbs02, with instances of V112A and V112B, respectively. We will be connecting to V112B for all RMAN operations.

Step 1. Build your auxiliary database directory structures:

```
mkdir /u02/32bit/app/oracle/oradata/aux1
mkdir /u02/32bit/app/oracle/oradata/aux1/arch
cd /u02/32bit/app/oracle/admin
mkdir aux1
cd aux1
mkdir pfile bdump udump cdump
ls
```

Step 2. Copy the target init.ora file to the auxiliary location. If your target database uses an SPFILE, you need to create a PFILE from the SPFILE to capture parameters to move over.

If you use an SPFILE at your target, enter the following:

```
SQL> connect / as sysdba
create pfile='/u02/32bit/app/oracle/admin/aux1/pfile/init.ora'
from spfile;
```

If you use an init.ora file at your target, enter the following:

```
cp /u02/32bit/app/oracle/admin/V112B/pfile/init.ora
   /u02/32bit/app/oracle/admin/aux1/pfile/init.ora
```

Step 3. Make all necessary changes to your aux1 init.ora file:

```
control_files=
   '/u02/32bit/app/oracle/oradata/aux1/control01.dbf'
core_dump_dest='/u02/32bit/app/oracle/admin/aux1/cdump'
background_dump_dest='/u02/32bit/app/oracle/admin/aux1/bdump'
user_dump_dest=/u02/32bit/app/oracle/admin/aux1/udump
log_archive_dest_1=
   'location=/u02/32bit/app/oracle/oradata/aux1/arch'
db_name='aux1'
instance_name='aux1'
remote_login_passwordfile=exclusive
```

```
db_file_name_convert=
 ('/dev/vx/rdsk/usupport_dg', '/u02/32bit/app/oracle/oradata/aux1')
```

You can remove the following parameters entirely, including those that refer to the other instance:

```
cluster_database_instances=2
cluster_database=true
V112A.instance_name='V112A'
V112B.instance_name='V112B'
V112B.instance_number=2
V112A.instance_number=1
V112B.thread=2
V112A.thread=1
V112B.undo_tablespace='UNDOTBS2'
V112A.undo_tablespace='UNDOTBS1'
```

You can replace them by just having the following:

```
undo_tablespace='UNDOTBS2'
```

Step 4. Build your aux1 password file. Refer to the "Building a Password File" RMAN Workshop in Chapter 19.

Step 5. Start the aux1 instance in NOMOUNT mode:

```
ORACLE_SID=aux1
export ORACLE_SID
SQLplus /nolog
SQL>connect / as sysdba
SQL>startup nomount
pfile=/u02/32bit/app/oracle/admin/aux1/pfile/init.ora
```

Step 6. Configure your network files for connection to aux1. After you make any changes to your listener.ora file, be sure that you bounce your listener, or the change will not take effect:

```
lsnrctl
LSNRCTL>stop
LSNRCTL>start
```

The tnsnames.ora file should have an entry like this:

```
AUX1 =
  (DESCRIPTION =
    (ADDRESS_LIST =
      (ADDRESS = (PROTOCOL = TCP)(HOST = opcbsol2)(PORT = 1526))
    )
    (CONNECT_DATA =
      (SID = aux1)
      (SERVER = DEDICATED)
    )
  )
```

The listener.ora file should have an entry like this:

```
(SID_DESC =
   (GLOBAL_DBNAME = aux1)
   (ORACLE_HOME = /u02/32bit/app/oracle/product/11.2.0/dbhome_1)
   (SID_NAME = aux1)
)
```

Step 7. From RMAN, connect to the target and auxiliary instance and run the **duplicate** command:

```
ORACLE_SID=V112B
export ORACLE_SID
rman
rman>connect target /
rman> connect auxiliary sys/password@aux1
rman>duplicate target database to aux1
  pfile=/u02/32bit/app/oracle/admin/aux1/pfile/init.ora
  logfile
  '/u02/32bit/app/oracle/oradata/aux1/redo1.dbf' size 100m,
  '/u02/32bit/app/oracle/oradata/aux1/redo2.dbf' size 100m,
  '/u02/32bit/app/oracle/oradata/aux1/redo3.dbf' size 100m;
```

The Single-Node Standby Database

Of course, if we can duplicate to a single node, then we can also use the **duplicate** command to create a standby database for our RAC cluster on a single node. Perhaps more so than even straight duplication, this feature gives us an excellent cost-to-performance strategy for providing a disaster recovery solution for our RAC database. Instead of purchasing all the hardware and software necessary to have a complete second RAC system set up but unused for a standby database, you can create the standby database on a single-node system. Obviously, it won't have the computing power or load-balancing features of the RAC database, but it gives a reasonable disaster recovery solution so that you can hobble along until the RAC database is restored.

As with the duplication process, the secret lies in using the DB_FILE_NAME_CONVERT parameter to switch the files from OCFS or ASM disk groups to normal, nonclustered file systems. In addition, the single-node standby database can receive archive logs from each of the nodes in the RAC cluster and apply them in the correct chronological order.

RMAN Workshop: *Creating a Single-Node Standby Database from a RAC Database*

Step 1. Use RMAN to create a standby control file:

```
ORACLE_SID=V112B
export ORACLE_SID
rman
```

```
rman> connect target /
rman> backup current controlfile for standby
   format= '/u02/backup/stby_cfile.%U';
```

You need to specify a point in time after you created this standby control file, so perform a few log switches, and then record the last log sequence number from V$ARCHIVED_LOG. It doesn't matter which thread you choose, because the following command will force a log switch at all nodes:

```
SQL> alter system archivelog current;
SQL> select sequence# from v$archived_log;
```

Step 2. Build your standby database directory structures:

```
mkdir /u02/32bit/app/oracle/oradata/stby
mkdir /u02/32bit/app/oracle/oradata/stby/arch
cd /u02/32bit/app/oracle/admin
mkdir stby
cd stby
mkdir pfile bdump udump cdump
ls
```

Step 3. Copy the target init.ora file to the auxiliary location. If your target database uses an SPFILE, you need to create a PFILE from the SPFILE to capture parameters to move over.
    If you use an SPFILE at your target, enter the following:

```
SQL> connect / as sysdba
create pfile='/u02/32bit/app/oracle/admin/stby/pfile/init.ora'
from spfile;
```

If you use an init.ora file at your target, enter the following:

```
cp /u02/32bit/app/oracle/admin/V112/pfile/init.ora
   /u02/32bit/app/oracle/admin/stby/pfile/init.ora
```

Step 4. Make all necessary changes to your stby init.ora file:

```
control_files= '/u02/32bit/app/oracle/oradata/stby/control01.dbf'
background_dump_dest=/u02/32bit/app/oracle/admin/stby/bdump
user_dump_dest=/u02/32bit/app/oracle/admin/stby/udump
log_archive_dest_1=
   'location=/u02/32bit/app/oracle/oradata/stby/arch'
standby_archive_dest=
   'location=/u02/32bit/app/oracle/oradata/stbyarch'
lock_name_space='stby'
remote_login_passwordfile=exclusive
db_file_name_convert=
 ('/dev/vx/rdsk/usupport_dg', '/u02/32bit/app/oracle/oradata/aux1')
log_file_name_convert=
 ('/dev/vx/rdsk/usupport_dg', '/u02/32bit/app/oracle/oradata/aux1')
```

You can remove the following parameters entirely, including those that refer to the other instance:

```
cluster_database_instances=2
cluster_database=true
V112A.instance_name='V112A'
V112B.instance_name='V112B'
V112B.instance_number=2
V112A.instance_number=1
V112B.thread=2
V112A.thread=1
V112B.undo_tablespace='UNDOTBS2'
V102A.undo_tablespace='UNDOTBS1'
```

You can replace them by just having the following:

```
instance_name='V112B'
undo_tablespace='UNDOTBS2'
```

Step 5. Build your stby password file. Refer to the "Building a Password File" RMAN Workshop in Chapter 19.

Step 6. Start the stby instance in NOMOUNT mode:

```
ORACLE_SID=stby
export ORACLE_SID
SQLplus /nolog
SQL>connect / as sysdba
SQL>startup nomount
pfile=/u02/32bit/app/oracle/admin/stby/pfile/init.ora
```

Step 7. Configure your network files for connection to stby. After making any changes to your listener.ora file, be sure that you bounce your listener, or the change will not take effect:

```
lsnrctl
LSNRCTL>stop
LSNRCTL>start
```

The tnsnames.ora file should have an entry like this:

```
STBY =
  (DESCRIPTION =
    (ADDRESS_LIST =
      (ADDRESS = (PROTOCOL = TCP)(HOST = opcbsol2)(PORT = 1521))
    )
    (CONNECT_DATA =
      (SID = stby)
      (SERVER = DEDICATED)
    )
  )
```

The listener.ora file should have an entry like this:

```
(SID_DESC =
  (GLOBAL_DBNAME = aux1)
  (ORACLE_HOME = /u02/32bit/app/oracle/product/11.2.0/dbhome_1)
  (SID_NAME = aux1)
)
```

Step 8.   From RMAN, connect to the target and auxiliary instance and run the **duplicate** command:

```
ORACLE_SID=V112B
export ORACLE_SID
rman
rman>connect target /
rman> connect auxiliary sys/password@stby
rman>run {
  set until sequence = 43 thread = 1;
  duplicate target database for standby
  dorecover;}
```

Backing Up the Multinode RAC Database

Once you have created the single-node standby database, you can take all of your backups from the standby database, just as you would in a normal environment. This means that you can offload your production RAC backups from the RAC cluster itself to the node that is set up and running as a standby database. This takes the load off the cluster, gives you a disaster recovery solution, and gives you a simplified backup solution for archive logs, because all the archive logs from all nodes will necessarily exist on the standby database.

Again, the secret is in the DB_FILE_NAME_CONVERT parameter. You are taking backups from the standby database that has the datafiles on a cooked file system, but even the standby database control file knows the original location of the files (the raw system). So, when you go to restore a backup taken from the standby on the production RAC database, RMAN checks with the control file, finds the raw locations, and places the files there.

For such a solution to work for you, you must use a recovery catalog. The recovery catalog acts as the transition agent for the metadata about the backups from the standby database control file to the primary database control file. After you take the backup from the standby database, RMAN resyncs with the recovery catalog, recording the backup metadata. Then, when you connect RMAN to the primary database and perform a manual resync, the backup metadata from the standby database control file is placed in the primary database control file records.

It is important to make sure that you connect to the standby database as the target database when performing backups from the standby database. Then, you connect to the primary database as the target database as well, to perform the resync. RMAN can do this smoothly because it sees no functional difference between the two databases: they have the same DB_NAME, the same DBID, and the same redo stream history.

Summary

In this chapter, we discussed the means by which RMAN interacts with databases in RAC clusters. We discussed how RMAN can allocate channels on each node for backup, but that recovery requires that all backups be accessible from a single node. We discussed the complications caused in archive log backups due to multiple threads of redo being generated at different nodes. We concluded with examples for duplicating a RAC database to a single-node database and for creating a single-node standby database from a RAC database.

CHAPTER
22

RMAN in Sync and Split Technology

ync and split technology is an example of an innovative (and challenging) solution for storage recovery that complements or duplicates many of the features RMAN can accomplish independently. Over the past five years, sync and split has become a widely used technology to provide immediate and very fast system recovery at the storage hardware level.

In this chapter, we will provide an overview of what sync and split technology refers to. We won't be discussing any single implementation in particular, but rather discussing the implications for RMAN and database backups. After the overview, we go into the specific steps required to integrate sync and split solutions into an RMAN backup strategy.

Sync and Split: Broken Mirror Backups

In the beginning, doing sync and split backups involved nothing more complicated than extending the functionality of hardware mirroring. The best way to explain this statement is through an example. Suppose we have a disk controller that has two hard drives. For redundancy, we set the RAID level to 0 + 1 so that we are mirroring everything on disk A to disk B. This gives us immediate protection against any kind of hardware failure on either disk A or disk B.

The next step, then, is to try to leverage the hardware mirror to provide logical fault tolerance. That is the goal of sync and split technology: to provide a fallback position in case of some failure that has occurred on both copies in the mirror. For example, suppose that a user has deleted the entire oracle software tree or the oradata directory. Such a deletion would immediately occur at both copies in our mirror, so having a mirrored copy would do us no good.

So, what is the solution? The innovation is that any mirrored disk group may have two mirror groups, but may only ever have one mirror currently writing the identical bits as the primary disk group. Let's build an example with three logical volumes, A, B, and C, all dedicated to the same data. Volumes A, B, and C are all mirrored copies of each other. However, at 2 P.M., volume A is split away from the mirror, leaving its bits "stuck" at the split time. Volumes B and C continue to be bit-for-bit copies. After four hours, at 6 P.M., volume C is split from volume B so that it no longer gets writes of data. At this point, there are three different copies of the data on the volume: a copy at 2 P.M., a copy at 6 P.M., and a current copy. There is also no redundancy to protect against a disk failure.

Where Are We in RAID?

Need a superfast, overly simplistic primer on RAID? We're here for you. There are hundreds of theories, from the radical to the traditional, that outline the best possible solution for disk failure protection. Typically, the Oracle "technorati" have long taken the position that nothing beats RAID 0 + 1, in which you have two disk groups, group 1 and group 2, both of which have two disks. The two disks on group 1 are striped, so that data is evenly spread across both disks. Group 2 is an exact copy, bit for bit, of group 1. This configuration gives us both performance, by striping across disks to avoid hot spots, and redundancy, by writing every bit twice.

Recently, we were reviewing the specs for a RAID 1 + 0 configuration, which is slightly different from 0 + 1. Instead of striping and then mirroring, a RAID 1 + 0 configuration mirrors and then stripes. The difference is best represented visually, as shown in the following illustration. Here, we mirror each disk separately so that we end up with four disk groups. After mirroring each disk, we then stripe across the four mirrors.

It might seem like a small difference, but RAID 1 + 0 has greater fault tolerance, because the failure of any one disk does not take down the other mirrored disks. In RAID 0 + 1, if any disk in group 2 fails, the whole group goes offline. So, RAID 1 + 0 provides greater tolerance than RAID 0 + 1 for multiple disk failure, instead of single disk failure.

To get back to our RAID 0 + 1 configuration, disk volume A will be "resilvered" up to disk B, which runs at the current point in time. This sync up is based on the fact that the volumes have a journaling mechanism in place that records all data changes. This journaling is more I/O on top of the multiple writes to each volume. Volume A will get access to the journals of changes on volume B and will apply all the changes until it is getting live writes at the same time as volume B. At this point, then, you have volumes A and B in redundant mode, and volume C is your fallback position, at 6 P.M. Figure 22-1 illustrates this process.

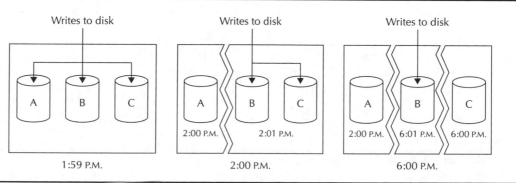

FIGURE 22-1 *Sync and split technology in action*

This sync and split cycle goes on and on, ad infinitum. Every four hours, a volume is synced up to the primary volume, and another volume is split away to provide a fallback position in case of a logical failure. What happens at the time you actually encounter the logical failure? In our example, let's assume that it is now 8 P.M. Volumes A and B are getting concurrent writes, and volume C is waiting idle at 6 P.M. At 8 P.M., a DBA is doing some system maintenance and deletes the system datafile from the production database. This is when the worrying begins.

Luckily, no unrecoverable data has been added to the database since the end of the day at 5 P.M. However, the nightly batch loads start in about 15 minutes. The DBA has a small window to get the production database back up and running.

With the database running entirely on the mirrored disk volumes A and B, the sync and split architecture has given our DBA an immediate solution. He immediately configures volume C, which was stuck at 6 P.M., as the primary volume and starts up the database. When the database looks for its datafiles, it finds all the files as they appear on volume C, at 6 P.M., and no deletes have taken place. By the time the DBA is finished, it is only 8:05 P.M. The batch processes will kick off on time. Figure 22-2 shows the process.

Oracle Databases on Sync and Split Volumes

The Oracle software files can reside on a sync and split volume and thus can help protect against logical corruption that occurs in the binaries themselves. No additional configuration is needed, from an Oracle perspective. The files associated with an Oracle database, on the other hand, come with some very specific caveats and disclaimers when you start putting them on sync and split volumes. These caveats and disclaimers relate to the fact that Oracle files are always open and always have active writes taking place (this being the primary importance of a good relational database). So, if you are actively writing to your database and it is mirrored on two drives, there will be consequences if you suddenly break the mirror, unbeknownst to the database.

Each vendor-specific solution is a bit different, but at some point, a volume that is getting active writes must turn off the writes to that volume while continuing to allow writes to another volume. And regardless of how a salesperson might pitch it, the process of breaking a mirror is not instantaneous. Breaking a mirror is more like peeling a banana—you start at the top and

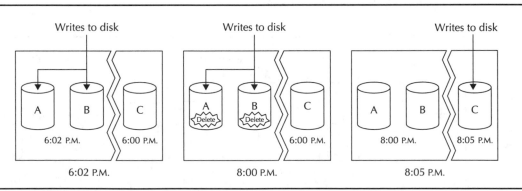

FIGURE 22-2 *Sync and split in action*

separate the peel from the fruit until you get to the bottom. Suppose your Oracle datafile is the fruit, and the mirrored copy of the datafile is the peel. If you peel away the mirror copy, you are starting at the beginning of the datafile, and the break is complete when you reach the end of the datafile. However, it is possible (likely) that Oracle will attempt to write to a block while the mirror is in the middle of peeling away. So, on the primary volume, nothing is wrong—the file header knows that an SCN has been advanced in the file and knows which block it was—but on the split mirror, the datafile header knows nothing about the written block. So, after the mirror break is complete, what do we have on the split mirror volume? One fuzzy datafile that is unrecoverable. Check out Figure 22-3 to see this.

Fear not, for there are ways to ensure that the split mirror is a healthy copy of the database. It just takes a bit of work first. How you configure Oracle database files in a sync and split environment depends on what type of files you are configuring: datafiles, control files, redo log files, or archive logs. The following sections address each in turn.

Datafiles

The previous section explained what happens to Oracle datafiles if a mirror split takes place without any preparation: the split volume copies of the files are left in a fuzzy, unusable state. This is precisely the same predicament you run into if you simply take a copy of an online datafile without first putting it into hot backup mode. So, before you break the mirror, you must put all datafiles into hot backup mode. This is not an optional step, regardless of which vendor product you are using. Because the split generally takes a very short time, the amount of time in hot backup mode is much shorter than it would be if you were doing a copy against the same datafiles. And the I/O hit of running in backup mode (and producing more archive logs) will be relatively small, as well.

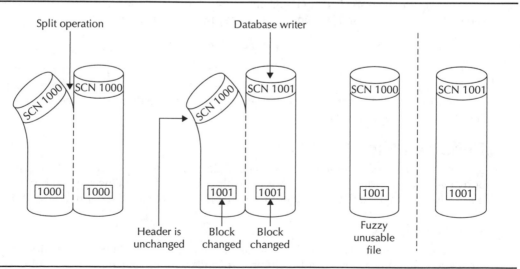

FIGURE 22-3 *Unrecoverable fuzzy datafile*

To alleviate the headaches of hot backup mode for those implementing sync and split architectures, Oracle has added syntax that allows you to put an entire database into hot backup mode with a single command:

```
alter database begin backup;
```

Previously, you had to put each tablespace into hot backup mode. If there is something preventing the file from going into backup mode, a warning is generated in the alert log, but the **begin backup** command proceeds anyway.

After the split is complete, you pull the database out of hot backup mode with the following command:

```
alter database end backup;
```

Control Files

A split mirror copy of a control file is in an unusable state immediately after the split mirror operation completes. The control file, in general, is up-to-date on the current state of all the datafiles. However, based on the total duration of the split itself, and the overall activity on the database at the time of the split, the control file at the split volume may not reflect much accurate data about the state of the datafiles.

Putting the database into hot backup mode cures most of these ills. With the database in hot backup mode, the control file is aware of a starting point at which recovery will be required, and from which it will be feasible. However, the control file is still at odds with reality: it thinks of itself as a current control file of an active database. This is hardly the case.

We've seen some implementations where a DBA insists on trying to keep the current control file available as such on the split volume, particularly if the split volume will be used for reporting purposes. However, when the time comes to put this control file into service for the sake of recovery, you have to use the **using backup controlfile** command so that the control file understands that some of its checkpoint and SCN information may not reflect reality:

```
recover database using backup controlfile until cancel;
```

If you will be mounting the Oracle database on the split mirror volume for reporting purposes, you may want to use the **using backup controlfile** command, even if you will not be applying any archive logs, just so the control file is flagged as a backup. We discuss this later in the section "Benefits of the Split Mirror Backup."

Redo Log Files

Split mirror copies of the online redo logs are useless in every way, shape, and form. If possible, don't even bother putting them on the volume that is going through the sync and split. There is no mechanism in the online redo logs to account for writes to the file during the split operation.

Archive Logs

Archive logs are an excellent candidate to be put on a sync and split volume. Doing so gives you a backup of existing archive logs on disk in a second location. Of course, if you split the archive log volume at the same time as the datafile volume, you do not get all the redo that you need to properly recover your database from the split volume. We suggest that you keep your archive logs on a separate set of sync and split volumes from the set on which you keep your datafiles and control files. That way, you can split the datafiles, take the database out of hot backup mode, force a log switch, and then split the archive log volumes. Then the split mirror volume with the archive logs contains all of the redo required to start the split mirror copy of the database.

One last note on archive logs on split mirror volumes. When the database begins to create an archive log on disk, the split operation may leave behind an unfinished archive log on the split mirror volume. This archive log would be unusable during any recovery operation. This poses a problem only for human-managed backup and recovery operations, where it is unknown if the archive log that is on-disk is complete or only half-written. Here's why it doesn't pose a problem for RMAN: When an archive log is being generated, the control file is not updated with a record that such an archive log exists until the archive log is complete. Therefore, in a split mirror scenario, if half of an archive log is generated on the split volume, the control file on the split volume has no record of that archive log. During an RMAN operation, then, the control file would be consulted for archive log records, and the half-written file would not exist in the metadata. To RMAN, the half-written file doesn't really exist.

Benefits of the Split Mirror Backup

We've discussed briefly the primary benefit of using the sync and split architecture: a nearly instantaneous fallback recovery point for all files on a particular set of disks. This benefit expands beyond the scope of this book (the Oracle database) to include a fallback point for all files that exist on the volume. There are also other primary benefits of the sync and split, which are discussed next.

Fast Point-In-Time Recovery

From the database perspective, sync and split provides a point-in-time recovery option that can take minutes instead of hours. You simply change the primary disk group to the split mirror, and the datafiles are ready. Then, apply archive logs up to the point where the failure occurred, and you can open the database.

Speedy-Looking Backups

Another benefit of the sync and split architecture is the relative speed of the backup operation itself. Properly generating copies of the database files at the split mirror side takes only a few moments with the database in hot backup mode. After that, a backup is ready to be pressed into service very quickly. Of course, there's no magic involved with sync and split. I/O is I/O is I/O. It might look like the backup is taking no time at all, but in reality the backup is being taken all the time at the hardware level, because prior to the split operation, the files are being written to simultaneously. However, handing the backups over to the hardware architecture can prove to be extremely powerful in many organizations, where the hardware can be responsible for backing up more than just the database.

Mounting a Split Mirror Volume on Another Server

Beyond the simplistic restore and recovery features, much of the true power of sync and split solutions currently in the marketplace comes from what you can do with the split copy of the database. Because the underlying hardware is likely to be a storage array with many computers connected to it, any volume on that storage array can theoretically be associated with any computer connected to it.

For example, let's take a database, PROD. PROD resides on disks in volume A, which is mirrored on volume B. Both volume A and B are connected to server Dex. Volumes A and B both exist on storage array Newton. At 2 P.M., volume B is split from volume A and disassociated from server Dex. Immediately after this, volume B is mounted on a different server, Proto, which is also connected to storage array Newton. After volume B is mounted on Proto, a copy of the database PROD that resided on Dex now resides on Proto, with almost real-time amounts of data. The database copy that is on volume B, and mounted by server Proto, can be recovered and then opened for testing, development, or reporting. Later, at 6 P.M., when it is time to resilver volume B with volume A, Proto can dismount volume B, and then it can be remounted by Dex. The sync operation takes place, overwriting any changes that occurred on volume B after the split at 2 P.M.

Note that before you can open a split mirror copy of the database on a different node, a new backup control file should be taken and used. When you resilver volume B with volume A, this new copy will be overwritten by the correct file on A.

Taking Backups from the Split Mirror

Another benefit of sync and split backups, within the framework of this book about RMAN, is the ability to mount the split volume on a different server and, from there, back up the database to tape for long-term backup storage. This allows you to offload the memory, CPU, and I/O operations of the RMAN backup to a completely different server and ensure that there is no impact to your production database.

RMAN and Sync and Split

There are a few different contact points that RMAN has with a sync and split implementation:

- If you use RMAN for recovery, you must make RMAN aware of the datafile copies that are created by the split operation.

- You can use RMAN to take backups from the split mirror volume instead of from the production database itself.

Registering Split Mirror Copies with RMAN

If you are a dedicated RMAN user, then you probably understand the benefits that come from executing all recovery statements from within RMAN, instead of from SQL*Plus or elsewhere. RMAN recovery provides access to the information in the control file so that you are not scrambling to uncover which backups exist where and trying to ensure that you are not missing any files. The control file also aids in archive log management during recovery. When a sync and split system is in place, RMAN doesn't know about everything. The act of splitting the mirror volumes effectively gives you a full datafile copy of every datafile in the database that can be used during a restore/ recovery operation, but RMAN has no idea these copies exist.

So, you have to make RMAN aware. You do this by registering the datafile copies with RMAN via the **catalog** command. The **catalog** command can be used against a single datafile copy:

```
catalog datafilecopy '/volumeA/oradata/system01.dbf';
```

Or, starting with 10g, you can catalog an entire directory by the directory name:

```
catalog start with '/volumeA/oradata';
```

By using the **catalog** command, you take the split mirror copies and make them part of any future restore or recovery operation that might be required.

You might be asking yourself, "Why do I need to make RMAN aware of the split mirror copies when I can just remount the entire volume as the primary volume and be up and running without RMAN's help?" A valid question. But what if it makes more sense to switch to only a single copy of the file? Perhaps doing a full database point-in-time recovery would be too expensive, but you still want to leverage the split mirror copy of a subset of files. Beyond that, RMAN also greatly simplifies the recovery stage of any operation, so it makes sense to make RMAN aware of the copies of the archive logs, as well.

Taking RMAN Backups from the Split Mirror

With increasing frequency, DBAs are realizing that with split mirror investments, an additional layer of protection is required, in the form of RMAN backups of the database. The split mirror backup is by definition a short-lived copy—sooner or later, it will be lost when the volume is resilvered with the primary database volume. But what about restoring from last night? Or last week? As you can see, a full-fledged media backup is still required.

With an idle copy of the database simmering on the back burner of the split mirror, a light bulb appears above the DBA's head: "I should just mount the split mirror drive onto a different server, and take the RMAN backup from the split mirror directly to tape (or to a different disk volume that can be mounted on the primary)." Great idea! Sounds simple enough, right? Well, a few tricky points need to get worked out first; otherwise, you will have the case of the mysteriously disappearing backups.

Here's the problem: RMAN accesses the control file to determine what to back up, and after the backup is complete, it updates the control file with the details of the backup. If you are connected to a split mirror copy of the control file, that copy gets updated with the details about the backup. So then, of course, when you go to resilver the split volume with the primary, the control file is overwritten with the data in the primary control file, and the backup data is lost forever.

The solution, you figure, is to use a recovery catalog when you back up at the split mirror. That is a sound, logical decision: after the backup is complete, the split volume control file is updated with the backup records, which are then synchronized to the catalog. Then, it's simply a matter of syncing the catalog with the primary volume so that the backups can be used. Too cool!

So, suppose that you back up from the secondary volume, you sync the backup records to your recovery catalog, and then, you connect RMAN to the primary volume database and to the catalog. You perform a resync. This is where things get really, really weird. Sometimes, when you try to perform an operation, you get this error:

```
RMAN-20035: invalid high recid
```

Other times, things work just fine, it seems, but the backups you took at the split mirror database have disappeared from the recovery catalog.

The problem, now, has become the internal mechanism of how RMAN handles record building in the control file and the recovery catalog. Every record that is generated gets a record ID (RECID), which is generated at the control file. When the backup occurs at the split mirror database, the control file gets its high RECID value updated, and this information gets passed to the catalog. But the RECID at the primary database control file has not been updated, necessarily. So, when you connect to the catalog and the primary database, if the catalog's high RECID is higher than the one in the control file, you get the "invalid high recid" error. If the RECID in the catalog is lower than the RECID of the primary database control file, RMAN initiates an update of the catalog that effectively eliminates all the records since the last sync operation with the primary control file. Poof! Backup records from the split volume are gone.

The solution to this problem is to set the control file at the split mirror to become a backup control file. If RMAN detects that it is backing up from a noncurrent control file (backup or standby), it does not increment the RECID in the catalog, so that the records are available after a resync with the current control file at the primary database.

You cannot use the control file autobackup feature if you will be taking backups from the split mirror volume. Because the control file in use is a backup control file, autobackup is disallowed.

RMAN Workshop: *Configure RMAN to Back Up from the Split Mirror*

Workshop Notes

This workshop assumes that you put all the tablespaces into hot backup mode (a requirement) during the period of the split. After the split, you connect the split volume to a new server that has 10*g* installed, and you now want to take an RMAN backup. Because RMAN will give an error if files are in backup mode, you need to manually end backup for every file, as described in this workshop. It's best to write a script for this. This workshop also assumes that you split the archive log destination and bring it across to the clone at the same time for archive log backup.

Step 1. Mount the database on the clone server, and prepare the control file for RMAN backup:

```
startup mount;
alter database end backup;
recover database using backup controlfile until cancel;
cancel
exit
```

Step 2. Connect RMAN to the clone instance (as the target) and the recovery catalog, and run the datafile backup:

```
rman target /
rman> connect catalog rman/password@rman_cat_db
rman> backup database plus archivelog not backed up two times;
```

Step 3. Connect RMAN to the production database (as the target) and the catalog, perform a sync operation and archive log cleanup, and then back up the control file:

```
rman target /
rman> connect catalog rman/password@rman_cat_db
rman> delete archivelog completed before sysdate -7;
rman> backup controlfile;
rman> resync catalog;
```

Getting Sync and Split Functionality from Oracle Software

There is considerable upside to having a hardware solution provide the architecture described in this chapter. Typically, any operation that can be done purely at the hardware level will have performance increases over the same operation done by software. By the same token, a hardware solution is always going to cost you more than a software solution. Sync and split solutions are no different—the more work that is being done at the storage array, the faster it will go…and the more it will cost.

Starting with Oracle Database 10*g* Release 2, Oracle includes a full solution to provide sync and split functionality without paying for any third-party hardware or software solutions. All you need is Oracle Database 10*g* Enterprise Edition, two servers (with the same OS), and a storage array.

Using a Standby Database, Flashback Database, and Incremental Apply for Sync and Split

To implement a sync and split solution using only Oracle software, you need to employ a different feature set within the RDBMS: a standby database, Flashback Database, and RMAN incremental backup and incremental apply. All of these features have already been discussed to some extent in previous chapters.

Here's how it works. First, you create a standby database of your production database (see the workshops in Chapter 20). Once you have the standby database fully operational as a disaster recovery solution, you need to implement Flashback Database on both production and standby databases:

```
alter database flashback on;
```

With Flashback Database enabled, you can set a restore point on the primary server:

```
create restore point chapter_20;
alter system switch logfile;
```

Apply changes through the restore point to the standby database. At this point, the standby database can be opened with reset logs for testing or reporting.

```
alter database activate standby database;
```

To resilver your standby database with the primary database, you need to take an incremental backup by using the **from scn** keywords to specify the SCN of the restore point. Once this backup is complete, move it to the standby database site.

```
backup database incremental from scn = 120000;
```

At the standby database, shut down and then remount the database again. Perform a flashback database to the restore point specified before the standby database was opened:

```
flashback database to restore point chapter_20;
```

Once the flashback completes, apply the incremental backup from the production database to the standby database, bringing it up to the point of the backup:

```
recover database until scn=1521321;
```

Then, the standby database can go back into managed standby mode and catch up to the production database. Or, it can simply be opened again for reporting, now with all of the latest data imported from the incremental backup. Figure 22-4 illustrates how this process might work.

Benefits of the Oracle Sync and Split Solution

Being less expensive isn't the only thing going for the Oracle sync and split solution. While most likely there are performance drop-offs related to using the standby database/Flashback Database/incremental apply solution, those drop-offs might be less dramatic than you think. This depends entirely on whether you are already using flashback logs for the inherent functionality provided by them. If you are, then you already have two journals of database changes: the flashback logs and the redo logs. Any more journaling at the file system level only adds additional—and redundant—journaling and can be eliminated.

In addition, you now have a standby database, which you can use for disaster recovery. Although disaster recovery is inherent in the hardware sync and split model as well, having a

FIGURE 22-4 *Using sync and split with a standby database and Flashback Database*

standby database at your disposal means that much of the manual footwork involved in failing over during an actual disaster is automated and simplified.

Ultimately, deciding between a fully Oracle solution and a hardware solution will come down to other factors, as well. Is the sync and split architecture needed for things other than the Oracle databases? Do you have licensing for the additional Enterprise Edition database? Do you have the expertise to use one solution over the other? You would need to address these questions, obviously. More than anything else, though, you would want to test the solutions. The good news about the Oracle solution is that you probably already have all the requirements to test it right now.

Oracle-Integrated Shadow Copy Services for Windows

An interesting example of the direction of sync/split type of hardware/OS integration can be seen in the integration Oracle 11*g* has down with the Volume Shadow Copy Service (VSS) functionality on the Windows platform. VSS is a capability that allows for background journaling, much like other vendors' mirroring functions, which can then be split off as a separate volume and moved to a different location on a storage array. VSS as a component of the Windows OS offers the ability to coordinate activities between storage writers (the Oracle database) and storage providers (the storage array technologies). It can coordinate component-based shadow copies, meaning that it doesn't have to understand the world only as a set of volumes; VSS can be informed of the components on the volume and act accordingly.

Oracle created a plug-in for VSS called the Oracle VSS Writer, a separate Windows service that runs independently from the Oracle Database service. The Oracle VSS Writer coordinates the specific activities required to take a VSS copy of the database.

Oracle VSS Writer is capable of making either component-level backups (i.e., file by file, such as datafiles and control files) or full volume backups. When making component-level backups of datafiles, the VSS Writer keeps track of redo generated separately from existing mechanisms, and then, during restore, it applies the redo automatically to the components that were backed up.

When VSS is making a full volume backup, nothing magical is occurring here. A database's data blocks can still be caught in mid-write, and therefore fuzzy, by the VSS Writer. So the Oracle VSS Writer still does the same things we've discussed so far in this chapter: it puts datafiles into hot backup mode for the duration of the datafile backup, so that the archive logs will have full copies of changed blocks to overwrite any fuzzy blocks.

The difference is the level of integration that we are starting to see—as the sync/split technologies offer better interface points for their technologies, as Microsoft has done, it allows Oracle to provide better automation of tasks that otherwise would have to be scripted separately by the system administrator or DBA.

Summary

In this chapter, we covered how a hardware sync and split architecture would impact your backup and recovery solutions. We discussed how to implement sync and split with the Oracle database and how to take RMAN backups from a split mirror copy of the database. Finally, we discussed how to use an existing Oracle RDBMS to implement a software-based sync and split environment.

CHAPTER
23

RMAN in the Workplace: Case Studies

e have covered a number of different topics in this book, and we are sure you have figured out that you might face almost an infinite number of recovery combinations. In this chapter, we provide various case studies to help you review your knowledge of backup and recovery (see if you can figure out the solution before you read it). When you do come across these situations, these case studies may well help you avoid some mistakes that you might otherwise make when trying to recover your database. You can even use these case studies to practice performing recoveries so that you become an RMAN backup and recovery expert.

Before we get into the case studies, though, the following section provides a quick overview about facing the ultimate disaster, a real-life failure of your database.

Before the Recovery

Disaster strikes. Often, when you are in a recovery situation, everyone is in a big rush to recover the database. Customers are calling, management is panicking, and your boss is looking at you for answers, all of which is making you nervous, wondering if your résumé is up to date. When the real recovery situation occurs, stop. Take a few moments to collect yourself and ask these questions:

1. What is the exact nature of the failure?
2. What are the recovery options available to me?
3. Might I need Oracle support?
4. Is there anyone who can act as a second pair of eyes for me during this recovery?

Let's address each of these questions in detail.

What Is the Exact Nature of the Failure?

Here's some firsthand experience from one of the authors. Back in the days when I was contracting, I was paged one night (on Halloween, no less!) because a server had failed, and once they got the server back up, none of the databases would come up. Before I received the page, the DBAs at this site had spent upward of eight hours trying to restart the 25 databases on that box. Most of the databases would not start. The DBAs had recovered a couple of the seemingly lost databases, yet even those databases still would not open. The DBAs called Oracle, and Oracle seemed unsure as to what the problem was. Finally, the DBAs paged me (while I was out trick-or-treating with my kids).

Within about 20 minutes after arriving at the office, I knew what the answer was. I didn't find the answer because I was smarter than all the other DBAs there (I wasn't, in fact). I found the answer for a couple of reasons. First, I approached the problem from a fresh perspective (after eight hours of problem solving, one's eyes tend to become burned and red!). Second, I looked to find the nature of the failure rather than just assuming the nature of the failure was a corrupted database.

What ended up being the problem, pretty clearly to a fresh pair of eyes, was a set of corrupted Oracle libraries. Once we recovered those libraries, all the databases came up quickly, without a problem. The moral of the story is that when you have a database that has crashed, or that will not open, do not assume that the cause is a corrupted datafile or a bad disk drive. Find out for sure what the problem is by investigative analysis. Good analysis may take a little longer to begin with, but, generally, it will prove valuable in the long run.

What Recovery Options Are Available?

Recovery situations can offer a number of solutions. Again, back when I was a consultant, I had a customer who had a disk controller drive fail over a weekend, and the result was the loss of file systems on the box, including files belonging to an Oracle database in ARCHIVELOG mode. The DBA at the customer site went ahead and recovered the entire database (about 150GB), which took, as I recall, a couple of hours.

The following Monday, the DBA and I had a discussion about the recovery method he selected. The corrupted file systems actually impacted only about five database datafiles (the other file systems contained web server files that we were not concerned with). The total size of the impacted database datafiles was no more than 8 or 10GB. The DBA was pretty upset about having to come into the office and spend several hours recovering the database. When I asked the DBA why he hadn't just recovered the five datafiles instead of the entire database, he replied that it just had not occurred to him.

The moral of this story is that it's important to consider your recovery options. The type of recovery you do may make a big difference in how long it takes you to recover your database. Another moral of this story is to really become a backup and recovery expert. Part of the reason the DBA in this case had not considered datafile recovery, I think, is that he had never done such a recovery. When facing a stressful situation, people tend to not consider options they are not familiar with. So, we strongly suggest you set up a backup and recovery lab and practice recoveries until you can do it in your sleep.

Might Oracle Support Be Needed?

You might well be a backup and recovery expert, but even the experts need help from time to time. This is what Oracle support is there for. Even though I feel like I know something about backup and recovery, I ask myself if the failure looks to be something that I might need Oracle support for. Generally, if the failure is something odd, even if I think I can solve it on my own, I "prime" support by opening a service request on the problem. That way, if I need help, I have already provided Oracle with the information they need (or at least some initial information) and have them primed to support me should I need it. If you are paying for Oracle support, use it now, don't wait for later.

Who Can Act as a Second Pair of Eyes During Recovery?

When I'm in a stressful situation, first of all it's nice to have someone to share the stress with. Somehow I feel a bit more comfortable when someone is there just to talk things out with. Further, when you are working on a critical problem, mistakes can be costly. Having a second, experienced pair of eyes there to support you as you recover your database is a great idea!

Recovery Case Studies

Now to the meat of the chapter, the recovery case studies. In this section, we provide you with a number of case studies listed next in the order they appear:

1. Recovering from complete database loss in NOARCHIVELOG mode with a recovery catalog

2. Recovering from complete database loss in NOARCHIVELOG mode without a recovery catalog

3. Recovering from complete database loss in ARCHIVELOG mode without a recovery catalog

4. Recovering from complete database loss in ARCHIVELOG mode with a recovery catalog

5. Recovering from the loss of the SYSTEM tablespace

6. Recovering online from the loss of a datafile or tablespace

7. Recovering from loss of an unarchived online redo log

8. Recovering through **resetlogs**

9. Completing a failed duplication manually

10. Using RMAN duplication to create a historical subset of the target database

11. Recovering from a lost datafile in ARCHIVELOG mode using an image copy in the flash recovery area

12. Recovering from running the production datafile out of the flash recovery area

13. Using Flashback Database and media recovery to pinpoint the exact moment to open the database with **resetlogs**

In each of these case studies, we provide you with the following information:

- **The Scenario** Outlines the environment for you

- **The Problem** Defines a problem that needs to be solved

- **The Solution** Outlines the solution for you, including RMAN output solving the problem

Now, let's look at our case studies!

Case #1: Recovering from Complete Database Loss (NOARCHIVELOG Mode) with a Recovery Catalog

The Scenario
Thom is a new DBA at Unfortunate Company. Upon arriving at his new job, he finds that his databases are not backed up at all, and that they are all in NOARCHIVELOG mode. Because Thom's manager will not shell out the money for additional disk space for archived redo logs, Thom is forced to do offline backups, which he begins doing the first night he is on the job. Thom also has turned on autobackups of his control file and has converted the database so that it is using an SPFILE. Finally, Thom has created a recovery catalog schema in a different database that is on a different database server.

The Problem
Unfortunate Company's cheap buying practices catch up to it in the few days following Thom's initial work, when the off-brand (cheap) disks that it has purchased all become corrupted due to a bad controller card. Thom's database is lost.

Thom's offline database backup strategy includes tape backups to a local tape drive. Once the hardware problems are solved, the system administrator quickly rebuilds the lost file systems, and Thom quickly gets the Oracle software installed. Now, Thom needs to get the database back up and running immediately.

The Solution

Thom's only recovery option in this case is to restore from the last offline backup. In this case, Thom's recovery catalog database was not lost (it was on another server), and his file systems are in place, so all he needs to do is recover the database. First, Thom needs to recover the database SPFILE, followed by the control file. Then, he needs to recover the database datafiles to the file systems.

The Solution Revealed   Based on the preceding considerations, Thom devises and implements the following recovery plan:

1. Restore a copy of the SPFILE. While you will be able to nomount the Oracle instance in many cases without a parameter file at all, to properly recover the database, Thom has to restore the correct SPFILE from backup. Because he doesn't have a control file yet, he cannot configure channels permanently. In this case, Thom has configured his autobackups of the control files to go to default disk locations. Thus, once Thom restored his Oracle software backups, he also restored the backup pieces to the autobackups of the control file. This makes the recovery of the SPFILE simple as a result:

   ```
   rman target sys/password catalog rcat_user/rcat_password@catalogdb
   startup force nomount;
   restore spfile from autobackup;
   shutdown immediate;
   startup nomount;
   ```

   NOTE
   If you are not using the FRA, you will need to set the DBID of the database before performing the restore of the SPFILE and the control file.

2. Restore a copy of the control file. Using the same RMAN session as in Step 1, Thom can do this quite simply. After the restore operation, he mounts the database using the restored control file:

   ```
   restore controlfile from autobackup;
   alter database mount;
   ```

3. Configure permanent channel parameters. Now that Thom has a control file restored, he can update the persistent parameters for channel allocation to include the name of the tape device his backup sets are on. This will allow him to proceed to restore the backup from tape and recover the database.

   ```
   configure default device type to sbt;
    configure channel 1 device type sbt
    parms = "env=(nb_ora_serv=mgtserv, nb_ora_client=cervantes)";
   ```

4. Perform the restore and recovery:

   ```
   restore database;
   recover database noredo;
   alter database open resetlogs;
   ```

NOTE
Thom used the **alter database open resetlogs** *command. He could have used the SQL command (***sql** *"alter database open resetlogs"), too. However, one benefit of using the RMAN* **alter** *command is that the catalog and the database will both be reset. Using the SQL version, only the database is reset.*

Case #2: Recovering from Complete Database Loss (NOARCHIVELOG Mode) Without a Recovery Catalog

The Scenario

Charles is the DBA of a development OLTP system. Because it is a development system, the decision was made to do RMAN offline backups and to leave the database in NOARCHIVELOG mode. Charles did not decide to use a recovery catalog when doing his backups. Further, Charles has configured RMAN to back up the control file backups to disk by default, rather than to tape.

The Problem

Sevi, a developer, developed a piece of PL/SQL code designed to truncate specific tables in the database. However, due to a logic bug, the code managed to truncate all the tables in the schema, wiping out all test data.

The Solution

If there were a logical backup of the database, this would be the perfect time to use it. Unfortunately, there is no logical backup of the database, so Charles (the DBA) is left with performing an RMAN recovery. Since his database is in NOARCHIVELOG mode, Charles has only one recovery option in this case, which is to restore from the last offline backup. Because all the pieces to do recovery are in place (the RMAN disk backups, the Oracle software, and the file systems), all that needs to be done is to fire up RMAN and recover the database.

The Solution Revealed   Based on the preceding considerations, Charles devises and implements the following recovery plan:

1.   Restore the control file. When doing a recovery from a cold backup, it is always a good idea to recover the control file associated with that backup (this prevents odd things from happening). In this case, Charles will be using the latest control file backup (since he doesn't back up the control file at other times). Since Charles uses the default location to create control file backup sets to, he doesn't need to allocate any channels. If Charles is not using the Oracle flash recovery area and not using a recovery catalog, he will need to set the DBID of the system, since he is not using a recovery catalog before he can restore the control file. If Charles is using a recovery catalog or the FRA, then setting the DBID would not be required. Once Charles restores the control file, he mounts the database:

```
rman target sys/password
startup nomount
set dbid=2540040039;
restore controlfile from autobackup;
sql 'alter database mount';
```

> **NOTE**
> *If you are using the FRA, you will not need to set the database DBID.*

2. The control file that Charles restored has the correct default persistent parameters already configured in it, so all he needs to do is perform the restore and recovery:

```
restore database;
recover database noredo;
sql "alter database open resetlogs";
```

Case #3: Recovering from Complete Database Loss (ARCHIVELOG Mode) Without a Recovery Catalog

The Scenario
We meet Thom from Case #1 again. Thom's company finally has decided that putting the database in ARCHIVELOG mode seems like a good idea. (Thom's boss thought it was his idea!) Unfortunately for Thom, due to budget restrictions, he was forced to use the space that was allocated to the recovery catalog to store archived redo logs. Thus, Thom no longer has a recovery catalog at his disposal.

The Problem
As if things have not been hard enough on Thom, we also find that Unfortunate Company is also an unfortunately located company. His server room, located in the basement as so many server rooms are, suffered the fate of a broken water main nearby. The entire room was flooded, and the server on which his database resides has been completely destroyed.

Thom's backup strategy has improved. It now includes tape backups to an offsite media management server. Also, he's sending his automated control file/SPFILE backups to tape rather than to disk. Again, he's salvaged a smaller server from the wreckage, which already has Oracle installed on the system, and now he needs to get the database back up and running immediately.

The Solution
Again, Thom has lost the current control file and the online redo logs for his database, so it's time to employ the point-in-time recovery skills. Thom still has control file autobackups turned on, so he can use them to get recovery started. In addition, he's restoring to a new server, so he wants to be aware of the challenges that restoring to a new server brings; there are media management, file system layout, and memory utilization considerations.

Media Management Considerations   Because he's restoring files to a new server, Thom must first make sure that the MML file has been properly set up for use on his emergency server. This means having the media management client software and Oracle Plug-In installed prior to using RMAN for restore/recovery. Thom uses the sbttest utility—a good way to check to make sure that the media manager is accessible.

Next, Thom needs to configure his tape channels to specify the client name of the server that has been destroyed. Thom will need to specify the name of the client from which the backups were taken. In addition, he needs to ensure that the media management server has been configured to allow for backups to be restored from a different client to his emergency server.

File System Layout Considerations   Thom's new system has a different file system structure from his original server. The production database had files manually striped over six mount points: /u02, /u03, /u04, /u05, /u06, and /u07. His new server has only two mount points: /u02 and /u03. Fortunately, Thom employed directory structure standards across his enterprise, and all data directories are /oradata/prod/ on all mount points. In addition, he has a standard that always puts the ORACLE_HOME on the same mount point and directory structure on every server.

Memory Utilization Considerations   Thom's emergency server has less physical memory than his lost production server. This means he will have to significantly scale back the memory utilization for the time being in order to at least get the database up and operational.

The Solution Revealed   Based on the preceding considerations, Thom devises and implements the following recovery plan:

1. Determine the DBID of the target database. Thom can do this by looking at the file handle for his control file autobackup. He needs to be able to view the media management catalog to do so. Even easier, Thom has every DBID for all his databases stored somewhere in a log—a notebook, a PDA, whatever. Whatever you decide to use, just make sure it's accessible in an emergency.

2. Restore a copy of the SPFILE. As you may remember, Thom will have to force an instance to be opened using a dummy SPFILE, and then restore the correct SPFILE from backup. Because Thom changed the default location for his control file/SPFILE autobackups to tape, he needs to manually configure the channel for this backup, because he doesn't have a control file yet; thus, he cannot configure channels permanently. Instead, he has to imbed **channel allocation** commands in a **run** block, and then issue the **startup** command to start the database with the correct SPFILE.

```
rman target /
set dbid=204062491;
startup force nomount;
run {
allocate channel tape_1 type sbt
parms='env=(nb_ora_serv=rmsrv, nb_ora_client=cervantes)';
restore spfile from autobackup;}
shutdown immediate;
startup nomount;
```

NOTE
If you are using the FRA, then you will not need to set the database DBID.

3. Make changes to the SPFILE. Thom must modify his SPFILE to take into account the new server configuration. This means changing memory utilization parameters and setting filename conversion parameters. He must connect to the newly started instance from SQL*Plus and make the necessary changes.

```
alter system set control_files= '/u02/oradata/prod/control01.dbf',
'/u03/oradata/prod/control02.dbf' scope=spfile;
alter system set db_file_name_convert= ('/u04' , '/u02' ,
'/u05' , '/u02' ,
```

```
'u06' , ' u03' ,
'u07' , 'u03') scope=spfile;
alter system set log_file_name_convert= ('/u04' , '/u02' ,
'/u05' , '/u02' ,
'u06' , ' u03' ,
'u07' , 'u03') scope=spfile;
alter system set log_archive_dest_1=
'location=/u02/oradata/prod/arch' scope=spfile;
alter system set db_cache_size=300m scope=spfile;
alter system set shared_pool_size=200m scope=spfile;
shutdown immediate;
startup nomount;
```

NOTE
You could also choose to use the **set newname** *option here.*

4. Restore a copy of the control file. Using the same RMAN session as the preceding, Thom can do this quite simply (he's already set the DBID). Then, mount the database using the restored control file.

```
run {
allocate channel tape_1 type sbt
parms='env=(nb_ora_serv=rmsrv, nb_ora_client=Cervantes)';
restore controlfile from autobackup; }
alter database mount;
```

5. Configure permanent channel parameters. Now that Thom has a control file restored, he can update the persistent parameters for channel allocation to include the name of the lost server as the media management client. This serves two purposes: it allows RMAN to access the backups that were taken from the lost server, and RMAN will pass this client name to the media management server when any backups are taken from the new server. That way, when the lost server is rebuilt, any backups taken from this stopgap system will be accessible at the newly reconstructed production server.

```
configure default device type to sbt;
configure device type sbt parallelism 2;
configure auxiliary channel 1 device type sbt parms
= "env=(nb_ora_serv=mgtserv, nb_ora_client=cervantes)";
configure auxiliary channel 2 device type sbt parms
= "env=(nb_ora_serv=mgtserv, nb_ora_cient=cervantes)";
```

6. Determine the last archive log for which there is a copy. Because Thom lost the entire server, he also lost any archive logs that had not yet been backed up by RMAN. So, he must query RMAN to determine what the last archive log is for which a backup exists.

```
list backup of archivelog from time = 'sysdate-7';
```

7. With the last log sequence number in hand, Thom performs his restore and recovery and opens the database:

```
restore database;
recover database until sequence=<number>;
alter database open resetlogs;
```

Case #4: Recovering from Complete Database Loss (ARCHIVELOG Mode) with a Recovery Catalog

The Scenario

Charles is taking over for Thom, because management recognized that Thom was a hero of a DBA and thus sent him and his wife to Hawaii for two weeks of R and R. Before he left, Thom's company added additional disk storage and decided that using the RMAN recovery catalog was probably a good idea.

Unfortunately for Charles, disaster seems to follow him around. At his last company, a huge electrical fire caused all sorts of mayhem, and this time, it's gophers. Yes, gophers. Somewhere outside the computer room, a lone gopher ate through the power cable leading to the computer room. This resulted in an electrical fire and a halon release into the computer room. As a result of the electrical fire, the server and disks on which his database resides have been completely destroyed...again.

The Problem

Charles reviews Thom's backup strategy. Again, Charles has salvaged a smaller server that survived the fiasco, which already has Oracle installed on the system, and now he needs to get the database back up and running immediately. Fortunately, the recovery catalog server is intact, so Charles can use it during the recovery.

The Solution

Again, Charles has lost the current control file and the online redo logs for his database, so it's time to employ his point-in-time recovery skills. The backup strategy still has control file autobackups turned on, so Charles can use them to get recovery started. In addition, he's restoring to a new server, so he wants to be aware of the challenges that restoring to a new server brings; there are media management, file system layout, and memory utilization considerations.

Media Management Considerations   Because Charles is restoring files to a new server, he must first make sure that the MML file has been properly set up for use on his emergency server. This means having the media management client software and Oracle Plug-In installed prior to using RMAN for restore/recovery. Charles uses sbttest to check to make sure that the media manager is accessible.

Next, Charles needs to configure his tape channels to specify the client name of the server that has been destroyed. Charles will need to specify the name of the client from which the backups were taken. In addition, he needs to ensure that the media management server has been configured to allow for backups to be restored from a different client to his emergency server.

File System Layout Considerations   On Charles's new system, the file system structure is different from that on his original server. The production database had files manually striped over six mount points: /u02, /u03, /u04, /u05, /u06, and /u07. His new server has only two mount points: /u02 and /u03. Luckily, directory structure standards exist across his enterprise, and all data directories are /oradata/prod/ on all mount points. In addition, he has a standard that always puts the ORACLE_HOME on the same mount point and directory structure on every server.

Memory Considerations   Charles's emergency server has less physical memory than his lost production server. This means he has to significantly scale back the memory utilization for the time being in order to at least get the database up and operational.

The Solution Revealed   Based on the preceding considerations, Charles devises and implements the following recovery plan:

1. Get a copy of the SPFILE restored. First, Charles will nomount the database instance without a parameter file, since Oracle supports this. Then, he will restore the correct SPFILE from backup. Because he doesn't have a control file yet, he cannot configure channels permanently. Instead, he has to embed **channel allocation** commands in a **run** block, and then issue the **startup** command to start the database with the correct SPFILE. Since he has a recovery catalog, he doesn't need to set the machine ID as he did earlier.

```
rman target / catalog rcat_user/rcat_password@catalog
startup force nomount;
run {
allocate channel tape_1 type sbt
parms='env=(nb_ora_serv=rmsrv, nb_ora_client=cervantes)';
restore spfile from autobackup;}
shutdown immediate;
startup nomount;
```

2. Make changes to the SPFILE. Charles must modify his SPFILE to take into account the new server configuration. This means changing memory utilization parameters and setting filename conversion parameters. He must connect to the newly started instance from SQL*Plus and make the necessary changes.

```
alter system set control_files= '/u02/oradata/prod/control01.dbf',
'/u03/oradata/prod/control02.dbf' scope=spfile;
alter system set db_file name convert= "('/u04' , '/u02' ,
'/u05' , '/u02' ,
'/u06' , '/u03' ,
'/u07' , '/u03')" scope=spfile;
alter system set log_file_name_convert= "('/u04' , '/u02' ,
'/u05' , '/u02' ,
'/u06' , '/u03' ,
'/u07' , '/u03')" scope=spfile;
alter system set log_archive_dest_1=
'location=/u02/oradata/prod/arch' scope=spfile;
alter system set db_cache_size=300m scope=spfile;
alter system set shared_pool_size=200m scope=spfile;
shutdown immediate;
startup nomount;
```

3. Restore a copy of the control file. Using the same RMAN session, Charles can do this quite simply (he's already set the DBID). Then, he must mount the database using the restored control file.

```
run {
allocate channel tape_1 type sbt
parms='env=(nb_ora_serv=rmsrv, nb_ora_client=Cervantes)';
restore controlfile from autobackup; }
sql 'alter database mount';
```

4. Configure permanent channel parameters. Now that Charles has a control file restored, he can update the persistent parameters for channel allocation to include the name of the lost server as the media management client. This serves two purposes: it allows RMAN to access the backups that were taken from the lost server, and RMAN will pass this client name to the media management server when any backups are taken from the new server. That way, when the lost server is rebuilt, any backups taken from this stopgap system will be accessible at the newly reconstructed production server.

```
configure default device type to sbt;
configure device type sbt parallelism 2;
configure auxiliary channel 1 device type sbt parms
= "env=(nb_ora_serv=mgtserv, nb_ora_client=cervantes)";
configure auxiliary channel 2 device type sbt parms
= "env=(nb_ora_serv=mgtserv, nb_ora_cient=cervantes)";
```

5. Determine the last archive log for which there is a copy. Because Charles lost the entire server, he also lost any archive logs that had not yet been backed up by RMAN. So, he must query RMAN to determine what the last archive log is for which a backup exists:

```
list backup of archivelog from time = 'sysdate-7';
```

6. With the last log sequence number in hand, Charles performs his restore and recovery and opens the database:

```
restore database;
recover database until sequence=<number>;
sql "alter database open resetlogs";
```

Case #5: Recovering from the Loss of the SYSTEM Tablespace

The Scenario
Nancy, an awesome DBA, is in charge of a large database installation. She shut down her database so the system administrators of her Unix system could do some file system maintenance.

The Problem
Unfortunately, during the maintenance operation, the system administrators at her company managed to drop a file system her database is sitting on. They have since restored the file system, but none of the files from her database are on it, so she must recover them. Nancy lost all datafiles from the following tablespaces: USERS, SYSTEM, and INDEX.

The Solution
Fortunately for Nancy, this is not a complete loss of her system. Her online redo logs and control file are all intact. Because she has to recover the SYSTEM tablespace, she has to do her recovery with the database closed, not open. Otherwise, the recovery is a pretty easy one.

The Solution Revealed   Based on the preceding considerations, the recovery plan that Nancy devises and implements simply requires her to restore the database, as follows:

```
rman target / catalog rcat_user/rcat_password@catalog
startup force mount;
restore tablespace users, system, index;
recover tablespace users, system, index;
alter database open;
```

Case #6: Recovering Online from the Loss of a Datafile or Tablespace

The Scenario

Yang was working on his database the other day when a power surge caused a media failure.

The Problem

Unfortunately for Yang, he lost one file system. This file system contained the following:

- All the datafiles for a tablespace called WORKING_DATA

- One datafile for a tablespace called HISTORICAL_DATA

Several other tablespaces in this database are not related to the tablespace he is recovering, so Yang needs to do this recovery with the database up and running.

The Solution

Yang will restore the WORKING_DATA tablespace and the lone datafile missing from the HISTORICAL_DATA tablespace via RMAN. He first will take offline the tablespace and datafile, so that others may continue to work.

The Solution Revealed   Based on the preceding considerations, Yang devises and implements the following recovery plan:

1. Take offline the WORKING_DATA tablespace:

   ```
   sql "alter tablespace working_data offline";
   ```

2. Take offline the HISTORICAL_DATA datafile needed to recover (Yang has already queried the V$DATAFILE view to determine that it is datafile 13):

   ```
   sql "alter database datafile 13 offline";
   ```

3. Restore and recover the tablespace and datafile using RMAN, and then bring them online:

   ```
   restore tablespace working_data;
   restore datafile 13;
   recover tablespace working_data;
   recover datafile 13;
   sql "alter tablespace working_data online";
   sql "alter database datafile 13 online";
   ```

NOTE
If either tablespace contains active rollback segments, this recovery case may not work. In the event of the loss of active rollback segment tablespaces, you may well be required to do an offline recovery of that tablespace or datafile.

Case #7: Recovering from Loss of an Unarchived Online Redo Log

The Scenario

Today is not Bill's day. A large thunderstorm is raging outside, and Bill has forgotten that his car's soft top is down. To make Bill's day worse, a strike of lightning hits the datacenter and fries several disk drives that Bill's database calls home.

The Problem

Once the hardware is repaired, Bill is horrified to find that he has lost all of his online redo logs, in addition to some of his datafiles. Fortunately, his control file is intact.

The Solution

Bill needs to restore his database by using incomplete recovery. Since the online redo logs are not available, Bill has to accept that there will be some data loss as a result of the recovery.

The Solution Revealed   Based on the preceding considerations, Bill devises and implements the following recovery plan:

1. Determine the last archive log for which there is a copy. Because Bill has to do incomplete recovery, he must query RMAN to determine the last archive log for which a backup exists.

   ```
   startup mount;
   List backup of archivelog from time = 'sysdate-7';
   ```

   The output will look something like the following output—note the log sequence number (log sequence number 3, in bold at the bottom of the report). Since this is the oldest backed up archived redo log, this is as far as Bill can recover to.

   ```
   List of Backup Sets
   ===================

   BS Key  Size        Device Type Elapsed Time Completion Time
   ------- ----------  ----------- ------------ ---------------
   216     48K         DISK           00:00:03     16-AUG-09
           BP Key: 247   Status: AVAILABLE   Tag: TAG20020816T095848
           Piece Name: D:\BACKUP\RECOVER\75E08R2P_1_1

     List of Archived Logs in backup set 216
     Thrd Seq     Low SCN    Low Time  Next SCN   Next Time
     ---- ------- ---------- --------- ---------- ---------
     1    2       1271924    16-AUG-09 1272223    16-AUG-09

   BS Key  Size        Device Type Elapsed Time Completion Time
   ------- ----------  ----------- ------------ ---------------
   218     2K          DISK           00:00:02     16-AUG-09
           BP Key: 249   Status: AVAILABLE   Tag: TAG20020816T100344
           Piece Name: D:\BACKUP\RECOVER\77E08RC1_1_1
   ```

```
List of Archived Logs in backup set 218
Thrd Seq     Low SCN    Low Time   Next SCN   Next Time
---- ------- ---------- ---------- ---------- ---------
  1    3      1272223    16-AUG-09  1272321    16-AUG-09
```

2. With the last log sequence number in hand, perform the restore and recovery and open the database. Bill first restores the database using the **until sequence** parameter. This ensures that all database datafiles will be restored to a point in time no later than log sequence 3. Also note the use of the **force** parameter, which ensures that all datafiles are restored. Recall that one of the requirements for point-in-time recovery is that all database datafiles must be restored to the same consistent point in time. Thus, it's important to restore all datafiles to at least a point in time prior to the point in time Bill wants to recover to.

    ```
    restore database until sequence=4 thread=1 force;
    ```

3. Recover the database until sequence 4 (since the **until sequence** recovers up to but not including the listed sequence number, Bill added one number to the last sequence number, and thus gets 4):

    ```
    recover database until sequence=4 thread=1;
    ```

4. Open the database:

    ```
    sql "alter database open resetlogs";
    ```

NOTE
*If Bill's database had been shut down normally (via **shutdown normal, immediate,** or **transactional***) before the online redo logs were lost, he may well have been able to open the database without needing to recover it.*

Case #8: Recovering Through resetlogs

The Scenario
Bill spent all night doing his recovery and then called in Tim to monitor the restore and finish the database recovery. Once the recovery was done, Tim was supposed to back up the database. One problem is that the business requirement demanded that the database be open and available during the backup.

Tim came in and finished the recovery. Following that, he opened the database using the **resetlogs** command (as previously described in Case #7). Following the business requirements, Tim began the backup, but allowed users access to the database.

The Problem
Unfortunately, on this troubled day, a power surge hit Tim's system, and one of the disk drives of Tim's database was damaged. After another hardware repair, Tim finds that several datafiles were lost. To make matters worse, he has no complete backup of these datafiles since he issued the **resetlogs** command. Fortunately for Tim, this database was upgraded to Oracle Database 11*g* about three months ago. So, Tim is in luck. Since Oracle Database 10*g*, Oracle has made recovery through the **resetlogs** command much easier.

When the database was upgraded to Oracle Database 11*g,* the LOG_ARCHIVE_FORMAT parameter was changed. The DBA added the new %R parameter so that LOG_ARCHIVE_ FORMAT now looks like this:

```
SQL> show parameter log_archive_format
NAME                                 TYPE        VALUE
------------------------------------ ----------- -----------
log_archive_format                   string      ARC%S_%R.%T
```

Now the LOG_ARCHIVE_FORMAT parameter includes the %R placeholder, which means the resetlogs ID is contained in the archived redo logs' filenames. This will save our intrepid DBAs much time during this recovery!

The Solution

Tim is going to use RMAN to recover the database through **resetlogs**. For the most part, this is a recovery that is easy to complete since Oracle Database 10*g.*

The Solution Revealed   Based on the preceding considerations, Tim devises and implements the following recovery plan:

1. Mount the database:

   ```
   /u01>Rman target=/
   RMAN>startup mount;
   ```

2. Tim knows that datafile 4 is missing. It is part of the USERS tablespace. He therefore restores datafile 4:

   ```
   restore datafile 4;
   ```

   NOTE
   *Tim didn't even have to reset the incarnation of the database! This is totally new since Oracle Database 10*g *and makes cross incarnation recovery so much easier.*

3. Having restored the datafile, Tim now recovers it, and then opens the database:

   ```
   recover datafile 4;
   alter database open resetlogs;
   ```

   NOTE
   Did it occur to you that Tim could have opened the database by just taking the datafile offline? He then could have restored the datafile and brought it online after the recovery. Here is an example of the commands he would have used to do an online recovery:

```
rman>startup mount
rman>sql 'alter database datafile 4 offline'
rman>alter database open;
rman>restore datafile 4;
rman>recover datafile 4;
rman>sql 'alter database datafile 4 online'
```

Case #9: Completing a Failed Duplication Manually

The Scenario
Tim decided to use RMAN duplication to create a clone of his production database on a different server. He ran the **duplicate** command, and the datafiles were successfully restored to the new server. The database is very large, and this file restore process took six hours to complete.

The Problem
Tim forgot to move the archive logs over to the auxiliary server for media recovery, so the duplication failed. This means that the cloned database is not fully recovered and does not have a new DBID.

The Solution
Tim isn't worried, though, and he certainly isn't going to take another six hours to perform the file restore. Tim can manually perform the media recovery and then use the DBNEWID utility on the clone database to create a new DBID and finish the duplication process without RMAN's assistance.

The Solution Revealed   Based on the solution he decided upon, Tim will implement the following action plan to complete his failed duplication:

1.   Move the archive logs from the production to the auxiliary site:

```
cd /space/oracle_user/OraHome1/oradata/sun92
tar -cvf arch.tar arch
gzip arch.tar
```

2.   Use FTP to move the arch.tar file to the auxiliary system, and then enter the following:

```
cd /space/oracle_user/OraHome1/oradata/sun92
gunzip arch.tar.gz
tar -xvf arch.tar
```

3.   Perform manual recovery on the database. Tim needs to note the sequence number of the last archive log available on his target database and then to set the recovery to stop at that sequence number. The %s variable in the LOG_ARCHIVE_FORMAT parameter signifies the sequence number and will be in the archive log name. Tim will perform manual recovery from SQL*Plus, connecting locally to his auxiliary database (at the auxiliary site).

```
ORACLE_SID=aux1
export ORACLE_SID
Sqlplus /nolog
SQL> connect / as sysdba
SQL> recover database using backup controlfile until sequence 11 thread 1;
```

4.   Use DBNEWID to create a new DBID for the clone database. Tim's auxiliary database has been mounted, but it has not yet been opened. This is the right state in which to use DBNEWID. If you are unsure of the database state, you can go ahead and remount it without doing any harm.

```
SQL> Shutdown immediate;
SQL> startup mount;
SQL> exit
$ nid target=/
$ sqlplus /nolog
```

```
SQL> connect / as sysdba
SQL> Shutdown immediate;
SQL> startup mount;
SQL> alter database open resetlogs;
```

Case #10: Using RMAN Duplication to Create a Historical Subset of the Target Database

The Scenario

Svetlana is a DBA at an online toy-train reseller. Her production database is under heavy load, with constant updates, inserts, and deletes. Over time, Svetlana has noticed that performance is starting to trail off for data-mining operations against certain inventory-tracking tables.

The Problem

She suspects foul play from the Cost-Based Optimizer, thinking that the Explain Plan might be changing in an adverse way. To test things, she is looking for a way to get a historical snapshot of a subset of production tables. She's considered duplication in the past, but doesn't have enough room on any server to clone the entire production database.

The Solution

Svetlana can use the Oracle Database 11*g* feature of being able to specify tablespaces to skip during duplication. In this way, she can include only tablespaces that are part of the subset that she needs to test. In addition to skipping tablespaces, she can specify an **until** clause in the **duplication** command itself to set the historical point in time that she would like to test against.

The Solution Revealed   Svetlana will be duplicating to the same server that runs her target database, so she needs to make sure that she has her file renaming strategy worked out. Then, she needs to get an auxiliary database started in NOMOUNT mode. After that, she runs her duplication code.

```
$ rman log=/space/backup/pitrdup.out
connect target /
connect auxiliary sys/password@aux1
duplicate target database to aux1
 pfile=/space/oracle_user/OraHome1/admin/aux1/pfile/init.ora
 skip tablespace 'CWMLITE' , 'USERS' , 'ODM' , 'TOOLS'
 until sequence = 11 thread = 1
 logfile
 '/space/oracle_user/OraHome1/oradata/aux1/redo01.dbf' size 5m,
 '/space/oracle_user/OraHome1/oradata/aux1/redo02.dbf' size 5m,
 '/space/oracle_user/OraHome1/oradata/aux1/redo03.dbf' size 5m;
```

The outcome would look something like the following RMAN log. This output has been truncated to save space; we've left the highlights that show what RMAN is doing to get rid of unneeded tablespaces. Remember that when you set an **until sequence** clause in RMAN, the sequence you specify is not included as part of the recover set. So, in Svetlana's code, she has archive logs through sequence 10, but not sequence 11.

```
Recovery Manager: Release 11.2.0.0.2 - Beta on Sun Aug 16 15:41:40 2009
Starting Duplicate Db at 16-AUG-09
using target database control file instead of recovery catalog
allocated channel: ORA_AUX_DISK_1
channel ORA_AUX_DISK_1: SID=280 device type=DISK
Checking that duplicated tablespaces are self-contained
Datafile 4 skipped by request
Datafile 5 skipped by request

contents of Memory Script:
{
   set until scn  945053;
   set newname for datafile  1 to
 "/home/oracle/app/oracle/oradata/aux1/system01.dbf";
   set newname for datafile  2 to
 "/home/oracle/app/oracle/oradata/aux1/sysaux01.dbf";
   set newname for datafile  3 to
 "/home/oracle/app/oracle/oradata/aux1/undotbs01.dbf";
   set newname for datafile  6 to
 "/home/oracle/app/oracle/oradata/aux1/fbs01.dbf";
   restore
   clone database
   skip forever tablespace  "USERS",
 "RECO_CAT"   ;
}
executing Memory Script
executing command: SET until clause
executing command: SET NEWNAME
executing command: SET NEWNAME
executing command: SET NEWNAME
executing command: SET NEWNAME

Starting restore at 16-AUG-09
executing script: Memory Script
executing command: SET until clause
executing command: SET NEWNAME
…
Starting recover at 16-AUG-09
datafile 3 not processed because file is offline
datafile 7 not processed because file is offline

starting media recovery
…
media recovery complete
Finished recover at 16-AUG-09
…
{   Alter clone database open resetlogs;}
executing script: Memory Script
database opened
```

```
printing stored script: Memory Script
{# drop offline and skipped tablespaces
sql clone "drop tablespace  USERS including contents";
# drop offline and skipped tablespaces
sql clone "drop tablespace  RECO_CAT including contents";

executing script: Memory Script
sql statement: drop tablespace  USERS including contents
sql statement: drop tablespace  RECO_CAT including content

Finished Duplicate Db at 16-AUG-09
Recovery Manager complete.
```

Case #11: Recovering from a Lost Datafile (ARCHIVELOG Mode) Using an Image Copy in the Flash Recovery Area

The Scenario

Tim, a senior DBA for a large manufacturing firm, has long lived by the maxim: "Just because you are paranoid doesn't mean they aren't out to get you." In this vein, he has fought hard up the management chain to garner the resources to keep a full database backup on disk, instead of streaming directly to tape. There is not enough room for every datafile backup on disk, so he has chosen those datafiles that represent the data that is most important to operations and that would be the most impacted by a prolonged outage.

After the database was migrated to 11.2, Tim set up his flash recovery area and created an image copy of his most important files in the FRA. He now takes a nightly incremental backup and applies the incremental to the image copy of those files.

The Problem

Disaster strikes, as it invariably does, near the end of month, when massive data processing is taking place. Tim's pager starts chirping only moments before a deluge of angry department heads start calling him. Tim turns off his phone and checks the database. He finds that one of the critical tablespaces has a corrupt datafile, file number 5. The file shows up on disk as 0 bytes. The end-of-month processing cannot continue until the file is recovered.

The Solution

Tim will switch to the datafile running in the FRA, which is current as of the level 1 incremental backup the night before. Then, it's just a matter of applying archive logs to the file to bring it up to the current point in time.

The Solution Revealed   Tim's preparation means his outage will be significantly minimized. Here is his action plan:

1. Switch datafile 5 to the copy in the FRA:

   ```
   [oracle@dex oracle]$ rman target /
   Recovery Manager: Release 11.2.0.0.0
   connected to target database: V112 (DBID=2188245167)

   RMAN> switch datafile 5 to copy;
   ```

```
using target database control file instead of recovery catalog
datafile 5 switched to datafile copy
"/u01/… /V102/datafile/o1_mf_payroll_21v9dhtp_.dbf"
```

2. Recover datafile 5:

```
RMAN> recover datafile 5;

Starting recover at 16-AUG-09
allocated channel: ORA_DISK_1
channel ORA_DISK_1: sid=124 devtype=DISK
allocated channel: ORA_DISK_2
channel ORA_DISK_2: sid=132 devtype=DISK

starting media recovery

archive log thread 1 sequence 208 is already on disk as file
/u01/app/oracle/flash_recovery_area/V102/archivelog/2006_03_19/o1_mf_1_208_
1v9hwr2_.arc
archive log thread 1 sequence 209 is already on disk as file
/u01/app/oracle/flash_recovery_area/V102/archivelog/2006_03_19/o1_mf_1_209_
1v9hzvb_.arc
archive log thread 1 sequence 210 is already on disk as file
/u01/app/oracle/flash_recovery_area/V102/archivelog/2006_03_19/o1_mf_1_210_
1v9j3ts_.arc
archive log thread 1 sequence 211 is already on disk as file
/u01/app/oracle/flash_recovery_area/V102/archivelog/2006_03_19/o1_mf_1_211_
1v9j4jz_.arc
archive log thread 1 sequence 212 is already on disk as file
/u01/app/oracle/flash_recovery_area/V102/archivelog/2006_03_19/o1_mf_1_212_
1v9j59g_.arc
archive log thread 1 sequence 213 is already on disk as file
/u01/app/oracle/flash_recovery_area/V102/archivelog/2006_03_19/o1_mf_1_213_
1v9jc07_.arc
archive log
filename=/u01/app/oracle/flash_recovery_area/V102/archivelog/2006_03_19/o1_
f_1_208_21v9hwr2_.arc thread=1 sequence=208
archive log
filename=
/…/flash_recovery_area/V102/archivelog/2006_03_19/o1_mf_1_209_21v9hzvb_.arc
thread=1 sequence=209
archive log
filename=
/…/flash_recovery_area/V102/archivelog/2006_03_19/o1_mf_1_210_21v9j3ts_.arc
thread=1 sequence=210
archive log
filename=
//flash_recovery_area/V102/archivelog/2006_03_19/o1_mf_1_211_21v9j4jz_.arc
thread=1 sequence=211
media recovery complete, elapsed time: 00:00:03
Finished recover at 16-AUG-09
```

3. Bring datafile 5 online:

```
sql>alter database datafile 5 online;
```

Case #12: Recovering from Running the Production Datafile Out of the Flash Recovery Area

The Scenario

Tim used his FRA setup to significantly minimize the outage due to a corrupted datafile 5. However, now he is running a production datafile out of the FRA, the bad disk has been replaced, and it is time to get the datafile properly restored to its normal location.

The Problem

Using the datafile switch methodology to decrease MTTR is, of course, a very good thing. But it means that the production database is running live with a datafile that is in the flash recovery area. This can hold for a short period, but ultimately the file has to be switched back to the correct, standard location.

The Solution

Tim needs to make a new backup of datafile 5, restore it to the original file location, and then take a temporary outage while he switches back to this datafile and recovers it.

For Tim to restore the production datafile to the production environment, he has to plan a temporary outage. One of the trade-offs of a quick recovery time is this preplanned temporary outage. But, Tim can plan for it to occur deep in the night, when few users will be affected, and can absolutely minimize the amount of time the outage requires.

The Solution Revealed   Tim will use the following action plan:

1. Take a new image copy backup of datafile 5. (Alternatively, Tim could use a previous backup of datafile 5 from tape, but Tim felt that taking a new backup of the file and restoring it from disk would actually be faster than trying to get the tape loaded and restored.)

```
RMAN>  backup as copy datafile 5 format
'/u01/app/oracle/oradata/v102/payroll01.dbf';

Starting backup at 16-AUG-09
using channel ORA_DISK_1
using channel ORA_DISK_2
channel ORA_DISK_1: starting datafile copy
input datafile fno=00005
name=/u01/app/oracle/flash_recovery_area/V102/datafile/o1_mf_payroll_21v9dh
p_.dbf
output filename=/u01/app/oracle/oradata/v102/payroll01.dbf
tag=TAG20060319T124728 recid=27 stamp=585492453
channel ORA_DISK_1: datafile copy complete, elapsed time: 00:00:07
Finished backup at 16-AUG-09
```

2. Restore datafile 5 to the original file location. In the code displayed previously, the file was backed up directly to the original location, so the restore is not required.

3. Switch datafile 5 to the copy in the original location:

```
RMAN> switch datafile 5 to copy;

datafile 5 switched to datafile copy
"/u01/app/oracle/oradata/v102/payroll01.dbf"
```

4. Recover datafile 5 and bring the file online:

```
RMAN> recover datafile 5;

Starting recover at 16-AUG-09
using channel ORA_DISK_1


starting media recovery

archive log thread 1 sequence 221 is already on disk as file
/u01/app/oracle/flash_recovery_area/V102/archivelog/2006_03_19/o1_mf_1_221_
1v9x6vv_.arc
archive log thread 1 sequence 222 is already on disk as file
/u01/app/oracle/flash_recovery_area/V102/archivelog/2006_03_19/o1_mf_1_222_
1v9xbvk_.arc
archive log thread 1 sequence 223 is already on disk as file
/u01/app/oracle/flash_recovery_area/V102/archivelog/2006_03_19/o1_mf_1_223_
1v9xjl5_.arc
archive log thread 1 sequence 224 is already on disk as file
/u01/app/oracle/flash_recovery_area/V102/archivelog/2006_03_19/o1_mf_1_224_
1v9xk6m_.arc
archive log
filename=/u01/app/oracle/flash_recovery_area/V102/archivelog/2006_03_19/o1_
f_1_221_21v9x6vv_.arc thread=1 sequence=221
media recovery complete, elapsed time: 00:00:02
Finished recover at 16-AUG-09
...
SQL> alter database datafile 5 online;

Database altered.

SQL> select name from v$datafile where file#=5;

/u01/app/oracle/oradata/v102/payroll01.dbf
```

Case #13: Using Flashback Database and Media Recovery to Pinpoint the Exact Moment to Open the Database with resetlogs

The Scenario
Farouk did not notice the problem for all of Monday and part of Tuesday morning, because it was not brought to his attention. Finally, Tuesday morning, one of the managers for the woodscrew department called him to say that the Woodscrew database was missing records for some of the most popular woodscrew models. Farouk checked the database and, sure enough, found that someone had deleted rows from a primary table.

The Problem
Finding out who did it, and why, would have to wait. First, it was time to act. The manager said he had noticed the problem around lunchtime on Monday. Farouk checked his Flashback Query option, but found that the transaction was already older than his undo segments. He checked his Flashback Database option and found that he could still flashback nearly 48 hours.

The Solution

Farouk will use Flashback Database to do a point-in-time recovery of his entire database. There is no other option at this time. However, Farouk does not know the exact moment of failure, so he needs to be able to move back and forth in time to pinpoint the very last transaction before the failure. He will use Flashback Database and archive log recovery to scroll back and forth until he finds the correct moment to open the database. He will open the database in READ ONLY mode to check the table.

The Solution Revealed Farouk devises the following plan:

1. Flashback the database to the approximated first point of the failure:

```
RMAN> run {
2> flashback database to time "to_date('2006-03-19 13:30:00',
'YYYY-MM-DDHH24:MI:SS')";
3> }
Starting flashback at 19-MAR-06
allocated channel: ORA_DISK_1

starting media recovery

archive log thread 1 sequence 225 is already on disk as file
/u01/app/oracle/flash_recovery_area/V102/archivelog/2006_03_19/o1_mf_1_225_
1vcwlnx_.arc
archive log thread 1 sequence 226 is already on disk as file
/u01/app/oracle/flash_recovery_area/V102/archivelog/2006_03_19/o1_mf_1_226_
1vcwnlv_.arc
archive log thread 1 sequence 227 is already on disk as file
/u01/app/oracle/flash_recovery_area/V102/archivelog/2006_03_19/o1_mf_1_227_
1vcwt8h_.arc
archive log thread 1 sequence 228 is already on disk as file
/u01/app/oracle/flash_recovery_area/V102/archivelog/2006_03_19/o1_mf_1_228_
1vczqgf_.arc
...
media recovery complete, elapsed time: 00:00:24
Finished flashback at 16-AUG-09
```

2. Select from the affected table to see if the values are in place:

```
sql> alter database open read only;
sql> select count(*) from ws_app.woodscrew where thread_cnt=30;
```

3. Farouk finds the values are not there, so he flashes back again:

```
sql> shutdown immediate;
sq> startup mount;

rman> run {
flashback database to time "to_date('2009-09-16 13:20:00',
'YYYY-MM-DD HH24:MI:SS')";}
```

4. He checks the values again:

```
sql> alter database open read only;
sql> select count(*) from ws_app.woodscrew where thread_cnt=30;
```

5. The values are there, but are missing a few rows that can be gained. So Farouk can shut down the database again and recover a bit further.

```
sql> shutdown immediate;
sql> startup mount;

RMAN> recover database until sequence=227 thread=1;

sql> alter database open read only;
sql> select count(*) from ws_app.woodscrew where thread_cnt=30;
```

6. The values are the best they can be, under the circumstances. Farouk opens the database in read/write mode.

```
sql> shutdown immediate;
sql> startup mount;
sql> alter database open resetlogs;
```

Summary

We hope you found these case studies helpful. We have done our best to provide you with a number of different circumstances that might come your way and solutions you can practice on a test system so that you will be ready to implement them in real life, should the occasion arise. This is also the last chapter in this book on RMAN. We had a ball putting it together, and we hope that you find it useful. Thanks for buying it, and please let us know if you found it to be helpful. We welcome any suggestions for the next revision!

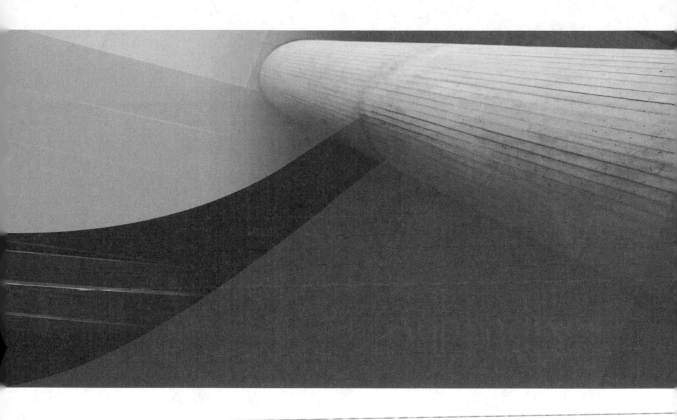

PART
V

Appendixes

APPENDIX
A

RMAN Syntax
Reference Guide

his appendix is a quick reference to the RMAN command set. For each command, you will find a quick description of the command, an associated syntax diagram, a chapter reference, and some examples on the use of that command. This reference also contains a list of the RMAN reserved words. We hope that you find this reference very useful. We expect that it will become very dog-eared from heavy use and will be the main reason you do not loan this book out to anyone!

RMAN Reserved Words

The following table provides a list of reserved words, which you should avoid using when performing RMAN operations:

,	#	(	)
/	{	}	\
<<<	>>>	;	&
–	'	=	^
@	.	:	abort
accessible	active	adviseid	Advise
AES128	AES192	AES256	Affinity
ater	algorithm	allocate	allow
All	alter	and	append
applied	archivelog	area	as
at	atall	autobackup	autoallocate
auxiliary	auxname	available	
backed	backuppiece	backupset	backups
backup	before	between	blockrecover
blocks	block	By	
cancel	catalog	change	channel
checksyntax	check	clear	clonename
clone	clone_cf	closed	cmdfile
command	comment	compatible	completed
compressed	compression	configure	connect
consistent	controlfilecopy	controlfile	Convert
copies	copy	corruption	create
critical	crosscheck	cumulative	current
database	datafile	datafilecopy	datapump
Days	dba	dbid	Db_file_name_convert
db_name	Db_recovery_file_dest	Db_unique_name	debug
decryption	default	Define	delete
deletion	destination	Detail	device
directory	diskratio	disk	Display
dorecover	drop	dump	Duplex
duplicate	duration		

echo	encryption	exclude	execute
exit	expired	export	
failover	failure	filesperset	Files
final	flashback	force	foreign
forever	format	for	from
full			
get	global	grant	group
guarantee	g		
header	high	host	
Identified	identifier	id	immediate
import	inaccessible	incarnation	include
Including	incremental	input	instance
io			
Job			
kbytes	keep	krb	k
Level	libparm	library	like
limit	list	load	logfile
logical	logseq	logs	log
logscn	Low	logseq	
maintenance	mask	maxcorrupt	maxdays
maxopenfiles	maxpiecesize	maxseq	maxsetsize
maxsize	method	minimize	misc
mount	msglog	Msgno	M
names	name	need	New-line
Newname	new	nocatalog	nofau
nochecksum	nodevals	noduplicates	noexclude
nofilenamecheck	nofileupdate	nokeep	nologs
nomount	none	noparallel	noprompt
noredo	normal	not	no
null			
obsolete	offline	off	of
only	on	open	optimization
option	orphan	or	
packages	parallelism	parallelmediarestore	parallel
parameter	Parameter_value_conversion	parms	partial
password	pfile	pipe	platform
plsql	plus	point	policy
pool	preview	primary	print
priority	privileges	proxy	put

Quit

rate	rcvcat	rcvman	readonly
readrate	recall	recoverable	recovery
recover	redundancy	register	release
reload	remove	renormalize	repairid
repair	replace	replicate	report
resetlogs	reset	restart	restore
restricted	resync	retention	reuse
revoke	rpctest	rpc	run
save	schema	scn	script
section	send	sequence	setlimit
setsize	set	shipped	show
shutdown	since	size	skip
slaxdebug	snapshot	spfile	spool
sql	standby	startup	start
step	summary	switch	
tablespaces	tablespace	tag	target
tdes168	tempfile	test	thread
timeout	times	time	to
trace	transactional	transport	type
uncatalog	undo	unlimited	unrecoverable
unregister	until	upgrade	up
using			
validate	verbose	virtual	
window	with		

RMAN Command List

The following table documents each RMAN command. Details on each command are provided in the upcoming section "RMAN Command List Syntax Details."

@	@@	ADVISE FAILURE	ALLOCATE CHANNEL
ALLOCATE CHANNEL FOR MAINTENANCE	BACKUP	CATALOG	CHANGE
CONFIGURE	CONNECT	CONVERT	CREATE CATALOG
CREATE SCRIPT	CROSSCHECK	DELETE	DELETE SCRIPT
DROP CATALOG	DROP DATABASE	DUPLICATE	EXECUTE SCRIPT
EXIT	FLASHBACK DATABASE	GRANT	HOST
IMPORT CATALOG	LIST	PRINT SCRIPT	QUIT

RECOVER	REGISTER DATABASE	RELEASE CHANNEL	REPAIR FAILURE
REPLACE SCRIPT	REPORT	RESET DATABASE	RESTORE
RESYNC_CATALOG	REVOKE	RMAN	RUN
SEND	SET	SHOW	SHUTDOWN
SPOOL	SQL	STARTUP	SWITCH
TRANSPORT TABLESPACE	UNREGISTER	UPGRADE CATALOG	VALIDATE

RMAN Specifier and Operands Lists

The following table provides the names of the various RMAN specifiers and operands.

allocOperandList	archivelogRecordSpecifier	completedTimeSpec
connectStringSpec	datafileSpec	deviceSpecifier
fileNameConversionSpec	forDbUniqueNameOption	foreignLogRecordSpecifier
formatSpec	keepOption	listObjList
maintQualifier	maintSpec	obsOperandList
recordSpec	tempfileSpec	untilClause

RMAN Command List Syntax Details

This section provides detailed information on each of the RMAN commands. For each command you will find

- A summary description of the command

- The syntax diagram for the command

- The relevant chapter in the book in which you can find more details on the command

- Examples of the use of the command

@ Command

The @ command executes a command file (RMAN script) from within RMAN or from within another RMAN command file.

Syntax Diagram

Chapter Reference

Chapter 16 provides more information on this command.

Example

```
@/usr/oracle/rman/script/rmanbackup.scr
```

@@ Command

The **@@** command executes a command file (RMAN script) from within RMAN or from within another RMAN command file. When the **@@** command is used, the script called will be executed from the same location as the calling script.

Syntax Diagram

Chapter Reference

Chapter 16 provides more information on this command.

Example

```
@@rmanbackup2.scr
```

advise failure Command

The **advise failure** command is used to display different repair options for the specified failures. The **advise failure** command displays a summary of the failures identified by the Data Recovery Advisor.

Syntax Diagram

Chapter Reference

Chapter 12 provides more information on this command.

Example

```
advise failure;
```

allocate channel Command

The **allocate channel** command establishes a channel, which is a connection between RMAN and a database instance. At least one channel must be allocated for any backup, recovery, or maintenance operation, though channels are often preconfigured.

Syntax Diagram

Chapter References

Several chapters reference the **allocate channel** command. Chapter 3 discusses automatic channel configuration, which eliminates the need for **allocate channel** most of the time. Chapters 11, 12, and 14 in particular provide direction on the use of the **allocate channel** command.

Examples

```
allocate channel c1 device type disk format '/u01/orabackup/robprod/robprod_%U';

allocate channel t1 DEVICE TYPE 'SBT_TAPE' PARMS
'ENV=(TDPO_OPTFILE=/opt/oraback/rman/delta_${ORACLE_SID}.opt)'
RATE 1 G FORMAT '${ORACLE_SID}_%U' MAXPIECESIZE 20 G MAXOPENFILES 64;
```

allocate channel for maintenance Command

The **allocate channel for maintenance** command is used to allocate a channel in preparation for issuing maintenance commands such as **change**, **crosscheck**, or **delete**. If you have automated channels configured, you should not need to use this command.

Syntax Diagram

Chapter Reference

We do not cover the **allocate channel for maintenance** command in this book, since we expect you are using automated channel allocation. Automated channel allocation is recommended by Oracle.

Example

```
allocate channel for maintenance device type sbt;
```

alter database Command

The **alter database** command allows you to mount or open the target database that RMAN is connected to.

Syntax Diagram

Chapter References

The **alter database** command is demonstrated in Chapters 11, 12, and 14.

Example

```
alter database open resetlogs;
```

backup Command

The **backup** command allows you to back up the database. The **backup** command supports online and offline backups and also supports backups of database files, copies of database files, archived logs, and backup sets.

Syntax Diagram

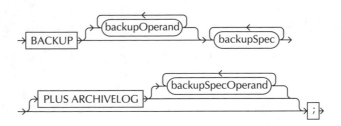

backupOperand Parameter Syntax Diagram

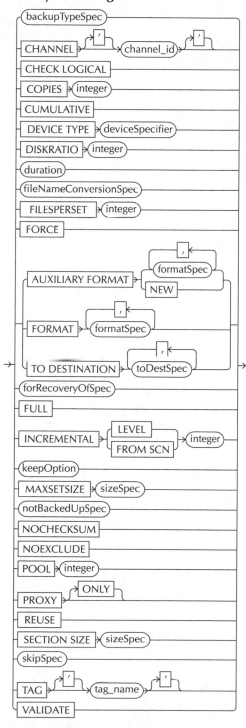

backupSpec Parameter Syntax Diagram

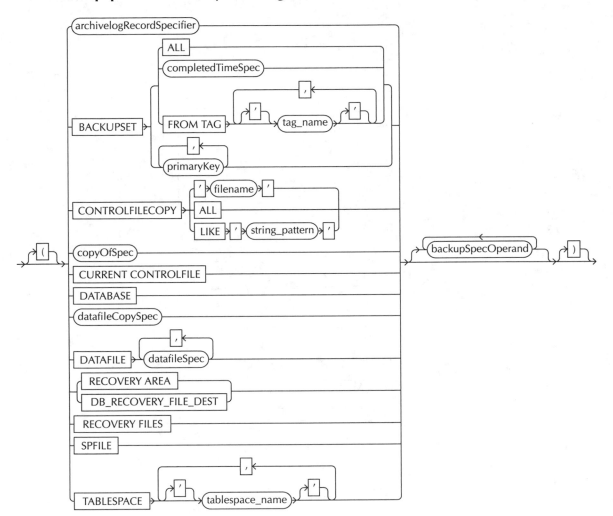

backupSpecOperand Parameter Syntax Diagram

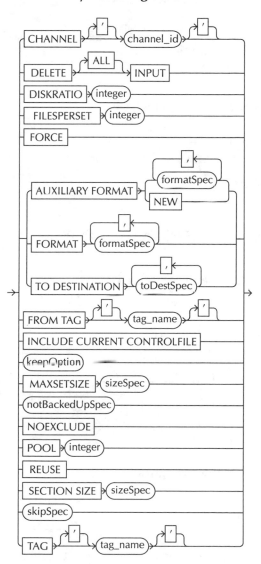

backupTypeSpec Parameter Syntax Diagram

copyOfSpec Parameter Syntax Diagram

datafileCopySpec Parameter Syntax Diagram

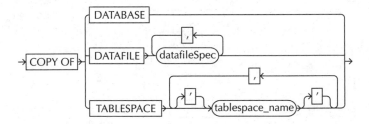

duration Parameter Syntax Diagram

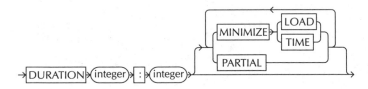

forRecoverOfSpec Parameter Syntax Diagram

notBackedUpSpec Parameter Syntax Diagram

sizeSpec Parameter Syntax Diagram

skipSpec Parameter Syntax Diagram

Chapter Reference

The **backup** command is covered in detail in Chapter 11.

Examples

```
backup database plus archivelog delete input;
backup tablespace users, system;
backup as copy datafile 1,2,3;
backup incremental level=0 check logical database plus archivelog;
```

catalog Command

The **catalog** command allows you to do the following:

- Add metadata about backup pieces and image copies to the database control file and recovery catalog

- Catalog valid backup sets, datafile copies, and archived redo logs in the flash recovery area (FRA)

- Catalog valid backups in ASM, OMF, and user-defined disk locations

- Record a datafile copy as a level 0 backup in the RMAN repository, so you can use that backup as the source of an incremental backup

Syntax Diagram

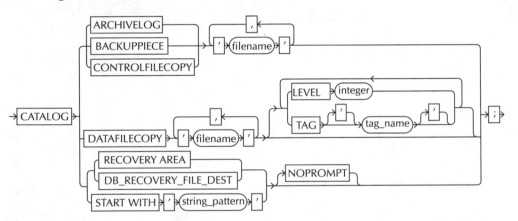

Chapter Reference

Chapter 16 provides more information on the **catalog** command.

Examples

```
catalog recovery area noprompt;

catalog datafilecopy 'd:\oracle\oraback\system01.bak'
'd:\oracle\oraback\users01.bak' level 0;
```

change Command

The **change** command is used to mark backup pieces, image copies, and archived redo logs with a status of AVAILABLE if they currently have a status of UNAVAILABLE. Additionally, this command can totally remove a backup or copy from a repository, and can also be used to modify the retention policy that is effective for a given backup or copy.

Syntax Diagram

maintSpec Parameter Syntax Diagram

forDbUniqueNameOption Parameter Syntax Diagram

resetDbUniqueNameOption Parameter Syntax Diagram

changeFailure Parameter Syntax Diagram

Chapter Reference

Chapter 16 contains a discussion on the use of the **change** command.

Example

```
change backup tag 'Gold_Backup' keep forever nologs;
```

configure Command

The **configure** command allows you to configure persistent RMAN configuration settings. These settings apply to all RMAN sessions, unless they are changed or disabled. These settings are stored in the database control file.

Syntax Diagram

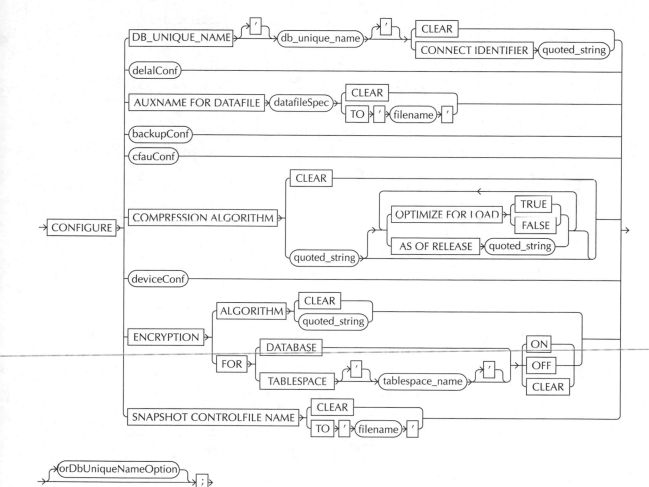

delalConf Parameter Syntax Diagram

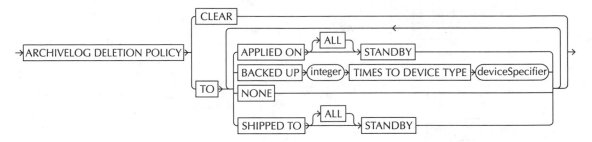

backupConf Parameter Syntax Diagram

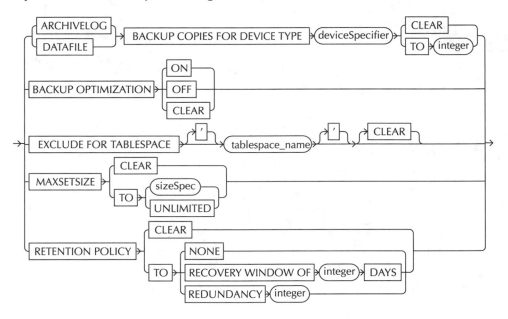

cfauConf Parameter Syntax Diagram

deviceConf Parameter Syntax Diagram

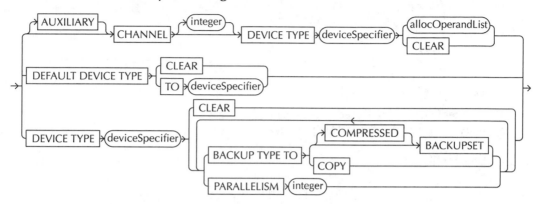

forDbUniqueNameOption Parameter Syntax Diagram

Chapter Reference
The **configure** command is covered in Chapter 3 in detail.

Examples

```
configure retention policy to recovery window of 180 days;
configure backup optimization off;
configure default device type to 'sbt_tape';
configure controlfile autobackup on;
configure controlfile autobackup format for
device type 'sbt_tape' ''%f'';
configure controlfile autobackup format for device type disk to
'/oradata/oraback/rman/robone/%f';
configure device type 'sbt_tape' parallelism 4;
configure device type disk parallelism 2;
configure datafile backup copies for device type 'sbt_tape' to 1;
configure datafile backup copies for device type disk to 1;
configure archivelog backup copies for device type 'sbt_tape' to 1;
configure archivelog backup copies for device type disk to 1;
configure channel device type 'sbt_tape' parms
'env=(tdpo_optfile=/opt/oracle/rman/tdpo_a273.opt)'
rate 9 g format   'a273_%u' maxpiecesize 20 g maxopenfiles 64;
configure channel device type disk format
'/oradata/orabck01/rman/a273/ora_a273_df%t_s%s_s';
configure auxiliary channel device type 'sbt_tape' parms
'env=(tdpo_optfile=/opt/oracle/rman/tdpo_a273_dup.opt)'
```

```
rate 99 g format  'a273_%u' maxpiecesize 20 g maxopenfiles 64;
configure maxsetsize to 20 g;
configure snapshot controlfile name to
'/oradata/orabck01/rman/a273/snapcf_a273.f';
configure channel 1 device type sbt
connect 'sys/robert@test1' parms 'env=(nsr_server=bktest1)';
```

connect Command

The **connect** command is used to connect to the target database, the recovery catalog, or the auxiliary instance from the RMAN prompt.

Syntax Diagram

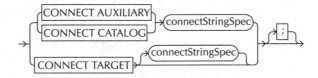

Chapter References

Examples of the **connect** command can be found in many of the chapters in this book.

Examples

```
connect target sys/Robert@maindb
connect catalog rman/rman@rmancat
```

convert Command

The **convert** command is used when moving tablespaces and databases across platforms. If the source and destination platforms are of a different byte-ordering format (endian), then the **convert** command must be used to make the datafiles compatible with the new platform. The **convert** command can also be used to move datafiles in and out of ASM storage.

Syntax Diagram

transportOptionList Parameter Syntax Diagram

skipSpec Parameter Syntax Diagram

convertOptionList Parameter Syntax Diagram

Chapter Reference

The **convert** command is covered in Chapter 14 in more detail.

Examples

```
-- Copy regular datafiles into ASM storage
convert datafile '/disk1/oracle/dbs/my_tbs_f1.df',
'/disk1/oracle/dbs/t_ax1.f'
format '+asmfile';

-- Copy a tablespace from ASM storage to disk.
convert tablespace tbs_2 format '/tmp/tbs_2_%U.df';

-- Convert a database, moving it to a new platform
convert database new database 'convdb'
transport script '/ora01/scripts/transport/transportscript'
to platform 'Microsoft Windows IA (32-bit)'
db_file_name_convert '/ora01/oracle/dbs' '/newora/converted';
```

create catalog Command

The **create catalog** command is used to create the recovery catalog schema.

Syntax Diagram

Chapter Reference

The **create catalog** command is covered in Chapter 10.

Example

```
create catalog tablespace rec_cat;
```

create script Command

The **create script** command allows you to create a stored command script within RMAN. You must have a recovery catalog to use this command.

Syntax Diagram

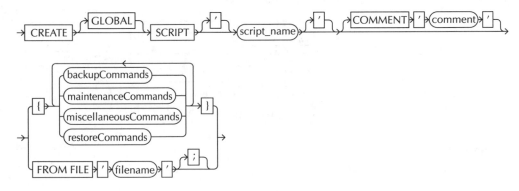

Chapter Reference

The **create script** command is referenced in Chapter 10.

Example

```
create script backup_db {backup database plus archivelog delete input;}
```

crosscheck Command

The **crosscheck** command is used to verify that existing backup sets and backup set pieces listed in the control file or recovery catalog exist on the backup media. Any physical backup file (backup set piece, copy, and so forth) that is not found on backup media is marked as EXPIRED and will not be considered by RMAN for recovery operations. If the backup file later appears, then it will be marked AVAILABLE during a subsequent **crosscheck** operation.

Syntax Diagram

maintSpec Parameter Syntax Diagram

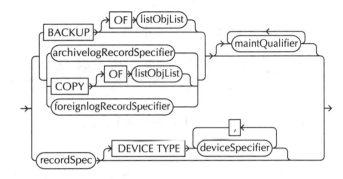

Chapter Reference
The **crosscheck** command is covered in Chapter 16.

Examples

```
crosscheck backup;
crosscheck backup completed between 'sysdate' and 'sysdate-30';
crosscheck archivelog all;
crosscheck archivelog time between 'sysdate' and 'sysdate-30';
```

delete Command
The **delete** command allows you to mark backups and copies in the recovery catalog or control file with a status of DELETED. Once backups or copies are marked DELETED, the status cannot be changed. Objects that are marked as EXPIRED (via the **crosscheck** command) or OBSOLETE (via predefined retention criteria) can be marked DELETED with the **delete** command.

Syntax Diagram

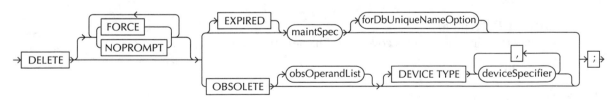

maintSpec Parameter Syntax Diagram

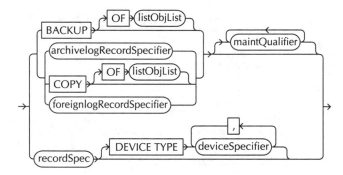

forDBUniqueNameOption Parameter Syntax Diagram

Chapter Reference
The **delete** command is covered in Chapter 16.

Examples

```
delete expired backup;
delete expired archivelog;
```

delete script Command

The **delete script** command allows you to delete any existing RMAN script stored in the recovery catalog.

Syntax Diagram

Chapter Reference
The **delete script** command is covered in Chapter 10.

Example

```
delete script backup;
```

drop catalog Command

The **drop catalog** command is used to drop the recovery catalog schema.

Syntax Diagram

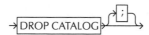

Chapter Reference

The **drop catalog** command is covered in Chapter 10.

Example

```
drop catalog;
```

drop database Command

The **drop database** command is used to remove the target database. If connected to a recovery catalog, the database will also be unregistered. When dropped, RMAN will remove all datafiles, online logs, and control files belonging to the target database.

Syntax Diagram

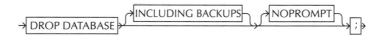

Chapter Reference

The **drop database** command is discussed in Chapter 16.

Example

```
drop database;
```

duplicate Command

The **duplicate** command is used to create either a duplicate database (with a new DBID) or a standby database (with the same DBID) using RMAN backups of a given target database.

Syntax Diagram

dupOptionList Parameter Syntax Diagram

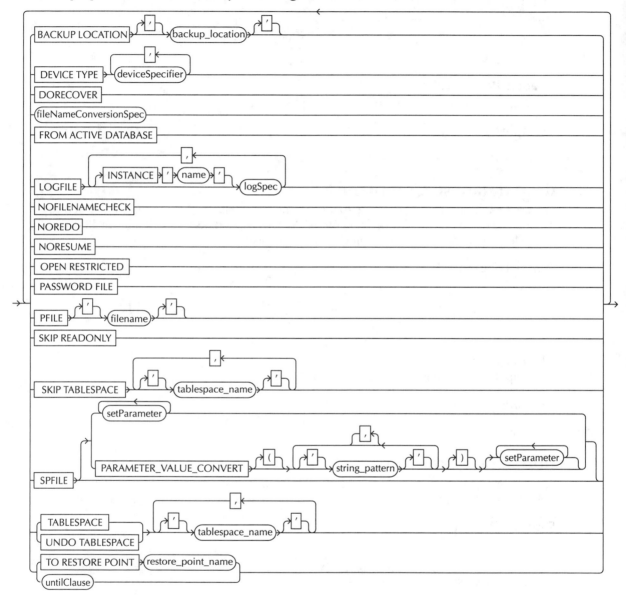

SetParameter Parameter Syntax Diagram

logSpec Parameter Syntax Diagram

dupOptionList Parameter Syntax Diagram

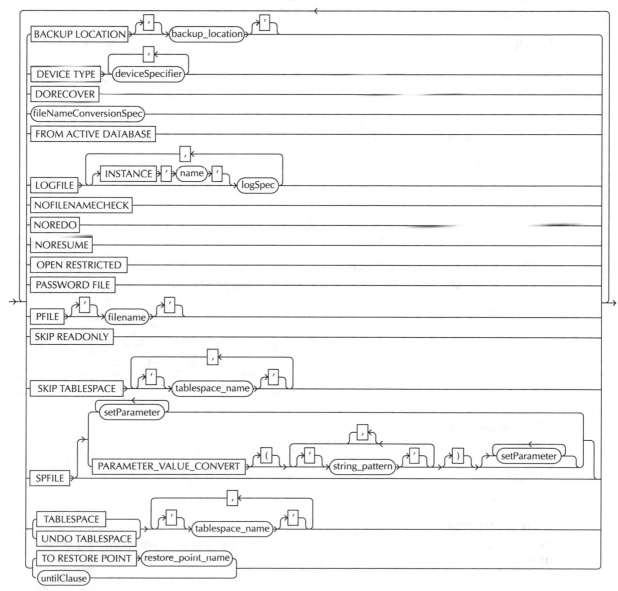

sizeSpec Parameter Syntax Diagram

Chapter References

The **duplicate** command is covered in Chapters 19 and 20.

Example

```
duplicate target database to copydb
db_file_name_convert=
('/ora01/oracle/oradata/olddb/','/ora02/oracle/oradata/newdb/')
    until time 'sysdate- 5'
    skip tablespace oldusers, test
    pfile = ?/dbs/initcopydb.ora
    logfile
      group 1 ('/ora01/oraredo/newdb/redo01_1.f',
               '/ora02/oraredo/newdb/redo01_2.f') size 200k,
      group 2 ('/ora01/oraredo/newdb/redo02_1.f',
               '/ora02/oraredo/newdb/redo02_2.f') size 200k,
      group 3 ('/ora01/oraredo/newdb/redo03_1.f',
               '/ora02/oraredo/newdb/redo03_2.f') size 200k reuse;
```

execute script Command

The **execute script** command is used to execute a stored RMAN script.

Syntax Diagram

Chapter Reference

The **execute script** command is covered in Chapter 10.

Example

```
execute script my_script;
```

exit Command

The **exit** command terminates the operation of your RMAN session and returns you to the OS prompt.

Chapter Reference
The **exit** command is covered in Chapter 3.

flashback database Command
The **flashback database** command allows RMAN to manage Oracle Flashback Database operations. This allows you to reset the database to some previous time or SCN.

Syntax Diagram

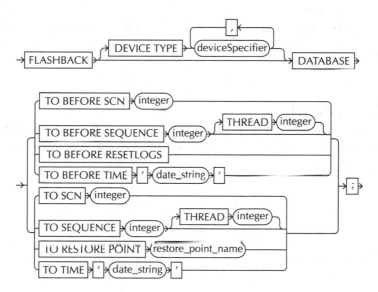

Chapter Reference
Chapter 15 contains a great deal of information on the **flashback** command.

Examples

```
flashback database to scn 669605;
flashback database to timestamp (sysdate-2);
flashback database to timestamp
   to_timestamp('2006-01-03 15:00:00', 'yyyy-mm-dd hh24:mi:ss');
flashback database to restore point "gold_copy";
flashback database to before resetlogs;
```

grant Command
The **grant** command is associated with the RMAN recovery catalog and a feature called a virtual private catalog. This feature provides the ability to restrict access to recovery catalog records by user. The **grant** command provides the means to grant privileges to users to see records in the recovery catalog when a virtual private catalog has been configured.

Syntax Diagram

Chapter Reference

Chapter 9 contains information on the **grant** command and on using a virtual private catalog.

Example

```
grant catalog for database mydb to operator1;
```

host Command

The **host** command invokes the OS command-line subshell from within RMAN. The **host** command also allows you to run a specific OS command from the RMAN prompt.

Syntax Diagram

Chapter Reference

Examples of the **host** command can be found in Chapter 16.

Examples

```
host 'dir';
Host 'ls -al';
host
```

import catalog Command

The **import catalog** command imports the metadata from one recovery catalog schema into a different catalog schema.

Syntax Diagram

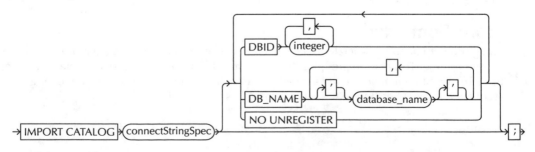

Chapter Reference
Examples of the **import catalog** command can be found in Chapter 10.

Example

```
import catalog cat_owner@oldcatdb;
```

list Command

The **list** command provides information on RMAN backups, such as when they occurred, what files they contain, and how long they took.

Syntax Diagram

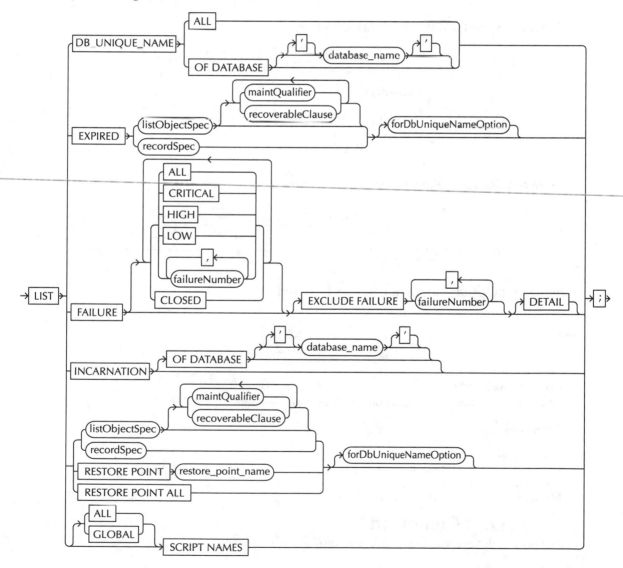

maintQualifier Parameter Syntax Diagram

listObjectSpec Parameter Syntax Diagram

recoverableClause Parameter Syntax Diagram

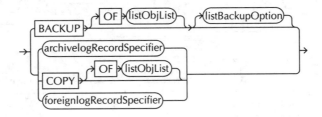

listBackupOption Parameter Syntax Diagram

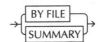

Chapter Reference

Chapter 17 contains information on the RMAN **list** command.

Examples

```
list backup of database;
list backup of database summary;
list backup of datafile;
list backup of archivelog all;
```

print script Command

The **print script** command allows you to display a stored script.

Syntax Diagram

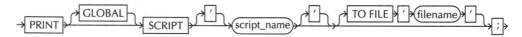

Chapter Reference
Chapter 10 provides more detail on the **print script** command.

Example

```
print script booga_booga;
```

quit Command
Use the **quit** command to exit the RMAN executable.

Chapter Reference
The **quit** command is covered in Chapter 3.

recover Command
The **recover** command is used after a restore to complete recovery of a database, tablespace, or datafile. The **recover** command will extract needed archived redo logs during the recovery process and apply the undo as required.

Syntax Diagram

recoverSpec Parameter Syntax Diagram

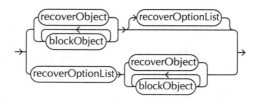

recoverObject Parameter Syntax Diagram

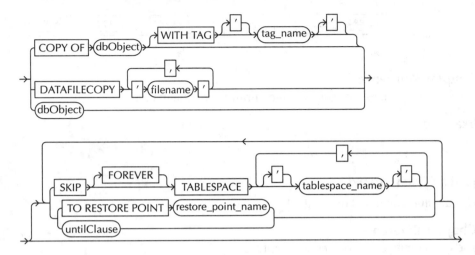

dbObject Parameter Syntax Diagram

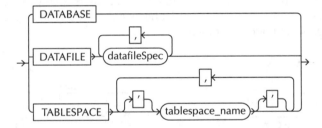

blockObject Parameter Syntax Diagram

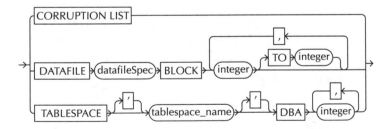

recoverOptionList Parameter Syntax Diagram

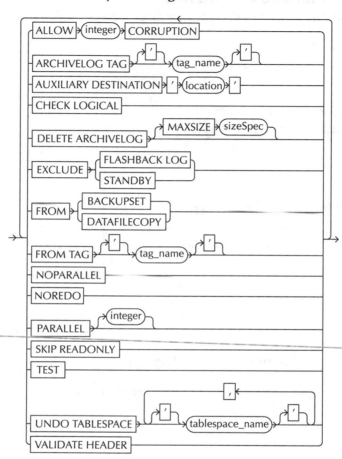

sizeSpec Parameter Syntax Diagram

Chapter References

The **recover** command is documented in several chapters, such as Chapters 12 and 14.

Examples

```
recover database;
recover tablespace users;
recover datafile 1;
```

register database Command

The **register database** command registers the target database in the recovery catalog.

Syntax Diagram

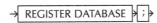

Chapter Reference

The **register database** command is covered in Chapter 10.

Example

```
register database;
```

release channel Command

The **release channel** command is used to release an allocated channel (regular and maintenance). Channels are generally released automatically by RMAN, so this command is rarely needed in practice.

Syntax Diagram

releaseForMaint Parameter Syntax Diagram

Example

```
release channel c1;
```

repair failure Command

The **repair failure** command is used to correct errors that are identified by the Data Recovery Advisor.

Syntax Diagram

Chapter Reference

The **repair failure** command is covered in Chapter 12.

Example

```
repair failure;
```

replace script Command

The **replace script** command is used to replace command scripts stored in the recovery catalog.

Syntax Diagram

Chapter Reference

Chapter 10 contains information on this command.

Example

```
replace script backup_full
{ backup device type sbt database plus archivelog; }
```

report Command

The **report** command is used to provide reporting functionality based on the metadata in the recovery catalog or the database control file. The output from the **report** command can be used to determine the recovery status of the database and its component parts.

Syntax Diagram

needBackupOption Parameter Syntax Diagram

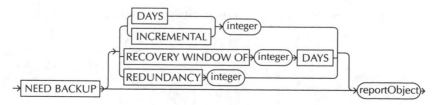

reportObject Parameter Syntax Diagram

atClause Parameter Syntax Diagram

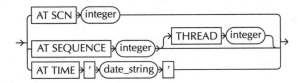

Chapter Reference

Chapter 17 provides information on the **report** command.

Examples

```
report need backup days=3;
report unrecoverable;
report obsolete;
```

reset database Command

The **reset database** command is used after you have created a new database incarnation via the use of the **alter database open resetlogs** command. The **reset database** command is also used to reset the database to a prior database incarnation for recovery purposes.

Syntax Diagram

Chapter Reference

Chapter 14 provides more details on the **reset database** command.

Examples

```
reset database to incarnation 3;
reset database;
```

restore Command

The **restore** command is used to restore database datafiles, datafile copies, archived redo logs, control files, or SPFILEs from backup media in preparation for recovery.

Syntax Diagram

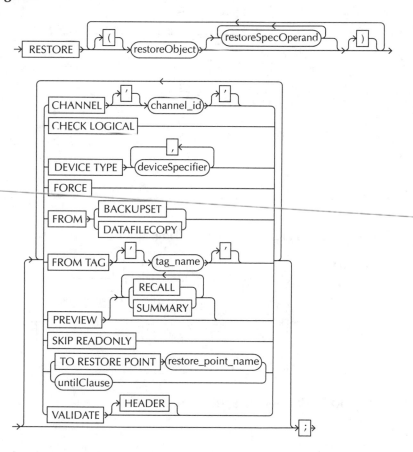

restoreObject Parameter Syntax Diagram

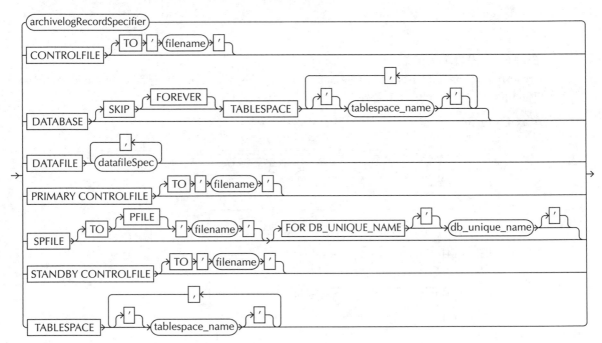

restoreSpecOperand Parameter Syntax Diagram

autoBackupOptList Parameter Syntax Diagram

Chapter References

The **restore** command is covered in detail in Chapters 12 and 14.

Examples

```
restore database;
restore tablespace user_data, user_index;
restore datafile 1,2,3,4,5;

CONNECT TARGET /
STARTUP NOMOUNT;
SET DBID 660055374;
RESTORE CONTROLFILE FROM TAG 'monday_cf_backup';
ALTER DATABASE MOUNT;

RMAN> RUN
{
  SET ARCHIVELOG DESTINATION TO '/oratmp/arch_restore';
  RESTORE ARCHIVELOG ALL;
}
```

resync catalog Command

The **resync catalog** command is used to resynchronize the recovery catalog with the database control file.

Syntax Diagram

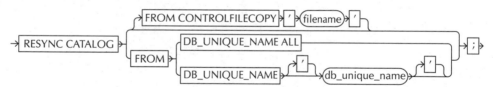

Chapter Reference

Chapter 10 contains information on the **resync** command.

Example

```
resync catalog;
```

revoke Command

The **revoke** command is associated with the RMAN recovery catalog and a feature called a virtual private catalog. This feature provides the ability to restrict access to recovery catalog records by user. The **revoke** command provides the means to remove previously granted privileges from users to see records in the recovery catalog when a virtual private catalog has been configured.

Syntax Diagram

Chapter Reference

Chapter 10 contains information on the **revoke** command and using a virtual private catalog.

Examples

```
revoke catalog for database mydb from operator1;
revoke all privileges from operator2;
```

run Command

The **run** command is used to compile and execute one or more RMAN commands. The commands to be executed are contained within a set of braces, called a **run** block. An opening brace is used, followed by RMAN commands. Once the final RMAN command is listed, a closing brace causes the entire set of commands to execute when you press ENTER.

Syntax Diagram

backupCommands Parameter Syntax Diagram

maintenanceCommands Parameter Syntax Diagram

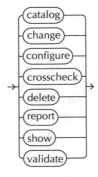

miscellaneousCommands Parameter Syntax Diagram

restoreCommands Parameter Syntax Diagram

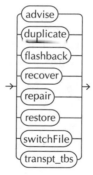

Chapter References

The **run** command is demonstrated in many chapters in this book, such as Chapter 11.

Example

```
RMAN> RUN
{
  set archivelog destination to '/oratmp/arch_restore';
  restore archivelog all;
}
```

send Command

The **send** command is used to send a vendor-specific string to one or more channels. Because these strings are vendor specific, they should be documented in your vendor-supplied media management layer documentation.

Syntax Diagram

Chapter References

See Chapters 4 through 9 for more on the MML layer and valid vendor strings.

Example

```
send 'env=serv_bck01';
```

set Command

The **set** command configures RMAN settings for the current RMAN session. It is used to configure settings that are not persistent, or to temporarily change persistent settings for a given session. The **set** command comes in two different flavors. The **set_run_option** parameters can be used within the confines of a **run** block. The **set_rman_option** parameters are set from the RMAN prompt.

Syntax Diagram

setRmanOption Parameter Syntax Diagram

setRunOption Parameter Syntax Diagram

setRmanOrRunOption Parameter Syntax Diagram

Chapter Reference

The **set** command is documented in Chapter 12.

Examples

```
set dbid 676549873;
set until time '1/10/2006 13:45:00';
set controlfile autobackup format for device type disk
to '/u01/oraback/cntrlf_%f.bak';
```

show Command

The **show** command is used to display the current persistent configuration settings for the database that RMAN is connected to. These settings come from the control file of that database.

Syntax Diagram

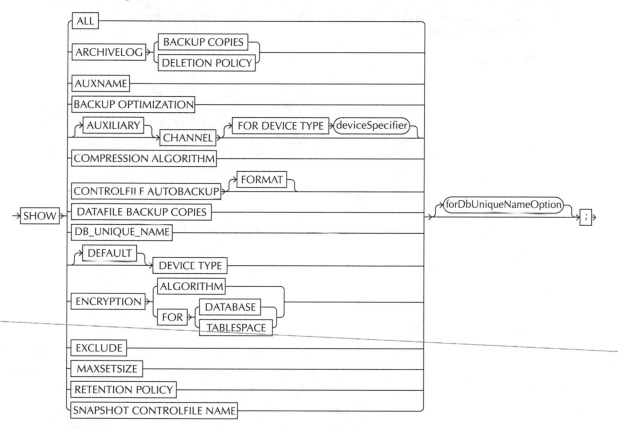

forDbUniqueNameOption Parameter Syntax Diagram

Chapter Reference

The **show** command is documented in Chapter 3.

Examples

```
show all;
show retention policy;
```

shutdown Command

The **shutdown** command is used to shut down the target database and is equivalent to the SQL*Plus **shutdown** command.

Syntax Diagram

Chapter References

The **shutdown** command is demonstrated in several chapters in this book.

Examples

```
shutdown abort;
shutdown immediate;
```

spool Command

The **spool** command is used to spool the output of RMAN operations to an operating system file.

Syntax Diagram

Example

```
spool log to 'rmanoutput.log'
```

SQL Command

The **SQL** command is used to execute a SQL statement from the RMAN prompt. Single SQL statements are placed within single quotes.

Syntax Diagram

Chapter References
This command is documented in many places in this book.

Example

```
sql 'alter tablespace mytbs offline immediate';
```

startup Command
The **startup** command is used to start the target database and is equivalent to the SQL*Plus **startup** command.

Syntax Diagram

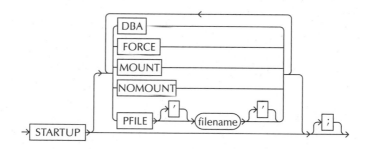

Chapter References
The **startup** command is documented in several chapters of this book.

Examples

```
startup nomount;
startup;
```

switch Command
The **switch** command causes an RMAN datafile copy to become the current database datafile. This command is used frequently if the database datafiles must be restored to a location other than their original location, and is generally associated with an RMAN **set newname** command. This command is equivalent to the SQL statement **alter database rename file** when applied to database datafiles.

Syntax Diagram

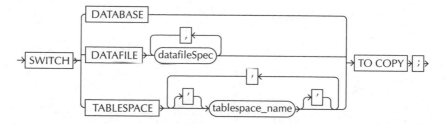

switchFile Parameter Syntax Diagram

Chapter Reference

Chapter 14 provides details on this command.

Example

```
run
{
  set newname for datafile '/disk7/oracle/tbs11.f'
    to '/disk9/oracle/tbs11.f';
  restore tablespace tbs_1;
  switch datafile all;
  recover tablespace tbs_1;
  sql "alter tablespace tbs_1 online";
}
```

transport tablespace Command

The **transport tablespace** command is used to create transportable tablespace sets from RMAN backups, instead of using the actual datafiles of the source database. You can also use the **transport tablespace** command to create transportable tablespace sets that can be recovered to a specific point in time.

Syntax Diagram

Transp_tbs_optlist Parameter Syntax Diagram

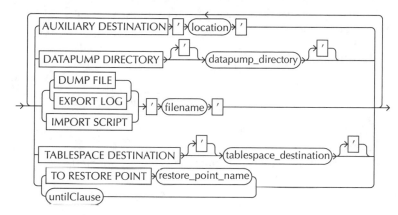

Chapter Reference

Chapter 14 covers transportable tablespaces and RMAN.

Example

```
transport tablespace tbs_2, tbs_3
    tablespace destination '/disk1/transportdest'
    auxiliary destination '/disk1/auxdest'
    UNTIL SCN 251982;
```

unregister database Command

The **unregister database** command removes a database and its associated records from the recovery catalog.

Syntax Diagram

Chapter Reference

The **unregister database** command is covered in Chapter 3.

Examples

```
unregister database;
unregister database oldprod;
```

upgrade catalog Command

The **upgrade catalog** command is used to upgrade the recovery catalog from an older version of RMAN to a newer version of RMAN.

Syntax Diagram

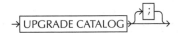

Chapter Reference

Chapter 10 contains information on the **upgrade catalog** command.

Example

```
upgrade catalog;
```

validate Command

The **validate** command is used to check and validate that a given backup set can be restored. All pieces of that backup set will be scanned by RMAN during the operation.

Syntax Diagram

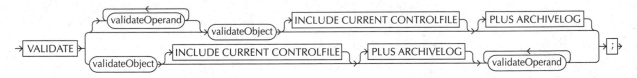

validateObject Parameter Syntax Diagram

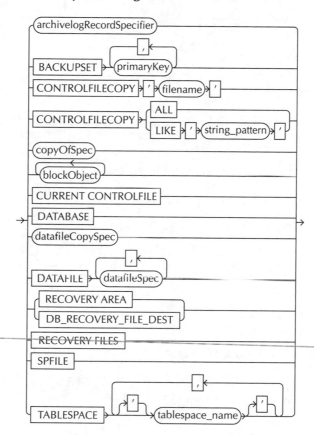

copyOfSpec Parameter Syntax Diagram

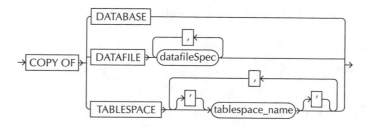

blockObject Parameter Syntax Diagram

validateOperand Parameter Syntax Diagram

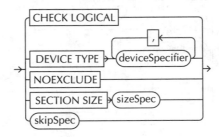

skipSpec Parameter Syntax Diagram

Chapter Reference

Chapter 16 contains information on the **validate** command.

Example

```
validate backup set 1330;
```

RMAN Subclauses Syntax Details

These subclauses appear in a number of different RMAN commands, so they are all listed in this common section for ease of reference. See the corresponding section of any related commands for examples on the use of these subclauses.

allocOperandList

This operand specifies control options related to a channel.

Syntax Diagram

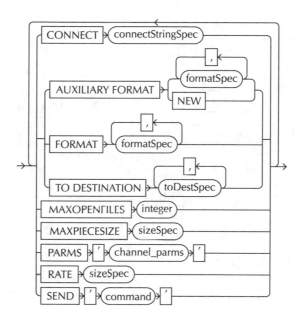

archivelogRecordSpecifier

This subclause is used to define the recovery period or archived redo logs to be applied during recovery.

Syntax Diagram

archlogRange Parameter Syntax Diagram

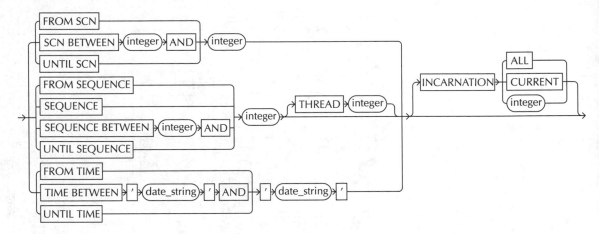

completedTimeSpec

This command is used to define when a backup or copy was completed. It is commonly used with the **list**, **crosscheck**, and **delete** commands.

Syntax Diagram

connectStringSpec

This subclause is used to define the username, password, and Oracle Net service name when connecting to a target database, a recovery catalog, or an auxiliary database.

Syntax Diagram

datafileSpec

This subclause is used to define a datafile by filename or datafile number for various operations, such as datafile recovery.

Syntax Diagram

deviceSpecifier

This subclause defines the type of storage to be used by the given RMAN operation.

Syntax Diagram

fileNameConversionSpec

This specification defines patterns that should be used to generate new datafile names based on old datafile names. See the sections for the **backup**, **convert**, and **duplicate** commands for more details.

Syntax Diagram

forDbUniqueNameOption

This subclause is used to specify if all databases or a specific database is being addressed in a specific RMAN-related Data Guard operation.

Syntax Diagram

foreignlogRecordSpecifier

This subclause defines a specific set of foreign archived redo logs to be used in the operation.

Syntax Diagram

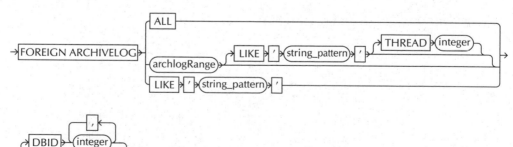

formatSpec

This specifier is used to define a specific filename format. This can include normal file names or ASM disk groups.

Syntax Diagram

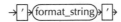

keepOption

This subclause is used to define the retention policy related to a given backup or copy.

Syntax Diagram

listObjList

This subclause is used to indicate specific datafiles and archived redo logs to be affected by the parent command.

Syntax Diagram

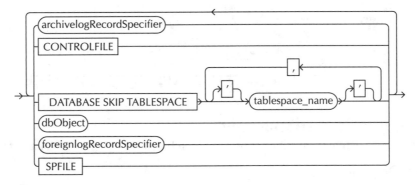

dbObject Parameter Syntax Diagram

maintQualifier

This subclause is used to define database files or archived redo logs in specific RMAN commands such as **list**, **crosscheck**, **delete**, and **switch**.

Syntax Diagram

maintSpec

This subclause is used to define database files or archived redo logs in specific RMAN commands such as **change**, **crosscheck**, and **delete**.

Syntax Diagram

obsOperandList

This subclause is used to define criteria used to mark backups and datafile copies as OBSOLETE.

Syntax Diagram

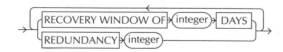

recordSpec

This subclause defines which objects that commands such as **change**, **crosscheck**, **delete**, and **list** will work on.

Syntax Diagram

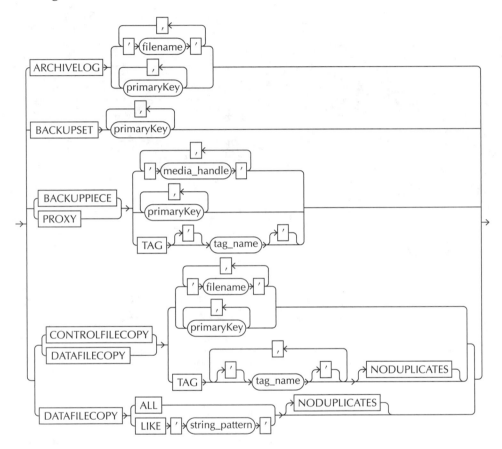

tempfileSpec

This subclause is used to define tempfiles by name or file number that should be operated on by the parent command.

Syntax Diagram

toDestSpec

This subclause is used to specify a directory or an Automatic Storage Management disk group for disk backups for the RMAN operation that the subclause is used in.

Syntax Diagram

untilClause

This subclause defines a limit based on time, SCN, restore point, or log sequence number that is referenced by the parent RMAN command.

Syntax Diagram

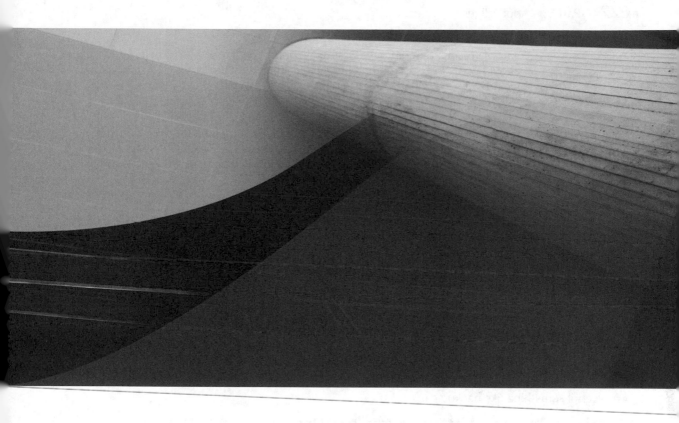

APPENDIX B

RMAN Scripting Examples

e have gotten a number of requests for scripts related to RMAN. The nice thing about RMAN is that scripting it is a pretty straightforward process. In this chapter, we provide you with some basic scripts for both Windows and Linux to get you started.

These scripts assume that you are using the Oracle flash recovery area (FRA), which will manage disk space and backup retention for you. If you are not using the FRA, perhaps you might want to customize these scripts for your own needs. We will leave that to your ingenuity and skill!

RMAN Scripts for Windows

These scripts were written and tested using Windows XP. First, we give you an example batch script that will call RMAN for a backup of the database and the archived redo logs. We will then show you a method of scheduling these scripts from the operating system. Note that this is just one method of scheduling automated backups. You might also choose to use Oracle Enterprise Manager (OEM) to schedule and manage your backups. Using Oracle Enterprise Manager is covered in Chapter 13, so you can reference that chapter for information on scheduling backups in OEM.

Creating a Windows Script to Schedule Backups

This is a pretty basic script; you might want to augment it for incremental backups, backup validation, or other operations. Note that the script will return an error message if the backup fails. To create this script, you might use Notepad, or some other text editor, and might call this script something like backup.bat.

```
rem ********************************************************************
rem * Script Name: backup.bat
rem * Script Purpose: This script will call RMAN and execute the command
rem * file specified on the command line.
rem * Usage backup.bat <oracle_sid> <backup|arch>
@echo off
rem
rem RMAN BACKUP SCRIPT
rem For WIN XP
rem
echo %1
set oracle_sid=%1
if "%2" == "backup" rman target=/ cmdfile=c:\oracle\scripts\backup.scr
if not ERRORLEVEL 0 echo "WARNING - FAILURE OCCURRED"
if "%2" == "arch" rman target=/ cmdfile= c:\oracle\scripts\arch.scr
if not ERRORLEVEL 0 echo "WARNING - FAILURE OCCURRED"
```

Note that this script calls two command files, backup.scr and arch.scr, which in this case are located in the c:\oracle\scripts directory.

Here is the backup.scr script:

```
Backup as compressed backupset database plus archivelog delete input;
```

This is the arch.scr script:

```
Backup as compressed backupset archivelog all delete input;
```

Again, each of these scripts would be created using a text editor and placed in the c:\oracle\ scripts directory. If you put them somewhere else, you will need to edit the backup.bat script to point to the correct location of these scripts.

Scheduling the Backup

Now, we want to schedule the backup. We will use the Windows schtasks utility to perform this operation. In our experience, schtasks is a rarely used but powerful scheduling utility. In this example, we are scheduling a daily database backup using the backup.bat file. We also have an example of scheduling the archived redo log backup and an example of how to remove a scheduled task:

```
schtasks /create /tn "database_backup" /sc weekly /d SUN /st 14:50:00 /tr
"c:\bc\rman\backup.bat rob10r2 backup>\>c:\bc\rman\backup.output"
rem schtasks /delete /tn "database_backup"
schtasks /create /tn "archivelog_backup" /sc daily /st 14:50:00 /tr
"c:\bc\rman\backup.bat rob10r2 arch>\>c:\bc\rman\backup.output"
```

You have a number of scheduling options when using the schtasks scheduler. The schtasks scheduler will request the login ID of the user that will be running the job.

RMAN Scripts for Unix

These scripts were written and tested on Red Hat Linux Version 5. In this section, we have a backup script (backup.ksh) and the related command-line files that will be used to execute the actual backup. You can use Cron or at to schedule this script in Unix. First, here is our example shell script for our Unix backup:

```
#/bin/ksh
# Script name: backup.ksh
# Usage: backup.ksh <ORACLE_SID> <backup|arch>
# Note: We assume the oracle environment is already setup except for
# ORACLE_HOME. If not, you will need to setup your environment correctly.
set ORACLE_SID=$1
if [ "$2"="backup" ]; then
    rman target=/ cmdfile=/home/oracle/scripts/backup.scr
fi
if [ "$2"="arch" ]; then
    rman target=/ cmdfile=/home/oracle/scripts/arch.scr
fi
```

The backup.scr script is the same as you saw earlier:

```
Backup as compressed backupset database plus archivelog delete input;
```

As is the arch.scr script:

```
Backup as compressed backupset archivelog all delete input;
```

APPENDIX C

Setting Up an RMAN Test Environment

s the complexity of production enterprise environments grows with each passing year, we DBAs are finding the same complexity creeping into our test environments. For example, in *Oracle9i RMAN Backup & Recovery,* the test environment was seemingly complex for us: a Windows laptop for minor tweaks and screen shots, another Windows server for more robust testing, and a Sun Blade 150 for multi-OS interaction and Unix commands. Among these three machines, we were able to do all technical reviews (combined with years of actual experience in the workplace, of course).

For the 10*g* RMAN book, the test environment included two Linux boxes with a shared FireWire disk drive (running RAC, of course), Matthew's trusty Windows laptop, that old Sun Blade, and a stand-alone Linux box. And Matthew still went hunting with his colleagues looking for other RAC clusters, tape storage jukeboxes, and Oracle Enterprise Manager repositories.

That being said, things have taken an interesting turn since the last book. We authors had to travel significantly during the production of this book, so the needs changed dramatically, from a tactical standpoint. Because of the up and down, thrashed and trashed nature of B&R testing, testing from a remote location can be difficult. And you can't connect to your datacenter from a plane yet. Yet. In addition, this was the first time that we wrote against Beta code (long story), so there are plenty of hiccups that simply prevented traditional solutions.

So, what did our test environment look like this time? One late-model Apple MacBook Pro, running VMWare Fusion, and an external hard drive. That's it. (Okay, Matthew still relied on those RAC clusters in the datacenter.) He installed RHEL 5, copied the VMWare slice, and had a multiserver environment running from his laptop—gotta love modern times. Now, Matthew had a completely mobile lab environment, with plenty of hard-drive space and a built-in way to trash everything and start over using his virtual snapshots. The only limit was that his late-model Mac had 3GB of memory, so he had to pick and choose environments carefully when running them simultaneously. With new models running up to 8GB, Matthew's looking forward to having that problem solved soon as well.

Granted, as discussed later in this appendix, this does not, in any way, come close to looking like a true production environment. Therefore, he can't do any performance benchmarking on his laptop, or expect that he has ensured that scripts are free of bugs in production. But, with the exact OS running (RHEL) and exact database version, he has gone a long way toward assurance that he knows what he's doing and how it will behave.

As stated back in *Oracle9i RMAN Backup & Recovery,* test environments can be tricky to describe or to provide advice about. Every shop has its own concept of what testing is required, and at what level, for application design, quality assurance, version control, and so forth. And with RMAN playing a more integral role in a wider array of DBA activities, it's increasingly difficult to separate an RMAN test environment from other test environments. But, you are looking at this book now, and we have opinions on testing backup strategies. As we like to say, everyone has a backup strategy. Few have a recovery strategy. Testing backups is only a fraction of the work. If you do not test your recovery strategies, then you don't have backups, no matter how many files you've written to how many thousands of dollars' worth of equipment.

A test environment for backup and recovery is different from other testing environments. First of all, you have to be able to remove datafiles, or even the entire database, on a whim, without having to clear it with other users. In other words, you need your own database. Or two. If you begin testing RMAN functionality on a shared database, pretty soon you'll either start getting angry phone calls from other users, or find yourself locked out of the machine by the SA.

A backup and recovery test environment is simply too volatile to share. Think about it from the other end: you're busy testing a backup yourself, when suddenly the backup aborts because someone started removing datafiles in order to test their own restore and recovery.

On the other hand, you need to test your strategies in an environment that most closely matches that of your production databases. Therefore, you can't always run in isolation, because you might need to tune your backup on a large, production-grade server that has the same kind of load as production.

What we suggest, then, is that you approach RMAN backup and recovery testing as a two-tiered investigation: First, get comfortable with functionality and behavior in the isolation of a small test server. Second, take the lessons you've learned, and schedule time to test on a larger, production-grade database server. That way, you can schedule time on a test box for a backup/recovery test outage, and avoid spending that valuable time trying to learn lessons that you could have figured out on your workstation.

So, what does this approach look like more specifically? The answer is provided in this appendix.

The Test Box

The first-level test machine for RMAN functionality doesn't need to be a supercomputer. In fact, you should think of the first level of testing as just a rehearsal—you're reading through your lines, getting the placement right, and talking through the steps with the other actors and the director.

Match Your Production Environment

If possible, your RMAN testing should take place on the same operating system that you run in production. This is a rather humorous thing to say, we know: who has a single OS in their environment anymore? Anyway, if you will be backing up only Solaris servers, it makes sense to invest a little money in a Sun workstation. That way, you can begin production environment matching as soon as possible.

Go Cheap

It's not that critical to have your first wave of testing take place on the same OS as your production environment. RMAN acts the same on all platforms, and the exercises in this book work on all platforms. So, if you're in the market for an RMAN test box, we have only two words: go cheap. Buy a commodity-priced computer that runs Windows or Linux. I've grown quite fond of my cut-rate Linux cluster that Scott Jesse outlined in the Oracle Press book *Oracle Database 10g High Availability with RAC, Flashback, and Data Guard* (2004). It is a two-node RAC tester for under $1,500, bought refurbished from Dell's Outlet. As far as what to look for in a cheap test environment, we provide the following advice:

- **Processor speed** Don't worry about processor speed at the RMAN proof-of-concept level. RMAN simply does not rely on CPUs that heavily. As you move into heavy parallelization in production, CPU speeds might grow in testing importance. Even if you monitor for performance at this level, the data is meaningless when compared with your production environment. Instead, spend money on other resources, mainly disk space and memory.

■ **Memory** You need enough memory to run three Oracle instances simultaneously, along with your media management software. If you will be testing with OEM or some other management software package, factor that in as well. This means that you need 2GB minimum. Don't cut corners on memory, or you will get sucked down into time-consuming swap rat holes from which there is no escape.

■ **Disk space** Disks are cheap, and you don't need some SCSI disk or anything, just space. Speed, again, is not important at this level. A 200GB hard drive should be sufficient. You're doing concept testing at this level, so you can limit the size of databases to keep things under control. But keep in mind that you're going to have more than one database, and you will also be backing up to disk (most likely), so you need space for RMAN backup pieces, as well. So load up on disk space if you can.

If you decide to do a RAC tester, you need an external SCSI or FireWire drive in addition to whatever you load internally into your box. Again, consult *Oracle Database 10g High Availability with RAC, Flashback, and Data Guard* for a blow-by-blow description of RAC home clusters.

The Oracle Configuration

After you get your test box up and running, you need to think about your Oracle installation and configuration. This step depends on what you need to test: Will you be backing up multiple versions of Oracle? Will you be using OEM?

Multiple Homes

If you will be testing multiple versions of Oracle, be sure to install them in chronological order from oldest to newest; for example, install version 9.2.0 before 10.1.0, and 10.1.0 before 10.2.0. Before you get very far, patch Oracle to the latest patch level. There are always RMAN bugs getting fixed, so it makes sense to be at the most recent patch level.

Creating Databases

Obviously, you need at least one database created in each ORACLE_HOME that you have installed. These databases may be default databases created during Oracle installation, but an even better scenario would be to use databases that are configured somewhat like production databases. From a size perspective, that may not be possible, but you can scale datafile sizes down while keeping the same number of datafiles and tablespaces.

In addition, try scaling down the memory utilization of these test boxes to be as low as possible. You won't actually be doing that much processing, so you don't need a lot of buffer cache available. The smaller you keep the System Global Area (SGA), the better off your little test box will be.

You also need a recovery catalog database that is separate from the target databases that you are using for testing. We always recommend that your recovery catalog database be the most recent version, so put this in a 11.2 home. In a pinch, this can also be used as a target database, but try to keep your recovery catalog database out of the mix of databases that you blow away and rebuild. It just makes life easier. If at all possible, put your recovery catalog database on a different server. Put it on a Windows workstation or an old Linux box. Keep it out of the crash-and-burn destruction path.

Using Oracle ASM

If you plan to test Oracle's volume manager, Automatic Storage Management (ASM), you have to make preparations when you first configure your RMAN test box. In a production environment, you would simply add full, raw disks to an ASM disk group. In a test environment, if you want to test multiple ASM disk groups, you can simply use logical partitions on a single disk. But this means you have to think ahead and create some unused, raw partitions on your disks before you get too far into your OS setup.

Oracle Enterprise Manager

If you plan to use OEM, make sure there is enough memory to do so. As you learned in Chapter 13, there are two flavors of OEM you can choose from: Database Control and Grid Control. From a testing perspective, it might make sense to go with Database Control to save on resources and administration headaches. However, make the choice that matches your production environment: if you deploy Grid Control management in production, use Grid Control to manage RMAN backups in the test environment.

That being said, try to avoid using production Grid Control for RMAN test environments. The databases will be down, up, down, lost, trashed, crashed, and lost. This means lots of alerts will be sent to the Oracle Management Service (OMS) and, consequently, e-mailed out to people. Avoid bot spam! If you have not already deployed a test Grid Control environment for your enterprise, get one set up for your RMAN backups, and then offer it to others for testing purposes.

For Database Control, expect a memory hit of 150 to 200MB per instance. Also, Database Control makes heavy use of CPUs and uses up database space. Database Control generates about 200MB of archive logs per day just by itself, with an idle database.

For Grid Control, you need a 2GB system all by itself for the repository database and OMS. Factor it in as a separate system. On the RMAN test system itself, the agent will use only about 60MB of memory and enough CPU to run its Perl scripts.

OEM, either Database or Grid Control, is highly dependent on a stable and predictable networking sublayer, which means you cannot constantly change the hostname or IP address. Sorry. It's just easier that way. If you have to, create your own subnet and manually assign dummy IP addresses in the hosts files. The easiest checks you can implement to ensure everything will operate correctly are the **nslookup** command on the hostname and a reverse lookup on the IP address.

Media Management Considerations

If possible, you should install a version of the media management client that you will be using in production. Then, install the Oracle Plug-In and do the backups to tape the same as you would in production. This gives you the best opportunity to anticipate what to expect when you implement your strategy in your enterprise.

If you can't get access to the media management product that is used for your enterprise, there is little alternative left. The best option is to try Oracle Secure Backup, as outlined in Chapter 5 of this book.

If you simply need to test tape channel allocations, or the process of staging the flash recovery area to tape, you still have access to the Oracle SBT API, which enables you to write "tape" backups to a disk location. This is described in the RMAN Workshop "Test Tape Channels with the Oracle Default SBT Interface" in Chapter 4.

The RMAN Configuration

Now that you have your system set up with Oracle installed and databases built, we have a few hints on the testing process:

■ *Have a cold backup that remains untouched.* Before you do any RMAN testing, shut down your database, take a cold OS copy backup, and place it in a folder that doesn't get touched. This is your last line of defense if you completely mess everything up during your RMAN testing.

■ *Switch your redo logs a lot.* One of the biggest mistakes that happens with RMAN testing is that the timeframe between the backup and restore is unrealistically short. Confusion sets in because there is no space between the completion time of the backup and the "until time" of the restore operation. So, after any backup, make sure you switch the log file three or four times, just to put a little "distance" between operations.

■ *Set the NLS_DATE_FORMAT environment variable.* This is good advice for RMAN in general, but particularly in a test situation, where the timeframe between a backup and a restore will be unrealistically short, and you will want to know the timeframe of a backup to the second. So, before starting RMAN, be sure to run the following:

```
export NLS_DATE_FORMAT='mon-dd-yyyy hh24:mi:ss'
```

Then, when you start RMAN and issue a **list backup** command, the time will always show details to the minute and second.

■ *Leave your catalog database alone.* You will be tempted to use the database that houses your catalog as a target and to perform some tests with it. That is fine—that's why it's called a test environment. But you can seriously undermine your testing if you foul up your catalog. Do yourself a favor and leave the catalog database alone. And export your catalog schema with a user-level export before any new test session begins.

■ *Keep up with catalog maintenance.* This may be your test environment, but you will be creating a lot of backups over time, and you have a limited amount of space on your little test box. Take the opportunity to test using retention policies to get rid of old backups.

■ *Remove clones as soon as possible.* Attack of the clones! If you use the **duplicate** command, you can end up with numerous different instances running and taking up precious memory and disk space. Hey, it's a clone, and you're in a test environment—get rid of it as soon as you make it.

■ *Leave a clone file system in place.* You don't need to go through the steps of building the file system and the init.ora file for your duplicate database every time you want to test the **duplicate** or **duplicate for standby** command. Leave the file system and supporting files in place, and use the same DB_NAME and SID. On Windows, be sure to leave the Oracleservice<sid> in place in the Services control panel.

■ *Don't get attached to your test environment.* Sometimes you need to just blow everything away and start over from scratch, particularly if you don't have good maintenance habits. Eventually, your database will get to the point that it has had tablespaces dropped; has had re-created, dropped, and forgotten files placed in the wrong directory; has had archive logs stored all over the place—basically it's a rambling mess. Don't worry. That's why they call it testing. Don't get too wrapped up in the environment you have; just whack everything and start over from the cold backup you took prior to testing.

You'll surely find some of your own valuable lessons after you've done a bit of testing. After you go through the conceptual learning, take the scripts you've built and the knowledge you've gained, and schedule some time on a production-grade system to make sure that everything is going to scale up to your enterprise. You'll be glad you took the time to learn it before you went live.

Index

GET YOUR FREE SUBSCRIPTION
TO *ORACLE MAGAZINE*

Oracle Magazine is essential gear for today's information technology professionals. Stay informed and increase your productivity with every issue of *Oracle Magazine*. Inside each free bimonthly issue you'll get:

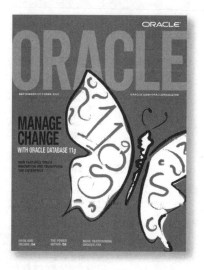

- Up-to-date information on Oracle Database, Oracle Application Server, Web development, enterprise grid computing, database technology, and business trends
- Third-party news and announcements
- Technical articles on Oracle and partner products, technologies, and operating environments
- Development and administration tips
- Real-world customer stories

If there are other Oracle users at your location who would like to receive their own subscription to *Oracle Magazine*, please photo-copy this form and pass it along.

Three easy ways to subscribe:

① Web
Visit our Web site at **oracle.com/oraclemagazine**
You'll find a subscription form there, plus much more

② Fax
Complete the questionnaire on the back of this card and fax the questionnaire side only to **+1.847.763.9638**

③ Mail
Complete the questionnaire on the back of this card and mail it to **P.O. Box 1263, Skokie, IL 60076-8263**

ORACLE

Want your own FREE subscription?

To receive a free subscription to *Oracle Magazine*, you must fill out the entire card, sign it, and date it (incomplete cards cannot be processed or acknowledged). You can also fax your application to +1.847.763.9638. **Or subscribe at our Web site at oracle.com/oraclemagazine**

O **Yes, please send me a FREE subscription** *Oracle Magazine.* O No.

O From time to time, Oracle Publishing allows our partners exclusive access to our e-mail addresses for special promotions and announcements. To be included in this program, please check this circle. If you do not wish to be included, you will only receive notices about your subscription via e-mail.

O Oracle Publishing allows sharing of our postal mailing list with selected third parties. If you prefer your mailing address not to be included in this program, please check this circle.

If at any time you would like to be removed from either mailing list, please contact Customer Service at +1.847.763.9635 or send an e-mail to oracle@halldata.com. If you opt in to the sharing of information, Oracle may also provide you with e-mail related to Oracle products, services, and events. If you want to completely unsubscribe from any e-mail communication from Oracle, please send an e-mail to: unsubscribe@oracle-mail.com with the following in the subject line: REMOVE [your e-mail address]. For complete information on Oracle Publishing's privacy practices, please visit oracle.com/html/privacy/html

X

signature (required)   date

name   title

company   e-mail address

street/p.o. box

city/state/zip or postal code   telephone

country   fax

Would you like to receive your free subscription in digital format instead of print if it becomes available? O Yes O No

---

YOU MUST ANSWER ALL 10 QUESTIONS BELOW.

① WHAT IS THE PRIMARY BUSINESS ACTIVITY OF YOUR FIRM AT THIS LOCATION? (check one only)

- □ 01 Aerospace and Defense Manufacturing
- □ 02 Application Service Provider
- □ 03 Automotive Manufacturing
- □ 04 Chemicals
- □ 05 Media and Entertainment
- □ 06 Construction/Engineering
- □ 07 Consumer Sector/Consumer Packaged Goods
- □ 08 Education
- □ 09 Financial Services/Insurance
- □ 10 Health Care
- □ 11 High Technology Manufacturing, OEM
- □ 12 Industrial Manufacturing
- □ 13 Independent Software Vendor
- □ 14 Life Sciences (biotech, pharmaceuticals)
- □ 15 Natural Resources
- □ 16 Oil and Gas
- □ 17 Professional Services
- □ 18 Public Sector (government)
- □ 19 Research
- □ 20 Retail/Wholesale/Distribution
- □ 21 Systems Integrator, VAR/VAD
- □ 22 Telecommunications
- □ 23 Travel and Transportation
- □ 24 Utilities (electric, gas, sanitation, water)
- □ 98 Other Business and Services _____

② WHICH OF THE FOLLOWING BEST DESCRIBES YOUR PRIMARY JOB FUNCTION? (check one only)

CORPORATE MANAGEMENT/STAFF
- □ 01 Executive Management (President, Chair, CEO, CFO, Owner, Partner, Principal)
- □ 02 Finance/Administrative Management (VP/Director/ Manager/Controller, Purchasing, Administration)
- □ 03 Sales/Marketing Management (VP/Director/Manager)
- □ 04 Computer Systems/Operations Management (CIO/VP/Director/Manager MIS/IS/IT, Ops)

IS/IT STAFF
- □ 05 Application Development/Programming Management
- □ 06 Application Development/Programming Staff
- □ 07 Consulting
- □ 08 DBA/Systems Administrator
- □ 09 Education/Training
- □ 10 Technical Support Director/Manager
- □ 11 Other Technical Management/Staff
- □ 98 Other

③ WHAT IS YOUR CURRENT PRIMARY OPERATING PLATFORM (check all that apply)

- □ 01 Digital Equipment Corp UNIX/VAX/VMS
- □ 02 HP UNIX
- □ 03 IBM AIX
- □ 04 IBM UNIX
- □ 05 Linux (Red Hat)
- □ 06 Linux (SUSE)
- □ 07 Linux (Oracle Enterprise)
- □ 08 Linux (other)
- □ 09 Macintosh
- □ 10 MVS
- □ 11 Netware
- □ 12 Network Computing
- □ 13 SCO UNIX
- □ 14 Sun Solaris/SunOS
- □ 15 Windows
- □ 16 Other UNIX
- □ 98 Other
- 99 □ None of the Above

④ DO YOU EVALUATE, SPECIFY, RECOMMEND, OR AUTHORIZE THE PURCHASE OF ANY OF THE FOLLOWING? (check all that apply)

- □ 01 Hardware
- □ 02 Business Applications (ERP, CRM, etc.)
- □ 03 Application Development Tools
- □ 04 Database Products
- □ 05 Internet or Intranet Products
- □ 06 Other Software
- □ 07 Middleware Products
- 99 □ None of the Above

⑤ IN YOUR JOB, DO YOU USE OR PLAN TO PURCHASE ANY OF THE FOLLOWING PRODUCTS? (check all that apply)

SOFTWARE
- □ 01 CAD/CAE/CAM
- □ 02 Collaboration Software
- □ 03 Communications
- □ 04 Database Management
- □ 05 File Management
- □ 06 Finance
- □ 07 Java
- □ 08 Multimedia Authoring
- □ 09 Networking
- □ 10 Programming
- □ 11 Project Management
- □ 12 Scientific and Engineering
- □ 13 Systems Management
- □ 14 Workflow

HARDWARE
- □ 15 Macintosh
- □ 16 Mainframe
- □ 17 Massively Parallel Processing
- □ 18 Minicomputer
- □ 19 Intel x86(32)
- □ 20 Intel x86(64)
- □ 21 Network Computer
- □ 22 Symmetric Multiprocessing
- □ 23 Workstation Services

SERVICES
- □ 24 Consulting
- □ 25 Education/Training
- □ 26 Maintenance
- □ 27 Online Database
- □ 28 Support
- □ 29 Technology-Based Training
- □ 30 Other
- 99 □ None of the Above

⑥ WHAT IS YOUR COMPANY'S SIZE? (check one only)

- □ 01 More than 25,000 Employees
- □ 02 10,001 to 25,000 Employees
- □ 03 5,001 to 10,000 Employees
- □ 04 1,001 to 5,000 Employees
- □ 05 101 to 1,000 Employees
- □ 06 Fewer than 100 Employees

⑦ DURING THE NEXT 12 MONTHS, HOW MUCH DO YOU ANTICIPATE YOUR ORGANIZATION WILL SPEND ON COMPUTER HARDWARE, SOFTWARE, PERIPHERALS, AND SERVICES FOR YOUR LOCATION? (check one only)

- □ 01 Less than $10,000
- □ 02 $10,000 to $49,999
- □ 03 $50,000 to $99,999
- □ 04 $100,000 to $499,999
- □ 05 $500,000 to $999,999
- □ 06 $1,000,000 and Over

⑧ WHAT IS YOUR COMPANY'S YEARLY SALES REVENUE? (check one only)

- □ 01 $500, 000, 000 and above
- □ 02 $100, 000, 000 to $500, 000, 000
- □ 03 $50, 000, 000 to $100, 000, 000
- □ 04 $5, 000, 000 to $50, 000, 000
- □ 05 $1, 000, 000 to $5, 000, 000

⑨ WHAT LANGUAGES AND FRAMEWORKS DO YOU USE? (check all that apply)

- □ 01 Ajax
- □ 02 C
- □ 03 C++
- □ 04 C#
- □ 05 Hibernate
- □ 06 J++/J#
- □ 07 Java
- □ 08 JSP
- □ 09 .NET
- □ 10 Perl
- □ 11 PHP
- □ 12 PL/SQL
- □ 13 Python
- □ 14 Ruby/Rails
- □ 15 Spring
- □ 16 Struts
- □ 17 SQL
- □ 18 Visual Basic
- □ 98 Other

⑩ WHAT ORACLE PRODUCTS ARE IN USE AT YOUR SITE? (check all that apply)

ORACLE DATABASE
- □ 01 Oracle Database 11*g*
- □ 02 Oracle Database 10*g*
- □ 03 Oracle9*i* Database
- □ 04 Oracle Embedded Database (Oracle Lite, Times Ten, Berkeley DB)
- □ 05 Other Oracle Database Release

ORACLE FUSION MIDDLEWARE
- □ 06 Oracle Application Server
- □ 07 Oracle Portal
- □ 08 Oracle Enterprise Manager
- □ 09 Oracle BPEL Process Manager
- □ 10 Oracle Identity Management
- □ 11 Oracle SOA Suite
- □ 12 Oracle Data Hubs

ORACLE DEVELOPMENT TOOLS
- □ 13 Oracle JDeveloper
- □ 14 Oracle Forms
- □ 15 Oracle Reports
- □ 16 Oracle Designer
- □ 17 Oracle Discoverer
- □ 18 Oracle BI Beans
- □ 19 Oracle Warehouse Builder
- □ 20 Oracle WebCenter
- □ 21 Oracle Application Express

ORACLE APPLICATIONS
- □ 22 Oracle E-Business Suite
- □ 23 PeopleSoft Enterprise
- □ 24 JD Edwards EnterpriseOne
- □ 25 JD Edwards World
- □ 26 Oracle Fusion
- □ 27 Hyperion
- □ 28 Siebel CRM

ORACLE SERVICES
- □ 28 Oracle E-Business Suite On Demand
- □ 29 Oracle Technology On Demand
- □ 30 Siebel CRM On Demand
- □ 31 Oracle Consulting
- □ 32 Oracle Education
- □ 33 Oracle Support
- □ 98 Other
- 99 □ None of the Above

08014004